Entrepreneurship

The International Library of Critical Writings in Economics

Series Editor: Mark Blaug
Professor Emeritus, University of London
Consultant Professor, University of Buckingham
Visiting Professor, University of Exeter

Entrepreneurship

Edited by

Mark Casson

Professor of Economics
University of Reading

An Elgar Reference Collection

Published by
Edward Elgar Publishing Limited
Gower House
Croft Road
Aldershot
Hants GU11 3HR
England

Edward Elgar Publishing Company
Old Post Road
Brookfield
Vermont 05036
USA

British Library Cataloguing in Publication Data

Entrepreneurship. – (The International Library of Critical Writings in Economics)
   1. Economics. Concepts: Entrepreneurship
   I. Casson, Mark, *1945*– II. (The International Library of Critical Writings in Economics)
   338.04

   ISBN 1 85278 209 9

Printed in Great Britain by Galliard (Printers) Ltd, Great Yarmouth

Contents

Acknowledgements

The editor and publishers wish to thank the following who have kindly given permission for the use of copyright material.

D.H. Aldcroft for his own article: (1964), 'The Entrepreneur and the British Economy, 1970–1914', *Economic History Review*, 2nd series, **17**, 113–34.

American Economic Association for articles: W.J. Baumol (1968), 'Entrepreneurship in Economic Theory', *American Economic Review* (Papers and Proceedings), **58**, 64–71; H. Leibenstein (1968), 'Entrepreneurship and Development', *American Economic Review*, **58**, 72–83; D.S. Evans and L.S. Leighton (1989), 'Some Empirical Aspects of Entrepreneurship', *American Economic Review*, **79**, 519–35.

Basil Blackwell for articles: F.A. von Hayek (1937), 'Economics and Knowledge', *Economica* (NS), **4**, 33–54; Z.J. Acs and D.B. Audretsch (1989), 'Small Firm Entry in US Manufacturing', *Economica* (NS) **56**, 255-65; P.S. Johnson and D.G. Cathcart (1979), 'The Founders of New Manufacturing Firms: A Note on the Size of Their Incubator Plants', *Journal of Industrial Economics*, **38** (2), 19–24; and for excerpt: M.C. Casson (1982), 'The Entrepreneur: An Economic Theory', Martin Robertson, 201–17.

Cambridge University Press for article: P.N. O'Farrell and R. Crouchley (1984), 'An Industrial and Spatial Analysis of New Firm Formation in Ireland', *Regional Studies*, **18**, 221–36; and for excerpts: L.G. Sandberg 'The Entrepreneur and Technological Change' from *The Economic History of Britain since 1700: 2. 1860 to the 1970s*, R. Floud and D. McCloskey (eds); M.J. Wiener (1981), Chapter 8 'An Overview and an Assessment' from *English Culture and the Decline of the Industrial Spirit*.

D.C. Heath & Co. for excerpt: I.M. Kirzner (1982), 'Uncertainty, Discovery and Human Action: A Study of the Entrepreneurial Profile in the Misesian System' from his edited book *Method, Process and Austrian Economics: Essays in Honour of Ludwig von Mises*, 139–59.

Elsevier Publishers B.V. for articles: R. Highfield and R. Smiley (1987), 'New Business Starts and Economic Activity: An Empirical Investigation', *International Journal of Industrial Organisation*, **5**, 51–66; Z.J. Acs and D.B. Audretsch (1987), 'Innovation, Market Structure and Firm Size', *Review of Economics and Statistics*, **69**, 567–74.

Harvard University Press for excerpt from: Joseph A. Schumpeter, *The Theory of Economic Development*, 65–94, copyright 1934 by the President and Fellows of Harvard College.

International Council for Small Business, Canada for article: R.M. Knight (1985), 'The Financing of Small High-Technology Firms in Canada', *Journal of Small Business and Entrepreneurship*, **3** (1), 5–17.

John Wiley & Sons Inc. for article: G.A. Calvo and S. Wellisz (1980), 'Technology, Entrepreneurs and Firm Size', *Quarterly Journal of Economics*, **95**, 663–77.

Longman for excerpt from: P. Mathias (1967), *Retailing Revolution: A History of Multiple Retailing in the Food Trades based upon the Allied Suppliers Group of Companies*, 96–108.

Macmillan, London and Basingstoke and St. Martin's Press, New York for excerpt: B. Loasby (1983), 'Knowledge, Learning and Enterprise' from *Beyond Positive Economics?*, J. Wiseman (ed.), 104–21; and Macmillan for excerpt: A. Marshall (1921), 'Transition to Present Problems of Industry and Trade' from *Industry and Trade*, 163–77.

New York University Press for excerpt from: R.D. Waldinger (1986), *Through the Eye of the Needle: Immigrants and Enterprise in New York's Garment Trades*, 19–47, 214–17.

Pinter Publishers for excerpt: R. Rothwell and W. Zegveld (1982), 'New Ventures and Large Firms: the Search for Internal Entrepreneurship' from *Innovation and the Small and Medium Sized Firm: Their Role in Employment and in Economic Change*.

Rand Corporation for article: R.R. Nelson and S.G. Winter (1978), 'Forces Generating and Limiting Concentration under Schumpeterian Competition', *Bell Journal of Economics*, **9**, 524–48.

Scottish Economic Society for article: D.J. Storey and A.M. Jones (1987), 'New Firm Formation – A Labour Market Approach to Industrial Entry', *Scottish Journal of Political Economy*, **34**, 37–51.

The Urban Institute Press for excerpt: D.R. Young (1986), 'Entrepreneurship and the Behaviour of Nonprofit Organisations: Elements of a Theory' from *The Economics of Nonprofit Institutions: Studies in Structure and Policy*, S. Rose-Ackerman (ed.), 161–84.

University of Chicago Press for articles: N.H. Leff (1978), 'Industrial Organisation and Entrepreneurship in the Developing Countries: The Economic Groups', *Economic Development and Cultural Change*, **26**, 661–75; R.E. Kihlstrom and J.J. Laffont (1979), 'A General Equilibrium Entrepreneurial Theory of Firm Formation based on Risk Aversion', *Journal of Political Economy*, **87**, 719–48.

University of Sydney, Australia for article: B.W. Ross (1987), 'The Leisure Factor in Entrepreneurial Success during the "Robber Baron" Era', *Department of Economics, University of Sydney Working Paper* No 96.

University of Toronto Press for excerpt from: J.S. Mill (1848), *Principles of Political Economy*, Variorum edition (ed. J.M. Robson), 131–40.

Every effort has been made to trace all the copyright holders but if any have been inadvertently overlooked the publishers will be pleased to make the necessary arrangement at the first opportunity.

In addition the publishers wish to thank the Library of the London School of Economics and Political Science for their assistance in obtaining these articles.

Introduction

Entrepreneurship is an important and, until fairly recently, sadly neglected subject. The literature is extremely diffuse. This book is intended to provide a basic resource, not only for libraries, but for all those engaged with the subject as teachers, students or practitioners. The book should be accessible to anyone with a reasonable grasp of basic economic principles. It attempts to synthesize some of the best literature on the subject. It contains the thinking of some of the most profound scholars in philosophy, sociology and history, as well as economics.

The readings are organized into three main sections, dealing respectively with Economic Theory, Empirical Evidence on Firm and Industry, and Culture and Economic Development. This structure is reflected in this introductory essay, which provides a commentary on the contents of the book.

The main omission is a section on government policy. Despite its topical relevance, the appraisal of specific policies would occupy a very large amount of space because international differences in institutional arrangements mean that too many separate studies on different countries would have to be included. The reader can readily infer, however – particularly from the empirical papers – that according to recent research special incentives and interventions to promote small firm start-ups, of the kind currently favoured by many governments, are unlikely to stimulate entrepreneurship to any significant extent. The literature suggests that improvements in basic education (both moral and scientific), coupled with wide-ranging fiscal reforms are likely to be more effective than special 'small firm' policies. These are only indications, however, and definite conclusions will have to wait on the results of future research.

Economic Theory

Four main approaches to entrepreneurship can be identified in economic theory. The first focuses on the factor distribution of income. It seeks to identify a factor for which profit is the reward. The second emphasizes market processes. It is a dynamic approach which emerges from a critique of the static Walrasian concept of perfect competition. Thirdly, there is the heroic Schumpeterian vision of the entrepreneur as an innovator whose 'creative destruction' regulates growth and fluctuation in the economy. The final approach concerns the relation between the entrepreneur and the firm. It focuses on the entrepreneur as decision-maker – in particular, his motivation and his perception of the environment. In this final approach, special attention is given to small and newly-founded firms, and to key issues of strategy formulation, building market share, managing growth through diversification, and so on.

Risk and uncertainty

Profit is defined as the surplus which remains once the wages of labour, the rent of land and the interest on capital have been paid out of revenue. In a static competitive economy anyone can purchase factors and combine them to generate ouput. With free entry and exit, and no economies of scale, competition between producers maintains long run economic profit at zero. There is simply no need for an entrepreneur.

One way of introducing entrepreneurship is to relax the assumption of a static environment. This is, however, of little consequence if the environment varies in a simple deterministic – and therefore quite predictable – manner. It does, however, become significant if the environment is unpredictable because this introduces elements of risk and uncertainty. Cantillon was the first economist to emphasize the significance of uncertainty. He argued that the speculative middleman, who buys in order to resell, cannot know for certain the market conditions prevailing at a later date. Yet the contract of purchase assures the seller of a fixed return independent of what the middleman can subsequently resell the commodity for. The assured nature of the contractual payment thus makes the middleman a specialized bearer of risk. The same point applies, of course, to a producer who incurs a non-recoverable set-up cost before he has been able to contract forward for the disposal of subsequent output; he is not merely a manager of production but also a specialized bearer of risk.

Cantillon's analysis of the middleman suggests that most economic agents can be divided into two groups: those who receive fixed incomes, and those who contract to pay these incomes even though their own incomes are uncertain. An important reason why these incomes are uncertain is that those living on fixed incomes, and indeed those living on variable incomes too, prefer to purchase goods in small amounts as and when they need them, rather than purchase according to a stable and predictable routine. Cantillon identifies those who live on uncertain incomes as the entrepreneurs whilst those who live on fixed incomes are either literally or metaphorically their employees.

Frank Knight refined this idea by distinguishing between risk and uncertainty. Risks, according to Knight, relate to recurrent situations in which, by repeated observation, it is possible to estimate the relative frequencies with which different outcomes will arise. Overall risk can be reduced by pooling risks which are imperfectly correlated. Indeed, according to Knight, the evolution of the joint-stock corporation can be understood in precisely these terms.

Knight argues that it is not measurable risk but unmeasurable uncertainty that constitutes the basis for pure profit. Uncertainty pertains to unique situations which have no precedent, and no analogy by which the probabilities of alternative outcomes can be assessed. Another way of putting this is to say that risks are unlikely to generate surprises which lead to a significant revaluation of the firm. The regular recurrence of a particular type of risky situation has a measurable effect on the volatility of the firm's profit stream, which can be incorporated, through a risk premium, into its valuation. So long as the underlying fundamentals do not change, there is no reason why the value of the firm should change either. The resolution of an uncertain situation may lead to revaluation of the firm, however, and so for the owner of the firm the unanticipated shock may provide a windfall gain which constitutes pure profit.

The ideas of Cantillon and Knight have been formalized by Kihlstrom and Laffont. Their analysis of the allocation of production risk in a competitive economy illustrates one of the great strengths of modern theory. By abstracting from institutional detail their model becomes amenable to rigorous mathematical analysis. It shows how the equilibrium distribution of income between entrepreneurs and their employees is governed by their relative degree of risk aversion, the marginal productivity schedule of the employees, and the magnitude of technological risk in production. Comparative static analysis shows how a change in technology which increases risks raises the risk premium paid by the employees to the entrepreneurs, and so reduces wages and raises profits.

The analysis also highlights several weaknesses of conventional theorizing. First, the approach is essentially reductionist because, despite the allusion to Knight, his distinction between risk and uncertainty is ignored, and all uncertainty is reduced to measurable risk in order to make the model tractable. Secondly, some crucial aspects of entrepreneurship are assumed away without any justification being given. Thus while in both Cantillon and Knight the most important uncertainties relate to future price levels in non-Walrasian markets, according to Kihlstrom and Laffont all uncertainties are technological and all markets Walrasian. Finally, some issues are simply fudged. Thus the entrepreneur, besides bearing risk, also owns an indivisible fixed factor which is necessary for the operation of a firm, but whose rationale is never properly explained. The provision of the fixed factor is united with risk-bearing because there is no equity market in the model that would permit the separation of these functions. Although the authors have considered such issues elsewhere, it is evident that the results of their model are highly sensitive to assumptions which have only an indirect bearing on the essential features of entrepreneurial activity.

Market process

One essential feature is the entrepreneur's role as an intermediary in a dynamic market process. Hayek argues that the market system is indispensable in motivating people to supply the kind of information that is needed to help decision-makers economize on the use of scarce resources. Markets provide decision-makers with price quotations which can be used to measure opportunity costs. In a competitive market the quotation corresponds to an average of the subjective valuations of the commodity by everyone in the society. The weights used in this average will, however, vary according to the distribution of personal income.

When information is scarce, different people are likely to hold different beliefs. Some people are confident enough to believe that other people's beliefs are wrong and theirs are right. They are also likely to believe that other people will eventually come round to their view, and that resources will be revalued as a result. This motivates people to intervene in markets for purely speculative purposes. But by intervening they tend to drive the price marginally against themselves, so that the current price begins to reflect what they believe they know about the future. The opinions of these confident individuals then become heavily weighted in the pricing process. By influencing price, these confident individuals indirectly contribute what they think they know to other people's perceptions of opportunity costs.

If several people hold the same opinion then their competition to purchase undervalued resources will drive up the price to eliminate any prospect of profit. All the benefit of the new information will accrue to the initial owners of the resources. To appropriate the full value from new information a temporary monopoly is required. According to Kirzner, it is the most alert individuals who will appropriate this profit. It is the prospect of monopoly profits which motivates people to search actively for new information, and so sustains the adaptive and innovative capacities of the economy.

Buying up undervalued resources to resell later is a form of intertemporal arbitrage. Arbitrage can also be effected over space, and between different types of goods. Arbitrage over space is exemplified by a merchant who transports goods between local markets in response to transitory price differentials. Arbitrage between goods is exemplified by the producer who transforms a low-value combination of inputs into a high-value output.

Kirzner's theory of the entrepreneur is commonly presented as part of a wider package of ideas generated by the renaissance of Austrian economics. A key element in Austrian thinking is the repudiation of objectivity in social science. All knowledge is provisional and subjective. The closest approximation to objective information is a strongly held belief that is common to everyone. Some approximation to objectivity is necessary, however, for certain steps in Kirzner's analysis to be valid. The efficiency of the market system, for example, clearly depends upon common perceptions of prices by transactors. If personal bias in perception distorted price communication then even within a market system anarchy would prevail.

Repudiation of objectivity is linked to the rejection of measurement, and through this to a rejection of the Popperian or 'positivist' methodology of attempting to falsify hypotheses by recourse to data. Thus while Austrian theory shares with conventional neoclassical theory a commitment to methodological individualism and the rationality of human action, it does not attempt to generate testable hypotheses. Rather it aims to show the impracticality of solving economic problems through centralized planning and the social ownership of capital. The centralized socialist approach is impractical because it fails to provide incentives for the collection and proper use of information and because the problems of motivating employees within a planning unit are insuperable.

Innovation

Schumpeter's view of the entrepreneur as innovator has widespread appeal. His early work, which highlights the romantic and visionary aspects of business, appeals to artists and individualists, whilst his later work appeals to scientists and collectivists because of its claim that innovation can be effectively programmed and coordinated within a large organization. His emphasis on the special psychology of the innovator, and his vision of how capitalism stimulates 'creative destruction', give his work a social and historical dimension which is lacking in most other theories of the entrepreneur.

Schumpeter's distinction between invention and innovation and his relation of innovation to credit creation permit his theory to integrate issues as diverse as long run economic development, business cycles, market structure and the growth of the firm. Because of its visionary nature, however, it is difficult to capture Schumpeter's analysis within formal models. Several writers have attempted this, however; some have siezed upon the Darwinian flavour of Schumpeter's work, in order to embed Schumpeter's analysis within an evolutionary approach to the subject (see Nelson and Winter).

From a Darwinian perspective, innovation is a source of potential diversity analogous to genetic variation. In one version of this analogy, the variation occurs within a population of firms when one of them adopts a new management practice or a new technology. The innovating firm then competes with established firms in a competitive struggle for survival. The industry constitutes an environmental niche in which the struggle goes on. Imitation constitutes a social mechanism by which the characteristics of the successful innovation are transmitted to rival firms. In the long run only the fittest firms in the industry – those using best practice techniques – earn a normal rate of profit and so survive.

The analogy can be further extended by noting that many inventions are generated by synthesizing ideas from previous innovations, rather like the way that genetic materials are synthesized from others during reproduction. Like all analogies, however, the evolutionary perspective becomes dangerous if pursued too far. The psychology of innovation involves a deliberate act of anticipation – an imagination of potential future consequences – which is lacking in the natural world. Entrepreneurs have a choice of what to innovate and, indeed, whether to innovate at all, and in many cases it is by no means obvious what this choice should be. Some people are better than others at anticipating the response of a complex environment, and it is people with this ability that are likely, in the long run, to be most successful. These people can transmit their successful practices to future generations by training their successors within the firm. The firm is an institution that can outlive any individual entrepreneur and thereby perpetuate his ideas without recourse to genetic mechanisms (see below). Whilst competition between innovators may have Darwinian aspects, therefore, the innovation decision itself presents the entrepreneur with opportunities for deliberate choice and for institution-building which are entirely missing from the Darwinian picture.

The entrepreneur and the firm

One of the most unsatisfactory aspects of entrepreneurial theory is its failure to distinguish properly between the entrepreneur and the firm. For example, until recent work by Reekie (1979), Ricketts (1987) and others, Austrian economists entirely fudged this issue. Austrians' aversion to planning in general means that they have failed to appreciate the obvious advantages of planning within the firm. These advantages stem from the avoidance of transaction costs in external markets, and are considered in more detail later.

Writers who focus on the role of the firm as an employer of labour tend to see the key role of the entrepreneur as supervision. Indeed, in contrast to early French writers such as Say (1803), who accorded the entrepreneur an active role in the promotion of ventures, early English writers such as Mill tended to identify the entrepreneur exclusively with this supervisory role. On this view, the size of the firm is governed chiefly by the supervisor's optimal span of control.

Marshall, by emphasizing management rather than merely supervision, widened the scope of analysis, and aligned it more closely with subsequent thinking which, following Coase (1937), regards the key aspect of the firm as the supercession of the market. Unfortunately, however, Marshall attempts to integrate his analysis into a static theory of income distribution by reducing entrepreneurship to a fourth factor of production. By implicitly treating entrepreneurship as a homogeneous factor service traded in a competitive market Marshall overlooks some of its most distinguishing characteristics.

A common mistake in the literature is to suppose that there can only be one entrepreneur per firm. This view is apparent not only in Marshall and Mill but in many business biographies, in which the operations of the firm are regarded merely as an extension of the personality of its founder. This tradition lives on today in the practice of applying entrepreneurial theory only to the 'entrepreneurial firm' in which a single owner-manager appears to be in absolute control (see below).

Postulating a single entrepreneur per firm creates an artificial problem, namely of deciding who exactly is the entrepreneur. The answer may be fairly obvious in the case of an owner-manager, but it is not so in the case of a large diversified corporation in which ownership and control are divorced. The difficulties this can entail are well illustrated by Knight's attempt to apply his theory of the entrepreneur to the large corporation.

As already noted, Knight argues that uncertainty-bearing is the true entre-preneurial function and that this is effected by the owner of the firm who receives the residual income. According to Knight, responsibility for the financial consequences of a decision can never, in an efficient system, be separated from responsibility for taking the decision. Since in a large corporation there are many owners, these owners must share not only in the financial consequences but also in the decision-making. The difficulty this creates – namely that possibly thousands of shareholders participate in decisions – is handled by Knight by arguing that management is a fairly routine activity. The really crucial decision concerns the selection of a chief executive who, if he is competent, will then select competent junior managers who will run the entire operation efficiently.

This argument fudges the issue of stockholder unanimity in the selection of the chief executive. But, quite apart from this, it is simply incompatible with the facts. The management of a firm is far less routine, and far more judgemental, than this picture suggests. The chief executive requires a reputation for integrity and good judgement, and he will be looking for similar qualities in the assistants he appoints. His reputation is an asset which he places at risk when he takes responsibility for decisions. It is this reputation that encourages shareholders to delegate decisions to him, confident in both his intrinsic personal qualities and in the fact that he knows that his own future salary earning power depends on maintaining the reputation he has acquired. Thus, contrary to what Knight asserts, reputation mechanisms allow a separation between decision making on the one hand and shareholders' financial responsibilities on the other. Delegation of decisions from shareholders to managers allows entrepreneurship to be shared; moreover, if it is distributed more to one group than another, then it is surely managers that take the larger share.

The view that the entrepreneurial role is unitary derives some support from the argument of Kaldor (1934, and also paper 9), which says that if the overall strategy of the firm is to be consistent then it must ultimately pass through a single 'brain'. But as Charles Babbage (1832) noted over 150 years ago, a division of labour in thought can be effected in decision-making, so that different aspects of a decision can be delegated to different people. If each of these people has genuine discretion then their decisions can affect the strategy of the firm in a material way. Thus the delegation of decisions from shareholders to a chief executive can be repeated within the organization, as the chief executive resolves his own problems into sub-problems which are delegated progressively further down the hierarchy. Of course, the chief executive who reconciles and synthesizes the delegates' decisions has the most important role. But nevertheless entrepreneurial decision-making is still an activity which can, in principle, permeate the whole organization.

Another problem with Kaldor's view is that it does not really explain what the firm is doing in the first place. It tends to take the existence of the firm as self-evident, and to explain the role of the entrepreneur in terms of the need to manage the firm in a particular way. An alternative approach is to take entrepreneurship as the primary concept and explain the creation of the firm as a deliberate and rational response to a problem encountered by the entrepreneur.

I have developed this approach elsewhere (paper 12). The entrepreneur, it is claimed, has superior judgement, which means that he can handle complex and ill-defined problems better than other people. No-one can be certain that their judgement is better than other people's, because other people may know things that they do not, but confident individuals may nevertheless act as if they had such assurance. The simplest example is of someone who believes that they possess relevant information not available to other people. The firm is then developed by this individual as an institution for reallocating resources in the more efficient manner suggested by this information. Transaction costs in external markets make it easier for the entrepreneur to exploit the information himself rather than to license it, and to exploit it within an institution rather than purely through arbitraging in arm's length trade.

The firm is not only a device for exploiting information but for gathering it too. Information can be used to test between alternative hypotheses concerning the state of the environment, prior to submitting the hypotheses to the ultimate test of whether they provide profitable strategies in the market place. The capacity of the firm to generate a feedback loop by monitoring the consequences of managerial decisions makes it possible to institutionalize the learning process (paper 13). Good internal communications within the firm allow it to function as an open-learning system, whereby the public good properties of information are exploited to allow all employees to draw their own inferences from information collected by the firm. The firm evolves into a social unit, in which decisions are delegated through an intellectual division of labour. Information fed back from the environment is disseminated widely as an internal public good. Free access to this information allows everyone to take entrepreneurial decisions effectively, wherever they have the authority and the confidence to do so.

Empirical Evidence on Firm and Industry

The theoretical confusion that prevails on the relation between the firm and the entrepreneur is reflected in the empirical literature. Entrepreneurship, it was suggested above, is a general phenomenon, reflected in the superior decision-making abilities of certain individuals. The empirical literature, however, takes a very narrow view of the field in which such abilities are revealed. It concentrates mainly upon *market entry through innovation effected by new small owner-managed firms*.

The emphasis on new firm formation directs attention to the occupational choice between self-employment and ordinary employment (see papers 14 and 15) and, to a lesser extent, between self-employment, unemployment and early retirement. The obvious way to analyse this choice is through the Cantillon-Knight theory that self-employment is inherently more risky because the self-employed person is contractually committed to uncertainty-bearing whereas the employee is not. The emphasis on market entry relates entrepreneurship to the question of barriers to entry and to changes in industrial concentration over time. Do macroeconomic prospects affect market entry, for example, by discouraging business start-ups at the onset of depression (see paper 16)? Is there any evidence that small firms face greater barriers to entry, or are more susceptible to cyclical influences (see paper 17)?

The emphasis on innovation means that Schumpeterian issues concerning the relation between size of firm, R & D expenditure and innovation are very much to the fore. Are small firms more innovative than large firms, and are the innovations they make in some sense the more fundamental ones (see paper 18)? Does the extremely speculative nature of high-technology research mean that small firms are heavily penalized by their limited access to capital markets; are their entrepreneurs more dependent, as a result, on borrowing from family and friends (see paper 19)? Finally, to what extent can innovative individuals obtain financial backing from their own employers rather than have to go independent to develop their ideas; in other words, is 'intrapreneurship' within the large firm an adequate substitute for small firm entry in high-technology industries (see paper 20)?

It would be premature to claim that definite answers can be given to questions of this kind. Indeed, some of the questions about the relative performance of large and small firms seem a little naive. For if theory is correct in suggesting that firms develop as instruments of the entrepreneur then each firm presumably develops to a scale which reflects the needs, and the capacities of its entrepreneur(s); thus there is no reason to believe that, in general, either large firms or small firms will perform better than the others. Indeed, to the extent that capital markets are efficient, any bias in favour of large firms will lead to small firms being swallowed up by acquisition or merger, whilst any bias in favour of small firms will lead to asset-stripping or management buy-outs. This suggests that if firms of different sizes are able to survive then, in the absence of market distortions, their performance will be roughly equivalent.

So far it has been implicitly assumed that firms of different sizes are to be regarded as competitors. There is, however, considerable evidence of a symbiotic relation between large and small firms; in many cases they are complements rather than substitutes, and collaborators rather than competitors. Many small firms begin life as subcontractors for larger firms, specializing in small-batch production of non-standard items required at short notice. The large firm frequently controls the small firm's marketing and distribution. Rivalry only develops once the small firm grows to a point where it can cut out the intermediating or 'merchant' activity of its larger partner. As the Emilian model shows (see paper 21), a large firm may be the hub of many such relationships within a locality. Relationships of this kind can arise naturally and harmoniously when intrapreneurs of the kind described in paper 20 move to an 'arm's length' contractual relation with their employer.

Previous employment experience with the client firm can be invaluable in developing entrepreneurial skills. Self-employed people with previous experience of their industry perform, on average, better than do outsiders. There is evidence that medium-size firms are better than very large firms at incubating relevant skills (see paper 22). Large capital-intensive continuous-flow plants relying on impersonal hierarchical control of semi-skilled labour do not encourage the kind of flexible thinking required of the entrepreneur. This seems to be one reason why workers made redundant by the closure of large plants appear to have less success in developing independent businesses than those who voluntarily quit smaller firms where they have enjoyed more responsibility. Such effects are, however, difficult to disentangle from the effects of the age, educational background and personal wealth of those involved, and from the general depression in a locality in which major plant closures have occurred.

The symbiotic relations described above often work most effectively over short distances. They rely upon informal contracts which are promoted by face-to-face communication. A successful large firm can therefore generate significant economies of agglomeration. Small firms are attracted to its locality through the selective immigration of enterprising people from more depressed areas. Such effects are strengthened by the 'invisible infrastructure' of the locality – good research and educational establishments and the absence of political interference, for example. The 'Silicon Valley' phenomenon suggests that such effects are particularly important in the high-technology field. There are also important historical precedents from the time of the first industrial revolution. It has been alleged by Myrdal (1957) and others that the combination of economies of agglomeration and selective migration generates widening regional disparities through a process of cumulation causation. There is certainly convincing evidence that regional differences in entrepreneurship help to generate spatial inequalities in employment, income and growth (see paper 23).

Culture and Economic Development

Personality and motivation

Evidence of entrepreneurship can be found in the records of most leading civilizations – in Mesopotamian tablets, in early contracts in the Nile grain trade, in the orations of Demosthenes relating to commercial disputes at Piraeus in Ancient Greece, and so on. The appearance of entrepreneurship as a driving force in modern industrialization is, however, usually traced back to the appearance of individualism in Western Europe. Individualism has both secular and religious manifestations. Whilst the former are most conspicuous today it is the latter which are, arguably, of the greater historical significance.

Secular individualism is perceived as liberating acquisitiveness and greed. It removes traditional taboos associated with indulgence, motivating effort by permitting gratification through consumption as its reward. It is this crude hedonism which underlies much utilitarian thinking, and has been incorporated into conventional economic theory. It fits nicely with the scientific and materialistic outlook of the contemporary West. It provides a convenient biologically-based account of the origin of consumer preferences. When resources are limited, the pursuit of self-gratification throughout a society inevitably leads to conflict, so that competition must be accepted as a natural part of life.

Despite its declining contemporary influence, it is nevertheless religious rather than secular individualism that is most important in understanding the origins of industrialism in the West. Historically, individualism appeared at a time when religious authority and influence was still strong. Individualism liberated conscience rather than greed – man's higher nature rather than his lower nature was affected. By encouraging people to develop a direct personal relation with their Creator, individualism stimulated the independence of judgement and the distrust of consensus views which is characteristic of the entrepreneur. People believed that their soul was destined for heaven provided they could avoid the snares and temptations of mortal life. What better way to avoid frivolous distractions than by hard work and frugal living, supported by regular habits? A life devoted to building up a family business for the benefit of one's descendants could, in this context, be considered a noble calling. Moreover the personal reputation acquired through this life-style would create a virtuous circle – honesty and frugality could be justified not only for moral ends, but as means to business success. Thus moral and economic considerations became entwined ambiguously within the ethos of commercially-oriented religious groups (see paper 24).

The impact of religious individualism is still discernible. As paper 25 indicates, a significant amount of entrepreneurial activity in the contemporary US is still directed to nonprofit objectives which are explicitly legitimated in social and moral terms. Studies of chief executives show that family-orientation and leadership by moral example still provide a formula for success in many firms. Indeed, a reappraisal of the careers of some of the best-known 'robber barons' of the past reveals a surprising portrait of naive religious conviction, wide-ranging philanthropic interest and –

perhaps most surprisingly – a recognition of the need for recreation in order to stimulate imagination (see paper 26).

Some of the most rational and sophisticated business strategies have been developed by businessmen who ultimately rejected (or at least neglected) the business world for other pursuits. Thus Thomas Lipton (27), one of the first British businessmen to recognize the growing sophistication of the working class consumer, the role of packaging in mass-marketing, and the advantages of backward integration in securing quality control, devoted his later years to buying his way into the social establishment through owning racehorses instead of expanding further his international chain of retail stores. Although some aspects of this behaviour could, of course, be explained in purely hedonistic terms, his efforts to win acceptance from people with far less acumen than himself is really only intelligible within the context of the culture of his time.

Immigrants, social mobility and culture

The entrepreneur, it would appear, is something of a nonconformist and so, as a result, he may tend to opt out of rigidly organized social groups to gain greater flexibility. In certain cases, indeed, he may be an outcast from such groups – or at least feel himself to have become one. Hence the search for respectability, noted above, may be an attempt to regain a social position which the entrepreneur believes he has lost. In a slightly different context, Brenner (1987) has in fact suggested that entrepreneurial risk-taking may be an attempt to regain a lost position by people belonging to nations or social groups which have suffered unanticipated decline.

In other cases the entrepreneur may be excluded from high-status groups at the outset. This seems to be true of religious minorities, who are often discriminated against, or even persecuted, for their beliefs. It may also be true of ethnic minorities and of immigrants. Avenues of social advancement through the establishment – church, armed forces, civil service, and the large hierarchical enterprise (see below) – are denied to them, and as a result they are pushed, rather than pulled, into self-employment.

The close social ties that exist within minority groups can give minority-group employers a strong advantage in labour recruitment (see paper 28). Such employers have many sanctions against poor employees through the family and community network. Indeed, many immigrant groups rely upon the extended family both for labour (involving intergenerational transfer of skills through on-the-job training) and finance (through an intergenerational capital market). Loan defaulters and slacking employees know that they will quickly gain a bad reputation in the community, and this encourages a high degree of integrity in relations with other members of the social group. Because minority groups are marginalized by society as a whole, however, the attitudes of their members towards outsiders may be distinctly hostile, Mafia entrepreneurship being a prominent example.

Unless minority enterprises have the same growth potential as ordinary enterprises, their employment opportunities will remain an inadequate substitute for other methods of personal advancement. Many immigrant firms seem to be limited by an inability to extend their customer base beyond the immigrant community, though in certain labour-intensive services, such as construction, restaurants and hotels, entry into the markets of established firms may well be possible.

Studies of business leadership in large corporations tend to suggest, however, that once a significant divorce between ownership and control has occurred, management teams become self-perpetuating oligarchies. Educated sons and daughters of professional managers have a better chance than others of being appointed to similar positions in large firms. Thus even if the immigrant enterprise should grow to become a large corporation, management will eventually be taken over by employees with different social origins. The establishment maintains its power by gradually assimilating the most successful enterprises which arise to challenge it. The Horatio Alger myth (see paper 29) that under capitalism everyone of similar ability has the same chance of getting rich is thus no more than a myth. Nevertheless, as previous remarks about culture have shown, such myths can still exercise a powerful influence on behaviour. They have a tendency towards self-fulfilment, in the sense that immigrants who believe in the myth acquire a confidence which makes them more likely to succeed than if they did not.

Development and decline

It is difficult to explain differences in the performance of national economies purely in terms of differential endowments of conventional factors of production such as land, labour and capital. It is often suggested that differences in indigenous entrepreneurship explain the residual variation. There is, however, a danger that entrepreneurship is introduced merely as a non-specific catch-all for the non-quantifiable factors involved.

It is fairly obvious, for example, that countries lacking a scientific outlook will fail to assimilate modern technology, and so experience lower productivity. There are, however, technologically advanced countries – such as the Soviet Union and, to some extent, China – which remain economically backward because of their failure to allocate resources efficiently. Entrepreneurial failure is manifest both in the X-inefficiency of large bureuacratic organizations and in high transactions costs in conventional markets. A major factor in the failure of both markets and hierarchies appears to be a lack of trust between the parties involved. This generates a high risk of default in arm's length contracts and severe agency problems in terms of the accountability of subordinates within an organization.

It is far easier for a person to be enterprising when surrounded with people they trust, not only because they can depend on the cooperation of colleagues and subordinates but because their superiors trust them sufficiently to devolve responsibility freely – they leave the person free to carry on their work in their own way. Neither impersonal markets mediated by formal contracts, nor rigid hierarchies with elaborate systems of supervision and control can provide this supporting environment. A social group with an outward-looking leadership that promotes high moral values within the group is most likely to sustain entrepreneurial cooperation of this kind (see paper 29). The existence of such groups can be detected in the progressive sectors of many societies – in contemporary Japan, France and Brazil, for example. The emergence of such groups, it can also be argued, is one of the characteristics of the take off period in the development of many economies. In particular, élite groups that span the fields of business and politics can be extremely influential in fashioning development strategy by coordinating high-level decisions in different sectors of the economy.

If the emergence of entrepreneurship can explain the economic rise of a nation then the obvious supplementary question is whether the disappearance of entrepreneurship can explain its relative decline. The British economy did, in fact, begin to go into decline at about the time that new groups (notably the general unions and the Fabian intellectuals of the Labour Party) began to challenge the power of business groups at both the municipal and national level. Whether the disappearance of business hegemony was a cause or effect of the decline is difficult to say, however.

The debate over the decline of the British economy (see papers 32, 33) highlights one of the methodological problems of entrepreneurial research, namely to operationalize entrepreneurial theory to the point where testable propositions can be devised. One of the difficulties is that entrepreneurial failure can always be rationalized in some other way – for example, as a collective change in the time-preference of business leaders which encourages them to liquidate their businesses rather than invest. Some Austrian economists would argue that, in fact, testing is impossible and that belief in entrepreneurial theory must ultimately be an act of faith.

It is, however, perfectly reasonable to attempt an exploration of the rise and decline of nations that embraces the totality of what we know (or think we know). It could be argued, for example, that the cultural values of late Victorian Britain reflected a romantic attachment to nature amongst the governing élite that was incompatible with sustained industrialization (see paper 34). These values may have encouraged business leaders to misperceive seriously their environment – to underestimate the potential strength of foreign competition, to misunderstand the growing social challenge to the legitimacy of private ownership of industry, and to ignore the improvements in efficiency available from new technologies and management methods. The literary legacy of the period, and the evidence of business archives and official statistics are all compatible with such an explanation, whereas more conventional economic explanations offer only a contrived interpretation of the statistics alone.

The debate over the rise and decline of the British economy illustrates both the strengths and weaknesses of entrepreneurial theory – its relevance to performance and policy on the one hand, and the difficulty of placing it on a scientific footing on the other. Entrepreneurship is a fascinating subject because it is ultimately concerned with some of the most exciting, and disturbing, aspects of human behaviour, as manifested in business life. This fascination is likely to remain for some considerable time, because the questions raised by entrepreneurship are difficult ones that can never be completely resolved.

Acknowledgements

The need for a book of this kind became apparent as a result of teaching on the MA course in entrepreneurship at the University of Reading.

Many people have provided advice on the selection of material, and I am grateful to them all. Special thanks are due to David Storey for his comments on an early outline, and for directing my attention to a number of the readings included in this volume. John Cantwell and Geoffrey Jones provided detailed comments on the final draft. Feedback from the MA students, and from the publisher, has also been very useful.

References

Babbage, C. (1832), *On the Economy of Machinery and Manufactures,* London: Charles Knight.
Brenner, R. (1987), *Rivalry: In Business, Science, among Nations,* Cambridge: Cambridge University Press.
Coase, R.H. (1937), 'The Nature of the Firm', *Economica* (New Series), **4,** 386–405.
Kaldor, N. (1934), 'The Equilibrium of the Firm', *Economic Journal,* **44,** 60–76.
Myrdal, G. (1957), *Economic Theory and Underdeveloped Regions,* London: Duckworth.
Reekie, W.D. (1979), *Industry, Prices and Markets,* Deddington, Oxon: Philip Allan.
Ricketts, M. (1987), *The Economics of Business Enterprise: New Approaches to the Firm,* Brighton: Wheatsheaf.
Say, J.B. (1803), *A Treatise on Political Economy: Or, the Production, Distribution and Consumption of Wealth,* New York: Augustus M. Kelley (1964).

Part I
Economic Theory

Risk and Uncertainty

Chapter XIII

*The circulation and exchange of goods and merchandise
as well as their production are carried on in
Europe by Undertakers, and at a risk*

The Farmer is an undertaker who promises to pay to the
Landowner, for his Farm or Land, a fixed sum of money

(generally supposed to be equal in value to the third of the produce) without assurance of the profit he will derive from this enterprise. He employs part of the land to feed flocks, produce corn, wine, hay, etc. according to his judgment without being able to foresee which of these will pay best. The price of these products will depend partly on the weather, partly on the demand; if corn is abundant relatively to consumption it will be dirt cheap, if there is scarcity it will be dear. Who can foresee the number of births and deaths of the people in a State in the course of the year? Who can foresee the increase or reduction of expense which may come about in the families? And yet the price of the Farmer's produce depends naturally upon these unforeseen circumstances, and consequently he conducts the enterprise of his farm at an uncertainty.

The City consumes more than half the farmer's produce. He carries it to Market there or sells it in the Market of the nearest Town, or perhaps a few individuals set up as Carriers themselves. These bind themselves to pay the Farmer a fixed price for his produce, that of the market price of the day, to get in the City an uncertain price which should however defray the cost of carriage and leave them a profit. But the daily variation in the price of produce in the City, though not considerable, makes their profit uncertain.

The Undertaker or Merchant who carries the products of the Country to the City cannot stay there to sell them retail as they are consumed. No City family will burden itself with the purchase all at once of the produce it may need, each family being susceptible of increase or decrease in number and in consumption or at least varying in the choice of produce it will consume. Wine is almost the only article of consumption stocked in a family. In any case the majority of citizens who live from day to day and yet are the largest consumers cannot lay in a stock of country produce.

For this reason many people set up in a City as Merchants or Undertakers, to buy the country produce from those who bring it or to order it to be brought on their account. They pay a certain price following that of the place where they purchase it, to resell wholesale or retail at an uncertain price.

Such Undertakers are the wholesalers in Wool and Corn, Bakers, Butchers, Manufacturers and Merchants of all kinds who buy country produce and materials to work them up and resell them gradually as the Inhabitants require them.

These Undertakers can never know how great will be the demand in their City, nor how long their customers will buy of them since their rivals will try all sorts of means to attract customers from them. All this causes so much uncertainty among these Undertakers that every day one sees some of them become bankrupt.

The Manufacturer who has bought wool from the Merchant or direct from the Farmer cannot foretell the profit he will make in selling his cloths and stuffs to the Merchant Taylor. If the latter have not a reasonable sale he will not load himself with the cloths and stuffs of the Manufacturer, especially if those stuffs cease to be in the fashion.

The Draper is an Undertaker who buys cloths and stuffs from the Manufacturer at a certain price to sell them again at an uncertain price, because he cannot foresee the extent of the demand. He can of course fix a price and stand out against selling unless he gets it, but if his customers leave him to buy cheaper from another, he will be eaten up by expenses while waiting to sell at the price he demands, and that will ruin him as soon as or sooner than if he sold without profit.

Shopkeepers and retailers of every kind are Undertakers who buy at a certain price and sell in their Shops or the Markets at an uncertain price. What encourages and maintains these Undertakers in a State is that the Consumers who are their Customers prefer paying a little more to get what they want ready to hand in small quantities rather than lay in a stock and that most of them have not the means to lay in such a stock by buying at first hand.

All these Undertakers become consumers and customers one in regard to the other, the Draper of the Wine Merchant and vice versa. They proportion themselves in a State to the Customers or consumption. If there are too many Hatters in a City or in a street for the number of people who buy hats there, some who are least patronised must become bankrupt: if they be too few it will be a profitable Undertaking which will encourage new Hatters to open shops there and so it is that the Undertakers of all kinds adjust themselves to risks in a State.

All the other Undertakers like those who take charge of Mines, Theatres, Building, etc., the Merchants by sea and land, etc., Cook-shop keepers, Pastry Cooks, Inn-keepers, etc. as well as the Undertakers of their own Labour who need no Capital to establish themselves, like Journeymen artisans, Copper-smiths, Needlewomen, Chimney Sweeps, Water Carriers, live at uncertainty and proportion themselves to their customers. Master Craftsmen like Shoemakers, Taylors, Carpenters, Wigmakers, etc. who employ Journeymen according to the work they have, live at the same uncertainty since their customers may forsake them from one day to another: the Undertakers of their own labour in Art and Science, like Painters, Physicians, Lawyers, etc. live in the like uncertainty. If one Attorney or Barrister earn 5000 pounds sterling yearly in the service of his Clients or in his practice and another earn only 500 they may be considered as having so much uncertain wages from those who employ them.

It may perhaps be urged that Undertakers seek to snatch all they can in their calling and to get the better of their customers, but this is outside my subject.

By all these inductions and many others which might be made in a topic relating to all the Inhabitants of a State, it may be laid down that except the Prince and the Proprietors of Land, all the Inhabitants of a State are dependent; that they can be divided into two classes, Undertakers and Hired people; and that all the Undertakers are as it were on unfixed wages and the others on wages fixed so long as they receive them though their functions and ranks may be very unequal. The General who has his pay, the Courtier his pension and the Domestic servant who has wages all fall into this last class. All the rest are Undertakers, whether they set up with a capital to conduct their enterprise, or are Undertakers of their own labour without capital, and they may be regarded as living at uncertainty; the Beggars even and the Robbers are Undertakers of this class. Finally all the Inhabitants of a State derive their living and their advantages from the property of the Landowners and are dependent.

It is true, however, that if some person on high wages or some large Undertaker has saved capital or wealth, that is if he have stores of corn, wool, copper, gold, silver or some produce or merchandise in constant use or vent in a State, having an intrinsic or a real value, he may be justly considered independent so far as this capital goes. He may dispose of it to acquire a mortgage, and interest from Land and from Public loans secured upon Land: he may live still better than the small Landowners and even buy the Property of some of them.

But produce and merchandise, even gold and silver, are

much more subject to accident and loss than the owner-ship of land; and however one may have gained or saved them they are always derived from the land of actual Proprietors either by gain or by saving of the wages destined for one's subsistence.

The number of Proprietors of money in a large State is often considerable enough; and though the value of all the money which circulates in the State barely exceeds the ninth or tenth part of the value of the produce drawn from the soil yet, as the Proprietors of money lend con-siderable amounts for which they receive interest either by mortgage or the produce and merchandise of the State, the sums due to them usually exceed all the money in the State, and they often become so powerful a body that they would in certain cases rival the Proprietors of Lands if these last were not often equally Proprietors of money, and if the owners of large sums of money did not always seek to become Landowners themselves.

It is nevertheless always true that all the sums gained or saved have been drawn from the land of the actual Proprietors; but as many of these ruin themselves daily in a State and the others who acquire the property of their land take their place, the independence given by the ownership of Land applies only to those who keep the possession of it; and as all land has always an actual Master or Owner, I presume always that it is from their property that all the Inhabitants of the State derive their living and all their wealth. If these Proprietors confined themselves to living on their Rents it would be beyond question, and in that case it would be much more difficult for the other Inhabitants to enrich themselves at their Expence.

I will then lay it down as a principle that the Pro-prietors of Land alone are naturally independent in a State: that all the other Classes are dependent whether Undertakers or hired, and that all the exchange and circulation of the State is conducted by the medium of these Undertakers.

[2]

With the introduction of uncertainty — the fact of ignorance and necessity of acting upon opinion rather than
knowledge — into this Eden-like situation, its character
is completely changed. With uncertainty absent, man's
energies are devoted altogether to doing things; it is
doubtful whether intelligence itself would exist in such a
situation; in a world so built that perfect knowledge was
theoretically possible, it seems likely that all organic readjustments would become mechanical, all organisms
automata. With uncertainty present, doing things, the
actual execution of activity, becomes in a real sense a
secondary part of life; the primary problem or function
is deciding what to do and how to do it. The two most
important characteristics of social organization brought
about by the fact of uncertainty have already been noticed.
In the first place, goods are produced for a market, on the
basis of an entirely impersonal prediction of wants, not for
the satisfaction of the wants of the producers themselves.
The producer takes the responsibility of forecasting the
consumers' wants. In the second place, the work of forecasting and at the same time a large part of the technological direction and control of production are still further
concentrated upon a very narrow class of the producers,
and we meet with a new economic functionary, the entrepreneur.

When uncertainty is present and the task of deciding
what to do and how to do it takes the ascendancy over that
of execution, the internal organization of the productive
groups is no longer a matter of indifference or a mechanical
detail.[1] Centralization of this deciding and controlling
function is imperative, a process of "cephalization," such

[1] See above, chapter IV, p. 106, note.

as has taken place in the evolution of organic life, is inevitable, and for the same reasons as in the case of biological evolution. Let us consider this process and the circumstances which condition it. The order of attack on the problem is suggested by the classification worked out in chapter VII of the elements in uncertainty in regard to which men may in large measure differ independently.

In the first place, occupations differ in respect to the kind and amount of knowledge and judgment required for their successful direction as well as in the kind of abilities and tastes adapted to the routine operations. Productive groups or establishments now compete for managerial capacity as well as skill, and a considerable rearrangement of personnel is the natural result. The final adjustment will place each producer in the place where his particular combination of the two kinds of attributes seems to be most effective.

But a more important change is the tendency of the groups themselves to specialize, finding the individuals with the greatest managerial capacity of the requisite kinds and placing them in charge of the work of the group, submitting the activities of the other members to their direction and control. It need hardly be mentioned explicitly that the organization of industry depends on the fundamental fact that the intelligence of one person can be made to direct in a general way the routine manual and mental operations of others. It will also be taken into account that men differ in their powers of effective control over other men as well as in intellectual capacity to decide what should be done. In addition, there must come into play the diversity among men in degree of confidence in their judgment and powers and in disposition to act on their opinions, to "venture." This fact is responsible for the most fundamental change of all in the form of organization, the system under which the confident and venturesome "assume the risk" or "insure" the doubtful and timid by guaran-

270   RISK, UNCERTAINTY, AND PROFIT

teeing to the latter a specified income in return for an assignment of the actual results.

Uncertainty thus exerts a fourfold tendency to select men and specialize functions: (1) an adaptation of men to occupations on the basis of kind of knowledge and judgment; (2) a similar selection on the basis of degree of foresight, for some lines of activity call for this endowment in a very different degree from others; (3) a specialization within productive groups, the individuals with superior managerial ability (foresight and capacity of ruling others) being placed in control of the group and the others working under their direction; and (4) those with confidence in their judgment and disposition to "back it up" in action specialize in risk-taking. The close relations obtaining among these tendencies will be manifest. We have not separated confidence and venturesomeness at all, since they act along parallel lines and are little more than phases of the same faculty — just as courage and the tendency to minimize danger are proverbially commingled in all fields, though they are separable in thought. In addition the tendencies numbered (3) and (4) operate together. With human nature as we know it it would be impracticable or very unusual for one man to guarantee to another a definite result of the latter's actions without being given power to direct his work. And on the other hand the second party would not place himself under the direction of the first without such a guaranty. The result is a "double contract" of the type famous in the history of the evasion of usury laws. It seems evident also that the system would not work at all if good judgment were not in fact generally associated with confidence in one's judgment on the part both of himself and others. That is, men's judgment of their own judgment and of others' judgment as to both kind and grade must in the large be much more right than wrong.[1]

[1] The statement implies that a man's judgment has in an effective

ENTERPRISE AND PROFIT   271

The result of this manifold specialization of function is *enterprise and the wage system of industry.* Its existence in the world is a direct result of the fact of uncertainty; our task in the remainder of this study is to examine this phenomenon in detail in its various phases and divers relations with the economic activities of man and the structure of society. It is not necessary or inevitable, not the only conceivable form of organization, but under certain conditions has certain advantages, and is capable of development in different degrees. The essence of enterprise is the specialization of the function of *responsible direction* of economic life, the neglected feature of which is the inseparability of these *two* elements, *responsibility* and *control.* Under the enterprise system, a special social class, the business men, direct economic activity; they are in the strict sense the producers, while the great mass of the population merely furnish them with productive services, placing their persons and their property at the disposal of this class; the entrepreneurs *also* guarantee to those who furnish productive services a fixed remuneration. Accurately to define these functions and trace them through the social structure will be a long task, for the specialization is never complete; but at the end of it we shall find that in a free society the two are essentially inseparable. Any degree of effective exercise of judgment, or making decisions, is in a free society coupled with a corresponding degree of uncertainty-bearing, of taking the responsibility for those decisions.

With the specialization of function goes also a differentiation of reward. The produce of society is similarly divided into *two kinds of income,* and two only, contractual income, which is essentially *rent,* as economic theory has described incomes, and residual income or *profit.* But the differentiation of contractual income, like that of profit, is

sense a true or objective value. This assumption will be justified by the further course of the argument.

never complete; neither variety is ever met with in a pure form, and every real income contains elements of both rent and profit. And with uncertainty present (the condition of the differentiation itself) it is not possible even to determine just how much of any income is of one kind and how much of the other; but a partial separation can be made, and the causal distinction between the two kinds is sharp and clear.

We may imagine a society in which uncertainty is absent transformed on the introduction of uncertainty into an enterprise organization. The readjustments will be carried out by the same trial-and-error methods under the same motives, the effort of each individual to better himself, which we have already described. The ideal or limiting condition constantly in view would still be the equalization of all available alternatives of conduct by each individual through the distribution of efforts and of expenditure of the proceeds of effort among the lines open. Under the new system labor and property services actually come into the market, become commodities and are bought and sold. They are thus brought into the comparative value scale and reduced to homogeneity in price terms with the fund of values made up of the direct means of want satisfaction.

Another feature of the new adjustment is that a condition of perfect equilibrium is no longer possible. Since productive arrangements are made on the basis of anticipations and the results actually achieved do not coincide with these as a usual thing, the oscillations will not settle down to zero. For all changes made by individuals relate to the established value scale and this price-system will be subject to fluctuations due to unforeseen causes; consequently individual changes in arrangements will continue indefinitely to take place. The experiments by which alone the value of human judgment is determined involve a proportion of failures or errors, are never complete, and in view of hu-

ENTERPRISE AND PROFIT   273

man mortality have constantly to be recommenced at the beginning.

We turn now to consider in broad outline the two types of individual income implied in the enterprise system of organization, contractual income and profit.[1] We shall try as hitherto to explain events by placing ourselves in the actual positions of the men acting or making decisions and interpreting their acts in terms of ordinary human motives. The setting of the problem is a free competitive situation in which all men and material agents are competing for employment, including all men at the time engaged as entrepreneurs, while all entrepreneurs are competing for productive services and at the same time all men are competing for positions as entrepreneurs. The essential fact in understanding the reaction to this situation is that men are acting, competing, on the basis of what they *think* of the *future*. To simplify the picture and make it concrete we shall as before assume that there exists some sort of grouping of men and things under the control of other men as entrepreneurs (a random grouping will do as a start) and that entrepreneurs and others are in competition as above stated.

The production-distribution system is worked out through offers and counter-offers, made on the basis of anticipations, of two kinds. The laborer asks what he thinks the entrepreneur will be able to pay, and in any case will not accept less than he can get from some other entrepreneur, or by turning entrepreneur himself. In the same way the entrepreneur offers to any laborer what he thinks he must in order to secure his services, and in any case not

---

[1] As already observed, the theoretical features of contractual income are those associated with rent in the conventional distributive analysis. From the point of view of our present assumptions, all productive goods being fixed in amount and in their distribution among the members of society, such incomes might naturally be called wages. As we have insisted that there is no significant causal or ethical difference in the sources of income it does not particularly matter what they are called.

more than he thinks the laborer will actually be worth to him, keeping in mind what he can get by turning laborer himself. The whole calculation is in the future; past and even present conditions operate only as grounds of prediction as to what may be anticipated.[1]

Since in a free market there can be but one price on any commodity, a general wage rate must result from this competitive bidding. The rate established may be described as the socially or competitively anticipated value of the laborer's product, using the term "product" in the sense of specific contribution, as already explained. It is not the opinion of the future held by either party to an employment bargain which determines the rate; these opinions merely set maximum and minimum limits outside of which the agreement cannot take place. The mechanism of price adjustment is the same as in any other market. There is always an established uniform rate, which is kept constantly at the point which equates the supply and demand. If at any moment there are more bidders willing to employ at a higher rate than there are employees willing to accept the established rate, the rate will rise accordingly, and similarly if there is a balance of opinion in the opposite direction. The final decision by any individual as to what to do is based on a comparison of a momentarily existing price with a subjective judgment of significance of the commodity. The judgment in this case relates to the indirect significance derived from a twofold estimate of the future, involving

---

[1] In actual society freedom of choice between employer and employee status depends normally on the possession of a minimum amount of capital. The degree of abstraction involved in assuming such freedom is not serious, however, since demonstrated ability can always get funds for business operations. A propertyless employer can make the contractual payments secure by insurance even when they may involve loss, and complete separation of the risk-taking and control function from that of furnishing productive services is possible if there is a high development of organization and a high code of business honor. But the conditions generally necessary in real life for the giving of effective guarantees must also be taken into account as we proceed.

both technological and price uncertainties. The employer in deciding whether to offer the current wage, and the employee in deciding whether to accept it, must estimate the technical or physically measured product (specific contribution) of the labor and the price to be expected for that product when it comes upon the market. The estimation may involve two sorts of calculation or estimate of probability. The venture itself may be of the nature of a gamble, involving a large proportion of inherently unpredictable factors. In such a case the decision depends upon an "estimate" of an "objective probability" of success, or of a series of such probabilities corresponding to various degrees of success or failure. And normally, in the case of intelligent men, account will be taken of the probable "true value" of the estimates in the case of all estimated factors.

The meaning of the term "social" or "competitive" anticipation will now be clear. The question in the mind of either party to an employment agreement relates simply to the fact of a difference between the current standard of remuneration for the services being bargained for and his own estimate of their worth, discounted by probability allowances. The magnitude of the difference is altogether immaterial. The prospective employer may know absolutely that the service has a value to him ever so much greater than the price he is paying, but he will have to pay only the competitively established rate, and his purchase will affect this rate no more than if he were ever so hesitant about the bargain, just so he makes it. It is the general estimate of the magnitudes involved, in the sense of a "marginal" demand price, which fixes the actual current rate.

[3]

A General Equilibrium Entrepreneurial Theory of Firm Formation Based on Risk Aversion

Richard E. Kihlstrom

University of Illinois, Urbana-Champaign

Jean-Jacques Laffont

Laboratoire d'Économetrie, L'Ecole Polytechnique, Paris

We construct a theory of competitive equilibrium under uncertainty using an entrepreneurial model with historical roots in the work of Knight in the 1920s. Individuals possess labor which they can supply as workers to a competitive labor market or use as entrepreneurs in running a firm. All entrepreneurs have access to the same risky technology and receive all profits from their firms. In the equilibrium, more risk averse individuals become workers while the less risk averse become entrepreneurs. Less risk averse entrepreneurs run larger firms and economy-wide increases in risk aversion reduce the equilibrium wage. A dynamic process of firm entry and exit is stable. The equilibrium is efficient only if all entrepreneurs are risk neutral. Inefficiencies in the number of firms and in the allocation of labor to firms are traced to inefficiencies in the risk allocation caused by institutional constraints on risk trading. In a second best sense which accounts for these constraints, the equilibrium is efficient.

I. Introduction

The recent work on the economics of uncertainty has failed to achieve general agreement as to the goals which motivate firm behavior under

Research support from the National Science Foundation under grant SOC-76-11583 is gratefully acknowledged. Much of this work was completed while Kihlstrom was a visitor at the Laboratoire d'Econometrie, L'Ecole Polytechnique. Their support for that visit is greatly appreciated. Finally, we also would like to thank Jean Michel Grandmont, Sergiu Hart, Glenn Loury, Robert Lucas, Ed Prescott, Sherwin Rosen, and Hugo Sonnenschein for helpful comments.

[*Journal of Political Economy*, 1979, vol. 87, no. 4]

uncertainty. The criteria guiding firm decision making which have been proposed and studied in the existing literature include expected profit maximization and expected utility of profit maximization as well as maximization of the firm's stock market value. Difficulties with each of these criteria have led to a discussion ("Symposium on the Optimality of Competitive Capital Markets" [1974]) of the conditions under which there exists a criteria for firm decision making which achieves unanimous approval of stockholders. They have also led to the study of other more sophisticated criteria for firm decision making. The paper of Drèze (1974) is one in which this latter approach is taken. Each of these subsequent approaches has achieved only limited success. For example, unanimity can be achieved only in limited technological circumstances. Similarly, the equilibria of Drèze are not always efficient in the "second best" sense of Diamond (1967).

In this paper we construct a competitive general equilibrium theory of the firm under uncertainty which is based on an entrepreneurial model having its historical roots in the work of Knight (1921). The entrepreneurial model permits us simultaneously to use the expected utility maximization criterion and to provide a justification for its use. This is accomplished by assuming that for each firm there is an expected utility maximizing entrepreneur who makes decisions for the firm. Furthermore, the model uses a free-entry assumption to endogenously determine the number of firms and the identity of the entrepreneurs who run them. It also permits us to identify the individual characteristics of individuals who choose to become entrepreneurs.

In the model, individuals are assumed to have a choice between operating a risky firm or working for a riskless wage. There are, of course, many factors which should influence this choice. The most important ones would include entrepreneurial ability, labor skills, attitudes toward risk, and initial access to the capital required to create a firm. The present paper focuses on risk aversion as the determinant which explains who becomes an entrepreneur and who works as a laborer. The equilibrium which is shown to exist has the property that less risk averse individuals become entrepreneurs, while the more risk averse work as laborers.

In addition to providing an explanation for the identity of entrepreneurs, the entrepreneurial model can also be used to study several issues of traditional interest to economists. One of these is the process of firm entry and exit.

Specifically, using the model described below, it is possible to analyze the dynamics of firm entry and exit in a general equilibrium context. This can be done using a formalization of a tâtonnement process which is analogous to that commonly used to study the stability of competitive equilibrium. While our stability analysis is less complete and more special than the analysis in the stability literature for competitive equilibrium, it nevertheless introduces an element, specifically firm entry and exit, which this literature was unable to incorporate. Furthermore, this element is introduced while retaining the general equilibrium framework and the basic price-adjustment process. In our general equilibrium process, as in the tâtonnement process used in the competitive equilibrium literature, prices (in our case, wages) adjust to (labor) market disequilibrium by rising when there is excess supply. Earlier formalizations of the entry-exit process, specifically, those in Quandt and Howrey (1968) and Brock (1972), were partial equilibrium models. They were also based on formalizations of the adjustment process which, while similar in spirit, differed in detail from the tâtonnement price-adjustment process used in the competitive equilibrium framework. For example, in the papers by Quandt and Howrey and by Brock, the dynamic variable is the number of firms in an industry. The industry grows when profits (or excess profits) are positive; it contracts when profits are negative.

Another traditional question which can be investigated using the entrepreneurial model concerns the determinants of the distribution of firm size. Specifically, an entrepreneur's attitude toward risk can be related to the size of the firm which he operates. While it might be conjectured that more risk averse entrepreneurs run smaller firms, this is not always true. However, it does follow when the production function satisfies certain conditions which are spelled out in theorem 3 below.

It is also possible to use this model to study one determinant of the distribution of income between workers and entrepreneurs. Specifically, it can be shown that, under certain conditions, the equilibrium wage level would be depressed if the economy's population became more risk averse.

Finally, it is possible to investigate the efficiency of the equilibrium of the entrepreneurial model. In general the equilibrium is inefficient and the inefficiency takes three forms: risks are maldistributed, firms are operated at the wrong levels, and there is an inappropriate number of firms. It is shown, however, that all of these forms of inefficiency occur because there are institutional constraints embodied in the model which prohibit an efficient allocation of risks when entrepreneurs are risk averse. This is seen in two ways. First, the equilibrium is efficient if, in equilibrium, all entrepreneurs are risk neutral. Second, we follow Diamond (1967) and Radner (1968) and investigate the efficiency of equilibrium in a second best or "limited" sense which permits a less than completely efficient allocation of risks. Although the "limited efficiency" approach taken in this paper is in the same spirit as those adopted by Diamond and by Radner, it employs a different concept of limited efficiency than the ones they employed. Thus we accept the specific institutional constraints imposed by our equilibrium model on the distribution of risk and ask only that, given these constraints, all other decisions be made efficiently (Pareto optimally). The constraints on risk trading imposed in taking this approach are, in fact, stronger than those introduced by Diamond and by Radner. It is possible, however, to show that if, in defining limited efficiency, these constraints are imposed, then the equilibrium is efficient in the limited sense.

Because all of the inefficiencies which may arise in an equilibrium can be traced to the institutional constraints on risk trading, it is reasonable to conjecture that the efficiency properties of the equilibrium will be substantially improved by the introduction of at least some market opportunities for risk sharing among entrepreneurs and between entrepreneurs and workers. The introduction of a stock market in which the entrepreneur can raise capital for the purpose of financing his input purchases would be one way of providing additional opportunities for risk sharing. Sharecropping arrangements provide another device by which risks are, in fact, often shared. This is especially true in agricultural economies. The present paper does not investigate the issues which arise when either of these risk sharing possibilities becomes available. In a subsequent paper (Kihlstrom and Laffont 1978), we have, however, succeeded in studying these extensions of the entrepreneurial model discussed here. The emphasis there is on the stock market as a device for risk sharing. It is specifically shown that the introduction of a stock market does, indeed, result in equilibrium allocations which are efficient in a stronger sense than that considered here. Specifically they are efficient in the sense of Diamond.

This paper concludes with a brief summary of our results and a discussion of their relationship to Knight's above-mentioned entrepreneurial theory.

II. The Model

The set of agents is identified with the interval $[0,1]$. If $\alpha \in [0,1]$, individual α has the von Neumann Morgenstern utility function $u(I,\alpha)$ where I represents income, and $I \in [0,\infty)$. For all $I \geq 0$, the first and second derivatives u_I and u_{II} exist and are continuous. The marginal utility u_I is positive and nonincreasing, that is, $\mu_{II} \leq 0$. Thus all agents are risk averse or indifferent to risk.

We also assume that the Arrow (1971)-Pratt (1964) absolute risk aversion measure is nondecreasing in α. More precisely, if α exceeds β, then agent α is at least as risk averse as agent β in the sense that

$$r(I,\alpha) = - \frac{u_{II}(I,\alpha)}{u_{I}(I,\alpha)} \geqq - \frac{u_{II}(I,\beta)}{u_{I}(I,\beta)} = r(I,\beta) \qquad (1)$$

for all $I \in (0, \infty)$.

Each agent can become an entrepreneur and use without cost a technology defined by a continuous production function $y = g(L,x)$ where $y \geqq 0$ is output, $L \geqq 0$ is the labor input, and x is the value taken by a nondegenerate random parameter $\tilde{x}$ with support $[0, \bar{x}]$, $0 < \bar{x} < +\infty$.

The marginal product g_L is assumed to be continuous and positive on $[0,+\infty) \times (0, \bar{x}]$. The second derivative is continuous and nonpositive on $[0,+\infty) \times [0, \bar{x}]$. Thus g exhibits nonincreasing returns to scale for each x. In addition, $g(0,x) = g(L,0) = 0$ for all $x \in [0, \bar{x}]$ and $L \in [0,+\infty)$, while $g(L,x) > 0$ on $(0,+\infty) \times (0, \bar{x}]$.

A variety of interpretations of the random variables $\tilde{x}$ is possible. In all of these interpretations, the stochastic distribution of $\tilde{x}$ is assumed to be the same for all firms. On the one extreme we can assume that the random variables which determine the output of each firm are stochastically independent. At the other extreme they can be perfectly correlated. In this case, not only is the distribution of $\tilde{x}$ the same for all firms, but the same random variable $\tilde{x}$ influences the output of all firms. Intermediate cases occur when the $\tilde{x}$'s are correlated but not perfectly correlated. In each of these alternative interpretations, all individuals are assumed to have the same beliefs about the distribution of $\tilde{x}$, that is, the distribution of $\tilde{x}$ is objective.

The price of output is 1 and labor is hired at a competitive wage w. It is assumed that the demands of entrepreneurship preclude additional work by agents who choose to operate a firm. Thus agents have a choice. They can become entrepreneurs and receive an uncertain income or they can work and receive the market wage w. If an individual becomes an entrepreneur and employs L workers he will receive profits equal to

$$g(L,\tilde{x}) - wL. \qquad (2)$$

To avoid the difficulties associated with the problem of bankruptcy we assume that all individuals begin with A units of income and that they are unable to hire workers who cannot be paid if $\tilde{x} = 0$. Thus L must be less than or equal to A/w.

An individual who becomes an entrepreneur will choose to employ

$L(w,\alpha)$ workers where $L(w,\alpha)$ is the L value in $[0, A/w]$ which maximizes

$$Eu\left(A + g(L,\tilde{x}) - wL, \alpha\right). \tag{3}$$

Our assumptions on u and g guarantee that $L(w,\alpha)$ exists. If either $u_{ll} < 0$ or $g_{LL} < 0$, then $L(w,\alpha)$ will be unique. When entrepreneur α faces the wage w and employs $L(w,\alpha)$ workers, his profits are random and equal to

$$\tilde{\pi}(w,\alpha) = g\left(L(w,\alpha), \tilde{x}\right) - wL(w,\alpha). \tag{4}$$

If the wage is w, agent α will choose to be an entrepreneur when

$$Eu\left(A + \tilde{\pi}(w,\alpha), \alpha\right) \geqq u(A + w,\alpha). \tag{5}$$

He will be a worker at wage w if

$$Eu\left(A + \tilde{\pi}(w,\alpha), \alpha\right) \leqq u(A + w, \alpha), \tag{6}$$

and he will be indifferent if the equality holds in (5) and (6).

Equilibrium is reached when the labor market clears. At the equilibrium wage, the labor demanded by all agents who choose to become entrepreneurs equals that supplied by agents who choose to enter the labor market.

Formally, an equilibrium is a partition $\{\Delta,\Gamma\}$ of $[0,1]$ and a wage w, that is, a pair $(\{\Delta,\Gamma\},w)$; for which

(E.1)   labor supply equals labor demand in the sense that

$$\int_\Delta L(w,\alpha)\mu(d\alpha) = \mu(\Gamma)$$

where μ is Lebesgue measure and

(E.2)   for all $\alpha \in \Delta$ (5) holds and for all $\alpha \in \Gamma$ (6) holds.

III.   The Existence and Uniqueness of Equilibrium

We can now prove that an equilibrium exists. The first step is to define $w(\alpha)$, the certainty equivalent wage which makes agent α indifferent between the two activities—work and entrepreneurship. Formally, $w(\alpha)$ is defined by

$$Eu\left(A + \tilde{\pi}\left(w(\alpha), \alpha\right), \alpha\right) = u\left(A + w(\alpha), \alpha\right). \tag{7}$$

The properties of $w(\alpha)$ are established in the lemma which follows. These properties will permit us to describe the structure of the equilibrium in a way which simplifies the existence proof. Further interpretive remarks follow the formal statement of the lemma.

Lemma

Assume that for each I, $r(I,\alpha)$ is an increasing function of α.[1] Also assume that either $g_{LL} < 0$ or $u_{II} < 0$. Then:

  i) For each $\alpha \epsilon [0,1]$, $Eu(A + \bar{\pi}(w,\alpha), \alpha) - u(A + w, \alpha)$ is a continuous monotonically decreasing function of w.
 ii) $w(\alpha)$ is a well-defined function of α, that is, for each $\alpha \epsilon [0,1]$, $w(\alpha)$ exists and is unique. In addition $w(\alpha) > 0$.
iii) If $w > (<) w(\alpha)$, then $Eu(A + \bar{\pi}(w,\alpha), \alpha) < (>) \mu(A + w, \alpha)$.
 iv) If $\alpha > \beta$, then $w(\alpha) < w(\beta)$.
  v) If $\beta > (<) \alpha$, then $Eu(A + \bar{\pi}(w(\alpha), \beta), \beta) < (>) u(A + w(\alpha), \beta)$.
 vi) If $0 < w < w(\beta)$, then $L(w,\beta) > 0$.

This is true, in particular, if $w = w(\alpha)$ where $\alpha > \beta$.

Remark 1

Result iv asserts that more risk averse individuals are induced to become workers at lower wages than less risk averse agents. In order to interpret result v, note that agent α will be the marginal entrepreneur if the equilibrium wage is $w(\alpha)$. Result v asserts that all individuals who are more (less) risk averse than the marginal entrepreneur will be workers (entrepreneurs). This result implies that in any equilibrium, there will be a marginal entrepreneur $\hat{\alpha}$ for whom $w(\hat{\alpha})$ is the equilibrium wage. The set of entrepreneurs Δ will be the interval $[0,\hat{\alpha}]$ and the set of workers Γ will be $(\hat{\alpha},1]$. The problem of finding an equilibrium then reduces to the problem of finding a marginal entrepreneur $\hat{\alpha}$ for whom E.1 holds when $w = w(\hat{\alpha})$, $\Delta = (0,\hat{\alpha}]$, and $\Gamma = (\hat{\alpha},1]$, that is, for whom $\int_0^{\hat{\alpha}} L(w(\hat{\alpha}),\alpha)\mu(d\alpha) = 1 - \hat{\alpha}$.

PROOF.—(i) The assumptions made about u and g guarantee that $Eu(A + g(L,\tilde{x}) - wL, \alpha)$ is a strictly concave continuous function of L and a continuous function of w.

To prove monotonicity, note first that for each nonnegative L, the monotonicity of u implies that

$$Eu(A + g(L,\tilde{x}) - wL, \alpha) < Eu(A + g(L,\tilde{x}) - w'L, \alpha) \qquad (8)$$

when $w > w'$. Maximizing over L on each side of inequality (8) implies the inequality

[1] If $r(I,\alpha)$ is nondecreasing but not strictly increasing the strict inequalities in iii, iv, and v are replaced by weak inequalities.

$$Eu\big(A + \tilde{\pi}(w,\alpha),\, \alpha\big) = \max_{\frac{A}{w} \geqq L \geqq 0} Eu\big(A + g(L,\tilde{x}) - wL,\, \alpha\big)$$

$$\leqq \max_{\frac{A}{w'} \geqq L \geqq 0} Eu\big(A + g(L,\tilde{x}) - w'L,\, \alpha\big) \qquad (9)$$

$$= Eu\big(A + \tilde{\pi}(w',\alpha),\, \alpha\big)$$

when $w > w'$. Thus $Eu\big(A + \tilde{\pi}(w,\alpha),\, \alpha\big)$ is nonincreasing and $Eu\big(A + \tilde{\pi}(w,\alpha),\, \alpha\big) - u(A + w,\alpha)$ is monotonically decreasing.

ii) It is easily seen that $Eu\big(A + \tilde{\pi}(w,\alpha),\, \alpha\big) - u(A + w,\alpha) > 0$ when $w \simeq 0$. If, on the other hand, w is large, then

$$g(L,x) - wL \leqq \max_{\substack{0 \leqq L \leqq \frac{A}{w} \\ 0 \leqq x \leqq \bar{x}}} g(L,x) \simeq 0 \qquad (10)$$

and equation (6) will hold. Because of the continuity established in i, the intermediate value theorem implies the existence of a positive wage $w(\alpha)$ which satisfies (7). The monotonicity established in i implies the uniqueness of $w(\alpha)$. Monotonicity also implies inequality iii. Figure 1 illustrates the situation.

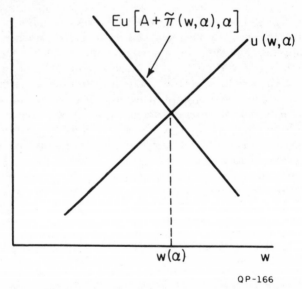

$$Eu\left[A + \tilde{\tilde{\pi}}(w,\alpha),\alpha\right]$$

$$u(w,\alpha)$$

$$w(\alpha) \qquad\qquad w$$

QP-166

Fig. 1

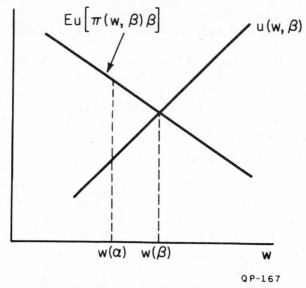

$$Eu\left[\pi(w, \beta)\beta\right]$$

$$u(w, \beta)$$

$$w(\alpha) \quad w(\beta)$$

$$w$$

QP-167

FIG. 2

iv) We use the fact that $w(\alpha)$ is the certainty equivalent of $\tilde{\pi}(w(\alpha), \alpha)$. We also define $w(\alpha,\beta)$ to be the certainty equivalent of $\tilde{\pi}(w(\alpha), \alpha)$ for agent β. Pratt's (1964) theorem 1 is now applied to prove that $\beta > (<) \alpha$ implies $w(\alpha,\beta) < (>) w(\alpha)$. The monotonicity of $u(w,\beta)$ in w then guarantees that

$$Eu\big(A + \tilde{\pi}(w(\alpha), \alpha), \beta\big) = u\big(A + w(\alpha,\beta), \beta\big) < (>) u\big(A + w(\alpha), \beta\big) \tag{11}$$

when $\beta > (<) \alpha$.

Now note that, by definition of $\tilde{\pi}(w,\beta)$,

$$Eu\big(A + \tilde{\pi}(w(\alpha), \beta), \beta\big) \geqq Eu\big(A + \tilde{\pi}(w(\alpha), \alpha), \beta\big). \tag{12}$$

When $\beta < \alpha$ inequalities (11) and (12) combine to yield

$$Eu\big(A + \tilde{\pi}(w(\alpha), \beta), \beta\big) > u\big(A + w(\alpha), \beta\big). \tag{13}$$

Figure 2 illustrates what is easily proven; that inequality iv is a consequence of inequality (13), the equality defining $w(\beta)$, and the fact that $Eu\big(\tilde{\pi}(w,\beta), \beta\big) - u(w,\beta)$ decreases monotonically in w.

v) Inequality v follows immediately from iii and iv.

vi) Since iii implies that $Eu\big(A + \tilde{\pi}(w, \beta)\beta\big) > u\big(A + w, \beta\big)$, if $w(\beta) > w$, $\tilde{\pi}(w, \beta) = g\big(L(w, \beta), \tilde{x}\big) - wL(w, \beta)$ must exceed $w > 0$ with positive probability. This is impossible if $L(w, \beta) = 0$. ||

In the discussion of existence, the analysis is restricted to cases which satisfy assumption A: $u(I,\alpha)$ is everywhere a continuous function of α.

THEOREM 1.[2]—Assume that for each I, $r(I,\alpha)$ is a nondecreasing function of α. Also assume that either $g_{LL} < 0$ or $u_{II} < 0$. Under assumption A an equilibrium exists.

PROOF.—Under assumption A it can be shown that our assumptions guarantee that $L(w,\alpha)$ and $w(\alpha)$ are continuous functions of α on $[0,1]$. Thus for each $w \in [w(0),w(1)]$ and $\hat{\alpha} \in [0,1]$, $\int_0^{\hat{\alpha}} L(w,\alpha)d\alpha$ exists. We can now find an $\hat{\alpha}^*$ such that

$$\int_0^{\hat{\alpha}^*} L(w(\hat{\alpha}^*), \alpha)d\alpha = 1 - \hat{\alpha}^*. \tag{14}$$

Note that $\int_0^{\hat{\alpha}} L(w(\hat{\alpha}), \alpha)d\alpha - (1 - \hat{\alpha})$ is a continuous function of $\hat{\alpha}$ which is negative when $\hat{\alpha} = 0$ and positive (by vi of the lemma) when $\hat{\alpha} = 1$. The intermediate value theorem implies the existence of an $\hat{\alpha}^*$ satisfying 14.

Now we can define

$$(\{\Delta,\Gamma\}, w) = (\{[0,\hat{\alpha}^*], (\hat{\alpha}^*,1], w(\hat{\alpha}^*)) \tag{15}$$

or

$$(\{\Delta,\Gamma\}, w) = (\{[0,\hat{\alpha}^*), [\hat{\alpha}^*,1], w(\hat{\alpha}^*)).$$

For these entrepreneur, worker, wage combinations v of the lemma implies that condition E.2 holds while E.1 reduces to (14). ||

The next theorem gives conditions under which the equilibrium is unique.

THEOREM 2.—Assume that for each I, $r(I,\alpha)$ is a nondecreasing function of α. Also assume that either $g_{LL} < 0$ or $u_{II} < 0$. If, in addition, $L(w,\alpha)$ is a decreasing function of w, then the equilibrium is unique.

PROOF.—Because of the lemma, and for reasons discussed in remark 1, the equilibrium occurs at an $\hat{\alpha}$ for which (14) holds. In addition, the lemma implies that $L(w,\alpha) > 0$ for all α and all $w \leqslant w(\alpha)$, and that $w(\hat{\alpha}) \geqslant w(\hat{\alpha}')$ if $\hat{\alpha} < \hat{\alpha}'$. Then since $L(w,\alpha)$ is a decreasing function of w, $\hat{\alpha} < \hat{\alpha}'$ implies

$$\int_0^{\hat{\alpha}'} L(w(\hat{\alpha}'),\alpha)d\alpha = \int_0^{\hat{\alpha}} L(w(\hat{\alpha}'),\alpha)d\alpha$$

$$+ \int_{\hat{\alpha}}^{\hat{\alpha}'} L(w(\hat{\alpha}'),\alpha)d\alpha > \int_0^{\hat{\alpha}} L(w(\hat{\alpha}),\alpha)d\alpha.$$

---

[2] This theorem can be proved without assumption A. The assumption is made solely to permit a simple existence proof.

Thus labor demand at $w(\hat{\alpha})$, $\int_0^{\hat{\alpha}} L(w(\hat{\alpha}),\alpha)d\alpha$, is a strictly increasing function of $\hat{\alpha}$. Furthermore, labor supply at $w(\hat{\alpha})$, $(1 - \hat{\alpha})$, is a strictly decreasing function of $\hat{\alpha}$. Therefore excess demand at $w(\hat{\alpha})$, $\int_0^{\hat{\alpha}} L(w(\hat{\alpha}),\alpha)d\alpha - (1 - \hat{\alpha})$, is a strictly increasing function of $\hat{\alpha}$ and there can be only one $\hat{\alpha}$ at which excess demand can equal zero, that is, at which (14) can hold. ‖

Conditions under which $L(w,\alpha)$ is a decreasing function of the wage w are discussed in remark 4 at the end of the following section on comparative statics.

IV. Comparative Statics

Having established the existence of an equilibrium, it is now possible to study its properties. Specifically, we can first ask how a firm's size, as measured by its labor demand, is related to the risk averseness of the entrepreneur running the firm. It might be expected that more risk averse entrepreneurs operate smaller firms, that is, use less labor than less risk averse entrepreneurs. Theorem 3 gives conditions under which this expected result obtains. The conditions require that a change in x must affect output and the marginal product of labor in the same way; if an increase in x raises output it must also raise the marginal product of labor. One important special case in which this condition holds occurs when the uncertainty enters multiplicatively

$$g((L, x) = xh(L).^3 \tag{16}$$

THEOREM 3.—Assume that $L(w,\alpha) < A/w$. If $g(L,x)$ and $g_L(L,x)$ are both monotonically increasing or both monotonically decreasing functions of x, then $L(w,\alpha)$ is a monotonically decreasing function of α.

The proof is essentially the same as that given in Baron (1970) and is not reproduced.

We can now ask to what extent it is possible to describe the influence of individual attitudes toward risk and of technological parameters on the equilibrium. In general, not much can be said about the effect of these parameters on the number of firms, a variable of particular interest. But for the purpose of studying the distribution of wealth between workers and entrepreneurs it is important to know how these parameters influence the wage. What can be shown is that, under certain reasonable conditions, an increase in individual risk aversion reduces the wage.

[3] This is the case considered by Baron (1970). In Baron's paper, x is interpreted as price. Equation (16) is also included in the class of cases studied by Diamond. In Diamond's terminology, (16) represents a case of stochastic constant returns to scale.

THEOREM 4.—If (i) in equilibrium, all entrepreneurs are identical, (ii) either $g_{LL} < 0$ or $u_{II} < 0$, (iii) $g(L,x)$ and $g_L(L,x)$ are both monotonically increasing (or decreasing) functions of x, and (iv) $L(w,\hat{\alpha})$ is an interior solution and a decreasing function of w, then an increase in the Arrow-Pratt absolute risk aversion measure $r(I,\hat{\alpha})$ for all I, lowers the equilibrium wage.

Remark 2

The intuitive basis for this result is as follows. Since, in equilibrium, workers are the most risk averse individuals, an economy-wide increase in risk aversion increases the supply of workers and this tends to lower the wage. This tendency is reinforced by demand changes implied by theorem 3 which applies because of assumption iii. Specifically, theorem 3 implies that an increase in the entrepreneurs' aversion to risk reduces the demand for labor.

PROOF.—If, in equilibrium, $L(w,\hat{\alpha})$ is an interior solution, the first-order maximization condition for the marginal entrepreneur is

$$Eu_I(A + g(L,\tilde{x}) - wL, \hat{\alpha})g_L(L,\tilde{x}) = Eu_I(A + g(L,\tilde{x}) - wL, \hat{\alpha})w \quad (17)$$

where $L = L(w,\hat{\alpha})$.

We also have

$$u(A + w, \hat{\alpha}) = Eu(A + g(L,\tilde{x}) - wL, \hat{\alpha}) \quad (18)$$

at $L = L(w,\hat{\alpha})$.

The equilibrium conditions (17) and (18) imply relationships between L and w which are described in figure 3. The relationship implied by (17) is downward sloping because of assumption iii. As indicated, (18) implies that w is a function of L which reaches its minimum when it intersects the line defined by (17). This is proved by differentiating (18) implicitly to obtain

$$\frac{dw}{dL} = -\frac{Eu_I(A + g(L,\tilde{x}) - wL, \hat{\alpha})\,[g_L(L,\tilde{x}) - w]}{u_I(A + w,\hat{\alpha}) + Eu_I(A + g(L,\tilde{x}) - wL, \hat{\alpha})L}. \quad (19)$$

The differentiation is justified by the implicit function theorem because the denominator in (19) is positive. The numerator is zero when (17) holds. The second order sufficient condition for the entrepreneurial maximization problem is satisfied because of condition ii. Thus, as reflected in figure 3, the numerator in (19) is positive (negative) and dw/dL is negative (positive) when $L < (>) L(w, \hat{\alpha})$.

Now suppose that $r(I,\hat{\alpha})$ increases for every I, then theorem 3 above guarantees that $L(w,\hat{\alpha})$ is lower for each w. Also, reasoning similar to that employed in the proof of the lemma guarantees that for each L,

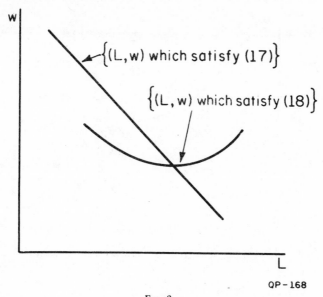

Fig. 3

the wage level w at which (18) holds is also reduced. Thus the r increase affects the relationships between L and w implied by (17) and (18) as shown in figure 4. As a result the equilibrium wage must decline. ||

We can now make several observations which we formalize as remarks.

Remark 3

A similar proof applies if $L(w,\hat{\alpha})$ is always an increasing function of w.

Remark 4

There are several important cases in which $L(w,\hat{\alpha})$ is indeed a decreasing function of w. These occur when either (a) $r(I,\hat{\alpha})$ is a constant function of I, (b) $g(L,x)$ and $g_L(L,x)$ are both increasing (or both decreasing) functions of x and $r(I,\hat{\alpha})$ is a nonincreasing function of I, or (c) $g(L,x)$ satisfies (16) and

$$-\frac{I u_{II}(A + I, \hat{\alpha})}{u_I(A + I, \hat{\alpha})} \leqq 1$$

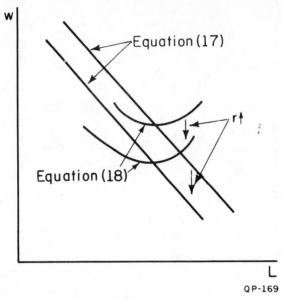

FIG. 4

for all I. The condition imposed on $u(\cdot, \hat{\alpha})$ in c asserts that when $u(A + I, \hat{\alpha})$ is considered as a function of I it has Arrow-Pratt relative risk aversion less than or equal to one.

PROOF OF REMARK 4.—Implicitly differentiating (17) we obtain

$$\frac{dL}{dw} = -\frac{-LEu_{II}(A + g(L,\tilde{x}) - wL, \hat{\alpha})[g_L(L,\tilde{x}) - w]}{D}$$
$$-\frac{-Eu_I(A + g(L,\tilde{x}) - wL, \hat{\alpha})}{D} \quad (20)$$

where $D = Eu_{II}(A + g(L,\tilde{x}) - wL, \hat{\alpha})[g_L(L,\tilde{x}) - w]^2 + Eu_I(A + g(L,\tilde{x}) - wL, \hat{\alpha})g_{LL}(L,\tilde{x})$. The second-order condition for the entrepreneur's maximization problem (which is implied by condition ii of theorem 4) guarantees that the implicit function theorem applies to justify the implicit differentiation. This condition also asserts that the denominator in (20) is negative. In general, the sign of the numerator in (20) is ambiguous since the first term is ambiguous. (The second term is negative.) In case a, however, the first term is

$$LEu_{II}(A + g(L,\tilde{x}) - wL,\hat{\alpha})[g_L(L,\tilde{x}) - w]$$
$$= -rLEu_I(A + g(L,\tilde{x}) - wL,\hat{\alpha})[g_L(L,\tilde{x}) - w] \quad (21)$$

which equals zero because of the first-order condition (17). Thus in case a, the numerator is negative as is dL/dw.

THEORY OF FIRM FORMATION 733

In case b, the first term can be shown to be nonpositive by an argument similar to that used by Baron (1970).

In case c, the fact that $h''(L) \leqq 0$ can be used to obtain

$$[h'(L)L\tilde{x} - wL] \leqq h(L)\tilde{x} - wL \tag{22}$$

and

$$\begin{aligned} -u_{II}(A + h(L)\tilde{x} - wL, \hat{\alpha})[h'(L)L\tilde{x} - wL] \\ \leqq -u_{II}(A + h(L)\tilde{x} - wL, \hat{\alpha})[h(L)\tilde{x} - wL]. \end{aligned} \tag{23}$$

When this inequality is combined with c, the numerator in (20) is negative. $||$

V. Dynamics

In this brief section, we consider the stability of a tâtonnement adjustment process similar to that used in studying the stability of competitive equilibrium. In this process, the wage is assumed to adjust to labor market disequilibrium by rising when there is excess demand and falling when there is excess supply. Specifically,

$$\frac{dw}{dt} = \phi\left[\int_0^{\hat{\alpha}(w(t))} L(w(t), \alpha)d\alpha - \left(1 - \hat{\alpha}(w(t))\right)\right] \tag{24}$$

where ϕ is a differentiable increasing function such that $\phi(0) = 0$ and where $\hat{\alpha}(w)$ satisfies the equation

$$Eu(\tilde{\pi}(w, \hat{\alpha}(w)), \hat{\alpha}(w)) = u(w, \hat{\alpha}(w)). \tag{25}$$

We define

$$V(w) = \left(\phi\left\{\int_0^{\hat{\alpha}(w)} L(w, \alpha)d\alpha - [1 - \hat{\alpha}(w)]\right\}\right)^2 \tag{26}$$

to be the Lyapunov function. Then[4]

$$\begin{aligned} \frac{d}{dt} V(w(t)) = 2\phi'\left[\int_0^{\hat{\alpha}(w)} L(w, \alpha)d\alpha - \left(1 - \hat{\alpha}(w)\right)\right] \\ \times \left\{\left[L(w(t), \hat{\alpha}(w(t))) + 1\right]\hat{\alpha}'(w(t))\right. \\ \left. + \int_0^{\hat{\alpha}(w(t))} \frac{\partial L}{\partial w}(w(t), \alpha)d\alpha\right\}\left(\frac{dw}{dt}\right)^2. \end{aligned} \tag{27}$$

Now $\phi' > 0$ by assumption, and $\alpha'(w(t))$ is negative because of the lemma. Thus if $\partial L/\partial w < 0$, $d/dt\, V(w(t))$ is negative and $w(t)$ converges to the equilibrium wage.

[4] If we assume that u_α and $u_{I\alpha}$ exist and are continuous, repeated application of the implicit function theorem implies that $\hat{\alpha}(w)$ is a differentiable function of w.

These results are summarized in the following theorem.

THEOREM 5.—Assume that for each I, $r(I,\alpha)$ is a decreasing function of α and that either $g_{LL} < 0$ or $u_{II} < 0$. Also assume that u_α and $u_{I\alpha}$ exist and are continuous. If $L_w(w,\alpha)$ exists and is negative, then $w(t)$ converges to the unique equilibrium wage.

Remark 5

In the standard explanation for firm entry and exit, which does not admit the possibility of uncertain profits, reductions (increases) in profits caused by falling (rising) demand or increases (decreases) in cost result in exit (entry). In our entrepreneurial model demand changes are not explicitly considered and cost changes are introduced by wage changes. In addition, changes in the return to nonentrepreneurial activities, specifically labor, also cause entry or exit. Again these changes are embodied in wage changes.

The fact that returns to nonentrepreneurial activities influence firm entry and exit is a reflection of the general equilibrium nature of our formalization. In this framework, an individual's decision to enter as an entrepreneur or exit to become a worker is made after the expected utility of the random profits available to entrepreneurs has been compared to the utility of the nonrisky wages earned by workers. In the formalizations of Quandt and Howrey (1968) and of Brock (1972), firms decide to enter if (excess) profits can be made. This is appropriate when there is no uncertainty and no opportunity cost to entry other than capital costs. In our model both of these complications are present. Profits are random and the opportunity cost of becoming an entrepreneur is lost wages.

Remark 6

Since the model of the adjustment process studied here is analogous to that employed in the literature on competitive equilibrium, it is subject to the same criticisms. Specifically, the dynamic wage change equations are not explained by an underlying model of maximizing behavior. In the paper by Smith (1974), the dynamic equations which describe the process of firm entry and exit are explicitly obtained from a maximization model.

VI. Efficiency of Equilibrium

In this section, two concepts of efficiency are studied. The first is unconstrained Pareto optimality in the sense of Arrow (1964) and

Debreu (1959). The second is a constrained version of Pareto optimality in which the institutional constraints on risk trading implicit in our concept of equilibrium are imposed on all allocations. The reasons for studying constrained optima will be suggested by the analysis of unconstrained optima. We will show that because of the institutional restrictions embodied in our equilibrium concept, asking for unconstrained optimality is, in general, clearly asking for too much. There are, nevertheless, interesting cases in which an equilibrium is efficient in an unconstrained sense. In addition, it is possible to specify the nature of the unconstrained inefficiencies.

Before proceeding to the formal discussion it is convenient to introduce special assumptions which are employed to simplify the analysis of unconstrained efficiency. Specifically, we now assume that $\tilde{x}$ is the same random variable for all firms, that is, that the random variations in the firms' outputs are perfectly correlated. This assumption will be sufficient to permit an intuitive explanation of the inefficiencies occurring in our model. Furthermore, a general treatment would take us beyond the scope of the paper. The reader should note however that this assumption is used only in the discussion of unrestricted efficiency. In the subsequent discussion of restricted efficiency, no assumptions are made about the dependence or independence of the returns to different firms.

As a preliminary to the formal discussion, we define an unrestricted feasible allocation as a specification of Γ and Δ and of functions $\nu : \Delta \to [0,\infty)$ and $y(\cdot, x) : [0,1] \to [0,\infty)$, for each x, which satisfy the conditions

$$\int_\Delta \nu(\alpha)\mu(d\alpha) = \mu(\Gamma) \tag{28}$$

and

$$\int_0^1 y(\alpha, x)\mu(d\alpha) = \int_\Delta g(\nu(\alpha), x)\mu(d\alpha) + A \tag{29}$$

for each x.

The ν specifies the allocation of labor to firms. Equation (28) asserts that labor supply equals demand. The function $y(\cdot, x)$ describes the allocation of income to individuals in each state. The constraints (29) require that, in each state x, the supply of the commodity equals demand.[5]

The Pareto-optimal allocations can be studied by introducing arbitrary linear social welfare functions. Specifically, let λ be an arbitrary

[5] Notice that the notation embodies the assumption that the output of all firms is affected by the same random variable $\tilde{x}$. Specifically, a "state of nature" is completely defined by x, the value taken by $\tilde{x}$. If different firms were affected by different random variables, the description of a "state" would have to specify the value taken by each of these variables.

Lebesgue measurable function $\lambda:[0,1] \to [0,1]$. The corresponding social welfare function is

$$\int_0^1 \lambda(\alpha)Eu\big(y(\alpha,\tilde{x}),\alpha\big)\mu(d\alpha). \tag{30}$$

If Γ, Δ, ν, and $y(\cdot,\cdot)$ are chosen to maximize (30) subject to the constraints (28) and (29), the result is a Pareto-optimal allocation. In order to describe the Pareto optimal allocations, we study the solutions to these maximization problems for arbitrary λ functions.

First notice that it is possible for a planner who wishes to maximize (30) subject to the constraints (28) and (29) to ignore the identity of individuals who become workers and entrepreneurs and concern himself only with the number of entrepreneurs, that is, the number of firms. A similar simplification is possible in choosing ν; only the distribution of labor to firms matters; it is unimportant which entrepreneur runs which firm. This makes it possible to establish a convention that facilitates the comparison of efficient allocations with equilibrium allocations. Specifically, we can assume that in making his choice of Γ and Δ, the planner simply chooses an individual $\hat{\alpha}$ ($\hat{\alpha}$ can also be interpreted as the number of firms) and then assigns $\Delta = [0,\hat{\alpha}]$ and $\Gamma = (\hat{\alpha},1]$.

The second simplification which is possible in the discussion of unconstrained optimality is introduced because g exhibits decreasing returns to scale. Under this assumption, efficiency requires that every firm produce the same amount. If this were not true, output in each state x could be increased if labor were transferred from a high output firm to a low output firm. This transfer would increase output because of the differences in labor's marginal productivity (in every state x) which would result from the initial inequality of the outputs of the two firms considered.[6]

Since $\gamma(\alpha)$ must be the same for all entrepreneurs (28) reduces to

$$\nu(\alpha) = \frac{1 - \hat{\alpha}}{\hat{\alpha}} \tag{31}$$

for all $\alpha \in [0,\hat{\alpha}]$. Using this result, (29) becomes

$$\int_0^1 y(\alpha,x)\mu(d\alpha) = \hat{\alpha}g\left(\frac{1 - \hat{\alpha}}{\hat{\alpha}}, x\right) + A. \tag{32}$$

---

[6] This result can be derived immediately by writing the Euler equation corresponding to the maximization with respect to $\nu(\cdot)$. We get $E\delta(\tilde{x})g_L(\nu(\alpha),\tilde{x}) = \delta_0$ where δ_0 is the multiplier associated with (28) and $\delta(x)$ are the multipliers associated with (29). Thus $E\delta(\tilde{x})g_L(\nu(\alpha),\tilde{x}) = E\delta(\tilde{x})g_L(\nu(\alpha'),\tilde{x})$ for all $\alpha \leq \hat{\alpha}$ and $\alpha' \leq \hat{\alpha}$. Since g_L is a decreasing function of L for each x, $\nu(\alpha') \neq \nu(\alpha)$ would make this equality impossible.

The program for obtaining Pareto-optimal allocations reduces to

$$\max_{(\hat{\alpha}, \mu(\cdot, \cdot))} \int_0^1 \lambda(\alpha) \, Eu \, \left(y(\alpha, \tilde{x}), \alpha \right) \mu(d\alpha)$$

subject to (32) for all x. The first-order conditions are

$$\lambda(\alpha)\pi(x)u_I\big(y(\alpha,x),\alpha\big) = \delta(x), \text{ for all } \alpha \text{ and all } x \tag{33}$$

and

$$\int_0^{\bar{x}} \delta(x) \, g\Big(\frac{1-\hat{\alpha}}{\hat{\alpha}}, x\Big)dx = \int_0^{\bar{x}} \frac{\delta(x)}{\hat{\alpha}} g_L\Big(\frac{1-\hat{\alpha}}{\hat{\alpha}}, x\Big)dx \tag{34}$$

where $\delta(x)$ is the multiplier associated with the resource constraint in state x, and $\pi(x)$ is the value of the objective probability density function at x.

Using the value of $\delta(x)$ defined by (33) and inserting in (34) we obtain, after taking the expectation over x,

$$\frac{1}{\hat{\alpha}} E \, u_I\big(y(\alpha,\tilde{x}),\alpha\big) g_L\Big(\frac{1-\hat{\alpha}}{\hat{\alpha}}, \tilde{x}\Big) = E \, u_I\big(y(\alpha,\tilde{x}),\alpha\big) g\Big(\frac{1-\hat{\alpha}}{\hat{\alpha}}, x\Big) \tag{35}$$

for every α.

Using (33) for two different x values, say x_1 and x_s, and for two different α values, say α and β, we also obtain

$$\frac{u_I\big(y(\alpha, x_s), \alpha\big)}{u_I\big(y(\alpha, x_1), \alpha\big)} = \frac{u_I\big(y(\beta, x_s), \beta\big)}{u_I\big(y(\beta, x_1), \beta\big)} \tag{36}$$

for all s and all α, β.

Condition (35) can be viewed as that which determines the efficient $\hat{\alpha}$, that is, the optimal division of individuals between workers and entrepreneurs. In the special case where (16) holds, that is, when there are stochastic constant returns to scale, (35) reduces to

$$\hat{\alpha} = \Big[h'\Big(\frac{1-\hat{\alpha}}{\hat{\alpha}}\Big)\Big]\Big/\Big[h\Big(\frac{1-\hat{\alpha}}{\hat{\alpha}}\Big)\Big] \tag{37}$$

which is the $\hat{\alpha}$ level which maximizes the output $\hat{\alpha}h\,((1-\hat{\alpha})/\hat{\alpha})x$ for every x. The input level $1-\hat{\alpha}/\hat{\alpha}$ is also the one which would be chosen in an allocation which is efficient in Diamond's second-best sense.

The conditions (36) are those which characterize efficient allocations of contingent claims to the output produced.

It is clear from the preceding discussion and from the conditions (35) and (36) that there will be several sources of inefficiency in an equilibrium of the type defined above. The most obvious relates to the point made earlier that in an efficient allocation all firms should be producing equal amounts if returns to scale are diminishing for each x. In general, the equilibrium will be characterized by entrepreneurs who have varying attitudes toward risk. For that reason different entrepreneurs will produce different outputs. This is one source of inefficiency. Note, however, that it will fail to arise if all entrepreneurs have the same utility function and therefore the same attitude toward risk.

A second type of inefficiency arises because of the fact that only entrepreneurs bear risks in equilibrium. This is the institutional constraint on the allocation of risk bearing of which we spoke earlier. Thus, in general, the conditions (36) cannot be satisfied if there are risk averse entrepreneurs. A special case in which this problem does not arise occurs when all entrepreneurs are indifferent to risk. In that case condition (36) holds in equilibrium because of the linearity of entrepreneurs' utility functions and the fact that workers bear no risk. We will return to discuss this case more completely later.

The third source of inefficiency which requires more discussion is the optimal choice of $\hat{\alpha}$. To discuss this problem in an appropriate setting it seems necessary to consider an equilibrium in which all entrepreneurs are the same and produce the same output. This eliminates inefficiencies of the first type mentioned and makes it possible to ask if (35) might be satisfied.

To study this question, recall that (17) is the necessary condition for entrepreneurial expected utility maximization. In general, (17) differs from (35) because, as we shall see below,

$$\hat{\alpha}Eu_I\left(A + g\left(\frac{1-\hat{\alpha}}{\hat{\alpha}},\tilde{x}\right) - w\left(\frac{1-\hat{\alpha}}{\hat{\alpha}}\right),\hat{\alpha}\right)g\left(\frac{1-\hat{\alpha}}{\hat{\alpha}},\tilde{x}\right)$$
$$\neq wEu_I\left(A + g\left(\frac{1-\hat{\alpha}}{\hat{\alpha}},\tilde{x}\right) - w\left(\frac{1-\hat{\alpha}}{\hat{\alpha}}\right),\alpha\right). \tag{38}$$

(In an equilibrium in which all entrepreneurs have the same utility function, $L\left(w(\hat{\alpha}),\,\hat{\alpha}\right) = \dfrac{1-\hat{\alpha}}{\hat{\alpha}}$ since supply equals demand.)

Also recall that, in equilibrium, w satisfies (18) where $L = \dfrac{1-\hat{\alpha}}{\hat{\alpha}}$. Thus w is the certainty equivalent of the random variable $g(\frac{1-\hat{\alpha}}{\hat{\alpha}},\tilde{x})$ $- w(\frac{1-\hat{\alpha}}{\hat{\alpha}})$. When entrepreneurs are risk averse, condition (18) implies that

$$w = Eg\left(\frac{1-\hat{\alpha}}{\hat{\alpha}},\tilde{x}\right) - w\left(\frac{1-\hat{\alpha}}{\hat{\alpha}}\right) - \rho \tag{39}$$

where ρ is a positive risk premium. Rearranging, we obtain that

$$\frac{1}{\hat{\alpha}}w = Eg\left(\frac{1-\hat{\alpha}}{\hat{\alpha}},\tilde{x}\right) - \rho. \tag{40}$$

THEORY OF FIRM FORMATION

Substituting (40) in (17) yields

$$\frac{1}{\hat{\alpha}} Eu_I(A + g(L,\tilde{x}) - wL, \hat{\alpha})g_L(L,\tilde{x}) = \frac{1}{\hat{\alpha}} wEu_I(A + g(L,\tilde{x}) - wL, \hat{\alpha})$$

$$= [Eg(L,\tilde{x})][Eu_I(A + g(L,\tilde{x}) - wL, \hat{\alpha})] - \rho Eu_I(A + g(L,\tilde{x}) - wL, \hat{\alpha}) \tag{41}$$

where $L = \dfrac{1 - \hat{\alpha}}{\hat{\alpha}}$. Risk aversion ($u_{II} < 0$) also implies that

$$0 > c = \text{cov}\big(g(L,\tilde{x}), u_I(A + g(L,\tilde{x}) - wL, \hat{\alpha})\big)$$

$$= Eg(L,\tilde{x})u_I(A + g(L,\tilde{x}) - wL, \hat{\alpha}) \tag{42}$$

$$-[Eg(L,\tilde{x})][Eu_I(A + g(L,\tilde{x}) - wL, \hat{\alpha})]$$

where, again $L = (1 - \hat{\alpha})/\hat{\alpha}$. Combining (41) and (42) we obtain

$$\frac{1}{\hat{\alpha}} Eu_I(A + g(L,\tilde{x}) - wL, \hat{\alpha})g_L(L,\tilde{x}) = Eg(L,\tilde{x})u_I(A + g(L,\tilde{x}) - wL, \hat{\alpha})$$

$$- c - \rho Eu_I(A + g(L,\tilde{x}) - wL, \hat{\alpha}), \tag{43}$$

with $L = (1 - \hat{\alpha})/\hat{\alpha}$. Note that (43) and (35) are the same if the covariance c equals the negative of $\rho u_I\big(A + g\big(\dfrac{1 - \hat{\alpha}}{\hat{\alpha}},\tilde{x}\big) - w\big(\dfrac{1 - \hat{\alpha}}{\hat{\alpha}}\big),\hat{\alpha}\big)$.

In this case the equilibrium is efficient. Otherwise, risk aversion causes two types of errors. One of these, measured by the term $-\rho u_I\big(A + g\big(\dfrac{1 - \hat{\alpha}}{\hat{\alpha}},\tilde{x}\big) - w\big(\dfrac{1 - \hat{\alpha}}{\hat{\alpha}}\big), \hat{\alpha}\big)$, is introduced by the "entry condition" (18) and tends to cause the right-hand side (RHS) of (35) to exceed the left-hand side (LHS). The other type of error is measured by c. It enters through the entrepreneurial maximization condition (17) and it tends to make the RHS of (35) smaller than the LHS in equilibrium. To identify the direction of the effect which each of these errors has on the choice of $\hat{\alpha}$ consider the case in which (16) holds so that the optimal choice of $\hat{\alpha}$ is independent of the preferences and the income distribution. Recall that in this case $\hat{\alpha}$ should be chosen to maximize output in each state and that (35) reduces to the first-order condition for this output maximization problem. It is also easy to verify that when the LHS of (35) exceeds the RHS in equilibrium, then the derivative, $h\big(\dfrac{1}{\hat{\alpha}} - 1\big)x - \dfrac{1}{\hat{\alpha}}h'\big(\dfrac{1}{\alpha} - 1\big)x$, of output with respect to $\hat{\alpha}$ is negative at the equilibrium. It is then clear from figure 5 that in this case the equilibrium $\hat{\alpha}$ is too large to be efficient. Thus there are too many firms in equilibrium when the error, $-c$, introduced by the

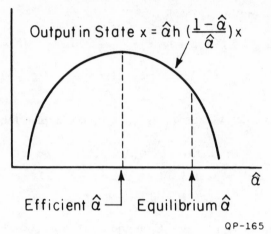

$$\text{Output in State } x = \hat{\alpha}h\left(\frac{1-\hat{\alpha}}{\hat{\alpha}}\right)x$$

Efficient $\hat{\alpha}$ Equilibrium $\hat{\alpha}$

QP-165

Fig. 5

entrepreneur's equilibrium condition, outweighs $-\rho E u_I\left(A + g\left(\frac{1-\hat{\alpha}}{\hat{\alpha}},\right.\right.$ $\left.\left.\tilde{x}\right) - w\left(\frac{1-\hat{\alpha}}{\hat{\alpha}}\right), \hat{\alpha}\right)$, the error introduced by the entry condition. Similar reasoning leads us to conclude that there are too few entrepreneurs when the error introduced by the entry condition outweighs the error introduced by the entrepreneurial first-order condition. These conclusions coincide with intuition. On the one hand risk aversion should cause too few individuals to become entrepreneurs and this should operate through the entry condition. On the other hand risk aversion on the part of those who become entrepreneurs reduces labor demand when (16) holds (recall theorem 3). The error caused by entrepreneurial risk aversion should reduce the equilibrium labor demand and the equilibrium wage. The low wage creates an incentive for too many individuals to become entrepreneurs.

We can now consider several important special cases. The first such case is that in which all entrepreneurs have constant absolute risk aversion in the sense of Arrow-Pratt, that is, $u(I,\alpha_1) = -e^{-rI}$, for some $r > 0$; and the production function is

$$g(L,x) = L^\gamma x \tag{44}$$

where $\gamma \in (0,1)$. In this case, (35) reduces to

$$\hat{\alpha} = 1 - \gamma, \tag{45}$$

and the efficient labor input per firm is

$$\frac{1-\hat{\alpha}}{\hat{\alpha}} = \frac{\gamma}{1-\gamma}. \tag{46}$$

The equilibrium conditions (17) and (18) combine to yield

$$0 = \frac{E\tilde{x}e^{-rL^{\gamma}\tilde{x}}}{Ee^{-rL^{\gamma}\tilde{x}}} + \frac{1}{r\gamma L^{\gamma-1}(1+L)} \log (Ee^{-r\tilde{x}L^{\gamma}}) \tag{47}$$

where $L = (1 - \hat{\alpha})/\hat{\alpha}$.

It can be shown that the RHS of (47) is a decreasing function of L and that it is negative if $\gamma/(1 - \gamma)$ is substituted for L. Thus the efficient L level exceeds the equilibrium level. As a result there are too many firms in equilibrium.

Note that in this class of examples the efficient number of firms approaches zero if γ approaches one, that is, if returns to scale become constant. The limiting case in which returns to scale are indeed constant is one in which, in general, there are too many entrepreneurs. The efficiency analysis just carried out does not apply to this case because it assumes that $g_{LL} < 0$ for all L. (The existence of equilibrium proof does apply if $u_{II} < 0$.) It is possible to analyze this case directly however by substituting

$$g(L,x) = h(L)x = kLx \tag{48}$$

in (34). The output in state x then becomes $k(1 - \hat{\alpha})x$ which is clearly maximized for each x when $\hat{\alpha} = 1$. Thus the measure of the optimal set of entrepreneurs is zero and almost all individuals should work. This result occurs because the technology set of the economy is the same if there is either one entrepreneur, some larger entrepreneur set of measure zero, or a set of positive measure.

There is one important case in which the equilibrium is efficient. That is the case already mentioned in which all entrepreneurs are indifferent to risk. Since the preceding discussion makes it clear that entrepreneurial risk aversion causes the errors which result in a nonoptimal equilibrium level for $\hat{\alpha}$, it should not now be surprising that the equilibrium is efficient when entrepreneurs are not risk averse. For that case, we have already noted that the distribution of risk is efficient, that is, condition (36) is satisfied. The linearity of the utility function implies then that $u_I(\cdot,\alpha)$ is independent of $y(\alpha,x)$, so that (35) reduces to

$$\hat{\alpha}Eg\left(\frac{1 - \hat{\alpha}}{\hat{\alpha}}, \tilde{x}\right) = Eg_I\left(\frac{1 - \hat{\alpha}}{\hat{\alpha}}, \tilde{x}\right). \tag{49}$$

For the same reason (17) reduces to

$$Eg_I\left(\frac{1 - \hat{\alpha}}{\hat{\alpha}}, \tilde{x}\right) = w. \tag{50}$$

In addition, risk indifference implies that $\rho = 0$ so that (40) becomes

$$w = \hat{\alpha}Eg\left(\frac{1 - \hat{\alpha}}{\hat{\alpha}}, \tilde{x}\right). \tag{51}$$

Taken together the equilibrium equations (50) and (51) imply (49) and the equilibrium therefore satisfies all of the conditions for efficiency.

The preceding discussion of efficiency suggests that entrepreneurial risk aversion is the source of all of the observed inefficiencies. When entrepreneurs are risk averse the equilibrium is not only characterized by an inefficient distribution of risk; there will, in general, also be too many or too few firms and they will not employ the correct number of workers. In fact, it is well known that an inefficient distribution of risk is inevitable with any equilibrium in which some subgroup of risk averse individuals (in this case, the entrepreneurs) bear all of the risks. Suppose, however, that we concede the inevitability of a maldistribution of risks and ask if, given this kind of inefficiency, the other aspects of the equilibrium might be efficient. Specifically, let us accept the fact that entrepreneurial risks cannot be shared and require only an optimal division of individuals between entrepreneurial activities and labor and of labor between firms. Is it then possible that in this restricted sense the equilibrium is efficient?

In order to pose this question formally we define a restricted feasible allocation to be a specification of Γ, Δ together with two functions $\nu : \Delta \rightarrow [0,\infty)$ and $\xi : [0,1] \rightarrow [-A,\infty)$ which satisfy the equations (28),

$$\int_0^1 \xi(\alpha)d\alpha = 0, \tag{52}$$

and $A + g(\nu(\alpha),x) + \xi(\alpha) \geq 0$ for all x and $\alpha \in \Delta$.

The function $\nu(\alpha)$ specifies the labor to be employed by entrepreneur α, that is, for each $\alpha \in \Delta$, $\nu(\alpha)$ is α's labor demand. Equation (28) expresses the equality of labor supply and demand. The function ξ specifies the amount of a certain payment made to each α. Equation (52) is a supply-demand equality for these payments. It guarantees that the resources exist to make all payments. The final condition rules out bankruptcy.

The difference between this concept of restricted feasibility and the notion of unrestricted feasibility should be noted. In the definition of unrestricted feasibility, the payments made to individuals are contingent on the state of nature x. As in an Arrow-Debreu economy, the only constraint on the allocation of contingent claims is that supply must equal demand in each state. As a result, risks can be completely reallocated. In contrast, a restricted feasible allocation specifies, for each α, a payment $\xi(\alpha)$ which is not state contingent; it does not permit a reallocation of risks. As a result, the distribution of risks implied by a restricted feasible allocation has two important features. First, as in equilibrium, workers bear no risks; entrepreneurs bear all risks. In addition, the distribution of risk among entrepreneurs is determined by the distribution of labor since, for entrepreneurs, $y(\alpha,x)$ is restricted to equal $A + g(v(\alpha),x) + \xi(\alpha)$. This feature is also shared with equilibrium allocations of risk since, in equilibrium, $y(\alpha,x) = g(L(w,\alpha), x) - wL(w,\alpha) + A$ if α is an entrepreneur. These considerations permit us to observe that the conditions defining restricted feasibility do indeed embody the institutional constraints on risk trading implicit in our equilibrium concept.

It should also be noted that this definition of restricted feasible allocations does not employ any explicit or implicit assumptions about the independence or dependence of the $\tilde{x}$'s which enter the production functions of different firms.

An allocation Λ which is restricted feasible is said to be restricted efficient if there is no other restricted feasible allocation Λ^* which Pareto dominates Λ.

We can now prove that an equilibrium is efficient in the restricted sense just defined. It should first be emphasized again that for this theorem we can and will drop the assumption that the $\tilde{x}$ is the same for all firms. In fact, it is not necessary for the theorem to make any assumptions about the dependence or independence of the random variables which enter different firm's production functions.[7]

THEOREM 6.—An equilibrium is restricted efficient.

PROOF.—In an equilibrium allocation

$$
\begin{aligned}
\Delta &= [0,\hat{\alpha}) \\
\Gamma &= [\hat{\alpha},1] \\
v(\alpha) &= L\big(w(\hat{\alpha}), \alpha\big) \text{ and} \\
\xi(\alpha) &= \begin{vmatrix} -wL\big(w(\hat{\alpha}), \alpha\big) & \text{if } \alpha \in \Gamma \\ w & \text{if } \alpha \in \Delta. \end{vmatrix}
\end{aligned}
\tag{53}
$$

Now consider some other allocation $\Lambda^* = (\Gamma^*, \Delta^*, v^*, \xi^*)$ which Pareto dominates the equilibrium. To express this domination formally it is necessary to first partition the set of individuals into four sets:

    i) those in $\Delta^* \cap \Delta$,
    ii) those in $\Delta^* \cap \Gamma$,
    iii) those in $\Gamma^* \cap \Gamma$, and
    iv) those in $\Gamma^* \cap \Delta$.

If α is in $\Delta^* \cap \Delta$, then Pareto dominance of Λ^* implies that

$$
Eu\big(A + g(L\big(w(\hat{\alpha}), \alpha\big), \tilde{x}\big) - w(\hat{\alpha})L\big(w(\hat{\alpha}), \alpha\big), \alpha\big)
$$
$$
\leq Eu\big(A + g\big(v^*(\alpha), \tilde{x}\big) + \xi^*(\alpha), \alpha\big).
\tag{54}
$$

---

[7] Note that unlike the definition of unrestricted feasibility, the definition of restricted feasibility embodies no implicit assumption about the dependence of the $\tilde{x}$'s faced by different firms.

By definition of $L(w(\hat{\alpha}), \alpha)$ then

$$\xi^*(\alpha) \geqq - w(\hat{\alpha})v^*(\alpha). \tag{55}$$

If α is in $\Delta^* \cap \Gamma$, then again Pareto dominance of Λ^* implies

$$Eu\big(A + g\big(L\big(w(\hat{\alpha}), \alpha\big), \tilde{x}\big) - wL\big(w(\hat{\alpha}), \alpha\big), \alpha\big)$$
$$\leqq u\big(A + w(\hat{\alpha}), \alpha\big) \tag{56}$$
$$\leqq Eu\big(A + g\big(v^*(\alpha), \tilde{x}\big) + \xi^*(\alpha), \alpha\big)$$

and again (55) holds.

If α is in $\Gamma^* \cap \Gamma$, then

$$u\big(A + w(\hat{\alpha}), \alpha\big) \leqq u\big(A + \xi^*(\alpha), \alpha\big) \tag{57}$$

and

$$w(\hat{\alpha}) \leqq \xi^*(\alpha). \tag{58}$$

Finally, if α is in $\Gamma^* \cap \Delta$, then

$$u\big(A + w(\hat{\alpha}), \alpha\big) \leqq Eu\big(A + g\big(L\big(w(\hat{\alpha}), \alpha\big), \tilde{x}\big) - w(\alpha)L\big(w(\hat{\alpha}), \alpha\big), \alpha\big)$$
$$\leqq u\big(\xi^*(\alpha), \alpha\big) \tag{59}$$

so that (58) holds in this case also.

We have established that for all $\alpha \, \epsilon \, \Delta^*$, (55) holds while for all $\alpha \, \epsilon$ Γ^*, (58) holds. In fact, a similar argument guarantees that since Λ^* Pareto dominates the equilibrium, there must either be a Δ^* subset of positive measure on which (55) holds with a strict inequality or a Γ^* subset of positive measure on which (58) holds with a strict inequality. Thus

$$\int_0^1 \xi^*(\alpha)d\alpha > \Big[-\int_{\Delta^*} v^*(\alpha)d\alpha + \mu(\Gamma^*)\Big]w(\hat{\alpha}). \tag{60}$$

Inequality (60) implies that Λ^* cannot be restricted feasible. Specifically, because of (60), equations (28) and (52) cannot hold simultaneously. We have therefore shown that the equilibrium is restricted efficient because it cannot be Pareto dominated by a restricted feasible allocation. $\|$

Restricted efficiency is similar in spirit to Diamond's (1967) constrained efficiency, that is, efficiency under the given constraints on the risk allocation. Here we have imposed more constraints than in Diamond's model of the stock market since, in our approach, entrepreneurs are not allowed to share any risk with workers or other entrepreneurs. However, we get restricted efficiency without any technological assumption such as those imposed by Diamond's assumption of stochastic constant returns to scale. A similar result is obtained in Kihlstrom and Laffont (1978), where risk sharing is introduced by the existence of markets for shares to firms. The resulting equilibrium is shown to be efficient in the sense of Diamond. The efficiency theorem involves no restrictive assumptions about technology. Specifically, it does not require stochastic constant returns to scale.

VII. Summary

In this paper we have introduced a simple general equilibrium model of firm formation in which production requires entrepreneurial as well as normal labor inputs. Workers receive fixed wages while entrepreneurs receive risky profits. Individuals decide whether to become entrepreneurs or workers by comparing the risky returns of entrepreneurship with the nonrisky wage determined in the competitive labor market. The wage adjusts to the point where the supply of workers is equal to the entrepreneurial demand for labor.

Although we have not discussed the interpretation of the entrepreneurs' contribution to the productive process we have implicitly or explicitly made assumptions about the nature of this contribution. The primary assumption is that the relationship between output and the entrepreneurial labor input is characterized by an indivisibility. Specifically, each firm requires a unit of entrepreneurial labor regardless of how much normal labor it employs and how much it produces. In this sense, the expenditure of entrepreneurial labor can be viewed as a set-up cost. Normally, the nonconvexities introduced by indivisibilities in general and set-up costs in particular cause problems when the existence of equilibrium is studied. In our model, this problem is avoided, as it can be in general (see, e.g., Aumann 1966), by assuming that the set of individuals is a continuum.

One possible interpretation of our model is that the entrepreneur contributes managerial and organizational skills. In Knight's words he performs the "function of exercising responsible control."[8] In fact, our entire model can be viewed as a formalization, for a special case, of Knight's discussion of the entrepreneur.[9] In our model, an entrepreneur is characterized by two activities. He supplies entrepreneurial inputs and bears the risks associated with production. In

---

[8] Knight (1921), p. 278.

[9] Knight's view of the entrepreneur as well as the view formalized here are rather different from that set forth by Schumpeter (1934, 1939). Schumpeter viewed the entrepreneur as an innovator. (See, e.g., the discussion on pp. 132–36 of Schumpeter [1934].) His view of the entrepreneur's contribution and of his compensation is in essence dynamic. He also specifically asserts on p. 137 of Schumpeter (1934) that "the entrepreneur is never a risk bearer." For a more modern discussion of the entrepreneur and his role (or lack of one) in economic theory, see Baumol (1968).

Knight's treatment the entrepreneur makes the same contributions "with the performance of his peculiar twofold function of (*a*) exercising responsible control and (*b*) securing the owners of productive services against uncertainty and fluctuation in their incomes."[10] Knight's view of the labor market and of an individual's decision to become a worker or an entrepreneur also appears to be similar to that formalized here. This is illustrated by the discussion on pages 273–74 of Knight (1921). Specifically, he asserts that, "the laborer asks what he thinks the entrepreneur will be able to pay, and in any case will not accept less than he can get from some other entrepreneur, or *by turning entrepreneur himself.* In the same way the entrepreneur offers to any laborer what he thinks he must in order to secure his services, and in any case not more than he thinks the laborer will be worth to him, *keeping in mind what he can get by turning laborer himself.*"[11] He continues: "Since in a free market there can be but one price on any commodity, a general wage rate must result from this competitive bidding."[12]

Our model represents only a special case of Knight's view because we assume that all individuals are equal in their ability to perform entrepreneurial as well as normal labor functions. They differ only in their willingness to bear risks. Knight emphasizes ability as well as "willingness [and] power to give satisfactory guarantees"[13] as factors determining the supply of entrepreneurs. In our model, the size of the initial income A can be interpreted as a measure of an individual's power to guarantee wages by bearing risk. We have assumed here that all individuals are alike in their possession of this "power." An interesting alternative interpretation can be made by explaining the differences in risk aversion as arising from differences in wealth. Suppose, for example, that all entrepreneurs have the same utility function which is decreasingly risk averse (in the absolute sense of Arrow-Pratt). Then the differences in the willingness to bear risk— that is, to "give satisfactory guarantees" in Knight's words—will be determined by initial wealth. Thus if A varies across individuals, the more risk averse individuals will also be those who initially are the poorest. Assuming that the constraints $L \le A/w$ are never binding in equilibrium our model can then be reinterpreted as predicting that entrepreneurs are those who are initially wealthy. (Of course the opposite prediction can be obtained by making the less generally accepted assumption that the common utility function is increasingly risk averse.) With this interpretation, the possession of wealth which

---

[10] Knight (1921, p. 278).
[11] Ibid., pp. 273–74 (emphasis added).
[12] Ibid., p. 274.
[13] Ibid., p. 283.

THEORY OF FIRM FORMATION   **747**

provides additional power to give satisfactory guarantees also makes an individual more willing to bear risk.

To complete the analogy between our results and Knight's discussion note that our theorem 4, which relates the equilibrium wage to the level of entrepreneurial risk aversion, was in a sense anticipated by the discussion of Knight (1921, p. 283) which concludes that "entrepreneur income, being residual, is determined by the demand for these other [productive] services, which demand is a matter of self-confidence of entrepreneurs as a class. . . ."[14]

This paper has extended the classical results concerning the existence and stability of equilibrium to the entrepreneurial model. We have also described the nature of the equilibrium's inefficiencies and identified the institutional constraints on risk trading as the source of these inefficiencies. These results establish that it is possible to construct an internally consistent general equilibrium model of entrepreneurially operated firms. In fact, this analysis should only be viewed as a first step in the construction of a general equilibrium entrepreneurial theory of the firm under uncertainty. As presented here it is perhaps best viewed as a description of equilibrium in a world of small businesses or farms.

The next step is to incorporate a stock market into our analysis. Once a stock market is embedded in the model, we can use it to ask interesting questions about the interaction between a modern firm's financial and productive decisions. Furthermore, the introduction of a stock market represents an institutional change that facilitates risk trading and thereby eliminates some of the inefficiencies that occur at an equilibrium. The extension of the model in this direction has been studied in a subsequent paper (Kihlstrom and Laffont 1978).

References

Arrow, Kenneth J. "The Role of Securities in the Optimal Allocation of Risk-Bearing." *Rev. Econ. Studies* 31 (April 1964): 91–96.
———. *Essays in the Theory of Risk Bearing.* Chicago: Markham, 1971.
Aumann, Robert J. "Existence of Competitive Equilibria in Markets with a Continuum of Traders." *Econometrica* 34 (January 1966): 1–17.
Baron, David P. "Price Uncertainty, Utility and Industry Equilibrium in Pure Competition." *Internat. Econ. Rev.* 11 (October 1970): 463–80.
Baumol, William J. "Entrepreneurship in Economic Theory." *A.E.R. Papers and Proc.* 63 (May 1968): 64–71.
Brock, William A. "On Models of Expectations That Arise from Maximizing Behavior of Economic Agents over Time." *J. Econ. Theory* 5 (December 1972): 348–76.

[14] Ibid.

Debreu, Gerard. *Theory of Value*. New York: Wiley, 1959.

Diamond, Peter A. "The Role of a Stock Market in a General Equilibrium Model with Technological Uncertainty." *A.E.R.* 57 (September 1967): 759–76.

Drèze, Jacques. "Investment under Private Ownership: Optimality, Equilibrium Stability." In *Allocation under Uncertainty: Equilibrium and Optimality*. London: Macmillan, 1974.

Kihlstrom, Richard E., and Laffont, Jean-Jacques. "A Competitive Entrepreneurial Model of the Stock Market." Mimeographed. Urbana, Ill.: Univ. Illinois, 1978.

Knight, Frank H. *Risk, Uncertainty and Profit*. New York: Harper & Row, 1965.

Pratt, John W. "Risk Aversion in the Small and in the Large." *Econometrica* 32 (January–April 1964): 122–36.

Quandt, Richard, and Howrey, E. Phillip. "The Dynamics of the Number of Firms in an Industry." *Rev. Econ. Studies* 35 (July 1968): 349–53.

Radner, Roy. "Competitive Equilibrium under Uncertainty." *Econometrica* 36 (January 1968): 31–58.

Schumpeter, Joseph A. *The Theory of Economic Development; An Inquiry into Profits, Capital, Credit, Interest, and the Business Cycle*. Cambridge, Mass.: Harvard Univ. Press, 1934.

———. *Business Cycles; A Theoretical, Historical, and Statistical Analysis of the Capitalist Process*. Abridged ed. New York: McGraw Hill, 1939.

Smith, Vernon. "Optimal Costly Firm Entry in General Equilibrium." *J. Econ. Theory* 9 (1974): 397–417.

"Symposium on the Optimality of Competitive Capital Markets." *Bell J. Econ. Management Sci.* 5 (Spring 1974): 125–86.

[4]

ENTREPRENEURSHIP IN ECONOMIC THEORY*

By William J. Baumol
Princeton University

The entrepreneur is at the same time one of the most intriguing and one of the most elusive characters in the cast that constitutes the subject of economic analysis. He has long been recognized as the apex of the hierarchy that determines the behavior of the firm and thereby bears a heavy responsibility for the vitality of the free enterprise society. In the writings of the classical economist his appearance was frequent, though he remained a shadowy entity without clearly defined form and function. Only Schumpeter and, to some degree, Professor Knight succeeded in infusing him with life and in assigning to him a specific area of activity to any extent commensurate with his acknowledged importance.

In more recent years, while the facts have apparently underscored the significance of his role, he has at the same time virtually disappeared from the theoretical literature. And, as we will see, while some recent theoretical writings seem at first glance to offer a convenient place for an analysis of his activities, closer inspection indicates that on this score matters have not really improved substantially.

This paper will undertake to examine three major matters. First, I will review briefly the grounds on which entrepreneurship should concern us. Second. I will seek to explain why economic theory has failed to develop an illuminating formal analysis of entrepreneurship and I shall conclude that it is unlikely to do so for the foreseeable future. Finally, I shall argue that theory can say a great deal that is highly relevant to the subject of entrepreneurship even if it fails to provide a rigorous analysis of the behavior of the entrepreneur or of the supply of entrepreneurship.

Before proceeding with the discussion I would like to make a distinction that is somewhat artificial but nevertheless important. It is necessary for us to differentiate between the entrepreneurial and the managerial functions. We may define the manager to be the individual who oversees the ongoing efficiency of continuing processes. It is his task to see that available processes and techniques are combined in proportions appropriate for current output levels and for the future outputs that are already in prospect. He sees to it that inputs are not wasted, that

* The author would like very much to thank his colleague W. A. Lewis, whose comments were used liberally in the revision of this paper. He must also thank the National Science Foundation whose grant greatly facilitated the completion of this paper.

schedules and contracts are met, he makes routine pricing and advertising outlay decisions, etc., etc. In sum, he takes charge of the activities and decisions encompassed in our traditional models.

The preceding description is not intended to denigrate the importance of managerial activity or to imply that it is without significant difficulties. Carl Kaysen has remarked that in practice most firms no doubt find themselves in a position well inside their production possibility loci and one of their most challenging tasks is to find ways of approaching those loci more closely; i.e., of increasing their efficiency even within the limits of known technology. This is presumably part of the job of the manager who is constantly on the lookout for means to save a little here and to squeeze a bit more there. But for many purposes the standard models would appear to provide an adequate description of the functions of the manager. Given an arrangement which calculation, experience, or judgment indicate to constitute a reasonable approximation to the current optimum, it is the manager's task to see that this arrangement is in fact instituted to a reasonable degree of approximation.

· The entrepreneur (whether or not he in fact also doubles as a manager) has a different function. It is his job to locate new ideas and to put them into effect. He must lead, perhaps even inspire; he cannot allow things to get into a rut and for him today's practice is never good enough for tomorrow. In short, he is the Schumpeterian innovator and some more. He is the individual who exercises what in the business literature is called "leadership." And it is he who is virtually absent from the received theory of the firm.

I. *On the Significance of the Entrepreneur*

If we are interested in explaining what Haavelmo has described as the "really big dissimilarities in economic life," we must be prepared to concern ourselves with entrepreneurship. For the really big differences are most usually those that correspond to historical developments over long periods of time or to the comparative states of various economies, notably those of the developed and the underdeveloped areas.

It has long been recognized that the entrepreneurial function is a vital component in the process of economic growth. Recent empirical evidence and the lessons of experience both seem to confirm this view. For example, some empirical studies on the nature of the production function have concluded that capital accumulation and expansion of the labor force leave unexplained a very substantial proportion of the historical growth of the nation's output. Thus, in a well-known paper, Solow [6, p. 320] has suggested on the basis of American data for the period 1909–49 that "gross output per man-hour doubled over the interval, with 87$\frac{1}{2}$ percent of the increase attributable to technical change and the remaining 12$\frac{1}{2}$ percent to increase in the use of capital."[1] But any such innovation, whether it is purely technological or it consists in a modification in the way in which an industry is organized, will require entrepreneurial initiative in its introduction. Thus we are led to suspect that by ignoring the entrepreneur we are prevented from accounting fully for a very substantial proportion of our historic growth.

Those who have concerned themselves with development policy have apparently been driven to similar conclusions. If we seek to explain the success of those economies which have managed to grow significantly with those that have remained relatively stagnant, we find it difficult to do so without taking into consideration differences in the availability of entrepreneurial talent and in the motivational mechanism which drives them on. A substantial proportion of the energies of those who design plans to stimulate development has been devoted to the provision of means whereby entrepreneurs can be trained and encouraged.

The entrepreneur is present in institutional and applied discussions of a number of other economic areas. For example, his absence is sometimes cited as a significant source of the difficulties of a declining industry, and a balance-of-payments crisis is sometimes discussed in similar terms. Thus both macro problems and micro problems offer a substantial place for him in their analysis. Whether or not he is assigned the starring role he would appear in practice to be no minor character.

II. *The Entrepreneur in Formal Models*

Contrast all this with the entrepreneur's place in the formal theory. Look for him in the index of some of the most noted of recent writings on value theory, in neoclassical[2] or activity analysis models of the firm. The references are scanty and more often they are totally absent. The theoretical firm is entrepreneurless—the Prince of Denmark has been expunged from the discussion of *Hamlet*.

It is not difficult to explain his absence. Consider the nature of the model of the firm. In its simplest form (and in this respect we shall see that the more complex and more sophisticated models are no better) the theoretical firm must choose among alternative values for a small number of rather well-defined variables: price, output, perhaps adver-

[1] Solow's result and other similar conclusions have recently been challenged in an article by Jorgenson and Griliches [3]. However, their contention does not necessarily imply any denigration of the role of the entrepreneur. They argue merely that entrepreneurship and innovation have achieved growth in outputs only with the aid of corresponding increases in input quantities.

[2] There is one residual and rather curious role left to the entrepreneur in the neoclassical model. He is the indivisible and non-replicable input that accounts for the U-shaped cost curve of a firm whose production function is linear and homogeneous. How the mighty have fallen!

tising outlay. In making this choice management is taken to consider the costs and revenues associated with each candidate set of values, as described by the relevant functional relationships, equations, and inequalities. Explicitly or implicitly the firm is then taken to perform a mathematical calculation which yields optimal (i.e., profit maximizing) values for all of its decision variables and it is these values which the theory assumes to be chosen—which are taken to constitute the business decision. There matters rest, forever or until exogenous forces lead to an autonomous change in the environment. Until there is such a shift in one of the relationships that define the problem, the firm is taken to replicate precisely its previous decisions, day after day, year after year.

Obviously, the entrepreneur has been read out of the model. There is no room for enterprise or initiative. The management group becomes a passive calculator that reacts mechanically to changes imposed on it by fortuitous external developments over which it does not exert, and does not even attempt to exert, any influence. One hears of no clever ruses, ingenious schemes, brilliant innovations, of no charisma or of any of the other stuff of which outstanding entrepreneurship is made; one does not hear of them because there is no way in which they can fit into the model.[3]

It must be understood clearly that what I have been saying constitutes no criticism, not even an attempt to reprove mildly the neoclassical model of the firm. I think that model does what it was designed to do and does it well. Like any respectable analysis, one hopes that it will be modified, amended, and improved with time. But not because it cannot handle an issue for which it is irrelevant. The model is essentially an instrument of optimality analysis of well-defined problems, and it is precisely such (very real and important) problems which need no entrepreneur for their solution.

Some readers may suspect that I am subtly putting forward as more appropriate candidates for the job some alternative models of the firm with which I have to some degree been associated. But this is certainly not my intention, because it seems clear to me that these models are

---

[3] The problem was recognized long ago by Thorstein Veblen. One may recall the characteristic passage in which he described the economic man as "a lightning calculator of pleasures and pains, who oscillates like a homogeneous globule of desire of happiness under the impulse of stimuli that shift him about the area, but leave him intact. He has neither antecedent nor consequent. He is an isolated, definitive human datum, in stable equilibrium except for the buffets of impinging forces that displace him in one direction or another. Self-imposed in elemental space, he spins symmetrically about his own spiritual axis until the parallelogram of forces bears down upon him, whereupon he follows the line of the resultant. When the force of the impact is spent, he comes to rest, a self-contained globule of desire as before. . . . [he] is not a prime mover. He is not the seat of a process of living, except in the sense that he is subject to a series of permutations enforced upon him by circumstances external and alien to him" [7, pp. 73–74].

no better for the purpose than the most hidebound of conventional constructs. For example, consider what Oliver Williamson has described as the "managerial discretion models." in which the businessman is taken to maximize the number of persons he employs, or sales, or still another objective distinct from profits. True, this businessman has (somewhere outside the confines of the model) made a choice which was no mere matter of calculation. He has decided, in at least some sense, to assign priority to some goal other than profit. But having made this choice he becomes, no less than the profit maximizer, a calculating robot, a programmed mechanical component in the automatic system that constitutes the firm. He makes and enforces the maximizing decision and in this the choice of maximand makes no difference.

Nor can the "practical pertinence" of the decision variables make the difference in carving out a place for the entrepreneur. Maximization models have recently been developed in which, instead of prices and outputs, the decision variables are the firm's real investment program, or its financial mix (the proportion of equity and debt in its funding), or the attributes of a new product to be launched by the company. These decisions seem to smell more of the ingredients of entrepreneurship. But though the models may be powerful and serve their objective well, they take us not a whit further in the analysis of entrepreneurship, for their calculations are again mechanistic and automatic and call for no display of entrepreneurial initiative.

Finally, it must be understood that the timeless nature of these models has nothing to do with the problem. Professor Evans [2] long ago developed a model in which the firm considered the consequence of its decisions for the time path of prices and where the calculus of variations served as his instrument of analysis. In one of my own models the firm was taken to choose not a stationary, once-and-for-all output level, but selected instead an optimal growth rate. None of these alternatives helps matters. In all these models, automaton maximizers the businessmen are and automaton maximizers they remain.

And this shows us why our body of theory, as it has developed, offers us no promise of being able to deal effectively with a description and analysis of the entrepreneurial function. For maximization and minimization have constituted the foundation of our theory, and as a result of this very fact the theory is deprived of the ability to provide an analysis of entrepreneurship. The terminology of game theory has been extremely suggestive; the willingness of the behaviorists to break away from traditional formulations has been encouraging; but I see no real breakthroughs in this area even on the distant horizon. At most I hope for more brilliant observations and descriptive insights such as those provided by Schumpeter and more recently by Leibenstein, but I foresee for the immediate future no more formal, manipulatable engine of calculation and analysis.[4]

III. *On the Supply of Entrepreneurship*

There is yet another reason why a marriage between theory and policy is not easily arranged in this area. In its discussions of inputs our formal analysis deals, by and large, with the way in which these inputs are used, and tells us relatively little about where they come from. In our growth models, for example, the behavior of the labor supply exerts a critical influence on the economy's expansion path. But the determination of the growth of the labor force itself is generally taken to be an exogenous matter. Similarly, in a neoclassical or a programming analysis of production one investigates how inputs should be used in the production process, but one assumes that their supply is somehow determined outside the system. Thus even if we were to develop a model which were successful in advancing the theory of entrepreneurship to the level of sophistication of our treatment of other inputs, we would have defined more effectively the entrepreneurial role, but we would have added relatively little to our understanding of the determinants of the level of output of entrepreneurship.

From the point of view of policy, however, the priorities would seem to be reversed. The first order of business in an economy which exhibits very little business drive is presumably to induce the appearance of increased supplies of entrepreneurial skills which would then be let loose upon the area's industry. The policy-maker thus is interested primarily in what determines the supply of entrepreneurship and in the means that can be used to expand it.

But there is reason to suppose that these issues are to a very considerable extent matters of social psychology, of social arrangements, of cultural developments and the like. And perhaps this is why many of the recent discussions of the theory of entrepreneurship have been contributed by the sociologists and the psychologists.[5] This may then be no

---

[4] My colleague, Professor Lewis, has adduced yet another reason why the current theory does not help us to understand the entrepreneur. He remarks in a note to me that "the entrepreneur is doing something new and is therefore to some extent a monopolist. . . . We have no good theory of entrepreneurship because we have no good theory of monopoly. Our theory that monopolists [act] to maximize profit is obviously absurd, given the low elasticity of demand of most monopolized products." I agree that this observation points to a most fundamental gap in the theory of the firm.

[5] For a remarkable study of entrepreneurship by a social psychologist, see McClelland [4]. While the book is not free of somewhat distracting jargon, and is naïve in spots, particularly in its literal interpretation of the role of the profit motive in economic analysis, it does offer a number of extremely interesting hypotheses and provides in their support quantities of psychological test results relating to a great variety of cultures. In what is perhaps the most interesting part of his discussion from our point of view, the author claims to show that entrepreneurs are motivated by n-achievement (the need for achievement) and not by desire for money (pp. 233–37). In his tests, people with high levels of n-achievement do no better when offered larger

fortuitous development. The very nature of the more pressing issues relating to entrepreneurship may invite more directly the attention of the practitioners of disciplines other than theoretical economics.

IV. *A Place for Theory and Entrepreneurship*

Given these difficulties besetting any attempt to construct a relevant economic theory in the area, I can offer only one suggestion for a theoretical approach to entrepreneurship, but one which I think is not without promise. We may not be able to analyze in detail the supply of entrepreneurship, the entrepreneur's strategy choices, his attitudes to risk, or the sources of his ideas. But one can hope to examine fruitfully what can be done to encourage his activity. Here an analogy is illuminating. The Keynesian analysis really bypasses the issue of expectations which is surely at the heart of the investment decision and yet the model succeeds in coming to grips with some means that can stimulate investment. In the same way one can undertake to grapple, assisted by theoretical instruments, with the policies that encourage entrepreneurship.

This can be done by considering not the means which the entrepreneur employs or the process whereby he arrives at his decisions but by examining instead the determinants of the payoff to his activity.[6] In his operations he must bear risks, never mind just how he does this, but let the theory consider how the marginal costs of his risk bearing can be reduced. He employs the results of work in research and development; very well, let us investigate what means make it easier, economically, to undertake R and D. Theoretical analysis of the effects of alternative tax arrangements, for example, should shed some light on these matters. The role of the structure of interest rates is no doubt also pertinent and we do have a powerful body of literature which treats of

---

amounts of money for success, whereas people with low *n*-achievement scores do much better when offered money. However, it should be noted that while a rise in absolute income levels does not seem to stimulate *n*-achievers, a rise in marginal returns does seem likely to spur them on, according to the author because it provides a clearer measure of accomplishment. (The economist would no doubt propose a different explanation.) He also claims to show that *n*-achievers choose smaller risks than the average man: they are not gamblers, but are calculators and planners. The entrepreneur is not essentially a man who chooses to bear risks—that is the speculator, a man with quite a different personality (pp. 210–25). Another interesting McClelland claim is that the *n*-achiever is not an individualist and does not depend for his success on private enterprise (pp. 292–300). He gets just as much satisfaction from the manipulation of a committee, or from working for a government, since his interest is in results rather than in these other considerations. This is perhaps the reason huge committee-run corporations can be successful.

[6] I believe the key element of Schumpeter's contribution to the theory of entrepreneurship is precisely of this variety. In its discussion of the functions of the entrepreneur, *The Theory of Economic Development* [5] offers us little more than a taxonomy. But enormous illumination is provided by Schumpeter's analysis of the process whereby the rewards of innovation are only gradually eroded by the competitive process and the corollary observation that some imperfection in the market mechanism is essential to permit some financial reward for innovation.

these matters. On all of these fronts analysis is well advanced and it is no heroic exercise to imagine rather complex and probing theoretical formulations capable of shedding light upon them.

It should be recognized, moreover, that such a theoretical analysis can be of enormous significance for policy. In a growth-conscious world I remain convinced that encouragement of the entrepreneur is the key to the stimulation of growth. The view that this must await the slow and undependable process of change in social and psychological climate is a counsel of despair for which there is little justification. Such a conclusion is analogous to an argument that all we can do to reduce spending in an inflationary period is to hope for a revival of the Prostestant ethic and the attendant acceptance by the general public of the virtues of thrift! Surely we have learned to do better than that, in effect by producing a movement along the relevant functional paths rather than undertaking the more heroic task involved in shifting the relationships. This is precisely why I have just advocated more careful study of the rewards of entrepreneurship. Without awaiting a change in the entrepreneurial drive exhibited in our society, we can try to learn how one can stimulate the volume and intensity of entrepreneurial activity, thus making the most of what is permitted by current mores and attitudes. If the theory succeeds in no more than showing us something about how that can be done,[7] it will have accomplished very much indeed.

[7] For a crude attempt at such an analysis, see the last chapter of [1].

REFERENCES

1. W. J. Baumol, *Business Behavior, Value and Growth* (revised ed., Harcourt, Brace and World, 1967).
2. G. C. Evans, "The Dynamics of Monopoly," *Amer. Math. Monthly*, Feb., 1924, pp. 77–83.
3. D. W. Jorgenson and Z. Griliches, "The Explanation of Productivity Change," *Rev. of Econ. Studies*, July, 1967, pp. 249–83.
4. D. C. McClelland, *The Achieving Society* (Princeton, 1961).
5. J. A. Schumpeter, *The Theory of Economic Development* (Cambridge, Mass., 1936).
6. R. M. Solow, "Technical Change and the Aggregate Production Function," *Rev. of Econ. and Statis.*, Aug., 1957, pp. 312–20.
7. T. B. Veblen, "Economics and Evolution," *The Place of Science in Modern Civilization* (New York, 1919).

Market Process

[5]

Economics and Knowledge[1]

By F. A. von Hayek

I

THE ambiguity of the title of this paper is not accidental. Its main subject is, of course, the rôle which assumptions and propositions about the knowledge possessed by the different members of society play in economic analysis. But this is by no means unconnected with the other question which might be discussed under the same title, the question to what extent formal economic analysis conveys any knowledge about what happens in the real world. Indeed my main contention will be that the tautologies, of which formal equilibrium analysis in economics essentially consists, can be turned into propositions which tell us anything about causation in the real world only in so far as we are able to fill those formal propositions with definite statements about how knowledge is acquired and communicated. In short I shall contend that the empirical element in economic theory—the only part which is concerned, not merely with implications but with causes and effects, and which leads therefore to conclusions which, at any rate in principle, are capable of verification[2]—consists of propositions about the acquisition of knowledge.

Perhaps I should begin by reminding you of the interesting fact that in quite a number of the more recent attempts made in different fields to push theoretical investigation beyond the limits of traditional equilibrium analysis, the answer has soon proved to turn on one question which, if not identical with mine, is at least part of it, namely the question of foresight. I think the field where, as one would expect, the discussion of the assumptions concerning foresight first attracted wider attention was the theory of risk.[3] The stimulus which was exercised in this connection

---

[1] Presidential Address to the London Economic Club, November 10th, 1936.
[2] Or rather falsification. Cf. K. Popper, *Logik der Forschung*, Vienna, 1935, *passim*.
[3] A more complete survey of the process by which the significance of anticipations was gradually introduced into economic analysis would probably have to begin with Professor Irving Fisher's *Appreciation and Interest* (1896).

by the work of Professor F. H. Knight may yet prove to have a profound influence far beyond its special field. Not much later the assumptions to be made concerning foresight proved to be of fundamental importance for the solution of the puzzles of the theory of imperfect competition, the questions of duopoly and oligopoly. And since then it has become more and more obvious that in the treatment of the more " dynamic " questions of money and industrial fluctuations the assumptions to be made about foresight and " anticipations " play an equally central rôle, and that in particular the concepts which were taken over into these fields from pure equilibrium analysis, like those of an equilibrium rate of interest, could be properly defined only in terms of assumptions concerning foresight. The situation seems here to be that before we can explain why people commit mistakes, we must first explain why they should ever be right.

In general it seems that we have come to a point where we all realise that the concept of equilibrium itself can be made definite and clear only in terms of assumptions concerning foresight, although we may not yet all agree what exactly these essential assumptions are. This question will occupy me later in this paper. At the moment I am only concerned to show that at the present juncture, whether we want to define the boundaries of economic statics or whether we want to go beyond it, we cannot escape the vexed problem of the exact position which assumptions about foresight are to have in our reasoning. Can this be merely an accident ?

As I have already suggested, the reason for this. seems to me to be that we have to deal here only with a special aspect of a much wider question which we ought to have faced at a much earlier point. Questions essentially similar to those mentioned arise in fact as soon as we try to apply the system of tautologies—those series of propositions which are necessarily true because they are merely transformations of the assumptions from which we start, and which constitute the main content of equilibrium analysis[1]—to the

---

[1] I should like to make it clear from the outset that I use the term " equilibrium analysis " throughout this paper in the narrower sense in which it is equivalent to what Professor Hans Mayer has christened the " functional " (as distinguished from the " causal- genetic ") approach, and to what used to be loosely described as the " mathematical school ". It is round this approach that most of the theoretical discussions of the past ten or fifteen years have taken place. It is true that Professor Mayer has held out before us the prospect of another, " causal-genetic " approach, but it can hardly be denied that this is still largely a promise. It should,

situation of a society consisting of several independent persons. I have long felt that the concept of equilibrium itself and the methods which we employ in pure analysis, have a clear meaning only when confined to the analysis of the action of a single person, and that we are really passing into a different sphere and silently introducing a new element of altogether different character when we apply it to the explanation of the interactions of a number of different individuals.

I am certain there are many who regard with impatience and distrust the whole tendency, which is inherent in all modern equilibrium analysis, to turn economics into a branch of pure logic, a set of self-evident propositions which, like mathematics or geometry, are subject to no other test but internal consistency. But it seems that if only this process is carried far enough it carries its own remedy with it. In distilling from our reasoning about the facts of economic life those parts which are truly *a priori*, we not only isolate one element of our reasoning as a sort of Pure Logic of Choice in all its purity, but we also isolate, and emphasise the importance of, another element which has been too much neglected. My criticism of the recent tendencies to make economic theory more and more formal is not that they have gone too far, but that they have not yet been carried far enough to complete the isolation of this branch of logic and to restore to its rightful place the investigation of causal processes, using formal economic theory as a tool in the same way as mathematics.

II

But before I can prove my contention that the tautological propositions of pure equilibrium analysis as such are not directly applicable to the explanation of social relations, I must first show that the concept of equilibrium *has* a clear meaning if applied to the actions of a single individual, and what this meaning is. Against my contention it might be argued that it is precisely here that the concept of equilibrium is of no significance, because, if one

however, be mentioned here that some of the most stimulating suggestions on problems closely related to those treated here have come from his circle. Cf., H. Mayer, "Der Erkenntniswert der funktionellen Preistheorien," *Die Wirtschaftstheorie der Gegenwart*, Vol. II, 1931 ; P. N. Rosenstein-Rodan, " Das Zeitmoment in der mathematischen Theorie des wirtschaftlichen Gleichgewichts," *Zeitschrift für Nationalökonomie*, Vol. I, No. 1, and " The Rôle of Time in Economic Theory," ECONOMICA (N.S.), Vol. I (1), 1934.

wanted to apply it, all one could say would be that an isolated person was always in equilibrium. But this last statement, although a truism, shows nothing but the way in which the concept of equilibrium is typically misused. What is relevant is not whether a person as such is or is not in equilibrium, but which of his actions stand in equilibrium relationships to each other. All propositions of equilibrium analysis, such as the proposition that relative values will correspond to relative costs, or that a person will equalise the marginal returns of any one factor in its different uses, are propositions about the relations between actions. Actions of a person can be said to be in equilibrium in so far as they can be understood as part of one plan. Only if this is the case, only if all these actions have been decided upon at one and the same moment, and in consideration of the same set of circumstances, have our statements about their interconnections, which we deduce from our assumptions about the knowledge and the preferences of the person, any application. It is important to remember that the so-called " data ", from which we set out in this sort of analysis, are (apart from his tastes) all facts given to the person in question, the things as they are known to (or believed by) him to exist, and not in any sense objective facts. It is only because of this that the propositions we deduce are necessarily *a priori* valid, and that we preserve the consistency of the argument.[1]

The two main conclusions from these considerations are, *firstly*, that since equilibrium relations exist between the successive actions of a person only in so far as they are part of the execution of the same plan, any change in the relevant knowledge of the person, that is, any change which leads him to alter his plan, disrupts the equilibrium relation between his actions taken before and those taken after the change in his knowledge. In other words, the equilibrium relationship comprises only his actions during the period during which his anticipations prove correct. *Secondly*, that since equilibrium is a relationship between actions, and since the actions of one person must necessarily take place successively in time, it is obvious that the passage of time is essential to give the concept of equilibrium any meaning. This deserves mention since many economists

---

[1] Cf., on this point particularly L. Mises, *Grundprobleme der Nationalökonomie*, Jena, 1933, pp. 22 *et seq.*, 160 *et seq.*

appear to have been unable to find a place for time in equilibrium analysis and consequently have suggested that equilibrium must be conceived as timeless. This seems to me to be a meaningless statement.

III

Now, in spite of what I have said before about the doubtful meaning of equilibrium analysis in this sense if applied to the conditions of a competitive society, I do not of course want to deny that the concept was originally introduced precisely to describe the idea of some sort of balance between the actions of different individuals. All I have argued so far is that the sense in which we use the concept of equilibrium to describe the interdependence of the different actions of one person does not immediately admit of application to the relations between actions of different people. The question really is what use we make of it when we speak of equilibrium with reference to a competitive system.

The first answer which would seem to follow from our approach is that equilibrium in this connection exists if the actions of all members of the society over a period are all executions of their respective individual plans on which each decided at the beginning of the period. But when we inquire further what exactly this implies, it appears that this answer raises more difficulties than it solves. There is no special difficulty about the concept of an isolated person (or a group of persons directed by one of them) acting over a period according to a preconceived plan. In this case, the execution of the plan need not satisfy any special criteria in order to be conceivable. It may of course be based on wrong assumptions concerning the external facts and on this account may have to be changed. But there will always be a conceivable set of external events which would make it possible for the plan to be executed as originally conceived.

The situation is, however, different with the plans determined upon simultaneously but independently by a number of persons. In the first instance, in order that all these plans can be carried out, it is necessary for them to be based on the expectation of the same set of external events, since, if different people were to base their plans on conflicting expectations, no set of external events could make the execution of all these plans possible. And, secondly, in a society based on exchange their plans will to a considerable extent refer to actions which require corresponding actions on the part of other individuals. This means that the plans of different individuals must in a special sense be compatible if it is to be even conceivable that they will be able to carry all of them out.[1] Or, to put the same thing in different words, since some of the " data " on which any one person will base his plans will be the expectation that other people will act in a particular way, it is essential for the compatibility of the different plans that the plans of the one contain exactly those actions which form the data for the plans of the other.

In the traditional treatment of equilibrium analysis part of this difficulty is apparently avoided by the assumption that the data, in the form of demand schedules representing individual tastes and technical facts, will be equally given to all individuals and that their acting on the same premises will somehow lead to their plans becoming adapted to each other. That this does not really overcome the difficulty created by the fact that one person's decisions are the other person's data, and that it involves to some degree circular reasoning, has often been pointed out. What, however, seems so far to have escaped notice is that this whole procedure involves a confusion of a much more general character, of which the point just mentioned is just a special instance, and which is due to an equivocation of the term " datum ". The data which now are supposed to be objective facts and the same for all people are evidently no longer the same thing as the data which formed the starting point for the tautological transformations of the Pure Logic of Choice. There " data " meant all facts, and only the facts, which were present in the mind of the acting person, and only this subjective interpretation of the term datum made those propositions necessary truths. " Datum " meant given,

---

[1] It has long been a subject of wonder to me why there should, to my knowledge, have been no systematic attempts in sociology to analyse social relations in terms of correspondence and non-correspondence, or compatibility and non-compatibility, of individual aims and desires. It seems that the mathematical technique of *analysis situs* (topology) and particularly such concepts developed by it as that of *homeomorphism* might prove very useful in this connection, although it may appear doubtful whether even this technique, at any rate in the present state of its development, is adequate to the complexity of the structures with which we have to deal. A first attempt made recently in this direction by an eminent mathematician (Karl Menger, *Moral, Wille und Weltgestaltung*, Vienna, 1934) has so far not yet led to very illuminating results. But we may look forward with interest to the treatise on exact sociological theory which Professor Menger has promised for the near future. (Cf.," Einige neuere Fortschritte in der exakten Behandlung sozialwissenschaftlicher Probleme," in *Neuere Fortschritte in den exakten Wissenschaften*, Vienna, 1936, p. 132.)

known, to the person under consideration. But in the transition from the analysis of the action of an individual to the analysis of the situation in a society the concept has undergone an insidious change of meaning.

IV

The confusion about the concept of a datum is at the bottom of so many of our difficulties in this field that it is necessary to consider it in somewhat more detail. Datum means of course something given, but the question which is left open, and which in the social sciences is capable of two different answers, is to whom the facts are supposed to be given. Economists appear subconsciously always to have been somewhat uneasy about this point, and to have reassured themselves against the feeling that they did not quite know to whom the facts were given by underlining the fact that they *were* given — even by using such pleonastic expressions as " given data ". But this does not solve the question whether the facts referred to are supposed to be given to the observing economist, or to the persons whose actions he wants to explain, and if to the latter, whether it is assumed that the same facts are known to all the different persons in the system, or whether the " data " for the different persons may be different.

There seems to be no possible doubt that these two concepts of " data ", on the one hand in the sense of the objective real facts, as the observing economist is supposed to know them, and on the other in the subjective sense, as things known to the persons whose behaviour we try to explain, are really fundamentally different and ought to be kept carefully apart. And, as we shall see, the question why the data in the subjective sense of the term should ever come to correspond to the objective data is one of the main problems we have to answer.

The usefulness of the distinction becomes immediately apparent when we apply it to the question of what we can mean by the concept of a society being at any one moment in a state of equilibrium. There are evidently two senses in which it can be said that the subjective data, given to the different persons, and the individual plans, which necessarily follow from them, are in agreement. We may merely mean that these plans are mutually compatible and that there is consequently a conceivable set of external events which will allow all people to carry out their plans and not cause any disappointments. If this mutual compatibility of intentions were not given, and if in consequence no set of external events could satisfy all expectations, we could clearly say that this is not a state of equilibrium. We have a situation where a revision of the plans on the part of at least some people is inevitable, or, to use a phrase which in the past has had a rather vague meaning, but which seems to fit this case perfectly, where endogenous disturbances are inevitable.

There is, however, still the other question of whether the individual subjective sets of data correspond to the objective data, and whether in consequence the expectations on which plans were based are borne out by the facts. If correspondence between data in this sense were required for equilibrium it would never be possible to decide otherwise than *ex post*, at the end of the period for which people have planned, whether at the beginning the society has been in equilibrium. It seems to be more in conformity with established usage to say in such a case that the equilibrium, as defined in the first sense, may be disturbed by an unforeseen development of the (objective) data, and to describe this as an exogenous disturbance. In fact it seems hardly possible to attach any definite meaning to the much used concept of a change in the (objective) data unless we distinguish between external developments in conformity with, and those different from, general expectations, and define as a " change " any divergence of the actual from the expected development, irrespective of whether it means a " change " in some absolute sense. Surely if the alternations of the seasons suddenly ceased and the weather remained constant from a certain day onward, this would represent a change of data in our sense, that is a change relative to expectations, although in an absolute sense it would not represent a change but rather an absence of change. But all this means that we can speak of a change in data only if equilibrium in the first sense exists, that is, if expectations coincide. If they conflicted, any development of the external facts might bear out somebody's expectations and disappoint those of others, and there would be no possibility of deciding what was a change in the objective data.[1]

[1] Cf. " The Maintenance of Capital," ECONOMICA (N.S.), Vol. II, 1935, p. 265.

V

For a society then we *can* speak of a *state* of equilibrium at a point of time—but it means only that compatibility exists between the different plans which the individuals composing it have made for action in time. And equilibrium will continue, once it exists, so long as the external data correspond to the common expectations of all the members of the society. The continuance of a state of equilibrium in this sense is then not dependent on the objective data being constant in an absolute sense, and is not necessarily confined to a stationary process. Equilibrium analysis becomes in principle applicable to a progressive society and to those inter-temporal price relationships which have given us so much trouble in recent times.[1]

These considerations seem to throw considerable light on the relationship between equilibrium and foresight, which has been somewhat hotly debated in recent times.[2] It appears that the concept of equilibrium merely means that the foresight of the different members of the society is in a special sense correct. It must be correct in the sense that every person's plan is based on the expectation of just those actions of other people which those other people intend to perform, and that all these plans are based on the expectation of the same set of external facts, so that under certain conditions nobody will have any reason to change his plans. Correct foresight is then not, as it has sometimes been understood, a precondition which must exist in order that equilibrium may be arrived at. It is rather

---

[1] This separation of the concept of equilibrium from that of a stationary state seems to me to be no more than the necessary outcome of a process which has been going on for a fairly long time. That this association of the two concepts is not essential but only due to historical reasons is to-day probably generally felt. If complete separation has not yet been effected, it is apparently only because no alternative definition of a state of equilibrium had yet been suggested which has made it possible to state in a general form those propositions of equilibrium analysis which are essentially independent of the concept of a stationary state. Yet it is evident that most of the propositions of equilibrium analysis are not supposed to be applicable only in that stationary state which will probably never be reached. The process of separation seems to have begun with Marshall and his distinction between long and short run equilibria. (Cf., statements like this : " For the nature of equilibrium itself, and that of the causes by which it is determined, depend on the length of the period over which the market is taken to extend." *Principles*, Vol. I, 6, 7th ed., p. 330.) The idea of a state of equilibrium which was not a stationary state was already inherent in my " Das intertemporale Gleichgewichtssystem der Preise und die Bewegungen des Geldwertes " (*Weltwirtschaftliches Archiv*, Vol. XXVIII, June, 1928) and is, of course, essential if we want to use the equilibrium apparatus for the explanation of any of the phenomena connected with " investment ". On the whole matter much historical information will be found in E. Schams, Komparative Statistik, *Zeitschrift für Nationalökonomie* II/1, 1930.

[2] Cf. particularly O. Morgenstern, " Vollkommene Voraussicht und Wirtschaftliches Gleichgewicht," *Zeitschrift für Nationalökonomie*, Vol. VI, p. 3.

the defining characteristic of a state of equilibrium. Nor need foresight for this purpose be perfect in the sense that it need extend into the indefinite future, or that everybody must foresee everything correctly. We should rather say that equilibrium will last so long as the anticipations prove correct, and that they need to be correct only on those points which are relevant for the decisions of the individuals. But on this question of what is relevant foresight or knowledge, more later.

Before I proceed further I should probably stop for a moment to illustrate by a concrete example what I have just said about the meaning of a state of equilibrium and how it can be disturbed. Consider the preparations which will be going on at any moment for the production of houses. Brickmakers, plumbers and others will all be producing materials which in each case will correspond to a certain quantity of houses for which just this quantity of the particular material will be required. Similarly we may conceive of prospective buyers as accumulating savings which will enable them at certain dates to buy definite quantities of houses. If all these activities represent preparations for the production (and acquisition) of the same amount of houses we can say that there is equilibrium between them in the sense that all the people engaged in them may find that they can carry out their plans.[1] This need not be so, because other circumstances which are not part of their plan of action may turn out to be different from what they expected. Part of the materials may be destroyed by an accident, weather conditions may make building impossible, or an invention may alter the proportions in which the different factors are wanted. This is what we call a change in the (objective) data, which disturbs the equilibrium which has existed. But if the different plans were from

---

[1] Another example of more general importance would, of course, be the correspondence between " investment " and " saving " in the sense of the proportion (in terms of relative cost) in which entrepreneurs provide producers' goods and consumers' goods for a particular date, and the proportion in which consumers in general will at this date distribute their resources between producers' goods and consumers' goods. (Cf. my " Preiserwartungen, monetäre Störungen und Fehlinvestitionen," *Ekonomisk Tidskrift*, Vol. 34, 1935 (French translation : " Prévisions de Prix, Perturbations Monétaires et Faux Investissements," *Revue des Sciences Economiques*, October, 1935) and " The Maintenance of Capital," ECONOMICA (N.S.), Vol. II, 1935, pp. 268–273.) It may be of interest in this connection to mention that in the course of investigations of the same field, which led the present author to these speculations, the theory of crises, the great French sociologist G. Tarde stressed the " contradiction de croyances " or " contradiction de jugements " or " contradictions des espérances " as the main cause of these phenomena (*Psychologie Economique*, Paris, 1902, Vol. II, pp. 128–9 ; Cf. also N. Pinkus, *Das Problem des Normalen in der Nationalökonomie*, Leipzig, 1906, pp. 252 and 275).

the beginning incompatible, it is inevitable that somebody's plans will be upset and have to be altered, and that in consequence the whole complex of actions over the period will not show those characteristics which apply if all the actions of each individual can be understood as part of a single individual plan he has made at the beginning.[1]

VI

When in all this I emphasise the distinction between mere inter-compatibility of the individual plans[2] and the correspondence between them and the actual external facts or objective data, I do not of course mean to suggest that the subjective inter-agreement is not in some way brought about by the external facts. There would of course be no reason why the subjective data of different people should ever correspond unless they were due to the experience of the same objective facts. But the point is that pure equilibrium analysis is not concerned with the way in which this correspondence is brought about. In the description of an existing state of equilibrium which it provides, it is simply assumed that the subjective data coincide with the objective facts. The equilibrium relationships cannot be deduced merely from the objective facts, since the analysis of what people will do can only start from what is known to them. Nor can equilibrium analysis start merely from a given set of subjective data, since the subjective data of different people would be either compatible or incompatible, that is, they would already determine whether equilibrium did or did not exist.

We shall not get much further here unless we ask for the reasons for our concern with the admittedly fictitious state of equilibrium. Whatever may occasionally have been said by over-pure economists, there seems to be no possible

[1] It is an interesting question, but one which I cannot discuss here, whether in order that we can speak of equilibrium, every single individual must be right, or whether it would not be sufficient if, in consequence of a compensation of errors in different directions, quantities of the different commodities coming on the market were the same as if every individual had been right. It seems to me as if equilibrium in the strict sense would require the first condition to be satisfied, but I can conceive that a wider concept, requiring only the second condition, might occasionally be useful. A fuller discussion of this problem would have to consider the whole question of the significance which some economists (including Pareto) attach to the law of great numbers in this connection. On the general point see P. N. Rosenstein-Rodan, "The Coordination of the General Theories of Money and Price," ECONOMICA, August, 1936.

[2] Or, since in view of the tautological character of the Pure Logic of Choice, "individual plans" and "subjective data" can be used interchangeably, between the agreement between the subjective data of the different individuals.

doubt that the only justification for this is the supposed existence of a tendency towards equilibrium. It is only with this assertion that economics ceases to be an exercise in pure logic and becomes an empirical science ; and it is to economics as an empirical science that we must now turn.

In the light of our analysis of the meaning of a state of equilibrium it should be easy to say what is the real content of the assertion that a tendency towards equilibrium exists. It can hardly mean anything but that under certain conditions the knowledge and intentions of the different members of society are supposed to come more and more into agreement, or, to put the same thing in less general and less exact but more concrete terms, that the expectations of the people and particularly of the entrepreneurs will become more and more correct. In this form the assertion of the existence of a tendency towards equilibrium is clearly an empirical proposition, that is, an assertion about what happens in the real world which ought, at least in principle, to be capable of verification. And it gives our somewhat abstract statement a rather plausible common-sense meaning. The only trouble is that we are still pretty much in the dark about (*a*) the *conditions* under which this tendency is supposed to exist, and (*b*) the nature of the *process* by which individual knowledge is changed.

VII

In the usual presentations of equilibrium analysis it is generally made to appear as if these questions of how the equilibrium comes about were solved. But if we look closer it soon becomes evident that these apparent demonstrations amount to no more than the apparent proof of what is already assumed.[1] The device generally adopted for this purpose is the assumption of a perfect market where every event becomes known instantaneously to every member. It is necessary to remember here that the perfect market which is required to satisfy the assumptions of equilibrium analysis must not be confined to the markets of all the individual commodities ; the whole economic system must be assumed

---

[1] This seems to be implicitly admitted, although hardly consciously recognised, when in recent times it is frequently stressed that equilibrium analysis only describes the conditions of equilibrium without attempting to derive the position of equilibrium from the data. Equilibrium analysis in this sense would, of course, be pure logic and contain no assertions about the real world.

to be one perfect market in which everybody knows everything. The assumption of a perfect market then means nothing less than that all the members of the community, even if they are not supposed to be strictly omniscient, are at least supposed to know automatically all that is relevant for their decisions. It seems that that skeleton in our cupboard, the " economic man ", whom we have exorcised with prayer and fasting, has returned through the back door in the form of a quasi-omniscient individual.

The statement that, if people know everything, they are in equilibrium is true simply because that is how we define equilibrium. The assumption of a perfect market in this sense is just another way of saying that equilibrium exists, but does not get us any nearer an explanation of when and how such a state will come about. It is clear that if we want to make the assertion that under certain conditions people will approach that state we must explain by what process they will acquire the necessary knowledge. Of course any assumption about the actual acquisition of knowledge in the course of this process will also be of a hypothetical character. But this does not mean that all such assumptions are equally justified. We have to deal here with assumptions about causation, so that what we assume must not only be regarded as possible (which is certainly not the case if we just regard people as omniscient) but must also be regarded as likely to be true, and it must be possible, at least in principle, to demonstrate that it is true in particular cases.

The essential point here is that it is these apparently subsidiary hypotheses or assumptions that people do learn from experience, and about how they acquire knowledge, which constitute the empirical content of our propositions about what happens in the real world. They usually appear disguised and incomplete as a description of the type of market to which our proposition refers ; but this is only one, though perhaps the most important, aspect of the more general problem of how knowledge is acquired and communicated. The important thing of which economists frequently do not seem to be aware is that the nature of these hypotheses is in many respects rather different from the more general assumptions from which the Pure Logic of Choice starts. The main differences seem to me to be two :

Firstly, the assumptions from which the Pure Logic of Choice starts are facts which we know to be common to all human thought. They may be regarded as axioms which define or delimit the field within which we are able to understand or mentally to reconstruct the processes of thought of other people. They are therefore universally applicable to the field in which we are interested—although of course where *in concreto* the limits of this field are is an empirical question. They refer to a type of human action (what we commonly call rational, or even merely conscious, as distinguished from instinctive action) rather than to the particular conditions under which this action is undertaken. But the assumptions or hypotheses, which we have to introduce when we want to explain the social processes, concern the relation of the thought of an individual to the outside world, the question to what extent and how his knowledge corresponds to the external facts. And the hypotheses must necessarily run in terms of assertions about causal connections, about how experience creates knowledge.

Secondly, while in the field of the Pure Logic of Choice our analysis can be made exhaustive, that is, while we can here develop a formal apparatus which covers all conceivable situations, the supplementary hypotheses must of necessity be selective, that is, we must select from the infinite variety of possible situations such ideal types as for some reason we regard as specially relevant to conditions in the real world.[1] Of course we could also develop a separate science, the subject matter of which was *per definitionem* confined to a "perfect market" or some similarly defined object, just as the Logic of Choice applies only to persons who have to allot limited means among a variety of ends. And for the field so defined our propositions would again become *a priori* true. But for such a procedure we should lack the justification which consists in the assumption that the situation in the real world is similar to what we assume it to be.

[1] The distinction drawn here may help to solve the old difference between economists and sociologists about the rôle which "ideal types" play in the reasoning of economic theory. The sociologists used to emphasise that the usual procedure of economic theory involved the assumption of particular ideal types, while the economic theorist pointed out that his reasoning was of such generality that he need not make use of any "ideal types". The truth seems to be that within the field of the Pure Logic of Choice, in which the economist was largely interested, he was right in his assertion, but that as soon as he wanted to use it for the explanation of a social process he had to use "ideal types" of one sort or another.

VIII

I must now turn to the question of what the concrete hypotheses are concerning the conditions under which people are supposed to acquire the relevant knowledge and the process by which they are supposed to acquire it. If it were at all clear what the hypotheses usually employed in this respect were, we should have to scrutinise them in two respects : we should have to investigate whether they were necessary and sufficient to explain a movement towards equilibrium, and we should have to show to what extent they were borne out by reality. But I am afraid I am now getting to a stage where it becomes exceedingly difficult to say what exactly are the assumptions on the basis of which we assert that there will be a tendency towards equilibrium, and to claim that our analysis has an application to the real world. I cannot pretend that I have as yet got much further on this point. Consequently all I can do is to ask a number of questions to which we shall have to find an answer if we want to be clear about the significance of our argument.

The only condition, about the necessity of which for the establishment of an equilibrium economists seem to be fairly agreed, is the " constancy of the data ". But after what we have seen about the vagueness of the concept of " datum " we shall suspect, and rightly, that this does not get us much farther. Even if we assume—as we probably must—that here the term is used in its objective sense (which includes, it will be remembered, the preferences of the different individuals) it is by no means clear that this is either required or sufficient in order that people shall actually acquire the necessary knowledge, or that it was meant as a statement of the conditions under which they will do so. It is rather significant that at any rate some authors[1] feel it necessary to add " perfect knowledge " as an additional and separate condition. And indeed we shall see that constancy of the objective data is neither a necessary nor a sufficient condition. That it cannot be a necessary condition follows from the facts, firstly, that nobody would want to interpret it in the absolute sense that nothing must ever happen in the world, and, secondly, that, as we have seen, as soon as we want to include changes which occur periodically or

---

[1] *Vide* N. Kaldor, " A Classificatory Note on the Determinateness of Equilibrium," *Review of Economic Studies*, Vol. I, No. 2, 1934, p. 123.

perhaps even changes which proceed at a constant rate, the only way in which we can define constancy is with reference to expectations. All that this condition amounts to then is that there must be some discernible regularity in the world which makes it possible to predict events correctly. But while this is clearly not sufficient to prove that people will learn to foresee events correctly, the same is true to a hardly less degree even about constancy of data in an absolute sense. For any one individual, constancy of the data does in no way mean constancy of all the facts independent of himself, since, of course, only the tastes and not the actions of the other people can in this sense be assumed to be constant. And as all those other people will change their decisions as they gain experience about the external facts and other people's action, there is no reason why these processes of successive changes should ever come to an end. These difficulties are well known[1] and I only mention them here to remind you how little we actually know about the conditions under which an equilibrium will ever be reached. But I do not propose to follow this line of approach further, though not because this question of the empirical probability that people will learn (that is, that their subjective data will come to correspond with each other and with the objective facts) is lacking in unsolved and highly interesting problems. The reason is rather that there seems to me to be another and more fruitful way of approach to the central problem.

IX

The questions I have just discussed concerning the conditions under which people are likely to acquire the necessary knowledge, and the process by which they will acquire it, has at least received some attention in past discussions. But there is a further question which seems to me to be at least equally important, but which appears to have received no attention at all, and that is how much knowledge and what sort of knowledge the different individuals must possess in order that we may be able to speak of equilibrium. It is clear that if the concept is to have any empirical significance it cannot presuppose that everybody knows everything. I have already had to use the undefined term " relevant

---

[1] On all this cf. N. Kaldor, loc. cit., *passim*.

knowledge ", that is, the knowledge which is relevant to a particular person. But what is this relevant knowledge ? It can hardly mean simply the knowledge which actually influenced his actions, because his decisions might have been different not only if, for instance, the knowledge he possessed had been correct instead of incorrect, but also if he had possessed knowledge about altogether different fields.

Clearly there is here a problem of the *Division of Knowledge* which is quite analogous to, and at least as important as, the problem of the division of labour. But while the latter has been one of the main subjects of investigation ever since the beginning of our science, the former has been as completely neglected, although it seems to me to be the really central problem of economics as a social science.[1] The problem which we pretend to solve is how the spontaneous interaction of a number of people, each possessing only bits of knowledge, brings about a state of affairs in which prices correspond to costs, *etc.*, and which could be brought about by deliberate direction only by somebody who possessed the combined knowledge of all those individuals. And experience shows us that something of this sort does happen, since the empirical observation that prices do tend to correspond to costs was the beginning of our science. But in our analysis, instead of showing what bits of information the different persons must possess in order to bring about that result, we fall in effect back on the assumption that everybody knows everything and so evade any real solution of the problem.

Before, however, we can proceed further, to consider this division of knowledge among different persons, it is necessary to become more specific about the sort of knowledge which is relevant in this connection. It has become customary among economists to stress only the need of knowledge of prices, apparently because—as a consequence of the confusions between objective and subjective data— the complete knowledge of the objective facts was taken for granted. In recent times even the knowledge of current prices has been taken so much for granted that the only connection in which the question of knowledge has been regarded as problematic has been the anticipation of future

[1] I am not certain, but I hope, that the distinction between the Pure Logic of Choice and economics as a social science is essentially the same distinction as that which Professor A. Ammon has in mind when he stresses again and again that a " *Theorie des Wirtschaftens* " is not yet a " *Theorie der Volkswirtschaft* ".

prices. But, as I have already indicated at the beginning, price expectations and even the knowledge of current prices are only a very small section of the problem of knowledge as I see it. The wider aspect of the problem of knowledge with which I am concerned is the knowledge of the basic fact of how the different commodities can be obtained and used,[1] and under what conditions they are actually obtained and used, that is, the general question of why the subjective data to the different persons correspond to the objective facts. Our problem of knowledge here is just the existence of this correspondence which in much of current equilibrium analysis is simply assumed to exist, but which we have to explain if we want to show why the propositions, which are necessarily true about the attitude of a person towards things which he believes to have certain properties, should come to be true of the actions of society with regard to things which either do possess these properties, or which, for some reason we shall have to explain, are commonly believed by the members of society to possess these properties.[2]

But to revert to the special problem I have been discussing, the amount of knowledge different individuals must possess in order that equilibrium may prevail (or the " relevant " knowledge they must possess), we shall get nearer to an answer if we remember how it can become apparent either that equilibrium did not exist or that it is being disturbed. We have seen that the equilibrium connections will be severed if any person changes his plans, either because his

---

[1] Knowledge in this sense is more than what is usually described as skill, and the division of knowledge of which we here speak more than is meant by the division of labour. To put it shortly, " skill " refers only to the knowledge of which a person makes use in his trade, while the further knowledge about which we must know something in order to be able to say anything about the processes in society, is the knowledge of alternative possibilities of action of which he makes no direct use. It may be added here that knowledge, in the sense in which the term is here used, is identical with foresight only in the sense in which all knowledge is capacity to predict.

[2] That all propositions of economic theory refer to things which are defined in terms of human attitudes towards them, that is, that for instance the " sugar " about which economic theory may occasionally speak, is not defined by its " objective " qualities, but by the fact that people believe that it will serve certain needs of theirs in a certain way, is the source of all sorts of difficulties and confusions, particularly in connection with the problem of " verification ". It is, of course, also in this connection that the contrast between the *verstehende* social science and the behaviourist approach becomes so glaring. I am not certain that the behaviourists in the social sciences are quite aware of *how* much of the traditional approach they would have to abandon if they wanted to be consistent, or that they would want to adhere to it consistently if they were aware of this. It would, for instance, imply that propositions of the theory of money would have to refer exclusively to, say, " round discs of metal, bearing a certain stamp," or some similarly defined physical object or group of objects.

tastes change (which does not concern us here) or because new facts become known to him. But there are evidently two different ways in which he may learn of new facts which make him change his plans, which for our purposes are of altogether different significance. He may learn of the new facts as it were by accident, that is in a way which is not a necessary consequence of his attempt to execute his original plan, or it may be inevitable that in the course of his attempt he will find that the facts are different from what he expected. It is obvious that, in order that he may proceed according to plan, his knowledge needs to be correct only on the points on which it will necessarily be confirmed or corrected in the course of the execution of the plan. But he may have no knowledge of things which, if he possessed it, would certainly affect his plan.

The conclusion then which we must draw is that the relevant knowledge which he must possess in order that equilibrium may prevail is the knowledge which he is bound to acquire in view of the position in which he originally is, and the plans which he then makes. It is certainly not all the knowledge which, if he acquired it by accident, would be useful to him, and lead to a change in his plan. And we may therefore very well have a position of equilibrium only because some people have no chance of learning about facts which, if they knew them, would induce them to alter their plans. Or, in other words, it is only relative to the knowledge which a person is bound to acquire in the course of the carrying out of his original plan and its successive alterations that an equilibrium is likely to be reached.

While such a position represents in one sense a position of equilibrium, it is however clear that it is not an equilibrium in the special sense in which equilibrium is regarded as a sort of optimum position. In order that the results of the combination of individual bits of knowledge should be comparable to the results of direction by an omniscient dictator, further conditions must apparently be introduced.[1] And while it seems quite clear that it is possible to define the amount of knowledge which individuals must possess in order that this result should be obtained, I know of no real attempt in this direction. One condition would

[1] These conditions are usually described as absence of " frictions ". In a recently published article (" Quantity of Capital and the Rate of Interest," *Journal of Political Economy*, Vol. XLIV/5, 1936, p. 638) Professor F. H. Knight rightly points out that " ' error ' is the usual meaning of friction in economic discussion ".

probably be that each of the alternative uses of any sort of resources is known to the owner of some such resources actually used for another purpose and that in this way all the different uses of these resources are connected, either directly or indirectly.[1] But I mention this condition only as an instance of how it will in most cases be sufficient that in each field there is a certain margin of people who possess among them all the relevant knowledge. To elaborate this further would be an interesting and a very important task, but a task that would far exceed the limits of this paper.

But although what I have said on this point has been largely in the form of a criticism, I do not want to appear unduly despondent about what we have already achieved in this field. Even if we have jumped over an essential link in our argument, I still believe that by what is implicit in its reasoning, economics has come nearer than any other social science to an answer to that central question of all social sciences, how the combination of fragments of knowledge existing in different minds can bring about results which, if they were to be brought about deliberately, would require a knowledge on the part of the directing mind which no single person can possess. To show that in this sense the spontaneous actions of individuals will under conditions which we can define bring about a distribution of resources which can be understood as if it were made according to a single plan, although nobody has planned it, seems to me indeed an answer to the problem which has sometimes been metaphorically described as that of the " social mind ". But we must not be surprised that such claims on our part have usually been rejected by sociologists, since we have not based them on the right grounds.

There is only one more point in this connection which

---

[1] This would be one, but probably not yet a sufficient, condition to ensure that, with a given state of demand, the marginal productivity of the different factors of production in their different uses should be equalised and that in this sense an equilibrium of production should be brought about. That it is not necessary, as one might think, that every possible alternative use of any kind of resources should be known to at least one among the owners of each group of such resources which are used for one particular purpose is due to the fact that the alternatives known to the owners of the resources in a particular use are reflected in the prices of these resources. In this way it may be a sufficient distribution of knowledge of the alternative uses, $m, n, o, \ldots y, z$, of a commodity, if A, who uses the quantity of these resources in his possession for m, knows of n, and B, who uses his for n, knows of m, while C who uses his for o, knows of n, *etc., etc.*, until we get to L, who uses his for z, but only knows of y. I am not clear to what extent in addition to this a particular distribution of the knowledge of the different proportions is required in which different factors can be combined in the production of any one commodity. For complete equilibrium additional assumptions will be required about the knowledge which consumers possess about the serviceability of the commodities for the satisfaction of their wants.

I should like to mention. This is that if the tendency towards equilibrium, which we have reason to believe to exist on empirical grounds, is only towards an equilibrium relative to that knowledge which people will acquire in the course of their economic activity, and if any other change of knowledge must be regarded as a " change in the data " in the usual sense of the term, which falls outside the sphere of equilibrium analysis, this would mean that equilibrium analysis can really tell us nothing about the significance of such changes in knowledge, and would go far to account for the fact that pure analysis seems to have so extraordinarily little to say about institutions, such as the press, the purpose of which is to communicate knowledge. And it might even explain why the preoccupation with pure analysis should so frequently create a peculiar blindness to the rôle played in real life by such institutions as advertising.

X

With these rather desultory remarks on topics which would deserve much more careful examination I must conclude my survey of these problems. There are only one or two further remarks which I want to add.

One is that, in stressing the nature of the empirical propositions of which we must make use if the formal apparatus of equilibrium analysis is to serve for an explanation of the real world, and in emphasising that the propositions about how people will learn, which are relevant in this connection, are of a fundamentally different nature from those of formal analysis, I do not mean to suggest that there opens here and now a wide field for empirical research. I very much doubt whether such investigation would teach us anything new. The important point is rather that we should become clear about what the questions of fact are on which the applicability of our argument to the real world depends, or, to put the same thing in other words, at what point our argument, when it is applied to phenomena of the real world, becomes subject to verification.

The second point is that I do not want of course to suggest that the sort of problems I have been discussing were foreign to the arguments of the economists of the older generations. The only objection that can be made against them is that they have so mixed up the two sorts of propositions, the *a priori* and the empirical, of which every realistic economist makes constant use, that it is frequently quite impossible to see what sort of validity they claimed for a particular statement. More recent work has been freer from this fault—but only at the price of leaving more and more obscure what sort of relevance their arguments had to the phenomena of the real world. All I have tried to do has been to find the way back to the common-sense meaning of our analysis, of which, I am afraid, we are apt to lose sight as our analysis becomes more elaborate. You may even feel that most of what I have said has been commonplace. But from time to time it is probably necessary to detach oneself from the technicalities of the argument and to ask quite naïvely what it is all about. If I have only shown that in some respects the answer to this question is not only not obvious, but that occasionally we do not even quite know what it is, I have succeeded in my purpose.

[6]

12

Uncertainty, Discovery, and Human Action: A Study of the Entrepreneurial Profile in the Misesian System

Israel M. Kirzner

A central element in the economics of Ludwig von Mises is the role played by the entrepreneur and the function fulfilled by entrepreneurship in the market process. The character of that process for Mises is decisively shaped by the leadership, the initiative, and the driving activity displayed and exercised by the entrepreneur. Moreover, in an intellectual edifice built systematically on the notion of individual *human action*—on the manner in which reasoning human beings interact while seeking to achieve their individual purposes—it is highly significant that Mises found it of relevance to emphasize that each human actor is always, in significant respects, an entrepreneur.[1] The present paper seeks to explore the character of Misesian entrepreneurship, with special reference to the influence exercised by the inescapable uncertainty that pervades economic life. Both at the level of isolated individual human action and at the level of entrepreneurial activity in market context, we shall be concerned to determine the extent to which the Misesian entrepreneur owes his very existence and his function to the unpredictability of his environment and to the ceaseless tides of change that undergird that unpredictability.

On the face of it, this question may not seem worthy of new research. Mises, it may be pointed out, expressed himself quite clearly on numerous occasions to the effect that the entrepreneurial function is inseparable from speculation with respect to an uncertain future. For example he wrote that "the entrepreneur is always a speculator."[2] Or, again, he wrote that "entrepreneur means acting man in regard to the changes occurring in the data of the market."[3] Moreover when Mises points out that every individual acting man is an entrepreneur, this is because "every action is embedded in the flux of time and thus involves a speculation."[4] In other words the entrepreneurial element cannot be abstracted from the notion of individual human action, because the "uncertainty of the future is already implied in the very notion of action. That man acts and that the future is uncertain are by no means two independent matters, they are only two different modes of establishing one thing."[5]

Thus it might seem that the essentiality of uncertainty for the Misesian entrepreneur hardly needs to be established anew. Certainly any thought of questioning that essentiality must, it might appear, be quickly dismissed.

What I shall argue in this chapter is not that the role of uncertainty in the function of the Misesian entrepreneur may be any less definitive than these clear-cut statements imply but that this role is a more subtle one than may on the surface appear to be the case. It is this subtlety in the role played by uncertainty in the Misesian system, I believe, that sets that system apart in significant respects from the views of other economists (such as Knight or Shackle) who have emphasized the phenomenon of uncertainty in the context of the market.

The Background of the Present Exploration

In earlier forays into the field of the Misesian entrepreneur, I developed an interpretation of the entrepreneurial function in which the role of uncertainty, while recognized and certainly not denied, was not emphasized. This failure to emphasize uncertainty was quite deliberate and was indeed explicitly acknowledged.[6] Instead of emphasizing the uncertainty in which entrepreneurial activity is embedded, these earlier treatments stressed the element of *alertness to hitherto unperceived opportunities* that is, I argued, crucial for the Misesian concept of entrepreneurship.[7] Since my position explicitly recognized the element of change and uncertainty, while it claimed to be able to explicate the elusive quality of entrepreneurship without need to emphasize the uncertainty element, it is perhaps not surprising that my treatment has drawn fire from two different perspectives. A number of critics have felt rather strongly that failure to emphasize the role of uncertainty renders my understanding of entrepreneurship fundamentally defective. At least one critic, on the other hand, has been persuaded by my exposition of entrepreneurship to the point that even my frugal references to uncertainty as an inescapable characteristic of the entrepreneurial scene appear altogether unnecessary and are seen as productive of confusion. Since all these critics are basically in agreement with me, I believe, on the broad accuracy of the general entrepreneurial character of the market process that I ascribe to Mises, it has for some time been my hope to delve into these questions more thoroughly. Some further brief recapitulation of these earlier discussions seems in order as an introduction to our present exploration.

My emphasis on alertness to hitherto unperceived opportunities as the decisive element in the entrepreneurial function stemmed from my pursuit of a didactic purpose. This purpose was to distinguish the analysis of the market *process* (a process in which the entrepreneur plays the crucial role)

Uncertainty, Discovery, and Human Action 141

as sharply as possible from the analysis of equilibrium states (in which all scope for entrepreneurial activity has been assumed away). In equilibrium, it turns out, all market decisions have somehow come already into complete mutual coordination. Market participants have been assumed to be making their respective decisions with perfectly correct information concerning the decisions that all other participants are making at the same time.[8] So long as the underlying present consumer attitudes and production possibilities prevail, it is clear that we can rely on the very same set of decisions being made in each of an indefinite number of future periods. On the other hand, in the absence of such complete equilibrium coordination of decisions, a market process is set in motion in which market participants are motivated to learn more accurately to anticipate the decisions of others; in this process the entrepreneurial, profit-motivated discovery of the gaps in mutual coordination of decisions is a crucial element. Entrepreneurial activity drives this market process of mutual discovery by a continually displayed alertness to profit opportunities (into which the market automatically translates the existing gaps in coordination). Whereas entrepreneurial activity is indeed speculative, the pursuit of profit opportunities is a purposeful and deliberate one, the "emphasis on the element of alertness in action [was] intended to point out that, far from being numbed by the inescapable uncertainty of our world, men *act upon their judgments of* what opportunities have been left unexploited by others."[9]

In developing this aspect of entrepreneurship I was led to emphasize the capture of pure entrepreneurial profit as reducible essentially to the exploitation of arbitrage opportunities. Imperfect mutual awareness on the part of other market participants had generated the emergence of more than one price for the same bundle of economic goods; the entrepreneur's alertness to the profit opportunity presented by this price discrepancy permits him to win these profits (and, in so doing, tends to nudge the prices into closer adjustment with each other). In so emphasizing the arbitrage character of pure profit, emphasis was deliberately withdrawn from the speculative character of entrepreneurial activity that wins pure profit by correctly anticipating *future* price movements.[10]

A number of (otherwise friendly) critics expressed serious reservations concerning my deliberate lack of stress on the speculative character of entrepreneurial activity. Henry Hazlitt pointed out that my repeated references to the entrepreneur's perceiving of opportunities fail to make clear that at best the entrepreneur *thinks* that he perceives opportunities; that what an entrepreneur "acts on may not be a perception but a *guess*."[11] Murray Rothbard has endorsed a discussion by Robert Hébert in which my definition of the entrepreneur is sharply distinguished from that of Mises: "Mises conceives of the entrepreneur as the uncertainty bearer. . . . To Kirzner, on the other hand, entrepreneurship becomes reduced to the quality of *alert-*

ness; and uncertainty seems to have little to do with the matter.''[12] Although conceding that my treatment of the entrepreneur has ''a certain amount of textual justification in Mises,'' Rothbard sees this not as providing genuine support for my reading of the Misesian entrepreneur but as being the result of a ''certain uncharacteristic lack of clarity in Mises' discussion of entrepreneurship.''[13]

In a most thoughtful paper by Lawrence H. White several years ago, he too deplored my deliberate failure to emphasize uncertainty in the analysis of entrepreneurship. This treatment White argues, fosters neglect of important features of entrepreneurial activity that arise precisely from the passage of time and from the uncertainty generated by the prospect of unanticipated changes bound to occur during the journey to the future. To compress entrepreneurial activity into an arbitrage box is, in particular, to fail to recognize the highly important part played by entrepreneurial *imagination.*[14]

On the other hand my treatment of entrepreneurship has been criticized by J. High from a diametrically opposite point of view. High accepts the definition of entrepreneurship in terms of alertness to opportunities for pure profit. He proceeds to point out that ''[n]othing in this definition requires uncertainty. The definition requires ignorance, because the opportunity has not been discovered earlier; it requires error, because the opportunity could have been discovered earlier, but the definition does not require uncertainty.''[15] High is therefore critical of passages in which uncertainty is linked specifically with entrepreneurship.[16]

Clearly the role of uncertainty in the entrepreneurial environment, and in particular its relationship to the entrepreneur's alertness to error, demands further explication. What follows may not satisfy my critics (from both wings). I trust, however, that my discussion of some of the perhaps less obvious links between uncertainty and alertness will, if it does not quite absolve me of the charge of intransigence, at least bear witness to my grateful acknowledgement of the very deep importance of the problems raised by my critics.

Our inquiry will be facilitated by a careful examination of the sense in which each individual engaging in human action is, as already cited from Mises, exercising entrepreneurship.[17] Or, to put the issue somewhat differently, it will be helpful to explore more precisely what it is that distinguishes human action from purely calculative, allocative, economizing activity.

I have argued in earlier work that the concept of human action emphasized by Mises includes an ineradicable entrepreneurial element that is absent from the notion of economizing, of the allocation of scarce resources among competing ends, that was articulated by Lord Robbins.[18] On the face of it there appear to be two distinct aspects of Misesian human action that might be considered to set it apart from Robbinsian economizing activity. We shall have to ask whether these are indeed two distinct aspects of human

Uncertainty, Discovery, and Human Action 143

action and how they relate to the entrepreneurial element that human action contains (but which Robbinsian allocative activity does not). These two aspects of human action (not present in economizing activity) may be identified as (1) the element in action that is beyond the scope of "rationality" as an explanatory tool, and (2) the element in action that constitutes discovery of error. Let us consider these in turn.

The Limits of Rationality

Perhaps the central feature of purely economizing activity is that it enables us to explain behavior by reference to the postulate of rationality. With a given framework of ranked goals sought, and of scarce resources available to be deployed, rationality (in the narrow sense of consistency of behavior with the relevant given ranking of ends) assures a unique pattern of resource allocation; decision making can be fully understood in the light of the given ends-means framework. There is no part of the decision that cannot be accounted for; given the framework, the decision taken is fully determined (and therefore completely explained); any other decision would have been simply unthinkable.

On the other hand the notion of Misesian human action embraces the very adoption of the ends-means framework to be considered relevant. The adoption of any particular ends-means framework is a step which is logically (although not necessarily chronologically) prior to that of allocating means consistently with the given ranking of ends. If the human decision is to be perceived as including the selection of the ends-means framework, then we have an element in that decision that cannot, of course, be explained by reference to rationality. Consistency in action is not sufficient to account for that ranking of ends in terms of which consistency itself is to be defined. So that the totality of human action cannot, even in principle, be explained on the basis of rationality. A science of human action cannot fail to acknowledge—even after full recognition of the formidable explanatory power of the postulate of rationality—that human history, depending as it does on unexplained adoption of goals and awareness of means, contains a strong element of the unexplained and even the spontaneous. These are themes that have, of course, been extensively developed by G.L.S. Shackle. "Choice and reason are things different in nature and function, reason *serves* the chosen purposes, not performs the selection of them."[19] "A man can be supposed to act always in rational response to his 'circumstances': but those 'circumstances' can, *and must,* be in part the creation of his own mind. . . . In this loose-textured history, men's choices of action being choices among thoughts which spring indeterminately in their minds, we can deem them to *initiate* trains of events in some real sense."[20]

In an earlier era, much criticism of the role of the rationality postulate

144   Method, Process, and Austrian Economics

in economic theory focused on the place of apparently nonrational behavior, behavior arising out of impetuous impulse or out of unthinking habit.[21] It is simply unrealistic, these criticisms ran, to assume that economic activity represents the exclusive result of deliberation. Man acts all too often without careful deliberation; he does not weigh the costs and benefits of his actions. This is not the place to evaluate these criticisms or deal with the debates that they engendered three-quarters of a century ago and more. But it is perhaps important to point out that limits of rationality discussed in this section have little to do with the arguments based on impulsiveness and on habit bondage. It is not at all being argued here that human action involves the *thoughtless* selection of goals. Human decision making may of course involve the most agonizingly careful appraisal of alternative courses of action to choose that which seems likely to offer the most estimable of outcomes. In emphasizing that the rationality postulate is unable to explain the selection of the relevant ends-means framework, we are not suggesting that that selection occurs without deliberation, but merely that the results of that deliberation cannot be predicted on the basis of the postulate of consistency; that deliberation is essentially creative. One may predict the answer that a competent mathematician will arrive at when he tackles a given problem in computation (in the same way that one may know in advance the answer to that problem that will be yielded by an electronic computer); but one cannot, in the same way, predict which computational problem the mathematician will deliberately choose to tackle (as one may not be able to predict which problems will be selected to be fed into the electronic computer).

The matter may be presented in an alternative version. One may always distinguish, within each human decision an element into which thought enters in self-aware fashion from an element into which thought enters without self-awareness. A man desires a specific goal with great eagerness; but deliberation persuades him, let us imagine, that it is in his interest not to reveal that eagerness to others (say, because others might then spitefully wish to deny that goal to him). The studied nonchalance with which he masks his pursuit of the goal exhibits scope for both elements: (1) his apparent nonchalance is indeed deliberate and studied, he knows precisely the reason why it is important that he pretend disinterest; but (2) he may not be at all self-aware as to how he arrived at this judgment to act on the assumption that others may spitefully seek to frustrate his achievement. He simply decides so to act. His decision is to refrain from naively pursuing with evident eagerness that which he eagerly desires; but his decision is yet naive in the sense that he has not, for example, sought (as reasons having to do with long-term strategy might well suggest) to ostentatiously pretend unawareness of the spitefulness of the others. No matter how calculative a man's behavior may be, it seems impossible to avoid having accepted, without cal-

Uncertainty, Discovery, and Human Action 145

culation, some framework within which to self-consciously engage in cost-benefit comparisons. A man decides to display behavior *a*. We may call the mental activity of making that decision, activity *b*. Now the man *may* have decided (in the course of decision-making activity *c*) to engage in decision-making activity *b*, (or he may have simply and impulsively engaged in decision-making activity *b*). But even if engaging in decision-making activity *b* (as a result of which behavior *a* was chosen) was itself the outcome of "higher" decisions, at some level our decision maker's highest decision was made quite unselfconsciously.

This extra-Robbinsian aspect of human action, the aspect which involves the creative, unpredictable selection of the ends-means framework, can also be usefully stated in terms of *knowledge*. Given his knowledge of the relevant ends-means framework, man's decision can be predicted without doubt; it is simply a matter of computation. To the extent, however, that man must "decide" what it is, so to speak, that he knows, and that this determination is not, in general, based ineluctably on other knowledge unambiguously possessed, man's behavior is not at all predictable. What a man believes himself to know is not itself the result of a calculative decision.[22] This expression of the notion of the existence of limits to rationality will facilitate our insight into the important linkage that exists between these limits and the phenomenon of uncertainty.

In the absence of uncertainty it would be difficult to avoid the assumption that each individual does in fact already know the circumstances surrounding his decision. Without uncertainty, therefore, decision making would no longer call for any imaginative, creative determination of what the circumstances really are. Decision making would call merely for competent calculation. Its results could, in general, be predicted without doubt. Human judgment would have no scope. "With uncertainty absent, man's energies are devoted altogether to doing things; . . . in a world so built . . . it seems likely that . . . all organisms [would be] automata. . . ."[23] "If man knew the future, he would not have to choose and would not act. He would be like an automaton, reacting to stimuli without any will of its own."[24] Thus the extra-Robbinsian aspect of human action, the aspect responsible for rendering human action unpredictable and incompletely explainable in terms of rationality, arises from the inherent uncertainty of human predicament. If, then, one chooses to identify entrepreneurship with the function of making decisions in the face of an uncertain present or future environment, it certainly appears that Misesian human action does (while Robbinsian economizing does not) include an entrepreneurial element.

But before making up our minds on this point, we must consider that second element, mentioned at the end of the preceding section, that distinguishes Misesian human action from Robbinsian allocative decision making.

The Discovery of Error

To draw attention to this element in human action I shall draw on an earlier paper in which I attempted to identify that which might represent "entrepreneurial profit" in successful individual action in a Crusoe context.[25] Entrepreneurial profit in the Crusoe context, it turned out, can be identified only where Crusoe discovers that he has up until now attached an erroneously low valuation to resources over which he has command. Until today Crusoe has been spending his time catching fish with his bare hands. Today he has realized that he can use his time far more valuably by building a boat or making a net. "He has discovered that he had placed an incorrectly low value on his time. His reallocation of his labor time from fishing to boat-building is an entrepreneurial decision and, assuming his decision to be a correct one, yields pure profit in the form of additional value discovered to be forthcoming from the labor time applied."[26] This (Crusonian) pure profit arises from the circumstance that at the instant of entrepreneurial discovery Menger's law is violated. Menger's law teaches that men value goods according to the value of the satisfactions that depend on possession of those goods. This law arises from man's propensity to attach the value of ends to the means needed for their achievement. At the moment of entrepreneurial discovery Crusoe realizes that the ends achievable with his labor time have higher value than the ends he had previously sought to achieve:

> The value Crusoe has until now attached to his time is *less* than the value of the ends he now seeks. This discrepancy is, at the level of the individual, pure profit. . . . Once the old ends-means framework has been completely and unquestionably replaced by the new one, of course, it is the value of the new ends that Crusoe comes to attach to his means. . . . But, during the instant of an entrepreneurial leap of faith . . . there is scope for the discovery that, indeed, the ends achieved are more valuable than had hitherto been suspected. *This,* is the discovery of pure (Crusonian) entrepreneurial profit.[27]

Scope for entrepreneurship thus appears to be grounded in the possibility of discovering error. In the market context, the state of general equilibrium, providing as it does absolutely no scope for the discovery of profitable discrepancies between prices and costs, affords no opportunity for entrepreneurial discovery and turns out to be populated entirely by Robbinsian maximizers. In the same way, it now appears, the situation in which Crusoe is errorlessly allocating his resources—with the value of ends being fully and faultlessly attached to the relevant means in strict accordance with Menger's law—affords no scope for the entrepreneurial element in human action. Human action, without scope for the discovery of error, collapses into Robbinsian allocative activity.

Uncertainty, Discovery, and Human Action 147

Clearly this way of identifying the entrepreneurial element that is present in Misesian human action but absent in Robbinsian economizing activity fits in well with the approach that defines enterpreneurship as alertness to hitherto unperceived opportunities.[28] In the market context entrepreneurship is evoked by the presence of as yet unexploited opportunities for pure profit. These opportunities are evidence of the failure of market participants, up until now, to correctly assess the realities of the market situation. At the level of the individual too, it is then attractive to argue, an entrepreneurial element in action is evoked by the existence of as-yet-unexploited private opportunities. To act entrepreneurially is to identify situations overlooked until now because of error.

Uncertainty and/or Discovery

Our discussion has led us to identify two apparently distinct elements in human action, each of which possesses plausible claims as constituting that entrepreneurial element in action that sets it apart from purely calculative economizing activity: (1) On the one hand we saw that it appears plausible to associate entrepreneurship with the department within human action in which the very framework for calculative economizing activity is, in an open-ended, uncertain world, selected as being relevant. It is here that we would find scope for the unpredictable, the creative, the imaginative expressions of the human mind—expressions that cannot themselves be explained in terms of the postulate of consistency. Thus entrepreneurship, at the Crusoe level, arises uniquely and peculiarly from the circumstance that, as a result of the inescapable uncertainty of the human predicament, acting man cannot be assumed to be sure of the framework relevant for calculative activity. He must, using whatever entrepreneurial gifts he can display, *choose* a framework. (2) On the other hand, as we have seen, it appears perhaps equally plausible to associate entrepreneurship with that aspect of human action in which the alert individual realizes the existence of opportunities that he has up until now somehow failed to notice. Scope for entrepreneurship, at the Crusoe level, arises then not from the present uncertainty that must now be grappled with in decision making but from earlier error from which entrepreneurial discovery must now provide protection.

We must emphasize that these alternative identifications of the entrepreneurial element in action do appear, at least on a first scrutiny, to be genuinely different from one another. It is of course true that past error (from which, on the one view, we look to entrepreneurial discovery to provide a rescue) may be attributed to the pervasive uncertainty that characterizes our world (and to the inevitably kaleidic changes responsible for that uncertainty.) But to discover hitherto unnoticed opportunities (unnoticed because of past failure to pierce correctly the fog of uncertainty) does not at all seem to be the same task as that of selecting between alternative present scenarios for the future within which calculative activity is to be undertaken. Moreover, whatever the possible reasons for past error, error itself implies merely ignorance, not necessarily uncertainty.[29] To escape ignorance is one thing; to deal with uncertainty is another.

This tension that we have discovered at the level of human action in the Crusoe context, between present uncertainty and earlier error as sources of entrepreneurship, is clearly to be linked immediately with our more general exploration in this chapter. This chapter is concerned with determining the extent to which the Misesian entrepreneur is to be perceived as the creature of uncertainty. The tension we have now discovered between present uncertainty and earlier error corresponds exactly to the disagreement that we encountered between those who see the Misesian entrepreneur as essentially the bearer of market uncertainty and those who see him as the discoverer of earlier market errors. It is my contention that our awareness of this apparent tension can in fact shed light on certain subtleties in the concept of entrepreneurship likely otherwise to be overlooked. Our procedure to develop this claim will be as follows: We will seek to show that, on a deeper understanding of the meaning of uncertainty and of the discovery of error at the level of individual action, the tension between them dissolves in a way that will reveal the full significance of entrepreneurial alertness at the level of the individual. Thereafter we will pursue the analogy between the scope of entrepreneurship at the individual level and that of the entrepreneurship at the level of the market, drawing on this analogy to identify precisely the relative roles, in market entrepreneurship, of uncertainty and of alertness.

Action and Alertness

Man acts, in the light of the future as he envisages it, to enhance his position in that future. The realized consequences of man's actions, however, flow from the impact of those actions on the actual (as contrasted with the envisaged) course of future events. The extent to which man's plans for the enhancement of his future prospects are fulfilled depends on the extent to which the future as he has envisaged it corresponds to the future as it in fact occurs. There is no natural set of forces or constraints assuring correspondence between the envisaged future and the realized future. The two may, it seems at first glance, diverge from one another with complete freedom. The future course of events is in general certainly not constrained by past forecasts; nor, unfortunately, are forecasts constrained by the actual future events these forecasts seek to foretell. On the face of it, then, with nothing to guarantee correspondence between the actual future and the future as it is

Uncertainty, Discovery, and Human Action

envisaged, it might seem as if successful action were entirely a matter of good fortune. Indeed, if man is aware of this apparent lack of ability to envisage the future correctly except as a matter of sheer good fortune, it is not clear why (apart from the joys of gambling itself) man bothers to act at all. But of course the overwhelming fact of human history is that man does act, and his choices are made in terms of an envisaged future that, although by no means a photographic image of the future as it will actually unfold, is yet not entirely without moorings in regard to that realized future. "To be genuine, choice must be neither random nor predetermined. There must be some grounds for choosing, but they must be inadequate; there must be some possibility of predicting the consequences of choice, but none of perfect prediction."[30] "The essence of the situation is action according to *opinion,* . . . neither entire ignorance nor complete and perfect information, but partial knowledge."[31] The genuine choices that do, we are convinced, make up human history express man's conviction that the future as he envisages it does hold correspondence, in some degree, to the future as it will in fact unfold. The uncertainty of the future reflects man's awareness that this correspondence is far from complete; the fact that he acts and chooses at all reflects his conviction that this correspondence is far from negligible. Whence does this correspondence, incomplete though it may be, arise? If there are no constraints assuring correspondence, how is successful action anything but the sheerest good fortune?

The answer to this dilemma surely lies in the circumstance that man is *motivated* to formulate the future as he envisages it, as accurately as possible. It is not a matter of two unfolding tapestries, one the realized future, the second a fantasized series of pictures of what the first might look like. Rather, acting man really does try to construct his picture of the future to correspond to the truth as it will be realized. He really does try to glimpse the future, to peer through the fog. He is thus motivated *to bring about* correspondence between the envisaged and the realized futures. Man's purposeful efforts to better his condition are responsible not only for his choices as constructed against a given envisaged future; that purposefulness is, perhaps even more importantly, responsible for the remarkable circumstance that that envisaged future does overlap significantly with the future as it actually unfolds. (Of course, these forecasts need not be made, explicitly, prior to action; they are embedded, possibly without self-awareness, in action itself.) We call this motivated propensity of man to formulate an image of the future man's *alertness.* Were man totally lacking in alertness, he could not act at all: his blindness to the future would rob him of any framework for action. (In fact, were man totally lacking in potential for alertness, it would be difficult to identify a notion of error altogether: were unalert man to act, it would not be on the basis of an erroneously forecast future. It would be on the basis of no relevant forecast at all. Not recogniz-

ing that he might—had he been more alert—have avoided the incorrect picture of the future, he could not in any meaningful sense blame himself for
having erred.)

It will surely be acknowledged that this alertness—which provides the
only pressure to constrain man's envisaged future toward some correspondence with the future to be realized—is what we are searching for under the
phrase "the entrepreneurial element in human action." Robbinsian allocation activity contains no such element, because within the assigned scope of
such defined activity no possible divergence between a future as envisaged
and a future to be realized is considered. What is incomplete in the notion
of purely allocative activity is surely to be found precisely in this abstraction
from the desperately important element of entrepreneurship in human
action.

It should be observed that the entrepreneurial alertness we have identified does not consist merely in "seeing" the unfolding of the tapestry of the
future in the sense of seeing a preordained flow of events. Alertness must,
importantly, embrace the awareness of the ways in which the human agent
can, by imaginative, bold leaps of faith, and determination, in fact *create*
the future for which his present acts are designed. As we shall argue in a
subsequent section, this latter expression of entrepreneurial alertness does
not affect its essential formal character—which remains that of assuring a
tendency for the future context envisaged as following present action to
bear some realistic resemblance to the future as it will be realized.

We must notice, in understanding this entrepreneurial element in
human action, two aspects of it: (1) We note what provides the scope for
entrepreneurship. This scope is provided by the complete freedom with
which the future as envisaged might, without entrepreneurial alertness,
diverge from the future as it will in fact be. Entrepreneurial alertness has a
function to perform. (2) We note what provides the incentive that switches
on entrepreneurial alertness. This incentive is provided by the lure of pure
entrepreneurial profit to be grasped in stepping from a less accurately
envisaged future to a more accurately envisaged one. Each step taken in
moving toward a vision of the future that overlaps more significantly with
the truth is not merely a step toward truth (that is, a positive entrepreneurial
success); it is also a profitable step (that is, a step that enhances the value of
the resources with which action is available to be taken).

Viewed from this perspective, the tension between the uncertainty-envi-
ronment in which action occurs, on the one hand, and the discovery-of-
error aspect of action, on the other, can be seen to dissolve at a glance.
These two aspects of action can be seen immediately as merely two sides of
the same entrepreneurial coin. If uncertainty were merely an unpleasant
condition of life to which man must passively adjust, then it would be reasonable to distinguish between the quite separate activities of bearing uncer-

Uncertainty, Discovery, and Human Action 151

tainty on the one hand and of discovering error on the other. Escaping from current errors is one thing; grappling with the uncertainty of the future is another. But, as we have noticed, to choose means to *endeavor,* under the incentive to grasp pure profit, to identify a more truthful picture of the future. Dealing with uncertainty is motivated by the profit to be won by avoiding error. In this way of viewing the matter the distinction between escaping current error and avoiding potential future error is unimportant. The discovery of error is an interesting feature of action because it offers incentive. It is this incentive that inspires the effort to pierce the fog of uncertainty that shrouds the future. To deal with uncertainty means to seek to overcome it by more accurate prescience; to discover error is merely that aspect of this endeavor that endows it with incentive attraction. The imagination and creativity with which man limns his envisaged future are inspired by the pure gains to be won in ensuring that that envisaged future is in fact no less bright than that which can be made the truth.

We shall find in the next section that these insights surrounding entrepreneurship at the level of individual action have their exact counterparts in entrepreneurship in the market context. It will be useful to summarize briefly the key points we have learned about individual entrepreneurship:

1. Entrepreneurship in individual action consists in the endeavor to secure greater correspondence between the individual's future as he envisages it and his future as it will in fact unfold. This endeavor consists in the individual's alertness to whatever can provide clues to the future. This alertness, broadly conceived, embraces those aspects of imagination and creativity through which the individual may himself *ensure* that his envisaged future will be realized.

2. Scope for entrepreneurship is provided by the uncertainty of the future. For our purposes uncertainty means that, in the absence of entrepreneurial alertness, an individual's view of the future may diverge with total freedom from the realized future. In the absence of entrepreneurial alertness it is only sheer chance that can be responsible for successful action.

3. Incentive for the "switching on" of entrepreneurial alertness is provided by the pure gain (or avoidance of loss) to be derived from replacing action based on less accurate prescience by action based on the more realistically envisaged future. The avoidance of entrepreneurial error is not merely a matter of being more truthful, it happens also to be profitable.

Entrepreneurship in the Market

Our examination of the entrepreneurial element in individual action permits us to see the role of entrepreneurship in the market in a fresh light. We shall

152   Method, Process, and Austrian Economics

discover, in the market context, elements that correspond precisely to their analogues in the individual context. Let us consider what happens in markets.

In a market exchanges occur between market participants.[32] In the absence of perfect mutual knowledge, many of the exchanges are inconsistent with one another. Some sales are made at low prices when some buyers are buying at high prices. Some market participants are not buying at all because they are unaware of the possibility of buying at prices low enough to be attractive; some are refraining from selling because they are unaware of the possibility of selling at prices high enough to be attractive. Clearly the actions of these buyers and sellers are, from the perspective of omniscience, uncoordinated and inconsistent. We notice that, although the assumption of perfect knowledge that is necessary for market equilibrium would constrain different transactions in the market to complete mutual consistency, the actuality of imperfect knowledge permits these different transactions in different parts of the market to diverge with apparently complete freedom. What alone tends to introduce a modicum of consistency and coordination into this picture, preventing a situation in which even the slightest degree of coordination could exist only as a matter of sheerest chance, is market entrepreneurship, inspired by the lure of pure market profit. We are now in a position to identify, in the market context, elements that correspond to key features already identified in the context of individual entrepreneurship.

Corresponding to uncertainty as it impinges on individual action we have market discoordination. The freedom with which an individual's envisaged future may diverge from the future to be realized, corresponds precisely to the freedom with which transactions made in one part of the market may diverge from transactions made elsewhere. In the absence of entrepreneurship it is only out of the purest chance that market transactions by different pairs of buyers and sellers are made on anything but the most wildly inconsistent terms. There is nothing that constrains the mutually satisfactory price bargain reached between one pair of traders to bear any specific relation to corresponding bargains reached between other pairs of traders.

Corresponding to error at the level of the individual, we have price divergence at the level of the market. Perfect knowledge (such as in Robbinsian individual allocative activity) precludes error. Market equilibrium (implied by universal perfect knowledge) precludes price divergences.

The individual entrepreneurial element permits the individual to escape from the distressing freedom with which divergences between envisaged futures and realized futures may occur; the entrepreneur fulfills the same function for the market. The function of the entrepreneur is to bring different parts of the market into coordination with each other. The market

Uncertainty, Discovery, and Human Action   153

entrepreneur bridges the gaps in mutual knowledge, gaps that would otherwise permit prices to diverge with complete freedom.

Corresponding to the incentive for individual entrepreneurship provided by more realistic views of the future, we have, at the market level, the incentive provided by opportunities for pure entrepreneurial profit. Market profit consists in the gap between prices generated by error and market inconsistency—just as the source for private gain is to be discovered in a present divergence between the imagined and the actual future.

The following are propositions, in the context of the market, that concern entrepreneurship; they correspond precisely to those stated at the conclusion of the preceding section:[33]

1.° Entrepreneurship in the market consists in the function of securing greater consistency between different parts of the market. It expresses itself in entrepreneurial alertness to what transactions are in fact available in different parts of the market. It is only such alertness that is responsible for any tendency toward keeping these transactions in some kind of mutual consistency.

2.° Scope for market entrepreneurship is provided by the imperfect knowledge that permits market transactions to diverge from what would be a mutually inconsistent pattern.

3.° Incentive for market entrepreneurial activity is provided by the pure gain to be won by noticing existing divergences between the prices at which market transactions are available in different parts of the market. It is the lure of market profits that inspires entrepreneurial alertness.

Time, Uncertainty, and Entrepreneurship

Our analogy between entrepreneurship at the level of the individual and entrepreneurship in the market emphasized only the most salient respects of the analogy. Certain additional features of the entrepreneurial function in the market need to be dealt with more extensively. In the individual context the divergence (which it is the function of entrepreneurship to limit) was a divergence between anticipated and realized future. Its source in uncertainty was immediately apparent. In the market context the divergence (which it is the function of entrepreneurship to limit) was a divergence between the transactions in different parts of the market. Its source was stated in terms of imperfect mutual knowledge among market participants. Its relationship to uncertainty was not asserted. This requires both amplification and modification.

Our statements concerning market entrepreneurship were couched in terms of the market for a single commodity within a single period. It should be clear that nothing essential is lost when our picture of the market is

expanded to include many commodities and, in particular, the passage of
time. This should of course not be understood to mean that the introduction
of the passage of time does not open up scope for additional insights. We
merely argue that the insights we have gained in the single-period context
for entrepreneurship are not to be lost sight of in the far more complex
multiperiod case.

When we introduce the passage of time, the dimensions along which
mutual ignorance may develop are multiplied. Market participants in one
part of today's market not only may be imperfectly aware of the transactions available in another part of that market; they also may be imperfectly
aware of the transactions that will be available in next year's market.
Absence of consistency between different parts of today's market is seen as
a special case of a more general notion of inconsistency that includes also
inconsistency between today's transactions and those to be transacted next
year. A low price today may be in this sense inconsistent with the high prices
that will prevail next year. Scope for market entrepreneurship, in the context of the passage of time, arises then from the need to coordinate markets
also across time. Incentive for market entrepreneurship along the intertemporal dimension is provided not by arbitrage profits generated by imperfectly coordinated present markets but, more generally, by the speculative
profits generated by the as yet imperfectly coordinated market situations in
the sequence of time. And, of course, the introduction of entrepreneurial
activity to coordinate markets through time introduces, for individual
entrepreneurs engaged in market entrepreneurship, precisely the considerations concerning the uncertain future that we have, until now, considered
only in the context of the isolated individual.

It is because of this last circumstance that we must acknowledge that
the introduction of the passage of time, although leaving the overall formal
function of market entrepreneurship unchanged, will of course introduce
substantial modification into the way we must imagine entrepreneurship to
be exercised concretely. It is still the case, as noted, that the entrepreneurial
function is that of bringing about a tendency for transactions in different
parts of the market (conceived broadly now as including transactions
entered into at different times) to be made in greater mutual consistency.
But whereas in the case of entrepreneurship in the single-period market
(that is, the case of the entrepreneur as arbitrageur) entrepreneurial alertness meant alertness to present facts, in the case of multiperiod entrepreneurship alertness must mean alertness to the future. It follows that market
entrepreneurship in the multiperiod case introduces uncertainty as facing
the entrepreneur not only as in the analogy offered in the preceding section—where the market analogue for uncertainty turned out to be the freedom with which transactions in different parts of today's market may
unconstrainedly diverge from being mutually consistent—but also as in the

Uncertainty, Discovery, and Human Action 155

simple sense of the entrepreneur's awareness of the freedom with which his own envisaged future (concerning future market transactions) may diverge from the realized future. In particular the futurity that entrepreneurship must confront introduces the possibility that the entrepreneur may, by his own creative actions, in fact *construct* the future as *he* wishes it to be. In the single-period case alertness can at best discover hitherto overlooked current facts. In the multiperiod case entrepreneurial alertness must include the entrepreneur's perception of the way in which creative and imaginative action may vitally shape the kind of transactions that will be entered into in future market periods.

Thus the exercise of entrepreneurial alertness in the multiperiod market context will indeed call for personal and psychological qualifications that were unneeded in the single-period case. To be a successful entrepreneur one must now possess those qualities of vision, boldness, determination, and creativity that we associated earlier with the entrepreneurial element in isolated individual action with respect to an uncertain future. There can be no doubt that in the concrete fulfillment of the entrepreneurial function these psychological and personal qualities are of paramount importance. It is in this sense that so many writers are undoubtedly correct in linking entrepreneurship with the courage and vision necessary to *create* the future in an uncertain world (rather than with merely seeing that which stares one in the face).

However, the function of market entrepreneurship in the multiperiod context is nonetheless still that spelled out in the preceding section. What market entrepreneurship accomplishes is a tendency for transactions in different parts of the market (including the market at different dates) to become coordinated. The incentive that inspires this entrepreneurial coordinaton is the lure of pure profit—the difference in market values resulting from hitherto less complete coordination. These insights remain true for the multiperiod case no less than for the arbitrage case. For some purposes it is no doubt important to draw attention to the concrete psychological requirements on which successful entrepreneurial decision making depends. But for other purposes such emphasis is not required; in fact such emphasis may divert attention from what is, from the perspective of the overall functioning of the market system, surely the essential feature of entrepreneurship: its market-coordinative properties.

Let us recall that at the level of the individual, entrepreneurship involved not merely the bearing of uncertainty but also the overcoming of uncertainty. Uncertainty is responsible for what would, in the absence of entrepreneurship, be a failure to perceive the future in a manner sufficiently realistic to permit action. Entrepreneurship, so to speak, pushes aside to some extent the swirling fogs of uncertainty, permitting meaningful action. It is this function of entrepreneurship that must be kept in view when we study the market process. The uncertainty that characterizes the environment within which market entrepreneurship plays its coordinative role must be fully recognized; without it there would be no need and no scope for entrepreneurship. But an understanding of what entrepreneurship accomplishes requires us to recognize not so much the extent to which uncertainty is the ineradicable feature of human existence but rather the extent to which both individual action and social coordination through the market can occur significantly despite the uncertainty of the future (and in spite also of the uncertainty-analogue that would, in the absence of the arbitrageur, fog up even the single-period market).

Further Reflections on Uncertainty and Alertness

Thus we can see how those writers who have denied that the pure entrepreneurial role involves the bearing of uncertainty were both correct and yet at least partly irrelevant. Both J.A. Schumpeter[34] and J.B. Clark insisted that only the capitalist bears the hazards of business; the pure entrepreneur has, by definition, nothing to lose.[35] No doubt all this is true, as far as it goes, But what is important about linking the entrepreneur with the phenomenon of uncertainty is not that it is the entrepreneur who accepts the disutilities associated with the assumption of the hazards of business in an uncertain world. What is important is that the entrepreneur, motivated by the lure of pure profits, attempts to pierce through these uncertainties and endeavors to see the truth that will permit profitable action on his part.

A number of economists may be altogether unwilling to accept the notion of alertness with respect to uncertain future. In fact many may wish to reject the very formulation we have employed to schematize the uncertainty of the future. For us uncertainty meant the essential freedom with which the envisaged future may diverge from the realized future. Entrepreneurial alertness means the ability to impose constraints on that freedom, so that the entrepreneur's vision of the future may indeed overlap, to some significant extent, with that future that he is attempting to see. But many will be unwilling to treat the future as something to be seen at all. "The present is uniquely determined. It can be seen by the eye-witness. . . . What is the future but the void? To call it the future is to concede the presumption that it is already 'existent' and merely waiting to appear. If that is so, if the world is determinist, then it seems idle to speak of choice."[36] Similarly many are unwilling to see the entrepreneur as "alert to opportunities" if this terminology implies that future opportunities already "exist" and are merely waiting to be grasped. "Entrepreneurial projects are not waiting to be sought out so much as to be thought up."[37]

What perhaps needs to be emphasized once again is that in using phrases such as "grasping future opportunities," "seeing the future correctly or incorrectly," or the "divergence between the envisaged future and the realized future," we do not wish to imply any determinacy regarding the future. No doubt, to say that one sees the future (with greater or lesser accuracy) is to employ a metaphor. No doubt the future that one "sees" is a future that may in fact be constructed significantly by one's action, which is supposed to be informed by that very vision. But surely these metaphors are useful and instructive. To dream realistically in a way that inspires successful, creative action is to "see correctly" as compared to the fantasies that inspire absurd ventures or the cold water poured by the unduly timid pessimist that stunts all efforts at improvement. "The future," we have learned, "is unknowable, though not unimaginable."[**] To acknowledge the unknowability of the future is to acknowledge the essential indeterminacy and uncertainty surrounding human existence. But surely in doing so we need not consign human existence to wholly uncoordinated chaos. To speak of entrepreneurial vision is to draw attention, by use of metaphor, to the formidable and benign coordinative powers of the human imagination. Austrian economists have, in principled fashion, refused to see the world as wholly knowable, as suited to interpretation by models of equilibrium from which uncertainty has been exhausted. It would be most unfortunate if, in pursuing this refusal, economists were to fall into a no-less-serious kind of error. This error would be the failure to understand how entrepreneurial individual action, and the systematic market forces set in motion by freedom for entrepreneurial discovery and innovation, harness the human imagination to achieve no less a result than the liberation of mankind from the chaos of complete mutual ignorance. Mises's concept of human action and his analysis of the role of entrepreneurial market processes surely remain, in this regard, unique and as yet insufficiently appreciated contributions to the profound understanding of human society.

Notes

1. L. von Mises, *Human Action* (New Haven: Yale University, 1949), p. 253.

2. Ibid., p. 288.

3. Ibid., p. 255.

4. Ibid., p. 254.

5. Ibid., p. 105.

6. I.M. Kirzner, *Competition and Entrepreneurship* (Chicago: University of Chicago, 1973), pp. 86–87.

7. Ibid., chap. 2. See also I.M. Kirzner, *Perception, Opportunity, and Profit* (Chicago: University of Chicago, 1979), chap. 10.

158   Method, Process, and Austrian Economics

8. F.A. Hayek, *Individualism and Economic Order* (London: Rout-ledege and Kegan Paul, 1949), p. 42.

9. Kirzner, *Competition and Entrepreneurship,* pp. 86-87. (Italics in original.)

10. Such activity was subsumed under arbitrage by pointing out the formal similarity between (1) buying and selling in different markets today and (2) buying and selling in different markets at different dates. (See Kirzner, *Competition and Entrepreneurship,* pp. 85-86.)

11. Henry Hazlitt, review of *Competition and Entrepreneurship,* in *Freeman* (December 1974):759. Similar concerns seem to be expressed in a review of *Competition and Entrepreneurship* by Percy L. Greaves, Jr. in *Wertfrei* (Spring 1974): especially pp. 18-19.

12. See unpublished paper by Murray N. Rothbard, "Professor Hébert on Entrepreneurship," pp. 1-2. Reprinted with permission.

13. Ibid., p. 7.

14. L.H. White, "Entrepreneurship, Imagination, and the Question of Equilibrium," unpublished paper (1976). See also L.H. White, "Entrepreneurial Price Adjustment" (Paper presented at Southern Economic Association meetings Washington, D.C., November, 1978), p. 36, n. 3.

15. J. High, review article on *Perception, Opportunity and Profit* in *Austrian Economics Newsletter* (Spring 1980):14.

16. High's criticisms of my references to uncertainty as a characteristic of the entrepreneurial environment focus most specifically on what he believes to be my use of uncertainty to "serve as the distinguishing characteristic between entrepreneurship and luck." (Ibid.) Here there seems to be a definite misunderstanding of my position. So far from the presence of the uncertainty surrounding entrepreneurship being what separates entrepreneurial profit from the lucky windfall, almost the exact reverse is the case. What marks entrepreneurial profit as different from the lucky windfall is that the former was, despite the (inevitable) uncertainty that might have discouraged the entrepreneur, in fact deliberately pursued. Where luck confers gain may well reflect the circumstance that the uncertainty of this gain deterred the actor from even dreaming of winning it. High's reading apparently resulted from his understanding a passage that he cites (from Kirzner, *Perception, Opportunity and Profit,* pp. 159-160) to represent the case of a purely lucky gain. In fact the passage cited does not refer to luck at all. If one knows that one's labor can convert low-valued leisure into high-valued apples, the apples one so gains through one's hard work does not constitute a lucky windfall. The point of the cited passages is that Menger's law shows how there is no value gain at all derived from that labor, since one would already have attached the higher value of the ends to the available means. Our discussion in this chapter, however, proceeds on the assumption that High's unhappiness at my treatment of uncertainty in entrepreneurship

Uncertainty, Discovery, and Human Action 159

does not rest solely on the validity of the way in which I distinguish entrepreneurial profits from windfall gains.

17. Mises, *Human Action,* p. 253.

18. See Kirzner, *Competition and Entrepreneurship,* pp. 32-35. See also Kirzner, *Perception, Opportunity and Profit,* pp. 166-168.

19. G.L.S. Shackle, *Epistemics and Economics* (Cambridge: Cambridge University, 1972), p. 136. (Italics in original.)

20. Ibid., p. 351.

21. See also Kirzner, *The Economic Point of View* (Princeton: Van Nostrand, 1960), p. 167.

22. See also Kirzner, *Perception, Opportunity and Profit,* chap. 9.

23. F.H. Knight, *Risk, Uncertainty and Profit* (New York: Houghton Mifflin, 1921), p. 268.

24. Mises, *Human Action,* p. 105.

25. See Kirzner, *Perception, Opportunity and Profit,* chap. 10, especially pp. 158-164.

26. Ibid., p. 162.

27. Idid., p. 163.

28. See, for example, Kirzner, *Competition and Entrepreneurship,* p. 39.

29. See note 15 of this chapter.

30. B.J. Loasby, *Choice, Complexity and Ignorance* (Cambridge: Cambridge University, 1976), p. 5.

31. Knight, *Risk, Uncertainty and Profit,* p. 199.

32. Our discussion proceeds in terms of the market for a single commodity. It could be couched, without altering the essentials in any respect, in more general terms. See also the subsequent section of this chapter.

33. The three pairs of statements may be viewed as additions to the two lists of twelve statements developing the analogy between the individual and the market, provided in Kirzner, *Perception, Opportunity and Profit,* chap. 10, pp. 170-172, 173-175.

34. J.A. Schumpeter, *The Theory of Economic Development* (Cambridge, Mass.: Harvard University, 1934), p. 137; J.A. Schumpeter, *History of Economic Analysis* (Oxford: Oxford University, 1954), p. 556. See also S.M. Kanbur, "A Note on Risk Taking, Entrepreneurship and Schumpeter," *History of Political Economy* 12 (Winter 1980):489-498.

35. J.B. Clark, "Insurance and Business Profit," *Quarterly Journal of Economics* 7 (October 1892):46 (cited in Knight, *Risk, Uncertainty and Profit,* p. 38.)

36. Shackle, *Epistemics and Economics,* p. 122.

37. White, "Entrepreneurship, Imagination," p. 7.

38. L.M. Lachmann, "From Mises to Shackle: An Essay," *Journal of Economic Literature* 14 (March 1976):59.

Innovation

[7]

Excerpt from J.A. Schumpeter (1934), 'The Theory of Economic Development', *An Inquiry Into Profits, Capital, Credit, Interest and the Business Cycle*, trans. R. Opie, Cambridge, Mass: Harvard University Press, 65–94.

II

These spontaneous and discontinuous changes in the channel of the circular flow and these disturbances of the centre of equilibrium appear in the sphere of industrial and commercial life, not in the sphere of the wants of the consumers of final products. Where spontaneous and discontinuous changes in consumers' tastes appear, it is a question of a sudden change in data with which the businessman must cope, hence possibly a question of a *motive* or an opportunity for other than gradual adaptations of his conduct, but not of such other conduct itself. Therefore this case does not offer any other problems than a change in natural data or require any new method of treatment; wherefore we shall neglect any spontaneity of consumers' needs that may actually exist, and assume tastes as "given." This is made easy for us by the fact that the spontaneity of wants is in general small. To be sure, we must always start from the satisfaction of wants, since they are the end of all production, and the given economic situation at any time must be understood from this aspect. Yet innovations in the economic system do not as a rule take place in such a way that first new wants arise spontaneously in consumers and then the productive apparatus swings round through their pressure. We do not deny the presence of this nexus. It is, however, the producer who as a rule initiates economic change, and consumers are educated by him if necessary; they are, as it were, taught to want new things, or things which differ in some respect or other from those which they have been in the habit of using. Therefore, while it is permissible and even necessary to consider consumers' wants as an independent and indeed the fundamental force in a theory of the circular flow, we must take a different attitude as soon as we analyse *change*.

To produce means to combine materials and forces within our reach (cf. *supra*, Chapter I). To produce other things, or the same things by a different method, means to combine these materials and forces differently. In so far as the "new combination" may in time grow out of the old by continuous adjustment in small steps, there is certainly change, possibly growth, but neither a

66   *THE THEORY OF ECONOMIC DEVELOPMENT*

new phenomenon nor development in our sense. In so far as this is not the case, and the new combinations appear discontinuously, then the phenomenon characterising development emerges. For reasons of expository convenience, henceforth, we shall only mean the latter case when we speak of new combinations of productive means. Development in our sense is then defined by the carrying out of new combinations.

This concept covers the following five cases: (1) The introduction of a new good — that is one with which consumers are not yet familiar — or of a new quality of a good. (2) The introduction of a new method of production, that is one not yet tested by experience in the branch of manufacture concerned, which need by no means be founded upon a discovery scientifically new, and can also exist in a new way of handling a commodity commercially. (3) The opening of a new market, that is a market into which the particular branch of manufacture of the country in question has not previously entered, whether or not this market has existed before. (4) The conquest of a new source of supply of raw materials or half-manufactured goods, again irrespective of whether this source already exists or whether it has first to be created. (5) The carrying out of the new organisation of any industry, like the creation of a monopoly position (for example through trustification) or the breaking up of a monopoly position.

Now two things are essential for the phenomena incident to the carrying out of such new combinations, and for the understanding of the problems involved. In the first place it is not essential to the matter — though it may happen — that the new combinations should be carried out by the same people who control the productive or commercial process which is to be displaced by the new. On the contrary, new combinations are, as a rule, embodied, as it were, in new firms which generally do not arise out of the old ones but start producing beside them; to keep to the example already chosen, in general it is not the owner of stage-coaches who builds railways. This fact not only puts the discontinuity which characterises the process we want to describe in a special light, and creates so to speak still another kind of discontinuity in addi-

FUNDAMENTALS OF ECONOMIC DEVELOPMENT 67

tion to the one mentioned above, but it also explains important features of the course of events. Especially in a competitive economy, in which new combinations mean the competitive elimination of the old, it explains on the one hand the process by which individuals and families rise and fall economically and socially and which is peculiar to this form of organisation, as well as a whole series of other phenomena of the business cycle, of the mechanism of the formation of private fortunes, and so on. In a non-exchange economy, for example a socialist one, the new combinations would also frequently appear side by side with the old. But the economic consequences of this fact would be absent to some extent, and the social consequences would be wholly absent. And if the competitive economy is broken up by the growth of great combines, as is increasingly the case to-day in all countries, then this must become more and more true of real life, and the carrying out of new combinations must become in ever greater measure the internal concern of one and the same economic body. The difference so made is great enough to serve as the water-shed between two epochs in the social history of capitalism.

We must notice secondly, only partly in connection with this element, that whenever we are concerned with fundamental principles, we must never assume that the carrying out of new combinations takes place by employing means of production which happen to be unused. In practical life, this is very often the case. There are always unemployed workmen, unsold raw materials, unused productive capacity, and so forth. This certainly is a contributory circumstance, a favorable condition and even an incentive to the emergence of new combinations; but great unemployment is only the consequence of non-economic events — as for example the World War — or precisely of the development which we are investigating. In neither of the two cases can its existence play a fundamental rôle in the explanation, and it cannot occur in a well balanced circular flow from which we start. Nor would the normal yearly increment meet the case, as it would be small in the first place, and also because it would normally be absorbed by a corresponding expansion of production within the circular flow, which, if we admit such increments, we must think of as adjusted

68   *THE THEORY OF ECONOMIC DEVELOPMENT*

to this rate of growth.[1] As a rule the new combinations must draw the necessary means of production from some old combinations — and for reasons already mentioned we shall assume that they *always* do so, in order to put in bold relief what we hold to be the essential contour line. The carrying out of new combinations means, therefore, simply the different employment of the economic system's existing supplies of productive means —which might provide a second definition of development in our sense. That rudiment of a pure economic theory of development which is implied in the traditional doctrine of the formation of capital always refers merely to saving and to the investment of the small yearly increase attributable to it. In this it asserts nothing false, but it entirely overlooks much more essential things. The slow and continuous increase in time of the national supply of productive means and of savings is obviously an important factor in explaining the course of economic history through the centuries, but it is completely overshadowed by the fact that development consists primarily in employing existing resources in a different way, in doing new things with them, irrespective of whether those resources increase or not. In the treatment of shorter epochs, moreover, this is even true in a more tangible sense. Different methods of employment, and not saving and increases in the available quantity of labor, have changed the face of the economic world in the last fifty years. The increase of population especially, but also of the sources from which savings can be made, was first made possible in large measure through the different employment of the then existing means.

The next step in our argument is also self-evident: command over means of production is necessary to the carrying out of new combinations. Procuring the means of production is one distinct problem for the established firms which work within the circular flow. For they *have* them already procured or else can procure them currently with the proceeds of previous production as was explained in the first chapter. There is no fundamental gap here

---

[1] On the whole it is much more correct to say that population grows slowly up to the possibilities of any economic environment than that it has any tendency to outgrow it and to become thereby an independent cause of change.

FUNDAMENTALS OF ECONOMIC DEVELOPMENT 69

between receipts and disbursements, which, on the contrary, necessarily correspond to one another just as both correspond to the means of production offered and to the products demanded. Once set in motion, this mechanism works automatically. Furthermore, the problem does not exist in a non-exchange economy even if new combinations are carried out in it; for the directing organ, for example a socialist economic ministry, is in a position to direct the productive resources of the society to new uses exactly as it can direct them to their previous employments. The new employment may, under certain circumstances, impose temporary sacrifices, privations, or increased efforts upon the members of the community; it may presuppose the solution of difficult problems, for example the question from which of the old combinations the necessary productive means should be withdrawn; but there is no question of procuring means of production not already at the disposal of the economic ministry. Finally, the problem also does not exist in a competitive economy in the case of the carrying out of new combinations, if those who carry them out have the necessary productive means or can get them in exchange for others which they have or for any other property which they may possess. This is not the privilege of the possession of property *per se*, but only the privilege of the possession of disposable property, that is such as is employable either immediately for carrying out the new combination or in exchange for the necessary goods and services.[1] In the contrary case — and this is the rule as it is the fundamentally interesting case — the possessor of wealth, even if it is the greatest combine, must resort to credit if he wishes to carry out a new combination, which cannot like an established business be financed by returns from previous production. To provide this credit is clearly the function of that category of individuals which we call "capitalists." It is obvious that this is the characteristic method of the capitalist type of society — and important enough to serve as its *differentia specifica* — for forcing the economic system into new channels, for putting its means at

---

[1] A privilege which the individual can also achieve through saving. In an economy of the handicraft type this element would have to be emphasised more. Manufacturers' "reserve funds" assume an existing development.

the service of new ends, in contrast to the method of a non-exchange economy of the kind which simply consists in exercising the directing organ's power to command.

It does not appear to me possible to dispute in any way the foregoing statement. Emphasis upon the significance of credit is to be found in every textbook. That the structure of modern industry could not have been erected without it, that it makes the individual to a certain extent independent of inherited possessions, that talent in economic life "rides to success on its debts," even the most conservative orthodoxy of the theorists cannot well deny. Nor is the connection established here between credit and the carrying out of innovations, a connection which will be worked out later, anything to take offence at. For it is as clear *a priori* as it is established historically that credit is primarily necessary to new combinations and that it is from these that it forces its way into the circular flow, on the one hand because it was originally necessary to the founding of what are now the old firms, on the other hand because its mechanism, once in existence, also seizes old combinations for obvious reasons.[1] First, *a priori*: we saw in the first chapter that borrowing is not a necessary element of production in the normal circular flow within accustomed channels, is not an element without which we could not understand the essential phenomena of the latter. On the other hand, in carrying out new combinations, "financing" as a special act is fundamentally necessary, in practice as in theory. Second, historically: those who lend and borrow for industrial purposes do not appear early in history. The pre-capitalistic lender provided money for other than business purposes. And we all remember the type of industrialist who felt he was losing caste by borrowing and who therefore shunned banks and bills of exchange. The capitalistic credit system has grown out of and thrived on the financing of new combinations in all countries, even though in a different way in each (the origin of German joint stock banking is especially characteristic). Finally there can be no stumblingblock in our speak-

---

[1] The most important of which is the appearance of productive interest, as we shall see in Chapter V. As soon as interest emerges somewhere in the system, it expands over the whole of it.

FUNDAMENTALS OF ECONOMIC DEVELOPMENT 71

ing of receiving credit in "money or money substitutes." We certainly do not assert that one can produce with coins, notes, or bank balances, and do not deny that services of labor, raw materials, and tools are the things wanted. We are only speaking of a method of procuring them.

Nevertheless there is a point here in which, as has already been hinted, our theory diverges from the traditional view. The accepted theory sees a problem in the existence of the productive means, which are needed for new, or indeed any, productive processes, and this accumulation therefore becomes a distinct function or service. We do not recognise this problem at all; it appears to us to be created by faulty analysis. It does not exist in the circular flow, because the running of the latter presupposes given quantities of means of production. But neither does it exist for the carrying out of new combinations,[1] because the productive means required in the latter are drawn from the circular flow whether they already exist there in the shape wanted or have first to be produced by other means of production existing there. Instead of this problem another exists for us: the problem of detaching productive means (already employed somewhere) from the circular flow and allotting them to new combinations. This is done by credit, by means of which one who wishes to carry out new combinations outbids the producers in the circular flow in the market for the required means of production. And although the meaning and object of this process lies in a movement of goods from their old towards new employments, it cannot be described entirely in terms of goods without overlooking something essential, which happens in the sphere of money and credit and upon which depends the explanation of important phenomena in the capitalist form of economic organisation, in contrast to other types.

Finally one more step in this direction: whence come the sums

---

[1] Of course the productive means do not fall from heaven. In so far as they are not given by nature or non-economically, they were and are created at some time by the individual waves of development in our sense, and henceforth incorporated in the circular flow. But every individual wave of development and every individual new combination itself proceeds again from the supply of productive means of the existing circular flow — a case of the hen and the egg.

72   *THE THEORY OF ECONOMIC DEVELOPMENT*

needed to purchase the means of production necessary for the new combinations if the individual concerned does not happen to have them? The conventional answer is simple: out of the annual growth of social savings plus that part of resources which may annually become free. Now the first quantity was indeed important enough before the war — it may perhaps be estimated as one-fifth of total private incomes in Europe and North America — so that together with the latter sum, which it is difficult to obtain statistically, it does not immediately give the lie quantitatively to this answer. At the same time a figure representing the range of all the business operations involved in carrying out new combinations is also not available at present. But we may not even start from total "savings." For its magnitude is explicable only by the results of previous development. By far the greater part of it does not come from thrift in the strict sense, that is from abstaining from the consumption of part of one's regular income, but it consists of funds which are themselves the result of successful innovation and in which we shall later recognise entrepreneurial profit. In the circular flow there would be on the one hand no such rich source, out of which to save, and on the other hand essentially less incentive to save. The only big incomes known to it would be monopoly revenues and the rents of large landowners; while provision for misfortunes and old age, perhaps also irrational motives, would be the only incentives. The most important incentive, the chance of participating in the gains of development, would be absent. Hence, in such an economic system there could be no great reservoirs of free purchasing power, to which one who wished to form new combinations could turn — and his own savings would only suffice in exceptional cases. All money would circulate, would be fixed in definite established channels.

Even though the conventional answer to our question is not obviously absurd, yet there is another method of obtaining money for this purpose, which claims our attention, because it, unlike the one referred to, does not presuppose the existence of accumulated results of previous development, and hence may be considered as the only one which is available in strict logic. This method of ob-

FUNDAMENTALS OF ECONOMIC DEVELOPMENT 73

taining money is the creation of purchasing power by banks. The form it takes is immaterial. The issue of bank-notes not fully covered by specie withdrawn from circulation is an obvious instance, but methods of deposit banking render the same service, where they increase the sum total of possible expenditure. Or we may think of bank acceptances in so far as they serve as money to make payments in wholesale trade. It is always a question, not of transforming purchasing power which already exists in someone's possession, but of the creation of new purchasing power out of nothing — out of nothing even if the credit contract by which the new purchasing power is created is supported by securities which are not themselves circulating media — which is added to the existing circulation. And this is the source from which new combinations *are* often financed, and from which they would have to be financed *always*, if results of previous development did not actually exist at any moment.

These credit means of payment, that is means of payment which are created for the purpose and by the act of giving credit, serve just as ready money in trade, partly directly, partly because they can be converted immediately into ready money for small payments or payments to the non-banking classes — in particular to wage-earners. With their help, those who carry out new combinations can gain access to the existing stocks of productive means, or, as the case may be, enable those from whom they buy productive services to gain immediate access to the market for consumption goods. There is never, in this nexus, granting of credit in the sense that someone must wait for the equivalent of his service in goods, and content himself with a claim, thereby fulfilling a special function; not even in the sense that someone has to accumulate means of maintenance for laborers or land-owners, or produced means of production, all of which would only be paid for out of the final results of production. Economically, it is true, there is an essential difference between these means of payment, if they are created for new ends, and money or other means of payment of the circular flow. The latter may be conceived on the one hand as a kind of certificate for completed production and the increase in the social product effected through it, and on the other hand as a kind of order upon, or claim to, part of this social product. The former have not the first of these two characteristics. They too are orders, for which one can immediately procure consumption goods, but not certificates for previous production. Access to the national dividend is usually to be had only on condition of some productive service previously rendered or of some product previously sold. This condition is, in this case, not yet fulfilled. It will be fulfilled only after the successful completion of the new combinations. Hence this credit will in the meantime affect the price level.

The banker, therefore, is not so much primarily a middleman in the commodity "purchasing power" as a *producer* of this commodity. However, since all reserve funds and savings to-day usually flow to him, and the total demand for free purchasing power, whether existing or to be created, concentrates on him, he has either replaced private capitalists or become their agent; he has himself become the capitalist par excellence. He stands between those who wish to form new combinations and the possessors of productive means. He is essentially a phenomenon of development, though only when no central authority directs the social process. He makes possible the carrying out of new combinations, authorises people, in the name of society as it were, to form them. He is the ephor of the exchange economy.

III

We now come to the third of the elements with which our analysis works, namely the "new combination of means of production," and credit. Although all three elements form a whole, the third may be described as the fundamental phenomenon of economic development. The carrying out of new combinations we call "enterprise"; the individuals whose function it is to carry them out we call "entrepreneurs." These concepts are at once broader and narrower than the usual. Broader, because in the first place we call entrepreneurs not only those "independent" businessmen in an exchange economy who are usually so designated, but all who actually fulfil the function by which we define

FUNDAMENTALS OF ECONOMIC DEVELOPMENT 75

the concept, even if they are, as is becoming the rule, "dependent" employees of a company, like managers, members of boards of directors, and so forth, or even if their actual power to perform the entrepreneurial function has any other foundations, such as the control of a majority of shares. As it is the carrying out of new combinations that constitutes the entrepreneur, it is not necessary that he should be permanently connected with an individual firm; many "financiers," "promotors," and so forth are not, and still they may be entrepreneurs in our sense. On the other hand, our concept is narrower than the traditional one in that it does not include all heads of firms or managers or industrialists who merely may operate an established business, but only those who actually perform that function. Nevertheless I maintain that the above definition does no more than formulate with greater precision what the traditional doctrine really means to convey. In the first place our definition agrees with the usual one on the fundamental point of distinguishing between "entrepreneurs" and "capitalists" — irrespective of whether the latter are regarded as owners of money, claims to money, or material goods. This distinction is common property to-day and has been so for a considerable time. It also settles the question whether the ordinary shareholder as such is an entrepreneur, and disposes of the conception of the entrepreneur as risk bearer.[1] Furthermore, the ordinary characterisation of the entrepreneur type by such expressions as "initiative," "authority," or "foresight" points entirely in our direction. For there is little scope for such qualities within the routine of the circular flow, and if this had been sharply separated

---

[1] Risk obviously always falls on the owner of the means of production or of the money-capital which was paid for them, hence never on the entrepreneur *as such* (see Chapter IV). A shareholder *may* be an entrepreneur. He may even owe to his holding a controlling interest the power to act as an entrepreneur. Shareholders *per se*, however, are never entrepreneurs, but merely capitalists, who in consideration of their submitting to certain risks participate in profits. That this is no reason to look upon them as anything but capitalists is shown by the facts, first, that the average shareholder has normally no power to influence the management of his company, and secondly, that participation in profits is frequent in cases in which everyone recognises the presence of a loan contract. Compare, for example, the Graeco-Roman *foenus nauticum*. Surely this interpretation is more true to life than the other one, which, following the lead of a faulty legal construction — which can only be explained historically — attributes functions to the average shareholder which he hardly ever thinks of discharging.

76   *THE THEORY OF ECONOMIC DEVELOPMENT*

from the occurrence of changes in this routine itself, the emphasis in the definition of the function of entrepreneurs would have been shifted automatically to the latter. Finally there are definitions which we could simply accept. There is in particular the well known one that goes back to J. B. Say: the entrepreneur's function is to combine the productive factors, to bring them together. Since this is a performance of a special kind only when the factors are combined for the first time — while it is merely routine work if done in the course of running a business — this definition coincides with ours. When Mataja (in Unternehmergewinn) defines the entrepreneur as one who receives profit, we have only to add the conclusion of the first chapter, that there is no profit in the circular flow, in order to trace this formulation too back to ours.[1] And this view is not foreign to traditional theory, as is shown by the construction of the *entrepreneur faisant ni bénéfice ni perte*, which has been worked out rigorously by Walras, but is the property of many other authors. The tendency is for the entrepreneur to make neither profit nor loss in the circular flow — that is he has no function of a special kind there, he simply does not exist; but in his stead, there are heads of firms or business managers of a different type which we had better not designate by the same term.

It is a prejudice to believe that the knowledge of the historical origin of an institution or of a type immediately shows us its sociological or economic nature. Such knowledge often leads us to understand it, but it does not directly yield a theory of it. Still more false is the belief that "primitive" forms of a type are also *ipso facto* the "simpler" or the "more original" in the sense that they show their nature more purely and with fewer complications than later ones. Very frequently the opposite is the case, amongst other reasons because increasing specialisation may allow functions and qualities to stand out sharply, which are more difficult to recognise in more primitive conditions when mixed with others.

---

[1] The definition of the entrepreneur in terms of entrepreneurial profit instead of in terms of the function the performance of which creates the entrepreneurial profit is obviously not brilliant. But we have still another objection to it: we shall see that entrepreneurial profit does not fall to the entrepreneur by "necessity" in the same sense as the marginal product of labor does to the worker.

FUNDAMENTALS OF ECONOMIC DEVELOPMENT 77

So it is in our case. In the general position of the chief of a primitive horde it is difficult to separate the entrepreneurial element from the others. For the same reason most economists up to the time of the younger Mill failed to keep capitalist and entrepreneur distinct because the manufacturer of a hundred years ago was both; and certainly the course of events since then has facilitated the making of this distinction, as the system of land tenure in England has facilitated the distinction between farmer and landowner, while on the Continent this distinction is still occasionally neglected, especially in the case of the peasant who tills his own soil.[1] But in our case there are still more of such difficulties. The entrepreneur of earlier times was not only as a rule the capitalist too, he was also often — as he still is to-day in the case of small concerns — his own technical expert, in so far as a professional specialist was not called in for special cases. Likewise he was (and is) often his own buying and selling agent, the head of his office, his own personnel manager, and sometimes, even though as a rule he of course employed solicitors, his own legal adviser in current affairs. And it was performing some or all of these functions that regularly filled his days. The carrying out of new combinations can no more be a *vocation* than the making and execution of strategical decisions, although it is this function and not his routine work that characterises the military leader. Therefore the entrepreneur's essential function must always appear mixed up with other kinds of activity, which as a rule must be much more conspicuous than the essential one. Hence the Marshallian definition of the enterpreneur, which simply treats the entrepreneurial function as "management" in the widest meaning, will naturally appeal to most of us. We do not accept it, simply because it does not bring out what we consider to be the salient point and the only one which specifically distinguishes entrepreneurial from other activities.

[1] Only this neglect explains the attitude of many socialistic theorists towards peasant property. For smallness of the individual possession makes a difference only for the petit-bourgeois, not for the socialist. The criterion of the employment of labor other than that of the owner and his family is economically relevant only from the standpoint of a kind of exploitation theory which is hardly tenable any longer.

78   *THE THEORY OF ECONOMIC DEVELOPMENT*

Nevertheless there are types — the course of events has evolved them by degrees — which exhibit the entrepreneurial function with particular purity. The "promoter," to be sure, belongs to them only with qualifications. For, neglecting the associations relative to social and moral status which are attached to this type, the promoter is frequently only an agent intervening on commission, who does the work of financial technique in floating the new enterprise. In this case he is not its creator nor the driving power in the process. However, he *may* be the latter also, and then he is something like an "entrepreneur by profession." But the modern type of "captain of industry" [1] corresponds more closely to what is meant here, especially if one recognises his identity on the one hand with, say, the commercial entrepreneur of twelfth-century Venice — or, among later types, with John Law — and on the other hand with the village potentate who combines with his agriculture and his cattle trade, say, a rural brewery, an hotel, and a store. But whatever the type, everyone is an entrepreneur only when he actually "carries out new combinations," and loses that character as soon as he has built up his business, when he settles down to running it as other people run their businesses. This is the rule, of course, and hence it is just as rare for anyone always to remain an entrepreneur throughout the decades of his active life as it is for a businessman never to have a moment in which he is an entrepreneur, to however modest a degree.

Because being an entrepreneur is not a profession and as a rule not a lasting condition, entrepreneurs do not form a social class in the technical sense, as, for example, landowners or capitalists or workmen do. Of course the entrepreneurial function will *lead* to certain class positions for the successful entrepreneur and his family. It can also put its stamp on an epoch of social history, can form a style of life, or systems of moral and aesthetic values; but in itself it signifies a class position no more than it presupposes one. And the class position which may be attained is not as such an entrepreneurial position, but is characterised as landowning or

---

[1] Cf. for example the good description in Wiedenfeld, Das Persönliche im modernen Unternehmertum. Although it appeared in Schmoller's Jahrbuch in 1910 this work was not known to me when the first edition of this book was published.

FUNDAMENTALS OF ECONOMIC DEVELOPMENT 79

capitalist, according to how the proceeds of the enterprise are used. Inheritance of the pecuniary result and of personal qualities may then both keep up this position for more than one generation and make further enterprise easier for descendants, but the function of the entrepreneur itself cannot be inherited, as is shown well enough by the history of manufacturing families.[1]

But now the decisive question arises: why then is the carrying out of new combinations a special process and the object of a special kind of "function"? Every individual carries on his economic affairs as well as he can. To be sure, his own intentions are never realised with ideal perfection, but ultimately his behavior is moulded by the influence on him of the results of his conduct, so as to fit circumstances which do not as a rule change suddenly. If a business can never be absolutely perfect in any sense, yet it in time approaches a relative perfection having regard to the surrounding world, the social conditions, the knowledge of the time, and the horizon of each individual or each group. New possibilities are continuously being offered by the surrounding world, in particular new discoveries are continuously being added to the existing store of knowledge. Why should not the individual make just as much use of the new possibilities as of the old, and, according to the market position as he understands it, keep pigs instead of cows, or even choose a new crop rotation, if this can be seen to be more advantageous? And what kind of special new phenomena or problems, not to be found in the established circular flow, can arise there?

While in the accustomed circular flow every individual can act promptly and rationally because he is sure of his ground and is supported by the conduct, as adjusted to this circular flow, of all other individuals, who in turn expect the accustomed activity from him, he cannot simply do this when he is confronted by a new task. While in the accustomed channels his own ability and experience suffice for the normal individual, when confronted with innovations he needs guidance. While he swims with the stream in the circular flow which is familiar to him, he swims against the

---

[1] On the nature of the entrepreneurial function also compare my statement in the article "Unternehmer" in the Handwörterbuch der Staatswissenschaften.

80   *THE THEORY OF ECONOMIC DEVELOPMENT*

stream if he wishes to change its channel. What was formerly a help becomes a hindrance. What was a familiar datum becomes an unknown. Where the boundaries of routine stop, many people can go no further, and the rest can only do so in a highly variable manner. The assumption that conduct is prompt and rational is in all cases a fiction. But it proves to be sufficiently near to reality, if things have time to hammer logic into men. Where this has happened, and within the limits in which it has happened, one may rest content with this fiction and build theories upon it. It is then not true that habit or custom or non-economic ways of thinking cause a hopeless difference between the individuals of different classes, times, or cultures, and that, for example, the "economics of the stock exchange" would be inapplicable say to the peasants of to-day or to the craftsmen of the Middle Ages. On the contrary the same theoretical picture [1] in its broadest contour lines fits the individuals of quite different cultures, whatever their degree of intelligence and of economic rationality, and we can depend upon it that the peasant sells his calf just as cunningly and egotistically as the stock exchange member his portfolio of shares. But this holds good only where precedents without number have formed conduct through decades and, in fundamentals, through hundreds and thousands of years, and have eliminated unadapted behavior. Outside of these limits our fiction loses its closeness to reality.[2] To cling to it there also, as the traditional theory does, is to hide an essential thing and to ignore a fact which, in contrast with other deviations of our assumptions from reality, is theoretically important and the source of the explanation of phenomena which would not exist without it.

[1] The same *theoretical* picture, obviously not the same sociological, cultural, and so forth.

[2] How much this is the case is best seen to-day in the economic life of those nations, and within our civilisation in the economics of those individuals, whom the development of the last century has not yet completely drawn into its stream, for example, in the economy of the Central European peasant. This peasant "calculates"; there is no deficiency of the "economic way of thinking" (Wirtschaftsgesinnung) in him. Yet he cannot take a step out of the beaten path; his economy has not changed at all for centuries, except perhaps through the exercise of external force and influence. Why? Because the choice of new methods is not simply an element in the concept of rational economic action, nor a matter of course, but a distinct process which stands in need of special explanation.

FUNDAMENTALS OF ECONOMIC DEVELOPMENT 81

Therefore, in describing the circular flow one must treat combinations of means of production (the production-functions) as data, like natural possibilities, and admit only small [1] variations at the margins, such as every individual can accomplish by adapting himself to changes in his economic environment, without materially deviating from familiar lines. Therefore, too, the carrying out of new combinations is a special function, and the privilege of a type of people who are much less numerous than all those who have the "objective" possibility of doing it. Therefore, finally, entrepreneurs are a special type,[2] and their behavior a special

---

[1] Small disturbances which may indeed, as mentioned earlier, in time add up to great amounts. The decisive point is that the businessman, if he makes them, never alters his routine. The usual case is one of small, the exception one of great (*uno actu* great), disturbances. Only in this sense is emphasis put upon "smallness" here. The objection that there can be no difference in principle between small and large disturbances is not effective. For it is false in itself, in so far as it is based upon the disregard of the principle of the infinitesimal method, the essence of which lies in the fact that one can assert of "small quantities" under certain circumstances what one cannot assert of "large quantities." But the reader who takes umbrage at the large-small contrast may, if he wishes, substitute for it the contrast adapting-spontaneous. Personally I am not willing to do this because the latter method of expression is much easier to misunderstand than the former and really would demand still longer explanations.

[2] In the first place it is a question of a type of *conduct* and of a type of *person* in so far as this conduct is accessible in very unequal measure and to relatively few people, so that it constitutes their outstanding characteristic. Because the exposition of the first edition was reproached with exaggerating and mistaking the peculiarity of this conduct, and with overlooking the fact that it is more or less open to every businessman, and because the exposition in a later paper ("Wellenbewegung des Wirtschaftslebens," Archiv für Sozialwissenschaft) was charged with introducing an intermediate type ("half-static" businessmen), the following may be submitted. The conduct in question is peculiar in two ways. First, because it is directed towards something different and signifies doing something different from other conduct. One may indeed in this connection include it with the latter in a higher unity, but this does not alter the fact that a theoretically relevant difference exists between the two, and that only one of them is adequately described by traditional theory. Secondly, the type of conduct in question not only differs from the other in its object, "innovation" being peculiar to it, but also in that it presupposes aptitudes differing *in kind* and not only in degree from those of mere rational economic behavior.

Now these aptitudes are presumably distributed in an ethically homogeneous population just like others, that is the curve of their distribution has a maximum ordinate, deviations on either side of which become rarer the greater they are. Similarly we can assume that every healthy man can sing if he will. Perhaps half the individuals in an ethically homogeneous group have the capacity for it to an average degree, a quarter in progressively diminishing measure, and, let us say, a quarter in a measure above the average; and within this quarter, through a series of continually increasing singing ability and continually diminishing number of people

82   THE THEORY OF ECONOMIC DEVELOPMENT

problem, the motive power of a great number of significant phenomena. Hence, our position may be characterised by three corresponding pairs of opposites. First, by the opposition of two real processes: the circular flow or the tendency towards equilibrium on the one hand, a change in the channels of economic routine or a spontaneous change in the economic data arising from within the system on the other. Secondly, by the opposition of two theoretical *apparatuses*: statics and dynamics.[1] Thirdly, by the opposi-

who possess it, we come finally to the Carusos. Only in this quarter are we struck in general by the singing ability, and only in the supreme instances can it become the characterising mark of the person. Although practically all men can sing, singing ability does not cease to be a distinguishable characteristic and attribute of a minority, indeed not exactly of a type, because this characteristic — unlike ours — affects the total personality relatively little.

Let us apply this: Again, a quarter of the population may be so poor in those qualities, let us say here provisionally, of economic initiative that the deficiency makes itself felt by poverty of their moral personality, and they play a wretched part in the smallest affairs of private and professional life in which this element is called for. We recognise this type and know that many of the best clerks, distinguished by devotion to duty, expert knowledge, and exactitude, belong to it. Then comes the "half," the "normal." These prove themselves to be better in the things which even within the established channels cannot simply be "dispatched" (erledigen) but must also be "decided" (entscheiden) and "carried out" (durchsetzen). Practically all business people belong here, otherwise they would never have attained their positions; most represent a selection — individually or hereditarily tested. A textile manufacturer travels no "new" road when he goes to a wool auction. But the situations there are never the same, and the success of the business depends so much upon skill and initiative in buying wool that the fact that the textile industry has so far exhibited no trustification comparable with that in heavy manufacturing is undoubtedly partly explicable by the reluctance of the cleverer manufacturers to renounce the advantage of their own skill in buying wool. From there, rising in the scale we come finally into the highest quarter, to people who are a type characterised by super-normal qualities of intellect and will. Within this type there are not only many varieties (merchants, manufacturers, financiers, etc.) but also a continuous variety of degrees of intensity in "initiative." In our argument types of every intensity occur. Many a one can steer a safe course, where no one has yet been; others follow where first another went before; still others only in the crowd, but in this among the first. So also the great political leader of every kind and time is a type, yet not a thing unique, but only the apex of a pyramid from which there is a continuous variation down to the average and from it to the sub-normal values. And yet not only is "leading" a special function, but the leader also something special, distinguishable — wherefore there is no sense in our case in asking: "Where does that type begin then?" and then to exclaim: "This is no type at all!"

[1] It has been objected against the first edition that it sometimes defines "statics" as a theoretical construction, sometimes as the picture of an actual state of economic life. I believe that the present exposition gives no ground for this opinion. "Static" theory does not assume a stationary economy; it also treats of the effects of changes in data. In itself, therefore, there is no necessary connection between static theory and stationary reality. Only in so far as one can exhibit the fundamental form of the

FUNDAMENTALS OF ECONOMIC DEVELOPMENT 83

tion of two types of conduct, which, following reality, we can picture as two types of individuals: mere managers and entrepreneurs. And therefore the "best method" of producing in the theoretical sense is to be conceived as "the most advantageous among the methods which have been empirically tested and become familiar." But it is not the "best" of the methods "possible" at the time. If one does not make this distinction, the concept becomes meaningless and precisely those problems remain unsolved which our interpretation is meant to provide for.

Let us now formulate precisely the characteristic feature of the conduct and type under discussion. The smallest daily action embodies a huge mental effort. Every schoolboy would have to be a mental giant, if he himself had to create all he knows and uses by his own individual activity. And every man would have to be a giant of wisdom and will, if he had in every case to create anew all the rules by which he guides his everyday conduct. This is true not only of those decisions and actions of individual and social life the principles of which are the product of tens of thou-

economic course of events with the maximum simplicity in an unchanging economy does this assumption recommend itself to theory. The stationary economy is for uncounted thousands of years, and also in historical times in many places for centuries, an incontrovertible fact, apart from the fact, moreover, which Sombart emphasised, that there is a tendency towards a stationary state in every period of depression. Hence it is readily understood how this historical fact and that theoretical construction have allied themselves in a way which led to some confusion. The words "statics" and "dynamics" the author would not now use in the meaning they carry above, where they are simply short expressions for "theory of the circular flow" and "theory of development." One more thing: theory employs two methods of interpretation, which may perhaps make difficulties. If it is to be shown how all the elements of the economic system are determined in equilibrium by one another, this equilibrium system is considered as not yet existing and is built up before our eyes *ab ovo*. This does not mean that its coming into being is genetically explained thereby. Only its existence and functioning are made logically clear by mental dissection. And the experiences and habits of individuals are assumed as existing. How just these productive combinations have come about is not thereby explained. Further, if two contiguous equilibrium positions are to be investigated, then sometimes (not always), as in Pigou's Economics of Welfare, the "best" productive combination in the first is compared with the "best" in the second. And this again need not, but may, mean that the two combinations in the sense meant here differ not only by small variations in quantity but in their whole technical and commercial structure. Here too the coming into being of the second combination and the problems connected with it are not investigated, but only the functioning and the outcome of the already existing combination. Even though justified as far as it goes, this method of treatment passes over our problem. If the assertion were implied that this is also settled by it, it would be false.

84   *THE THEORY OF ECONOMIC DEVELOPMENT*

sands of years, but also of those products of shorter periods and of a more special nature which constitute the particular instrument for performing vocational tasks. But precisely the things the performance of which according to this should involve a supreme effort, in general demand no special individual effort at all; those which should be especially difficult are in reality especially easy; what should demand superhuman capacity is accessible to the least gifted, given mental health. In particular within the ordinary routine there is no need for leadership. Of course it is still necessary to set people their tasks, to keep up discipline, and so forth; but this is easy and a function any normal person can learn to fulfil. Within the lines familiar to all, even the function of directing other people, though still necessary, is mere "work" like any other, comparable to the service of tending a machine. All people get to know, and are able to do, their daily tasks in the customary way and ordinarily perform them by themselves; the "director" has his routine as they have theirs; and his directive function serves merely to correct individual aberrations.

This is so because all knowledge and habit once acquired becomes as firmly rooted in ourselves as a railway embankment in the earth. It does not require to be continually renewed and consciously reproduced, but sinks into the strata of subconsciousness. It is normally transmitted almost without friction by inheritance, teaching, upbringing, pressure of environment. Everything we think, feel, or do often enough becomes automatic and our conscious life is unburdened of it. The enormous economy of force, in the race and the individual, here involved is not great enough, however, to make daily life a light burden and to prevent its demands from exhausting the average energy all the same. But it is great enough to make it possible to meet the ordinary claims. This holds good likewise for economic daily life. And from this it follows also for economic life that every step outside the boundary of routine has difficulties and involves a new element. It is this element that constitutes the phenomenon of leadership.

The nature of these difficulties may be focussed in the following three points. First, outside these accustomed channels the individual is without those data for his decisions and those rules of

FUNDAMENTALS OF ECONOMIC DEVELOPMENT 85

conduct which are usually very accurately known to him within them. Of course he must still foresee and estimate on the basis of his experience. But many things must remain uncertain, still others are only ascertainable within wide limits, some can perhaps only be "guessed." In particular this is true of those data which the individual strives to alter and of those which he wants to create. Now he must really to some extent do what tradition does for him in everyday life, viz. consciously plan his conduct in every particular. There will be much more conscious rationality in this than in customary action, which as such does not need to be reflected upon at all; but this plan must necessarily be open not only to errors greater in degree, but also to other kinds of errors than those occurring in customary action. What has been done already has the sharp-edged reality of all the things which we have seen and experienced; the new is only the figment of our imagination. Carrying out a new plan and acting according to a customary one are things as different as making a road and walking along it.

How different a thing this is becomes clearer if one bears in mind the impossibility of surveying exhaustively all the effects and counter-effects of the projected enterprise. Even as many of them as could in theory be ascertained if one had unlimited time and means must practically remain in the dark. As military action must be taken in a given strategic position even if all the data potentially procurable are not available, so also in economic life action must be taken without working out all the details of what is to be done. Here the success of everything depends upon intuition, the capacity of seeing things in a way which afterwards proves to be true, even though it cannot be established at the moment, and of grasping the essential fact, discarding the unessential, even though one can give no account of the principles by which this is done. Thorough preparatory work, and special knowledge, breadth of intellectual understanding, talent for logical analysis, may under certain circumstances be sources of failure. The more accurately, however, we learn to know the natural and social world, the more perfect our control of facts becomes; and the greater the extent, with time and progressive rationalisation, within which things can be simply calculated, and indeed quickly and reliably calculated, the more the significance of this function decreases. Therefore the importance of the entrepreneur type must diminish just as the importance of the military commander has already diminished. Nevertheless a part of the very essence of each type is bound up with this function.

As this first point lies in the task, so the second lies in the psyche of the businessman himself. It is not only objectively more difficult to do something new than what is familiar and tested by experience, but the individual feels reluctance to it and would do so even if the objective difficulties did not exist. This is so in all fields. The history of science is one great confirmation of the fact that we find it exceedingly difficult to adopt a new scientific point of view or method. Thought turns again and again into the accustomed track even if it has become unsuitable and the more suitable innovation in itself presents no particular difficulties. The very nature of fixed habits of thinking, their energy-saving function, is founded upon the fact that they have become subconscious, that they yield their results automatically and are proof against criticism and even against contradiction by individual facts. But precisely because of this they become drag-chains when they have outlived their usefulness. So it is also in the economic world. In the breast of one who wishes to do something new, the forces of habit rise up and bear witness against the embryonic project. A new and another kind of effort of will is therefore necessary in order to wrest, amidst the work and care of the daily round, scope and time for conceiving and working out the new combination and to bring oneself to look upon it as a real possibility and not merely as a day-dream. This mental freedom presupposes a great surplus force over the everyday demand and is something peculiar and by nature rare.

The third point consists in the reaction of the social environment against one who wishes to do something new. This reaction may manifest itself first of all in the existence of legal or political impediments. But neglecting this, any deviating conduct by a member of a social group is condemned, though in greatly varying degrees according as the social group is used to such conduct

FUNDAMENTALS OF ECONOMIC DEVELOPMENT 87

or not. Even a deviation from social custom in such things as dress or manners arouses opposition, and of course all the more so in the graver cases. This opposition is stronger in primitive stages of culture than in others, but it is never absent. Even mere astonishment at the deviation, even merely noticing it, exercises a pressure on the individual. The manifestation of condemnation may at once bring noticeable consequences in its train. It may even come to social ostracism and finally to physical prevention or to direct attack. Neither the fact that progressive differentiation weakens this opposition — especially as the most important cause of the weakening is the very development which we wish to explain — nor the further fact that the social opposition operates under certain circumstances and upon many individuals as a stimulus, changes anything in principle in the significance of it. Surmounting this opposition is always a special kind of task which does not exist in the customary course of life, a task which also requires a special kind of conduct. In matters economic this resistance manifests itself first of all in the groups threatened by the innovation, then in the difficulty in finding the necessary cooperation, finally in the difficulty in winning over consumers. Even though these elements are still effective to-day, despite the fact that a period of turbulent development has accustomed us to the appearance and the carrying out of innovations, they can be best studied in the beginnings of capitalism. But they are so obvious there that it would be time lost for our purposes to dwell upon them.

There is leadership *only* for these reasons — leadership, that is, as a special kind of function and in contrast to a mere difference in rank, which would exist in every social body, in the smallest as in the largest, and in combination with which it generally appears. The facts alluded to create a boundary beyond which the majority of people do not function promptly by themselves and require help from a minority. If social life had in all respects the relative immutability of, for example, the astronomical world, or if mutable this mutability were yet incapable of being influenced by human action, or finally if capable of being so influenced this type of action were yet equally open to everyone, then there would be no special function of leadership as distinguished from routine work.

The specific problem of leadership arises and the leader type appears only where new possibilities present themselves. That is why it is so strongly marked among the Normans at the time of their conquests and so feebly among the Slavs in the centuries of their unchanging and relatively protected life in the marshes of the Pripet. Our three points characterise the nature of the *function* as well as the *conduct* or behavior which constitutes the leader type. It is no part of his function to "find" or to "create" new possibilities. They are always present, abundantly accumulated by all sorts of people. Often they are also generally known and being discussed by scientific or literary writers. In other cases, there is nothing to discover about them, because they are quite obvious. To take an example from political life, it was not at all difficult to see how the social and political conditions of France at the time of Louis XVI could have been improved so as to avoid a breakdown of the *ancien régime*. Plenty of people as a matter of fact did see it. But nobody was in a position to *do* it. Now, it is this "doing the thing," without which possibilities are dead, of which the leader's function consists. This holds good of all kinds of leadership, ephemeral as well as more enduring ones. The former may serve as an instance. What is to be done in a casual emergency is as a rule quite simple. Most or all people may see it, yet they want someone to speak out, to lead, and to organise. Even leadership which influences merely by example, as artistic or scientific leadership, does not consist simply in finding or creating the new thing but in so impressing the social group with it as to draw it on in its wake. It is, therefore, more by will than by intellect that the leaders fulfil their function, more by "authority," "personal weight," and so forth than by original ideas.

Economic leadership in particular must hence be distinguished from "invention." As long as they are not carried into practice, inventions are economically irrelevant. And to carry any improvement into effect is a task entirely different from the inventing of it, and a task, moreover, requiring entirely different kinds of aptitudes. Although entrepreneurs of course *may* be inventors

FUNDAMENTALS OF ECONOMIC DEVELOPMENT 89

just as they may be capitalists, they are inventors not by nature of their function but by coincidence and vice versa. Besides, the innovations which it is the function of entrepreneurs to carry out need not necessarily be any inventions at all. It is, therefore, not advisable, and it may be downright misleading, to stress the element of invention as much as many writers do.

The entrepreneurial kind of leadership, as distinguished from other kinds of economic leadership such as we should expect to find in a primitive tribe or a communist society, is of course colored by the conditions peculiar to it. It has none of that glamour which characterises other kinds of leadership. It consists in fulfilling a very special task which only in rare cases appeals to the imagination of the public. For its success, keenness and vigor are not more essential than a certain narrowness which seizes the immediate chance and *nothing else*. "Personal weight" is, to be sure, not without importance. Yet the personality of the capitalistic entrepreneur need not, and generally does not, answer to the idea most of us have of what a "leader" looks like, so much so that there is some difficulty in realizing that he comes within the sociological category of leader at all. He "leads" the means of production into new channels. But this he does, not by convincing people of the desirability of carrying out his plan or by creating confidence in his leading in the manner of a political leader — the only man he has to convince or to impress is the banker who is to finance him — but by buying them or their services, and then using them as he sees fit. He also leads in the sense that he draws other producers in his branch after him. But as they are his competitors, who first reduce and then annihilate his profit, this is, as it were, leadership against one's own will. Finally, he renders a service, the full appreciation of which takes a specialist's knowledge of the case. It is not so easily understood by the public at large as a politician's successful speech or a general's victory in the field, not to insist on the fact that he seems to act — and often harshly — in his individual interest alone. We shall understand, therefore, that we do not observe, in this case, the emergence of all those affective values which are the glory of all other kinds of social leadership. Add to this the precariousness of the

90   THE THEORY OF ECONOMIC DEVELOPMENT

economic position both of the individual entrepreneur and of entrepreneurs as a group, and the fact that when his economic success raises him socially he has no cultural tradition or attitude to fall back upon, but moves about in society as an upstart, whose ways are readily laughed at, and we shall understand why this type has never been popular, and why even scientific critique often makes short work of it.[1]

We shall finally try to round off our picture of the entrepreneur in the same manner in which we always, in science as well as in practical life, try to understand human behavior, viz. by analysing the characteristic motives of his conduct. Any attempt to do this must of course meet with all those objections against the economist's intrusion into "psychology" which have been made familiar by a long series of writers. We cannot here enter into the fundamental question of the relation between psychology and economics. It is enough to state that those who on principle object to *any* psychological considerations in an economic argument may leave out what we are about to say without thereby losing contact with the argument of the following chapters. For none of the results to which our analysis is intended to lead stands or falls with our "psychology of the entrepreneur," or could be vitiated by any errors in it. Nowhere is there, as the reader will easily satisfy himself, any necessity for us to overstep the frontiers of observable behavior. Those who do not object to *all* psychology but only to the *kind* of psychology which we know from the traditional textbook, will see that we do not adopt any part of the time-honored picture of the motivation of the "economic man."

In the theory of the circular flow, the importance of examining motives is very much reduced by the fact that the equations of the system of equilibrium may be so interpreted as not to imply any psychic magnitudes at all, as shown by the analysis of Pareto

---

[1] It may, therefore, not be superfluous to point out that our analysis of the rôle of the entrepreneur does not involve any "glorification" of the type, as some readers of the first edition of this book seemed to think. We do hold that entrepreneurs *have* an economic function as distinguished from, say, robbers. But we neither style every entrepreneur a genius or a benefactor to humanity, nor do we wish to express any opinion about the comparative merits of the social organisation in which he plays his rôle, or about the question whether what he does could not be effected more cheaply or efficiently in other ways.

FUNDAMENTALS OF ECONOMIC DEVELOPMENT   91

and of Barone. This is the reason why even very defective psychology interferes much less with results than one would expect. There may be rational *conduct* even in the absence of rational *motive*. But as soon as we really wish to penetrate into motivation, the problem proves by no means simple. Within given social circumstances and habits, most of what people do every day will appear to them primarily from the point of view of duty carrying a social or a superhuman sanction. There is very little of conscious rationality, still less of hedonism and of *individual* egoism about it, and so much of it as may safely be said to exist is of comparatively recent growth. Nevertheless, as long as we confine ourselves to the great outlines of constantly repeated economic action, we may link it up with wants and the desire to satisfy them, on condition that we are careful to recognise that economic motive so defined varies in intensity very much in time; that it is society that shapes the particular desires we observe; that wants must be taken with reference to the group which the individual thinks of when deciding his course of action — the family or any other group, smaller or larger than the family; that action does not promptly follow upon desire but only more or less imperfectly corresponds to it; that the field of individual choice is always, though in very different ways and to very different degrees, fenced in by social habits or conventions and the like: it still remains broadly true that, within the circular flow, everyone adapts himself to his environment so as to satisfy certain *given* wants — of himself or others — as best he can. In *all* cases, the *meaning* of economic action is the satisfaction of wants in the sense that there would be no economic action if there were no wants. In the case of the circular flow, we may also think of satisfaction of wants as the normal *motive*.

The latter is not true for our type. In one sense, he may indeed be called the most rational and the most egotistical of all. For, as we have seen, conscious rationality enters much more into the carrying out of new plans, which themselves have to be worked out before they can be acted upon, than into the mere running of an established business, which is largely a matter of routine. And the typical entrepreneur is more self-centred than other types, because he relies less than they do on tradition and connection and because his characteristic task — theoretically as well as historically — consists precisely in breaking up old, and creating new, tradition. Although this applies primarily to his economic action, it also extends to the moral, cultural, and social consequences of it. It is, of course, no mere coincidence that the period of the rise of the entrepreneur type also gave birth to Utilitarianism.

But his conduct and his motive are "rational" in no other sense. And in *no* sense is his characteristic motivation of the hedonist kind. If we define hedonist motive of action as the wish to satisfy one's wants, we may indeed make "wants" include any impulse whatsoever, just as we may define egoism so as to include all altruistic values too, on the strength of the fact that they also mean something in the way of self-gratification. But this would reduce our definition to tautology. If we wish to give it meaning, we must restrict it to such wants as are capable of being satisfied by the consumption of goods, and to that kind of satisfaction which is expected from it. Then it is no longer true that our type is acting on a wish to satisfy his wants.

For unless we assume that individuals of our type are driven along by an insatiable craving for hedonist satisfaction, the operations of Gossen's law would in the case of business leaders soon put a stop to further effort. Experience teaches, however, that typical entrepreneurs retire from the arena only when and because their strength is spent and they feel no longer equal to their task. This does not seem to verify the picture of the economic man, balancing probable results against disutility of effort and reaching in due course a point of equilibrium beyond which he is not willing to go. Effort, in our case, does not seem to weigh at all in the sense of being felt as a reason to stop. And activity of the entrepreneurial type is obviously an obstacle to hedonist enjoyment of those kinds of commodity which are usually acquired by incomes beyond a certain size, because their "consumption" presupposes leisure. Hedonistically, therefore, the conduct which we usually observe in individuals of our type would be irrational.

FUNDAMENTALS OF ECONOMIC DEVELOPMENT 93

This would not, of course, prove the absence of hedonistic motive. Yet it points to another psychology of non-hedonist character, especially if we take into account the indifference to hedonist enjoyment which is often conspicuous in outstanding specimens of the type and which is not difficult to understand.

First of all, there is the dream and the will to found a private kingdom, usually, though not necessarily, also a dynasty. The modern world really does not know any such positions, but what may be attained by industrial or commercial success is still the nearest approach to medieval lordship possible to modern man. Its fascination is specially strong for people who have no other chance of achieving social distinction. The sensation of power and independence loses nothing by the fact that both are largely illusions. Closer analysis would lead to discovering an endless variety within this group of motives, from spiritual ambition down to mere snobbery. But this need not detain us. Let it suffice to point out that motives of this kind, although they stand nearest to consumers' satisfaction, do not coincide with it.

Then there is the will to conquer: the impulse to fight, to prove oneself superior to others, to succeed for the sake, not of the fruits of success, but of success itself. From this aspect, economic action becomes akin to sport — there are financial races, or rather boxing-matches. The financial result is a secondary consideration, or, at all events, mainly valued as an index of success and as a symptom of victory, the displaying of which very often is more important as a motive of large expenditure than the wish for the consumers' goods themselves. Again we should find countless nuances, some of which, like social ambition, shade into the first group of motives. And again we are faced with a motivation characteristically different from that of "satisfaction of wants" in the sense defined above, or from, to put the same thing into other words, "hedonistic adaptation."

Finally, there is the joy of creating, of getting things done, or simply of exercising one's energy and ingenuity. This is akin to a ubiquitous motive, but nowhere else does it stand out as an independent factor of behavior with anything like the clearness with which it obtrudes itself in our case. Our type seeks out difficulties, changes in order to change, delights in ventures. This group of motives is the most distinctly anti-hedonist of the three.

Only with the first groups of motives is private property as the result of entrepreneurial activity an essential factor in making it operative. With the other two it is not. Pecuniary gain is indeed a very accurate expression of success, especially of *relative* success, and from the standpoint of the man who strives for it, it has the additional advantage of being an objective fact and largely independent of the opinion of others. These and other peculiarities incident to the mechanism of "acquisitive" society make it very difficult to replace it as a motor of industrial development, even if we would discard the importance it has for creating a fund ready for investment. Nevertheless it is true that the second and third groups of entrepreneurial motives may in principle be taken care of by other social arrangements not involving private gain from economic innovation. What other stimuli could be provided, and how they could be made to work as well as the "capitalistic" ones do, are questions which are beyond our theme. They are taken too lightly by social reformers, and are altogether ignored by fiscal radicalism. But they are not insoluble, and may be answered by detailed observation of the psychology of entrepreneurial activity, at least for given times and places.

[8]

Forces generating and limiting concentration under Schumpeterian competition

Richard R. Nelson
Professor of Economics
Yale University

and

Sidney G. Winter
Professor of Economics
Yale University

Stochastic theories of the firm size distribution explain observed size differences among firms as the consequence of random growth rate differences, accumulated over time. Little attention has thus far been paid, however, to economic interpretation of the abstract stochastic processes explored. This paper investigates the implications for size distribution phenomena of a model of industry evolution in which the stochastic elements reflect the uncertainties attending firms' efforts to advance productivity. A simulation experiment establishes that the development of concentration in the model industry is significantly affected by the rate of growth of potential ("latent") productivity, the effectiveness of technological imitation efforts, and the extent to which firms restrain investment in response to perceived market power.

1. Introduction

■ Competition, in the everyday sense of the term, is an active process, not a structural state. Ordinarily, a competitive process does not continue indefinitely, and when it is over, there are identifiable winners and losers. That there are winners—or a single winner—does not usually come as a surprise to the onlookers; in fact, they may view the identification of a winner as the main point of the process. An apparent winner is sometimes disqualified for infractions of the rules, but being lucky is not grounds for disqualification. Indeed, a situation that is regarded as "highly competitive" is typically one in which luck

The authors are indebted to Ramy Goldstein and Larry Spancake for invaluable research assistance. The participants in the Yale microeconomics workshop provided useful comments on an earlier version of the paper. Helpful suggestions were also received from Paul Joskow, Richard Levin, and two anonymous referees. Financial support from the Sloan Foundation and the National Science Foundation is gratefully acknowledged.

is the principal factor that finally distinguishes winners from near-winners — although vast differentials of skill and competence may separate contenders from noncontenders.

In the literature of economics, it is Schumpeter's work that presents us with an account of competition closely related to the everyday meaning of the term. Schumpeter not only describes a dynamic process, but even goes so far as to suggest that the joys of the struggle and the hope of recognition as a winner may be more significant motivational considerations than the pecuniary rewards on which economists normally focus (1934, p. 93). And, although Schumpeterian competitive processes do not have such clearly defined termination times as football games and football seasons, they are nevertheless punctuated, divided into a series of episodes, each of which involves the introduction and diffusion of a particular innovation.

In the study of industrial organization, the Schumpeterian notion of competition survives in uneasy coexistence with the refined concept of competition that is standard in economic theory — the concept that reduces, in most cases, to that of pricetaking behavior. It is plain, especially in policy-oriented discussion, that neither of these conceptualizations can be dispensed with without the loss of important insights. Equally plainly, it is not a simple matter to relate the two concepts in an effective way, so as to employ them in tandem in a single analysis. Prominent among the many obstacles to success in such an undertaking is the difficulty of raising Schumpeterian discussion to a level of abstraction and formalization comparable to that of standard price theory.

In the present paper we use an explicit formal model of Schumpeterian competition in an investigation of the relationships linking the development of industrial concentration to characteristics of the technological environment of the industry, and to firms' perceptions of their market power. Most theoretical and empirical studies in this general area have sought to reveal the causal linkage running from the level of concentration to the pace and pattern of innovation. Yet it is apparent that there are forces running in the reverse direction as well, and it is with these that our discussion is concerned. Under a regime of Schumpeterian competition, temporary supranormal profits are the reward to successful innovation. To the extent that growth is keyed to profitability, successful innovators grow relative to other firms. If a firm is a successful innovator frequently enough, or if one of its innovations is dominant enough, the consequences of successful innovation may be a highly concentrated industrial structure. In this sense, a clear "winner" may emerge from the competitive struggle.

2. Background and description of the model

■ A few studies have been concerned with this line of causation. Mansfield (1962) has examined empirically the question of whether successful innovators tend to grow faster than do other firms and, if so, the persistence of their advantage. He found out that they do tend to grow faster, but that their advantage tends to damp out over time. Since his exploration was empirical, not theoretical, he did not explore the factors that would make the growth rate differential between innovators and noninnovators large rather than small, or persistent rather than transient. Relatedly, he did not consider the effect of these kinds of variables on the size distribution of firms that would evolve. There are some propositions about this. Phillips (1971) has proposed that in an industry, like the producers of commercial aircraft, where opportunities for major technological advance occur infrequently and there are significant and durable advantages to the firm that makes an advance first, a high degree of concentration is likely to develop. Williamson (1972) has discussed antitrust problems that may result from a circumstance in which the past innovative prowess of a firm has led to its market domination and blockaded entry, but in which that firm no longer is creative.

The perspectives on the sources of industrial concentration in these studies, and in the present one, are very different from those contained within the standard textbooks in microeconomic theory. There the analysis generally assumes a constant technology, and concentrated industrial structure is viewed as stemming from economies of scale in production, or if there are none, is unexplained. In the discussions oriented around the Schumpeterian concept of competition, technology is most certainly not a constant, and concentration is viewed as resulting (at least in part) from successful innovation, with no requirement for or presumption of economies of scale in production. The two different perspectives of course also focus attention of different costs and benefits of concentrated as compared with less concentrated structure, but these are not the concern of this paper.[1]

Our theoretical treatment of Schumpeterian competition owes as much to Herbert Simon as to Schumpeter, and we are therefore particularly pleased that our analysis is here published in a symposium in Simon's honor. There are, in fact, two distinguishable areas in which we are drawing heavily on ideas that Simon pioneered. First, our model can be considered a member of the class of stochastic models of the size distribution of firms, a literature to which Simon made seminal contributions. Secondly, our model is based on a characterization of firm behavior that clearly shows the influence of Simon, Cyert, and March. We shall discuss each of these connections in turn.

Simon has helped clarify how the various stochastic models of the firm size distribution can be seen as involving various deviations from "Gibrat's law." If the population of firms is constant and if the probability distribution of growth rates from one period to the next is the same for all firms and over all periods—in particular, there are no relation between firm size and the distribution of growth rates and no serial correlation—the distribution of firm sizes will asymptotically approach log normal. As Simon has pointed out, the log-normal distribution fits the actual distribution of firm sizes reasonably well, except at the "tails." Also, Gibrat's formulation predicts that the variance of firm size continues to grow over time, and the data do not show this occurring, at least not at the rate Gibrat's law would predict. Various modifications of Gibrat's law have been suggested to take care of these problems.

Simon, himself (1955), and with colleagues Bonini (1958) and Ijiri (1964, 1974), has proposed three significant modifications. One of these is to admit entry into the population of firms. Under his particular model specification, he shows that the effect of entry upon a model where the "firms in being"

---

[1] As we have suggested, the Schumpeterian viewpoint receives more attention in the industrial organization literature than in the microeconomics texts, but that attention has largely been focused on the idea that large firm size and/or monopoly power may be favorable to technological progressiveness, to the virtual exclusion of other aspects of Schumpeterian competitive process.

follow Gibrat's law is that the asymptotic distribution is Yule rather than log normal. The Yule distribution approximately follows Pareto's law—that the log of size is a negative linear function of the log of rank—in the upper tail. This "fits" actual size distributions somewhat better than the upper tail of the log normal. Regarding "firms in being," Simon's models have departed from Gibrat's law in two important ways. One is to build in serial correlation of the growth rates on the grounds that this is realistic and empirically observed. The other, played down by Simon but highlighted by Vining in a recent note (1976), is to have the average growth rate of firms tend to decline as a firm ages. With the vision of hindsight (aided by Vining's analysis) one can see that the latter assumption builds into the model a negative correlation between the growth rate and size, at least after some critical size. This both further improves the "fit" at the upper tail, by providing a bit of concavity to the log size-log rank plot, and keeps the variance of the distribution from exploding.

Our model, while capable of admitting entry, has been run with entry excluded in the runs reported here. As will be stressed later, our purpose is not so much to "fit" any actual distribution of firm sizes as to explore the effect of various conditions of Schumpeterian competition on the evolution of concentration. While entry obviously is an important factor determining concentration, it seemed analytically cleaner to consider the particular questions we examined in a context of a constant group of "firms in being." In discussing our results, however, we do comment briefly on the differences it would make if entry were permitted.

Our model does incorporate the other two modifications to Gibrat's law proposed by Simon—serial correlation of growth rates and restraints on growth as firms grow large. However, these are built into the model in a manner quite different from that employed by Simon and colleagues, or the other architects of stochastic growth models. A weakness of this genre of models, even Simon's, is that the models' grounding in a theory of firm behavior tends to be rather superficial and the specification of the competitive environment is left implicit. Such assumptions as serial correlation and decline in growth rate with firm age or size are introduced as characteristics of stochastic processes, and not particularly well justified in terms of the behavior of the economic actors. Even the central stochastic forces which drive the model tend not to be rationalized in any detail. Our own model is more complete and explicit on these matters.

In the spirit of Simon, Cyert, March, and other behavioral theorists, we argue that firms cannot optimize in any formal sense because their decision problems are too complicated for them to comprehend fully. The actions of our model's firms at any time are governed by a set of decision rules, and we do not regard these rules as deducible from any "optimization" calculations. However, as evolutionary theorists, we expect the rules actually employed to be sensible and plausibly responsive to conditions in the firms' environment. This perspective, and empirical observation, guide our specification, which also is constrained by considerations of analytic tractability and transparency.

There are three major decision rules that our firms employ. (1) Given the techniques they have (characterized in terms of output per unit of capital and constant returns to scale), firms produce at capacity levels regardless of prices. It is assumed that other inputs are proportional to capital inputs, and that total costs are a constant times capital. (2) Investment is triggered if product price is such that firms earn more than a target markup over production costs.

The target markup is higher for large firms than for small ones, reflecting their appraisal of their market power. The investment of a firm also is limited by its access to finance, assumed equal to revenues minus costs augmented by bank credit. (3) The amount firms spend on R & D, which involves both exploring new technological opportunities and scanning what other firms are doing, is proportional to their size (capital stock).[2]

The firms in the industry face a constant, unit-elastic demand curve for the product of the industry as a whole.[3] Input prices are constant. At any time, the stock of capital of each firm and its technology determine the output of each firm and for the industry as a whole. Output price then is determined by the demand curve and hence so is the actual mark-up over cost that each firm will earn. Investment decisions—which will influence the next period's stock of capital—then are regulated by the relationship of actual and target markup, and by financing constraints.

The R & D of a firm gives it a chance to find a better technique for use in the next period. Technological opportunities are expanding over time, in the sense that the distribution of techniques (characterized in terms of input per unit of capital) that a firm "samples" by doing R & D is improving. And, as other firms find and adopt new techniques, the distribution of techniques that are targets for imitation improves as well. The chance of actually drawing from these improving populations is proportional to R & D spending.[4] Of course, a technique found by R & D will only be adopted if it is better than the one that firm currently is using. (The firm may be faced with a choice among a triplet: its current technique, the new one it has found, and the technique used by a competitor.)

If R & D expenditures were insensitive to firm size, and if target markups also were unrelated to firm size, the model would involve Gibrat's law modified by serial correlation. The serial correlation would stem from the fact that a firm with a significantly better than average (worse than average) technology today is likely to have a better (worse) one tomorrow.

But R & D expenditures are not insensitive to firm size, nor are investment policies. Large firms spend more on R & D than do small firms. The

[2] For a more complete discussion of the rationale of our general approach to firm behavior and of the specific decision rules imputed to firms, see Nelson and Winter (1977b). The model common to the 1977 paper and the present one contrasts with that in Nelson, Winter, and Schuette (1976) in a number of respects. For example, the firms in the earlier model satisfice on their current techniques and seek improvements only when under pressure, whereas in the more recent model they pursue "level of effort" R & D policies that may produce technical change even when they are prospering. (We think of them as satisficing on the R & D policies.) We would not commit ourselves to either representation to the exclusion of the other; each seemed appropriate in the light of the objectives of the particular investigation.

[3] There is a special significance to the stationary, unit-elastic demand curve: declining costs and prices, as a result of technical change, do not of themselves create pressures for adjustment of the industry capital stock in either direction. Much the same results would occur if demand were inelastic but growing, or elastic but shrinking, provided the demand growth rate (γ), the rate of productivity growth (λ), and the demand elasticity (η) maintained the relation $\gamma + \lambda(\eta - 1)$ = constant. We have not really explored the question of what an overlay of capital-stock adjustment considerations would do to our results, but it is clear that, for example, the significance of the physical depreciation constraint on capital stock decline would be enhanced if the industry were declining; the significance of external financing constraints would be enhanced if it were expanding.

[4] We use R & D to refer collectively to all of a firm's efforts to obtain new technology; "research" refers to efforts that draw on sources exogenous to the industry and "imitation" refers to efforts that draw on the experience of other firms in the same industry.

probability that a firm will come up with an innovation is proportional to its R & D spending. Larger firms thus have a higher probability of coming up with a new technique in any period, and on average they tend to be closer to the frontier of techniques and to experience more steady progress than do smaller firms which come up with innovations less frequently. Also, the chances that a firm will be able to imitate the best technology used by other firms is proportional to its R & D spending. This further accentuates the tendency of large firms to stay close to the frontier and to experience relatively steady progress. Counteracting these advantages of size, and the consequent tendency of large firms to grow relative to small firms, is the fact that large firms have higher target markups than small firms. They restrain their plans for expansion in recognition that one of the consequences of expansion will be to drive down price. Given this formulation, one might expect a variance of growth rates that declines with firm size, and an average growth rate that first increases and then flattens out or decreases with firm size.

The modifications to Gibrat's law built into our model are similar to those of Simon's models. Each seems to square with empirical evidence. As mentioned above, Mansfield found serial correlation and showed that this was related to successful innovation. He also showed that the variance of growth rates declined with firm size. Singh and Whittington (1975) in a recent article report serial correlation, smaller variance of growth rates for large firms than for small, and a positive correlation between growth rates and size for a large sample of firms in the United Kingdom. While their study does not show the non-linearity between average growth rates and firm size apparently built into our model, their "largest size" group has a considerable range. A number of researchers who have explored growth rate differences among quite large firms in some detail have proposed that after some point, there is negative correlation between size and the growth rate. See, for example, Steindl (1965) and, of course, Simon *et al.*

Further detail about the model can be found in Appendix 1. (See Nelson and Winter (1977b) for a more detailed presentation.) For our purposes here it suffices to remark that the model will generate a size distribution of firms. In contrast with other such models, ours is based on an explicit submodel of firm behavior and an explicit specification of competition in the sense of Schumpeter. The stochastic element stems from the uncertainty regarding what a firm will find when it is doing R & D.

These commitments about the sources of industrial concentration imply, of course, some limit on the intended range of applications of the model. It relates to the size distribution, not of all firms, but of the firms in an "industry." Two features make the "industry" a significant unit in the analysis: the demand curve that sets a limit to the aggregate size of all firms and the imitation process that presumes the relevance of the technical advances achieved by one firm to the problems of another. Relatedly, the essential concept of a "firm" in the model is implicitly characterized by the assumption that the processes by which technical information comes to be more widely used are markedly different, and less costly, when the information transfer occurs within the boundaries of a firm than when the transfer is firm-to-firm. The intended reference of our model is further limited to industries in which ordinary economies of scale in production clearly do not suffice to explain observed concentration; we do not mean to imply that this is universally the case.

The fact that the only form of innovation in the model is reduction in the production cost of a single product may appear to be yet another consideration that sharply restricts its possible empirical relevance. In this case we argue that appearances are, at least in part, deceiving. The model can equally well be interpreted in terms of product innovation. In this alternative interpretation, product improvement involves an equiproportional increase in the effectiveness of the product in every use; when such an improvement can be achieved with a smaller proportional increase in unit production cost, there has been an effective reduction in the cost at which "efficiency units" are produced. To put it another way, the firms in the model may be thought of as producing physically heterogeneous products that embody varying amounts of a single Lancasterian "characteristic" per physical unit. The demand curve of the model is then to be interpreted as the demand curve for the characteristic, and prices of different products will vary in relation to the amount of the characteristic they contain.

Thus, mere physical heterogeneity of the products of different firms does not necessarily render our model inapplicable. And, to the extent patterns of that buyer preference among products are dominated by the variation in a single quality dimension, the "cost reduction" approach may, at a minimum, be a useful approximation. Nevertheless, it is certainly true that products often have more than one significant characteristic; the structure of demand is truly multidimensional. Our model, in its present form, cannot handle such cases. It is worth emphasizing, however, that the conceptual problems here must be faced in the first instance in the modeling of demand, not in the modeling of innovation.

3. Hypotheses and experimental set-up

■ Our primary concern in this inquiry is with concentration as an outcome of Schumpeterian competitive processes. We touch only briefly on the question of our model's performance in the role for which most stochastic models of the firm size distribution were intended, namely, the generation of predicted firm size distributions that conform in significant respects to empirically observed distributions. We therefore employ, in most of the analysis, a simple measure of concentration—the Herfindahl index of concentration of the industry's capital stock.

In a recent paper, Hause (1977) has presented an argument, based on an extention of Cournot oligopoly theory, as to why the Herfindahl index should be correlated with a gap between price and average marginal costs in an industry. Dansby and Willig (1976) also have addressed the question of theoretical rationales for various concentration measures, including the Herfindahl index. In our model there is also a theoretical rationale for use of the Herfindahl index of (capital) concentration, different from those put forward by Hause and by Dansby and Willig: it is a measure of the expected percent of the industry's capital stock that can be "modernized" by a successful R & D project.[5]

Consider a successful R & D project occurring at a moment in time. The project could have been the work of any of the firms in the industry. The

---

[5] Stephen Horner made the same use of the Herfindahl index in his doctoral dissertation (University of Michigan, 1977). The dissertation is concerned with the analytical treatment of the stochastic processes arising in models of technical change akin to our own.

probability that any particular firm came up with the successful project is, in our model, proportional to its share of R & D spending in the industry's total; in turn this is simply equal to the share of the firm's capital stock in the industry's total. The percent of industry capital which can be "modernized" by that project also is the percent of that firm's capital in total industry capital. Thus, the expected fraction of industry capital which can be modernized by a successful R & D project is simply:

$$H = \sum_i \left(\frac{K_i}{K} \cdot \frac{K_i}{K} \right) = \sum_i \left(\frac{K_i}{K} \right)^2.$$

This is the Herfindahl index of capital concentration. In much of our analysis we employ the inverse of the Herfindahl index or "Herfindahl numbers equivalent"—which has an interpretation as the number of equal-sized firms which would have the same Herfindahl index as the actual size distribution of firms.

One of the advantages of working with a model that is grounded on an explicit and relatively detailed theory of firm and industry behavior is that one can explore the effects of economically meaningful parameters on industry concentration. The model is transparent enough so that it is possible to discern a number of relations between institutional characteristics of an industry, including the character of innovation opportunities, and the tendency for concentration to develop. For example, the above-noted propositions due to Mansfield, Phillips, and Williamson are either built into the model or are readily interpreted as hypotheses about its behavior.

We focus here on a number of key variables that influence the evolution of market structure. The logic of the model would appear to imply that the more rapid the pace at which technological opportunities extend over time, the more uncertain the outcome of a research project aimed at seizing new opportunities, the harder it is to imitate successful innovation, and the less the tendency of firms to restrain their output growth as they grow larger, the *greater* the tendency of significant concentration to develop out of a situation that originally started out with many equal-sized firms. While the same factors would tend to operate in the same direction in an industry that originally started out with a few large equal-sized firms, there are considerations that lead us to expect greater stability in the latter situation. The fact that the firms originally are large means that they spend more on both research and imitation and thus tend to stay close to each other in technologies, as well as close to the frontier. Further, output-growth restraint is operative always, not just when a firm grows large.

The foregoing propositions about the model's behavior seem highly plausible in view of the underlying logic of the model. They are so plausible, in fact, that they may be regarded as conjectures for which deductive proofs may one day be provided. (Since the model is stochastic, the theorems would, of course, have to be stated in probabilistic terms.) One of the reasons that we have kept the model relatively simple in structure, and constrained it to a Markov process framework, is the hope that a body of analytical technique adequate to the theorem-proving task may be located or developed. At present, we do not have such a body of analytical technique at hand,[6]

---

[6] However, we made some progress on the analytical tack in dealing with another Markov model of industry evolution. See Nelson and Winter (1975). Also, recent work by Futia looks promising in this connection.

and we need an alternative tool for exploring the validity of conjectures about the model's behavior. Simulation is such a tool. While corroboration of conjectures by simulation experiments does not have the force of a theorem, it does raise one's confidence in the conjectures and in one's general understanding of the model's logic. Conversely, discovery of results inconsistent with the conjectures will force one to review the arguments that produced them, and perhaps direct attention to neglected implications of the model's logic. Simulation results have, in addition, at least one advantage that general theorems do not: provided that the model's parameters are set to plausible values, a simulation experiment provides at least a rough indication of the possible *quantitative* significance of the effects being explored. Since reasonable approximations to the quantitative behavior of stochastic processes are notoriously difficult to achieve by intuitive judgment alone, this is a consideration of some importance. Overall, we consider that simulation techniques, properly used, can serve effectively the same objectives that analytical techniques serve—to expand and strengthen our understanding of a simplified model, the better to judge how, and whether, the model relates to a more complex reality.[7]

Our experimental design was to set two different levels for each of four experimental factors—the pace of latent productivity growth, the variance of research "draws" around latent productivity, the difficulty of imitation, and the aggressiveness of investment policies—and to run each of the 16 possible combinations in a context starting with four equal-sized firms, and 16 equal-sized firms. To get some indication of the variability of outcomes for a given combination of factor settings, we ran each setting at least twice in the 16-firm cases.

4. Results

■ We report first on the striking differences between the runs which started out with four equal-sized firms and those which started out with 16 equal-sized firms. We had conjectured that the initial distribution in the former case would be more stable than in the latter case, and the ultimate distribution of firm sizes would be less sensitive to such factors as the rate of advance of latent productivity, or the ease of imitation. We confess surprise at the strength with which these conjectures were confirmed.

Table 1 presents the figures for the Herfindahl numbers equivalent at period 101, after 25 years of simulated industry evolution. The contrast between the two parts of the table is dramatic. Over a run of 101 quarterly periods (during which, even in the runs with "slow" growth of latent productivity, average output per unit of capital increased by more than half), for virtually every parameter setting, the four initially equal-sized firms preserved close to their initial shares of industry output. One principal factor which bound the firms together was that all of them had numerous successes in their R & D efforts looking at new technological possibilities and at the techniques their competitors were using. As a result, over time they tended to have roughly the same (in many cases identical) productivity levels. Figure 1 presents the time path of productivity for each of the four firms in a representative case (1000).

---

[7] We have discussed the methodological issues associated with the use of simulation techniques in another paper (1977a).

Entrepreneurship

TABLE 1

FINAL—PERIOD CONCENTRATION

	EXPERIMENTAL CONDITION BINARY NO.	HERFINDAHL NUMBERS EQUIVALENT	EXPERIMENTAL CONDITION BINARY NO.	HERFINDAHL NUMBERS EQUIVALENT
FOUR—FIRM RUNS	0000	4.000	1000	3.976
	0001	3.995	1001	3.719
	0010	3.998	1010	3.611
	0011	3.973	1011	3.794
	0100	4.000	1100	3.701
	0101	3.997	1101	3.849
	0110	3.978	1110	2.353
	0111	3.998	1111	2.489
SIXTEEN—FIRM RUNS	0000	14.925	1000	12.937
		15.060		13.158
	0001	14.347	1001	13.550
		14.286		13 228
	0010	12.005	1010	7.429
		12.019		7.788
	0011	12.516	1011	6.361
		13.514		4.938
	0100	13.072	1100	10.893
		13.495		11.001
	0101	14.045	1101	10.091
		10.741		8.058
	0110	10.776	1110	6.150
		9.579		5.102
	0111	11.050	1111	2.856
		8.418		4.686

BINARY CODE: EXPERIMENTAL FACTORS ARE REPRESENTED BY BINARY DIGITS IN THE FOLLOWING ORDER (LEFT TO RIGHT): AGGRESSIVENESS OF INVESTMENT POLICIES, DIFFICULTY OF IMITATION, RATE OF LATENT PRODUCTIVITY GROWTH, VARIABILITY OF RESEARCH OUTCOMES. THE "ONE" (OR "HIGH") SETTING OF A FACTOR IS EXPEC- TED TO LEAD TO HIGHER CONCENTRATION THAN THE "ZERO" (OR "LOW") SETTING. FOR EXAMPLE, 0101 DENOTES THE CONDITION IN WHICH INVESTMENT POLICIES ARE UNAGGRESSIVE, IMITATION IS DIFFICULT, THE RATE OF LATENT PRODUCTIVITY GROWTH IS LOW, AND THE VARIABILITY OF RESEARCH OUTCOMES IS HIGH; 1100 DENOTES THE CONDITION IN WHICH INVESTMENT POLICIES ARE AGGRESSIVE, IMITATION IS DIFFICULT, THE RATE OF PRODUCTIVITY GROWTH IS LOW, AND THE VARIANCE OF RESEARCH OUTCOMES IS LOW.

Another factor at work, in half the cases, was the investment restraint exercised by firms with substantial market shares, even when they gained a productivity advantage over their competitors. The Herfindahl numbers equivalent is systematically smaller in the right half of Table 1, which records runs in which firms viewed demand as infinitely elastic, than in the left half of the table, which records runs where firms did restrain investment in new capacity.

The last two of the four-firm runs, where firms exercised no restraint, latent productivity growth was rapid, and imitation was difficult, show a markedly more concentrated end structure than the other runs. Figure 2 presents the productivity time paths associated with the final run, condition 1111. There is obviously more dispersion among firms than is displayed in Figure 1. This, plus aggressive investment policies, clearly led to the growth of concentration. But this case was rather exceptional. To our eyes the most striking feature of the four-firm runs was that through thick and thin, and in spite of the fact that long-run output policies were noncooperative or even competitive, productivity levels

FIGURE 1

TIME PATHS OF FIRM PRODUCTIVITY LEVELS IN ONE FOUR–FIRM RUN
(EXPERIMENTAL CONDITION 1000)

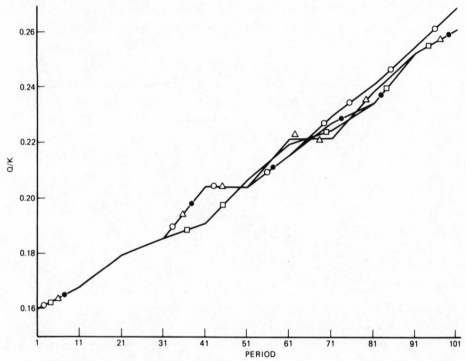

of the firms tended to stay close and the initial division of the market tended to be preserved.[8]

In the 16-firm runs, the situation was quite different. Two runs at each parameter setting are reported in the lower section of Table 1. As the table indicates, there was variation between the two runs at the same parameter settings, but these differences were small compared with those related to different parameter settings.

One simple but effective way to test the hypotheses about the model that we put forth in Section 3 is to make a set of binary comparisons of the Herfindahl numbers equivalent in the period 101 for runs that are identical in their parame-

---

[8] It should be emphasized that the size of the market and the industry totals of research and imitation draws are the same in the four-firm and 16-firm cases. This seemed to us to provide the most interesting sort of comparison, but it should be noted that the two mechanisms tending to stabilize the situation in the four firm cases operate in rather different ways. The investment restraint mechanism involves market shares; it would function in the same manner regardless of the size of the market. On the other hand, the tendency of firms to stay close in productivity levels reflects the fact that they obtain absolutely larger samples of possible new techniques over a given time period. This mechanism thus reflects the fact that firms are absolutely larger in the four-firm cases: It would also operate if the firms had smaller shares, but the market and the number of draws were larger.

FIGURE 2

TIME PATHS OF FIRM PRODUCTIVITY LEVELS IN ANOTHER FOUR–FIRM RUN
(EXPERIMENTAL CONDITION 1111)

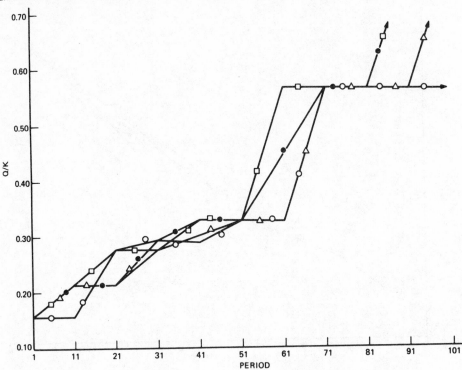

ter settings except for one variable. Thus, one can compare final concentration
in runs with the same parameter settings for ease of imitation, rate of latent
productivity growth, variability of research outcomes, but with different investment policy parameters and similarly for other differences.

Careful scrutiny of Table 1 discloses that most of our hypotheses are confirmed by the binary comparisons. In every comparison in which a run with
investment restraint is compared with one in which there was aggressive investment policy, the end concentration is greater in the latter. Similarly, in every
binary comparison in which a run with a high rate of latent productivity
growth is compared with a run with a lower rate of growth of latent productivity,
or a run in which easy imitation is compared with one in which imitation was
harder (all other factors being held constant), the results are in the predicted direction.

In contrast, comparison among runs that differed only in terms of the
variance of research draws around latent productivity yields ambiguous results.
It now is apparent to us that we did not fully think through the implications of the
fact that before adopting a new technique that it has "found" through research,
a firm compares the productivity of that technique against the productivity of
the technique it already is using. One implication is that an increase in the

536 / THE BELL JOURNAL OF ECONOMICS

dispersion of research outcomes always increases the expected productivity advance associated with a research draw: outcomes inferior to existing practice are irrelevant regardless of the margin of inferiority, and the increased likelihood of large advances always makes a positive contribution to the expectation. Table 2 shows that this implication is reflected in substantial overall productivity differences between runs of high and low variance in research outcomes.

A corollary implication is that no simple connection exists between the dispersion of research outcomes and interfirm variability in productivity levels. Hence, our hypothesized causal linkage running from research outcome variability to interfirm productivity differences to interfirm growth rate differences and finally to the growth of concentration is problematic at the first link. Because research outcomes inferior to existing technique are disregarded, the effective distribution of next-period productivity levels facing a firm has smaller variance than the research outcome distribution; furthermore, the better the firm's initial position, the more the truncation matters. And, as Table 2 confirms, the average "initial position" itself changes when the research outcome variance rises. Through additional calculations that are too detailed to report here, we have confirmed that the interplay of these considerations can be such as to substantially attenuate the effect of the research outcome variance on the final concentration figures. A likely explanation for the ambiguous experimental results has therefore been identified.

Another way we explored our hypotheses was to run least squares regressions with the Herfindahl equivalent number of firms as the dependent variable, and the various experimental conditions represented as binary-valued dummies. Table 3 displays the results of such calculations on a data set where all the sixteen-firm runs were pooled (making 32 observations in all). The coefficients on the dummy variables in regression 1 are simply the *differences* between the average value of the Herfindahl equivalent number of firms in the relevant binary comparisons. The interpretation of the coefficients in regression 2, where interaction terms are included, is somewhat more complex.

Not surprisingly, the results of the first regression confirm those of the binary comparisons. The coefficients relating to investment policy, the rate of latent productivity growth, and the ease of imitation, all have the right sign. From the binary comparisons we know something stronger: that in each binary comparison these variables worked in the expected direction. The lack of sensitivity of concentration to the variance of research outcomes shows up in the regression. (The t-statistics should be interpreted as descriptive. The distribution of error assumptions required for them to serve as the basis of

TABLE 2

GEOMETRIC AVERAGE RATIO OF INDUSTRY PRODUCTIVITY TO LATENT PRODUCTIVITY: COMPARISONS OF SOME SIXTEEN—FIRM RUNS DIFFERING IN RESEARCH OUTCOME VARIANCE FACTOR ONLY

	CONDITION							
	000X	001X	010X	011X	100X	101X	110X	111X
LOW VARIANCE (X = 0)	0.977	0.933	0.965	0.898	0.981	0.966	0.969	0.936
HIGH VARIANCE (X = 1)	1.022	1.108	1.004	1.068	1.049	1.191	1.033	1.102

TABLE 3

REGRESSIONS OF HERFINDAHL NUMBERS EQUIVALENT ON DUMMY VARIABLES
FOR EXPERIMENTAL FACTORS AND INTERACTION TERMS

EQUATION	CONSTANT	X_4	X_3	X_2	X_1	X_1X_2	X_1X_3	X_1X_4	X_2X_3	X_2X_4	X_3X_4
(1)	16.19	−3.85	−2.38	−4.23	−0.79						
$R^2 = 0.86$	(30.07)	(8.00)	(4.94)	(8.78)	(1.65)						
(2)	14.78	−1.39	−1.84	−2.62	0.23	−0.04	−0.94	−1.08	0.27	−3.43	−0.38
$R^2 = 0.94$	(24.70)	(1.94)	(2.56)	(3.64)	(0.33)	(0.05)	(1.30)	(1.50)	(0.037)	(4.76)	(0.53)

VARIABLES: X_1 = DUMMY VARIABLE FOR VARIANCE OF RESEARCH DRAWS FACTOR
X_2 = DUMMY VARIABLE FOR RATE OF LATENT PRODUCTIVITY GROWTH FACTOR
X_3 = DUMMY VARIABLE FOR EASE OF IMITATION FACTOR
X_4 = DUMMY VARIABLE FOR AGGRESSIVE INVESTMENT POLICY FACTOR
IN ALL CASES THE "1" LEVEL OF THE FACTOR IS HYPOTHESIZED
TO LEAD TO HIGHER CONCENTRATION (LOWER NUMBERS EQUIVALENT).
FIGURES IN PARENTHESES ARE ABSOLUTE VALUES OF t–RATIOS.

significance tests are violated because of the nature of the dependent variable—
if not otherwise.)

The regression format has certain advantages over the binary comparison
format for probing at interaction effects. Regression 2 displays a variety of
interaction effects. The strong interaction between rate of latent productivity
growth and investment restraint does not come as a surprise. If the rate of
latent productivity growth is slow, one firm does not have a significant chance
of suddenly getting a major productivity advantage over other firms, which it
then could exploit competitively. When the rate of latent productivity growth
is high, the chances of this are much greater. But if the firm with a competitive
advantage is concerned about growing too much, it exerts less pressure on
the lower productivity firms, and gives them a chance to recover. On the other
hand, where the productivity leader invests aggressively, the effect of its growth
will be to force low-productivity firms to decline. As they decline and cut back
their R & D spending, their chances of ever catching up are diminished. This
reasoning suggests that the "ease of imitation" variable should also be playing
a role in the interactions. However, it is not easy to discern such a role in the
regression displayed in Table 3.

The above discussion suggests an alternative way of analyzing interaction effects. What we did was to split the sample in two ways. We separated
the runs with aggressive investment policies from those in which there was
investment restraint. And we separated the runs in which the rate of latent
productivity growth was high from those in which it was low. Table 4 presents
regressions of the Herfindahl equivalent number of firms against the three remaining dependent variables, in the case where firms exercised investment
restraint and where they behaved aggressively. The rate of latent productivity
growth has a much greater effect on the extent to which concentration develops in the latter case than in the former. And, while the evidence is far
from sharp, one can faintly discern that the ease of imitation also matters
more in the case of aggressive investment than in the case where firms

TABLE 4

HERFINDAHL NUMBERS EQUIVALENTS: COMPARISON OF REGRESSION RESULTS FOR SUBSAMPLES WITH DIFFERENT INVESTMENT POLICIES

			INVESTMENT RESTRAINT ($X_4 = 0$)				
EQUATION	CONSTANT	X_3	X_2	X_1	X_1X_2	X_1X_3	X_2X_3
(3) $R^2 = 0.77$	14.97 (28.77)	−2.19 (4.20)	−2.51 (4.83)	−0.25 (0.48)			
(4) $R^2 = 0.82$	14.84 (20.65)	−1.40 (1.47)	−2.67 (2.84)	−0.36 (0.39)	1.06 (0.98)	−0.83 (0.76)	−0.74 (0.68)
			AGGRESSIVE INVESTMENT ($X_4 = 1$)				
(5) $R^2 = 0.94$	13.57 (28.55)	−2.57 (5.41)	−5.95 (1.25)	−1.33 (2.81)			
(6) $R^2 = 0.96$	13.34 (23.21)	−2.68 (3.56)	−6.01 (7.8)	−0.73 (0.32)	−1.14 (1.31)	−1.06 (1.21)	1.28 (1.47)

VARIABLES: AS IN TABLE 3.

FIGURES IN PARENTHESES ARE ABSOLUTE VALUES OF *t*–RATIOS.

restrain their growth. The same results appeared when separate regressions were run for cases in which the rate of latent productivity growth is high and for cases where it is low.

It is clear enough from the above analysis that one would expect a positive relationship to develop over time between the size of a firm and its productivity level; firms grow big because they are productive. One also would expect the variance of productivity to be smaller among large firms than among smaller ones. The simulation data confirm these expectations. Figure 3 displays a good

FIGURE 3

PLOT OF PRODUCTIVITY LEVEL AGAINST CAPITAL STOCK FOR FIRMS IN ONE SIXTEEN–FIRM RUN (EXPERIMENTAL CONDITION 0110, PERIOD 81)

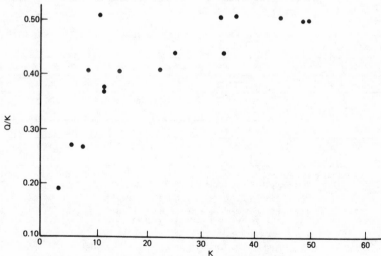

illustration of these relationships. In addition to advantages of higher average productivity, large firms (in our model) have a higher expectation of discovering a new technique. One would expect, therefore, a positive relationship between expected growth rates and firm size, at least up to some critical size level, beyond which point restraint on further growth might flatten the relationship or make it turn down. This suggests regressing growth rates as a quadratic function of firm size and separating the sample between those runs where firms exercised investment restraint as they grew large, and those runs where they did not. The results are displayed in Table 5. All expectations are confirmed, including that the curvature of the relationship is much greater in the runs where firms restrained growth than in those where they did not.

The logic of the model also would seem to imply a rather strong serial correlation of growth rates in the short run, with the extent of correlation diminishing as longer time intervals are considered. This expectation also was confirmed.

As stressed earlier, the model we are exploring was designed to give insight into the nature of Schumpeterian competition, and the experiments reported here were focused on forces generating and limiting the growth of concentration. Unlike many of the stochastic models of firm growth discussed in Section 2, this one was not developed for the specific purpose of generating a distribution that fits actual data. We should report, however, that the firm size distributions generated by the model have at least a family resemblance to empirical distributions. In some cases the simulated distributions closely approximate the log normal. Figure 4 shows the cumulative distribution for log K_i in run 0110, plotted on normal probability paper (so that an actual cumulative normal would trace out a straight line). This particular run produced one of the closer approximations to log normal. When we focused attention on the validity of the Pareto law for the upper tail of the distribution (the large firms) the log size/log rank plot typically displayed concavity for the investment restraint cases.

Qualitatively, the simulation model clearly behaves in ways that correspond for the most part to our hypotheses; the model also illustrates and exemplifies

TABLE 5

REGRESSIONS RELATING FIRM GROWTH RATES, PERIOD 81—PERIOD 101, TO FIRM SIZE IN PERIOD 81

INVESTMENT RESTRAINT ($X_4 = 0$)			
EQUATION	CONSTANT	K_{81}	K_{81}^2
(7) $R^2 = 0.13$	−1.957 (3.59)	0.1204 (2.96)	−0.0017 (2.56)
AGGRESSIVE INVESTMENT ($X_4 = 1$)			
(8) $R^2 = 0.64$	−3.014 (15.01)	0.0659 (5.83)	−0.0002 (2.37)

VARIABLES: DEPENDENT VARIABLE IS PERCENTAGE RATE OF FIRM GROWTH, PER QUARTER, PERIOD 81 TO PERIOD 101.

K_{81} IS FIRM SIZE (CAPITAL STOCK) IN PERIOD 81.

SAMPLE: ALL SIXTEEN FIRMS IN RUNS CODED 0011 AND 0111 (FOR EQUATION (7)) OR 1011 AND 1111 (EQUATION (8)).

N = 64 IN EACH CASE.

FIGURES IN PARENTHESES ARE ABSOLUTE VALUES OF t–RATIOS.

FIGURE 4

PLOT OF STANDARDIZED CUMULATIVE DISTRIBUTION OF LOG K ON NORMAL
PROBABILITY PAPER (EXPERIMENTAL CONDITION 1110, FINAL PERIOD)

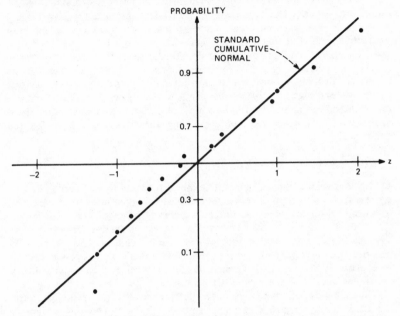

various mechanisms and patterns that empirical studies of industrial concentration have brought to light. It remains to consider, briefly, the *quantitative* import of our simulation results.

It seems clear that the differences between 14 or 15 firms and four or five firms would be generally conceded to be an "interesting" difference in industrial market structure. This is the difference, by the Herfindahl numbers equivalent measure, between our 0000 and 1111 experimental conditions, after 25 years of simulated change from essentially identical initial conditions. We are not, of course, in a position to support any bold claims that these simulated effects are of a realistic magnitude. We have stressed above that this is essentially a theoretical exercise, and that no serious calibration effort has been made. If we had chosen different parameter settings, the results would have been different.

On the other hand, the model is fairly simple as simulation models go; its parameters are not numerous, and most of them can be interpreted and checked against known empirical magnitudes.[9] We chose unity for our elasticity of

---

[9] This observation constitutes our basic reply to a type of criticism often leveled against simulation studies of the present sort, that the model has so many parameters that it can be made to produce any set of quantitative results whatsoever. No doubt there are simulation models (and forecasting models) that are so rich in parameters (and "bumping constants") that this criticism has substantial validity. But considered as a complaint against simulation models generically, it is mere prejudice. Sometimes this prejudice is "supported" by reference to the proposition that $N + 1$ points (x,y) can be perfectly fit by an Nth order polynomial in x—a proposition that has

Entrepreneurship

demand; we had no particular industry in mind, but the value is not bizarre. The capital-output ratio in value terms—which determines how unit cost advantages translate into excess returns and hence into firm growth rates—is 1.6 on an annual basis. Our two conditions for latent productivity growth are 2 percent and 6 percent per year; there are empirical measures of observed productivity growth below our low value and above our high value. And so it goes, through most of the parameter list. To the best of our ability, we have chosen parameter values and levels of experimental factors to be at least "in the ball park." In our view, therefore, the quantitative results do carry some weight; they are at least suggestive of the sorts of effects that might arise in the stochastic processes of economic reality. A critic skeptical of even this rather timid assertion faces the challenge of explaining where we might have left the ball park.[10]

5. Summary and conclusions

■ Schumpeterian competition is, like most processes we call competitive, a process that tends to produce winners and losers. Some firms track emerging technological opportunities with greater success than other firms; the former tend to prosper and grow, the latter to suffer losses and decline. Growth confers advantages that make further success more likely, while decline breeds technological obsolescence and further decline. As these processes operate through time, there is a tendency for concentration to develop even in an industry initially composed of many equal-sized firms.

In the logic of our model, we have attempted to reflect the principal causal mechanisms operative in Schumpeterian competition. In choosing parameter values, we have tried to give our numerical examples a claim to attention as illustrations of realistic possibilities. Our experimental results indicate that the tendency to increasing concentration, arising from the workings of the competi-

---

minimal relevance to a model with an independently defined logical structure, even if all the parameter values are totally unconstrained. Finally, it may be worth mentioning that we did not, in fact, engage in an extensive preliminary investigation of the model's behavior to find a region of the parameter space that would yield desired or interesting effects on concentration. We chose parameters, experimented, and have here reported the results.

[10] We can offer such a critic a little help. There is one important segment of the model in which the abstractions we employ are relatively hard to interpret, and hence to check, in terms of observable magnitudes. This is the characterization of the form of the results of R & D activity in terms of probabilities of obtaining research and imitation "draws" on certain probability distributions. The indivisibility of a "draw" is an important feature of the model. If parameters are set so that draws are rare in the industry as a whole, each successful research draw will tend to have a large transforming effect on industry structure. Latent productivity will have increased substantially since the last draw, and imitation will be slow. The lucky firm will surely grow rapidly and for an extended period, perhaps to the point where little luck will be needed for it to get the next draw as well. By contrast, a steady, gentle rain of technological advances on the industry will tend to make all firms move forward together—each individual success will matter less, and the larger total number of successes will reduce the variability among firms.

We explored this issue by doing two additional runs under the 1111 experimental condition, except that the rates of both research and imitation draws were at least three times the levels of that condition. The resulting Herfindahl numbers equivalents were 5.4 and 8.3; as expected, these values are well above those obtained in the 1111 condition itself. At the higher rates, a firm of average size gets (by research or imitation) a new technique to consider more than one quarter in three, on the average. According to our intuitions, such rates are unrealistically high—and although the tendencies to concentration are diminished, they remain very substantial.

tive process itself, is quite strong—strong enough to be interesting from a policy point of view. They indicate also that there is interesting variation in the strength of this tendency as a function of industry characteristics. We think of our results concerning this variation as a set of propositions that might ultimately provide a basis for an empirical test of some descendant of the present model, but there is obviously much work to be done before such testing would be feasible or appropriate.

The results linking the growth of concentration to the investment policies of firms seem particularly deserving of emphasis. They can be summarized succinctly in a proposition that at first appears paradoxical: The actual exercise of market power by the larger firms in an industry may be an important factor tending to limit the growth of concentration in the industry. In spite of the note of paradox, the proposition is quite an obvious consequence of the logic of our model. There is nothing mysterious in the fact that the effect shows up clearly in our experimental contrast between a pricetaking and a Cournot model of investment decisions in the individual firm. It would be incorrect to say that this perspective on concentration is absent from the industrial organization literature—for example, the theorem that "a dominant firm tends to decline" (Scherer, 1970, p. 217) is a close relative of our proposition. But it does seem that this perspective is seriously underemphasized relative to the proposition that an existing state of high concentration signifies the existence of market power.

Our experiments also yielded striking illustrations of the relationships noted by Phillips (1971). What Phillips proposed, and illustrated in a convincing case study, was that an environment that offers abundant opportunities for technological advance, and where advances are not easily imitated, is one of high uncertainty for the individual firm. Hence, by the working of the mechanisms of stochastic firm growth, it is an environment in which concentration tends to rise. Our model offers a specific formalization of his account of this mechanism, and the experimental results concerning latent productivity growth and imitation corroborate his judgment on the implications for concentration. It turned out, however, that the corroboration was weakest where, *a priori*, one might have expected it to be strongest: an increase in the dispersion of research outcomes did not produce a strong and unambiguous effect, apparently because the direct impact is partly absorbed in a general rise of productivity.

Not surprisingly, in view of its antecedents in the stochastic models of Simon *et al.*, our model also does a respectable job of generating firm size distributions that are at least superficially realistic. We have not emphasized this point in our discussion, and we certainly could not assert it as a distinctive virtue of our model as against those other stochastic models. However, we take the point more seriously as a virtue of the class of stochastic models, as against other contenders. There are strong and reliable regularities in empirical firm size distributions. To disregard those regularities when modeling firm size or industry structure phenomena is, in our view, to waste one of the rare opportunities to guide theorizing by firm empirical constraints. Only the models involving random differences in firm growth rates seem, at present, capable of satisfying those empirical constraints in a parsimonious fashion.

To appreciate the empirical strength of the stochastic models is not, of course, to deny the importance of systematic determinants of industry structure. Our own stochastic model illustrates the point—presumably obvious—

that the explicit recognition of random elements in a class of phenomena is not antithetical to the causal explanation of regularities in those phenomena. A model like ours is stochastic, but not to the exclusion of systematic causation; it does not portray industry evolution as "merely random." The model would be improved if it were generalized to reflect more of the systematic influences on industry structure—for example, technological economies of scale, product differentiation, and entry conditions. But there is no reason to think that when thus modified, it would somehow become unresponsive to the considerations that we have explored in our experiments—or that the basic empirical strength of the stochastic approach would be forfeited.

The role of entry conditions deserves more than passing mention in this connection, since entry and the barriers thereto figure so importantly in the industrial organization literature on concentration. The degree to which our results might be sensitive to the exclusion of entry depends critically on the model of entry one has in mind. More specifically, it depends on how the model answers questions in three critical areas; the scale at which entry occurs, the technological progressiveness of entrants, and the operative incentives for entry, i.e., the nature of the calculation on which an entry decision is presumed to depend. We would expect our results to be little changed if the entry model restricted entry to relatively small scales (initial firm scales or smaller) and to small percentages of industry capacity in any single period, made the typical entrant merely imitative (at best) of prevailing technology, and allowed entry processes to be triggered only if entry appeared to be profitable on the basis of simple calculations based in industry experience over a short period of time. Under these conditions, the situation of a new entrant would be quite comparable to the situation of a small firm already in existence. Informational economies of scale would still favor the large established firms, and one would expect entrants to have a hard time of it. However, things would clearly be different if entrants came in at large scale, as technological leaders, and motivated by subtle, long-run strategic calculations.

As this brief discussion of entry illustrates, there are many difficult problems to be wrestled with before we can hope to put forward a coherent general model of the forces generating and limiting concentration. What we have presented in this paper is only a partial view of the matter, but it is a partial view that is clearly quite distinct from the other partial views that currently dominate discussion in this area. It offers a novel perspective on a wide range of positive and normative issues in industrial organization. For example, our model could be taken as the basis for an alternative interpretation of the sort of empirical data found in the "survivor technique" approach to assessing economies of scale. In the antitrust area it offers a possible basis for formal analysis of the "dominant firm" problems discussed by Williamson, including specifically that of the firm that achieves dominance through its innovative prowess and then stops innovating. And, as our discussion of the Phillips hypothesis illustrates, both the empirical and normative discussions of the relationship between concentration and innovation can usefully be illuminated by an explicit model of the causal forces running from the latter to the former. It is beyond the scope of this paper to probe further into these possible applications, but the common guiding principle we propose for these inquiries may be stated by way of conclusion: Industrial concentration is to be understood as a dynamic, historical phenomenon, endogenous to the market system in which it appears.

Appendix 1

Summary of the simulation model

■ **Firm state variables and industry states.** The state of firm j in period t is characterized by the pair (K_{jt}, A_{jt}), where K_{jt} is the size of the firm's physical capital stock, and A_{jt} is the productivity of its capital. The *industry state* is the list of firm states (four or 16 in number, in the runs reported here). The model simulates a time dependent Markov process in the set of industry states. From period to period firm state transitions occur. The transitions of different firms are interdependent for two reasons: (i) total industry output determines price, which determines profitability and thus partially determines firm investment rates, and (ii) a firm may imitate the best technique (highest productivity) currently displayed by other firms in the industry.

□ **Single period output and price determination.** The production technology is of the fixed-coefficients type, and firms always produce to full capacity. Hence, the output of firm j in period t is given by $Q_{jt} = K_{jt} A_{jt}$. Price is then determined by reference to a unit-elastic demand-price function, specifically,

$$PRICE_t = \frac{64}{QSUM_t},$$

where, of course,

$$QSUM_t = \sum_j K_{jt} A_{jt}.$$

The physical capital unit is the *numeraire*.

□ **Costs and profits.** There are three categories of costs, variable costs (associated with noncapital inputs), physical depreciation of capital, and returns to capital. All are assumed to be incurred in fixed proportion to capital; this implies, in particular, a dividend payout rule that simply equates combined interest and dividends to the give rate of return times physical capital. The cost parameters are

variable cost factor $(VCFAC)$ = 0.10 per period
depreciation rate $(DEPR)$ = 0.03 per period
interest rate $(RATE)$ = 0.03 per period.

One period in the simulation model is interpreted as a quarter year. R & D costs are assumed included in the $VCFAC$ category; in the simulations reported here, all firms have the same policies toward R & D.

Firm "net income" in the model is current economic profits (excess returns) from production operations:

$$NET_{jt} = (PRICE \cdot A_{jt} - RATE - DEPR - VCFAC) \cdot K_{jt}.$$

□ **Latent productivity and research draws.** Latent productivity increases at a constant exponential rate. The log of latent productivity, in a particular time period, is the mean of a normal distribution of outcomes of research draws in that period; an "outcome" is here understood to be a value of $\log(A)$, the logarithm of a productivity level. Each firm, in each period, has a probability of getting a "research draw" that is proportional to its capital stock. In the runs reported here, the probability of a research draw is $0.0025 \cdot K_{jt}$ per period, which corresponds to an average rate of about one research draw per period in the industry as a whole. The rate of latent productivity increase and the dispersion of research outcomes are among the factors manipulated in the experiments.

☐ **Imitation draws.** Similarly, a firm has, in a given period, a probability proportional to its capital stock of getting an "imitation draw." An imitation draw makes best practice technique available to the firm; i.e., the firm j obtains $Max_k(A_{kt})$ as a possible value of $A_{j(t+1)}$. The rate of imitation draws is a factor manipulated in the experiments.

☐ **Productivity change.** Firm j may have from one to three different productivity levels available to it as possible values for $A_{j(t+1)}$. The first, which is always available, is the current value, A_{jt}. In addition, it may have the outcomes of research and imitation draws, if it chances to obtain such in period t. Its actual productivity level in $(t + 1)$ is the largest of the available ones—with occasional exceptions generated by a mechanism producing a small random error in the productivity level comparison process.

☐ **Constraints on gross investment.** The gross investment of a firm in a particular period is bounded below by zero and above by a financing constraint. (It may happen that the financing constraint implies a negative value, in which case the zero bound is determinative.) The value of financable gross investment, FIN_{jt}, is determined differently depending on whether the firm is making economic profits or not. If it is not, the financable amount is the sum of depreciation charges and net income, the latter being negative:

$$FIN_{jt} = DEP_{jt} + NET_{jt}, \quad (\text{if } NET_{jt} \leq 0),$$

where $DEP_{jt} = DEPR \cdot K_{jt}$. Thus, a firm that earns a negative economic profit always contracts. Up to the constraint imposed by depreciation, its (negative) rate of growth is equal to its (negative) rate of excess return. For firms earning positive excess returns, the financable amount of investment is increased by "matching funds" obtained by borrowing:

$$FIN_{jt} = DEP_{jt} + (1 + BANK) \cdot NET_{jt}, \quad (\text{if } NET_{jt} > 0).$$

In the runs reported here, parameter $BANK = 1$, so the "matching" of excess returns is dollar-for-dollar.

☐ **Desired investment.** Firms desire positive net investment if the ratio of price to unit cost exceeds a target markup factor. In general, the target markup factor is an increasing function of the firm's market share $(Q_{jt}/QSUM)$, and equal to one when the share is zero. In the runs reported here the target markup formula is $MU = PDEL/(PDEL - SHR)$, where $PDEL$ is "perceived demand elasticity" and SHR is the market share. When $PDEL$ is set equal to the true market demand elasticity (as it is in one of our experimental conditions), this formula corresponds to "Cournot behavior" in the sense that the resulting price is profit maximizing on the assumptions that other firms' outputs do not change and unit costs are constant. Note, however, that the Cournot assumption here is relevant not to short-run output determination, but rather to the adequacy of existing capacity, given the price/cost relationship. The desired investment calculation is made after the productivity level of the following period is determined, and the unit cost employed is the one derived from the new productivity level. Desired *gross* investment is desired net investment plus depreciation. The specific formula is

$$DESIN_{jt} = \left[DEPR + \left(1 - \frac{MU \cdot UNCOST_{j(t+1)}}{PRICE_t} \right) \right] \cdot K_{jt},$$

where $UNCOST_{j(t+1)} = (RATE + DEPR + VCFAC)/A_{j(t+1)}$. On this assumption the carrying out of desired investment behavior by *identical* firms would result in the elimination in a single step of any small discrepancy between their existing position and long-run Cournot equilibrium.

☐ **Gross investment.** Actual gross investment relates to desired gross investment and the constraints in the manner already described. Formally, gross investment is given by

$$GRIN_{jt} = \text{Max}[0, \text{Min}(DESIN_{jt}, FIN_{jt})].$$

Hence,

$$K_{j(t+1)} = (1 - DEPR) \cdot K_{jt} + GRIN_{jt}.$$

Since the foregoing account describes how a list of firm states in period t is stochastically transformed into the list at $(t + 1)$, the system is now completely characterized—apart from the initial conditions and values of experimental factors, which are described in Appendix 2.

Appendix 2

Experimental factors and initial conditions

■ **Binary numbering of experimental conditions:** $X_4 X_3 X_2 X_1$.

☐ **Variability of research outcomes (X_1).** Different levels of this factor are distinguished according to the number of years of latent productivity growth corresponding to a given probability point on the cumulative distribution of research outcomes. Specifically, the low variability condition is defined by a standard deviation equal to one year of latent productivity growth, and the high variability condition by a standard deviation equal to three years of latent productivity growth. Research outcomes ($\log(A)$) are normally distributed with mean equal to log of latent productivity and standard deviation, *SIGR*, as follows:

$X_1 = 0$:

If $X_2 = 0$, $SIGR = 0.019840$.

If $X_2 = 1$, $SIGR = 0.059408$.

$X_1 = 1$:

If $X_2 = 0$, $SIGR = 0.059408$.

If $X_2 = 1$, $SIGR = 0.178224$.

☐ **Rate of latent productivity growth (X_2).** The two levels of this factor correspond to rates of latent productivity growth of 2 percent and approximately 6 percent per year. The quarterly increment in the logarithm of latent productivity, *FXLINC*, is as follows:

$X_2 = 0$, $FXLINC = 0.004951$

$X_2 = 1$, $FXLINC = 0.014852$.

☐ **Difficulty of imitation** (X_3). Under the easy imitation condition, the expected number of imitation draws in the industry as a whole is about two per quarter. In the difficult imitation condition, the expected number is about one per quarter—the same as the expected number of research draws:

$X_3 = 0$, Imitation draw probability = $0.005\ K_{jt}$

$X_3 = 1$, Imitation draw probability = $0.0025\ K_{jt}$.

☐ **Aggressiveness of investment policy** (X_4). At the zero level of this factor, the perceived demand elasticity is set to the true value of the market demand elasticity, so that the target markup formula corresponds to Cournot behavior in the sense described in Appendix 1. The one level involves a very large value of the perceived elasticity, with the result that the desired investment mechanism of the model is virtually irrelevant; only the constraints matter:

$X_4 = 0$, $PDEL = 1$

$X_4 = 1$, $PDEL = 1000$.

☐ **Initial conditions.** In all cases, initial productivity levels of all firms equal the initial level of latent productivity, 0.16. Initial capital stocks of the firms are adjusted according to the level of experimental factor four, so that the industry is initially in equilibrium at the prevailing productivity levels:

$X_4 = 0$ *(investment restraint):*
      In four-firm runs, $K_{j1} = 75.094$
      In 16-firm runs, $K_{jt} = 23.466$.
$X_4 = 1$ *(aggressive investment):*
      In four-firm runs, $K_{j1} = 100.0$
      In 16-firm runs, $K_{j1} = 25.0$.

References

CYERT, R. M. AND MARCH, J. G. *A Behavioral Theory of the Firm.* Englewood Cliffs, New Jersey: Prentice Hall, Inc., 1963.

DANSBY, R. E. AND WILLIG, R. D. "Welfare Theory of Concentration Indices." Paper presented to the Econometric Society, Atlantic City, New Jersey, September 1976.

FUTIA, C. "Schumpeterian Competition." Mimeo, Bell Labs, 1977.

HAUSE, J. "The Measurement of Concentrated Industrial Structure and the Size Distribution of Firms." *Annals of Economic and Social Measurement,* Vol. 6 (Winter 1977), pp. 73–108.

HORNER, S. *Stochastic Models of Technology Diffusion.* Unpublished Ph.D. dissertation, University of Michigan, Ann Arbor, 1977.

IJIRI, Y. AND SIMON, H. A. "Business Firm Growth and Size." *The American Economic Review,* Vol. 54, No. 1 (March 1964), pp. 77–89.

———— AND ————. "Interpretations of Departures from the Pareto Curve Firm-Size Distributions." *Journal of Political Economy,* Vol. 82 (March-April 1974), pp. 315–331.

KAMIEN, M. I. AND SCHWARTZ, N. L. "Market Structure and Innovation: A Survey." *Journal of Economic Literature,* Vol. 8 (March 1975), pp. 1–37.

MANSFIELD, E. "Entry, Gibrat's Law, Innovation and the Growth of Firms." *The American Economic Review,* Vol. 52, No. 5 (December 1962), pp. 1023–1051.

NELSON, R. R. AND WINTER, S. G. "Factor Price Changes and Factor Substitution in an Evolutionary Model." *The Bell Journal of Economics,* Vol. 6 (Autumn 1975), pp. 466–486.

548 / THE BELL JOURNAL OF ECONOMICS

———— AND ————. "Simulation of Schumpeterian Competition." *The American Economic Review*, Vol. 67 (February 1977a), pp. 271–276.

———— AND ————. "Dynamic Competition and Technical Progress," Chapter 3 in B. Balassa and R. Nelson, eds., *Economic Progress, Private Values and Public Policy: Essays in Honor of William Fellner*, Amsterdam: North-Holland, 1977b.

NELSON, R. R., WINTER, S. G. AND SCHUETTE, H. L. "Technical Change in an Evolutionary Model." *The Quarterly Journal of Economics*, Vol. 90 (February 1976), pp. 90–118.

PHILLIPS, A. *Technology and Market Structure: A Study of the Aircraft Industry*. Lexington, Mass.: D. C. Heath and Co., 1971.

SCHERER, F. M. *Industrial Market Structure and Economic Performance*. Chicago: Rand McNally & Co., 1970.

SCHUMPETER, J. A. *The Theory of Economic Development*. Cambridge: Harvard University Press, 1934.

————. *Capitalism, Socialism and Democracy*, 3rd ed. New York: Harper & Brothers, 1950.

SIMON, H. A. "On a Class of Skew Distribution Functions." *Biometrika*, Vol. 42 (December 1955), pp. 425–440.

————. "Theories of Decision Making in Economics." *The American Economic Review*, Vol. 49 (June 1959), pp. 253–283.

———— AND BONINI, C. P. "The Size Distribution of Business Firms." *The American Economic Review*, Vol. 48 (September 1958), pp. 607–617.

SINGH, A. AND WHITTINGTON, G. "The Size and Growth of Firms." *Review of Economic Studies*, Vol. 42 (January 1975), pp. 15–26.

STEINDL, J. *Random Processes and the Growth of Firms*. New York: Hafner, 1965.

VINING, D. R., JR. "Autocorrelated Growth Rates and the Pareto Law: A Further Analysis." *Journal of Political Economy*, Vol. 84 (April 1976), pp. 369–380.

WILLIAMSON, O. E. "Dominant Firms and the Monopoly Problem: Market Failure Considerations." *Harvard Law Review*, Vol. 85 (June 1972), pp. 1512–1531.

[9]

TECHNOLOGY, ENTREPRENEURS, AND FIRM SIZE*

GUILLERMO A. CALVO AND STANISLAW WELLISZ

We analyze Schumpeterian entrepreneurship within a general equilibrium model of a competitive economy patterned after Lucas. All individuals have access to exogenously growing knowledge. Those who acquire sufficient knowledge become entrepreneurs. If learning is only a function of ability, the faster the progress, the fewer the entrepreneurs, and the higher their pay relative to workers' wages. If knowledge is only a function of lifetime, the faster the progress is, the earlier the entry will be into the entrepreneurial group. When age and ability are considered together, the individuals (if any) who become entrepreneurs with faster progress are younger and more able than those (if any) who drop out of the group.

In this paper we explore the role of entrepreneurship by introducing Schumpeterian concepts into the general equilibrium analysis of a competitive economy.[1] We derive the optimal number of entrepreneurs and the characteristics of the marginal members of the entrepreneurial group under alternative assumptions concerning the ability and age structure of the population and the rate of technical progress. We also draw inferences concerning income distribution and the size distribution of firms.[2]

Our analysis is closely related to that of Lucas [1978]. Like him, we are concerned with the problem of efficient allocation of resources within a closed economy with a workforce that is homogeneous with respect to productivity as employees, but heterogeneous with respect to managerial ability.[3] Our model is compatible with his and, to facilitate cross-references, we adopt a similar notation. We differ from Lucas, however, in two important respects. First, while Lucas "does not say anything about the nature of tasks performed by managers, other than that whatever managers do, some do it better than others" [Lucas, 1978, p. 511], we concentrate on specific entrepreneurial functions. Second, in Lucas' model individuals with sufficient inborn ability become managers immediately upon entering the labor force,

*We wish to acknowledge the helpful comments of an anonymous referee. This work was supported by a grant from the National Science Foundation.

1. For an alternative mode of attack on the problem of the firm, more closely related to the Schumpeterian system, see Nelson and Winter [1977, 1978].
2. This problem is the principal focal point of Kaldor [1960], Mayer [1960], and Lucas [1978].
3. However, we omit the problem of allocation of homogeneous capital that enters Lucas' analysis, and focus our attention exclusively on human resources.

whereas in our model they acquire the necessary knowledge through a learning process.

We model entrepreneurship in the spirit of Schumpeter and of Kaldor. We take from the former the notion that the function of entrepreneurs is to apply general technical knowledge to firm-specific purposes [Schumpeter, 1939, pp. 84–87, 130–31 and passim]. From the latter we borrow the justification of the assumption that every firm has only one entrepreneur. Decisions that affect the firm as a whole "should be made on a comparison with all other decisions already made or likely to be made" and "must therefore pass through a single brain" [Kaldor, 1960, p. 43]. We do not exclude, of course, the possibility of delegation of certain managerial functions, but in this paper we are concerned with the captains, and draw no distinction between the officers and the crews.[4]

We assume that all individuals have access to a common pool of general knowledge. Those who acquire sufficient knowledge become entrepreneurs. As we shall show, the rate of increase of technical knowledge is an important determinant in the selection of entrepreneurs. However, creation of knowledge as such is not a concern of ours. We shall assume that technological knowledge is exogenous, and we shall concentrate on the relation between technology and entrepreneurship.

Individuals may differ as to their ability, which we define as the rate at which they are capable of acquiring new knowledge. We assume that an individual who has an entrepreneurial position applies his knowledge to firm-specific purposes as soon as he acquires it. These assumptions simplify the general equilibrium analysis. Acquisition of specific knowledge through learning-by-doing lends itself more readily to the partial approach (see Prescott and Visscher [1978]).

This paper falls into three parts. In the first we state our model and apply it to the problem of selecting entrepreneurs from among a population with heterogeneous abilities. In the second we concentrate on the age factor in order to study the life cycle problem. Part III is devoted to a discussion of the interaction of age and ability.

I. ABILITY, MANAGERIAL SELECTION, AND FIRM SIZE

In this section we shall explore the consequences of the assumption that individuals vary in terms of ability; that is, in terms

4. For a discussion of problems of managerial hierarchy, see Williamson [1967] and Calvo and Wellisz [1978, 1979]. We shall utilize some of our results to justify "span of control" assumptions made in this paper.

of the rate at which they acquire and apply technical knowledge. We shall show that at steady state the faster the technical progress is, the higher will be the ability required of the marginal entrepreneur. It follows that with a given distribution of abilities, the faster the progress, the smaller the entrepreneurial group, and the larger the average firm size. On the other hand, a single "burst" of progress leads initially to a more stringent entrepreneurial selection (and to greater concentration), followed by a return to the initial situation that occurs when the laggards adopt the new technology. If technology is stationary, and if there are no random shocks, entrepreneurial ability does not determine firm size. If knowledge does not accumulate, everybody eventually acquires it, and nobody has entrepreneurial advantage even if there is a wide dispersion of abilities.[5]

As a framework of our analysis, we shall first present a simplified version of a model recently studied by Lucas [1978]; we shall subsequently expand and adapt the model to suit our needs.

Let x denote an individual's ability. We shall assume, with Lucas, that the distribution of abilities over individuals can be represented by a (continuous) cumulative distribution function that we denote $\Gamma(x)$, $0 \le x$. Thus, $\Gamma(x)$ is the share of total active population with ability less than or equal to x. We assume that $\Gamma(x)$ is independent of time.

The *productive effectiveness* of a type-x individual is denoted E_x, and is assumed to affect his productivity as entrepreneur in the following manner. Output in a firm run by a type-x individual is given by

(1) $E_x f(n_x),$

where n_x is the number of workers employed in his firm, and f is a strictly concave, increasing, and twice differentiable function defined on the nonnegative real line, such that

(2) $\lim_{n \to 0} [f(n) - (1+n)f'(n)] < 0$

(3) $\lim_{n \to \infty} [f(n) - (1 + n)f'(n)] > 0.$

---

5. Kaldor conjectured that in a full long-period equilibrium "the task of management is reduced to pure supervision, co-ordinating ability [which corresponds to our definition of entrepreneurship] becomes free good and the optimum size of the individual firm becomes infinite (or indeterminate)" [1960, p. 45]. Supervision per se may, however, set a limit to firm size, as shown by Williamson [1967] and by Calvo and Wellisz [1978].

Notice that conditions (2) and (3) are slightly more general than Inada's conditions.

What (1) is asserting is that productive effectiveness operates as "Hicks-neutral" technical progress. Notice, incidentally, that we are assuming that productive effectiveness is the same for all individuals of type x independent of their age. The case where age is emphasized will be the subject of the next section. The properties of f are essentially those assumed in Lucas [1978], and they could be thought of as reflecting what has been termed "loss of control" [Williamson, 1967, and Calvo and Wellisz, 1978].

Firms are profit-maximizers; hence, in equilibrium,

$$(4) \qquad E_x f'(n_x) = w,$$

where w (>0) is the wage rate. Inverting (4), we get

$$(5) \qquad g(w/E_x) = \text{demand for labor by each type-}x\text{ individual}$$
$$\textit{if} \text{ he owns a firm,}$$

where $g \equiv f'^{-1}$. Therefore, the quasi rent of a type-x individual if he owns a firm is

$$(6) \qquad E_x f(g(w/E_x)) - wg(w/E_x).$$

In equilibrium, a type-x individual will prefer to be an entrepreneur or a worker depending on whether (6) is greater or less than w, while those for which (6) equals w would be indifferent between the two courses of action. We assume that E_x is a nondecreasing function of x, although this assumption will in fact become an implication of this and the next section.

Let z be a type for which (6) equals w. By (4) and the conditions that quasi rent of a z-type equals the wage, we get

$$(7) \qquad E_z \frac{f(n_z)}{1 + n_z} = w = E_z f'(n_z),$$

which, by (2) and (3) and the other assumptions on f, uniquely determines employment in firms run by type-z individuals independently of E_z and z. Let us denote the equilibrium level of employment in a z-type firm by $\bar{n}$. Thus, (7) implies that

$$(8) \qquad w = E_z f'(\bar{n}).$$

Therefore, there is a one-to-one correspondence between E_z and w. Thus, recalling (5) and (8), we can compactly characterize a general equilibrium by the condition that demand equals supply in the labor market:

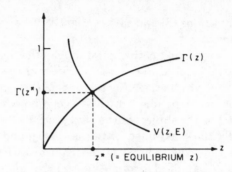

FIGURE I

$$(9) \qquad V(z,E) \equiv \int_z^\infty g\left(\frac{E_z}{E_x} f'(\overline{n})\right) d\Gamma(x) = \Gamma(z),$$

where E denotes the entire function E_x, $x \geq 0$, and z is the type below which everybody is a worker. (We shall refer to z as the "marginal type.") The determination of equilibrium is shown in Figure I, which is essentially Figure 2 of Lucas [1978]. The equilibrium solution is clearly a function of the distribution of productive effectiveness. A change in the distribution of E that shifts the V-curve to the right, for example, will imply a higher equilibrium z; more people will prefer to become workers in equilibrium, and thus the *average size of firms* (measured by the average number of workers per firm = $\Gamma(z)/(1 - \Gamma(z))$) will increase.

Thus far we have been going over the ground covered by Lucas [1978]. We now depart from him to investigate the dynamic behavior of E_x.

We assume that

$$(10) \qquad \dot{E}_x(t) = x[\overline{E}(t) - E_x(t)].$$

In other words, the productive effectiveness grows in proportion to the gap between an exogenous technological level and the actual productive efficiency.[6] The proportion, in turn, is given by the learning ability of the individual, x. So for the same gap, the higher the abilities, the greater the individual's increase in effectiveness will be. But if the gap becomes zero, productive effectiveness will cease to grow, no matter what the level of ability. In a simple manner, this captures the hypothesis referred to at the outset.

---

6. Nelson and Phelps [1966] used a formulation similar to (10) to analyze the impact of education on growth.

Now we are prepared to study the implications of the model. Let us assume

$$(11) \qquad \alpha = \dot{\overline{E}}(t)/\overline{E}(t) = \text{a nonnegative constant.}$$

Suppose that we compare two economies of this type, identical except that the exogenous rate of technical progress α is greater in one economy than in the other. For this comparison we shall assume that the economies have reached their steady-state equilibria; thus we must have

$$(12) \qquad \dot{E}_x(t)/E_x(t) = \alpha, \qquad \text{all } t \text{ and } x.$$

It follows from (10) and (11) that

$$\alpha = x[\overline{E}(t)/E_x(t) - 1]$$

or

$$(13) \qquad \overline{E}(t)/E_x(t) = 1 + \alpha/x.$$

So for each t, $E_x(t)$ is a nondecreasing function of x, implying that at each point of the steady-state path (8) is satisfied. Hence, in steady state

$$(14) \qquad \frac{E_z(t)}{E_x(t)} = \frac{1 + \alpha/x}{1 + \alpha/z} \leq 1 \qquad \text{for } x \geq z.$$

It is easy to verify that (14) decreases with α. Thus, recalling (9) and that $g' < 0$, it follows that an increase in α will produce an outward shift of the V function in Figure I, which, as noted before, implies that the average size of firms will increase. Therefore, the economy with a higher rate of exogenous technical progress will have, on the average, larger firms and more able entrepreneurs.

Convergence to the steady state is no problem here, because the dynamic behavior of the economy is governed by (10). Solving (10), the reader can verify that $\overline{E}(t)/E_x(t)$ approaches the expression given in (13) as t grows large. Hence, $E_z(t)/E_x(t)$ will converge to (14) and, by (9), the average firm size will tend toward that associated with the steady state. It is an open question, although perhaps of rather marginal interest, whether the approach is monotonic or not.

Another experiment in the spirit of Schumpeter is to examine the case where $\overline{E}$ suffers a discontinuous and, say, a once-and-for-all upward jump. Let the initial and new levels of $\overline{E}$ be denoted $\overline{E}_1$ and $\overline{E}_2$, respectively. Suppose that we start from the steady state corresponding to $\overline{E}_1$. Clearly, then, $\overline{E}_x(0) = E_1$ for all $x > 0$, that is to say, everybody (except for $x = 0$) has the same productive efficiency at the start, and equal to the exogenously given technological level of the past $\overline{E}_1$. Suppose that $\overline{E}$ jumps to $\overline{E}_2$ at $t = 0$. Obviously, the distribution of $E_x(0)$ is unaffected, so the size of the firms remains equal to that in the past. In fact, at $t = 0$, every individual with $x > 0$ would be indifferent between being a worker or an entrepreneur, firms would be of identical size $= \overline{n}$, and by (9), z would be determined by the condition

$$(15) \qquad g(f(\overline{n})) = \Gamma(z)/(1 - \Gamma(z)).$$

After the technical discovery, however, fast learners will start taking the lead because, by (10),

$$(16) \qquad \dot{E}_x(0) = x[\overline{E}_2 - \overline{E}_1].$$

Consequently,

$$(17) \qquad \left. \frac{d}{dt} \frac{E_z(t)}{E_x(t)} \right|_{t=0} < 0, \qquad x > z,$$

which implies an outward shift in the V function in the first stages of the process. In turn, this implies that firms will initially tend to become larger on the average. Eventually, however, everybody (except for $x = 0$) will catch up with the new technology and, except for a higher wage rate, the system will have the same characteristics that it had before the change. Empirical evidence is compatible with this conclusion: Mansfield [1962] found that successful innovators tend to grow faster than other firms, but that their advantage was eroded with time.

Our model can also be used to explore the impact of the rate of technical progress on income distribution. Let us define $D(\alpha)$ as the steady-state *ratio of average entrepreneurial income to the wage rate when the rate of technical progress equals* α. From previous considerations we know that $D(0) = 1$ and $D(\alpha) > 1$ for all $\alpha > 0$. Therefore, it follows that there are instances where an increase in the rate of technical progress leads to greater inequality between entrepreneurs and workers (as measured by D). This proposition can be strengthened if one is ready to make more specific assumptions on $f(\cdot)$. A class of functions that, as shown by Lucas [1978], is of particular interest because it is closely associated with the validity of Gibrat's Law, is characterized as follows:

$$f(n) = An^\beta, \qquad A > 0, \qquad 0 < \beta < 1.$$

Let $\pi(x)$ denote the equilibrium profit of a type-x entrepreneur (in general π will be a function of α). Under the above Cobb-Douglas type function we have

$$\frac{\pi(x)}{n_x w} = 1 - \beta$$

and, hence, in equilibrium

$$D(\alpha) = \frac{1}{1 - \Gamma(z)} \int_z^\infty \frac{\pi(x)}{w} \, d\Gamma(x) = \frac{1 - \beta}{1 - \Gamma(z)} \Gamma(z).$$

Since we previously showed that steady-state z rises with α, it follows that $D(\alpha)$ increases with α. Thus, more rapid progress brings about a shrinkage of the entrepreneurial group (the less able entrepreneurs become "proletarized"), and increases the relative income of the remaining members of the group. These conclusions, derived within a neoclassical framework, have a slightly Marxian flavor.

In a similar fashion one can show that, for the Cobb-Douglas case, a once-and-for-all jump in the level of technology will initially result in an increase in D, as defined above; however, in the long run D will return to 1. This provides a clue to the Kuznets curve puzzle. When a relatively backward, static society begins to catch up with technologically more advanced systems, there is generation of entrepreneurial profits. As the gap between theoretical knowledge and its applications decreases, and as the laggards catch up with the leaders, the size of the entrepreneurial group grows but unit entrepreneurial profits decrease. Thus, growth in its early phases may be associated with increased income distribution inequality, and in its later phases with a tendency toward income equalization.

II. AGE AND LEARNING

In this section we focus our attention on the life cycle problems. We assume that individuals have identical inherent abilities, but at a given point of time their effectiveness is a function of their lifetime learning. More specifically

(18) $A(t,v)$ = productive inefficiency at time t of an individual born at time v,

and we assume (here $\dot{A} \equiv \partial A/\partial t$) that

(19) $$\dot{A}(t,v) = \gamma[\overline{E}(t) - A(t,v)] \qquad \gamma > 0$$

with

(20) $$A(v,v) \equiv 0, \qquad \text{all } v.$$

In other words, individuals are a *tabula rasa* the day they first set foot (head?) on the earth (equation (20)), and steadily learn as the years pass by, at a rate proportional to the gap between the current technological knowledge and their actual productive efficiency (equation (19)). In contrast with the previous section, however, the factor of proportionality is the same for everybody.

We shall first characterize the steady state. Solving (19) for initial condition (20), and taking (11) into account, we get

(21) $$A(t,v) = \overline{E}(0)e^{\alpha t}\gamma/(\gamma + \alpha)[1 - e^{-(\gamma+\alpha)(t-v)}].$$

In fact, in order to utilize the static portion of the model developed in the previous section, it will be convenient to define

(22) $\quad E_h(t) =$ productive efficiency of an individual of age h at time t.

Thus, by (21) and (22), at the steady state

(21′) $$E_h(t) = \overline{E}(t)\gamma/(\gamma + \alpha)[1 - e^{-(\gamma+\alpha)h}].$$

Since by (11) and (21′) $E_{h''}(t) > E_{h'}(t)$ if $h'' > h'$, assumption (8) with h substituted for x is satisfied at all times. There, (9)—with h substituted for x—characterizes a general equilibrium if $\Gamma(h)$ is interpreted as the proportion of individuals whose age is less than or equal to h and z is understood to be the age of the youngest entrepreneur. For the present purposes we shall assume, as in the previous section, that $\Gamma(h)$ is constant over time.

By (21′)

(23) $$\frac{E_z(t)}{E_h(t)} = \frac{1 - e^{-(\gamma+\alpha)z}}{1 - e^{-(\gamma+\alpha)h}}, \qquad h > 0.$$

So we are now in the position of comparing average firm size across steady states. In formal terms this involves studying the expression in (23) for $h > z$ as a function of α. As we show in the Appendix, it turns out that the latter increases with α which, by (9), permits us to show that, in contrast with the previous section, z decreases with α. Thus, the age of the youngest entrepreneur, and consequently the average firm size, decreases with the rate of technical progress. The intuition is that a higher rate of technical progress tends to wash out the relative advantage of being older. We shall be able to see this in a more straightforward manner when we study the second experiment of this section.

Convergence to the steady state is again shown very simply, but we shall not take up space to prove it. A much more interesting aspect of the present set of assumptions is the nature of the transition. To facilitate comparison, we shall again study the case where there is a once-and-for-all jump in $\overline{E}$ at $t = 0$, from $\overline{E}_1$ to $\overline{E}_2$ ($>\overline{E}_1$). The economy is assumed to start at the steady state corresponding to $\overline{E}_1$.

By (19) and (20)

$$(24a) \quad A(t,v) = \overline{E}_1 e^{-\gamma t}[1 - e^{\gamma v}] + \overline{E}_2[1 - e^{-\gamma t}], \qquad \text{for } v \leq 0$$

$$(24b) \qquad A(t,v) = \overline{E}_2[1 - e^{-\gamma(t-v)}], \qquad \text{for } v \geq 0.$$

Hence, if we recall (22),

$$(25a) \quad E_h(t) = \overline{E}_2 - \overline{E}_1 e^{-\gamma h} - (\overline{E}_2 - \overline{E}_1)e^{-\gamma t}, \qquad \text{for } t - h \leq 0$$

$$(25b) \qquad E_h(t) = \overline{E}_2[1 - e^{-\gamma h}], \qquad \text{for } t - h \geq 0.$$

As is familiar to us now, the shift in the V-function in Figure I depends on the behavior of $E_z(t)/E_h(t)$. The first simple observation in this respect is that, by (25b), the above ratio equals that of (23) for $\alpha = 0$ if t is sufficiently large so that there is no one alive who was born before time zero. Thus, in normal circumstances the economy will revert back in finite time to the same steady state from which it started.

To study the transition, let us consider the case where $z > t$, i.e., when the youngest entrepreneur was born before $t = 0$. Then, by (25a)

$$(26) \qquad \frac{E_z(t)}{E_h(t)} = \frac{\overline{E}_2 - \overline{E}_1 e^{-\gamma z} - (\overline{E}_2 - \overline{E}_1)e^{-\gamma t}}{\overline{E}_2 - \overline{E}_1 e^{-\gamma h} - (\overline{E}_2 - \overline{E}_1)e^{-\gamma t}}.$$

This ratio is less than 1 for $h > z$ and increases over time. This will necessarily be the relevant situation at $t = 0$ and shortly thereafter. So it follows that shortly after the technical change (which occurs at $t = 0$), z will fall below its steady state (and also, by assumption, initial) level. This means that during the early stages of the transition, the age of the youngest entrepreneur will decrease, and also the average firm size will become smaller. This contrasts with the situation in Section I, where we showed that a similar experiment would initially result in a larger, not smaller, average firm size.

Since the economy eventually returns to the steady state, z will necessarily recover its initial level but, as can easily be checked using (25), at no point in time will z overshoot that level.

The intuition behind this result is not difficult to find. By (19) we see that at $t = 0$ the learning of an individual (his $\dot{A}$) will have an exogenous component ($= \gamma(\overline{E}_2 - \overline{E}_1)$), which is the same for all individuals. Thus, it is to be expected that the relative efficiency of two individuals of different ages will initially shift closer to 1, and thus the relative advantage of being older will tend to disappear. For this reason, the minimum age for joining the entrepreneurial ranks initially declines, reducing the average firm size.

The analysis of "learning by aging" yields two conclusions, one trivial and one not so obvious. The trivial conclusion is that, in a society in which all individuals have the same inherent ability, you will get to the top if you live long enough: in time, you will become a village elder. It is less obvious, however, that you will join the top ranks faster if technology grows more quickly, even if you are no more able (and have less accumulated learning) than your elders. Thus, even if we disregard ability, we conclude that youth is favored by progress.

Another conclusion is that in the present model entrepreneurial quasi rents do not tend to disappear even when technology is stationary. This result, an easy implication of our assumptions, acquires greater significance considering the widely accepted view that technological progress is an essential ingredient for the existence of such entrepreneurial income. It also shows that Lucas' [1978] setup is not necessarily inconsistent with a stationary technology.

III. Ability, Age, and Learning

We shall now take a small analytic step, and a giant one in the direction of greater realism: we shall combine our two models and consider the age and ability factors simultaneously.

We shall indicate by $A_x(t,v)$ the productive efficiency at time t of an individual of ability x and who was born at time v. We assume that

$$(27) \qquad \dot{A}_x(t,v) = x[\overline{E}(t) - A_x(t,v)].$$

If we recall (13) and (21′) it is quite obvious that, at a steady state,

$$(28) \quad \frac{E_{xh}(t)}{\overline{E}(t)} = \frac{1 - e^{-(x+\alpha)h}}{1 + \alpha/x} \equiv R(x,h;\alpha) \equiv \quad \text{``relative efficiency'' of an } (x,h)\text{-type,}$$

where

$E_{xh}(t) = $ productive efficiency of an individual of quality x and age h at time t.

Figure II depicts a typical map of iso-"relative efficiency" curves for a given α. Letting $\Gamma(x,h)$ denote the (time-independent) cumulative distribution over quality x and age h, we can now express the equilibrium condition (i.e., the analogue of (9)) as follows:

674 QUARTERLY JOURNAL OF ECONOMICS

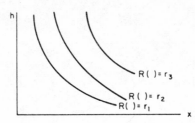

FIGURE II
Isoefficiency Curves ($r_1 < r_2 < r_3$)

$$(9') \quad \int_{B_\alpha(r)} g\left(\frac{r}{R(x,h;\alpha)} f'(\overline{n})\right) d\Gamma(x,h) = 1 - \int_{B_a(r)} d\Gamma(x,h),$$

where

$$(29) \qquad B_\alpha(r) = \{(x,h):R(x,h;\alpha) \geq r\}.$$

Thus, r denotes the relative efficiency of the least efficient entrepreneur in equilibrium, and it takes the place of the variable z of our previous analysis. We shall therefore call r the *marginal relative efficiency*.

We shall now show that isoefficiency curves become "steeper" as α increases.

The slope of an isorelative efficiency curve is given by

$$(30) \quad \frac{dh}{dx}\bigg|_{R=\text{const.}}$$

$$= -\frac{R_x}{R_h}\left\{\frac{h}{x+\alpha} + \frac{\alpha}{x(x+\alpha)^2}\left[e^{(x+\alpha)h} - 1\right]\right\} \equiv s(x,h;\alpha).$$

Now,

$$(31) \quad \frac{\partial s}{\partial \alpha} = \frac{h}{(x+\alpha)^2} - \frac{(x+\alpha)^2 - 2(x+\alpha)\alpha}{x(x+\alpha)^4}$$

$$\times \left[e^{(x+\alpha)h} - 1\right] - \frac{\alpha h}{x(x+\alpha)^2} e^{(x+\alpha)h}$$

$$= \frac{1}{(x+\alpha)^2}\left\{\left[h - \frac{e^{(x+\alpha)h} - 1}{x+\alpha}\right] + \frac{\alpha}{x}h\left[\frac{e^{(x+\alpha)h} - 1}{(x+\alpha)h} - e^{(x+\alpha)h}\right]\right\} < 0$$

when $(x + \alpha) > 0$ and $h > 0$.

Now we can characterize what happens in a steady state with α'' compared to one with α', $\alpha'' > \alpha'$. This is shown in Figure III, where r' and r'' are the marginal relative efficiencies associated with α' and

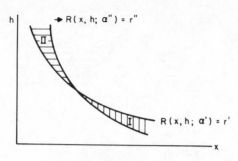

FIGURE III
Effect of Change in α

α'', respectively. Shaded area I indicates the set of (x,h) pairs that become entrepreneurs as α shifts from α' to α''. On the other hand, area II corresponds to the set of pairs that cease to be entrepreneurs under the same circumstances. We have found, therefore, that *as the rate of* (exogenous) *technical progress increases, the quality of the "new" entrepreneurs is higher and their age is lower than those of any individual who ceases to be an entrepreneur in the new equilibrium.*[7] In the present case, however, the effect of the average size of firms cannot be ascertained without further knowledge of the production and distribution functions.

A similar result would obtain during the transition from stationary levels $\overline{E}_1 < \overline{E}_2$. One can easily show (the proof is left for the interested reader) that the steady state is the same for $\overline{E}_1$ as for $\overline{E}_2$ (except for a higher wage in the second situation); however, during the first stages of the transition, entrepreneurs who relinquish their helms will be older and less able than the new entrepreneurs.

Finally, by (30) we see that isoefficiency curves tend to become perfectly vertical as $\alpha \to \infty$, indicating that the ranking of productive efficiencies will tend to depend exclusively on quality, and not on age, as the (exogenous) rate of technical progress becomes very large.

In this section we have shown that the acceleration of technical progress eliminates older, less inherently able individuals from the entrepreneurial ranks, and adds younger, more inherently capable ones to these ranks. This result was obtained without appealing to the argument that ability to learn declines with age. We also dispensed with the cost of acquisition of human capital argument which states

---

7. Notice that the r' and r'' lines in Figure III do not necessarily intersect, and even if they do, areas I or II could be null according to the probability measure induced by $\Gamma(\cdot,\cdot)$. This implies that as α increases, there may be no "new" entrepreneurs or, alternatively, that no one ceases to be an entrepreneur.

that, if learning involves costs, rational calculus indicates that younger people should learn more than older ones. It is clear that either one of those considerations strengthens our results.

We have also provided a theoretical explanation of the often-observed phenomenon that age and experience matter more in relatively static societies, while inherent ability matters more in societies where technology evolves at a rapid pace. Going beyond the model, we may speculate on the relation between the structure of leadership and the rate of progress. If we assume that power derived from leadership is valued for itself, it seems plausible that elderly leaders are likely to oppose progress which represents a threat to their supremacy for the same reason progress is likely to be championed by younger, more able individuals. This self-interest may provide one explanation for the conservatism of older leaders and the radicalism of the younger challengers.

APPENDIX

Let us define

(A1)
$$\psi(\alpha) = \frac{1 - e^{-(\gamma+\alpha)z}}{1 - e^{-(\gamma+\alpha)x}}, \qquad 0 < z < x.$$

We shall show that $\psi(\alpha)$ is monotonically increasing for all $\alpha \geq 0$, which is what was asserted in Section II. For present purposes, however, it will be convenient to think of ψ as being defined on the interval $[-\gamma, \infty)$, where

(A2)
$$\psi(-\gamma) = \lim_{\alpha \downarrow -\gamma} \psi(\alpha) = \frac{z}{x}.$$

We shall show the (stronger) proposition that $\psi(\alpha)$ is monotonically increasing over $[-\psi, \infty)$. The proof is by contradiction.

First note that

(A3)
$$\lim_{\alpha \to \infty} \psi(\alpha) = 1 > \frac{z}{x}$$

and

(A4)
$$\psi(\alpha) < 1 \qquad \text{for all } \alpha \geq -\gamma.$$

Furthermore, by (A1),

(A5)
$$\text{If } \alpha \geq -\gamma \quad \text{and} \quad \psi'(\alpha) = 0,$$
$$\text{then} \quad \psi(\alpha) = z/x \, e^{(\gamma+\alpha)(x-z)}.$$

One implication of the above is

(A6)
$$\psi(\alpha) \geq z/x \qquad \text{for all } \alpha \geq -\gamma,$$

because if the latter were contradicted, by (A2) and (A3), there would exist an α such that $\psi(\alpha) < z/x$ and $\psi'(\alpha) = 0$. But this contradicts (A5), according to which

$$\psi(\alpha) = z/x \; e^{(\gamma+\alpha)(x-z)} > z/x$$

[because $\gamma + \alpha > 0$ and $x - z > 0$].

Therefore, by (A2)–(A4) and (A6) if $\psi(\alpha)$ were not monotonically increasing, we should have $\alpha_2 > \alpha_1 > -\gamma$ such that α_1 is a local maximum, α_2 is a local minimum and

(A7) $\psi(\alpha_1) > \psi(\alpha_2);$

but, by (A5),

$$\psi(\alpha_1)/\psi(\alpha_2) = e^{(\alpha_1-\alpha_2)(x-z)} < 1,$$

contradicting (A7). This proves the proposition.

COLUMBIA UNIVERSITY

REFERENCES

Calvo, Guillermo A., and Stanislaw Wellisz, "Supervision, Loss of Control, and the Optimum Size of the Firm," *Journal of Political Economy*, LXXXVI (Oct. 1978), 943–52.
——, and ——, "Hierarchy, Ability, and Income Distribution," *Journal of Political Economy*, LXXXVII (Oct. 1979), 991–1010.
Kaldor, Nicholas, "The Equilibrium of the Firm," in *Essays on Value and Distribution* (London: Gerald Duckworth and Co. Ltd., 1960), Ch. 2.
Lucas, Robert E., Jr., "On the Size Distribution of Business Firms," *Bell Journal of Economics*, IX (Autumn 1978), 508–23.
Mayer, Thomas, "The Distribution of Ability and Earnings," *Review of Economics and Statistics*, XLII (May 1960), 189–95.
Nelson, Robert R., and Sidney G. Winter, "Simulation of Schumpeterian Competition," *American Economic Review*, LXVII (Feb. 1977), 271–76.
——, and ——, "Forces Generating and Limiting Concentration under Schumpeterian Competition," *Bell Journal*, IX (Autumn 1978), 524–48.
Prescott, Edward C., and Michael Visscher, "Organization Capital," Carnegie-Mellon University, mimeographed, 1978.
Schumpeter, Joseph A., *Business Cycles* (New York and London: McGraw-Hill Book Co., 1939).
Williamson, Oliver E., "Hierarchical Control and Optimum Firm Size," *Journal of Political Economy*, LXXV (April 1967), 123–38.

The Entrepreneur and the Firm

[10]

CHAPTER IX

Of Production on a Large, and Production on a Small Scale

§ 1. [*Advantages of the large system of production in manufactures*] From the importance of combination of labour, it is an obvious conclusion, that there are many cases in which production is made much more effective by being conducted on a large scale. Whenever it is essential to the greatest efficiency of labour that many labourers should combine, even though only in the way of Simple Co-operation, the scale of the enterprise must be such as to bring many labourers together, and the capital must be large enough to maintain them. Still more needful is this when the nature of the employment allows, and the extent of the possible market encourages, a considerable division of labour. The larger the enterprise, the *farther* the division of labour may be carried. This is one of the principal causes of large manufactories. Even when no additional subdivision of the work would follow an enlargement of the operations, there will be good economy in enlarging them to the point at which every person to whom it is convenient to assign a special occupation, will have full employment in that occupation. This point is well illustrated by Mr. Babbage.*

"If machines be kept working through the twenty-four hours," (which is evidently the only economical mode of employing them,) "it is necessary that some person shall attend to admit the workmen at the time they relieve each other; and whether the porter or other *person* so employed admit one person or twenty, his rest will be equally disturbed. It will also be necessary occasionally to adjust or repair the machine; and this can be done much better by a workman accustomed to machine-making, than by the person who uses it. Now, since the good performance and the duration of machines depend, to a very great extent, upon correcting every shake or imperfection in their parts as soon as they appear, the prompt attention of a workman resident on the spot will considerably reduce the expenditure arising from the wear and tear of the machinery. But in the case of a single

*Page 214 et seqq. [Pp. 214–6.]

*a–a*MS, 48, 49, 52   further   *b–b*Source, MS, 48, 49, 52, 57, 62   servant lace-frame, or a single loom, this would be too expensive a plan. Here then arises another circumstance which tends to enlarge the extent of a factory. It ought to consist of such a number of machines as shall occupy the whole time of one workman in keeping them in order: if extended beyond that number, the same principle of economy would point out the necessity of doubling or tripling the number of machines, in order to employ the whole time of two or three skilful workmen.

"*c*When*c* one portion of the workman's labour consists in the exertion of mere physical force, as in weaving, and in many similar arts, it will soon occur to the manufacturer, that if that part were executed by a steam-engine, the same man might, in the case of weaving, attend to two or more looms at once: and, since we already suppose that one or more operative engineers have been employed, the number of looms may be so arranged that their time shall be fully occupied in keeping the steam-engine and the looms in order. *d*

"Pursuing the same principles, the manufactory becomes gradually so enlarged, that the expense of lighting during the night amounts to a considerable sum: and as there are already attached to the establishment persons who are up all night, and can therefore constantly attend to it, and also engineers to make and keep in repair any machinery, the addition of an apparatus for making gas to light the factory leads to a new extension, at the same time that it contributes, by diminishing the expense of lighting, and the risk of accidents from fire, to reduce the cost of manufacturing.

"Long before a factory has reached this extent, it will have been found necessary to establish an accountant's department, with clerks to pay the workmen, and to see that they arrive at their stated times; and this department must be in communication with the agents who purchase the raw produce, and with those who sell the manufactured article." It will cost these clerks and accountants little more time and trouble to pay a large number of workmen than a small number; to check the accounts of large transactions, than of small. If the business doubled itself, it would probably be necessary to increase, but certainly not to double, the number either of accountants, or of buying and selling agents. Every increase of business would enable the whole to be carried on with a *e*proportionately*e* smaller amount of labour.

As a general rule, the expenses of a business do not increase by any means proportionally to the quantity of business. Let us take as an example, a set of operations which we are accustomed to see carried on by one great establishment, that of the Post Office. Suppose that the business, let us say

c–cSource, MS, 48, 49, 52, 57   Where
*d*MS   [*ellipsis indicated by*] . . . .
e–eMS, 48, 49, 52, 57, 62, 65   proportionally

only of the London letter-post, instead of being centralized in a single concern, were divided among five or six *competing companies*. Each of these would be obliged to maintain almost as large an establishment as is now sufficient for the whole. Since each must arrange for receiving and delivering letters in all parts of the town, each must send letter-carriers into every street, and almost every alley, and this too as many times in the day as is now done by the Post Office, if the service is to be as well performed. Each must have an office for receiving letters in every neighbourhood, with all subsidiary arrangements for collecting the letters from the different offices and re-distributing them. *To this must be added* the much greater number of superior officers who would be required to check and control the subordinates, implying not only a greater cost in salaries for such responsible officers, but the necessity, perhaps, of being satisfied in many instances with an inferior standard of qualification, and so failing in the object.

Whether or not the advantages obtained by operating on a large scale preponderate in any particular case over the more watchful attention, and greater regard to minor gains and losses, usually found in small establishments, can be ascertained, in a state of free competition, by an unfailing test. Wherever there are large and small establishments in the same business, that one of the two which in existing circumstances carries on the production at greatest advantage will be able to undersell the other. The power of permanently underselling can only*, generally speaking,* be derived from increased effectiveness of labour; and this, when obtained by a more extended division of employment, or by a classification tending to a better economy of skill, always implies a greater produce from the same labour, and not merely the same produce from less labour: it increases not the surplus only, but the gross produce of industry. If an increased quantity of the particular article is not required, and *ᶦ* part of the labourers in consequence lose their employment, the capital which maintained and employed them is also set at liberty; and the general produce of the country is increased by some other application of their labour.

Another of the causes of large manufactories, however, is the introduction of processes requiring expensive machinery. Expensive machinery supposes a large capital; and is not resorted to except with the intention of producing, and the hope of selling, as much of the article as comes up to the full powers of the machine. For both these reasons, wherever costly machinery *is* used, the large system of production is inevitable. But the

f-f+48, 49, 52, 57, 62, 65, 71
*g-g*MS, 48, 49, 52, 57   I say nothing of
h-h+52, 57, 62, 65, 71
*i*MS, 48, 49   a
*j-j*MS, 48   are

134					BOOK I, CHAPTER ix, § 1

power of underselling is not in this case so unerring a test as in the former, of the beneficial effect òn the total production of the community. The power of underselling does not depend on the absolute increase of produce, but on its bearing an increased proportion to the expenses; which, as was shown in a former chapter,* it may do, consistently with even a diminution of the gross annual produce. By the adoption of machinery, a circulating capital, which was perpetually consumed and reproduced, has been converted into a fixed capital, requiring only a small annual expense to keep it up: and a much smaller produce will suffice for merely covering that expense, and replacing the remaining circulating capital of the producer. The machinery therefore *ᵏ*might*ᵏ* answer perfectly well to the manufacturer, and *ˡ* enable him to undersell his competitors, though the effect on the production of the country *ᵐ*might*ᵐ* be not an increase but a diminution. It is true, the article will be sold cheaper, and therefore, of that single article, there will probably be not a smaller, but a greater quantity sold; since the loss to the community collectively has fallen upon the work-people, and they are not the principal customers, if customers at all, of most branches of manufacture. But though that particular branch of industry may extend itself, it will be by replenishing its diminished circulating capital from that of the community generally; and if the labourers employed in that department escape loss of employment, it is because the loss will spread itself over the labouring people at large. If any of them are reduced to the condition of unproductive labourers, supported by voluntary or legal charity, the gross produce of the country is to that extent permanently diminished, until the ordinary progress of accumulation makes it up; but if the condition of the labouring classes enables them to bear a temporary reduction of wages, and the superseded labourers become absorbed in other employments, their labour is still productive, and the breach in the gross produce of the community is repaired, though not the detriment to the labourers. I have restated this exposition, which has already been made in a former place, to impress more strongly the truth, that a mode of production does not of necessity increase the productive effect of the collective labour of a community, because it enables a particular commodity to be sold cheaper. The one consequence generally accompanies the other, but not necessarily. I will not here repeat the reasons I formerly gave, nor anticipate those which will be given more fully hereafter, for deeming the exception to be rather a case abstractedly possible, than one which is frequently realized in fact.

A considerable part of the saving of labour effected by substituting the

*Supra, chap. vi. p. 94.

*ᵏ⁻ᵏ*MS may
*ˡ*MS may
*ᵐ⁻ᵐ*MS may

OF PRODUCTION ON A LARGE, AND ON A SMALL SCALE 135

large system of production for the small, is the saving in the labour of the capitalists themselves. If a hundred producers with small capitals carry on separately the same business, the superintendence of each concern will probably require the whole attention of the person conducting it, sufficiently at least to hinder his time or thoughts from being disposable for anything else: while a single manufacturer possessing a capital equal to the sum of theirs, with ten or a dozen clerks, could conduct the whole of their amount of business, and have leisure too for other occupations. The small capitalist, it is true, generally combines with the business of direction some portion of the details, which the other leaves to his subordinates: the small farmer follows his own plough, the small tradesman serves in his own shop, the small weaver plies his own loom. But in this very union of functions there is, in a great proportion of cases, a want of economy. The principal in the concern is either wasting, in the routine of a business, qualities suitable for the direction of it, or he is only fit for the former, and then the latter will be ill done. I must observe, however, that I do not attach, to this saving of labour, the importance often ascribed to it. There is undoubtedly much more labour expended in the superintendence of many small capitals than in that of one large capital. For this labour however the small producers have generally a full compensation, in the feeling of being their own masters, and not servants of an employer. It may be said, that if they value this independence they will submit to pay a price for it, and to sell at the reduced rates occasioned by the competition of the great dealer or manufacturer. But they cannot always do this and continue to gain a living. They thus gradually disappear from society. After having consumed their little capital in prolonging the unsuccessful struggle, they either sink into the condition of hired labourers, or become dependent on others for support.

§ 2. [*Advantages and disadvantages of the joint-stock principle*] Production on a large scale is greatly promoted by the practice of forming a large capital by the combination of many small contributions; or, in other words, by the formation of joint stock companies. The ᵃadvantagesᵃ of the joint stock principle are numerous and important.

In the first place, many undertakings require an amount of capital beyond the means of the richest individual or private partnership. No individual could have made a railway from London to Liverpool; it is doubtful if any individual could even work the traffic on it, now when it is made. The government indeed could have done both; and in countries where the practice of co-operation is only in the earlier stages of its growth, the government can alone be looked to for any of ᵇtheᵇ works for which a great combination of means is requisite; because it can obtain those means

ᵃ⁻ᵃMS recommendations   ᵇ⁻ᵇMS, 48, 49, 52, 57, 62 those by compulsory taxation, and is already accustomed to the conduct of large operations. For reasons, however, which are tolerably well known, and of which we shall treat fully hereafter, government agency for the conduct of industrial operations is generally one of the least eligible of resources, when any other is available.

Next, there are undertakings which individuals are not absolutely incapable of performing, but which they cannot perform on the scale and with the continuity which *are* ever more and more required by the exigencies of a society in an advancing state. Individuals are quite capable of despatching ships from England to any or every part of the world, to carry passengers and letters; the thing was done before joint stock companies *for the purpose* were heard of. But when, from the increase of population and transactions, as well as of means of payment, the public will no longer content themselves with occasional opportunities, but require the certainty that packets shall start regularly, for some places once or even twice a day, for others once a week, for others that a steam ship of *great* size and expensive construction shall depart on fixed days twice in each month, it is evident that to afford an assurance of keeping up with punctuality such a circle of costly operations, requires a much larger capital and a much larger staff of qualified subordinates than can be commanded by an individual capitalist. There are other cases, again, in which though the business might be perfectly well transacted with small or moderate capitals, the guarantee of a great subscribed stock is necessary or desirable as a security to the public for the fulfilment of pecuniary engagements. This is especially the case when the nature of the business requires that numbers of persons should be willing to trust the concern with their money: as in the business of banking, and that of insurance: to both of which the joint stock principle is eminently adapted. It is an instance of the folly and jobbery of the rulers of mankind, that until *a late period* the joint stock principle, as a general resort, was in this country interdicted by law to these two modes of business; to banking altogether, and to insurance in the department of sea risks; in order to bestow a lucrative monopoly on particular establishments which the government was pleased exceptionally to license, namely the Bank of England, and two insurance companies, the London and the Royal Exchange.

*Another advantage of joint stock or associated management, is its incident of publicity. This is not an invariable, but it is a natural consequence of the joint stock principle, and might be, as in some important cases it

c–cMS is
d–d+48, 49, 52, 57, 62, 65, 71
e–eMS enormous
f–fMS, 48, 49, 52, 57 very lately
g–g137+65, 71

OF PRODUCTION ON A LARGE, AND ON A SMALL SCALE   137

already is, compulsory. In banking, insurance, and other businesses which depend wholly on confidence, publicity is a still more important element of success than a large subscribed capital. A heavy loss occurring in a private bank may be kept secret; even though it were of such magnitude as to cause the ruin of the concern, the banker may still carry it on for years, trying to retrieve its position, only to fall in the end with a greater crash: but this cannot so easily happen in the case of a joint stock company, whose accounts are published periodically. The accounts, even if cooked, still exercise some check; and the suspicions of shareholders, breaking out at the general meetings, put the public on their guard.*g*

These are some of the advantages of joint stock over individual management. But if we look to the other side of the question, we shall find that individual management has also *h*very great*h* advantages over joint stock. The chief of these is the much keener interest of the managers in the success of the undertaking.

The administration of a joint stock association is, in the main, administration by hired servants. Even the committee, or board of directors, who are supposed to superintend the management, and who do really appoint and remove the managers, have no pecuniary interest in the good working of the concern beyond the shares they individually hold, which are always a very small part of the capital of the association, and in general but a small part of the fortunes of the directors themselves; and the part they take in the management usually divides their time with many other occupations, of as great or greater importance to their own interest; the business being the principal concern of no one except those who are hired to carry it on. But experience shows, and proverbs, the expression of popular experience, attest, how inferior is the quality of hired *i*servants*i*, compared with the ministration of those personally interested in the work, and how indispensable, when hired service must be employed, is "the master's eye" to watch over it.

The successful conduct of an industrial enterprise requires two quite distinct qualifications: fidelity, and zeal. The fidelity of the hired managers of a concern it is possible to secure. When their work admits of being reduced to a definite set of rules, the violation of these is a matter on which conscience cannot easily blind itself, and on which responsibility may be enforced by the loss of employment. But to carry on a great business successfully, requires a hundred things which, as they cannot be defined beforehand, it is impossible to convert into distinct and positive obligations. First and principally, it requires that the directing mind should be incessantly occupied with the subject; should be continually laying schemes by

*h–h*MS enormous
*i–i*MS, 48, 49, 52 service

138   BOOK I, CHAPTER ix, § 2

which greater profit may be obtained, or expense saved. This intensity of interest in the subject it is seldom to be expected that any one should feel, who is conducting a business as the hired servant and for the profit of another. There are experiments in human *ʲaffairs which areʲ* conclusive on the point. Look at the whole class of rulers, and ministers of state. The work they are entrusted with, is among the most interesting and exciting of all occupations; the personal share which they themselves reap of the national benefits or misfortunes which befal the state under their rule, is far from trifling, and the rewards and punishments which they may expect from public estimation are of the plain and palpable kind which are most keenly felt and most widely appreciated. Yet how rare a thing is it to find a statesman in whom mental indolence is not stronger than all these inducements. How infinitesimal is the proportion *ᵏ* who trouble themselves to form, or even to attend to, plans of public improvement, unless *ˡwhenˡ* it is made still more troublesome to them to remain inactive; or who have any other real desire than that of rubbing on, so as to escape general blame. On a smaller scale, all who have ever employed hired labour have had ample experience of the efforts made to give as little labour in exchange for the wages, as is compatible with not being turned off. The universal neglect by domestic servants of their employer's interests, wherever these are not protected by some fixed rule, is matter of common remark; unless where long continuance in the same service, and reciprocal good offices, have produced either personal attachment, or some feeling of a common interest.

Another of the disadvantages of joint stock concerns, which is in some degree common to all concerns on a large scale, is disregard of small gains and small savings. In the management of a great capital and great transactions, especially when the managers have not much interest in it of their own, small sums are apt to be counted for next to nothing; they never seem worth the care and trouble which it costs to attend to them, and the credit of liberality and openhandedness is cheaply bought by a disregard of such trifling considerations. But small profits and small expenses often repeated, amount to great gains and losses: and of this a large capitalist is often a sufficiently good calculator to be practically aware; and to arrange his business on a *system*, which if enforced by a sufficiently vigilant superintendence, precludes the possibility of the habitual waste, otherwise incident to a great business. But the managers of a joint stock concern seldom devote themselves sufficiently to the work, to enforce unremittingly, even if introduced, through every detail of the business, a really economical system.

From considerations of this nature, Adam Smith was led to enunciate as

---

ʲ⁻ʲMS, 48, 49   nature which are quite
ᵏMS   of them
ˡ⁻ˡ+49, 52, 57, 62, 65, 71

OF PRODUCTION ON A LARGE, AND ON A SMALL SCALE 139

a principle, that joint stock companies could never be expected to maintain themselves without an exclusive privilege, except in branches of business which, like banking, insurance, and some others, admit of being, in a considerable degree, reduced to fixed rules. This, however, is one of those over-statements of a true principle, often met with in Adam Smith. In his days there were few instances of joint stock companies which had been permanently successful without a monopoly, except the class of cases which he referred to; but since his time there have been many; and the regular increase both of the spirit of combination and of the ability to combine, will doubtless produce many more. Adam Smith fixed his observation too exclusively on the superior energy and more unremitting attention brought to a business in which the whole stake and the whole gain belong to the persons conducting it; and he overlooked various countervailing considerations which go a great way towards neutralizing even that great point of superiority.

Of these one of the most important is that which relates to the intellectual and active qualifications of the directing head. The stimulus of individual interest *m*is some security for*m* exertion, but *n* exertion is of little avail if the intelligence exerted is of an inferior order, which it must necessarily be in the majority of concerns carried on by the persons chiefly interested in them. Where the concern is large, and can afford a remuneration sufficient to attract a class of candidates superior to the common average, it is possible to select for the general management, and for all the skilled employments of a subordinate kind, persons of a degree of acquirement and cultivated intelligence which more than compensates for their inferior interest in the result. Their greater perspicacity enables them, with even a part of their minds, to see probabilities of advantage which never occur to the ordinary run of men by the continued exertion of the whole of theirs; *o*and their superior knowledge,*o* and *p* habitual rectitude of perception and of judgment, *q*guard*q* them against blunders, the *r*fear*r* of which would prevent the others from hazarding their interests in any attempt out of the ordinary routine.

It must *s*be further*s* remarked, that it is not a necessary consequence of joint stock management, that the persons employed, whether in superior or in subordinate offices, should be paid wholly by fixed salaries. There are modes of connecting more or less intimately the interest of the employés with the pecuniary success of the concern. There is a long series of intermediate positions, between working wholly on one's own account, and

*m–m*MS, 48, 49   secures the greatest amount of
*n*MS, 48, 49   that
o–o+57, 62, 65, 71
*p*MS, 48, 49, 52   their   *q–q*MS, 48, 49, 52   guards
*r–r*MS, 48, 49, 52, 57   apprehension   *s–s*MS, 48, 49   further be

working by the day, week, or year for an invariable payment. Even in the case of ordinary unskilled labour, there is such a thing as task-work, or working by the piece: and the superior efficiency of this is so well known, that judicious employers always resort to it when the work admits of being put out in definite portions, without the necessity of too troublesome a surveillance to guard against inferiority in the execution. In the case of the managers of joint stock companies, and of the superintending and controlling officers in many private establishments, it is a common enough practice to connect their pecuniary interest with the interest of their employers, by giving them part of their remuneration in the form of a percentage on the profits. The personal interest thus given to hired servants is not comparable in intensity to that of the owner of the capital; but it is sufficient to be a very material stimulus to zeal and carefulness, and, when added to the advantage of superior intelligence, often raises the quality of the service much above that which the generality of masters are capable of rendering to themselves. The ulterior extensions of which this principle of remuneration is susceptible, being of great social as well as economical importance, will be more particularly adverted to in a subsequent stage of the present inquiry.

As I have already remarked of large establishments generally, when compared with small ones, whenever competition is free its results will show whether individual or joint stock agency is best adapted to the particular case, since that which is most efficient and most economical will always in the end succeed in underselling the other.

§ 3. [*Conditions necessary for the large system of production*] The possibility of substituting the large system of production for the small, depends, of course, in the first place, on the extent of the market. The large system can only be advantageous when a large amount of business is to be done: it implies, therefore, either a populous and flourishing community, or a great opening for exportation. Again, this as well as every other change in the system of production is greatly favoured by a progressive condition of capital. It is chiefly when the capital of a country is receiving a great annual increase, that there is a large amount of capital seeking for investment: and a new enterprise is much sooner and more easily entered upon by new capital, than by withdrawing capital from existing employments. The change is also much facilitated by the existence of large capitals in few hands. It is true that the same amount of capital can be raised by bringing together many small sums. But this (besides that it is not equally well suited to all branches of industry) supposes a much greater degree of commercial confidence and enterprise diffused through the community, and belongs altogether to a more advanced stage of industrial progress.

[11]

CHAPTER IX

TRANSITION TO PRESENT PROBLEMS OF INDUSTRY AND TRADE

1. *The foundations of modern business in general confidence and credit.*

The present chapter is designed to afford a link between Book I and Book II by applying some indications, furnished by observation of past phases of industry and trade, as part of the basis for a study of business under present conditions.

A chief feature of economic evolution has been the gradual emergence of the notion of a "business point of view" in regard to the affairs of life. That phrase could not have been understood in a primitive society: and there is a sense in which it may be argued that business operations are merely one drift of a tendency to adapt means to ends, which is universal throughout all forms of life. Biology is indeed discovering numerous ways in which inheritance and natural selection--supplemented by the imitation of the successful actions of parents and other older individuals, and by other post-natal influences—have enabled even low grade animals so to adjust their structure and their operations to their environment, that they may be able to utilize it for their own benefit with ever increasing ease, efficiency and certainty[1].

---

[1] This remark does not assume that acquired faculties are inherited from parents by children at their birth: it is sufficient for the argument that children automatically imitate the actions of those by whom they are surrounded, and are especially sensitive to suggestions from the examples of mother and father: while acquired skill and faculty in small matters, as well as in large, pass from parents to children by definite instruction. But a protest may be permissible against the pretensions of some exponents of Mendelian doctrine that arithmetical averages of observation of inheritance by mice and vegetables afford

164   TRANSITION TO PRESENT INDUSTRIAL PROBLEMS

I, IX, 1.   Most of these adjustments are in regard to the functions of
individual members of a species separately: but one large part
of them has to do with the military organization of the various
members of a group, and another and yet larger part with their
business organization. It is probable that anthills and beehives
have been highly organized business concerns during very many
more centuries, than those which have seen human business
organizations of equal complexity and efficiency: but, so far as
we know, the organization of ants and bees has been automatic
and unconscious, without direction by foresight and deliberate
contrivance. On the other hand there has been some element
of conscious adaptation of means to ends in nearly every organization of human business. And, though the automatic elements
preponderated greatly over the conscious and deliberate elements
in early phases of economic growth, yet changing conditions
were gradually met by quiet adjustments. Elementary, partial
division of labour grew up between individual members of the
same family, between families, and between neighbouring villages,
or clans. Here were the origins of business trust and confidence,
which were indeed enforced within each group by the social
penalty of ostracism: an offender against his neighbours became
an outcast, often without refuge.

As small communities merged and increased in size, an
offender could more easily move from the scene of his trans-
gression. The extension of neighbourliness lowered its intensity;
and in consequence the trust between neighbours became less
habitual and instinctive. In other words life became in some
degree "business-like"; and ere long the transactions between
neighbours began to be governed by arithmetical comparisons

conclusive proof that the characters which children bring into the world with
them, are incapable of being affected by the past mode of life of their parents.
Mendelians do not claim to know what causes originate differences between
elementary germs: it seems to be certain that changes in the mental and moral
habits of a human being are reflected in his face: and Mendelian arithmetic
has little direct bearing on the question whether the nutrition supplied to
germs in the body of a person excessively addicted to drink or other sensual
indulgences may not result in the birth of a child with less firm character than
it would have had, if the parent had lived soberly and chastely. Some Mendelians
concede that it does: and the gradual development of trustworthy statistics
of inherited mental and moral characters may ultimately lead to further ad-
missions in the same direction.

between the value of that which was given, and that which was   I, ix, 1.
received in exchange.

The traders who bought goods in one locality and sold them
in another were distinctively business men. But the greater
number even of them seldom needed to look long ahead or
very far afield: partly because they were in personal touch with
those from whom they bought, and to whom they sold; and
were thus directly cognisant of nearly all changes (except those
arising out of war, famine and plague) which were likely to
upset their calculations in the short time over which each such
transaction generally ran. On the other hand a broad confidence
in the steadfastness and efficiency of large and various markets
is a necessary condition of the highly complex modern division
of labour among producers, and between producers and middlemen: for indeed almost every considerable operation of business
involves some speculation based on well-informed confidence.
The whole mechanism of society rests on confidence: it per-
meates all life, like the air we breathe: and its services are apt to
be taken for granted and ignored, like those of fresh air, until
attention is forcibly attracted by their failure. When confidence
is shaken by a rumour of war or of civil commotion, or of disturbing financial legislation, or of extensive frauds or rash trading
by important firms, then business life is stifled; and men yearn
for the wholesome atmosphere that is associated with the general
re-establishment of confidence[1].

This trust contains a personal element: but it contains
much more. For most of those on whose actions anyone
relies are personally unknown to him. It is sometimes called
"commercial credit." But that term seems not to cover the
whole of it: we may call it "*social credit*." It is analogous to
personal credit. But it is also, and for the larger part, trust in

---

[1] The methods of business in the remoter districts of New England a century ago throw much light on those of Mediaeval England: the light is all the
brighter, because high intelligence and cultured thought were being brought to
bear on crude material conditions. Professor Sherwood (*Quarterly Journal
of Economics*, viii. p. 157) tells how his grandfather used to dress flax for the
ropes and grain bags needed on his farm, and to make his own shoes; but slowly
gave up the habit, as the growth of markets around him gave him a double
confidence that he could advantageously dispose of his grain to one set of people,
and obtain his ropes and shoes from another.

166   TRANSITION TO PRESENT INDUSTRIAL PROBLEMS

I, ɪx, 1.   the character of society; in the stability of public order, in
freedom from disturbance at home and from foreign attack; in
the gradual and harmonious development of economic conditions; in the probity and reasonableness of people generally,
and especially business men and legislators; and—to lay special
stress on one important detail—in the solidity and good working
of that currency which acts as a medium of exchange and a
standard measure for gauging economic obligations and transactions of all kinds. The breadth, persistency, and fluidity
of modern markets enable the producer to make things on
the "speculative" chance of selling them, with a reasonable
confidence that he knows beforehand approximately the price
at which he will be able to sell them; whether they be finished
or half-finished commodities, or raw materials, or implements
that have no value except to people engaged in other industries
—people whom he has perhaps never seen, but with whom the
wide ramifications of business keep him in constant, if unconscious contact.

The modern producer throws all his energies into one
particular group of operations, trusting that the same market
organization, which secures for him in advance approximately
known prices for his sales, will enable him to buy at approximately known prices such things as he may want; whether they
be small supplies of personal necessaries and luxuries drawn
from distant regions of the earth, or relatively large supplies of
just those highly specialized kinds of raw material and implements which are used in his work.

The merchant, the broker, and the financier are those who
are most directly concerned with the machinery of modern
marketing, and with the stability of the social credit; just as
fire insurance companies are most directly concerned in provision against fire. But a general reduction in the risks of fire,
which would be an unmixed gain to the general public, would
bring loss as well as profit to the insurance companies: and
those who have profited most in the aggregate by the growing
efficiency and stability of social credit, and market organization
are the producing class rather than the trading class; and the
general public has gained most of all.

GROWING SELF-SUFFICIENCY OF GIANT BUSINESSES   **167**

2. *A preliminary review of changes, which sometimes*   I, IX, 2.
render a very large manufacturing or mining business in a
measure independent of other industries in its neighbour-
hood. A note on the meaning of the word "productive."

Economic progress has at last undermined some of the
foundations of Petty's great rule that "Each country flourisheth
in the manufacture of its own native commodities." But yet
most of them remain, though changed in form; and they are
now, as formerly, intermingled with, and sometimes confused
with, the advantages which an industry derives from a large
home market. In Petty's time, and very much later, people
worked of course much for themselves in their own houses on
whatever materials Nature supplied liberally to their hands:
and, when a specialized industry began to take the work over, it
found a large home demand ready to encourage its development.
Abundant raw material, and a large market for the finished
products, developed ever more highly specialized skill in the
main industry, and ever stronger subsidiary industries to supply
its incidental requirements, and to work up its waste products.
Each single business was on a small scale; and though it had
access to many of the economies of production on a large scale,
these were *external* to it, and common to the whole district.

For long ages industrial leadership depended mainly on the
number and extent of centres of specialized skill in which these
external economies abounded: a relatively small importance
attached to those *internal* economies which any single business
could attain by the elaboration of its own plant, and to the
subtle division of labour between its own employees. But with
the growth of capital, the development of machinery, and the
improvement of the means of communication, the importance
of internal economies has increased steadily and fast; while
some of the old external economies have declined in importance;
and many of those which have risen in their place are national,
or even cosmopolitan, rather than local.

Associated with this change there has been some shifting
in the relative importance of different orders of industrial
capacity relatively to one another and to capital. The supply
of skilled labour has increased: but, partly under American

I, ix, 2. influence, machinery has covered so large a range of work that a comparatively short training enables a youth, who is naturally alert, to control a manufacturing process that not long ago would have required the work of a great number of artisans.

Skilled labour is indeed better remunerated than ever before. But while the earlier stages of machine production tended to raise the wages of skilled labour even faster than those of unskilled; the later stages have tended to diminish, relatively at least, the volume of the demand for that sort of highly developed manual skill, which requires special training from boyhood upwards. There are a few industries in which a considerable supply of skill of this kind is as imperatively necessary as ever: and an attempt to start such an industry in a new home has great difficulties and risks. But the chief need of the large majority of modern industries is for alert intelligence, good judgment, promptness and trustworthiness in conduct on the part of the more responsible employees. Where this need has been met, resolute and capable men and women can generally be found who will quickly acquire adequate familiarity with the materials, the plant, and the operations of the industry. Such an industry can be started by a powerful firm; if it imports a considerable staff of leading men into a district, the population of which is energetic and has a fair share of alert intelligence. Modern facilities of communication by railway, and motor traffic; by post, telegraph and telephone facilitate this independence of local aid: and a powerful firm can sometimes set up a railway siding of its own.

Another disruptive influence, which helps a strong business in able hands to be independent of its surroundings, is the certainty with which business success attracts capital. It is often more difficult for a small business to borrow a thousand pounds than for one, which is ten times as large, to borrow fifty thousand: and there is practically no limit to the amount of capital that the public is ready to place at the command of a joint-stock company, which has already done great things, and is believed to be in strong hands. For indeed the stock of capital has grown so much faster even than the scope for its use in industry, that capital is always at the command of those who have I, ɪx, 2. both the mental faculty and the moral character needed for turning it to good account.

The keynote of this change was struck by the American Francis Walker, who said as early as 1876 that the man who has the faculties required "to shape and direct production, and to organize and control the industrial machinery...rises to be master of the situation. It is no longer true that a man becomes an employer because he is a capitalist. Men command capital because they have the qualifications to profitably employ labour. To these captains of industry...capital and labour resort for opportunity to perform their several functions[1]."

The drift of capital and labour to the control of the best business faculty within a country is gaining force, and is being accompanied by a similar drift from one country to another. The great business energy of Germany attracts to her industrial districts labour from countries in Europe equally well endowed by Nature. The great business energy of the United States has caused her population to increase very rapidly, even after her best natural resources have passed into private ownership, and the new comer might be able to obtain elsewhere better opportunities of becoming the owner of rich land with but little outlay. It is true that these countries have not recently borrowed very much external capital for public and private investment to match the increase of this population; but the reason is that indigenous capital has been growing very fast in Germany, and at a stupendous rate in the United States.

And again a new keynote is struck:—"A few managing Britons or Americans can now readily be obtained to establish manufactures in any part of the world, and educate nations to become satisfactory workers....The seat of manufacturing is now, and will continue to be more and more, simply a question where the requisite materials are found under suitable conditions. Capital and labour have lost the power they once had to attract raw materials; these now attract labour and capital[2]." This keynote may perhaps have been struck a little too sharply. But it is certainly true that manufactures on a large scale can

---

[1] *The Wages Question*, ch. xɪv.
[2] Carnegie, *Rectorial Address at St Andrew's*, 1902, pp 7, 8.

6—5

170   TRANSITION TO PRESENT INDUSTRIAL PROBLEMS

I, IX, 2. be created, wherever the resources of nature are favourable,
much more quickly than was possible before the recent developments of mechanical processes of production. It is no longer
necessary that several generations of workers should successively
be trained to a gradually higher pitch of specialized skill. And,
what is in many cases almost as important, a new industry
is not as dependent as formerly on the parallel development
of subsidiary industries in its neighbourhood, which may supply
its minor wants and turn its by-products to account. Machinery
and other implements can now be brought from almost any
distance in standardized shapes; and the other services, many
of which used to be rendered by subsidiary industries, can now
be performed in subsidiary workshops, erected for the purpose
by a single vast factory.

The great business, which is set up far from cognate industries, has to trust very much to its own resources not only on its
"productive" side, but also in regard to marketing; that is in regard to buying what it needs and selling what it produces. This
points to the facts, which will receive much attention later on,
that an increasing part of the activity of a manufacturing firm
is now given to marketing; and that indeed the line of division
between production and marketing is increasingly blurred.

According to popular usage agriculture, fishing, mining and
manufacture are productive, because they produce new goods
into the field of business: while transport and commerce merely
change the positions and the ownership of goods which are
already in that field. But man does not make coal, he merely
transports it from its bed to the surface; and thus makes it
potentially useful; its usefulness is nearly complete when
delivered by carrier and merchant into a private cellar; and is
quite complete when delivered by a domestic servant to the
fireplace. Thus the common distinction between "productive"
industries and others rests on no scientific basis. But it corresponds to a division, which plays a considerable part in economic
studies; the objections to coining a new term to take its place
are very great; and for the present at least we must be content
to use it[1].

[1] The student of science whose discoveries promote the advance of manu-

THE EVER-RISING PRESTIGE OF MANUFACTURE

3. *General causes which have given to the leaders of* *productive industry much of the prominence and responsibility, that formerly belonged almost exclusively to great merchants.*

The chief beginnings of bold capitalistic speculation were in the long distance trade, and especially in that between different countries. As has already been noted, it was relatively small in volume, being confined mainly to a few fine and costly manufactures; and to things, which could be obtained only by special favour of Nature in particular places: but, slight as it was, this trade was the chief training ground for those faculties which distinguish the master minds in business at the present day. In it alone was there large scope for economic initiative and far-reaching foresight; for the power of controlling great numbers of subordinates of all ranks, from the unskilled porter to the highly responsible officer who was often at once captain of a ship and chief administrator of a large moving storehouse of valuable goods. During long ages the land and the authority of Government were indeed the chief sources of great accumulations of wealth: but gradually even powerful rulers began to lean for financial support on the shoulders of those who had reaped the harvests of large mercantile business[1].

facture has as good a right in the abstract to be called productive, as the commanding officer has to be called a soldier, though he may not handle any weapon.

[1] Of course every great empire of early as well as of recent times has afforded a training ground for the faculties of organization and administration in regard to the affairs of Government in peace and war; and, in the hands of a man possessing business genius and aptitude, the work sometimes reached a high standard of technical excellence. But the proceedings were based on force rather than on free bargaining: arbitrary decisions governed incomings and outgoings alike; and those who amassed large fortunes from handling the public revenues, from selling privileges, and even from the ownership of large tracts of land, were not always endowed with high constructive faculty. The resemblance of the fortunes of Richelieu, Mazarin and Fouquet to those of predatory Roman Proconsuls has been made familiar by Dumas. The large share of the fortunes of eminent merchants, which was derived from the necessities of King and State on the Continent generally, is indicated by Ehrenberg, *Das Zeitalter der Fugger.* M. d'Avenel (in *Les riches depuis sept cent ans*; and the suggestive chapter "De quoi se composaient les anciennes fortunes," of his *Découvertes d'histoire sociale*) discusses the importance of ransoms as a source of wealth; and observes (p. 260) that a prisoner served as a sort of negotiable bill of exchange, according to his ransom, with which a debt might be paid.

172   TRANSITION TO PRESENT INDUSTRIAL PROBLEMS

I, IX, 3.   Merchants were the "Venturers" or "Adventurers" from
whom modern enterprise descended. They had a large part in
the coordination and the finance of localized manufacture, as
soon as it began to outgrow the capacity of the small master
working with two or three assistants. The clothiers and other
merchants, who let out wool to be spun and woven to their
orders on the Yorkshire streams at the end of the eighteenth
century, were men of a larger scope than the "manufacturers":
and Liverpool Merchants looked down upon the Manchester
cotton spinners, even after a hundred years of mechanical
inventions had raised the capitalist manufacturer up to the
level of leading merchants in regard to the magnitude of his
operations, and had entrusted to him a greater responsibility
than theirs as a leader of men. It may possibly be true that
no industrial leader of recent times has excelled Watt and
Stephenson in creative faculty, or Boulton in administrative:
for they were forced to rely mainly on their own strength;
whereas only a small percentage of those ideas, which are turned
to account in any existing business, were created in that business.
But yet the work of some great manufacturing and other productive businesses in the present age has demanded a combination of faculties almost as rare as those of Watt and Boulton;
together with other acquirements and resources which were not
in demand, and were not forthcoming, in the earlier age.

This development is the result of many causes: most of
which are connected with the magnitude and complexity of
modern industrial operations, and their intricate relations to
and dependence on one another. The stage has been passed
at which a great idea is almost self-sufficing: it has to be
elaborated in connection with others already in possession of
the same or neighbouring parts of the industrial field; and
its application is therefore not an act, but a long process,
needing patience and large resources of mind and perhaps of
capital. For instance, when a new mechanical idea has been
created, its translation into a smoothly-working business
machine generally involves a long series of experimental stages:
the constant increase in the size and complexity of the machine-
unit often causes such an experimental stage to need the
consideration of many more side issues than formerly; and

THE EVER-RISING PRESTIGE OF MANUFACTURE

perhaps to cost hundreds or thousands of pounds, where tens
or hundreds would have sufficed for the simpler and smaller
appliances of a few generations ago. There is therefore a large
class of improvements, of which prominent examples may be
found in the heavy steel industry and again in the manufacture
of monster printing presses or other machines, which are beyond
the range of anyone who does not unite the command of a great
business concern, with the possession of high faculty for appre-
ciating new inventions, if not for creating them. Again, most
of the so-called "chemical" industries, together with others in
some of those connected with metals, glass, oil, explosives and
other things, which are not commonly regarded as chemical,
offer exceptional opportunities for those great business men
in Germany and elsewhere, whose genius is partly scientific, and
who have founded laboratories within their own works. So
far as these considerations are concerned, the growth of large
industrial capitals tends to promote technical progress: the
inclination of the great manufacturer to take a direct interest
in engineering chemical and other studies works wholly for good
in raising the prestige of industry.

Again, a progressive business must sometimes rouse an
interest in its improved and new-fashioned products: and if they
are very expensive, as for instance electrical power plants are, the
marketing side of the business must be very strong and enterprising and courageous: he who can discharge these functions
adequately must include among his qualities and aptitudes those
of a great merchant.

Lastly the administrative head of a giant business must hold
together several thousands of employees of various grades in
an order which, while harmonious and disciplined, yet elicits
their individual and spontaneous enterprise: and for this he
must have some of the chief qualities that are required of the
commander of an army. He is not a "captain" of industry;
he is a "general" in control of several regiments.

Thus it appears that the term a "large business" has become
ambiguous. Not very long ago a business was almost always
concentrated in one place: it might have agencies and branch
offices elsewhere; but they were under the control of the central
bureau. Now, however, a single company frequently owns

174   TRANSITION TO PRESENT INDUSTRIAL PROBLEMS

I, IX, 4. several large establishments engaged in the same or allied
branches of a great industry; each of them being self-contained
as regards plant, material and executive, though all are under
the same supreme financial control. So far as technical efficiency
is concerned, each of these establishments is a separate business.
But the central control can bring the experience of each part to
bear in guiding the whole: and can defray the costs of large
experiments, the benefit of which will be available to the whole.
Again, each may have some advantage in being secure either of
a good market for its products, or of a good supply of its own
requirements in half-finished products, from some of its sister
establishments acting under orders from the directors of the one
financial business that includes them all. Further the technique
of each establishment may be indirectly strengthened by the
opportunity afforded to it of keeping expensive specialized
plant in nearly continuous activity on a relatively small range
of work; while other parts of orders, coming to the central
bureau, are told off to different establishments, which also work
intensively within a narrow range. In so far as this can be done
the technical efficiency of the business as a whole appears to
correspond rather to its aggregate capital than to that which is
invested in any one of its establishments.

In fact, however, the question is much more complex than
this. "No one is so wise as all the world"; and no single
business is as powerful as the whole industry to which it belongs.
A large open market effects an automatic distribution of tasks
to those establishments which are severally best fitted for them.
The domination of a few large businesses may impair the efficiency
of the open market; and the aggregate technical efficiency of the
country may be less than if each large establishment had been
less independent[1].

4. *Some observations on the assumption that social and
economic tendencies, which are general and seem natural, are
to be accepted as inevitable and beneficial.*

Increasingly throughout our coming study we shall be concerned to inquire how far industrial progress is dependent on

---

[1] The subjects of this Section are considered more fully in Book II; and
reference is made to some of them in the last chapter of the volume.

individual and how far on collective action: how far it depends I, IX, 4
on ceaseless initiative; and how far on broad ideas and knowledge, which when once acquired pass speedily into common
ownership; and become part of the collective wealth, in the first
instance of the countries to which the industries specially
affected belong, and ultimately of the whole world. We must
consider how the embodiment of a new knowledge or a new idea
in a new or improved industrial implement or method is likely
to require the control of a large capital. We must examine
the limitation which this condition imposes on the utilization
of the world's stores of creative faculty in the development of
the material sources of well-being. We must inquire how far the
gains, which accrue to a giant business as the apparent results
of its fine initiative and its prudent courage in taking financial
risks, are really its own; how far such gains are increasing the
dominance of large capitals; and lastly how far the tendencies
thus resulting are desirable, and how far they are inevitable.

Even thoughtful men are still often in some measure under
the dominion of the old notions that those changes, which are
general, are probably irresistible; and that to resist them is
flying in the face of nature. But subordination to natural
tendencies, when pushed to its extreme logical issue, is blind
fatalism. It is true that capitalistic aggregations, approximating
to the mechanical routine of a socialistic bureaucracy, have so
far been most prominent where economic progress has been most
rapid; but so also have the pallid faces caused by a scarcity of
fresh air and sunlight. Sources of individual or social decay are
sometimes most dangerous, when they are associated with great
achievements, and rich benefits.

Darwin's "law of the survival of the fittest" is often mis-
understood; Nature being supposed to secure, through competition, that those shall survive who are fittest to benefit the
world. But the law really is that those races are most likely
to survive, who are best fitted to thrive in their environment:
that is, to turn to their own account those opportunities which
the world offers to them. A race of wolves that has well organized
plans for hunting in packs is likely to survive and spread;
because those plans enable it to catch its prey, not because they
confer a benefit on the world.

176   TRANSITION TO PRESENT INDUSTRIAL PROBLEMS

I, IX, 4.   The common opinion is, however, not as wholly false in
substance as it is in form. For almost every increase in power,
which any race of men has acquired, can be traced to some social
qualities which have enabled that race to overcome the difficulties that lie in the way of obtaining the necessaries and comforts
of life; or to overcome its human enemies, or both. Success in
war may indeed be partly due to ferocity of character. But,
though it could perhaps not have been predicted *à priori*, the
social qualities, habits and institutions of a conquering race
have in the past generally been of a stronger fibre than those
of the conquered. The temper which enables wolves to maintain
the discipline of the pack, has in it something that is noble; and
the world has in fact gained a good deal from those qualities
which have enabled the dog, a domesticated wolf, to take a high
rank among living creatures. But man is not bound to follow
the slow steps by which the race of wolves has passed through
disciplined ferocity to higher things.

Again, by aid of "natural selection" certain insects, and
flowers from which they gather honey, mutually modify one
another, till the insects ensure themselves an abundance of
food by the untiring efficiency with which they fertilize the
flowers. And in like manner, while it is true that those institutions tend to survive which have the greatest faculty for
utilizing the environment in developing their own strength;
it is also true that, in so far as they in return benefit the environment, they strengthen the foundations of their own strength,
and thereby increase their chance of surviving and prospering.
On this account then we may admit that the mere existence of
broad tendencies towards the dominance of the joint-stock form
of administration and towards combinations of semi-monopo-
listic scope, affords some reason for thinking that these tendencies
make for the public good. But it is only a *primâ facie* reason,
and not a very strong one.

The earlier socialists, neglecting the teachings of history,
constructed ideal societies, which probably would have been unstable even in a world consisting solely of people, whose unselfish
love of humanity was as eager and unalloyed as their own.
Marx and his followers resolved to be practical, and argued that
history showed a steadily hastening growth of large businesses

GENERAL TENDENCIES ARE NOT ALWAYS BENEFICIAL 177

and of mechanical administration by vast joint-stock companies: I, ix, 4.
and they deduced the fatalistic conclusion that this tendency is
irresistible; and must fulfil its destiny by making the whole
State into one large joint-stock company, in which everyone
would be a shareholder. But no one would have much scope
for independent initiative, and a glib tongue would be likely to
give a man more prominence and influence than could often be
attained by originality and energy: while those, who just escaped
discipline as sluggards, might often have an unduly easy existence.

[12]
11

The Market for Information

11.1 INTRODUCTION

An important application of the theory of market-making costs is to the market for information. It can be shown that there is a strong incentive for an entrepreneur to internalize the exploitation of the commercial information upon which his superior judgment is based. It is the internalization of commercial information that leads the entrepreneur to acquire control of assets, and hence links the entrepreneur to the management of a firm. In analysing this, it will be assumed that the entrepreneur is certain of the accuracy of the information at his disposal.

There are five main ways in which an entrepreneur can exploit commercial information:

(1) He can license the information.

(2) He can enter into bets with those who do not have the information and whose judgment as a result differs from his own.

(3) He can buy up assets which, given his information, are currently undervalued, with a view to reselling later. Once the information becomes public, other transactors will revalue the assets and he will make a capital gain. This strategy relies upon other people coordinating the use of resources once the information becomes public. It also depends upon other entrepreneurs creating the market for the assets.

(4) He can initiate the coordination himself. He can intermediate any additional transactions which the information indicates are required. He can also acquire control of any multi-purpose goods which need to be reallocated to another use.

(5) He can act as coordinator, but as delegate rather than principal. He can offer his services as a delegate to someone who is liable to make the wrong decision – or whose existing delegate is inept – and rely upon the incentive system of his employer to reward a correct decision.

11.2 THE LICENSING OPTION

Consider an entrepreneur who believes that he has privileged information. He is absolutely convinced of its accuracy. He also believes that it is relevant to other people. If made available to them it will change their decisions and as a result improve their welfare. Under these conditions it seems perfectly reasonable to regard the item of information as a commodity which should command a positive price, and to market it as such. Given a perfect market in information, the entrepreneur should be able to sell his information for an amount equal to the capitalized value of its use.

However information is not just like any other good and its market, far from being perfect, is in many cases prohibitively costly to organize. Recall from Chapter 6 that to sell any good it is necessary to be able to exclude people from it. Because information is a public good with practically infinite capacity it is difficult to enforce custody of it. Partly because of this difficulty, the law regards most information as being in common ownership. With the exception of certain items of information which are patentable, and others which are covered by the right to personal privacy, exclusion from information is not legally enforceable. Thus the problems of *de facto* exclusion are compounded by the absence of legal sanctions. In these circumstances the right of exclusion can only be upheld by secrecy.

It is an unfortunate fact that the very act of marketing information is likely to undermine its secrecy. The reason is that, where information is concerned, it is difficult to separate the product itself from its specification. As a result the information is given away as soon as the specification is announced. Separation of specification and product can be achieved in a few cases: newspaper vendors have developed the art of separating the description of news from the news itself. 'Famous film star dies' or 'Shock election result' describes what the news is without describing precisely what it is about. Even in these cases, though, people who have read the description may be able to make a reasonable guess at what the news item is, and in other cases it may be possible to infer the information from the specification with reasonable certainty. It follows that a vendor of information always runs a risk of giving his product away through the very act of specifying it to buyers. This in itself would not matter if information were not a satiation good. In some markets, sellers regularly give away samples of their product to stimulate future demand. But because information is a satiation good fulfilling demand just once destroys all subsequent demand from the same source.

If the seller decides to enforce exclusion by keeping the specification secret, then he creates uncertainty in the mind of the buyer. As a result the buyer cannot appraise the value of the information properly. His demand price will reflect a strong subjective probability that the information is worthless to him – he may know it already or it may simply be irrelevant to his needs. This makes it likely that the buyer will be unable to offer anything like what the seller believes the information to be worth. If the seller fails to recognize the buyer's uncertainty problem, then he may hold out for too a high price, and negotiations may break down.

Given the asymmetry in the perception of the situation between buyer and seller, it would be mutually advantageous for the seller to insure the value of the information to the buyer. The buyer would pay the seller only if the information is novel and relevant to him. The buyer would be willing to pay more if the payment were contingent upon the novelty and relevance of the information being proven, and the seller, being confident of this, would regard this payment as being just as assured as an unconditional payment. Unfortunately this arrangement runs into the difficulties described in Section 10.3; for it is essentially a contingent contract, and one contingent upon factors – novelty and relevance – which are to some extent subjective. Unless the contract is very carefully specified, there will be ample opportunity for the buyer to default, by dishonestly claiming that he already had the information or that he could have done just as well without it. If in addition the information relates to a future state of the world, then the problem of default is magnified, for the contingent contract then becomes a forward contract too.

Information also poses severe problems of quality control. With most products a defect simply means that the buyer has wasted his payment. But with some products defects in quality can impose severe penalties on the buyer. Information typically comes into the latter category. This is because information is commonly used in decision-making and mistaken decisions can result in severe losses due to resource misallocation. Just as correct information leads to coordination, so the use of incorrect information may lead to dislocation.

It has already been noted that the use of guarantees to insure the buyer is not usually reliable when severe losses are possible. Neither can the buyer satisfy himself of the quality by supervising the researching of the information, for this would destroy the seller's secrecy, and so eliminate the basis for the market. The best that can probably be hoped for is that the seller can offer to provide the buyer with corroborative evidence before the information is used. Effectively this transforms the information from an experience good to an inspection good and so makes it easier for the buyer to control the risk that the information will actually prove a liability.

Finally, it is necessary to return to the problem of enforcing exclusion from a public good. It is apparent that if two or more people already have access to a public good then they are both in a weak position when selling access to a third party. If each can offer access then neither can ensure exclusion unless they collude. Competition between them will drive down the price of access to zero. So far as information is concerned, this means that it normally has to be sold with restrictions upon resale by the buyer. If the buyer attempts to resell the information in competition with the original seller, then together they will bid away any reward from a subsequent sale. Restrictions on resale are notoriously difficult to police, and so the risk of default by the buyer is considerable. Furthermore it is doubtful if such restrictions would be enforceable in law. Given the widespread view that information is in common ownership, restrictions on resale are liable to be regarded as illegal restraints of trade. Thus even if offenders could be detected, penalties could not be enforced in law.

11.3 THE BETTING OPTION

If an entrepreneur cannot sell his information to other people, then the obvious alternative is to exploit it himself. This is equivalent to internalizing the market for information. As exploiter of the information, he buys it from himself; as the possessor of the information, he sells it to himself.

In a world of perfect markets, betting would be the best way of exploiting information. The entrepreneur offers to bet with other people upon the event whose occurence is uncertain, or upon the state of the world − or the aspect of it − which is in doubt. The betting method was explained in detail in Chapter 5.

Betting can operate in cases where licensing cannot. It can generate a private reward even to information which is quite irrelevant to personal welfare. All that is necessary for betting to succeed is that the parties with whom the entrepreneur seeks to bet are not totally risk-averse. Since the entrepreneur is by assumption convinced of the accuracy of his information he perceives no risk, and is therefore restricted in his bets mainly by the risk-aversion of other parties. The other constraint is his wealth, which restricts the payments he can offer to make if he is wrong.

However, betting is not without its problems. One of them is that offering to bet with people may actually change their beliefs. This problem is particularly acute when betting upon events which are known to be irrelevant. If an event is irrelevant to the entrepreneur then his motive for betting cannot be insurance. It must be speculation. This signals to other people that the entrepreneur believes he has superior information. If he offers very large bets this suggests, furthermore, that he feels certain of his information. This in turn may persuade other people that he is probably right. The fact that the entrepreneur offers a bet may therefore change the mind of the people with whom he plans to bet. As a result, there may be nobody with whom he can bet on favourable terms.

Note that this problem is the reverse of the problem with licensing. Licensing rests upon the assumption that other people will believe the information when they are told it, and encounters problems because they may not. More precisely, licensing relies upon people believing the claims that are made for the information, and not challenging them once it has been supplied. Betting rests on the principle that people would not believe the information on which the entrepreneur acts even if they were told it. Indeed the nature of the bet virtually tells them what it is the entrepreneur believes. Problems arise when other people actually believe that the entrepreneur's information is correct!

This problem with betting is somewhat reduced if the information relates to a relevant event or to a future one. When the entrepreneur bets upon a relevant event, it is conceivable that his motive is insurance. It is therefore possible that he does not have privileged information, and so it is less likely that other people will change their beliefs. Almost by definition, the entrepreneur cannot know the outcome of a future event, however strong his beliefs about it. Consequently it is always possible that he is wrong. Furthermore, if the event lies in the future, it is more difficult for people to check out the entrepreneur's information for themselves, and so there is less likelihood of his privileged access to it being eliminated. However, betting on a future event involves a forward contract and so incurs a risk of default. This implies, amongst other things, that the entrepreneur must have a reputation for integrity if his bets on future events are to prove acceptable to others.

Finally, betting shares a problem with licensing in respect of the multiplicity of markets that are required. Information is a very heterogeneous good, and so each item of information, and each bet, incurs its own market-making costs. Even if contact-making, monitoring and enforcement costs can be shared between them, each item, and each bet, incurs its own specification and negotiation costs. The gains from exploiting some items of information may be sufficiently large to warrant the establishment of a special market, but generally this will not be so. On the whole, the market-making costs for information and bets are so high, and the possibilities of sharing them so limited, that it is uneconomic for specific items of information to be sold and specific bets to be placed.

11.4 PORTFOLIO SPECULATION

The problems of betting are largely overcome by portfolio speculation. Portfolio speculation, like licensing, applies only to the exploitation of information about relevant events. Also like licensing, it applies to information which will be believed once people gain access to it. The principle of portfolio speculation is that because the information is relevant, resources will be reallocated once the information becomes public. In a market system this reallocation will be guided by prices. The entrepreneur can back his judgment by making spot purchases of assets which he believes will appreciate once prices change.

An asset is of course just a forward claim, or a bundle of such claims. It might be argued, therefore, that the method is similar to betting. However there is one crucial difference, which is that portfolio speculation relies upon the revaluation of claims that already exist rather than upon the creation of purpose-made claims.

This has several advantages. First, there is the obvious advantage that no additional markets need to be created. The speculator enters markets that already exist for other purposes. The market-making costs incurred are marginal costs only: the fixed costs of market-making are avoided altogether.

Second, the information upon which the entrepreneur is acting is masked by the remaining volume of trade in the market. This will be governed by other, possibly quite different, motives. Even in a purely speculative market there may be many people present, each speculating upon some different item of information. This makes it very difficult for those with whom the entrepreneur is trading to ascertain upon which event he is speculating, and to modify their own beliefs accordingly. Thus the confidentiality of the information is maintained by trading in a market where price is determined by other factors besides beliefs about the particular event concerned.

Finally it is possible for the entrepreneur to trade in markets where forward claims are relatively secure. For example, it was noted earlier that durable goods may be regarded as an embodiment of forward claims on user services. Custody of a durable good – especially a private good – provides a very secure forward claim on a user service. If user services are liable to be revalued whe the information becomes public, then an entrepreneur can take a speculative position in the spot market for durable goods. By working out which user services will become scarcer, he can determine which durables are liable to appreciate. If he concentrates his portfolio upon these then he can anticipate a capital gain.

Of course, portfolio speculation has its disadvantages too. First it is necessary for the entrepreneur to think through the implications of the event concerned before he can speculate upon it. This means that he must have considerable background knowledge about the way the economy works. Unless he invests time and effort in analysing its implications, lack of background information – or simply faulty logic – may lead him to the wrong conclusion. Thus his information about the event may be right, but his speculative position wrong. Rather ironically, it is possible that in this situation two wrongs could make a right. If his information is misleading, and his interpretation of it incorrect then his speculation may turn out successful. Obviously though it is impossible to rely upon such coincidence when undertaking speculation.

The main problem with portfolio speculation is that it relies upon other people responding to the information when it becomes public. It is other people that actually reallocate resources: the entrepreneur just sits back and takes a capital gain. If publication of the information is delayed, then coordination will be postponed and the potential reward from the information will be reduced. If information were costless to transmit there would be no problem. The entrepreneur would transmit the information right away, as soon as he had formed his speculative portfolio. Everyone would interpret the information in the same way as the entrepreneur, and his conjectures would be completely validated. Resources would be reallocated immediately.

But in practice, information is costly to transmit, particularly if the message has to be forceful and clear. This is very important in the present instance because the entrepreneur is relying upon his conjectures about how other people will respond to the information to achieve his capital gain. If they misunderstand the message, or fail to recognize its implications then coordination will be delayed and some of the value of the information lost. If the cost of reliable publication is very high, then the only alternative is to rely upon the accidental rediscovery of the information by other people. For the entrepreneur this means uncertainty about exactly when, and by whom, implementation will be initiated. Under these circumstances portfolio speculation becomes a much less attractive option.

11.5 FORWARD INTEGRATION INTO COORDINATION

The problem of predicting other people's discovery of information, and their reaction to it, is avoided if the entrepreneur implements coordination himself. The entrepreneur still needs some background information to ensure that he does not miss any of the implications for coordination. But he does not need to make detailed predictions about other people's collective response to its announcement. Indeed, the boot is now very much on the other foot. Given his commitment to effect coordination himself, the entrepreneur desires protection against competition. He therefore wishes to inhibit the diffusion of information rather than to promote it.

The significance of the competitive threat depends upon whether there is a once-for-all opportunity for coordination, or a continuing one. Typically a once-for-all opportunity involves stock adjustment, while a continuing opportunity involves the adjustment of flows (see Chapter 8). A once-for-all opportunity is easy to pre-empt simply by being the first in the field. The fact that the entrepreneur has a temporary lead in the implementation of the information guarantees his success.

Where a continuing opportunity is concerned, the entrepreneur must reconcile himself to the fact that eventually his successful exploitation of it will attract the attention of others. Even if they would not normally have discovered the information for themselves, they can do so now simply by studying his method of operation. There are two main strategies available to the entrepreneur for preventing the erosion of his profit. One is to use his temporary lead to invest in creating barriers to entry. This has already been analysed in detail in Section 8.12. The other is to supplement coordination with portfolio speculation. The principle underlying this strategy is as follows.

The entry of competitors will cause selling prices to be bid down and buying prices to be bid up as the entrepreneur's monopoly is destroyed. The benefits will accrue not to the competitors but to those with whom they trade. If, for example, the entrepreneur is buying user services which are in less than perfectly elastic supply, then the price of these services will be bid up. As a result the durable goods which generate them will appreciate in value. If the entrepreneur owns the durable goods whose services he uses then, as an owner, he stands to gain from the entry of competitors. To exploit this opportunity fully, the entrepreneur will wish to own as many units of the durables as he can, and not just the units whose services he uses. In this way the entrepreneur can recover some of his losses by speculating upon the entry of his competitors.

Even if the entrepreneur does not anticipate competition, the ownership of inputs is a method of minimizing risk. It offers partial insurance not only against competition but against any other factor which could raise the price of inputs and reduce the gains from coordination. The principle applies most strongly to inputs which are in inelastic supply, since it is these inputs whose prices are most sensitive to disturbances.

It is apparent that forward integration into coordination is as much a complement to portfolio speculation as it is a substitute for it. Nevertheless forward integration is not without its problems, the chief of which is that it requires a diversity of skills to be exercised by the entrepreneur.

The two main forms of coordination are production – in which choice of technique has to be coordinated with the state of nature – and the creation of trade, in which the plans of one individual have to be coordinated with the plans of another. Successful production requires not only privileged information about the state of nature, but detailed knowledge of how to implement the appropriate technique. Successful trade-creation requires not only privileged information about transactors' willingness to trade, but also knowledge of market-making techniques. The entrepreneur must either have this know-how himself, or he must know where to hire it. But hiring know-how is difficult for the very reasons considered above. The same problems the entrepreneur encounters in selling his information to others will cause problems for an entrepreneur who wishes to buy information from others. If the entrepreneur cannot hire the know-how then he must supply it himself. It is this excessive demand upon the entrepreneur's knowledge and ability that constitutes the main disadvantage of forward integration.

11.6 FINANCING THE ENTREPRENEUR

The exploitation of information in the ways discussed above is liable to be constrained by the wealth of the entrepreneur. An exception may have to be made for licensing, but that option is usually excluded on other grounds. Betting is constrained by the entrepreneur's ability to pay up if he is proved wrong. Unless those who bet against him are irrational, they will not accept bets that could not be honoured. Portfolio speculation requires capital in order to buy up the appropriate assets. As noted above, forward integration into coordination is often an adjunct to portfolio speculation rather than an alternative to it. It also imposes its own capital requirements. Because of market-making costs, a producer may have to buy outright a producer durable whose services he would like to hire. For reasons explained in Chapter 12, to create trade efficiently, an entrepreneur may have to hold an inventory of the goods in which he trades, and an inventory of the means of payment to go with it. Furthermore there are often economies of integrating production and market-making, so that the entrepreneur is obliged to finance not only the purchase of producer durables but the creation of inventory as well.

It is tempting to suggest that if there were a perfect market in capital then the wealth constraint would disappear. The entrepreneur could borrow as much as he wished at the prevailing rate of interest. But this is false, and only illustrates the dangers of carrying over the logic of perfect competition into the realm of the entrepreneur. Entrepreneurship has its own logic, which is equally simple.

The entrepreneur who believes that he has relevant information believes that other people have got the allocation of resources wrong. If he cannot license the information, then he exploits it by backing his own judgment against theirs. This entire policy rests on the fact that other people think differently to him. He cannot expect people who think differently to lend him money to back his judgment against theirs, when if their judgment is proved correct he will be unable to repay the loan.

It might appear that to lend any money to an entrepreneur is a denial of the logic of the situation. But this is an overstatement. Certainly the lender perceives greater risks than does the entrepreneur. These risks would be reduced if the lender were better informed. To obtain a loan the entrepreneur must make his information available to the lender, together with any corroborative evidence that is available. The danger is that in doing so the entrepreneur builds up a competitor. Indeed it is worse than that, for it is likely that the potential lender has far more capital than does the entrepreneur. The entrepreneur needs the lender, but once the lender has the information he no longer needs the entrepreneur. He can cut out the entrepreneur and exploit the opportunity himself.

Wherever there is an obstacle to trade, people will seek to develop market-making institutions to overcome it. That is the moral of entrepreneurship. Loans are a form of intertemporal trade, and the information assymetry between borrower and lender is an obstacle to trade. The obstacle can be overcome if there is a market-making institution which has a reputation for integrity and confidentiality. The institution invites applications for loans and considers them in confidence using information supplied by the proposer (the entrepreneur). The institution voluntarily commits itself not to undertake on its own behalf projects of the kind for which loan applications are submitted. It also debars itself from approaching other people with proposals based upon those that have been submitted. It honours these commitments because it finds the loan business it can attract using its reputation for integrity is more valuable in the long-term than any gains it could make in the short-term by breaching this commitment. The type of institution which normally assumes this role is of course, the bank – in particular, the merchant bank.

This is in fact a special case of a more general phenomenon, namely the contribution that reputation makes to the creation of markets. An alternative to the bank's reputation for integrity is the entrepreneur's reputation for accuracy. If the entrepreneur has a record of successful judgment in similar projects, then the lender may be willing to accept that the entrepreneur is correct without knowing precisely what his information is. This preserves the entrepreneur's confidentiality while keeping down the lender's perception of risk. It provides privileged access to capital for the experienced and successful entrepreneur. But it does nothing to solve the strategic problems faced by the first-time entrepreneur.

Finally it is important to consider the case in which there are several like-minded individuals, each of whom has insufficient wealth to exploit the information properly. If the individuals can establish contact with one another, then they can pool their resources. Effectively they agree not to compete, but to collude, in backing their collective judgment against that of everyone else. The fact that each party has limited wealth affords security to the others that he will not drop out of the group and go it alone in competition with them. This concept of pooling entrepreneurial wealth is of course the basis of the joint-stock company. It is of particular importance when the implementation of coordination involves economies of scale.

11.7 REDUCING LENDER'S RISK

There are various ways in which a lender can reduce the risks involved in backing an entrepreneur. The first is to assess the entrepreneur's general knowledge and his basic business skills. If he is ignorant of even basic information then it is likely that his difference of judgment emanates not from knowing more than others but from knowing less. If he does not possess basic business skills, then whether or not his information is correct he is unlikely to translate it successfully into profit. Other relevant attributes of the entrepreneur include his ability to reason, to communicate and to cross-check information. It has even been claimed that qualities such as imagination and foresight can be assessed by studying behaviour in the simulated situations which appear in business games. If this claim were entirely correct, then many of the problems characteristic of entrepreneurship could be easily solved. In practice it is quite likely that entrepreneurs have more imagination than the people who devise the games. On the other hand, the potential reward to devising a successful method of screening for entrepreneurship is so great that continual improvement of technique is likely even if complete success cannot ever be attained.

Another method of controlling risk is to exploit the fact that the implementation of any activity always generates information as a by-product. Where the activity is designed to exploit privileged information, the information thrown up by the activity can be used to validate the initial claim. The sooner the information becomes available, the sooner errors can be detected and corrective action taken. So far as the lender is concerned, full and accurate reporting of the information is crucial in minimizing the risk of loss.

A lender is not automatically entitled to information of this kind. Even if he were to contract to receive such information, he would still need to check that there was no concealment, or deliberate distortion. Nor can the lender rely upon the entrepreneur agreeing to the correction of errors in the way that he would desire. To check that the entrepreneur is not concealing information, the lender needs to be able to monitor the implementation of the activity himself. He must have unrestricted access to the premises where the activity is carried on. As new information becomes available he must have the right to consult with the entrepreneur and, if things turn out badly, the right to overrule the entrepreneur in the interests of reducing the loss and protecting the repayment of his loan.

This suggests that the lender should participate in the project as one of its principals, with the entrepreneur assuming the role of delegate. Naturally the arrangement must provide for the entrepreneur to be rewarded if his judgment is correct. This can be achieved by the entrepreneur acting as joint principal with the lender and receiving a fixed reward for his work as delegate, or by the entrepreneur acting as delegate under an incentive system which pays delegates by their results.

Finally, it is possible for the lender to use the fact that collateral for his loan may be available in the form of durable goods and inventory owned by the entrepreneur. Given the additional risks perceived by the lender it is unlikely that his valuation of the collateral will be as high as the entrepreneur's. Nevertheless the lender can reduce his risk either by purchasing the assets himself and renting them on a long-term basis to the entrepreneur, or by acquiring a first charge on the assets so that should the project fail the lender can obtain custody of them. If the assets can be mortgaged to the lender then his potential loss is limited to the excess of the loan over a conservative, or pessimistic, valuation of the assets.

11.8 THE ENTREPRENEUR AS EMPLOYEE

The simplest way for the entrepreneur to act as delegate is to become an employee. The entrepreneur's principal provides him with the necessary finance. The entrepreneur continues to bear some of the risks because he is paid by results. But the risks that he cannot afford to bear are borne by somebody else.

Employment, however, is implicitly a long-term arrangement. Although an entrepreneur may become an employee in order to obtain financial backing for a project, can he continue as an entrepreneur and originate subsequent projects whilst remaining employed? This depends very much upon the nature of the post to which the entrepreneur is appointed.

Who would wish to hire an entrepreneur specifically to act in that capacity? The answer is another entrepreneur who believes that there is a gap in the market for entrepreneurship. An entrepreneur may believe that there is an entire field of economic activity in which there are many unexploited opportunities for coordination, and will continue to be so for some time. His judgment is that if only the right people were directed to these areas, then very large profits could be made. He does not have the depth of information required to recognize and exploit these opportunities himself. What he does have is information which, if made available to people with more specialized knowledge, would enable them to exploit them.

Given the problems of licensing information of this sort, it is probably easier to advertise for prospective entrepreneurs to come forward. The entrepreneurs are screened for ability in the manner indicated above and offered employment under an incentive system. The incentive system may be a formal one in which each employee is constituted as a separate 'profit centre' and receives a proportion of his profits as salary. Or it may be an informal system in which the employees' decisions are monitored and those who are most successful relative to the others are promoted, while those who are least successful are demoted or fired.

The delegate entrepreneurs are provided with information by their employer. They may also be expected to pool information among themselves. Typically each delegate is expected to put forward proposals for comments by the other delegates and, after suitable revision, for assessment by his employer. At each stage the proposal goes before a panel, or committee, in which the delegate advocates the implementation of his proposal. If he can persuade the others of its value then it proceeds to the next stage. If he cannot persuade them then his proposals will be vetoed. A proposal is implemented when it receives the final assent of the employer, or in the case of small proposals, the assent of those delegated to give approval.

The arrangement described above effectively makes a market in entrepreneurship itself. It is an entrepreneurial response to the problems of quality control in the market for entrepreneurs. In fact it has a dual role in improving quality and in checking it. It improves the quality of judgment by giving delegate entrepreneurs free access to the judgments and skills of other delegates as well as those of the employer. It checks quality both by assessing the delegate's personal qualities before he is hired, and by probing the proposals he puts up from the many different angles adopted by his fellow-entrepreneurs. The logic of linking the improvement of quality to the checking of it is quite simple. It exploits the fact that information gained from investigating one proposal may be useful in developing some other proposal. Thus having one entrepreneur screen another entrepreneur's proposals allows information to be 'captured' and put to further use.

Another way of explaining this is to say that the employer—entrepreneur internalizes the capital market. He performs a function similar to the banks, and other 'honest brokers' in the capital market, in allocating finds between alternative risky projects. But he lends to his own delegates rather than to independent borrowers. Because he can supervise and if necessary overrule his delegates, the risk of large losses is reduced. Furthermore, because his reward is directly related to the performance of the projects, he has a strong incentive to provide his delegates with information that will not only help to avoid losses, but will help to make large profits on their projects even larger.

The advantages of this system cannot really be questioned. The only question is how the employer–entrepreneur can get it to work. From whom does he get his own funds in the first place? How does he prevent his delegates from quitting once they have learnt their employer's secrets? How does he ensure that the different delegates co-operate with each other rather than compete?

The short answer is that the employer–entrepreneur can do these things only with difficulty. He must have an exceptional reputation in the capital market. He must be extremely good at organizing delegation. He can prevent delegates from learning too many of his secrets by compartmentalizing the system so that no delegate has access to all compartments at once. Thus at any one time each delegate may know a few secrets, but not sufficient to provide him with the overall perspective of the situation, which must remain unique to his employer. To retain his most able delegates, he must reward their judgment appropriately. This involves making a careful assessment of what they could expect to earn by exercising their judgment elsewhere. Finally he must devise incentives which, while rewarding individual success, also reward cooperative contributions to the success of other people's projects, and penalize success which is achieved at their expense.

11.9 THE SIGNIFICANCE OF THE FIRM

The contractual arrangements discussed above between entrepreneurs and lenders, and between one entrepreneur and another, are typically institutionalized in the firm. The firm is a legal fiction. The firm can own resources on its own behalf, and is in turn owned by other people (or by other firms). The capital structure of the firm, together with its contracts with employees, determine the allocation of risk. In principle the firm could issue many different kinds of contingent forward claims upon its output, and hold many different contingent forward claims upon its inputs. In practice, because of market-making costs, firms typically buy their inputs in spot markets and issue just two main kinds of forward claim. One is an unconditional claim, promising repayment of principal with interest, and the other is a residual claim on the profits of the firm. Within these two categories a number of variations occur. Some claims are transferable between lenders and some are not. Some claims are short-term, others long-term, and some perpetual. Some short-term claims may be renewable on demand, and some may not. Within the term of the loan, interest rates may be fixed or variable.

The most common forms of claim are: equity, which is a transferable perpetual residual claim; debenture, which a transferable long-term or perpetual fixed interest unconditional claim; a mortgage, which is a nontransferable long-term unconditional claim (normally at variable interest); and a bank loan, which is a nontransferable short-term unconditional claim, sometimes renewable on demand and normally at variable interest. Transferable claims are normally divided into shares so that each unit can be traded independently.

The existence of different types of claim enables lenders to specialize in insuring different types of risk. Holders of unconditional claims are exposed mainly to a risk of default, while holders of residual claims are exposed to the risk that profit will be less than the amount anticipated. By and large a more limited range of factors influence default than influence profitability, so that less judgment is involved in the valuation of unconditional claims than in the valuation of residual claims. Those who are best at assessing the factors which influence default will specialize in holding unconditional claims, while those who have the wider knowledge required to assess the factors which influence profit will specialize in holding residual claims. Similarly lenders who believe themselves to be farsighted will specialize in holding long-term nontransferable claims while those who are relatively near-sighted will specialize in holding short-term or transferable claims.

The risks associated with unconditional debt are obviously lower than the risks associated with residual debt. The division of capital between high-risk and low-risk claims facilitates unilateral insurance. It enables the least risk-averse to specialize their portfolios in residual claims and so provide insurance to the most risk-averse, who specialize their portfolios in unconditional claims. It should be emphasized, however, that the insurance is not complete. There is no guarantee that the holders of residual claims have sufficient personal wealth to guarantee the repayment of unconditional claims. Moreover, company law offers the privilege of limited liability to those who desire it, which means that in any case the residual claimants' personal wealth may be unavailable as security to the unconditional claimants.

The holders of risk capital also provide a measure of unilateral insurance to the employees. In particular, where an employee has discretion, the owners of capital will bear some of the loss incurred if the employee makes the wrong decision. The employee will bear some of the loss too, as he will be penalized by the incentive system. It does not follow, though, that the employee is necessarily seeking insurance. He may be risking as much through the incentive system as he could afford to risk if he were self-employed. He chooses to be an employee only because the incentive system offers a bigger potential reward for the same degree of risk. Because risk is subjective, the owners of capital believe they are providing insurance, while the employee simply believes that he is circumventing a failure in the capital market.

The existence of different types of firm whose risks are influenced by different factors facilitates both mutual insurance and portfolio speculation. In the absence of markets in specific contingent claims, individual investors can substitute into markets for corporate debt. An individual insuring against, or speculating upon, a particular event can work out which types of corporate debt are most likely to appreciate relative to the others when the event occurs, and concentrate his portfolio upon them in the expectation of a capital gain.

Small scale insurance and speculation is promoted by the availability of transferable shares in small denominations. It has already been established that share ownership allows like-minded entrepreneurs to cooperate in finding large scale projects. As originally formulated, the argument does not depend upon the shares beings transferable. But transferability and small denominations allow the principle to be applied more widely.

NOTES

This chapter has brought together a number of different strands of the preceding analysis to show that the entrepreneur who has gained privileged access to information must normally internalize its exploitation. For example the entrepreneur may integrate forward into market-making, or into production. He may become the owner of a firm, or one of its employees. The internalization of the market for information explains why entrepreneurship is rarely observed in a completely pure form; it is usually integrated with other functions as well. If external trade in information were common then the instutional structure of the economy would be quite different from what it is in practice. It is difficult to visualize an economy of this kind because the advantages of internalizing information are so overwhelming that almost every facet of economic organization takes this internalization for granted.

The problems associated with external markets in information, and with the organization of the contingent contracts that would be required, are considered by Arrow (1975) and Radner (1968).

7 Knowledge, Learning and Enterprise

BRIAN LOASBY

Although there is no intention, here or elsewhere in this volume, to develop an extended critique of conventional microeconomic analysis, it is appropriate to begin by indicating the problems which seem to provide the opportunity for a new approach. These problems are associated with the concepts of equilibrium and production.

EQUILIBRIUM AND KNOWLEDGE

The equilibrium of an economy is normally defined in terms of a set of prices and quantities (or, in growth models, rates of change in these variables) which, in the absence of any outside disturbance, would persist indefinitely. G. B. Richardson (1960) has drawn attention to the dependence of such equilibria on assumptions about the knowledge and expectations of economic agents, and emphasised the inadequacy of perfect competition as a plausible justification for the kind of assumptions which are needed. More recently, Professor Hahn (1973) has proposed a definition of equilibrium in terms, not of prices and quantities, but of *theory* and *policy*. An agent's *theory* is a procedure for deriving predictions (which may take the form of a probability distribution) from information; his *policy* is a procedure for deriving decisions from predictions. An appropriate example would be the use of a specific econometric model to forecast demand each month, together with a production-scheduling technique which generates output plans from the forecasts thus produced. A less formal example is a theory which predicts that it is safe to cross the road at a controlled crossing when a green light is showing to pedestrians, and a policy to cross only under such conditions.

Knowledge, Learning and Enterprise   105

Rational decisions appear to require both theory and policy. Indeed, it is difficult to see how policy can exist without theory, though the converse is often true: cosmological theories, for example, are not usually associated with decisions. Professor Hahn offers the following definition (1973, p. 25): 'an economy is in equilibrium when it generates messages which do not cause agents to change the theories which they hold or the policies which they pursue'. But although he introduces notions of knowledge and decision into his definitions, Professor Hahn follows conventional practice by confining his attention to the conditions which will sustain equilibrium; he explicitly renounces any attempt to cope with learning. Thus his further analysis is of no direct help to us here; his concepts, however, will serve as a reference point for our discussion. What should be noted immediately is that equilibrium, so defined, does not necessarily depend on the truth of a theory: someone who (in this country) will never have honey in the house because honey attracts bears is unlikely to receive any messages from his environment which will cause him to change either his theory or his policy.

Professor Hahn's definition of equilibrium is an unconscious paraphrase of that advanced over forty years ago by Professor Hayek (1937, p. 41). Professor Hayek, however, was addressing himself precisely to the problem of the acquisition and use of knowledge in an economy. Interest in processes of adjustment through a sequence of human decisions which improve knowledge is characteristic of the Austrian School of economists, and has been effectively developed by Professor Kirzner in his *Competition and Entrepreneurship* (1973). A market in which prices and quantities are out of equilibrium offers profit opportunities to entrepreneurs; they formulate plans to buy and sell particular quantities at particular prices on the basis of their expectations. These plans are then tested in the market, and the results may confirm plans and expectations or cause them to be modified.

The economy thus, it is claimed, moves towards an equilibrium of both plans and prices, through a market process that seems to parallel the sequence of conjecture and exposure to refutation which is at the heart of Sir Karl Popper's (1972) theory of scientific progress. Now Sir Karl has written extensively about the difficulties involved in deciding whether a conjecture has been effectively refuted, and what should be done if it is. Professor Kirzner, however, discusses no such difficulties. Knowledge, in his original model, lies waiting to be discovered; an entrepreneur simply recognises a change in preferences or technology which has already happened. (In a recent (1981) paper, Professor Kirzner has allowed uncertainty into his analysis; but he does not consider this problem.) As he defines it, Professor Kirzner's model is therefore of limited applicability; this can be seen by contemplating some of the implications of production.

PRODUCTION AND ORGANISATION

Austrians and conventional microequilibrium theorists both start with the analysis of exchange. Production is then introduced as a special case of exchange – the exchange of inputs for outputs – by adding technology to preferences and resource endowments, either (for conventional theorists) as the basic data from which an equilibrium configuration of prices and quantities is to be derived, or (for Professor Kirzner) as the set of knowledge which is open to entrepreneurial perception. In a formal sense, production functions are closely anaiogous to preference functions, converting inputs into outputs just as the latter convert commodities into utilities.

But this simple theoretical extension entails a formidable increase in the knowledge attributed to economic agents. Not only is the requirement that technologies be available, and known to be available, a good deal more demanding than the requirement that consumers should know their own preferences; these preferences must now cover not just those commodities which currently exist but those which might be brought into existence. Although many potential objects of exchange may have no place in the equilibrium solution, yet they exist independently of that solution; but commodities which result only from production have to be included in the equilibrium production set in order to come into existence at all. Even Professor Kirzner's entrepreneurs will need to be extremely alert in order to perceive production technologies and consumer preferences for goods which can be brought into existence only by their own decisions.

The opportunity may arise only from a combination of perceptions. Consider, for example, the opportunity created by juxtaposing the realisation that fluorine compounds might well prove effective anaesthetics and the recognition that all existing inhalant anaesthetics had significant disadvantages. These two perceptions occurred in different divisions of ICI; but it was some time before they were combined to stimulate the search which led to the introduction of a superior and profitable new anaesthetic. They also occurred, separately, to a number of people outside the company, but these perceptions were never combined into a productive opportunity (Bradbury *et al.*, 1972). Nor is such a search bound to succeed, even in inventing a product with the desired properties; a profitable outcome will require active management, and in many instances, numerous further instances of creative imagination. To confine entrepreneurship, as Professor Kirzner does, to the exploitation of ready-made opportunities, and thereby to exclude the problems of management in complex organisations, is to impose severe potential restrictions on the applicability of his theory.

Since the time of Adam Smith, production has been associated in economic theory with the division of labour; and the division of labour produces most of its benefits through differentiation, which enhances specific skills but narrows the range of competence. Thus individual firms cannot have effective access to the known set of technologies within the economy, but are favourably placed to initiate, or to adopt, improvements within certain specific technologies. Nor can they possibly be well informed about all actual or potential products but they may be quick to perceive, or to create, opportunities in particular markets. A firm, like an individual, possesses specialised knowledge, and pays for it by limitations on its flexibility.

Similar conclusions follow from the analysis, pioneered by Professor Coase (1937), of the firm as an alternative to the market, avoiding some of the information- and transaction-costs of using the market by substituting administrative arrangements for the internal allocation of resources. Within the firm, the advantages of division of labour are sought through organisational design. The specialisation of function thus prescribed may also be thought of as a means of accommodating the constraints of bounded rationality, which have provided a foundation for Professor Simon's (1976) analysis of organisational behaviour. But these constraints will affect behaviour as well as structure. Members of an organisation will thus give selective attention to phenomena, both internal and external, and will learn from their own particular patterns of experience. Their theories and their plans will be influenced by their own situation and their own history.

INTERPRETATIVE FRAMEWORKS AND THE METHODS OF SCIENCE

Whether, or in what condition, such theories and plans might be roughly consistent, is, in the broadest sense, the question underlying the analysis of general equilibrium theorists and of the Austrians. However, neither come very close to the issues which have been raised in the last few pages. The Austrians, it is suggested, are right to think in terms of processes, but avoid many of the difficulties by considering only how individuals interact through the market, and by assuming, in effect, that such individuals acquire knowledge by perceiving the truth. The purpose of this paper is to explain, and to begin to apply, a method of analysing human understanding and human action — the theories that people hold and the policies that they pursue — which, although unfamiliar to most economists, seems particularly appropriate to the problems of knowledge, learning and enterprise. The method was proposed by an American psychologist, George Kelly, and this is now well known in the analysis of personality (to which it was originally directed) and in studies of consumer behaviour. Those familiar with the work of Lakatos (1970) will recognise many similar ideas, expressed in a different language; but there is no space here to consider the attractive notion of a firm's 'research programme'.

Kelly's fundamental proposal is to analyse human beings as scientists: that is, as people whose *'ultimate aim is to predict and control'* (1963, p. 5). This, we may note, is the obverse of Sir Karl Popper's conception of scientific method as a carefully designed version of human trial and error: people learn (imperfectly and inefficiently) from their mistakes; science attempts to discover mistakes quickly and efficiently. A detailed comparison between the two views might be very rewarding; but in this paper we shall attempt no more than a few passing observations.

The selection of data, and its interpretation in the light of both theory and experience — the latter either natural or contrived — are central issues for anyone seeking to predict and control, whether as professional scientists or as human being. Why this is so emerges from the confrontation between the limits of human rationality and the interconnectedness of all phenomena, as Kelly explains. 'The universe that we presume exists . . . is integral. By that we mean it functions as a single unit with all its imaginable parts having an exact relationship to each other' (1963, p. 6). That, of course, is a general equilibrium concept, with the scope of the equilibrium far wider than has been essayed by any economist. Kelly can afford such a wide conception because he is not concerned to offer any general equilibrium solution. In fact, he argues that since anything like a total comprehension of this interdependent system is far beyond our powers, every discipline must necessarily take a partial view, and, recognising that the view is partial,

Knowledge, Learning and Enterprise 109

should be wary of making claims outside the realm thus (roughly) defined.

> Man looks at his world through transparent patterns or templets which he creates and then attempts to fit over the realities of which the world is composed. The fit is not always very good . . . Even a poor fit is more helpful to him than nothing at all. (1963, pp. 8–9)

Notice that these patterns, or theories, are created; they are neither perceived, nor derived in any simple way from the phenomena to which they are subsequently applied. Such a concept of theory-creation, and a similar explanation in terms of the desire to impose order on the unimaginable complexity of phenomena, is developed in Adam Smith's remarkable, though little known, early 'History of Astronomy' (1979), and is the key to Professor Shackle's account of the development of economic thought in *The Years of High Theory* (1967); Professor Skinner of Glasgow has examined Smith's ideas and their modern counterparts in a recent article (1979). Sir Karl Popper's rejection of induction as logically impossible has led him to emphasise the importance of imaginative conjecture in providing theories worth testing: however, he is primarily − though far from exclusively − concerned with the ways in which such conjectures may be exposed to possible refutation, whereas Smith, Shackle and Kelly all emphasise the defensive use of theories to accommodate experience. Sir Karl has persistently attacked such defensive uses as an impediment to the progress of knowledge; but they do appear to give a kind of security, even though it may be false. Moreover, as Kelly argues, it is necessary to close off some avenues of enquiry, if necessary by a theoretical fudge, in order to improve our understanding at all.

> We limit the *realm* and try to ignore, for the time being, the intransigent facts just outside the borders of that *realm* . . . For the time being we shall have to content ourselves with a series of miniature systems, each with its own realm or limited range of convenience . . . (1963, p. 10).

That such a strategy should gain even modest success requires that almost all interdependencies are of no significance almost all the time. In Professor Simon's (1969) phraseology, the universe is decomposable into a hierarchy of systems which for the most part interact only weakly. Kelly assumes this to be true within the human time-scale; Professor

Simon argues that complex systems are unlikely to evolve or to survive, unless they are nearly decomposable. But near decomposability is not identical with complete decomposability; and if the latter is assumed, as it has to be in order to construct miniature systems, then the theory embodied in these systems must be, to some extent, false. Two consequences should be noted. Not only are these systems unreliable beyond a limited range of application; they are liable to unsuspected collapse wherever the assumption of decomposability is falsified. Past performance is no guarantee of future success, either for a theory or for a firm which uses it. This inevitable fallibility is a good reason for possessing alternative structures of interpretation, even if they appear less immediately useful.

Kelly's analysis is intended to apply both to the discipline of psychology and to the behaviour of people trying to make sense of their situation. Since psychologists are, one presumes, people trying to make sense of the world, it should indeed apply to both — and to economists and managers also. But, as has been observed, any usable pattern must be incomplete and distorted — at least at the boundaries, where it necessarily denies connections which we believe to exist, and to matter; and it therefore follows that whatever pattern we happen to be using has no claim to exclusivity. 'The same event may be construed simultaneously and profitably within various disciplinary systems' (1963, p. 10). Alternative constructions may be profitable, not because they lead to similar conclusions, but because they do not. 'It is not a matter of indifference which of a set of alternative constructions one chooses to impose upon his world' (1963, p. 15) . . . 'often the facts assume their particular shapes only in the light of a certain theory' (1963, p. 26).

Like Kelly, I wish to use this argument at two levels. The underlying justification for this paper is the belief that by looking at firms in a different way from those employed either in the prevalent kinds of equilibrium theory or in Austrian theories, we can discover different interpretations which offer something additional to anything that the prevalent interpretations can provide. These prevalent interpretations, as was true of psychology when Kelly wrote, are based on theories of situational determinism and an experimental method of external observation. Economists and psychologists alike had reacted against introspection, and denied the relevance of personal testimony. Behaviour was all that mattered; knowledge and motivation, if used at all, appeared as conscious fictions. But the preference for behaviourism is a subjective preference, and even if it were — as it may be — the

Knowledge, Learning and Enterprise   111

best single principle of selection, it must, like any other principle, have a limited range of convenience. An approach which leaves room for human initiative, human experimentation and human interpretation, as do several modern theories of scientific development, seems worth exploring.

That is the argument for using alternative methods of analysis. But the view of firms as organisations being explored here uses this argument for alternative frameworks as its core. Managers, like scientists, or any other person who wishes to predict and control, must impose some pattern on events. No single pattern can claim any exclusive rights, yet different patterns may lead to different interpretations, and possibly to different decisions. It is part of the 'perfect knowledge' assumption which is never more than slightly attenuated in standard theories that all firms would have the same perception of any given situation; by abandoning that assumption one can gain some understanding of the behaviour of firms.

EVENTS AND FRAMEWORKS

The focus of Kelly's analysis is the interaction between events and the frameworks which are used to interpret them. These events are of two kinds. First, there are those which impinge on a passive observer. 'The universe is continually changing with respect to itself. Within our universe something is always going on. In fact, that is the way the universe exists; it exists by happening' (Kelly, 1963, p. 7). Thus the passage of time generates a stream of events to be interpreted by the use of whatever patterns people use. 'Experience is made up of the successive construing of events. It is not constituted merely by the events themselves' (p. 73). It is the recipient of the data who converts it into information; and this conversion may involve the use of existing theory to make fresh predictions, or a revision of theory to accommodate recalcitrant data. Since the events which are observed depend upon the time period, and a variety of patterns may be used, the lessons of experience are not common to all, even within a single industry. Different events (at different times, or in different places) and different interpretations are each capable of producing different conclusions about both theory and policy. It is of course possible that a variety of events and a variety of patterns should all lead to similar conclusions. Indeed, if this never happened, human behaviour would no doubt be much less coherent than it is. But there are no logical reasons for assuming that this will be generally true, and some fairly persuasive evidence that it is not. Our data rarely meets the requirements of sampling theory, and our interpretative frameworks are incomplete.

The passage of time gives us a chance to check the serviceability of the patterns which we use by testing them against subsequent events, either by the rigorous method of making explicit predictions before-hand, or by the more dangerous − but still quite often effective − method of seeing whether the new events can be accommodated within the currently-accepted framework. By either route, there is a presumption that the serviceability of a person's constructs will tend to improve over time, provided that the nature of the phenomena being observed is changing more slowly than he is able or willing to revise his interpretative framework − in particular that neglected interdependencies do not become significant − and furthermore that he does not seek to apply his interpretations to phenomena of a different kind. Both qualifications will be taken up later.

The second class of events are, at least in part, internal to the analysis. People do not simply observe and interpret; they also act. Agents have policies as well as theories. What happens in the universe is partly the result of human action, based on interpretations, and providing material for fresh interpretations − not only by the originating actors. The outcome of one set of entrepreneurial decisions provides opportunities for other entrepreneurs. Thus interpretations and decisions produce an interactive (but not closed) system which evolves over time. Whether this system moves towards some sort of equilibrium is an open question. That it should reach a static equilibrium is incompatible with the conception of the universe employed here. This is not to deny that static equilibrium concepts may sometimes offer a useful scheme of interpretation, provided one remembers that, like any other scheme, it is incomplete.

ORGANISATION AND INTERPRETATION

Let us now begin to apply these ideas to the firm as an organisation. A firm is composed of a group of people who all, in varying ways and to varying extents, interpret what they observe and take decisions according to their interpretation. We will follow convention by concentrating on those people who are usually called managers, though we should not forget that much of what follows applies also to those usually called workers.

Knowledge, Learning and Enterprise 113

If a new firm is created, and staffed by people who are unfamiliar with the line of business which the firm has chosen to enter, its managers are likely to be ill-equipped with constructs which will help them to understand what is happening and to take good decisions; but, provided that the firm does not collapse as a result of their inexperience, they will learn from events and their own mistakes, and will eventually acquire a set of frameworks which proves serviceable for that line of business. Indeed, the danger of collapse before the minimum amount of learning has been achieved is so generally recognised that it is unusual to staff a new organisation with people who have no knowledge of the business area; even those with such experience will probably need to modify their constructs to accommodate the somewhat different circumstances of the new firm.

It is even more certain that before things can run fairly smoothly, there will be a need for the alignment of the constructs used by different members of the firm. Even within a particular kind of business, different constructs may be employed, and people moving between organisations — be they two universities, two government departments, two consultancy firms or two manufacturing firms — will usually find some differences in the way things are done, and will have to spend time learning how the system into which they have entered works. Thus, even if there were no need to learn about the technology or the market, there would still be the need to learn about the working style of other members of the organisation.

While the learning process continues it consumes managerial resources; indeed, in the early stages it may consume a great many, and long hours and frequent meetings may be the price even of survival; but as people gradually learn to develop and to use interpretative frameworks which not only seem to offer a satisfactory fit to the data but are reasonably compatible with the systems used by other people within the organisation, so the effort required diminishes. Resources are thus released, and may be used to increase the throughput of the organisation, if necessary by bringing in additional people, who will also need to learn and to be assimilated, at some cost both to old and new members of the organisation.

In this process of learning, organisational design plays an important part, in two major ways. First, it determines the flow of events which will come to the attention of each manager, and thus the material which his developing constructs will have to fit. This sets limits to the interpretative possibilities, but, by the arguments advanced earlier, does not fix them. Second, by defining the extent, and the limits, of responsibility, it prescribes what the constructs must accomplish, and what they need not — the kinds of policy models which the theories are required to serve. As Kelly observes (1963, pp. 9–10), 'when one limits the realm of facts, it is possible to develop a detailed system without worrying about the inconsistencies in the system which certain peripheral facts would reveal'. What inconsistencies would matter depends on how the periphery is defined; constructs which would suit a functional manager may be quite inadequate for a product manager. The policy requirements, and thus the theoretical requirements, are very different. Indeed, the redrawing of organisational boundaries is usually intended to invalidate old constructs which were thought to be leading to decisions that are now judged to be undesirable when assessed from some higher viewpoint. Restructuring is intended to improve policy through the use of more appropriate theories.

A successful organisational design is one that generates a stream of events for each manager which enables him to develop quickly an effective set of constructs. Effectiveness is here assessed by the decisions which result from the use of these constructs: they must be consistent both with the world outside, and with those decisions taken by other members of the organisation. Consistency between decisions does not necessarily require similar constructs. For good organisational design not only brings some kinds of people together; it also keeps other kinds of people apart. Partial insulation may allow the development of simpler constructs within each field of interest, making management more effective within those limits. The art of organisational design requires the creation of such insulating barriers where they will facilitate good and low-cost local decision-making, while maintaining a sufficient commonality of framework to ensure (if assurance is indeed possible) that the outcomes of local decisions are not disastrous — for example, that products designed to replace the existing range are not totally outside the manufacturing competence of the existing equipment and workforce.

The speed of learning depends on what it is desired to learn. As Burns and Stalker (1961) taught us twenty years ago, in a very stable environment a mechanistic system of management, in which functions are narrowly defined, is very effective in developing the skills for dealing with that environment. Simple interpretative frameworks with very narrow ranges of convenience may be perfectly adequate. But its effectiveness depends on that environment remaining stable; and the great danger is of a failure to recognise how limited is the range of convenience of the simplified frameworks to which everyone has become accustomed. The structure reflects an assumption that neither theory nor policy will require more than minor amendment; no innovations are called for. Professor Hahn's self-imposed restriction of theory to the examination of equilibrium conditions may likewise lead to a specification which is quite incapable of adjusting to unforeseen events. At the other extreme, an organic system, providing for interaction anywhere within the organisation, slows down learning by providing only small samples of each kind of phenomenon and requires the development of many different patterns to fit different situations (or, improbably, some elaborate pattern which fits them all). The release of managerial resources from such a system is not likely to be rapid; on the other hand, those resources which are released are likely to have a far wider range of use than the resources released by a mechanistic system – not least because managers are likely to realise that new circumstances may require the creation of new schemes of interpretation.

GROWTH AND ADJUSTMENT

This apparent trade-off between the rate at which spare managerial resources are generated and their applicability suggests that the most rapid growth of firms may occur by simple expansion within an existing field, with additional output being supplied to existing customers, or to new customers with similar characteristics. Of course, if the total market is not expanding, or expanding only slowly, such growth must be at the expense of other firms, which might be expected to have similar potential for growth (though we should be careful not to assume that all will have similar ambitions). Thus one might expect to find fairly bitter battles in such circumstances, with little scope for avoiding direct confrontation by way of diversification. Control over customers or sources of supply might suggest itself as a competitive tactic.

There will also clearly be differences between firms with different patterns of experience (and experience, remember, depends both on events and their interpretation) in the rate at which resources are released and in their applicability. Even within the same industry, different firms may develop different capabilities; between industries there are liable to be wide differences. Nor is the release of resources an irreversible process. A drastic change in the environment of a firm (for example, through the development of new technology or a new source

116   *Beyond Positive Economics?*

of competition) may impose a need for relearning how to conduct its own business — a need which has proved beyond the powers of some organisations which were only too well adapted to their familiar circumstances. Too strong an assumption of convergence towards a state approximating to equilibrium is dangerous both for the theorist and for the manager.

Adjustment to new circumstances is not often easy. For what is required is often more than the revision of some local constructs in response to environmental change. Local constructs must be mutually compatible, at least to the extent that they impinge upon each other; and revisions in response to external events may disrupt that compatibility. The difficulty of adjustment may well be aggravated by the need to revise also the inter-relations between local constructs, so that some need to be more closely interlocked than before. As Kelly remarks (1963, p. 9), 'in seeking improvement [a person] is repeatedly halted by the damage to the system that apparently will result from the alteration of a subordinate construct'. We can all see how difficult it is for well-trained economists to give up a particular theoretical approach; but the difficulty is not peculiar to our discipline. Such a threat to a person's thought-system helps to explain why some people continue to make the same mistakes; any adequate response seems to them to require an adjustment of their ways of thinking which threatens their way of life — even, in the last resort, their personality. Kelly's professional interest in developing his theory was in fact to provide a better interpretative framework for the analysis of personality disorders.

Of course, this problem of maintaining one's personality applies directly to managers as to anyone else (to practitioners of an academic discipline, for example). But there is in addition the requirement to maintain some kind of working system for the organisation; and it may seem impossible to maintain that system if those adjustments are made which would permit more effective handling of particular problems. Thus learning, at a personal or an organisation level, may be impossible. For example, both management and union representatives in some firms may simply be incapable of changing their approach to industrial relations, despite the repeated failure of their current methods, because a more effective method would require so radical a change in their conceptions of the 'opposition' as to threaten their whole interpretation of the economic and social system. Chandler (1962) has explained how Du Pont's attempts to come to terms with the needs of a diversified business were agonisingly protracted by the company's devotion to the accepted practices of good management; and Burns and Stalker (1961) have shown how a deep-rooted belief in certain fundamental notions of orderliness frustrated the attempts of some Scottish firms to break into a new and technically-progressive industry. The history of British Rail, of British Leyland and its predecessors, the fate of AEI and BSA, are just a few instances of the appalling difficulty experienced by people and by organisations in abandoning well-confirmed theories and policies which have been carried by events far beyond the limits of their applicability. Some principles an organisation must have, if it is to remain an organisation; some principles of behaviour a person must cling to, whatever the evidence, if he is to remain a person. Some changes are simply not possible, even if the alternative is death.

GROWTH AND THE THEORY OF THE FIRM

The kind of analysis which has just been outlined may be used to add some detail to Penrose's (1959) treatment of the growth of firms. Penrose, like Coase (though she does not refer to him), regards the firm as an administrative framework which serves as an alternative to the market for the purposes of resource allocation: it is 'an autonomous administrative planning unit, the activities of which are interrelated and are coordinated by policies which are framed in the light of their effect on the enterprise as a whole' (Penrose, 1959, pp. 15–16). A feasible plan for the firm requires compatibility – not, we may repeat, identity – of interpretative frameworks between the component elements of the organisation.

These plans are derived jointly from its expectations – 'the way in which it interprets its environment' (p. 41) – and from its appraisal of its own internal resources. Its expectations, in the language of Professor Hahn, are generated by the theory which it holds; and among its own internal resources Penrose lays especial emphasis on managerial services, which we can now interpret as a well-validated set of constructs for selecting and interpreting data and for making effective and timely decisions. Perceived resources and expectations are brought together in the firm's '"productive opportunity", which comprises all of the productive possibilities that its "entrepreneurs" see and can take advantage of' (p. 31); and this productive opportunity, as Penrose makes clear, exists in the imaginations of entrepreneurs, not in the world outside. (The resemblance to Professor Shackle's ideas should need no emphasis.) The more imaginative the entrepreneur, the greater the productive opportunity.

Penrose pays very little attention to the relationship between perception and reality. She does not choose, like Professor Kirzner, to restrict entrepreneurs to the perception — selective and incomplete — of opportunities which already exist, as consequences of changes in preferences or technology which have already taken place. Instead she contents herself with observing that if the productive opportunities are a mirage, then the firm's plans will not be successful, and disclaiming any interest in such firms. Her theory is explicitly designed for successful firms; but might it not be helpful to have a theory which can help to explain the difference between success and failure?

Though success is not guaranteed, it does not necessarily depend on the choice of one particular course of action. The firm's own action may change its environment — a point also made by Kelly about individual actions (1963, p. 8). Both authors provide much more scope for originative choice than do the behaviourist traditions of situational determinism in psychology and economics. This analytical recognition of alternative possible futures adds to the significance of entrepreneurial versatility, which not only widens the range of perception but augments creativity. Within Kelly's system, versatility requires either constructs with a very wide range of convenience, or, more likely, a range of constructs with different foci of application. It certainly implies the capacity, and willingness, to adapt constructs as circumstances change.

The application of Kelly's mode of analysis to Penrose's theory reinforces the latter's argument for the heterogeneity of firms. Heterogeneity has important theoretical uses. It provides a basis for an assumption which Professor Kirzner needs but does not explain: the assumption that a few entrepreneurs will perceive an opportunity which is hidden from everyone else. As Richardson (1960, p. 57) has pointed out, 'a general profit opportunity, which is both known to everyone and equally capable of being exploited by everyone, is, in an important sense, a profit opportunity for no one in particular'. If every individual has his own pattern of experience, mediated by his own interpretative framework, then each may have a slightly different perception; thus relatively few will recognise any particular change in the environment. (For the great majority, it will not be within their own environment that the change occurs.) If the profitable exploitation of that change requires the use of a pool of resources within an administrative framework, then some of those who see the possibilities will feel unable to take advantage of them. Barriers to the entry of most firms may be necessary to give confidence to the remainder. Such barriers may thus, contrary to the presumptions of static theory, contribute to economic welfare.

COMPETITION

In welfare economics, any departure from the conditions of perfect competition is still likely to be condemned as a violation of Pareto optimality. Strictly speaking, of course, both Pareto optimality and perfect competition are valid only for equilibrium, and are not appropriate for the analysis of adjustment processes. Something close to perfect competition might perhaps be appropriate for adjustment, if we could somehow avoid the paralysing criticism of Richardson, and if we could assume that we all knew where to search for the equilibrium configuration: in Kelly's terms, we would be certain that there was no need to stray beyond the range of convenience of a single, commonly-shared set of constructs. But this is to assume a far greater degree of knowledge than we can hope to possess. Within an economy, just as within academia, we need a variety of interpretative frameworks; indeed we need them within an industry as we need them within an academic discipline. Possibilities of intellectual and of economic progress will not all be envisioned within any single framework.

The adjustment of constructs − of theories and of policies − is facilitated by their subordination to a higher-level construct which is formulated sufficiently loosely to accommodate a variety of subordinate constructs, not necessarily mutually compatible. The permeability of superordinate constructs, to use Kelly's term (p. 79) confers resilience. Such permeability is desirable within any organisation which has to cope with change; but, as we have argued above, it is necessarily limited. Successful adaptation within an industry may therefore be dependent on the existence of a number of firms, with substantially different sets of constructs, and (quite possibly) different organisational arrangements which permit different kinds of permeability. Attempts to compel all firms within an industry to conform to a single best pattern, as judged by the perceived requirements of the current situation, may prove disastrous. However successful that pattern may presently be, we must not forget that its range of applicability is limited, and, the more closely it is tailored to contemporary circumstances (and therefore apparently the more efficient), the narrower is that range.

120   *Beyond Positive Economics?*

Sir Karl Popper reminds us that no amount of corroboration can immunise a theory against falsification. There can be no assurance that alternative conjectures will never be required; and alternative conjectures arise most readily from alternative frameworks. If we are to react effectively to the stream of events by which the universe exists (some of them the product of human action) we must avoid misguided attempts to stabilise low-level constructs, either within individuals or within firms. It is the attempt to preserve detailed subordinate constructs in the face of their growing inadequacy to cope with the phenomena which they are required to interpret which leads to human breakdown. Similarly, an attempt to preserve every firm within an industry, or even every industry within an economy, is less likely to succeed in that object than to destroy a superordinate structure which could have been preserved by greater permeability.

REFERENCES

Bradbury, F. R., McCarthy, M. C., and Suckling, C. W. (1972) 'Patterns of innovation: Part ii – the Anaesthetic Halothane', *Chemistry and Industry*, pp. 105–10.

Burns, T., and Stalker, G. M. (1961) *The Management of Innovation* (London: Tavistock).

Chandler, A. D. (1962) *Strategy and Structure* (Cambridge, Mass.: MIT Press).

Coase, R. H. (1937) 'The Nature of the Firm', *Economica* (N.S.), iv, 386–405.

Hahn, F. H. (1973) *On the Notion of Equilibrium in Economics* (Cambridge University Press).

Hayek, F. A. (1937) 'Economics and Knowledge', *Economica* (N.S.), iv, 33–54.

Kelly, G. A. (1963) *A Theory of Personality* (New York: W. W. Norton).

Kirzner, I. M. (1973) *Competition and Entrepreneurship* (University of Chicago Press).

Kirzner, I. M. (1982) 'Uncertainty, Discovery and Human Action', in I. M. Kirzner (ed.), *The Contributions of Ludwig von Mises to Economics* (Lexington, Mass.: Lexington Books).

Lakatos, I. (1970) 'Falsification and the Methodology of Scientific Research Programmes', in I. Lakatos and A. Musgrove (eds), *Criticism and the Growth of Knowledge* (Cambridge University Press).

Penrose, E. T. (1959) *The Theory of the Growth of the Firm* (Oxford: Basil Blackwell).

Popper, K. R. (1972) *The Logic of Scientific Discovery*, 6th impression (London: Hutchinson).

Richardson, G. B. (1960) *Information and Investment* (Oxford University Press).

Shackle, G. L. S. (1967) *The Years of High Theory* (Cambridge University Press).

Knowledge, Learning and Enterprise 121

Simon, H. A. (1969) *The Sciences of the Artificial* (Cambridge, Mass.: MIT Press).

Simon, H. A. (1976) *Administrative Behavior*, 3rd edn (New York: The Free Press).

Skinner, A. S. (1979) 'Adam Smith: an Aspect of Modern Economics?' *Scottish Journal of Political Economy*, 26, 109–26.

Smith, A. (1979) 'History of Astronomy', in W. P. D. Wightman (ed.), *Essays on Philosophical Subjects* (Oxford University Press).

Part II
Empirical Evidence on Firm and Industry

New Firms and Market Entry

[14]

Some Empirical Aspects of Entrepreneurship

By DAVID S. EVANS AND LINDA S. LEIGHTON*

About 4.2 million men and women operate businesses on a full-time basis. Comprising more than a tenth of all workers, they run most of our nation's firms and employ about a tenth of all wage workers. The fraction of the labor force that is self-employed has increased since the mid-1970s after a long period of decline.[1] This paper examines the process of selection into self-employment over the life cycle and the determinants of self-employment earnings using data from the *National Longitudinal Survey of Young Men* (NLS) for 1966–1981 and the *Current Population Surveys* for 1968–1987.

Small-business owners are central to several recent lines of research.[2] First, the static models of entrepreneurial choice developed by Robert Lucas (1978) and Richard Kihlstrom and Jean-Jacques Laffont (1979) have renewed interest in a topic to which the last seminal contributions were made by Frank Knight (1921) and Joseph Schumpeter (1950).[3] David Blau (1985), William Brock and David Evans (1986), and Hedley Rees

and Anup Shah (1986) use these models to motivate their empirical work on self-employment selection and earnings. Second, current research on industry dynamics focuses on smaller firms which, because they tend to be younger, have faster and more variable growth, and fail more frequently than larger firms, are a major source of industry changes. For example, Boyan Jovanovic's (1982) model of industry evolution in which heterogeneous entrepreneurs learn about their abilities over time has stimulated empirical work by Timothy Dunne, Mark Roberts, and Larry Samuelson, 1987, Evans, 1987a, b, and Ariel Pakes and Richard Ericson, 1987. These authors analyze entry, exit, and growth of primarily small firms. Third, David Birch's (1979) claim that small firms create a disproportionate share of new jobs has generated much interest in the role of small businesses in the labor market.[4] Many states have programs designed to stimulate small-firm formation. Great Britain, France, Belgium, and the Netherlands have programs that help unemployed workers start small businesses.[5]

While recent studies have enhanced our empirical knowledge of the role of small businesses in the economy, data limitations have forced these studies to sidestep a number of issues that are basic to an economic understanding of firm formation, dissolution, and growth. Several studies (for example, George Borjas, and Stephen Bronars, 1987, Rees and Shah, 1986, and Brock and Evans, 1986, have used cross-sectional data on self-employed and wage workers to esti-

*Fordham University, Department of Economics, Bronx, NY 10458-5158. We are grateful to Christopher Flinn, Boyan Jovanovic, Jules Lichtenstein, Edward Starr, Hideki Yamawaki, participants of the International Conference on Small Business Economics held at the International Institute of Management, West Berlin, November 1988, and the referee for helpful comments and suggestions. Portions of our research were supported by the U.S. Small Business Administration under Contract No. SBA-1067-AER-86 to Fordham University and by faculty research fellowships provided by Fordham University to both authors. We retain responsibility for the views expressed below. We will provide a copy of a statistical appendix and the data set used in this paper on AT-compatible diskettes upon request for 1 year after the publication date of this paper.

[1] See David Evans and Linda Leighton (1987), William Brock and Evans (1989), Eugene Becker (1984), and David Blau (1987) for details. Evans and Leighton find that self-employment rates peaked in about 1983 and have decreased since.

[2] See Brock and Evans (1989) for a review of recent research.

[3] See Brock and Evans (1986) for a survey.

[4] For criticisms of this argument see Jonathan Leonard (1986) and Dunne, Roberts, and Samuelson (1987).

[5] See Mark Bendick and Mary Egan (1987). The U.S. Department of Labor is planning to conduct an experiment in which a sample of unemployment insurance recipients will be given the option to receive business startup funds in lieu of unemployment benefits.

mate static models of self-employment selection and earnings. But these studies are limited by their lack of data on such important factors as the length of time in business and previous business experience. Recent dynamic studies (for example, Evans, 1987a, b and Pakes and Ericson, 1987, rely on crude firm characteristics such as size and age but lack information on the entrepreneur himself.[6]

We use longitudinal data that permit a closer examination of some key aspects of entrepreneurship. We focus on white men who comprised 76 percent of all full-time self-employed workers in 1985.[7] Our main source of data is the *National Longitudinal Survey of Young Men* which contains detailed information on a sample of almost 4,000 white men who were between the ages of 14 and 24 in 1966 and who were surveyed 12 times between 1966 and 1981. The self-employed include all sole proprietors, partners, and sole owners of incorporated businesses.

These data permit several innovations over previous research. First, they allow us to track business starts and stops as the cohort of men ages. Second, they enable us to determine the length of time an individual has operated his current business and previous businesses and thereby to distinguish business and wage experience. Third, they permit us to evaluate several theories of entrepreneurship that have been proposed by psychologists and sociologists.[8]

We also use data for about 150,000 white men from *Current Population Surveys* for 1968–1987 as a check on and supplement to our NLS findings. These men were in contiguous years of the CPS March surveys giving us a 2-year panel for each individual. To keep our inquiry open ended—an important consideration given the limited empirical information on this topic—we do not develop and estimate structural models of entrepreneurship in this paper. The reader should exercise caution in placing behavioral interpretations on our results.

We report seven key findings. (1) The probability of switching into self-employment is roughly independent of age and total labor-market experience. This result is not consistent with standard job-shopping models such as William Johnson (1978) and Robert Miller (1984) which predict that younger workers will try riskier occupations first. (2) The probability of departing from self-employment decreases with duration in self-employment, falling from about 10 percent in the early years to 0 by the eleventh year in self-employment. About half of the entrants return to wage work within seven years.[9] (3) The fraction of the labor force that is self-employed increases with age until the early 40s and then remains constant until the retirement years. This relationship results from the process of entry and exit over the life cycle. (4) Men with greater assets are more likely to switch into self-employment all else equal. This result is consistent with the view that entrepreneurs face liquidity constraints.[10] (5) Wage experience has a much smaller return in self-employment than in wage work while business experience has just about the same return in wage work as in self-employment. These differences may

---

[6]For example, taken literally Jovanovic's model (1979) assumes that an individual learns about his entrepreneurial ability over time. Firm age is a crude proxy for the duration and intensity of entrepreneurial learning.

[7]We concentrate on white males for several reasons. The self-employment rate differs substantially between sex and race groups. The rate for women and blacks is only about a third that for white men. Investigating the source of these disparities would take us too far afield. (See George Borjas and S. Bronars, 1987, for a recent analysis of race differences). Moreover, because blacks and women have low self-employment rates, available longitudinal data sets provide too few observations on self-employment entry and exit for these demographic groups.

[8]There is an extensive theoretical and empirical literature on entrepreneurship in our sister disciplines. But

the empirical work generally does not control for anything more than rudimentary demographic characteristics.

[9]This is probably an underestimate because short spells of self-employment (under 1 year) are underrepresented in the data.

[10]See Evans and Joyanovic (1989) for an estimated structural model of entrepreneurship with liquidity constraints using the NLS data.

reflect some combination of true productivity differences and the results of selection into and out of self-employment over time. (6) Poorer wage workers—that is, unemployed workers, lower-paid wage workers, and men who have changed jobs a lot—are more likely to enter self-employment or to be self-employed at a point in time, all else equal. These results are consistent with the view of some sociologists that "misfits" are pushed into entrepreneurship.[11] (7) As predicted by one of the leading psychological theories, men who believe their performance depends largely on their own actions—that is, have an internal locus of control as measured by a psychologist test known as the Rotter Scale—have a greater propensity to start businesses.[12]

Section I describes the data. Section II presents aggregate statistics on self-employment entry and exit over the life cycle and reports estimates of the probability of entering into and exiting out of self-employment. Section III examines the determinants of self-employment earnings. It focuses on the relative returns to business and wage experience and education in self-employment versus wage work. Section IV suggests avenues for further research.

I. Data Sources

The *National Longitudinal Survey* is based on a national probability sample of men who were between the ages of 14 and 24 in 1966 and who were surveyed yearly between 1966 and 1971 and in 1973, 1975, 1976, 1978, 1980, and 1981.[13] There were 3,918 white men in the initial survey of whom 2,731 were still in the survey in 1981. The appendix presents definitions for the variables used in this paper. Because the data are described in

detail in Evans and Linda Leighton (1987), we focus on the advantages of these data over those used in previous research.

(1) Using information on employment status and tenure we have calculated total experience in wage work and self-employment for each year of the sample.[14] Previous studies that rely on cross-sectional data have not disaggregated experience. (2) We have found that workers who report themselves as self-employed often have no self-employment earnings and substantial wage earnings which suggests that either the workers are misclassified or their earnings are misclassified. We have found that it is possible to explain most of these inconsistencies using available data on dual jobs, tenure, and incorporation status. Our findings suggest some caution in taking reported self-employment earnings at face value.[15] (3) The panel data on employment status allow us to track entry and exit over time. Previous studies of self-employment selection that rely on cross-sectional data confound the entry and exit decisions. In a cross section, self-employed workers are workers who entered and remained in self-employment. (4) Data on assets, job changes, unemployment, and some standard psychological test scores enable us to look at a number of issues which cannot be examined with the data sets used by previous researchers. It turns out that these variables are important determinants of self-employment selection and earnings.

One disadvantage of the NLS is that the sample sizes for analyzing self-employment entry and exit are small. For example, the number of entrants into self-employment averages about 50 per year. Another disadvantage is that data are available only for men who are all younger than 40 by the end of the survey. A further problem is that there

---

[11]See Pyong Gap Min (1984) for a review of the major sociological theories.

[12]An internal locus of control is also a characteristic of individuals who have a high need for achievement which David McClelland (1964) has argued is a key determinant of entrepreneurship.

[13]Blacks were oversampled. About 25 percent of the initial respondents were black or other minorities.

[14]Some imputations, especially for workers with pre-1966 experience, were necessary. See Evans and Leighton (1987).

[15]On the other hand, the fact that most of the individuals who report themselves as being self-employed either report self-employed earnings or report themselves as having an incorporated business suggests that errors in reporting self-employment status are not substantial.

is substantial attrition—almost a third—between 1966 and 1981. To obtain larger and more representative samples for analyzing self-employment entry and exit we use data drawn from the March Supplement to the *Current Population Surveys* for 1968–1987. Each CPS survey contains information on the employment status of each respondent for the survey week and for the previous year. About half of all respondents are in contiguous surveys for most survey years.[16] We have matched these respondents for the pairs of years where this was possible. The resulting data set contains up to 2.33 years of employment information for about 150,000 white men who were between the ages of 18 and 65 at the time of the first observation on them and who were full-time labor-market participants in the first observation year. For each individual, we have information pertaining to the survey week for two years and information pertaining to the longest-held job in the preceding year. We have used the data to calculate entry and exit rates between jobs held as of the survey week and between the longest-held jobs in each year.[17] A deficiency of the CPS data is that individuals who operate incorporated businesses were included with wage workers for the survey-week job in all years and for the longest-held job for the surveys before 1976. For this reason we concentrate on unincorporated self-employment for the CPS data.

II. Entry and Exit

The probability that an individual operates a business T years after entering the labor force equals the probability that he started a business at time t, $t \leq T$, times the probability that he remained self-employed from time t to time T.[18] We examine several

aspects of this process of entry and exit over the life cycle in this section. We begin by summarizing the rates of entry into and exit out of self-employment for the NLS cohorts and for the matched CPS data. We show that a simple time-homogeneous Markov model in which entry and exit rates are constant over time provides a helpful first approximation to the cross-sectional relationship between self-employment and age. We then investigate whether the entry or exit rates exhibit duration dependence. We find that entry is time-homogeneous—it is constant in both age and labor-market experience—but that exit decreases sharply with time in business. Finally, we report estimates of the hazard into entrepreneurship that control for a variety of characteristics suggested by social science theories of the entrepreneur.

An Overview of Entry and Exit. Table 1 reports summary statistics on the evolution of self-employment for the NLS white men. The fraction of labor-force participants who enter self-employment exceeds the fraction who exit self-employment thereby increasing the fraction who are self-employed from 3.9 percent in 1966 to 17.7 percent in 1981. Since 1971, when the average age of the labor-market participants was 25 years, the entry rate—the percent of wage workers who enter self-employment—has been about 4.0 percent per year and the exit rate—the fraction of self-employed workers who return to wage work—has been about 13.8 percent per year. The entry rate was lower and the exit rate was somewhat higher prior to 1971.

A simple time-homogeneous Markov model provides a helpful first approximation to this process. Denote the probability of entering self-employment by e and the probability of exiting self-employment by x. Assume that e and x are independent of time or age. Then the probability that an individual will operate a business T years after entering the labor force is (see, for example, William Feller, 1968, p. 432),

$$\frac{e}{x+e}\left[1-(1-x-e)^T\right].$$

---

[16] The exceptions being 1971–1972, 1972–1973, 1976–1977, and 1985–1986.

[17] The construction of these data is described in Evans and Leighton (1987).

[18] Note that survival in self-employment is not necessarily equivalent to survival of a business since an individual may remain self-employed as he opens and closes successive businesses.

VOL. 79 NO. 3   *EVANS AND LEIGHTON: ENTREPRENEURSHIP*   523

TABLE 1—SELF-EMPLOYMENT ENTRY AND EXIT, 1966–1981

Survey Year	Percent of Labor Force Participants Who Enter Self-Employment Between Survey Years	Exit Self-Employment Between Survey Years	Percent of Labor Force Participants Who Are in Self-Employment as of the Survey Year	Percent of Self-Employed Workers Who Exit Self-Employment Between Survey Years
1966	1.92	1.49	3.89	30.36
1967	2.78	0.97	4.50	18.03
1968	2.43	1.71	5.54	25.30
1969	2.93	1.41	5.92	19.59
1970	2.35	2.10	7.04	27.50
1971[a]	5.24 (3.67)	1.83 (0.92)	6.64	24.06 (12.86)
1973[a]	4.77 (3.13)	2.91 (1.47)	9.16	26.73 (14.40)
1975	4.22	2.33	10.74	19.09
1976[a]	6.89 (4.82)	3.18 (1.60)	12.00	23.08 (12.30)
1978[a]	6.24 (4.37)	3.76 (1.90)	14.71	20.82 (11.02)
1980	4.04	2.68	16.68	12.93
1981	–	–	17.73	–

Source: White males drawn from the *National Longitudinal Survey of Young Men.*

[a] Denotes a two-year transition. We obtained annual rates that are comparable to the one-year transitions under the following assumptions. For entry we assumed that 40 percent of new entrants fail in the first year so that the average annual rate of entry is 1.4 times the two-year entry rate divided by 2. For failure we assumed that the annual rate of survival is s so that the probability of surviving two years is s^2. The annual rate of failure is simply $1 - s$. These adjusted rates are reported in parentheses beside the actual rate.

This simple model has two predictions. The first is that the probability of self-employment increases at a diminishing rate with the length of time in the labor force.[19] The second prediction is that the probability of self-employment converges to a plateau given by $e/x + e$ for older men. We check these predictions with the CPS data which contain many more observations and a broader age range than do the NLS data. The relationship between unincorporated self-employment and age found in the CPS data is displayed in Figure 1 for 150,275 white men who were between the ages of 18 and 65 between 1968 and 1987.[20] The rate of

self-employment increases at a diminishing rate with age and approaches a plateau at about age 40 which lasts until about age 60. The average rate of unincorporated business formation (entry into self-employment between successive March survey weeks) was 2.5 percent per year and the average rate of unincorporated business dissolution (exit out of self-employment between successive March survey weeks) was 21.6 percent per year for the CPS sample.[21] The predicted asymptote of 10.4 percent is close to the plateau of about 11.6 percent shown in Figure 1.

The Time-Dependence of Entry and Exit. The Markov model assumes that the probabilities of forming or dissolving a business are independent of time in the labor force.[22] We examined the dependence of entry on

[19] This prediction is consistent with cross-sectional studies by Brock and Evans (1986), Rees and Shah (1986), and Borjas (1987) which find that the probability of self-employment is convex in age. For the NLS men the probability of self-employment increases linearly with age for each of the 12 cross sections. The lack of convexity is probably due to the fact that these men are all under 40 even at the end of the sample period.
[20] The underlying data are reported in the Appendix.

[21] Entry rates are substantially lower for men under 25 and higher for men over 60 (see below). Excluding these two extremes we obtain a predicted asymptote of 11.0 percent.
[22] Because the probability of leaving a job decreases with age, the probability of starting a business condi-

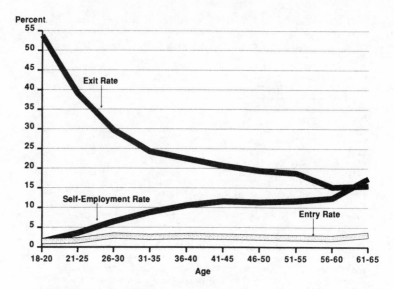

FIGURE 1. SELF-EMPLOYMENT AND AGE, WHITE MEN, AGES 21–65. BASED ON
DATA OF 150,275 EMPLOYED WHITE MEN FROM THE *CURRENT POPULATION
SURVEYS*, 1968–87

time in the labor force in several ways. First, we estimated the probit for entering self-employment as a function of age or labor-market experience for the NLS sample for each year. We can reject the hypothesis that entry depends upon age or labor-market experience at conventional levels of significance for all specifications and years.[23] This finding suggests that the probability of starting a business is independent of age or experience at least until age 40. Second, Table 2 and Figure 1 report entry rates by 5-year age categories for the CPS white men. The rate of entry is fairly constant between ages 25 and 50 and then decreases somewhat between ages 50 and 60.[24]

TABLE 2—SELF-EMPLOYMENT ENTRY RATE
BY AGE, WHITE MEN AGES 21–65[a]

Ages	Entry Rate (Percent)	Ages	Entry Rate (Percent)
21–25	1.7	46–50	2.5
26–30	2.9	51–55	2.4
31–35	2.6	56–60	2.3
36–40	2.8	61–65	3.1
41–45	2.7	21–65	2.5

Source: Based on data on 135,752 employed white men from the *Current Population Surveys*, 1968–1987.

[a]Entry rate is the percent of men who were wage workers as of the March survey week who were unincorporated self-employed during the March survey week of the following year.

tional upon leaving a job must increase with age. We would like to thank Jacob Mincer for this point.

[23]Results are available upon request.

[24]It increases after age 60, a reflection of the tendency of older men to switch to self-employment upon retirement. See Victor Fuchs (1982) for an analysis of this phenomenon.

We examined the dependence of exit from self-employment on the length of time in business by estimating the probability that an individual will survive T years in continuous self-employment and the probability of leaving self-employment during the next year, given that the individual has been em-

TABLE 3—ESTIMATED SURVIVAL AND HAZARD RATES
FOR SELF-EMPLOYMENT[a]

Self-Employment Duration in Years	Survival Rate (Percent)	Hazard Rate[b] (Percent)
0	100.0	–
2	79.4	10.3
4	61.5	11.3
6	51.4	8.2
8	47.0	4.3
10	41.2	6.2
12	39.9	1.6
14	39.9	0.0

[a] Based on estimates obtained from the Kaplan-Meier procedure using LIMDEP.

[b] Annual hazard rate based on the estimated survivorship function.

ployed for T years. We used data for 460 NLS white men who were observed from the time of entry to the end of the survey.[25] Table 3 summarizes life-table estimates of the survivorship and hazard rates obtained from the Kaplan-Meier procedure.[26] About a third of the entrants leave self-employment within the first 3 years of entry, about a half within 7 years, and about three-fifths within 10 years. The hazard rate decreases with duration in self-employment, falling from about 10 percent in the early years to 0 by the eleventh year in self-employment.[27]

[25] There were a total of 396 individuals, some of whom entered more than once (i.e., entered, failed, and reentered).

[26] We also attempted to control for individual characteristics using parametric hazards formulations. None of the characteristics such as education, wage experience, previous job tenure, or marital status was substantively or statistically important.

[27] The survivorship function is probably biased upward because short spells of self-employment are underrepresented in our sample since many of our observations are 1–2 years apart. Using the *Current Population Survey* data on the unincorporated self-employed we estimated the failure rate over a one-year period of white men who were wage workers on their longest-held job in the previous year (generally a period of at least six months) and who were self-employed in the survey week. Generally these people would have been self-employed less than nine months as of the survey week. Of these individuals, 41.4 percent were no longer self-employed in the subsequent survey week.

Estimates of the Probability of Entering Self-Employment. Individuals will switch from self-employment to wage work if the expected utility of self-employment exceeds the expected utility of wage work. The difference between these expected values depends upon the difference between expected earnings in the two occupations and upon relative tastes for the two. Expected wage earnings depend upon current wage earnings, education, job tenure, and wage experience. Expected self-employment earnings depend upon education and experience. We therefore conjecture that the probability of switching into self-employment will decline with current wage earnings but may increase or decrease with education and experience depending upon whether these characteristics are more important in self-employment or wage work. Another observable characteristic, which psychologists and sociologists have found to be correlated with selection into entrepreneurship, is the extent to which individuals have an internal locus of control.[28] We measure the internal locus of control by the individual's score on the Rotter test (which was administered in 1976). Finally, an individual will be more likely to switch into self-employment the greater his net worth if there are liquidity constraints as in Evans and Jovanovic (1989). As additional measures of worker quality we include the frequency of job changes (number of changes divided by total labor-market experience), unemployment as a fraction of time in the labor force, marital status, and whether the individual has a health problem.[29]

Table 4 reports probit estimates of a basic specification of the determinants of entry into self-employment for 1976–1978, 1978–

[28] See, for example, J. Schere (1982) and Janak Pandey and N. B. Tewary (1979) for empirical studies of the relationship between the internal locus of control and small-business ownership. The hypothesis that entrepreneurs have a high need for achievement is due to McClelland's (1964) pioneering study. Also see McClelland and David Winter (1969).

[29] Ivan Light (1979) has argued that these sorts of disadvantages push minorities into self-employment. For a recent study of self-employment of disadvantaged workers see Steven Balkin (in press).

TABLE 4—PROBABILITY OF ENTERING SELF-EMPLOYMENT FROM
WAGE WORK PROBIT ESTIMATES[a], 1980–81

National Longitudinal Survey of Young Men White Men
1980–1981

Variable	Coefficient	Std. Error	t	Prob > |t|	Mean
Enter					.0252039
Tenure	−.0238353	.0081510	−2.924	0.004	43.54411
Tenure^2	.0001638	.0000619	2.645	0.008	3096.182
Income	−.5163689	.2901084	−1.780	0.075	2.063929
Income^2	.0663933	.0541532	1.226	0.220	5.139952
Wage Exp.	.0462285	.0285732	1.618	0.106	13.3198
Prev. Self	.9107385	.2171792	4.193	0.000	.1030393
Education	.055382	.0434853	1.274	0.203	13.88288
Unemploy	.0478407	.0187881	2.546	0.011	2.361186
Changes	.3698019	.3711313	0.996	0.319	.3244283
Assets^{a,b}	.0985545	.0228677	4.310	0.000	4.645619
Assets^2	−.0010812	.0003849	−2.809	0.005	89.78229
Married	−.5815598	.2076951	−2.800	0.005	.7916976
Urban	.0516553	.2181547	0.237	0.813	.7249815
Handicap	−.0494911	.3936484	−0.126	0.900	.0518903
Constant	−2.909767	.9611979	−3.027	0.003	1

Number of obs = 1349   chi2(14) = 101.53
Log likelihood = −107.94862   Prob > chi2 = 0.0000

F-Tests	F	P-value
Income = 0	2.27	.1041
Asset = 0	11.12	.0000
Tenure = 0	4.28	.0141

1978–1980

Variable	Coefficient	Std. Error	t	Prob > |t|	Mean
Enter					.0526658
Tenure	−.0025117	.0060118	−0.418	0.676	37.36151
Tenure^2	.0000356	.0000573	0.621	0.535	2345.797
Income	−.2613197	.234179	−1.116	0.265	1.678607
Income^2	.0327625	.0491364	0.667	0.505	3.379527
Wage Exp.	−.0322216	.0197113	−1.635	0.102	11.60596
Prev. Self	.6916842	.153986	4.492	0.000	.0838752
Education	.0217275	.0256107	0.848	0.396	13.70546
Unemploy	−.020861	.0155898	−1.338	0.181	2.55832
Changes	.3529475	.2204601	1.601	0.110	.3494789
Assets^b	.0609102	.0246713	2.469	0.014	1.617229
Assets^2	−.0007327	.0004154	−1.764	0.078	21.10421
Married	−.0153407	.1432351	−0.107	0.915	1.210663
Urban	−.1589805	.1215175	−1.308	0.191	.7041612
Handicap	−.0253471	.2350554	−0.108	0.914	.0643693
Constant	−1.381862	.561222	−2.462	0.014	1

Number of obs = 1538   chi2(14) = 53.69
Log Likelihood = −290.4314   Prob > chi2 = 0.0000

F-Tests	F	P-value
Income = 0	1.14	.3215
Asset = 0	3.39	.0338
Tenure = 0	0.26	.7741

TABLE 4—CONTINUED

National Longitudinal Survey of Young Men White Men
1976–1978

Variable	Coefficient	Std. Error	t	Prob > |t|	Mean
Enter					.0563978
Tenure	−.0188406	.0059464	−3.168	0.002	32.44633
Tenure^2	.0001893	.0000577	3.278	0.001	1783.905
Income	−.0027703	.2210893	−0.013	0.990	1.307402
Income^2	.0148635	.0522132	0.285	0.776	2.088686
Wage Exp.	.0282834	.0188645	1.499	0.134	9.883356
Prev. Self	.6944128	.1503571	4.618	0.000	.0794421
Education	.0121024	.0245543	0.493	0.622	13.58702
Unemploy	.0036077	.0118607	0.304	0.761	2.796006
Changes	.4891922	.1692598	2.890	0.004	.3675908
Assets	.0787118	.0394622	1.995	0.046	1.52344
Assets^2	−.0023117	.0017761	−1.302	0.193	15.06044
Married	−.3480157	.1239067	−2.809	0.005	.7671316
Urban	.0254816	.1227831	0.208	0.836	.7064888
Handicap	−.1958478	.2220587	−0.882	0.378	.0721649
Constant	−1.976281	.4987808	−3.962	0.000	1

Number of obs = 1649
Log Likelihood = −324.18232

chi2(14) = 67.10
Prob > chi2 = 0.0000

F-Tests	F	P-value
Income = 0	0.19	.8268
Asset = 0	2.21	.1105

CURRENT POPULATION SURVEYS, 1968–86
LINEAR-PROBABILITY MODEL ESTIMATES
Current Population Surveys, 1968–1986
White Men, Ages 25–60[a]

Variable	Coefficient	Std. Error	t	Prob > |t|
Enter				
Income	−7.06372E−06	2.5543E−06	−2.765	.0057
Income^2	5.05253E−05	8.7298E−06	5.788	.0000
Liquidity	7.75240E−07	1.1777E−07	6.583	.0000
Age	−2.42493E−04	3.9411E−04	−.615	.5384
Age^2	2.71727E−06	4.4914E−06	.605	.5452
High School Drop	−6.72032E−04	.0013228	−.506	.6127
College Dropout	.003173	.001376	2.306	.0211
College Graduate	.006408	.001628	3.936	.0001
Post Graduate	.013793	.001651	8.352	.0000
Urban	−.005001	9.9962E−04	−5.003	.0000
Married	.002432	9.6085E−04	2.531	.0114
Veteran	−.002762	.001019	−2.710	.0067
Constant	.027483	.008177	3.361	.0008

Number of jobs | .106239
R-Square | .00286
F-Statistic | 12.7062

[a] Estimates obtained using STATA.
[b] Assets are for 1976.
[c] Estimates obtained using SPSSX.

1980, and 1980–1981 for the NLS. For comparison, we also report linear probability model estimates for the 1968–1986 matched CPS data. The samples consist of individuals who were in the labor force in both survey weeks. Several findings are robust. (1) The probability of switching into self-employment increases with net worth (measured by assets for the NLS and by the difference between family earnings and family income for the CPS). This finding is consistent with Evans and Jovanovic (1989) and suggests that individuals face liquidity constraints.[30] (2) Individuals with low wages are more likely to switch into self-employment. This relationship is highly significant when we control for assets but not for other labor-market characteristics. It remains but is much less statistically significant when we also condition on labor-market characteristics. (3) Wage experience is neither statistically nor substantively significant.[31] Thus, as we found earlier, the hazard into self-employment from wage work is independent of the length of time in wage work. (4) Individuals with longer job tenures are less likely to switch into self-employment.[32] (5) The probability of entry is higher for individuals who have had prior self-employment experience. (6) Individuals who have changed jobs frequently are more likely to switch into self-employment. (7) The effect of previous unemployment on the probability of entering self-employment is not consistent across the years: it is positive and significant for 1980–1981, positive and insignificant for 1976–1978, and negative and insignificant for 1978–1980. But we have found that men

who are unemployed are more likely to enter self-employment. For the CPS white men observed, entry rate was 4.7 percent for men who were unemployed (5,664 men) as of the initial survey week and 2.4 percent for men who were employed wage workers (126,750 men) as of the initial survey week.[33] (8) There is a negative relationship between the Rotter score and entry for most years but the relationship is generally not statistically significant.[34]

The general message of these results is that relatively poor wage workers—that is, workers with low wages and a history of instability—are most likely to switch to self-employment holding assets and education constant.

III. Self-Employment Selection and Earnings

In this section we report cross-sectional estimates of the probability that an individual is self-employed rather than a wage worker and estimates of self-employment and wage earnings for individuals who were self-employed workers or wage workers in 1981. Several other authors report estimates of self-employment selection and earnings models. Borjas and Bronars (1987), Evans (1985), and Brock and Evans (1986) use 1980 Census data, Rees and Shah (1985) use U.K. data on a small cross section, and Blau (1985) uses data on Malaysian farmers. These previous estimates suffer from two data problems. First, these studies have no information on self-employment versus wage experience. Indeed, all of these studies use proxies for aggregate experience (age less years of education). Second, they have rather sparse information on personal characteristics. The NLS data permit us to estimate a much more refined model and to investigate

---

[30] Evans and Jovanovic test and reject the alternative hypothesis that high-asset individuals are high-entrepreneurial ability individuals. For further evidence that small firms face liquidity constraints see Steven Fazzari, R. Glenn Hubbard, and Bruce Petersen (1987). For the 1980–1981 entrants we used 1981 assets.

[31] The fact that wage experience is not important is consistent with the comparative advantage model since the coefficient on this term reflects the difference in the returns to wage experience in self-employment versus wage work.

[32] The coefficients on wage experience are smaller and less significant when we do not condition on job tenure.

[33] We get similar results for the NLS men although the sample sizes are very small.

[34] Below, however, we report estimates that show that the Rotter score has a statistically significant negative effect on the probability of being self-employed at a point in time—and therefore having entered and survived up to a point in time. The results reported in the text are qualitatively the same when the Rotter score is included.

VOL. 79 NO. 3   *EVANS AND LEIGHTON: ENTREPRENEURSHIP*   529

the effects of wage and self-employment experience on wage and self-employment earnings.

The results reported in this section are primarily descriptive. It is very difficult to place behavioral interpretations on cross-sectional estimates of self-employment selection and earnings. For example, the probability of being self-employed at time T depends upon the underlying probability of switching into self-employment at some previous time and surviving until time T. The cross-sectional estimates confound the determinants of switching and survival. To take another example, the effect of wage experience on self-employment earnings confounds the productivity-enhancing effects of wage experience on business earnings and a variety of potential selection problems, for example, the possibility that workers who accumulated more wage experience before switching into self-employment had higher opportunity costs of switching into self-employment and therefore must have discovered unusually good self-employment opportunities to induce them to switch.[35] Nevertheless, the results reported here are helpful because they place some restrictions on the behavioral models of entrepreneurial selection and earnings that might be entertained.

The data for the analysis consist of 2,405 white men who were in the 1981 NLS survey, were employed as of the 1981 survey week, and were not enrolled in school full time. To have a clean comparision of the choice between self-employment and wage work we deleted individuals who held both wage and self-employment jobs. We found a number of possible errors in the self-employment status and earnings information and made several adjustments and deletions to minimize the effects of such errors. Some incorporated self-employed individuals reported wage earnings but no self-employment earnings; we assumed their wage earn-

ings were from their incorporated business. Some individuals switched into self-employment or wage work during the year; we prorated their earnings according to the proportion of the year they spent in the type of job held as of the survey week. Individuals who had inconsistent information—for example, who reported wage earnings but who were unincorporated self-employed and who had not switched during the year—were deleted. A total of 272 individuals were deleted either because they held both wage and self-employment jobs or because information was inconsistent.[36] A few other individuals were deleted for some of the analyses because of missing information.

Table 5 reports probit estimates of the probability that an individual is self-employed rather than a wage worker in 1981. We report estimates both with and without the Rotter score and an indicator of whether the individual's father held a managerial job since there were a substantial number of missing values on these variables. Several findings are notable. First, the probability of being self-employed increases with labor-market experience.[37] This result is consistent with the simple Markov model of self-employment: Individuals who have been in the labor market a longer time are more likely to have switched to self-employment. Second, the probability of being self-employed is higher for individuals who have changed jobs frequently. This finding is consistent with our entry estimates which also indicated that men with more unstable work histories were more likely to enter self-employment. Third, the probability of self-employment is higher for individuals with relatively more unemployment experience. This result is consistent with our earlier finding that unemployed workers are more likely to enter self-employment. Fourth, the

---

[35] These kinds of problem are analogous to those found in the recent labor-economics literature on the returns to seniority. See Joseph Altonji and Shakotko (1987), Robert Topel (1986), and Katherine Abraham and Henry Farber (1987) for discussion.

[36] The probit results reported below are similar when these individuals are included.

[37] The second-order term in experience was not significant. We would not expect the concave relationship found by Brock and Evans (1986), Rees and Shah (1986), and Borjas (1987) because our sample only includes individuals under the age of 40 in 1981.

TABLE 5—ESTIMATED PROBABILITY OF BEING SELF-EMPLOYED IN 1981,
WHITE MEN PROBIT ESTIMATES[a]

Variable	Coefficient	Model 1 Std. Error	t	Prob > |t|	Mean
Self-Employed					.161165
Urban	−.1845696	.0788463	−2.341	0.019	.7067961
Married	.0705539	.0923126	0.764	0.445	.776699
Divorced	.1504005	.101406	1.483	0.138	.1446602
Handicapped	−.2205851	.1354426	−1.629	0.104	.0859223
Experience	.0631149	.011388	5.542	0.000	14.45653
Education	.0468791	.0159466	2.940	0.003	13.83447
Unemployment	.0008846	.0001591	5.561	0.000	138.5192
Changes	.0129181	.0027347	4.724	0.000	16.87336
Farmer	1.852521	.1674885	11.061	0.000	.038835
Professional	1.318865	.1805655	7.304	0.000	.0286408
Military	.2254239	.1098127	2.053	0.040	.3504854
Mil. Exp.	−.0039777	.0032259	−1.233	0.218	9.865049
Constant	−3.077114	.3627388	−8.483	0.000	1

Number of obs = 2060   chi2(12) = 293.63
Log Likelihood = −762.87545   Prob > chi2 = 0.0000

Variable	Coefficient	Model 2 Std. Error	t	Prob > |t|	Mean
Self-Employed					.1618435
Urban	−.2040773	.0838386	−2.434	0.015	.7073955
Married	.0178929	.0986787	0.181	0.856	.7808146
Divorced	.0951484	.1097263	0.867	0.386	.142015
Handicapped	−.2174593	.142506	−1.526	0.127	.0846731
Experience	.0553762	.0123014	4.502	0.000	14.60937
Education	.0179523	.017547	1.023	0.306	13.86549
Unemployment	.0008873	.0001769	5.016	0.000	131.2435
Changes	.013667	.0029617	4.615	0.000	16.71073
Farmer	1.908768	.1732564	11.017	0.000	.0401929
Military	.3334698	.1235012	2.700	0.007	.3494105
Mil. Exp.	−.0111616	.0042291	−2.639	0.008	9.019829
Professional	1.364592	.197819	6.898	0.000	.0273312
Rotter Score	−.0216171	.0073045	−2.959	0.003	21.8612
Manager Father	.3363427	.0962543	3.494	0.000	.1709539
Constant	−2.102342	.442666	−4.749	0.000	1

Number of obs = 1866   chi2(14) = 303.83
Log Likelihood = −674.18848   Prob > chi2 = 0.0000

[a] Estimates obtained using STATA.

probability of being self-employed is higher for more highly educated individuals even after we control for individuals in professional occupations. Fifth, as suggested by psychologists, individuals who have a more internal locus of control are more likely to become entrepreneurs. Controlling for the internal locus of control renders the coefficient on education small and statistically insignificant. Sixth, men whose fathers were managers are more likely to be self-employed.

Using the probit selection equation reported above we were not able to reject the hypothesis that the correlation between selection and earnings is zero; controlling for selection had little effect on the coefficient estimates.[38] On the basis of a Chow test it

[38] The selection correction was performed using James Heckman's (1976) Lambda method using LIMDEP. Evans and Leighton (1987) report statistically significant negative selection but also find little effect on

TABLE 6—ESTIMATED LOG EARNINGS EQUATIONS FOR SELF-EMPLOYED
AND WAGE WORKERS', REGRESSION ESTIMATES[a]

Variable	Self-Employed Workers				
	Coefficient	Std. Error	t	Prob $> |t|$	Mean
Log Annual Earnings					9.722387
Urban	.2984078	.0959255	3.111	0.002	.5886525
Married	.1426724	.1182799	1.206	0.229	.8262411
Handicapped	− .7237983	.1653379	− 4.378	0.000	.0744681
Wage Exp.	.0212041	.0106104	1.998	0.047	8.838993
Bus. Exp.	.1127724	.0267228	4.220	0.000	6.831969
Bus. Exp.^{2}	− .0048672	.0012519	− 3.881	0.000	78.364
Prev. Bus.	.2638763	.1084132	2.434	0.016	.2234043
Education	.102862	.0187483	5.486	0.000	13.85816
Unemploy Wks	− .0076448	.0023534	− 3.248	0.001	12.71631
Changes	− .0019309	.0039824	− 0.485	0.628	18.22286
Farmer	.0088565	.1262476	0.070	0.944	.1950355
Professional	.1607639	.1705543	0.943	0.347	.0957447
Military	− .1787064	.122895	− 1.454	0.147	.3439716
Mil. Exp.	.0065334	.0037604	1.737	0.083	7.723404
Constant	7.547442	.3774288	19.997	0.000	1

Number of obs	=	282	F(14,267)	= 10.69
R-Square	= 0.3591		Prob $> F$	= 0.0000
Adj R-Square	= 0.3255		Root MSE	= .71254

Variable	Wage Workers				
	Coefficient	Std. Error	t	Prob $> |t|$	Mean
Log Earnings					9.888144
Urban	.2116573	.0287379	7.365	0.000	.7239521
Married	.2301503	.0304746	7.552	0.000	.7694611
Handicapped	− .180494	.0451322	− 3.999	0.000	.0874251
Wage Exp.	.0984876	.0198633	4.958	0.000	13.97031
Wage Exp.^{2}	− .0024167	.0006396	− 3.778	0.000	210.6699
Self Exp.	.0447571	.011243	3.981	0.000	.3203938
Education	.0706433	.0054855	12.878	0.000	13.82814
Unemploy Wks	− .0042027	.0005479	− 7.670	0.000	16.44012
Changes	− .0035781	.0009934	− 3.602	0.000	16.32626
Farmer	− .4048178	.1277192	− 3.170	0.002	.0101796
Professional	.15914	.1064927	1.494	0.135	.0149701
Military	.0213733	.0400467	0.534	0.594	.3556886
Mil. Exp.	.0018262	.0010989	1.662	0.097	10.36886
Constant	7.818336	.1790618	43.663	0.000	1

Number of obs	=	1670	F(13,1656)	= 49.85
R-Square	= 0.2813		Prob $> F$	= 0.0000
Adj R-Square	= 0.2756		Root MSE	= .51578

[a]Estimates obtained using STATA.

was also possible to reject the hypothesis that self-employed and wage workers have the same earnings equation at the 1 percent level.

coefficient estimates. The difference in the importance of the selection term appears to be due to the inclusion of blacks in our earlier work.

Table 6 reports regression estimates of log-earnings equations for self-employed workers and wage workers for our final specification. There are several important differences and similarities in the earnings functions. First, the return to wage experience in self-employment (2.1 percent) is lower than the return to wage experience in wage work (5.6 percent) and lower than the return to self-employment experience in self-employment (4.6 percent).[39] One interpretation of these differences is that human-capital accumulated through wage work is less valuable in self-employment than wage work. Another interpretation is that individuals who switch into self-employment later in their careers (and who have thereby accumulated more wage experience) are relatively poorer wage workers. Second, the return to self-employment experience in wage work (4.5 percent) is higher than the return to wage experience in wage work (3.1 percent) although the difference is not statistically significant. This result suggests that workers who fail at self-employment return to wage work at roughly the same wages they would have received had they not tried self-employment.[40] It is not possible to determine the extent to which this result reflects the value of business experience in wage work or the fact that those self-employed workers with the best wage opportunities will tend to switch. Third, even after controlling for professional workers the returns to education are somewhat higher in self-employment than in wage work—10.3 percent per year versus 7.1 percent. Fourth, unemployment experience carries a substantially larger penalty in self-employment than in wage work—0.8 percent per week vs. 0.4 percent per week. This result suggests that unemployed workers with the poorest opportunities in the wage sector switch to and remain in self-employment.

IV. Conclusions and Suggestions for Further Research

Economists have a lot to learn about entrepreneurship. Our results suggest some avenues to pursue. An interesting finding is that the probability of entering self-employment is independent of age or experience for the first 20 years of employment. This result is contrary to popular wisdom and inconsistent with imperfect-information models of occupational choice. Behavioral models of entrepreneurial selection that can explain this relationship would be helpful. One possible explanation examined by Evans and Jovanovic (1989) is that individuals face liquidity constraints and have to accumulate assets in order to start viable businesses. Another possible explanation is that it takes time to discover a business opportunity. Older people might be more likely to have identified an opportunity but less likely to choose to exploit it.[41]

Our results suggest that some theories are more consistent with the data than others. The disadvantage theory which views entrepreneurs as misfits cast off from wage work is consistent with many of our findings. People who switch from wage work to self-employment tend to be people who were receiving relatively low wages, who have changed jobs frequently, and who experienced relatively frequent or long spells of unemployment as wage workers.[42] The psychological theory based on the internal locus of control is also consistent with our findings. Self-employed workers at a point in time tend to have a more internal locus of control (a result which is statistically significant) and individuals with a more internal locus of control are more likely to enter self-employment (a result which is generally not statistically significant). The sociological and psychological literature on entrepreneurship contains many insights that economists might consider incorporating in their models.

---

[39] Evaluated at the mean experience levels for self-employed workers.

[40] There is a selection bias here too. Workers who leave self-employment for wage work will tend to be workers who were receiving relatively low wages in self-employment or who receive relatively high offers from wage employers.

[41] The fact that wage experience carries a higher return in wage work than in self-employment is consistent with this explanation.

[42] Of course it is easy enough to restate the sociologist's disadvantage theory in terms of the economist's comparative advantage model. See Table A for the definition of Variables for the NLS *Survey of Young Men*.

TABLE A—DEFINITION OF VARIABLES FOR *National Longitudinal
Survey of Young Men*[a]

Variable	Definition
	Categorial Variables[b]
Entry	Dummy for Individual Who Was a Wage Worker in the Survey Week and Self-Employed in the Next Survey Week Observed
Handicapped	Dummy for Individuals Who Have Poor Health
Veteran	Dummy for Individuals Who Served in the Military
Urban	Dummy for Individuals Who Live Within an SMSA
Professional	Dummy for Individuals in Professional Occupations
Farmer	Dummy for Individual in Farm Occupation
Manager Father	Dummy for Individuals Whose Fathers Were in a Managerial Occupation When Individual Was 14
Married	Dummy for Individual Who Is Married
Divorced	Dummy for Individual Who Has Been Divorced
	Continuous Variables
Income	Total Earnings in the Previous Year
Education	Years of Education
Business Experience	Years in Current Business
Previous Business	Years in Previous Business
Wage Experience	Years of Wage Experience
Liquidity	Net Family Assets
Military Experience	Weeks of Military Experience
Tenure	Years in Current Job
Rotter Score	Total Score on Rotter Test for 1976
Job Changes	Number of Jobs Held by Individual Since 1966 Divided by Wage Experience
Unemployment	Weeks of Unemployment Divided by Wage Plus Unemployment Experience Times 100.
Unemployment Weeks	Weeks of Unemployment Since 1966
Wage Earnings	Wage Earnings of Wage Workers
Self Earnings	Self-Employment Earnings of Self-Employed Workers or Wage Earnings of Incorporated Self-Employed Workers Who Report Wage But No Self-Employment Earnings
Assets	Net Worth (Assets Minus Liabilities) of Family

[a] Further details are provided in Evans and Leighton (1987).
[b] Dummy equal to 1 if condition holds and zero otherwise.

REFERENCES

Abraham, Katherine and Farber, Henry, "Job Duration, Seniority, and Earnings," *American Economic Review*, June 1987, *77*, 278–97.

Altonji, Joseph and Shakotko, Robert, "Do Wages Rise with Job Seniority?," *Review of Economic Studies*, July 1987, *54*, 437–60.

Blau, David, "Self-Employment and Self-Selection in Developing Country Labor Markets," *Southern Economic Journal*, October 1985, *52*, 351–63.

_____, "A Time-Series Analysis of Self-Employment," *Journal of Political Economy*, June 1987, *95*, 445–67.

Balkin, Steven, *Self-Employment for Low Income People*, New York: Praeger Press, in press.

Becker, Eugene H., "Self-Employed Workers: An Update to 1983," *Monthly Labor Review*, July 1984, *107*, 14–18.

Bendick, Mark and Egan, Mary, "Transfer Payment Diversion for Small Business Development: British and French Experience," *Industrial and Labor Relations Review*, July 1987, *40*, 132–57.

Birch, David, *The Job Generation Process*, Cambridge, MA: Center for the Study of Neighborhood and Regional Change, Cambridge: MIT Press, 1979.

Borjas, George, "The Self-Employment of Immigrants," *Journal of Human Resources*, Fall 1986, *21*, 485–506.

_____ and Bronars, S., "Self-Employment and Consumer Discrimination," University of California at Santa Barbara, unpublished manuscript, August 1987.

Brock, William A. and Evans, David S., *The Economics of Small Businesses: Their Role and Regulation in the U.S. Economy*, New York: Holmes and Meier, 1986.

_____ and _____, "Small Business Economics," *Small Business Economics: An International Journal*, January 1989, *1*, 7–20.

Dollinger, Marc J., "Use of Budner's Intolerance of Ambiguity Measure for Entrepreneurial Research," *Psychological Reports*, May 1983, *53*, 1019–21.

Dunne, Timothy, Roberts, Mark and Samuelson, Larry, "The Impact of Plant Failure on Employment Growth in the U.S. Manufacturing Sector," unpublished manuscript, Pennsylvania State University, January 1987.

Durand, Douglas and Shea, Dennis, "Entrepreneurial Activity as a Function of Achievement Motivation and Reinforcement Control," *Journal of Psychology*, June 1974, *88*, 57–63.

Evans, David S., *Entrepreneurial Choice and Success*, Washington: U.S. Small Business Administration, 1985.

_____, (1987a) "Firm Growth, Size, and Age: Estimates for 100 Manufacturing Industries," *Journal of Industrial Economics*, June 1987, *35*, 567–82.

_____, (1987b) "Tests of Alternative Theories of Firm Growth," *Journal of Political Economy*, August 1987, *95*, 657–74.

_____ and Leighton, Linda, *Self-Employment Selection and Earnings Over the Lifecycle*, Washington: U.S. Small Business Administration, December 1987.

_____ and Jovanovic, Boyan, "Estimates of a Model of Entrepreneurial Choice under Liquidity Constraints," *Journal of Political Economy*, forthcoming August 1989, in press.

Fazzari, Steven, Hubbard, R. Glenn and Petersen, Bruce, "Financing Constraints and Corporate Investment," NBER Working Paper No. 2387, Cambridge, MA: NBER, September 1987.

Feller, W., *An Introduction to Probability Theory and its Applications*, New York: Wiley & Sons, 1968.

Fuchs, Victor, "Self-Employment and Labor-Force Participation of Older Males," *Journal of Human Resources*, Fall 1982, *18*, 339–57.

Heckman, James J., "The Common Structure of Statistical Models of Truncation, Sample Selection, and Limited Dependent Variables, and a Simple Estimator for Such Models," *Annals of Economic Measurement*, Fall 1976, *5*, 475–92.

Johnson, William, "A Theory of Job-Shopping," *Quarterly Journal of Economics*, May 1978, *22*, 261–78.

Jovanovic, Boyan, "Job Matching and the Theory of Turnover," *Journal of Political Economy*, October 1979, *87*, 972–90.

_____, "The Selection and Evolution of Industry," *Econometrica*, May 1982, *50*, 649–70.

Kihlstrom, Richard and Laffont, Jean-Jacques, "A General Equilibrium Theory of Firm Formation Based on Risk-Aversion," *Journal of Political Economy*, August 1979, *87*, 719–48.

Knight, Frank, *Risk, Uncertainty, and Profit*, New York: Houghton Mifflin, 1921.

Leonard, Jonathan, "On the Size Distribution of Employment and Establishment," NBER Working Paper No. 1951, 1986.

LeRoy, Stephen and Singell, Larry, D. Jr., "Knight on Risk and Uncertainty," *Journal of Political Economy*, April 1987, *95*, 394–407.

Light, Ivan, *Ethnic Enterprise in America: Business and Welfare among Chinese, Japanese, and Blacks*, Berkeley, CA: University of California Press, 1972.

_____, "Disadvantaged Minorities in Self-Employment," *International Journal of Comparative Sociology*, March 1979, *20*, 31–45.

Lucas, Robert E., "On the Size Distribution of Business Firms," *Bell Journal of Economics*, Autumn 1978, *9*, 508–23.

McClelland, David C., *The Achieving Society*, Princeton, NJ: D. Van Nostrand, 1964.

_____ **and Winter, David G.,** *Motivating Economic Achievement*, New York: Free Press, 1969.

Miller, Robert, "Job Matching and Occupational Choice," *Journal of Political Economy*, December 1984, *92*, 1086–120.

Min, Pyong Gap, "From White-Collar Occupations to Small Business: Korean Immigrants Occupational Adjustment," *Sociological Quarterly*, Summer 1984, *11*, 333–52.

Pakes, Ariel and Ericson, Richard, "Empirical Implications of Alternative Models of Firm Dynamics," unpublished manuscript, Department of Economics, University of Wisconsin, December 1987.

Pandey, Janak and Tewary, N.B., "Locus of Control and Achievement Values of Entrepreneurs," *Journal of Occupational Psychology*, February 1979, *52*, 107–11.

Rees, Hedley and Shah, Anup, "An Empirical Analysis of Self-Employment in the U.K.," *Journal of Applied Econometrics*, Spring 1986, *1*, 95–108.

Schere, J., "Tolerance of Ambiguity as a Discriminating Variable between Entrepreneurs and Managers," in *Proceedings*, New York: Academy of Management, 1982.

Schumpeter, Joseph, *Capitalism, Socialism, and Democracy*, 3rd ed., New York: Harper and Row, 1950.

Shapero, Albert, "The Displaced, Uncomfortable Entrepreneur," *Psychology Today*, November 1975, *9*, 83–88.

Topel, Robert, "Job Mobility, Search, and Earnings Growth: A Reinterpretation of Human Capital Earnings Functions," in Ronald Ehrenberg, *Research in Labor Economics*, Greenwich, CT: JAI Press, 1986.

Wicker, Alan and King, Jean, "Employment, Ownership, and Survival in Microbusiness: A Study of New Retail and Service Establishments," unpublished manuscript, Department of Psychology, Claremont Graduate School, 1987.

[15]

Scottish Journal of Political Economy, Vol. 34, No. 1, February 1987
© 1987 Scottish Economic Society

NEW FIRM FORMATION—A LABOUR MARKET APPROACH TO INDUSTRIAL ENTRY*

D. J. STOREY AND A. M. JONES

University of Newcastle upon Tyne and University of York

I

INTRODUCTION

Although entrants play a central role in the structure/performance paradigm it is apparent that such firms are only indirectly included in the major empirical work on the topic. The central theme of the bulk of these studies is that variations in profitability, at an industry level, can be explained in terms of concentration, and a variety of barriers to entry (Sawyer, 1981). This barrier-orientated approach commonly features the concept of a queue of potential entrants, what Bain (1956) termed the "general condition of entry". However, due to a tendency to concentrate on the diversification of existing enterprises, the socio-economic determinants of new firm founders are invariably neglected.

There has been little attempt to directly test for a relationship between the number of entrants and perceived future profits. This is primarily a consequence of the difficulty of obtaining suitable data on entrants, whether they are wholly new firms or existing enterprises shifting or diversifying their operations.

This paper uses data for new manufacturing businesses created in Northern England between 1965 and 1978 and the East Midlands between 1968 and 1975 with a view to testing the validity of the conventional theory of entry. It is recognised that self-employment is an alternative to unemployment (or to paid employment) and an attempt is made to integrate industrial entry and labour search into a single model. This theoretical and empirical development requires that a distinction be made between entrants by transfer or diversification and wholly new firms.

II

THEORY

Much of the conventional entry theory has been built upon the concept of the limit price (Waterson 1984, Clarke 1985). This refers to industries in

* We are grateful for the many helpful suggestions made by Mike Waterson and an anonymous referee. We also thank Steve Fothergill and Graham Gudgin for allowing us access to their data on establishments in the East Midlands, but the opinions expressed are those of the authors alone.

Date of receipt of final manuscript: 21 April 1986.

37

38   D. J. STOREY AND A. M. JONES

which there are increasing returns to scale up to a level of output which is a significant proportion of the total market. The impact on aggregate supply of an entrant, of at least minimum efficient scale, will be to depress market price and consequently the level of profit. Post-entry profits rather than existing profit levels should therefore be the decision-making criterion for potential entrants. This fact allows existing firms to achieve actual profits at a level (above "normal") such that the level of expected post-entry profits is sufficient to discourage potential entrants.[1] The central thrust of the model is to render outcomes determinate in terms of price.[2]

As noted by Gorecki (1979), a major weakness of the limit pricing hypothesis lies in its inability to distinguish between entrants which are wholly new and existing enterprises which have diversified or transferred from other sectors. The importance of this distinction is that the two categories of firms are likely to respond to different stimuli.[3]

Total entrants into industry i (E_i) are therefore defined to be both wholly new businesses (NF_i) and existing businesses moving into i (TD_i), where wholly new businesses are independent enterprises setting up their first plant;

$$E_i = NF_i + TD_i \tag{1}$$

An existing business, currently operating in industry j, is expected to view a move to i (whether a transfer or a diversification) primarily on the basis of expected post-entry profits in i (π_i) and expected profits in j (π_j), subject to entry barriers (X_i) and any miscellaneous factors (Z_i). An example of the latter could be the reduction in uncertainty gained by vertical integration.

$$TD_i = f(\pi_i,\ \pi_j,\ X_i^T,\ Z_i) \tag{2}$$

where,

$$\frac{\partial TD_i}{\partial \pi_i} > 0 \ \frac{\partial TD_i}{\partial \pi_j} < 0 \ \frac{\partial TD_i}{\partial X_i^T} < 0$$

In equation (2) X is a vector representing barriers to entry, whether they are economies of scale, product differentiation or absolute cost advantages, and X_i^T refers only to those barriers which apply to this particular group of entrants. Those readers interested in a recent examination of cross entry are referred to Deutsch (1984).

[1] It is worth noting that the most appropriate measure of profitability in a profit maximisation model of limit pricing is the price-cost margin, equivalent to the profit-sales ratio.

[2] This simple determinancy was criticised by Caves and Porter (1977). They argued that structural barriers to entry, seen by Bain (1956) as exogenous, are in fact subject to the endogenous behaviour of incumbent firms.

[3] In developing their theory of barriers to mobility, Caves and Porter (1977) hypothesise the existence of subgroup structures within industries accompanied by group-specific entry barriers. An implication of this model is that potential entrants may also be distinguishable on the basis of the group they intend to enter. Caves and Porter define these groups primarily in terms of marketing strategies and they are therefore not strictly comparable with the distinction we propose to make between established and wholly new firms. However their approach does illustrate that much may be gained by abandoning assumptions of homogeneity.

NEW FIRM FORMATION   39

Wholly new firms are formed by individuals all of whom will have the
option of obtaining employment in the formal labour market or of being
unemployed.[4] Two contrasting views of this process may be offered. The first
argues that individuals currently employed in industry i are faced by the
alternatives of continued employment in i, possible employment in j,
unemployment, or of establishing a new venture. Similarly, in the event of
redundancies in industry i, the individuals involved may remain unemployed,
gain employment in industry j or become self-employed.[5] Of those who
exercise the latter option it is assumed that the majority will remain in
industry i, primarily because their "contacts", so important in starting a new
firm, will be in that industry. Individuals are more likely to be aware of
market gaps, suppliers and the technology of production in the industry in
which they were formerly employed.[6]

The majority of new firm founders in the ith industry begin their
operations with "second-hand" equipment. The price of this equipment
depends, in the short-term, primarily upon the extent to which falls in final
demand result in reductions in capacity in that industry. A reduction in final
demand thus increases spare capacity in the industry leading to plant and
machinery being sold off by liquidators and, to a lesser extent, by existing
enterprises. In recessionary conditions reductions in capacity by larger
enterprises will result in a major increase in the availability of second-hand
equipment, dwarfing the increased demand by entrepreneurs starting in
business. These characteristics of the second-hand capital market are clearly
shown by Binks and Jennings (1986). This reduces the price of second-hand
equipment which is the major entry barrier that the entrepreneur faces. The
effect, therefore of depressed market conditions in industry i may be both to
make self-employment relatively more attractive *and* to reduce an important
barrier to new firm formation in that industry.

A second view argues that whilst unemployment reduces the opportunity
cost of business formation it also depletes the assets of the entrepreneur so
making entry more difficult. Indeed the conventional view would be that
reduced labour demand reflects poor expected profitability, so discouraging
entry. It is therefore an essentially empirical question as to which of these
"explanations" is more powerful.

An entry function for wholly new businesses can now be proposed. The

---

[4] "The labourer asks what he thinks the entrepreneur will be able to pay, and in any case
will not accept less than he can get from some other entrepreneur, or by turning
entrepreneur himself. In the same way the entrepreneur offers to any labourer what he
thinks he must in order to secure his services and in any case will not offer more than he
thinks the labour will be worth to him, keeping in mind what he can get by turning labourer
himself." (Knight, 1921.)

[5] In a survey, carried out in the area which is now Cleveland county, 26 per cent of new
firm founders claimed to have been unemployed prior to to starting their business (Storey,
1982). Other authors who have seen unemployment as a stimulus of new firm formation
include Dahmen (1970), Wedervang (1965) and Oxenfeldt (1943).

[6] The Cleveland survey, which covered all industries except retailing, found that 60 per
cent of new firm founders had remained in the same industrial order (Storey, 1982). The
comparable figure produced by Johnson and Cathcart (1979) was 50 per cent.

40 D. J. STOREY AND A. M. JONES

independent variables again include expected post-entry profitabillity in industry i (π_i^1) and a specific set of barriers to entry (X_i^N). But they are now joined by an index of labour shedding (L_i), a specific indicator of employment opportunities in i. This variable plays a central role in subsequent analysis,[7] but the two hypotheses outlined above lead to conflicting signs. Two specific characteristics of L_i are possible. The first is net employment change in the ith industry i.e. gross job gains minus gross job losses, whilst the second is simply gross employment loss defined as job loss through closures and contractions. Take, now, two industries i and j, identical in size, in terms of employment and in terms of employment change over time. It is argued that if gross job losses in industry i are significantly higher than in j, then industry i will, *ceteris paribus*, have the higher rates of new firm formation since more individuals will have lost their jobs in that industry and so will be "forced" to consider the entrepreneurial option.[8]

$$NF_i = f(\pi_i^1, X_i^N, L_i) \qquad \frac{\partial NF_i}{\partial \pi_i^1} > 0 \qquad \frac{\partial NF_i}{\partial X_i^N} < 0 \tag{3}$$

The net effect of an exogenous reduction in demand for products of industry i on the number of entrants in subsequent periods therefore depends on the magnitude of two conflicting influences. A fall in profitability can be expected to lead to closures and a transfer of existing enterprises out of i but at the same time redundancies may stimulate the formation of wholly new businesses, as former employees find this more attractive than either unemployment or the possibility of obtaining work in industry j. The latter will depend upon the extent to which reduced job prospects reduce their assets and the extent to which these new and small firms can be expected to fill "niches" within the existing markets.

III

THE EXISTING WORK

The main empirical study using number of entrants as the dependent variable was carried out by Mansfield on a multiplicative model of the form:

$$E_{it} = \alpha_0 \pi_{it}^{\alpha_1} X_{it}^{-\alpha_2} Z_{it} \tag{4}$$

where

$$\frac{\partial E_{it}}{\partial \pi_{it}} > 0; \quad \frac{\partial E_{it}}{\partial X_{it}} < 0$$

---

[7] In the empirical section of this paper it is assumed that NF_i is a multiplicative function, log-linear in terms, X and L.

[8] Another factor, explored by Kihlstrom and Laffont (1979) is the degree of risk aversion amongst entrepreneurs, whilst differences in wage rates in i and j could also affect the model specification.

This model was tested with data for four industries over a variety of periods, yielding 10 data points. Mansfield showed that a significant and positive relationship existed between profitability and entry rates. The latter are defined as the number of firms that entered the ith industry during the tth period (and survived until the end of the period) as a proportion of the number in the industry at the beginning of the period. This is only one of the indices of entry since it neglects those entrants which failed to survive the given period. The difference between total entrants and surviving entrants may be considerable since in most of the industries covered by Mansfield the period used is a decade. An examination of data by Dun and Bradstreet for the U.S.A. suggests that approximately half of a given year's new manufacturing firms fail to survive for a decade. Mansfield would therefore seem to be underestimating the *total* number of entrants by this amount. Since however he is attempting to explain cross-industry differences this under-enumeration may not be so important, but the absence of a reliable control sample makes even this hypothesis untestable.

The formulation of entry rates used by Mansfield differs in several respects from that used in subsequent attempts to use entries as the dependent variable in regression equations. For example the work by Orr (1974) does not use the gross surviving entry rate favoured by Mansfield, but instead uses the net entry rate. This is defined to be:

$$E_i = 1/4 \sum_{t=1964}^{1967} N_{it} - N_{i(t-1)} \tag{5}$$

where:

$E = E_i \ldots E_{71}$ industries;

N_{it} = number of reporting corporations in the ith industry in the tth year (Canada);

$N_{it} - N_{i(t-1)}$ is defined as ≥ 0.

Orr therefore selects only those industries where there are more firms in year t than in year $t-1$, consequently his data includes wholly new firms, firms transferring from other industries, and exits. Orr admits that the data may also, in some cases, include firms where the ownership has changed. Finally it has to be recognised that the data source from which Orr draws, only includes firms which have sales exceeding $500,000, at 1967 prices. This means that only firms with at least 50 workers would be included in his sample. If the size distribution of new firms in Canada during the period was the same as in the Northern region of England then only 6 per cent of all new firms would be included in Orr's data.

The study by Gorecki (1975) also uses a net entry rate, examining the increased (decreased) number of enterprises in 51 industries in the U.K. between 1958 and 1963. Gorecki attempts to distinguish between the net change in specialist and in diversifying firms. His sample includes exits, yet there are strong reasons for believing that there is an asymmetry between

42   D. J. STOREY AND A. M. JONES

factors affecting rates of entry and exit. For example, whilst gross entries are postulated to be affected by profitability and entry barriers, empirical studies of gross exits have included profitability and the number of enterprises at risk because of their size (Mansfield 1962, Marcus 1963). Furthermore the study by Henderson (1980) has shown there to be no association between an industry's profitability and the propensity of its establishments to close. More recently Van Herck (1984) has attempted to explain the interrelationships between entry and exit but his empirical work does not make clear the definitions of entry used.

It is clear that a number of formulations of entry rates are theoretically justifiable for testing the relationship between entry and profitability. However, to test for a relationship between the choices open to the individual all new businesses have to be charted, including those which have diversified from other industries. Ideally such data should include all sizes of new firms, not simply those which reach a given (usually high) minimum size, and finally it should also include all new firms rather than only those which survive until the end of the period. Such data does not exist for the U.K. economy as a whole but is available to the authors for Northern England. Valuable data is also available for the East Midlands of England, but on the slightly different basis discussed in the next Section.

Finally it seems likely that the entrepreneur's view of expected post-entry profitability and of the actual height of entry barriers may vary from one location to another. For example, some areas may specialise in the "small" specialist end of a given market whilst other areas may specialise in large scale mass production. Recently two studies have examined the locational differences in *actual* profit rates in broadly comparable firms. Bayldon, Woods and Zafiris (1984) question whether differences exist between inner city and new town locations, whilst Fothergill, Gudgin, Kitson and Monk (1984) show that such differences do exist between conurbations and other areas.

IV

SOURCES OF DATA

Data on wholly new manufacturing firms in Northern England were derived from records constructed for the County Councils of Cleveland, Durham and Tyne and Wear.[9] Coverage is virtually complete, subject to the limitations of government statistics and the data base contains nearly 5,000 manufacturing establishments which existed at any stage between 1965 and 1978. For each establishment, data on employment are available for most years. In addition further data on, for example, name, address, location, industry (MLH), ownership, date of establishment (if after 1965) and date of closure (where applicable), are available.

[9] The construction is described in detail in Storey, Keasey, Watson and Wynarczyk (1987).

The East Midlands data were kindly supplied by Graham Gudgin and Steve Fothergill. The source for this data is the Factory Inspectorate and full details are available in Fothergill and Gudgin (1982). The numbers of wholly new firms existing in 1975 which had been created since 1968 were provided. It must be emphasised that these include only new firms which survived until 1975, and in this important aspect the data differs from that available on the Northern Region.

From this population of manufacturing establishments in the two regions it is possible to identify a group which consists of new independent businesses and to identify the years in which they began operations. In principle it would also be possible to identify existing establishments which switched their industry (cross-entry). However these cases are not included in subsequent analysis because in several cases a change in MLH is a reflection of the industrial classification being initially incorrect, rather than a genuine change of activity.

Finally it would therefore be desirable to have data on profitability and entry barriers specifically for the North and for the East Midlands but unfortunately such data does not exist. It has therefore proved necessary to use national data for both of these measures.

V

The Variables

(i) *Entry rates*

Four New Firm formation rates are used in this analysis.

(a) NF_i^N; takes the total number of wholly new firms in the ith industry (locally-owned sole proprietorships, partnerships, or private limited companies) which traded for the first time between 1965 and 1978 in the counties of Durham, Cleveland or Tyne and Wear. Such firms must be legally independent enterprises, i.e. not subsidiaries of existing enterprises. To identify a formation rate, the number of such wholly new firms is divided by the number of single plant independent firms in the ith industry in Durham, Cleveland and Tyne and Wear in 1965. Hence NF_i^N represents the gross proportionate increase in the number of single plant independent firms in the three counties over the 1965–1978 period.

(b) NF_i^{NUK}; if the number of single plant independent firms in the three counties existing in industry i in 1965 were low for some temporary reason then NF_i^N would be an an inappropriate index. Instead it may be better to divide the number of wholly new firms in the ith industry by the number of enterprises in the ith industry in the U.K. since this is less likely to be affected by "exceptional" values. Data for numbers of enterprises do not exist for 1965 but the U.K. data from "Census of Production" is used for 1968 to derive NF_i^{NUK}.

44   D. J. STOREY AND A. M. JONES

(c) NF_i^{EM}; since the North of England has been shown by Fothergill and Gudgin to have a rate of new firm formation significantly below the national average, data on formation rates in the East Midlands are used to determine whether the cross section formation rates in the North are correlated with those of a region with a formation rate more typical of the U.K. as a whole. NF_i^{EM} takes the data supplied by Steve Fothergill and Graham Gudgin on wholly new firms in the East Midlands between 1968 and 1975 for each MLH. This is divided by the number of single plant independent firms in that industry in 1968. It must be emphasised, however, that the East Midlands data includes firms starting after 1968 but which *survived* until 1975. It does not include, unlike the Northern data, new firms starting after 1968 but which failed to survive until 1975.

(d) NF_i^{EMUK}; This index takes the number of wholly new firms formed in the East Midlands in the ith industry between 1968 and 1975 and divides by the number of U.K. enterprises in the ith industry in 1968 according to the Census of Production.

(ii) *Profitability index*

The concept of expected post-entry profitability is, in practice, unquantifiable and a suitable proxy is required. Empirical studies have generally used ex-post profits (See Waterson, 1984). There may also be a lag between the observed opportunity for profit and an individual forming a firm to take advantage of that opportunity. The extent of this lag is likely to vary from a matter of days to years depending partly upon the individual and partly upon the industry to be entered. It seems likely that industries where initial capital requirements are high will experience a longer period between the perception of profit and actual entry than an industry where capital requirements are small. Neither we, nor other empirical studies, are able to take this into account except through the entry barriers index. Furthermore it could be argued that is is *not* the general level of profitability in industry i which affects the willingness of the individual to form his own firm since profitability in the industry as a whole may be affected by the presence of large firms. Of more relevance is the expected return which the individual could expect to obtain by forming a new firm and this will, at least initially, be more closely related to the profitability of smaller firms in the industry. The only useable data on corporate profitability is national and taken from Census of Production, so that in the model *Regional* entry rates will be compared with *National* ex-post profitability data.

$$\pi_i = \frac{\text{(Net output} - \text{Wages and Salaries)}}{\text{Net Output}}$$

From this general index a number of possible indices can be formed.

π^{68} = Gross Profits in 1968 in ith industry in U.K.
π^{70} = Gross Profits in 1970 in ith industry in U.K.
π^{73} = Gross Profits in 1973 in ith industry in U.K.
π^{76} = Gross Profits in 1976 in ith industry in U.K.

$^{99}\pi_i^{70}$ = Gross Profits in 1970 in U.K. ith industry in firms employing less than 100 workers.

$^{99}\pi_i^{73}$ = Gross Profits in 1973 in U.K. ith industry in firms employing less than 100 workers.

$^{99}\pi_i^{76}$ = Gross Profits in 1976 in U.K. ith industry in firms employing less than 100 workers.

In determining entry rates the change in the level of profit may be more important than the absolute level of profit. For example, an industry may have high entry barriers and high profits and a zero entry rate. In the event of an exogeneous increase in profitability entry could be stimulated. It could also be argued that changes in the profitability of small firms, rather than the profitability of all firms in the industry, are most likely to affect expectations.

Two types of index of change in profitability have therefore been constructed:

$\Delta\Pi_i^{t,t+1}$ = Change in U.K. profitability in ith industry between year t and year $t + 1$.

$^{99}\Delta\Pi_i^{t,t+1}$ = Change in U.K. profitability in ith industry between year t and year $t + 1$ in firms employing less than 100 workers.

(iii) *Labour market variables*

It was argued above that a factor influencing the likelihood of an individual becoming the founder of a new firm is the availability or otherwise of work locally in his/her industry.

Ceteris paribus it would be expected that those industries which were major net shedders of labour would also have the highest rates of new firm formation. However, these *net* employment changes conceal the growth in employment in some firms and the loss of employment in others. Since it is those workers in firms either *contracting* their labour forces or *closing* that are particularly "at risk", the index should express gross job losses as a proportion of total employment in industry i.

The labour market indices used are:

$L_i^{t,t+1}$ = % change in U.K. Employment in ith industry between year t and year $t + 1$, so that if $E_t > E_{t+1}$ then $L^{t,t+1} < 0$

L_i^N = Job Losses through Contractions + Closures in Northern England 1965–78 in ith industry

Total Employment in ith industry in 1965 in Northern England.

To estimate L^N, job losses through closure are defined as employment in 1965 in establishments which had closed by 1978. Job losses through contractions are defined as job losses in establishments which although trading in both 1965 and 1978 had *less* jobs in 1978 than in 1965. Gross Job Losses are defined as the summation of closures and contractions.

(iv) *Barriers to entry* (X_i^L)

Scherer (1980) reviews the variety of entry barriers used in empirical studies, but the index adopted in this paper is that formulated by Lyons

(1980). It estimates, for a variety of industries, the minimum efficient plant-size as a percentage of industry size (MEP/S) on the basis of a firm's decision to set up a second plant. Using the 1968 Standard Industrial Classification, Lyons provides estimates for 144 industries at MLH and sub-MLH level but he specifically excludes industries which have "miscellaneous" in their title. This is unfortunate in the present study since these industries frequently contain a large number of wholly new firms. Nevertheless, the advantages of having entry barrier data constructed at MLH level transcends these disadvantages.

VI

THE RESULTS

Difficulties arose in testing due to incomplete data for all industries and variables. During the period there was a major change in the Standard Industrial Classification in 1968 and a reallocation of some establishments in 1970, both of which raise problems of comparability over the time periods. Secondly, in many instances the number of wholly new firms in an MLH was less than five and so were excluded because of the risk of introducing "extreme" values. Finally, as noted above, the Lyons data does not cover all industries. Given these constraints only 31 MLH's were able to provide observations on all variables.

As noted earlier the existing empirical work has been unclear on the functional form of a relationship between entry and profitability. It is also unclear from a theoretical standpoint whether a linear or more complex functional form is appropriate. For this reason Table 1 presents a simple correlation matrix between the four endogenous variables (NF_i^N, NF_i^{NUK}, NF_i^{EM}, NF_i^{EMUK}), and the 15 exogenous variables. Table 2 identifies the correlation between endogenous variables. Table 3 presents similar data to Table 1 but with all variables subjected to a logarithmic transformation. Similarly Table 4 shows the correlation between the logarithmic transformed endogenous variables. Only after these tables are regression results presented in Tables 5 and 6.

The most striking feature of Tables 1 and 3 is the absence of any association between the absolute level of profit in a given year and entry rates, however defined, in either Northern England or the East Midlands. This statement applies to the absolute level of profit in any given year in all enterprises within that MLH and to profitability in the smaller enterprises, i.e. those with less than 100 employees.

The second group of variables shows the correlation between the two entry rates for each of the two Regions and the change in profitability for a number of time periods. A variety of different time periods was in fact tested but only three are shown here. Again there is no evidence of any association.

The third group of variables refer to labour shedding, the first three of

TABLE 1

Simple correlation matrix

	NF_i^N	NF_i^{NUK}	NF_i^{EM}	NF_i^{EMUK}
Π_i^{68}	0·0982	0·1681	0·1329	0·1405
Π_i^{70}	0·1124	0·0821	0·0753	−0·0484
Π_i^{73}	0·1049	0·1147	0·1473	0·0441
Π_i^{76}	0·0693	0·2131	0·0420	−0·0080
$^{99}\Pi_i^{70}$	−0·0091	−0·0212	−0·1003	0·0530
$^{99}\Pi_i^{73}$	0·0418	−0·0057	0·0063	0·1424
$^{99}\Pi_i^{76}$	0·1388	0·1694	0·1507	0·0071
$\Delta\Pi_i^{6876}$	0·1016	0·0391	0·0746	0·1879
$\Delta\Pi_i^{6873}$	0·0609	0·0654	−0·0145	0·1031
$^{99}\Delta\Pi_i^{7076}$	−0·1616	−0·2471	−0·2668	0·0246
L_i^{6873}	0·1101	−0·2188	0·1395	−0·0243
L_i^{6870}	0·0694	−0·2690	0·1490	−0·0717
L_i^{6876}	0·0064	−0·3429*	0·2585	0·0715
L_i^N	0·4752**	−0·1518	0·2594	−0·0803
X_i^L	−0·1158	−0·2927	−0·1542	0·2152

** Significant at 1% level.
* Significant at 5% level.

which are based on national data taken from the Census of Production whilst the fourth identifies the gross job losses in Northern England. For the first time in Table 1 the correlation coefficient for the Northern entry rates are significant at the 5 per cent level. Thus the index of gross job losses in Northern England L_i^N is positively associated with new firm formation rates in the Region NF_i^N. On the other hand L_i^{6876} is negatively associated with NF_i^{NUK} which is the opposite to that predicted by the labour shedding theory. To determine whether these relationships are robust when subject to logarithmic transformations it can be seen from Table 3 that the significantly positive relationship between L_i^N and NF_i^N continues whereas that between NF_i^{NUK} and L_i^{6876} disappears. This suggests that labour shedding is a factor "explaining" the sectoral variations in new firm formation rates in Northern England. It is not possible to construct a similar index for the East Midlands 1968–75, but for completeness the Table shows the insignificant association between East Midlands formation rates and L^N.

TABLE 2

Correlation matrix

	NF_i^N	NF_i^{NUK}	NF_i^{EM}	NF_i^{EMUK}
NF_i^N	1·0000			
NF_i^{NUK}	0·4833	1·0000		
NF_i^{EM}	0·1671	0·1763	1·0000	
NF_i^{EMUK}	0·0846	−0·1684	−0·0555	1·0000

TABLE 3

Correlation matrix: logarithmic transformations

	NF_i^N	NF_i^{NUK}	NF_i^{EM}	NF_i^{EMUK}
Π_i^{68}	0·1580	0·1694	0·0645	0·2316
Π_i^{70}	−0·0145	0·1916	−0·0209	0·1880
Π_i^{73}	−0·0314	0·2250	0·0434	0·2186
Π_i^{76}	0·0813	0·2518	0·0814	0·1620
$^{99}\Pi_i^{70}$	−0·0819	0·0201	−0·1054	0·1880
$^{99}\Pi_i^{73}$	0·0932	0·0564	0·0424	0·2582
$^{99}\Pi_i^{76}$	0·1230	0·1660	0·0392	0·0457
$\Delta\Pi_i^{6876}$	0·1630	0·1595	0·1463	−0·0421
$\Delta\Pi_i^{6873}$	−0·1461	−0·1774	0·1041	−0·0232
$^{99}\Delta\Pi_i^{7076}$	−0·2234	−0·0600	−0·2009	0·1271
L_i^{6876}	−0·0546	0·2791	0·0460	−0·0292
L_i^{6870}	−0·0276	0·0245	0·1855	0·3148*
L_i^{6873}	−0·0513	0·0158	−0·3308*	−0·2246
L_i^N	0·4171**	−0·1950	0·0610	−0·1439
X_i^L	−0·2062	−0·3704*	−0·1149	0·1997

** Significant at 1% level.
* Significant at 5% level.

TABLE 4

Correlation matrix: logarithmic transformations

	NF_i^N	NF_i^{NUK}	NF_i^{EM}	NF_i^{EMUK}
NF_i^N	1·0000			
NF_i^{NUK}	0·2632	1·0000		
NF_i^{EM}	0·4410	0·3044	1·0000	
NF_i^{EMUK}	−0·0169	−0·0945	0·2252	1·0000

Finally, the barriers to entry index X_i^L is shown to be significantly negatively correlated with NF_i^{NUK}, after the logarithmic transformation. This accords with the expectations from the theoretical model.

Tables 2 and 4 show the correlation between the four entry rates used in this analysis. They demonstrate the generally weak relationship between these variables, and this must be a matter of concern since it is not clear which index is the most appropriate.

Tables 5 and 6 show the "best" OLS equations, in terms of adjusted $\bar{R}^2$, using both a linear and logarithmic form. Only about 20 per cent of the variation in industry formation rates is explained by the included variables, but the values of $\bar{R}^2$ are significantly higher for NF_i^N where it is possible to identify a local index of job shedding than for other indices of formation. Of all variables included, the relationship between L_i^N and NF_i^N is the most striking. Of secondary interest is that in Table 5 there appears to be some

TABLE 5
Best fit equations: linear form[1]

	NF_i^N	NF_i^{NUK}	NF_i^{EM}	NF_i^{EMUK}
C	2·853 (2·969)	0·0362 (5·434)	0·9167 (5·256)	−0·053 (1·26)
π_i^{68}				0·1123 (1·91)
$^{99}\Delta\pi^{7076}$	−4·575 (1·135)	−0·023 (1·191)	−1·1053 (1·5064)	
L_i^{6876}		−0·0295 (1·844)	0·8671 (1·458)	
L_i^N	469·52 (2·974)			
X_i^L		−0·003 (1·176)		0·0161 (1·67)
$\bar{R}^2$	0·2599	0·2202	0·1368	0·1331

Notes: 1. 't' values in parenthesis.

TABLE 6
"Best" fit equations: log form[1]

	NF_i^N	NF_i^{NUK}	NF_i^{EM}	NF_i^{EMUK}
C	2·025 (2·142)	−3·653 (33·788)	−0·6916 (5·452)	−3·062 (6·553)
$^{99}\pi_i^{73}$				1·1103 (1·741)
$^{99}\Delta\pi_i^{7076}$	−0·3667 (1·4628)			
L_i^{6873}			−0·1143 (1·887)	
L_i^{6870}				0·1192 (1·802)
L_i^{6876}		0·0851 (1·358)		
L_i^N	0·2583 (2·582)			
X_i^L		−0·1331 (1·5665)		
$\bar{R}^2$	0·2326	0·1522	0·1094	0·2352

Notes: 1. 't' values in parenthesis.

50   D. J. STOREY AND A. M. JONES

support for the view that *increases* in industrial profitability in smaller business between 1970 and 1976 are associated with higher formation rates. However none of the coefficients in the equations is statistically significant, although each has a negative sign.

VII

CONCLUSIONS

This paper argues that a major local factor influencing the rate of new firm formation is the rate at which jobs are shed in that locality. The evidence presented shows that, at least for the Northern Region, there appears to be no association between changes in, or absolute national levels of, profitability in the *i*th industry and new firm formation rates in that industry. On the other hand formation rates in the *i*th industry in the Northern Region are positively correlated with job shedding in the region. It is not possible to identify an identical index of job shedding in the East Midlands where new firm formation rate data are also available, but the absence of any association between formation rates and national profitability data is again clear.

Even with stronger statistical associations, it could be argued that such an analysis is still compatible with conventional theory since the employment status of those starting the businesses is not given. However work undertaken by one of the present authors (Storey 1982) and by Binks and Jennings (1986) shows that between 25 per cent and 50 per cent of those starting new businesses claim to have been unemployed immediately prior to starting in business. Furthermore since these businesses were defined as being wholly new, i.e. not having more than 50 per cent of their share capital owned by any other enterprise, then their founders are certainly not existing asset holders buying up undervalued companies.

The evidence presented in this paper is not conclusive but it does suggest that local labour market conditions are of greater importance in influencing local rates of new firm formation than national indices of profitability.

REFERENCES

BAIN, J. S. (1956). *Barriers to New Competition.* Cambridge, U.S.A.: Harvard University Press.

BAYLDON, R., WOODS, A. and ZAFIRIS N. (1984). Inner City versus New Towns: A Comparison of Manufacturing Performance. *Oxford Bulletin of Economics and Statistics*, Vol. 46, No. 1, pp. 21–30.

BINKS, M. and JENNINGS A. (1986). *Small Firms as a source of Industrial Regeneration,* in J. CURRAN, J. STANWORTH and D. WATKINS (ed) *"The Survival of the Small Firm"*, Aldershot, Gower.

CAVES, R. E. and PORTER, M. E. (1977). From Entry Barriers to Mobility Barriers: Conjectural Decisions and Contrived Deterrence to New Competition. *Quarterly Journal of Economics*, Vol. 91, pp. 241–261.

CLARKE, R. (1985). *Industrial Economics.* Oxford: Basil Blackwell.

DAHMEN, E. (1970). *Entrepreneurial Activity and the Development of Swedish Industry 1919–1939.* Homewood, Illinois: Richard D. Irwin.

DEUTSCH, L. L. (1984). Entry and the extent of multiplant operations. *Journal of Industrial Economics,* Vol. 32, No. 4, June, pp. 477–487.

FOTHERGILL, S. and GUDGIN, G. (1982). *Unequal Growth.* London: Heinemann Educational Books.

FOTHERGILL, S., GUDGIN, G., KITSON, M. and MONK S. (1984). Differences in the Profitability of the U.K. Manufacturing Sector between conurbations and other Areas. *Scottish Journal of Political Economy,* Vol. 31, No. 1, February, pp. 72–91.

GORECKI, P. K. (1975). The Determinants of Entry by New and Diversifying Enterprises in the U.K. Manufacturing Sector 1958–1963: Some Tentative Results. *Applied Economics,* Vol. 7, pp. 139–147.

HENDERSON, R. A. (1980). An Analysis of Closures among Scottish Manufacturing Plants between 1966 and 1975. *Scottish Journal of Political Economy,* Vol. 27, pp. 152–174.

HYMER, S. and PASHIGAN, P. (1962). Firm Size and Rate of Growth. *Journal of Political Economy,* Vol. 70, pp. 556–569.

JOHNSON, P. S. and CATHCART, D. G. (1979). New Manufacturing Firms and Regional Development: Some Evidence from the Northern Region. *Regional Studies,* Vol. 13, pp. 269–280.

KIHLSTROM, R. E. and LAFFONT, J. (1979). A General Equilibrium Entrepreneurial Theory of Firm Formation Based on Risk Aversion. *Journal of Political Economy,* Vol. 87, pp. 719–748.

KNIGHT, F. H. (1921). *Risk, Uncertainty and profit.* New York: Houghton Mifflin.

LYONS, B. (1980). A New Measure of Minimum Efficient Plant Size in U.K. Manufacturing Industry. *Economica,* Vol. 47, pp. 19–34.

MANSFIELD, E. (1962). Entry, Gibrat's Law, Innovation and the Growth of Firms. *American Economic Review,* Vol. 52, pp. 1023–1051.

MARCUS, M. (1967). Firms' Exit Rates and their Determinants. *Journal of Industrial Economics,* Vol. 16, pp. 10–22.

ORR, D. (1974). The Determinants of Entry: a Study of the Canadian Manufacturing Industries. *The Review of Economics and Statistics,* Vol. 56, pp. 58–65.

OXENFELDT, A. R. (1943). *New Firms and Free Enterprise.* Washington, American Council on Public Affairs.

SAWYER, M. C. (1981). *The Economics of Industries and Firms.* London: Croom Helm.

SCHERER, F. M. (1980). *Industrial Market Structure and Economic Performance.* Chicago: Rand McNally.

STOREY, D. J. (1982). *Entrepreneurship and the New Firm.* London: Croom Helm.

STOREY, D. J., KEASEY, K., WATSON, R. and WYNARCZYK, P. (1987). The Performance of Small Firms. London: Croom Helm.

VAN DERCK, G. (1984). Entry, Exit and Profitability. *Managerial and Decision Economics,* Vol. 5, No. 1, pp. 25–31.

WATERSON, M. (1984). *Economic Theory of the Industry.* London: Cambridge University Press.

WEDERVANG, F. (1965). *Development of a Population of Industrial Firms.* Oslo: Scandinavian University Books.

[16]

International Journal of Industrial Organization 5 (1987) 51–66. North-Holland

NEW BUSINESS STARTS AND ECONOMIC ACTIVITY

An Empirical Investigation

Richard HIGHFIELD and Robert SMILEY*

Cornell University, Ithaca, NY 14853–4201, USA

Final version received November 1986

This paper identifies two types of factors that influence the rate of creation of new firms; macroeconomic and microeconomic. The macroeconomic climate that appears to be most conducive to the formation of small businesses is what might loosely be called sluggish. Lower rates of growth of GNP, lower inflation rates, and greater growth in the unemployment rate were followed by increases in the rate of new incorporations. The cross-sectional or micro-economic factors which lead to higher rates of entry into different industries include higher growth rates in sales, higher research and development intensity, and higher profit rates. We do not find any of the traditional barriers to entry to be related to the rate of new firm creation.

1. Introduction

What factors influence the rate of the new business starts? This question has been studied in some detail for other economies such as Sweden [Hause and DuRietz (1984)], and for sectors of the U.S. economy such as food [MacDonald (1986)], but never for the U.S. economy as a whole and never for a long period of time. This study presents the analysis of factors influencing the rate of new business starts in a large number of industries, and over a long period of time for the U.S. economy. A number of difficult methodological issues are confronted, and several improvements in empirical estimation techniques are presented.

The importance of understanding the determinants of new business activity should be obvious. An understanding of the dynamics of entry requires an understanding of the determinants of new firm creation as well as entry by existing firms [Caves and Porter (1977)]. Although there are some disputes about the exact numbers, recent empirical work indicates that new small

*Financial assistance for Robert Smiley was provided by the United States Small Business Administration under contract SBA-9241-OA-85. Robert Frank, Paul Geroski, Robert Hutchens, Bruce Phillips, and especially Robert Masson provided helpful comments on an earlier draft. We would like to thank Margaret Forster for excellent research assistance. The conclusions are the authors' and do not reflect official positions of the Small Business Administration.

business starts account for a large proportion of new job creation [Birch (1981)]. Furthermore, small business accounts for a disproportionately large amount of technical innovation [Scherer (1980, pp. 407–438)]. Finally, if economic policy makers should want to influence the rate of new business starts, they must first understand the interrelationships between policy variables and this rate.

In section 2 we present an analysis of the aggregate rate of new business starts (the new incorporations series) for the period 1947–1984. Section 3 presents an analysis of the determinants of new business starts across four-digit industries over the time period 1976–1981. A short conclusion section follows.

2. Time series analysis of new firm startups

One of the potentially confounding problems in cross-sectional industry studies of economic phenomena like entry is the existence of economy-wide factors that can affect behavior in all industries. The preferred method of examining such effects would be analysis of a pooled cross-section–time-series data set covering a sufficient number of data periods to allow modelling and testing of both the macro and industry-specific factors determining entry. In the present case our industry data are available for three two-year periods only, making inference regarding macro effects a practical impossibility. As an alternative we will present a basic analysis of economy-wide effects in this section using aggregate macro data, and will turn to the examination of industry-specific effects in the following section.

Our economy-wide entry variable to be explained is the quarterly growth rate (seasonally adjusted at annual rates) of the number of new U.S. incorporations over the period 1948 to 1984.[1] We use the growth rate in preference to the levels for two reasons. The first is that the number of new incorporations displays a strong upward trend that is quite similar to that of most real activity measures, and it is the deviations from this trend that are of interest. The second reason is a statistical one. The growth rate is approximately stationary[2] over the period studied and our techniques rely on the assumption of stationarity.

For potential explanatory variables we have gathered corresponding time series data on several macro variables which might reasonably be related to

---

[1]This data series is compiled monthly by Dun and Bradstreet from State government data. We compute the growth rate from as follows: $[\ln(INC_t) - \ln(INC_{t-1})] * 400$, where INC_t is the quarterly total.

[2]The concept of weak stationarity (or covariance stationarity) is all that is required here. A time series is weakly stationary if it has constant mean, constant variance and if the covariance between any two points in the series depends only on the amount of time separating them. These properties allow consistent estimation of the time series mean, variance, autocorrelations and cross-correlations with other stationary time series.

the rate of entry of new firms. These are the growth rate of real GNP, the growth rate of real expenditures on new plant and equipment,[3] the change in the unemployment rate, the inflation rate[4] and the real interest rate.[5] Again, all of these series are approximately stationary.

What type of business climate leads to a greater increase in the rate of formation of new firms? At least two different macroeconomic scenarios can be constructed that could lead to increases in new business activity. In a 'naive forecasting' scenario, individuals look at present rates of change and levels of important macroeconomic variables and forecast that these trends will continue. Further, individuals would prefer to start new business when the economy is robust. In this case, high rates of growth of new incorporations would accompany (or would lag by several quarters, since the process of incorporation requires some time) high rates of real GNP growth, low real interest rates, high inflation rates, high new plant and equipment expenditure growth and decreases in the unemployment rate.

An alternative scenario, with very different results, might be called an 'opportunistic' scenario. In this case entrepreneurs begin new business ventures when they sense an opportunity or vacuum in current economic activity. For example, a decrease in expenditures on new plant and equipment might present an opportunity or niche into which a new firm, with a newly constructed plant, might move. Similarly an increasing unemployment rate might indicate a lower cost of attracting qualified workers to a new venture, or even a lower opportunity cost of an entrepreneur's own salary foregone. In this scenario we would also expect low growth rates of real GNP, low rates of inflation, and high real interest rates to lead to increases in the rate of formation of new firms. 'Opportunity' and 'necessity' often have similar symptoms.

In our search for causal determinants of entry at the economy-wide level we will propose no structural model. Rather we will employ methods of statistical time series analysis and engage in a simple forecasting experiment. The concept is that models that incorporate data on causal factors should be able to forecast the growth of entry more accurately than models that do not. This is Granger's (1969) notion of causality, and it is based on the simple (albeit restrictive)[6] rule that the future cannot cause the past. It has been implemented extensively in macroeconomic studies on the role of money[7] and by Ashley, Granger and Schmalensee (1980) to examine the relationship between advertising and consumption.

As a first step in our analysis we have tabulated the sample cross-

---

[3] From the Bureau of Economic Analysis quarterly P&E survey.
[4] The rate of change in the implicit GNP deflator.
[5] Calculated as the quarterly average 90-day Treasury Bill rate less inflation.
[6] For a comprehensive discussion of causality in econometrics and economic theory, see Zellner (1978).
[7] See, for example, Sims (1972, 1977), Pierce (1977) and Feige and Pearce (1976).

correlations between our new incorporation growth time series and our macro data series. The cross-correlation between two stationary data series is

$$\rho_{XY} = \text{cov}(Y_{t+k}, X_t)/[\text{var}(X_t)\,\text{var}(Y_t)]^{\frac{1}{2}}, \tag{1}$$

i.e., $\rho_{XY}(k)$ is the correlation between Y and X, k periods earlier in time. In general $\rho_{YX}(k) \neq \rho_{YX}(-k)$. If X 'causes' Y but Y does not cause X we expect to find $\rho_{YX}(k) = 0$ for $k \leq -1$ (Y uncorrelated with future X's) but we also expect to find $\rho_{YX}(k) \neq \emptyset$ for some $k \geq 0$ (Y correlated with past X's).

Sample estimates of (1) were calculated according to Box and Jenkins (1976) and are tabulated in table 1 for data for the period 1948:3 through 1977:4. The remaining data were held back for a forecasting test discussed below. The picture painted is an interesting one. The growth rate of new incorporations is negatively correlated with measures of real activity in the prior year (real GNP and new plant expenditure growth) and positively

Table 1

Sample cross correlations of *DLINC* with various macro variables; period 1948:3 to 1977:4.[a]

	k	$SE(\hat{\rho}(k))$	Real GNP growth $\hat{\rho}(k)$	Real P&E exp. growth $\hat{\rho}(k)$	Unemp. rate changes $\hat{\rho}(k)$	Real int. rate $\hat{\rho}(k)$	Inflation $\hat{\rho}(k)$
Macro	−12	0.10	0.04	−0.05	−0.08	−0.08	0.05
variables	−11	0.10	0.04	−0.14	−0.01	−0.06	0.05
lagging	−10	0.10	−0.09	−0.24[b]	0.15	0.00	0.03
incorpora-	−9	0.10	−0.22[b]	−0.19	0.27[b]	0.16	−0.08
tion	−8	0.10	−0.30[b]	−0.09	0.23[b]	0.16	−0.09
growth	−7	0.10	−0.20	−0.03	0.18	0.10	−0.01
	−6	0.09	−0.18	0.09	0.07	0.04	0.05
	−5	0.09	−0.02	0.22[b]	0.01	0.07	0.04
	−4	0.09	−0.05	0.29[b]	−0.07	−0.09	0.15
	−3	0.09	0.13	0.31[b]	−0.21[b]	−0.13	0.16
	−2	0.09	0.23[b]	0.34[b]	−0.44[b]	−0.07	0.09
	−1	0.09	0.34[b]	0.11	−0.43[b]	−0.08	0.07
	0	0.09	0.25[b]	−0.13	−0.16	0.11	−0.14
Macro	1	0.09	0.00	−0.31[b]	0.25[b]	0.19[b]	−0.22[b]
variables	2	0.09	−0.31[b]	0.40[b]	0.45[b]	0.02	−0.09
leading	3	0.09	−0.32[b]	−0.44[b]	0.47[b]	0.09	−0.10
incorpora-	4	0.09	−0.30[b]	−0.10	0.21[b]	−0.02	0.04
tion	5	0.09	−0.07	0.01	−0.06	−0.11	0.15
growth	6	0.09	0.03	0.03	−0.06	−0.14	0.20[b]
	7	0.10	0.04	0.11	−0.07	−0.14	0.22[b]
	8	0.10	−0.03	0.04	−0.04	−0.16	0.23[b]
	9	0.10	−0.03	0.03	−0.01	−0.12	0.19
	10	0.10	−0.10	0.11	−0.07	0.01	0.07
	11	0.10	0.04	0.20	−0.08	−0.02	0.03
	12	0.10	0.06	0.11	−0.06	−0.04	0.05

[a] The large sample standard error of $\hat{\rho}(k)$ is $1/\sqrt{n-k}$, here $n = 118$.
[b] $\hat{\rho}(k)$ is greater than two standard deviations from zero.

correlated with these measures in the succeeding year.[8] The same picture is apparent in the cross correlations with the change in the unemployment rate and, somewhat weakly, with the real interest rate. Growth in the incorporation rate is positively associated with growing unemployment rates and higher real interest rates in the preceding year and with falling unemployment and lower interest rates in succeeding years. The cross-correlations with the inflation rate also indicate that periods of incorporation growth follow periods of lower inflation. Taken at face value, these results are generally consistent with the 'opportunistic' scenario. Firms may enter to fill the vacuum created by sluggish economic activity, with the result being that activity increases in later periods.[9]

The notion that slowing real activity causes incorporation growth should, however, not be accepted too readily. The fact that incorporation growth is correlated with real variables at both leads and lags suggests that these variables may in fact be jointly determined. This possibility was examined by computing the cross-correlations between the residuals from an ARMA model for each of the macro variables and the variable resulting when the incorporations series is filtered by the same model.[10] This procedure is designed to remove from the incorporation series any systematic movement that might be induced by the macro variable. If the remaining variation is still correlated at leads but uncorrelated at lags of the macro variable then a tentative inference of causality is possible. Only the inflation rate appears to lead (with the same signs as above) but not lag. Knowledge of the inflation rate may help increase the accuracy of forecasts of the incorporation growth rate, but the reverse is not expected to be true.

As was mentioned at the beginning of this section, one test of the notion that the macro variables discussed above play a role in determining incorporation growth is the predictive test. Indeed Ansley (1977) and Ashley,

[8]As our incorporation series represents all incorporations, both new firms and some established firms changing ownership structure, we cannot rule out the possibility that some of this relationship is attributable to owners acting to shield assets in bad times.

[9]The sample was also split in half and the analog to table 1 computed on both the earlier and later periods. The results for both periods give essentially the same impression as that given in table 1, with the earlier period results being slightly stronger than those above, and the later period slightly weaker. The real interest rate results are the only exception. The weak result above does not appear in the later period.

[10]This is called 'prewhitening' the series by Box and Jenkins (1976). Suppose $\phi(B)X_t = \theta(B)e_t$ represents a standard ARMA (p,q) for a model covariance stationary series X_t (one of our macro variables), where $\phi(B) = 1 - \phi_1 B - \cdots - \phi_p B_t^p$, $\theta(B) = 1 - \theta_1 B - \cdots - \theta_q B_t^q$, B is the backshift (or lag) operator such that $BX_t = X_{t-1}$ and e_t represents a zero mean, constant variance noise process. The prewhitened incorporation growth series a_t is calculated as $a_t = \theta^{-1}(B)\phi(B)(\text{incorporation growth})_t$. Thus systematic variation in incorporation growth directly induced by systematic variation in X_t is removed. What remains includes systematic variation induced by even random variation in X_t. Of course, if the only channel by which X_t affects or 'causes' incorporation growth is through its systematic (forecastable) variation then we are throwing the baby out with the bath.

Granger and Schmalensee (1980) have argued quite convincingly that cross-correlation analysis is better viewed as a tool for identifying forecasting models (in the sense that a time series analyst identifies the best forecasting model from within a class of possible models) and that post-sample forecasting tests are more appropriate for investigating causality. Here some simple models for forecasting incorporation growth have been devised. The first, which can be considered a benchmark, is a univariate ARMA model for incorporation growth. Such a model will set a level of predictive accuracy that can be expected from forecasting this variable on the basis of its own past alone. Of course, since an ARMA model is a purely statistical model, the form of the model chosen may depend indirectly on all factors determining incorporation growth.[11] To the extent that the factors we have chosen to focus on here are particularly important in determining entry, we would expect to improve upon the performance of the ARMA model.

The evidence from a simple forecasting competition is presented in table 2. One-step-ahead out-of-sample forecasts of the growth rate of incorporations were made for the 28 quarters 1978:1 through 1984:4 using several simple forecasting models.[12] The results of the ARMA forecasts are given on line 1 of the table. The competing models attempted are a univariate transfer function model involving the inflation rate as an exogenous explanatory variable (an idea supported by the cross-correlation analysis above), three

Table 2

Summary of forecasting results; one-step-ahead out-of-sample forecasts of incorporation growth for the period 1978:1 through 1984:4.

Forecasting model	Mean absolute forecast error	Root mean squared forecast error
1. Univariate ARMA model	12.05	14.78
2. Transfer function model input variable: inflation rate	11.85	14.64
3. Bivariate ARMA model incorporation growth and real GNP growth	11.37	14.67
4. Bivariate ARMA model incorporation growth and unemployment rate changes	11.03	14.48
5. Bivariate ARMA model incorporation growth and growth in new plant and equipment expenditures	12.41	16.17
6. Vector autoregression involving incorporation growth, inflation, real GNP growth, unemployment rate changes and growth in new plant and equipment expenditures	11.29	14.93

[11]This fact often goes unrecognized as an explanation of the fact that ARMA forecasts are often competitive with or even superior to forecasts from complex econometric models.

[12]I.e., each model was estimated using data from the period 1948:3 to 1977:4. Future incorporation growth was then predicted, the model updated to include data for 1978:1, another prediction was made, the model updated again, and so on.

separate bivariate ARMA models relating incorporation growth to real GNP growth, the change in the unemployment rate and new plant and equipment expenditure growth, and a vector autoregression involving all five variables. Only the transfer function model involving the inflation rate reflects a strict causal ordering. All of the other models assume joint causation (i.e., they include no exogeneity restrictions).[13] No model relating the real interest rate and incorporation growth was suggested by our analysis.

As seen, none of the models achieves dramatic improvements over the univariate model for incorporation growth. The best model, the bivariate ARMA model with unemployment rate changes, achieves about a 9% reduction in mean absolute forecast error, but a somewhat smaller reduction in root mean squared error, indicating the presence of some large forecasting errors. The second best model, the bivariate ARMA model with real GNP growth, achieves a 6.4% reduction in mean absolute forecast error, and also reduces the root mean squared error by a smaller amount. The coefficients in both models imply the same relationship as indicated by the cross-correlation results. Increases in the unemployment rate and decreases in real GNP growth lead increases in incorporation growth. While a tentative causal relationship appeared in the cross-correlation analysis of the inflation rate, the forecasting improvement achieved by the transfer function model is quite slight.

Although the evidence is by no means overwhelming, the business climate apparently most hospitable to new firm incorporation has not been a robust one: sluggish economic growth seems more likely to spur creation of new firms. The magnitude of the forecasting improvements indicates, however, that most of the variation in growth in incorporations remains unexplained and that none of the macro variables appears to be strongly causal in the sense of Granger. Policy implications are not strong in this setting. Certainly few would suggest the bizarre policy of slowing the economy down in order to create a better climate for new business. What is apparent, however, is an indication that higher incorporation growth goes hand in hand with an economy changing from the worse to the better. This might suggest that further incentives for new business formation could speed recoveries, but we have made no attempt to examine causality in this direction.

3. Entry determinants at the micro level – Cross-sectional relationships

The factors affecting the rate of entry by new firms into different industries are discussed in this section. The section is organized as follows: a model of

---

[13]In identifying and estimating the transfer function models and bivariate ARMA models we have followed the suggestions of Box and Jenkins (1976) and Tiao and Box (1981), respectively. To estimate the vector autoregression, which involves eight lags of each of the five variables, we employ the Bayesian techniques of Litterman (1984) and Highfield (1984).

the entry process is presented first, followed by a discussion of the measurement of the variables. The empirical results are presented last.

3.1. A model of entry

The rate of entry E_{it} by new firms into industry i in time period t is modeled as a function of the predicted future profit rate Π_{it} and the entry forestalling profit rate Π_{it}^N,

$$E_{it} = f(\Pi_{it} - \Pi_{it}^N) + \mu,\tag{2}$$

where

$f(0) = 0$ by the definition of entry forestalling,
$\Pi_{it} = \Pi(\Pi_{it}^{PAST}, GROWTH, RDEXP)$,
$\Pi_{it}^N = \Pi^N ADS, EXCAPEXP, MESMKT, CAPREQ, RISK, CONC, RDEXP)$,
μ = all entry orthogonal to excess profits.

Π_{it}^{PAST}:	past profit rates in industry i,
GROWTH:	past sales growth,
RDEXP:	research and development expenditures as a percentage of sales,
ADS:	advertising expenditures as a percentage of sales,
MESMKT:	the ratio of the plant size necessary to achieve minimum efficient scale, to the size of the market,
CAPREQ:	the investment necessary to build a plant of minimum efficient scale,
CAPEXP:	new capital expenditures as a percentage of net plant,
EXCAPEXP:	*CAPEXP—GROWTH*,
RISK:	a measure of the risk of entry,
CONC:	the four firm concentration ratio.

3.2. Discussion

Π_{it}: Predicted post-entry profits are a positive function (Π) of past profits, growth in sales and research and development expenditures. We will test different functional forms for the relationship between past and predicted future profit rates in the paper, but we would expect the overall relationship to be positive. We would expect future profits to be greater and entry more frequent in industries that are growing more rapidly (*GROWTH*).

A high rate of technical progress in an industry will also indicate a dynamic and evolving situation, and thus might attract new entrants seeking to discover and develop new products and processes. A high ratio of expenditure on research and development to sales ($RDEXP$) would indicate a technologically dynamic industry and signal new entrants.

Π_{it}^N: The entry forestalling profit rate is the highest long run profit rate that will not attract entry. Barriers to entry would positively affect the entry forestalling profit rate, and negatively affect the rate of entry, ceteris paribus.[14] The traditional barriers are the ratio of advertising expenditures to sales (ADS), the proportion of industry sales required to operate a plant of minimum efficient scale ($MESMKT$), and the amount of capital required to build a plant of minimum efficient scale ($CAPREQ$).

We also attempt to account for the possibility that some incumbent firms may be attempting to preempt the market through capacity expansion [Spence (1977)]. $CAPEXP$ measures capital expenditures lagged one year divided by net plant. Preemption attempts should be indicated when expenditures on plant and equipment exceed industry growth ($EXCAPEXP$).

Risk averse potential entrants will be deterred by high investment risk. We measure risk in two ways. $RISK$ is the average variance for industry firms in profits (after taxes as percentage of stockholder's equity) over the five years prior to the period in question. The second risk variable, $BAYRISK$, is a measure of the variability in predicted profits derived from a profit forecasting model discussed below. These are reasonable risk measures for individuals whose investment portfolios are *not* well diversified, which would seem an appropriate description of an individual starting up a new business.[15]

Concentration ($CONC$) and research intensity ($RDEXP$) could, in theory, attract or deter entry. Orr (1974) feels that '... when entering highly concentrated industries, the potential entrant must also consider the possibility that established firms may collude to thwart his entry.' Baron's (1973) model predicts that *lower* concentration may deter entry since a symmetric post entry equilibrium would imply smaller size and a higher likelihood that the entrant will be forced to operate below minimum efficient scale.[16] The possibility that high R&D expenditures might be correlated with frequent entry is discussed above. But new entrants into research intensive industries must also raise more risky financial capital, and the difficulty and cost of assembling the necessary human capital may also deter entry.

3.3. Measures of the variables

The U.S. Small Business Administration has been compiling entry statistics by four-digit industries only since 1976. The data, which originate from Dun

---

[14]See Bain (1956) and Demsetz (1982) for different points of view regarding barriers to entry.

[15]If an individual is perfectly well diversified, we would want to use the industry beta.

[16]See Masson and Shaanan (1986, pp. 4–5) for a thorough discussion of concentration and entry.

and Bradstreet, are available in two-year increments – 1976–77, 1978–79 and 1980–81.[17] Our entry measures are taken for these three time periods.

The entry rate ($Entry_{it}$) is simply the number of new firms formed in industry i within the time period t, divided by the number of firms in existence in the industry at the beginning of the period. This variable is then transformed as follows:

$$\text{Relative entry rate}_{it} = Entry_{it} - \overline{Entry_t}, \tag{3}$$

where $\overline{Entry_t}$ is the average entry rate across all industries i for period t. This transformation should control for any economy-wide factors (in the separate time periods) affecting entry rates. Problems of econometric estimation are also avoided since (unlike $Entry_{it}$), the Relative entry rate is unbounded.

The independent variables $PROFIT_{it}$, ADS_{it}, $RDEXP_{it}$, $CAPEXP_{it}$ and $RISK_{it}$ are taken from the Compustat tape. In the case of the first four variables, the observations are lagged one year (i.e., for the 1980–1981 period, ADS_{it} is observed in 1979). $PROFIT_{it}$ is after tax income less extraordinary items and discontinued operations, summed for each firm in industry i, and then divided by the sum of equity capital for industry i firms. $RDEXP_{it}$ and ADS_{it} are the sums of research and development expenditures and advertising expenditures as a proportion of sales. $CAPEXP_{it}$ is the sum of capital expenditures divided by the sum of net plant for firms in the ith industry.

In addition to using a simple lagged profits variable to predict future profits (and thus to signal entry), we have developed a somewhat more sophisticated measure of expected profitability.[18] We have formulated a simple forecasting model for profits which has been applied to each industry.

$$PROFIT_{it} = C + \alpha_1 PROFIT_{it-1} + \alpha_2 PROFIT_{it-2} + e_t. \tag{4}$$

The model is a Bayesian implementation of an autoregressive model in which profits in any period are related in a linear way to profits in the two preceding periods: where e_t is a zero mean, normally distributed error term. Forecasts from this model were generated iteratively[19] beginning in 1974, using annual data, and the forecasts for the years 1976, 1978 and 1980 (called $BAYPROF_{it}$)[20] were used as independent variables.

---

[17]The problems of classifying multiproduct firms into four-digit industries are well known. Aside from modifying national concentration ratios as discussed below, we have made no modifications to the official SIC classification scheme since we were (ultimately) constrained by Dun and Bradstreet's use of existing codes.

[18]Expectations regarding future profitability are also affected by $GROWTH$ and $RDEXP$, in addition to past profit rates.

[19]By 'iterative' we mean that no future data were used in the generation of the profit forecasts. They are true forecasts, not fitted values from the model.

[20]Our profit series for each industry begins in 1971, leaving very few observations with which to estimate the model. A Bayesian method of estimation was employed to overcome this

$BAYRISK_{it}$ is the variance of the predictive distribution of profits (where $BAYPROF_{it}$ is the mean). Due to its autoregressive nature, the model (3) will account for any time trend in profits. $BAYRISK_{it}$ will then be a risk measure taken after accounting for any underlying time trend.

The sources for the remaining variables are the various censuses.[21] $GROWTH_{it}$ is the annual growth rate in sales or value of shipments from 1972–1977. $MESMKT$ is the ratio of the average sales per establishment for establishments in the median size class, to sales for the industry for the year 1977. $CAPREQ$ is $MESMKT$ multiplied by total assets for the industry, for the year 1977. $CONC_{it}$ is the four firm concentration ratio. We have modified $CONC_{it}$ according to Schwartzman and Bodoff (1971) by first identifying the industries for which a national concentration ratio is not appropriate, since markets are regional or local. For these seven industries, we then added Schwartzman and Bodoff's estimates of the difference between average regional (or local) and national rates to our 1977 national rates. The resulting $CONC_{it}$ should adequately reflect national, regional and local concentration, where appropriate.

3.4. Estimation techniques and results

The basic results reported in this section are regressions in which we have pooled observations from the three time periods in our sample. As the independent variable is cross-sectional in nature, there is the possibility that omitted macroeconomic factors can bias the results. To the extent that these economy-wide factors affect entry in a similar way in all industries, we can control for these macro effects by subtracting the mean entry rate $Entry_t$ from the observed, industry specific, entry rate $Entry_{it}$.

The results for the data set that includes measures for all independent variables are presented in table 3. Data are available for one or more time periods for forty industries (four-digit), nearly all of which are manufacturing.[22]

The hypothesis tests are consistent with the finding that high industry growth strongly attracts entry by new firms. This finding is similar to the results of Hause and DuRietz (1984) for Swedish manufacturing industries. Although the F test indicates that the regression equation is clearly significant, the significance of the remaining coefficients is quite limited.

---

problem. Given the data through 1973 we assume a normal prior distribution on profits in 1974. The mean of this distribution being zero and its standard deviation being 0.5 (i.e., a profit or loss rate of 50% of equity capital is one standard deviation from the mean). Using this very spread out distribution as our starting point we infer a prior distribution for the parameters of eq. (3).

[21]Source: U.S. Bureau of the Census (1972, 1977).

[22]See table A.1 in the appendix for the industries included.

Table 3

115 observations; dependent variable: relative entry rate$_{it}$.

Independent variable	Coefficient	Standard error	T statistic
Constant	−0.035987	0.016084	−2.237475
BAYPROF	−0.244044	0.564525	−0.432300
ADS	−0.184650	0.175784	−1.050439
EXCAPEXP	0.029984	0.038803	0.772736
RDEXP	0.374736	0.24009	1.560756
RISK	−0.013461	0.008561	−1.572244
GROWTH	0.360785	0.072860	4.951744[a]
CONC	−0.000262	0.000187	−1.398997
MESMKT	0.311990	0.225176	1.385541
CAPREQ	0.000042	0.000081	0.519121

$$\bar{R}^2 = 0.322,\ F(10, 105) = 7.0241$$

[a]Statistically significant at 1%.

There is marginal support for the hypothesis that industries characterized by high R&D expenditures to sales ratios also experience higher rates of entry. Rather than acting as a barrier to entry, research intensity in an industry seems to attract entry by new firms. *RISK*, which measures the variance of past profits, also has the hypothesized sign and is marginally significant ($P = 11.9\%$, two tailed test). High profit rates in the periods prior to the time period of observation do not appear to signal new entry. None of the other coefficients on the deterrents or barriers to entry are statistically significant.[23]

Alternative methods for estimating expected future profits and investment risk were described above. When the equation in table 3 was estimated using *PROFIT*$_{it}$ (lagged profits) and *BAYRISK*$_{it}$ (the predicted variance in profits), neither coefficient was significantly different from zero, and the only major result affected was that *RDEXP* was no longer even marginally significant.

The sample size can be substantially enlarged by eliminating independent variables with missing values. In table 4, the variables *ADS, CONC* and *CAPREQ* have been dropped and 20 industries (61 observations) have been added, mostly in natural resource extraction and services. The findings are much stronger than those in table 3: entry occurs much more frequently in research intensive, rapidly growing industries.

There is also a substantial difference in the explanatory power of the profit variable. The Bayesian profit forecast, *BAYPROF*, is positively and significantly related to the subsequent rate of entry by new firms. The profit forecast using simple lagged profits (*PROFIT*$_{it}$) and the alternative risk measure

[23]These observations are consistent with most of the findings of MacDonald (1986) for food industries.

Table 4

176 observations; dependent variable: relative entry rate$_{it}$.

Independent variable	Coefficient	Standard error	T statistic
Constant	−0.029400	0.007565	−3.886144
BAYPROF	0.257411	0.056791	4.532634[a]
EXCAPEXP	0.003874	0.007649	0.506519
RDEXP	0.219136	0.096291	2.275763[b]
GROWTH	0.295167	0.044189	6.679606[a]
MESMKT	−0.067678	0.112233	−0.603017
RISK	−0.001167	0.006799	−0.171614

$$\bar{R}^2 = 0.316, \; F(7, 169) = 14.5$$

[a]Statistically significant at 1%.
[b]Statistically significant at 5%.

were substituted for *BAYPROF* and *RISK* in regressions not reported here. Neither was significantly different from zero at the 10% level. So with this more extensive industry coverage, the Bayesian autoregressive forecasting technique dominates a simple lagged profit forecast.[24] Entrepreneurs do use previously available profit information in deciding whether to risk their capital, but they use it in a sophisticated fashion.

4. Summary and conclusions

This paper contributes to the industrial organization literature on entry through enabling us to better understand what economic conditions are more hospitable to the creation of new firms, and through application of new methods to better understand these complex relationships. We have identified two types of factors that influence the rate of creation of new firms: macroeconomic and microeconomic factors. Although the evidence is somewhat weak, the macroeconomic climate that appears to be most conducive to the formation of small businesses is what might loosely be called sluggish. Lower rates of growth of GNP, lower inflation rates, and greater growth in the unemployment rate were followed by increases in the rate of new incorporations. These new incorporations in turn tend to lead periods of more robust economic activity. The cross-sectional or microeconomic factors which affect rates of entry into different industries include higher growth rates in sales, higher research and development intensity, and higher profit

[24]The regression in table 4 was also run with the smaller data set used in table 3. I.e., the table 3 regression was run with *ADS, CONC* and *CAPREQ* eliminated. The results for the remaining variables are quite similar to those reported in table 3 indicating that the significance of *BAYPROF* in table 4 is due to the expanded data set, not the elimination of the three variables.

rates. We do not find any of the traditional barriers to entry to be related to the rate of new firm creation.

Putting the time series and cross-sectional results together, we have a consistent and interesting picture of entry through the creation of new firms. Individuals decide to form new firms when economic conditions are relatively poor – but they decide to enter industries which are dynamic and robust, as measured by technical progressivity and profitability.

We have utilized some time series techniques which appear to be new to the industrial organization literature. After observing the patterns of leads and lags of new incorporation activity as they are correlated with leads and lags of important macroeconomic variables, we investigate whether knowledge of these macroeconomic variables will allow us to improve on forecasts of the new incorporations growth rate. In the cross-sectional study, we conclude that the lack of relationship in other studies [e.g., McDonald (1986), Orr (1974)] between the profit rate and subsequent new business creation is the result of lack of sophistication in modeling entrepreneurs' expectations about future profit rates.[25] The Bayesian autoregressive model we used to forecast future profit rates seems to indicate quite clearly that present profit rates do influence future entry.

[25]But see Masson and Shaanan (1986).

Appendix

Table A.1

Industries used in analysis.

SIC code	Industry description
Industries used in table 3	
2041	Flour and other grain mill products
2046	Wet corn milling
2065	Confectionary products
2082	Malt beverages
2086	Bottled and canned soft drinks
2121	Cigars
2711	Newspapers
2761	Manifold business forms
2834	Pharmaceutical preparations
2841	Soap and other detergents
2844	Toilet preparations
2911	Petroleum refining
3079	Miscellaneous plastic products
3221	Glass containers
3241	Cement, hydraulic
3443	Fabricated plate work, boiler shops
3444	Sheet metal work
3452	Bolts, nuts, rivets, and washers

R. Highfield and R. Smiley, Rate of new business starts 65

Table A.1 (continued)

SIC code	Industry description
3494	Valves and pipe fittings
3531	Construction machinery
3533	Oilfield machinery
3622	Industrial controls
3651	Radio and TV receiving sets
3662	Radio and TV communication equipment
3674	Semiconductors and related devices
3693	X-ray apparatus and tubes
3711	Motor vehicle and car bodies
3714	Motor vehicle parts and accessories
3721	Aircraft
3811	Engineering and scientific instruments
3823	Process control instruments
3825	Instruments to measure electricity
3841	Surgical and medical instruments
3842	Surgical appliances and supplies
3861	Photographic equipment and supplies
3914	Silverware and plated ware
3931	Musical instruments
5012	Automobiles and other motor vehicles
5065	Electronic parts and electronic communication equipment
8911	Engineering and architectural services

Additional industries used in table 4

1021	Copper ores
1211	Bituminous coal and lignite
1311	Crude petroleum and natural gas
1381	Drilling oil and gas wells
1382	Oil and gas exploration services
2111	Cigarettes
3442	Metal doors, sash, and trim
3661	Telephone and telegraph apparatus
5093	Scrap and waste materials – wholesale
5211	Lumber and other building materials – retail
5411	Grocery stores – retail
5712	Furniture stores
5812	Eating places – retail
7011	Hotels, rooming houses, camps, and other lodging places
7372	Computer programming and other software services
7374	Data processing and computer facilities management
7391	Research and development laboratories
7392	Consulting services
7393	Protective services
7395	Photofinishing laboratories

References

Ansley, C.F., 1977, Report on the NBER–NSF seminar on time series, Mimeo. (Graduate School of Business, University of Chicago, IL).

Ashley, R., C.W.J. Granger and R. Schmalensee, 1980, Advertising and aggregate consumption: An analysis of causality, Econometrica 48, no. 5, 1149–1167.

Bain, Joe S., 1956, Barriers to new competition (Harvard University Press, Cambridge, MA).

Baron, David, 1973, Limit pricing, potential entry and barriers to entry, American Economic Review, Sept., 666–674.

Birch, David L., 1981, Who creates jobs?, The Public Interest.

Box, G.E.P. and G.M. Jenkins, 1976, Time series analysis – Forecasting and control (Holden-Day, San Francisco, CA).

Caves, Richard and Michael Porter, 1977, From entry barriers to mobility barriers: Conjectural decisions and contrived deterrence to new competition, Quarterly Journal of Economics 91, 241–261.

Demsetz, Harold, 1982, Barriers to entry, American Economic Review, March, 47–57.

Feige, E.L. and D.K. Pearce, 1976, Economically rational expectations: Are innovations in the rate of inflation independent of innovations in measures of monetary and fiscal policy?, Journal of Political Economy 84, June, 449–552.

Granger, C.W.J., 1969, Investigating causal relations by econometric models and cross-spectral methods, Econometrica 37, July, 424–438.

Hause, John C. and Gunnar DuRietz, 1984, Entry, industry growth and the microdynamics of industry supply, Journal of Political Economy 92, no. 4.

Highfield, R.A., 1984, Forecasting with Bayesian state space models, Technical report (H.G.B. Alexander Research Foundation, Graduate School of Business, University of Chicago, IL).

Litterman, Robert B., 1984, Specifying vector autoregressions for macroeconomic forecasting, Research Department Staff Report no. 92 (Federal Reserve Bank of Minneapolis, Minneapolis, MN).

MacDonald, James M., 1986, Entry and exit on the competitive fringe, Southern Economic Journal 52, no. 3.

Masson, Robert T. and Joseph Shaanan, 1986, Optimal pricing and the threat of entry: Canadian evidence, Working paper (Cornell University, Ithaca, NY).

Orr, Dale, 1974, The determinants of entry: A study of the Canadian manufacturing industries, Review of Economics and Statistics, Feb., 58–66.

Pierce, D.A., 1977, Relationships – and the lack thereof – between economic time series, with special reference to money and interest rates, Journal of the American Statistical Association 72, March, 11–21.

Scherer, Frederic M., 1980, Industrial market structure and economic performance, 2nd ed. (Rand McNally, Chicago, IL).

Schwartzman, David and Joan Bodoff, 1971, Concentration in regional and local industries, Southern Economic Journal 37, Jan., 343–348.

Sims, C.A., 1972, Money, income and causality, American Economic Review LXII, Sept., 540–552.

Sims, C.A., 1977, Exogeneity and causal ordering in macroeconomic models, in: C.A. Sims, ed., New methods in business cycle research: Proceedings from a conference (Federal Reserve Bank of Minneapolis, Minneapolis, MN) 23–43.

Spence, A. Michael, 1977, Entry, capacity, investment and oligopolistic pricing, Bell Journal of Economics 8, Autumn, 534–544.

Standard and Poor's, 1984, Annual industrial compustat tape.

Tiao, G.C. and G.E.P. Box, 1981, Modeling multiple time series with applications, Journal of the American Statistical Association 76, 802–816.

U.S. Bureau of the Census, Census of manufacturers – 1972, Census of retail trade – 1972, Census of wholesale trade – 1972, Census of mineral industries – 1972, Census of construction industries – 1972, Census of service industries – 1972 (Washington, DC).

U.S. Bureau of the Census, Census of manufacturers – 1977, Census of retail trade – 1977, Census of wholesale trade – 1977, Census of mineral industries – 1977, Census of construction industries – 1977, Census of service industries – 1977 (Washington, DC).

Zellner, Arnold, 1978, Causality and econometrics, in: K. Brunner and A.H. Meltzer, eds., Three aspects of policy and policymaking, Carnegie–Rochester Conference Series on Public Policy, Vol. 10 (North-Holland, Amsterdam) 9–54.

[17]

Economica, **56**, 255-65

Small-firm Entry in US Manufacturing

By Zoltan J. Acs and David B. Audretsch

Wissenschaftszentrum für Sozialforschung Berlin

Final version received 9 May 1988. Accepted 12 July 1988.

A cross-section empirical analysis examining the entry behaviour of small firms is provided in this paper. While we find that certain traditional market structure characteristics and entry barriers have a strong impact on small-firm entry behaviour, the reliance upon innovative strategy by small firms also explains a significant amount of the variation in the pattern of entry by small firms. We conclude that small-firm entry is at least partially determined by entry barriers, industry-specific characteristics facilitating retaliatory conduct by incumbent firms, and the reliance upon innovative strategy by small firms.

INTRODUCTION

Despite the emergence of an empirical literature (Geroski, 1983) regarding the importance of entry, most of these studies either have focused on the entry of relatively large firms or else have not distinguished between different firm sizes.[1] That is, the determinants of small-firm entry have not been examined as a distinct entity from that of large firms. Because a growing field in the literature suggests that small firms, considered in an absolute rather than a relative sense, may be behaviourly distinct and unique from their larger counterparts (Mills and Schumann, 1985; Carlsson, 1986), there is little reason to assume that small-firm entry is an exact replica of that of larger rivals. The purpose of this paper is to fill this gap in the literature and to examine the extent and determinants of small-firm entry in manufacturing industries.[2]

There are three contributions in this study. First, we examine the pattern of small-firm entry, as distinct from entry by all firms or by large firms, over manufacturing industries. Second, while most of the empirical studies have been restricted to examining market structure characteristics in explaining entry, we are able to include measures of small-firm strategy, and in particular the small-firm innovation rate, as a determinant of small-firm entry. Finally, we are able to implement the empirical analysis utilizing a complete cross-section of 247 manufacturing industries for small-firm net entry between 1978 and 1980. This is facilitated by using data newly released by the US Small Business Administration. We are able to test for the robustness of our econometric results and inferences with respect to different definitions and measures of what constitutes a small firm, ranging from fewer than 10 employees to just under 500 employees.

In Section I below, we briefly review the general results of the studies examining the determinants of entry for all firm sizes and suggest why small-firm entry may be a distinct phenomenon. In Section III we use six different measures of what constitutes a small firm to test the hypothesis that small-firm entry emanates from three major sources: (1) the positive inducement from industries with high growth and a high technological opportunity; (2) the absence of barriers impeding entry; and (3) the reliance of small firms on strategies enhancing the ease of entry. Finally, in Section IV a summary and conclusions are presented. We find that small-firm entry is facilitated in those industries where the inherent scale disadvantages of small firms have been diminishing over time and where small firms have been able to implement a strategy of innovation. While other studies have found that R and D intensity actually promotes the entry of firms in general, we find that it clearly hinders the entry of small firms. In addition, while small-firm entry is not influenced by advertising expenditures, lagged profitability has no apparent effect on the entry behaviour of the smallest firms. Thus, small-firm entry is found to vary considerably from the pattern of large-firm entry that has emerged in the empirical entry literature. Finally, small firms tend to enter industries that are not dominated by small firms.

I. ENTRY BY LARGE AND SMALL FIRMS

Virtually every empirical study examining entry behaviour has considered the entry either of all new firms in an industry (generally approximated by the changes in the numbers of firms over a specific period or net entry) or else only of larger firms. While the results of these studies have not been unequivocal, certain tendencies have emerged. Theoretical models have predicted entry to be positively induced by high profits and growth (Bhagwati, 1970) and deterred in the presence of structural barriers such as capital intensity (Bain, 1956), and 'behavioural' barriers such as advertising intensity (Stone-breaker, 1976).

In fact, entry has been found to be positively related to growth in most studies (Orr, 1974; Gorecki, 1975; Duetsch, 1984; Khemani and Shapiro, 1986; and Highfield and Smiley, 1987). Most of these studies also found lagged profits to exert a positive influence on subsequent entry, with the exception of Orr (1974), who considered only the net entry of firms with either sales exceeding $5 million or assets exceeding $25 million, and Highfield and Smiley (1987). While Duetsch (1984) and Khemani and Shapiro (1986) found capital intensity to exert a negative influence on the entry of firms of all sizes, Highfield and Smiley (1987) found no such relationship. Similarly, both Orr (1974) and Khemani and Shapiro (1986) found advertising to be a significant barrier to entry of firms of all sizes, but neither Duetsch (1984) nor Highfield and Smiley (1987) identified the existence of a significant relationship. While market concentration is generally predicted to exert a negative influence on entry, most studies have not substantiated this.[3] Similarly, the existence of a high technological opportunity class has been hypothesized to induce entry[4] (Smiley, 1988), but only Highfield and Smiley (1987) have found evidence supporting this. Based on a number of empirical studies, it can reasonably be concluded that the entry of all firm sizes appears to take place in rapidly growing industries with relatively high price–cost margins and low advertising intensity, and where there is a relatively high level of technological opportunity or R and D intensity.

Although there has been to date no examination of the determinants of small-firm entry, several distinctions from the general pattern of entry might be expected to emerge.[5] First, while there is ambiguity between the pattern of entry for large firms or all firm sizes and capital intensity, small-firm entry would be expected to be impeded in the presence of high capital barriers. As White (1982) found, the existence of small firms is negatively related to capital intensity. Similarly, while Highfield and Smiley (1987) argue that the start-up of new firms is induced in high R and D industries, small-firm entry would be expected to be deterred in high R and D industries. As virtually every empirical study has shown, small firms face a severe scale disadvantage with respect to R and D (Mansfield, 1981; Kamien and Schwartz, 1975). Nor does it seem likely that profitability and advertising intensity would play as large a role in inducing and deterring small-firm entry as for large firms, since the entry of small firms is often in certain product niches within the industry. This is supported by Storey and Jones (1987), who found that local labour market conditions are more decisive than profitability in influencing local rates of new-firm formation.

There is some evidence that small firms pursue different strategies from their larger counterparts in order to survive in the same industries with larger firms (Caves and Pugel, 1980; Mills and Schumann, 1985). Implementing such strategies enables small firms to compensate for size-inherent disadvantages and the entry-deterring strategies by existing firms (Yip, 1982). One such example is the strategy of product innovation, which Caves and Pugel (1980) find to be one important strategy that small firms deploy to overcome inherent scale disadvantages.

Finally, a recent literature has emerged arguing that, through the application of 'flexible specialization' in certain industries, small firms have been able to enter and exist in markets where they previously would have experienced severe scale disadvantages (Mills and Schumann, 1985; Carlsson, 1987; Piore and Sabel, 1984).[6] To the extent to which small firms are able to employ 'flexible production' techniques, the inherent scale disadvantage of small firms would be reduced, enabling them to enter the industry more easily.

II. EMPIRICAL MODEL

The empirical model to be estimated is

$$SFE = \beta_1 GR + \beta_2 PCM + \beta_3 KL + \beta_4 AD + \beta_5 RD + \beta_6 SKILL + \beta_7 CR$$
$$+ \beta_8 SFIR + \beta_9 UNION + \beta_{10} CRSFP + \beta_{11} SFP + \mu$$

where the dependent variable is defined as the change in the number of firms with fewer than 500 employees between 1978 and 1980, divided by the average total number of firms in the industry in 1978 and 1980.[7] Unlike most other empirical entry studies, the US Small Business Administration data refer only to new enterprises (firms) and not just to new subsidiaries or branches (establishments) of existing firms.[8] Highfield and Smiley (1987), using the same data set for all firm sizes, used a similar net entry rate measure.[9]

Several qualifications must be made concerning the use of the net change in the number of firms over a specified time period as a measure of entry. First, this is a measure of net entry, which obscures the actual amount of gross entry occurring in each industry by adding in the number of firms that exited. The extent to which net entry deviates from actual entry depends upon the extent of exit in the industry. However, as for Orr (1974) and Duetsch (1984), data constraints do not enable us to control for industry exit. While Duetsch controlled for industry size by including the value-of-shipments as an explanatory variable in his regression analysis estimating the number of new entrants (of all sizes), we control for size by transforming the net entry measure into a net entry rate measure by dividing the dependent variable by the average number of firms, of all sizes, in the industry. This is the identical procedure used by Highfield and Smiley (1987). Thus, the small-firm entry rate measures the amount of small-firm net entry as a percentage of the total number of firms in the industry.[10] Using just the number of firms in the industry in either 1978 or 1980 in the denominator produced virtually identical regression results. The small-firm entry rate varies between -1 and 1, but because it approximates a normal distribution, with no industries taking on either of the extreme values, the method of ordinary least squares would not result in any considerable inefficient estimation (Judge *et al.*, 1980).

   GR refers to the 1972-77 industry growth rate of value-of-shipments. As has been found in the empirical literature for large firms, we expect that a positive relationship should emerge between lagged market growth and small-firm entry. *PCM* is defined as the 1977 industry price–cost margin and has generally been found to exert a positive influence on subsequent entry of large firms. However, as Storey and Jones (1987) found for new-firm formation, *PCM* may not exert a strong influence on small-firm entry. Since most small and new firms are in local rather than national markets, the profitability of the industry at the national level may be less important than variations in price–cost margins across different regions (Storey and Jones, 1987).

   KL is the 1977 capital–labour ratio, defined as the total capital stock divided by total employment (in thousands of dollars), and β_3 is expected to be less than zero for reasons explained above. *AD* is defined as advertising intensity, measured as advertising expenditures divided by value-of-shipments, 1977, and has been found to have a negative effect on entry in general.

   RD is defined as the ratio of industry total R and D expenditures-to-sales, 1977; and, while Highfield and Smiley (1987) found it to be positively related to entry of all firms, we expect it to be negatively related to small-firm entry for the reasons discussed above. We also include a measure of the extent to which the industry relies upon skilled labour, *SKILL*, which is defined as the number of professional and kindred workers as a percentage of total employment, and provides an alternative measure of the technological opportunity class. *CR* is defined as the four-firm concentration ratio in 1977, and is expected to exert a negative influence on small-firm entry.

   SFIR is defined as the small-firm innovation rate, measured as the number of innovations in the industry contributed by firms with fewer than 500 employees, divided by small-firm employment (thousands of employees) in 1982. Because the innovations are the result of inventions made, on average, 4·2 years earlier (Acs and Audretsch, 1987, 1988), in some sense *SFIR* represents the invention rate in 1977 of inventions that subsequently proved to be commercially viable by 1982. Since small-firm innovation strategy is hypothesized to be a mechanism for compensating for the presence of entry barriers, we expect that *SFIR* should be positively related to small-firm entry. *UNION* is defined as the percentage of employees in the industry that belong to a union, measured in 1975. Because unionization has been found to exert a positive influence upon wage rates, we expect that small firms, which typically can avoid becoming unionized by virtue of their size, would be induced to enter industries in which their larger counterparts have relatively high wages. Thus, we predict a positive relationship between *UNION* and small-firm entry.

CRSFP is defined as the relative change in small-firm productivity and is measured as the small-firm change in sales-per-employee between 1976 and 1982, divided by the industry average change in sales-per-employee over the same period. Thus, a value of CRSFP exceeding one suggests that the productivity change of small firms over this period has been greater than that of large firms, while a value of CRSFP of less than one implies that the productivity change of small firms has been less than that of their larger counterparts. Since this measure should reflect the change in the inherent cost disadvantage faced by small firms, we expect a positive relationship to emerge between CRFSP and small-firm entry. That is, the greater small-firm productivity has increased relative to that of large firms, the greater should be small-firm entry, *ceteris paribus*. Finally, SFP is defined as the small-firm presence in the industry, measured as the share of industry sales accounted for by firms with fewer than 500 employees. Including this variable enables us to test whether small firms tend to enter those industries where small firms already dominate the industry or industries with only a low small-firm presence. All of the variables are defined and further data explanations are provided in the Appendix. The linear form of the model follows in the tradition of virtually every empirical entry paper (Geroski, 1983).[11]

III. Empirical Results

Using the 1978–80 small-firm net entry rate, SFE, as the dependent variable, the regression model was estimated for 247 four-digit SIC industries. Equation (1) in Table 1 shows that the lagged growth rate has a statistically significant and positive effect on small-firm entry. The positive and statistically significant coefficient of PCM suggests that small firms are induced to enter those industries that have been profitable, even after controlling for other major influences. Although the coefficients of KL and AD are negative, neither is statistically significant, implying that advertising intensity and capital intensity do not represent substantial entry barriers for firms with fewer than 500 employees. However, the negative and significant coefficient of RD implies that R and D intensity does present an entry barrier to small firms.

While the level of market concentration generally has not been found in the literature to exert a negative effect on the entry of firms of all sizes, the negative and significant coefficient of CR suggests that small firms are, in fact, deterred from entering industries that are highly concentrated. The positive and statistically significant coefficient of SFIR implies that innovation is a strategy that small firms can undertake to facilitate entry. Small-firm entry is, therefore, found to be positively related to the small-firm innovation rate. As expected, the coefficient of UNION is positive and significant, implying that small firms tend to prefer to enter highly unionized industries over non-unionized industries, *ceteris paribus*. Similarly, the positive and significant coefficient of CRSFP suggests that the greater the increase in small-firm productivity, relative to that of large firms, the greater is the rate of entry. Finally, the negative and significant coefficient of SFP suggests that, in fact, after controlling for other influences, small firms do not tend to enter those industries in which there is already a considerable presence of small firms. Rather, the negative relationship between small-firm presence and small-firm

TABLE 1

REGRESSION RESULTS FOR MODELS OF SMALL-FIRM ENTRY

(*t*-ratios listed in parentheses)[a]

	Equation			
Variable	(1)	(2)	(3)	(4)
Intercept	−0·185	−6·460	−6·597	−1·630
	(−0·042)	(−1·734)*	(−1·759)*	(−0·505)
GR	41·803	41·047	39·588	39·654
	(3·361)**	(3·258)**	(3·126)**	(3·096)**
PCM	0·016	0·017	0·017	0·015
	(1·854)*	(1·971)**	(1·962)**	(1·699)*
KL	−0·043	−0·031	−0·043	−0·035
	(−1·003)	(−0·735)	(−1·005)	(−0·820)
AD	−1·397	1·320	1·898	0·484
	(−0·275)	(0·262)	(0·375)	(0·095)
RD	−1·133	−1·067	−1·042	−1·031
	(−2·019)**	(−1·874)*	(−1·822)*	(−1·784)*
SKILL	−0·088	7·745	10·170	7·113
	(−0·004)	(0·368)	(0·481)	(0·333)
CR	−0·121	−0·101	−0·101	−0·075
	(−3·108)**	(−2·592)**	(−2·576)**	(−1·959)*
SFIR	1·497	1·544	1·605	1·453
	(2·067)**	(2·105)**	(2·175)**	(1·953)*
UNION	0·085	0·098	1·088	—
	(1·991)**	(2·271)**	(2·523)**	—
CRSFP	0·527	0·505	—	—
	(2·191)**	(2·071)**	—	—
SFP	−0·070	—	—	—
	(−2·694)**	—	—	—
R^2	0·184	0·159	0·143	0·120
F	4·811**	4·448**	4·405**	4·068**

[a] The small-firm entry rate is measured as the net change in the number of firms with fewer than 500 employees between 1978 and 1980, divided by the average of the total number of firms in 1978 and 1980. The dependent variable has been multiplied by 100, and the coefficient of *AD* has been divided by 100.
* Statistically significant at the 90 per cent level of confidence for a two-tailed test.
** Statistically significant at the 95 per cent level of confidence for a two-tailed test.

entry suggests that small firms tend to enter industries that are not dominated by small firms, supporting the hypothesis of Piore and Sabel (1984).

Estimation bias arising from multicollinearity is obviously a concern in a cross-section regression analysis of the type reported in Table 1. Because the simple correlation is −0·39 between *SFP* and *CR*, and −0·20 between *SFP* and *KL*, *SFP* was omitted from equation (2). The effect on the coefficient of *CR* is only slight, and the coefficients of *GR, PCM, RD, SFIR, UNION* and *CRSFP* remain virtually unchanged, while the coefficients of *KL, AD* and *SKILL* are still statistically insignificant.[12] Because the simple correlation between *UNION* and *CR* is 0·28, and between *UNION* and *KL* is 0·18,

UNION is dropped in equation (4), and CRSFP is omitted in equation (3). As with SFP, deleting UNION and CRSFP from the regression equations leaves the results virtually unchanged. While deleting these variables does not have much of an impact on the estimated coefficients of the remaining variables included in the regressions, the omission of each of these variables causes an additional substantial reduction in R^2, along with a decrease in the F-ratio. Thus, it is concluded that multicollinearity does not appear to present severe estimation problems and that the regression results remain robust with respect to either the inclusion or omission of these variables.[13]

To consider how robust the regression results are with respect to varying definitions of what constitutes a small enterprise, the regression equations

TABLE 2

REGRESSION RESULTS FOR ALTERNATIVE MEASURES OF SMALL-FIRM ENTRY

(t-ratios in parentheses)[a]

Variable	Equation (and small-firm measure)				
	(1)	(2)	(3)	(4)	(5)
Intercept	−1·531	−1·173	−0·904	−0·018	−0·485
	(−0·548)	(−0·384)	(−0·238)	(−0·004)	(−0·114)
GR	24·335	34·363	37·698	39·633	39·356
	(2·766)**	(3·642)**	(3·351)**	(3·372)**	(3·201)**
PCM	0·007	0·009	0·010	0·014	0·014
	(1·312)	(1·304)	(1·212)	(1·672)*	(1·661)*
KL	−0·066	−0·059	−0·101	−0·080	−0·055
	(−2·229)**	(−1·844)*	(−2·644)**	(−2·002)**	(−1·322)
AD	1·601	3·678	1·260	0·474	−0·607
	(0·444)	(0·942)	(0·274)	(0·099)	(0·121)
RD	−0·717	−0·778	−1·097	−1·020	−1·100
	(−1·808)*	(−1·829)*	(−2·160)**	(−1·921)*	(−1·982)**
SKILL	−5·366	−1·226	8·678	0·603	3·698
	(−0·365)	(−0·078)	(0·460)	(0·031)	(0·179)
CR	−0·071	−0·067	−0·097	−0·118	−0·111
	(−2·520)**	(−2·225)**	(−2·662)**	(−3·133)**	(−2·853)**
SFIR	0·648	0·896	1·026	1·362	1·354
	(1·260)	(1·625)	(1·561)	(1·987)**	(1·892)*
UNION	0·063	0·054	0·078	0·071	0·079
	(2·096)**	(1·681)*	(2·016)**	(1·745)*	(1·875)*
CRSFP	0·108	−0·037	0·371	0·409	0·405
	(0·739)	(−0·205)	(2·089)**	(2·024)**	(1·778)*
SFP	−0·020	−0·057	−0·063	−0·078	−0·066
	(−0·185)*	(−0·880)	(−1·338)	(−2·171)**	(−2·262)**
R^2	0·149	0·141	0·183	0·193	0·165
F	3·740**	3·507**	4·796**	5·094**	4·229**

[a] Small-firm net entry is defined as the change in the number of firms with fewer than 10 employees (1), 20 employees (2), 50 employees (3), 100 employees (4) and 250 employees (5). The dependent variables have been multiplied by 100, and the coefficient of AD has been divided by 100.
* Statistically significant at the 90 per cent level of confidence for a two-tailed test.
** Statistically significant at the 95 per cent level of confidence for a two-tailed test.

shown in Table 2 substitute narrower measures defining a small firm, ranging from fewer than 10 employees in equation (1) to fewer than 250 employees in equation (5).[14] For the variables *GR, CR, RD, AD, SKILL* and *UNION* the results are virtually identical, regardless of the small-firm measure used. However, the coefficients of *PCM, SFIR* and *SFP* are not statistically significant for the three narrowest definitions of a small firm (less than 10, 20 and 50 employees), while the coefficient of *CRFSP* is not statistically significant for the narrowest two measures of a small firm. Further, the coefficient of *KL* is statistically significant only in equations (1)-(4) but not in equation (5), suggesting that capital intensity may serve as an entry barrier to firms with more than 100 but less than 250 employees. However, as equation (5) implies, along with the results from Table 1, entry by firms with at least 250 employees does not appear to be deterred by capital intensity, after controlling for other important factors. It is interesting that *PCM* is not statistically significant in the first three equations in Table 2, suggesting that profitability and entry are not related for firms with fewer than 100 employees. This result confirms the findings of Storey and Jones (1987).[15] The observed positive relationship for slightly larger firms suggests that entry by larger firms is positively related to industry profitability, as has typically been identified in the literature.

In general, the results from Tables 1 and 2 suggest that the entry behaviour of small firms is positively and strongly related to the lagged industry growth rate while it is negatively related to R and D intensity and market concentration. Further, beyond a certain minimal size, small-firm entry tends to be promoted by lagged profitability, small-firm innovation activity and the extent to which the productivity of small firms has increased relative to that of larger firms, while it is deterred from industries in which small firms already constitute a large share of the industry.

IV. CONCLUSION

The findings of our paper suggest that the entry behaviour of small firms may be distinct in some respects from that of large firms. As for large firms, past growth rates provide a strong incentive for small-firm entry. On the other hand, past profit rates induce entry only in firms with at least 250 employees but not the smallest enterprises. This may be because a very small firm often operates in a market niche or a very small market segment.[15] Similarly, capital intensity deters the entry of the smallest firms, but apparently does not impede the entry of slightly larger firms. In contrast to the studies examining entry behaviour in general, we find very strong evidence that R and D intensity and market concentration serve as deterrents.

Three additional variables which have never been included in any entry study suggest that small firms can at least partially compensate for their inherent size disadvantages by pursuing a strategy of product innovation, entering industries that are highly unionized, and industries in which the scale disadvantage of small firms has been diminishing. While we have found that considering the entry patterns of small firms yields a pattern remarkably distinct from that of large firms, subsequent research should consider the interdependence between entry behaviour and the ability of firms to expand and contract across different firm-size classes within an industry.

ACKNOWLEDGMENTS

We wish to thank Michael Karge for his computational assistance, George Bittling-mayer, Paul Geroski, Joachim Schwalbach, three anonymous referees and the editors of this Journal for their helpful comments, and Bruce D. Phillips of the US Small Business Administration for providing some of the data. All errors and omissions remain our responsibility.

APPENDIX

Data on small-firm entry (SFE), small-firm presence (SFP), and $CRSFP$ come from the US Small Business Administration (SBA), Office of Advocacy, Small Business Database. Since 1979 the SBA has maintained a major micro-database. The US Enterprise and Establishment Microdata (USEEM) file is a bi-annual database containing observations on employment, sales, organizational relationship and location for nearly all US firms (enterprises) and their component establishments (individual business locations). The data are derived from the DUNS Market Identifier (DMI) file leased from the Dun and Bradstreet Corporation. For a description of the data see Boden and Phillips (1985).

The data on the small-firm innovation rate ($SFIR$) are from the US Small Business Administration, Office of Advocacy. The data are described in Edwards and Gordon (1984).

The US Department of Commerce, Bureau of the Census, Annual Survey of Manufactures, 1977, *Industry Profiles* (Washington DC: US Government Printing Office, issued 1981) is the source for the capital–labour ratio (KL), the growth rate (GR), the price–cost margin (PCM) and concentration (CR). The advertising–sales (AD) ratio was derived by using the value-of-shipments data described above and advertising expenditures, from the 1972 United States Input–Output Table. The union participation rates ($UNION$) are from Freeman and Medoff (1979). The percentage of total employment that is unionized for three-digit SIC industries between 1973 and 1975 is reported. We repeat those three-digit values at the four-digit level. The 1977 R and D–sales ratio (RD) comes from the US Federal Trade Commission, *Annual Line of Business Report*, Washington, DC.

NOTES

1. A very recent example of a study examining net entry patterns but not distinguishing between different firm sizes is Highfield and Smiley (1987). We use the same database that they do, but by examining only the entry of small firms we find results that are quite different from theirs.
2. While no precise definition of a small firm exists, the US Small Business Administration defines a small firm as one with less than 500 employees. In Europe this definition may include small- and medium-sized firms.
3. One notable exception is Khemani and Shapiro (1986) for Canadian manufacturing industries.
4. While Smiley (1988) and Highfield and Smiley (1987) found evidence that R and D intensity is positively related to entry, Orr (1974) argues and finds evidence that R and D intensity discourages entry.
5. There are two interrelated questions with regard to small-firm entry that cannot be easily separated: the causes (determinants) of small-firm entry, and the effects of small-firm entry. The effect of small-firm entry and exit has been recently explored by Beesley and Hamilton (1984). The effect of small-firm entry is two-fold in industrial organization. First, small firms, often armed with different strategies from their larger counterparts, can revitalize existing industries. A good example of this has been the recent entry of small firms into the US steel industry (Crandall and Barnett, 1986). Second, small-firm entry plays a vital role in the creation of new industries through the venture process. Innovation, for example, by small firms has been important in the creation of the US semi-conductor industry.
6. In his empirical finding that markets in the United States now appear to be 'far more competitive than at any time during the modern industrial period', Shepherd (1982, p. 613) attributes some of this increase in competition to a reduction in the minimum efficient scale (MES) in at least some industries. Although Shepherd was unable to quantify the impact, he concluded that 'There is a strong general evidence and a growing belief that scale economies have

dwindled since the 1950s as computers and electronics have replaced cruder manufacturing processes' (1982, p. 620).

7. As one of the anonymous referees pointed out, entrepreneurs founding new firms are often motivated by the lack of alternative employment prospects. Thus, the characteristics of firms formed in the expansion phase of the business cycle might vary considerably from those formed during the trough phase. In 1978 real US output grew by 5·3 per cent, while in 1980 it slightly declined by 0·2 per cent. However, in the data available to us, a more stable period was not available. Further research should consider more carefully how entry varies over the business cycle.

8. The data are from the US Establishment Longitudinal Microdata (USELM) and the US Enterprise and Establishment Microdata (USEEM) files, which have been derived from the DUNS (Dun and Bradstreet) Market Identifier File (DMI). For further explanations and qualifications concerning limitations of the data, see Boden and Phillips (1985).

9. Although the US Small Business Administration has found that 'lagged updating of records for existing establishments or enterprises is probably not a problem for most USEEM data applications', there still remain weaknesses in the data base: 'Some firms and establishments are not included in the DMI (and, hence, USEEM) data until several years after they are born.... This phenomenon sometimes depresses the number of firms and establishments represented in each USEEM below the actual count, and is likely to be presented in fast-growing industries (such as certain types of services) as well as in new industries (such as microcomputer hardware and software related industries' (Boden and Phillips, 1985, p. 7). For other qualifications regarding formation of the Small Business Database see US Small Business Administration (1984).

10. Dividing the net change in the number of firms for each size class by the number of firms in that size class, rather than of the entire industry, would provide a better measure of the impact that entry has had on the existing stock of small firms. However, standardizing the amount of entry in each firm size class by the total number of firms in the industry reveals more about the subsequent price and output effects, or the overall industry effects, as a result of the entry.

11. It should be noted that the model specifies a flow measure, net entry, resulting from stock measures such as capital intensity, advertising and market concentration. This specification was first adopted by Bain (1956) and subsequently used in virtually every empirical study of entry. Essentially, an industry will be in equilibrium with no net change in the number of firms if, for a given level of profitability, the configuration of market structure characteristics does not result in either net entry or net exit. That is, the level of profitability is such that the cost to a new firm of entering the market exceeds the expected profitability. If, however, there is a change in either the level of expected profitability or the cost of entering, which is directly related to the entry barrier conditions, a net inflow (or outflow) of firms into the industry is expected, until equilibrium is again restored. Thus, entry (exit), which is a flow measure, occurs when the cost of entering associated with a particular configuration of market structure conditions (entry barriers), which are stock measures by nature, is not equal to the expected profitability subsequent to entry.

12. An anonymous referee pointed out that the highly unionized industries also tend to be composed predominantly of large firms. Since these large firms may not be interested in covering each new market niche that develops, there are continual opportunities for small firms to exploit. This would be consistent with the positive relationship observed between small-firm entry and unionization.

13. A more extensive analysis of multicollinearity was performed and revealed results similar to those discussed above.

14. Because *CRFSP* and *SFP* are specific to the small-firm measure used, they also were recalculated in each regression equation to coincide with the definition of *SFE*. This was not done for *SFIR* owing to data constraints.

15. This point was brought to our attention by one of the anonymous referees.

REFERENCES

Acs, Z. J. and Audretsch, D. B. (1987). Innovation, market structure, and firm size. *Review of Economics and Statistics*, **69**, 567–74.

—— (1988). Innovation in Large and Small Firms: An Empirical Analysis. *American Economic Review*, **78**, 678–90.

Bain, J. (1956). *Barriers to New Competition*. Cambridge, Mass.: Harvard University Press.

Beesley, M. E. and Hamilton, R. E. (1984). Small firms' seedbed role and the concept of turbulence. *Journal of Industrial Economics*, **33**, 217–32.

Bhagwati, J. (1970). Oligopoly theory, entry-prevention and growth. *Oxford Economic Papers*, **22**, 297–310.

BODEN, R. and PHILLIPS, B. R. (1985). Uses and limitations of USEEM/USELM data. US Small Business Administration, November.

CARLSSON, B. (1986). Flexibility in the theory of the firm. *International Journal of Industrial Organization,* forthcoming.

—— (1987). Manufacturing technology and US trade performance. Presented at the European Association for Research in Industrial Economics (EARIE) Conference, Madrid, August.

CAVES, R. E. and PUGEL, T. A. (1980). *Intra-industry Differences in Conduct and Performance: Viable Strategies in US Manufacturing Industries.* New York: New York University Press.

CRANDALL, W. and BARNETT, S. (1986). *Up From the Ashes: The Rise of the Steel Minimills in the United States.* Washington, DC: Brookings Institution.

DUETSCH, L. L. (1984). Entry and the extent of multiplant operations. *Journal of Industrial Economics,* **32,** 477–87.

EDWARDS, K. L. and GORDON, T. J. (1984). Characterization of innovations introduced on the US market in 1982 (The Futures Group). Prepared for the US Small Business Administration under Contract no. SB-6050-0A-82, March.

FREEMAN, R. B. and MEDOFF, J. L. (1979). New estimates of private sector unionism in the United States. *Industrial and Labor Relations Review,* **32,** 143–74.

GEROSKI, P. (1983). The empirical analysis of entry: a survey. Discussion Paper no. 8318, University of Southampton, October.

GORECKI, P. K. (1975). The determinants of entry by new and diversifying enterprises in the UK manufacturing sector, 1958–1963: some tentative results. *Applied Economics,* **7,** 139–47.

HIGHFIELD, R. and SMILEY, R. (1987). New business starts and economic activity: an empirical investigation. *International Journal of Industrial Organization,* **5,** 51–66.

JUDGE, G. C., GRIFFITHS, E., CARTER-HILL, R. and TSOUNG-CHAO LEE (1980). *The Theory and Practice of Econometrics.* New York: John Wiley.

KAMIEN, M. I. and SCHWARTZ, N. L. (1975). Market structure and innovation: a survey. *Journal of Economic Literature,* **13,** 1–37.

KHEMANI, R. S. and SHAPIRO, D. M. (1986). The determinants of new plant entry in Canada. *Applied Economics,* **18,** 1243–57.

MANSFIELD, E. (1981). Composition of R and D expenditures: relationship to size of firm, concentration, and innovative output. *Review of Economics and Statistics,* **63,** 610–15.

MILLS, D. E. and SCHUMANN, L. (1985). Industry structure with fluctuating demand. *American Economic Review,* **75,** 758–67.

ORR, D. (1974). The determinants of entry: a study of the Canadian manufacturing industries. *Review of Economics and Statistics,* **56,** 58–66.

PIORE, M. J. and SABEL, C. F. (1984). *The Second Industrial Divide: Possibilities for Prosperity.* New York: Basic Books.

SHEPHERD, W. G. (1982). The causes of increased competition in the economy, 1939–1980. *Review of Economics and Statistics,* **64,** 613–26.

SMILEY, R. (1988). Empirical evidence on strategic entry deterrence. *International Journal of Industrial Organization,* **6,** 167–80.

STONEBREAKER, R. (1976). Corporate profits and the risk of entry. *Review of Economics and Statistics,* **58,** 33–39.

STOREY, D. J. and JONES, A. M. (1987). New firm formation—a labor market approach to industrial entry. *Scottish Journal of Political Economy,* **34,** 37–51.

US SMALL BUSINESS ADMINISTRATION (1984). The derivation of the US establishment longitudinal microdata (USELM): the weighted integrated USEEM 1976–1982 sample. Washington, DC, November.

WHITE, L. J. (1982). The determinants of the relative importance of small business. *Review of Economics and Statistics,* **64,** 42–49.

YIP, G. (1982). *Barriers to Entry: A Corporate-Strategy Perspective.* Lexington, Mass.: Lexington Books.

Innovation and Size of Firm

[18]

The Review *of* Economics *and* Statistics

VOL. LXIX   NOVEMBER 1987   NUMBER 4

INNOVATION, MARKET STRUCTURE, AND FIRM SIZE

Zoltan J. Acs and David B. Audretsch*

Abstract—The hypothesis that the relative innovative advantage between large and small firms is determined by market concentration, the extent of entry barriers, the composition of firm size within the industry, and the overall importance of innovation activity is tested. We find that large firms tend to have the relative innovative advantage in industries which are capital-intensive, concentrated, highly unionized, and produce a differentiated good. The small firms tend to have the relative advantage in industries which are highly innovative, utilize a large component of skilled labor, and tend to be composed of a relatively high proportion of large firms.

I. Introduction

WHILE the two fundamental tenets of the Schumpeterian hypothesis—that innovative activity is promoted by large firms[1] and by imperfect competition—have been subjected to several empirical tests,[2] most studies have examined only one aspect in isolation from the other (Link, 1980). That is, the exact interaction between these two tenets has been largely overlooked, mainly because of the availability of data. However, as we show in the second section of this paper, large firms, in fact, are not more innovative than their smaller counterparts in every industry. While large firms have proven to be more innovative in a number of industries, the opposite is true in still others. In considering what accounts for these differences in innovative activity between large and small firms, we provide an empirical test of a somewhat modified Schumpeterian hypothesis which combines both of the central tenets. That is, we test the hypothesis that large firms have the innovative advantage in markets characterized by imperfect competition, but that small firms have

Received for publication September 4, 1986. Revision accepted for publication May 8, 1987.

*Wissenschaftszentrum Berlin für Sozialforschung.

We thank George Bittlingmayer, Al Link, J.-Matthias Graf von der Schulenburg, Joachim Schwalbach, Hideki Yamawaki, Klaus Zimmermann and two anonymous referees for their helpful comments, and Michael Karge for his computational assistance. Any errors or omissions remain our responsibility.

[1] Kamien and Schwartz (1975, p. 15) characterize the Schumpeterian debate as, "A statistical relationship between firm size and innovative activity is most frequently sought with exploration of the impact of firm size on both the amount of innovational effort and innovational success."

[2] For an excellent survey of this literature, see Kamien and Schwartz (1975).

the innovative advantage in markets more closely approximating the competitive model.

A particularly unique feature of this paper is that, by using data newly released from the U.S. Small Business Administration, we are able to apply a direct measure of innovation, for both large and small firms, over a broad sample of four-digit standard industrial classification (SIC) industries. After describing these new data in the second section of the paper, we present in the third section the hypothesis that market imperfections account for the relative innovative superiority of large firms over their smaller counterparts. In the fourth section, two different samples consisting of 172 innovative and 42 highly innovative industries are used in a model estimating the difference between large- and small-firm innovative rates. We find that large firms tend to have the relative innovative advantage in industries which are capital-intensive, concentrated, and advertising-intensive. By contrast, small firms tend to have the relative innovative advantage in highly innovative industries and in industries which tend to be composed of a relatively high proportion of large firms. Thus, in the last section, we conclude that the results support the hypothesis that large firms have the relative innovative advantage in markets characterized by imperfect competition, while small firms have the relative advantage in markets more closely approximating the competitive model.

II. Innovative Activity and Firm Size

Virtually all of the empirical studies testing the Schumpeterian hypotheses, or the relationships between firm size and innovative activity, and between market structure and innovative activity, have had to rely on relatively deficient measures of innovative activity. Typically, these measures have involved either some measure of an input into the innovative process, such as R & D (Scherer, 1965), or else a proxy measure of innovative output, such as patented inventions (Mansfield, 1968). While R & D measures suffer from indicating only the budgeted resources allocated towards trying to produce innovative activity, but not the actual amount of resulting innovations, the measures of patents suffer because not all patented inventions prove to be innovations, and many innovations are never patented.[3]

We are able to avoid these inherent problems in the traditional measures of innovation activity by using a new direct measure of innovation (Acs and Audretsch, 1987). The innovative measure we adopt in this paper is the number of innovations in each four-digit SIC industry recorded in 1982. The U.S. Small Business Administration identified innovations which were introduced in 1982 and appeared in the sections listing new innovations from over 100 technology, engineering, and trade journals, spanning every manufacturing industry. The entire list of trade journals used to compile these data is available from the authors. Although the innovations were recorded in 1982, the Small Business Administration found that they were the result of inventions made, on average, 4.2 years earlier. Thus, the innovation data in some sense represent inventions occurring around 1978. The Small Business Administration defines an innovation as "...a process that begins with an invention, proceeds with the development of the invention, and results in the introduction of a new product, process or service to the marketplace" (Edwards and Gordon, 1984, p. 1). The innovation data were classified into two firm-size categories, according to the employment level of the innovating firm. Innovations from firms with fewer than 500 employees were considered to constitute "small-firm innovations," while innovations from firms with at least 500 employees constitute "large-firm innovations." Unfortunately, these definitions of large and small firms by employment level are fixed and do not enable alternative measures of firm size to be constructed for comparison. Because not all of the innovations could be classified according to firm size, the number of total innovations does not always equal the sum of large- and small-firm innovations.

Table 1 shows the twenty four-digit SIC industries where the large-firm innovation rate

most greatly exceeds the small-firm innovation rate, and the twenty four-digit industries where the small-firm innovation rate most greatly exceeds the large firm innovation rate. The large-firm innovation rate (LIE) is defined as the number of innovations made by firms with at least 500 employees, divided by the number of employees (thousands) in large firms.[4] The small-firm innovation rate (SIE) is defined as the number of innovations made by firms with fewer than 500 employees, divided by the number of employees (thousands) in small firms.

The innovation rate, or the number of innovations per employee, is used because it measures innovative activity relative to the industry size. The absolute number of innovations contributed by an industry may be a misleading measure of innovative activity, since it is not standardized by some equivalent measure of industry size. The innovation rate is presumably a more reliable measure of innovation activity because it is weighted by industry and firm size. Thus, while large firms in manufacturing produced 2,608 innovations in 1982, and small firms contributed slightly fewer, 1,923, small-firm employment was only about half as great as large-firm employment, yielding an average small-firm innovation rate in manufacturing of 0.322, compared to a large-firm innovation rate of 0.225.

Of course, standardizing the innovation measures on the basis of employment may introduce bias to the extent that large firms might differ from their smaller counterparts in the capital-intensity of their production process. That is, if large firms tend to be more capital-intensive, their innovation rates will tend to be overstated, and the small-firm innovation rates will tend to be understated. Similarly, the extent to which small firms in the Bureau of Census SIC industry classification actually manufacture different product class lines than the larger firms also introduces bias into the measures. A third source of bias may be that innovation rates affect firm size (see Acs and Audretsch, 1986). While no adjustments can be made to address the second two sources of bias, an alternative measure of the innovation rates, defined as the number of innovations divided by sales (divided by 10,000), provides a

---

[3]According to Shepherd (1979, p. 400), "patents are a notoriously weak measure. Most of the eighty thousand patents issued each year are worthless and are never used. Many are of moderate value, and a few are bonanzas. Still others have negative social value. They are used as "blocking" patents to stop innovation, or they simply are developed to keep competition out."

[4] The employment data are from 1977 (see appendix A).

INNOVATION, MARKET STRUCTURE, AND FIRM SIZE   569

TABLE 1.—THE INDUSTRIES WITH THE LARGEST DIFFERENCES BETWEEN THE
LARGE- AND SMALL-FIRM INNOVATION RATES[a]

	LIE	SIE	DIE	DIS
Tires and inner tubes	8.4615	0.0000	8.4615	2.5090
Agricultural chemicals	2.2642	0.0000	2.2642	1.7940
General industrial machinery	2.2041	0.3939	1.8101	3.9210
Food products machinery	2.0109	0.6704	1.3405	3.6520
Ammunition, except for small arms	1.2281	0.0000	1.2281	5.2764
Cottonseed oil mills	1.1111	0.0000	1.1111	1.9342
Cheese, natural and processed	1.1258	0.0862	1.0396	1.9667
Wet corn milling	1.0000	0.0000	1.0000	0.1301
Storage batteries	0.9649	0.0000	0.9649	4.6968
Converted paper products	0.9848	0.0617	0.9231	5.2486
Truck and bus bodies	0.7643	0.0000	0.7643	0.9384
Paper industries machinery	0.8696	0.1053	0.7643	2.5401
Metal office furniture	1.1628	0.4000	0.7628	0.9827
Woodworking machinery	0.7500	0.0000	0.7500	2.5641
Building paper and board mills	0.6452	0.0000	0.6452	1.1468
Pens and mechanical pencils	0.6154	0.0000	0.6154	0.3194
Flat glass	0.5882	0.0000	0.5882	0.4395
Raw cane sugar	0.5455	0.0000	0.5455	0.6967
Industrial furnaces and ovens	1.6667	1.1250	0.5417	0.1242
Primary metal products	1.3793	0.9375	0.4418	0.8299
Scales and balances, except laboratory	0.8511	8.7500	− 7.8989	− 6.8472
Electronic computing equipment	0.9570	8.2246	− 7.2676	− 8.3290
Process control instruments	1.8785	9.0291	− 7.1507	− 3.8790
Synthetic rubber	0.0000	6.6667	− 6.6667	− 1.3788
Fluid meters and counting devices	0.4380	4.5455	− 4.1075	− 5.1517
Engineering and scientific instruments	1.5751	5.5333	− 3.9582	− 2.9035
Measuring and controlling devices	0.1442	3.9130	− 3.7688	− 4.2051
Gum and wood chemicals	0.2500	3.7500	− 3.5000	− 1.6155
Primary copper	0.0000	3.3333	− 3.3333	− 8.9286
Industrial controls	0.3538	3.5385	− 3.1847	− 3.6549
Surface active agents	0.5405	3.4483	− 2.9077	− 2.0639
Power driven handtools	0.5512	3.0435	− 2.4923	− 1.4856
Instruments to measure electricity	0.5534	2.9560	− 2.4026	− 2.4434
Surgical and medical instruments	0.9524	3.0769	− 2.1245	− 1.7433
Plastics materials and resins	0.5894	2.3810	− 1.7916	− 0.5038
Transformers	0.1344	1.8033	− 1.6689	− 0.9757
Electric lamps	0.0000	1.5789	− 1.5789	− 0.2908
Industrial trucks and tractors	0.6701	2.1277	− 1.4576	− 1.0488
Measuring and dispensing pumps	0.0000	1.4286	− 1.4286	− 1.1884
Environmental controls	0.6452	2.0408	− 1.3957	− 0.5742

[a] The twenty industries where the large-firm innovation rate (*LIE*) most greatly exceeds the small-firm innovation rate (*SIE*), and the twenty industries where the small-firm innovation rate most greatly exceeds the large-firm innovation rate. The innovation rate is measured as the number of innovations divided by total employment for *LIE*, *SIE*, and *DIE*, and by sales for *DIS*.

comparative measure of innovative activity. The last column in table 1 lists the corresponding differences in innovation rates, *DIS*, when the innovations are standardized by the sales accounted for by large and small firms. As table 1 shows, the correspondence between the innovation measures standardized by employment (*DIE*) and by sales (*DIS*) is fairly strong. In fact, for the entire sample of 247 four-digit SIC manufacturing industries, the simple correlation between the two measures is 0.707. While this is somewhat reassuring, standardizing the innovation rates by sales is susceptible to bias from differences in the vertical

level at which the sales are made between large and small firms. For example, if the large firms tend to sell products which are further downstream, then the innovation rates would tend to be overstated for small firms and understated for the large firms.

That the average innovation rate for small firms was about 43% higher than that of large firms in 1982 does not imply that the answer to the question, "Which firm size is more innovative?" is unequivocally "the small firm." Rather, table 1 suggests that the correct answer ·is: "it depends—on the particular industry." For example, in the tires industry, the large-firm innovation rate exceeded the small-firm innovation rate by 8.46, or by about eight innovations per thousand employees. Just as the innovation rate is relatively higher for the large firms in the tires, chemicals, industrial machinery, and food machinery industries, it is relatively higher for the small firms in the scales and balances, computing equipment, control instruments, and synthetic rubber industries.

III. The Hypothesis

While the Schumpeterian position has generally been interpreted as asserting that large firms are more innovative than their smaller counterparts,[5] this is clearly not validated in every manufacturing industry, as table 1 suggests. However, considering the other major tenet of the Schumpeterian hypothesis, that markets characterized by imperfect competition are particularly conducive to innovation activity, a modified Schumpeterian hypothesis is that the large firms should have the relative innovative advantage in concentrated markets imposing significant entry barriers, while the small firms should have the innovative advantage in markets more closely resembling the competitive model. In particular, the literature has identified three aspects of market structure which have been suggested to affect significantly the relative innovative advantage of large and small firms—the size distribution of firms, the existence of certain barriers to entry, and the stage of the industry in the product life-cycle.

Galbraith (1956) and Scherer (1980), among others, have noted that scale economies in production may provide scope economies for research and development (R & D).[6] To the extent that this view that innovative activity is positively related to the extent of scale economies is correct, the existence of capital-intensity in an industry should tend to provide a barrier to small-firm innovation, while relatively promoting large-firm innovation. Simply put, large firms, rather than small firms, are in a better position to exploit the gains yielded from innovation in an industry requiring capital-intensity.

Similarly, the extent of product differentiation through advertising intensity has been considered to yield a greater innovative advantage to large firms, while inhibiting the innovative activity of smaller firms (Comanor, 1967). Scherer (1980) notes that economies of scale in promotion facilitate the market penetration of new products, thus enabling larger firms with a greater profit potential from innovation in advertising-intensive industries.

The most obvious index measure for the extent of imperfect competition in a market is the degree of concentration.[7] As Kamien and Schwartz (1975) summarize the Schumpeterian hypothesis, market power and the potential for accruing economic rents is a necessary condition for innovation. Only firms that are large enough to attain at least temporary market power will therefore choose innovation as a means for profit-maximization. Concentration, in particular, should provide the large firms with an innovative advantage over their smaller counterparts because, according to Galbraith (1956, p. 87), innovation can occur only in the presence of such market power and "...only by a firm that has the resources which are associated with considerable size."[8]

On the other hand, the extent of unionization in an industry might be considered to be more of a barrier to large-firm innovation than to small-firm innovation. Hirsch and Link (1986) provide a model and empirical evidence suggesting that, through the rent-seeking activities of unions, rents accruing from innovation are captured to some extent by strong unions (see also Connolly et al., 1986). Since employees in small firms tend to have lower union participation rates than do employees in large firms (Hirsch and Addison, 1986), a high

---

[5] According to Schumpeter, "What we have got to accept is that (the large-scale establishment) has come to be the most powerful engine of progress..." (1950, p. 106).

[6] According to Scherer "(R)esearch and development projects may benefit from scale economies realized in other parts of the large firm's operations" (1980, p. 414).

[7] As Scherer (1980) notes, caution must be applied when interpreting the actual meaning of market concentration. Concentration ratios are a weak measure of market power at best, and in practice contain substantial error.

[8] It should be noted that Phillips (1965) argued that concentration should promote the innovative activity of small firms more than that of large firms. He reasoned that if concentration inhibits price competition, it is also likely to deter non-price competition, such as product innovation. However, the smaller firms are less likely to be bound by such tacit agreements restraining innovation. This argument runs contradictory to the literature in the Schumpeterian and Galbraithian tradition.

degree of unionization in an industry might adversely impact large-firm innovation relative to small-firm innovation.

Finally, several studies, including Pavitt and Wald (1971), suggest that the opportunity for small-firm innovation tends to be the highest when the industry is in the early stages of the product life-cycle. The introduction and growth stages of the life-cycle are defined by Vernon (1966) as the absence of a standardized product concept in the market. Because the product design is subject to rapid change and evolution, a relatively high level of skilled labor is required, while the production process remains fairly labor-intensive. Thus, the innovative opportunities for the small firms are presumably the greatest during the early life-cycle stages, and the least in the mature and declining stages, when product innovation plays a relatively minor role but capital-intensity becomes a more prominent feature.

To test the hypothesis that the difference between the large- and small-firm innovation rates is attributable to the extent of imperfect competition in the market, we estimate the following model:

$$DIE = \beta_0 + \beta_1 CAPVS + \beta_2 PROD \\ + \beta_3 CON + \beta_4 CB + \beta_5 GROWTH \\ + \beta_6 LFI + \beta_7 HK + \beta_8 TIE + \mu \quad (1)$$

where the dependent variable, DIE, is defined as the difference between the large-firm innovation rate (LIE) and the small-firm innovation rate (SIE), $DIE = LIE - SIE$, and the innovation rate is defined as the number of innovations per employee (thousands) in a four-digit SIC industry. An alternative measure of the difference between large- and small-firm innovation rates, DIS, is also estimated, where the innovation rates are defined as the number of innovations per sales (ten thousand dollars) in a four-digit SIC industry. To measure the discussed barriers, we include as explanatory variables the 1977 capital-output ratio ($CAPVS$), the percentage of employees in the industry covered by collective bargaining between 1973 and 1975 (CB), the 1977 four-firm concentration ratio (CON), and the 1977 advertising-to-sales ratio ($PROD$). A substitute measure of product differentiation is also used ($PRODC$), where $PRODC = PROD \times D$, and D is a dummy variable taking on the value of one in consumer

industries which are also convenience goods and zero otherwise. This follows the procedure used by Porter (1976) and Pugel (1978), who argue that product differentiation plays a more significant role only in these industries.

To measure the stage of the industry life-cycle we also include the percentage growth rate between 1972 and 1977, divided by five ($GROWTH$), a measure of human capital (HK), defined as the professional and kindred workers, as a percentage of total employment, 1970, and the total innovation rate (TIE), defined as the total number of innovations, divided by total industry employment. Since an industry tends to rely on the highest component of skilled labor during the early stages of the life-cycle, and the least amount of skilled labor after the product has become standardized in the mature and declining phases, HK is expected to be negatively related to DIE. Similarly, since industries in the early life-cycle stages tend to be the most innovative, and small firms are presumably relatively more innovative during the early life-cycle stages, high levels of TIE are expected to be conducive to small-firm innovation relative to large-firm innovation, implying a negative relationship between TIE and DIE. Finally, the percentage of an industry which is accounted for by firms with at least 500 employees in 1977 (LFI) is included as an explanatory variable. Caves and Pugel (1980) have argued that small firms can perhaps offset their inherent size disadvantage through pursuing a strategy of product innovation. That is, after controlling for the negative influences of entry barriers on small-firm innovation, small firms may tend to rely on a strategy of innovation in the presence of an industry dominated largely by large firms, suggesting a negative relationship between LFI and DIE. All variable sources and further data explanations are provided in appendix A.[9]

IV. Regression Results

Although 247 four-digit SIC industries were compatible for estimating the above model, a large number (170 or 38%) of four-digit industries experienced no innovation. In these industries the

---

[9]Quadratic terms for CON, $GROWTH$, HK, and TIE were also included in the model but did not lead to a qualitative change in the results.

TABLE 2.—ESTIMATES OF MODEL FOR THE DIFFERENCE IN LARGE- AND SMALL-FIRM INNOVATION RATES

Independent Variable	High Innovative Industries				Innovative Industries	
	(1) (DIE)	(2) (DIE)	(3) (DIS)	(4) (DIS)	(5) (DIE)	(6) (DIE)
Intercept	1.737	2.093	11.245	13.758	0.780	0.748
	(1.602)	(1.575)[a]	(17.921)	(17.504)	(0.361)[b]	(0.355)[b]
CAPVS	5.972	5.371	68.252	64.329	0.684	0.651
	(3.382)[b]	(3.332)[a]	(37.843)[b]	(37.034)[b]	(0.671)	(0.666)
PROD	169.970	—	12.480	—	61.614	—
	(117.890)[a]		(13.191)		(50.816)	
PRODC	—	148.620	—	11.509	—	74.630
		(125.580)		(13.959)		(58.360)[a]
CON	0.029	0.031	0.301	0.317	−0.004	−0.003
	(0.021)[a]	(0.021)[a]	(0.234)[a]	(0.237)[a]	(0.006)	(0.005)
CB	0.023	0.023	0.189	0.187	−0.001	−0.001
	(0.017)[a]	(0.018)[a]	(0.195)[a]	(0.197)[a]	(0.006)	(0.006)
GROWTH	4.196	3.329	62.952	56.882	1.565	1.556
	(4.632)	(4.581)	(51.825)	(50.927)	(1.458)	(1.457)
LFI	−6.601	−6.776	−57.038	−58.599	−0.797	−0.893
	(2.451)[b]	(2.518)[b]	(27.424)[b]	(27.994)[b]	(0.571)[a]	(0.577)[a]
HK	2.123	1.658	9.867	7.010	−2.934	−2.883
	(5.244)	(5.266)	(58.671)	(58.537)	(2.016)[a]	(2.019)[a]
TIE	−1.789	−1.753	−14.067	−13.827	−1.021	−1.007
	(0.409)[b]	(0.411)[b]	(4.576)[b]	(4.565)[b]	(0.183)[b]	(0.181)[b]
Sample Size	42	42	42	42	172	172
R^2	0.524	0.515	0.376	0.372	0.295	0.296
F	4.538[b]	4.371[b]	2.448[b]	2.446[b]	8.527[b]	8.556[b]

Note: The dependent variables are the industry difference between large- and small-firm innovation rates (DIE and DIS). Standard errors are listed in parentheses. The coefficients of PROD and PRODC have been divided by 100 in equations (3) and (4).
[a] Statistically significant at the 90% level of confidence for a one-tailed test.
[b] Statistically significant at the 95% level of confidence for a one-tailed test.

difference between the large- and small-firm innovation rates is, of course, zero. Hence, the sole determinant of DIE in these industries is the lack of innovation. That is, when considering what determines the differences in innovation rates between large and small firms, it seems appropriate only to examine industries where a difference can possibly exist—industries with at least some innovation activity. Thus, the above model is estimated for two different samples: (1) high innovative industries, which include the highest-fourth of industries that had at least some innovative activity; and (2) innovative industries, which include those industries that had some innovative activity.

Using the 1982 differences between the large- and small-firm innovation rates as the dependent variables, the cross-section regressions were estimated for the different samples of innovative intensity, and are shown in table 2. Equation (1) includes DIE as the dependent variable for the high innovative industries. The positive and statistically significant coefficient of $CAPVS$ indicates that, ceteris paribus, large firms tend to

have the relative innovative advantage over their smaller counterparts in the more capital-intensive industries. Conversely, the smaller firms tend to be relatively more innovative in the less capital-intensive industries. This lends support to a slightly reinterpreted Schumpeterian view: Where capital-intensity plays an important role in the industry, innovation tends to be promoted in large firms and impeded in small firms.

The coefficient of $PROD$ is also positive and statistically significant. This suggests that, like capital-intensity, advertising-intensity deters innovation by smaller firms. The coefficient of CON is also positive and significant, suggesting that the larger firms tend to have the relative innovative advantage in the highly concentrated industries, and that the smaller firms tend to have the relative innovative advantage in the less concentrated industries. The positive and statistically significant coefficient of CB suggests that large firms tend to have the innovative advantage in industries that are highly unionized, while small firms tend to have the innovative advantage in industries that are relatively non-unionized. The coefficient of

GROWTH is not statistically significant, implying that, among the high innovative industries, the growth rate has a similar effect on large- and small-firm innovation rates. Because the coefficient of *LFI* is negative and statistically significant, it appears that the less an industry is composed of small firms, the greater is the relative innovative advantage of those existing small firms over their larger counterparts. Perhaps this reflects the use of a strategy of innovation by small firms to remain viable in industries dominated by large firms.

The statistical insignificance of *HK* is somewhat surprising; the explanation may lie in the fact that virtually all of the industries in the high innovative industry sample are skilled-labor intensive. Thus, the lack of variation in *HK* may explain its statistical insignificance in equation (1). Finally, the negative and statistically significant coefficient of *TIE* implies that, even among the high innovative industries, the relative innovative advantage of the small firms increases as the total innovation rate of the industry also increases.

In equation (2), the high innovative industry sample is again used, but *PRODC* is substituted for *PROD*. The results remain virtually unchanged, except that the coefficient of *PRODC* is statistically insignificant, whereas the coefficient of *PROD* is statistically significant in equation (1). It appears, therefore, that advertising-intensity is a significant barrier to small-firm innovation across manufacturing in the high innovative industries and not just in the consumer goods industries.

In equations (3) and (4), the innovative measure standardizing large- and small-firm innovation by sales, *DIS*, is substituted for *DIE*. While the regression results remain mostly unchanged, the major difference is that the coefficient of *PROD* and *CB* are no longer significant. Accordingly, the coefficient of determination falls to 0.376 in equation (3) from 0.524 in equation (1), and to 0.372 in equation (4) from 0.515 in equation (2). However, while the results are somewhat weaker for *DIS* than for *DIE*, the signs and significance of the coefficient of *CAPVS, CON, LFI,* and *TIE* remain similar between the different sets of regressions.

The same model is estimated using the sample of innovative industries—where there was at least some innovative activity—in equations (5) and (6), which use *DIE* as the dependent variable. The coefficients of *CAPVS, CON,* and *CB* are not

statistically significant, although all are significant in equations (1) and (2). However, the coefficients of *LFI* and *TIE* remain statistically significant, and *HK* emerges as a statistically significant variable in both equations (5) and (6). Thus, when a broader spectrum of skilled-labor industries is considered, *HK* is found to have a significant effect on the differential between large-firm and small-firm innovation rates. The smaller firms tend to have the relative innovative advantage in the industries utilizing a fairly high component of skilled labor, whereas the large firms tend to have the relative innovative advantage in the industries utilizing less skilled labor. Since the regression results using *DIS* as the dependent variable were virtually identical to those in equations (5) and (6), they were not included in table 2 to save space.

V. Conclusion

In general, the empirical results support the modified Schumpeterian hypothesis that the relative innovative advantage of large and small firms is determined by the extent to which a market is characterized by imperfect competition. Industries which are capital-intensive, concentrated, and advertising-intensive tend to promote the innovative advantage in large firms. The small-firm innovative advantage, however, tends to occur in industries in the early stages of the life-cycle, where total innovation and the use of skilled labor play a large role, and where large firms comprise a high share of the market. At least for these industries, the conclusion of Scherer (1980) that markets composed of a diversity of firm sizes are perhaps the most conducive to innovative activity is reinforced.

Our findings suggest that the focus of the Schumpeterian debate should perhaps be redirected. Rather than posing the issue as, "Which firm size is most conducive to innovation?" the more relevant question may be, "Under which circumstances do large firms have the relative innovative advantage, and under which circumstances do small firms have the relative innovative advantage?" The evidence presented here implies that both sides of the debate—those arguments supporting the innovative superiority of large firms and those supporting the superiority of small firms —are, in fact, correct. However, neither side is correct universally across manufacturing industries. Although the mean manufacturing innovation rate of small firms exceeds that of large firms, in many industries the large firms are more innovative, just as in many others, the small firms are more innovative. We have found that the extent to which the market is characterized by imperfect competition accounts for at least some of this disparate innovation activity between large and small firms. Because innovation rates may also have a significant effect on firm size and market structure, these results must be somewhat qualified. An important topic for future research is the extent to which the firm size distribution is influenced by the relative innovative activity of large and small firms.

REFERENCES

Acs, Zoltan J., and David B. Audretsch. "Entrepreneurial Strategy, Entry Deterrence, and the Presence of Small Firms in Manufacturing," discussion paper IIM/IP 86-28, Wissenschaftszentrum Berlin für Sozialforschung (Oct. 1986).

――――. "Innovation in Large and Small Firms," *Economic Letters* 23 (1987), 109–112.

Caves, Richard E., and Thomas A. Pugel, *Intraindustry Differences in Conduct and Performance: Viable Strategies in U.S. Manufacturing Industries* (New York: New York University Press, 1980).

Comanor, William S., "Market Structure, Product Differentiation and Industrial Research," *Quarterly Journal of Economics* (Nov. 1967), 639–657.

Connolly, Robert A., Barry T. Hirsch, and Mark Hirschey, "Union Rent Seeking, Intangible Capital, and Market Value of the Firm," this REVIEW 68 (Nov. 1986), 567–577.

Edwards, Keith L., and Theodore J. Gordon, "Characterization of Innovations Introduced in the U.S. Market in 1982," prepared for the U.S. Small Business Administration under contract no. SBA-6050-A-82, Mar. 1984.

Galbraith, John K., *American Capitalism*, revised edition (Boston: Houghton Mifflin, 1956).

Hirsch, Barry T., and John T. Addison, *The Economic Analysis of Unions: New Approaches and Evidence* (Boston: George Allen and Unwin, 1986).

Hirsch, Barry T., and Albert N. Link, "Labor Union Effects on Innovative Activity," mimeo (June 1986).

Kamien, Morton I., and Nancy L. Schwartz, "Market Structure and Innovation: A Survey," *The Journal of Economic Literature* 13 (Mar. 1975), 1–37.

Link, Albert N., "Firm Size and Efficient Entrepreneurial Activity: A Reformulation of the Schumpeterian Hypothesis," *Journal of Political Economy* 88 (Aug. 1980), 771–782.

Mansfield, Edwin, *Industrial Research and Technological Change* (New York: W.W. Norton, 1968).

Pavitt, K., and S. Wald, "The Conditions for Success in Technological Innovation," OECD, Paris, 1971.

Phillips, A., "Market Structure, Innovation and Investment," in W. Alderson, B. Terpstra and J. Shapiro (eds.), *Patents and Progress: The Sources and Impact of Advancing Technology* (Homewood, Ill.: Irwin, 1965), 37–58.

Porter, Michael E., *Interbrand Choice, Strategy and Bilateral Market Power* (Cambridge: Harvard University Press, 1976).

Pugel, Thomas A., *International Market Linkages and U.S. Manufacturing: Prices, Profits, and Patterns* (Cambridge, MA: Ballinger, 1978).

Scherer, F. M., "Size of Firm, Oligopoly and Research: A Comment," *Canadian Journal of Economics and Political Science* 31 (May 1965), 256–266.

――――, *Industrial Market Structure and Economic Performance*, 2nd edition (Chicago: Rand McNally, 1980).

Schumpeter, Joseph A., *Capitalism, Socialism and Democracy*, third edition (New York: Harper and Row, 1950).

Shepherd, William G., *The Economics of Industrial Organization* (Englewood Cliff, N.J.: Prentice Hall, 1979).

Vernon, Raymond, "International Investment and International Trade in the Product Life Cycle," *Quarterly Journal of Economics* 80 (May 1966), 190–207.

APPENDIX A

Data Sources

DIE, LIE, SIE, TIE, DIS, LIS, SIS, and *LFI* are calculated from the innovation and employment data from the U.S. Small Business Administration (Edwards and Gordon, 1984). *HK* was constructed by the U.S. International Trade Commission and is reported in U.S. International Trade Commission, *Industrial Characteristics and Trade Performance Data Base,* Washington, D.C., 1975. A description of the data base can be found in Edward J. Ray, "The Determinants of Tariffs and Nontariff Trade Restrictions in the U.S.," *Journal of Political Economy* 89 (Feb. 1981), 105–121.

CAPVS, CON, and *GROWTH* are from U.S. Department of Commerce, Bureau of the Census, Annual Survey of Manufacturers, 1977, *Industry Profiles* (Washington, D.C.: U.S. Government Printing Office, issued 1981). (The same source for 1972 is also used to calculate *GROWTH.*) *PROD* uses the value-of-shipments data from the above source along with advertising expenditures from the 1972 United States Input-Output Table. *PRODC* is based on the classification of consumer goods industries which are also convenience goods, identified by Pugel (1978) and Porter (1976). *CB* is from Richard B. Freeman and James L. Medoff, "New Estimates of Private Sector Unionism in the United States," *Industrial and Labor Relations Review* 32 (Jan. 1979), 113–174. The percentage of total employment that is unionized for three-digit SIC industries is reported. We repeat these three-digit SIC values at the four-digit level.

[19]

THE FINANCING OF SMALL HIGH-TECHNOLOGY FIRMS IN CANADA

Russell M. Knight School of Business Administration
The University of Western Ontario
London, Ontario.

ABSTRACT

This paper describes the process whereby 124 small technical firms in Canada finance their growth. This includes the development of business plans to raise venture capital at various stages in their development, how they finance the move from developing a prototype in a research and development environment to mass-manufacture of a product, and how they finance the marketing of these products to very specialized markets. The financial management expertise required at each stage to successfully facilitate the growth and development of the high-technology firm is examined, especially their problems in bridging the gap between technically trained entrepreneurs and the general and financial management skills needed to facilitate these phases.

SOMMAIRE

Cet article décrit la façon dont 124 petites entreprises canadiennes de haute technologie financent leur croissance. Il y est notamment question de l'élaboration des plans destinés à recueillir des capitaux de risque à différentes étapes de leur développement, des moyens de financer le passage du stade du prototype à celui de la production en série et également de la façon de financer la pénétration des marchés très spécialisés auxquels s'adressent ces produits. L'article traite en outre des compétences en gestion financière dont les entreprises de haute technologie ont besoin pour promouvoir leur croissance et leur développement à chaque étape, avec accent sur le problème des entrepreneurs de formation technique qui ne possèdent souvent pas ces compétences en gestion financière et en administration générale.

ACKNOWLEDGEMENTS

Sponsorship by the following research programs of this research is gratefully acknowledged:
- The Social Science and Humanities Research Council of Canada
- The Canadian Industrial Innovation Centre at Waterloo
- The Management Excellence in Small Business Program, Department of Regional Economic Expansion
- The Technology Studies Branch, Department of Regional Economic Expansion
- The cooperation of the 124 companies researched in the study, all of whom must remain anonymous, is also acknowledged.

INTRODUCTION

Canada has lagged significantly behind much of the Western world, in terms of both industrial research and development, and incentives for fostering the growth of the small-business sector (1). Many people contend that the two issues are linked closely, since incentives for small technical firms will likely mean more research and development (2).

Recent government policy initiatives have helped spawn an infant high-technology "Silicon Valley North" outside Ottawa, and both research and development and small

5

business have received much attention from government at all levels, as the recent federal and provincial budgets illustrate.

Little research has been undertaken regarding high-technology entrepreneurship and innovation in Canada (3), but what has been done points to a need for more venture financing (4), better general management of small technical firms, especially in the finance and marketing areas (5) and the need for more market research for innovations in Canada (6). It is therefore the objective of this research to examine these issues in detail and to generate recommendations to business, government and the academic sector for action in this area.

PURPOSE OF THE RESEARCH

This research project was proposed to study the process of innovation and management (or entrepreneurship) in small technical firms in Canada. Phase One, An Investigation of the Financing of High-Technology Ventures in Canada, involved a survey of 124 high-technology firms in Canada using a questionnaire similar to one which has been developed for a previous study involving those firms rejected by venture capitalists. The original sample of 500 firms was obtained from a variety of sources including *The Canadian Manufacturer's Trade Index* and *Scott's Directory*. This first phase investigated the process used by those high-technology firms to finance their operations from start-up through expansion to the public-company stage.

Issues explored included the development of business plans, venture-capital financing, other sources of capital and the financial management abilities of these firms. Through questionnaires or an interview with each firm, the researchers attempted to assess the process whereby high-technology firms seek financing in Canada and needed improvements in the system whereby such firms are funded. (The author had previously researched similar issues (4) (5) and authored a book on small business in Canada (7).)

Phase Two, Manufacturing by High-Technology Ventures in Canada, explored the problems and process of producing for a mass market those high-technology innovations which have been developed in the laboratory. The same 124 firms were examined as in Phase One. Many new technical ventures have failed because of the problems of mass-producing a prototype. (This phase is described in a separate paper (8).)

Phase Three, Marketing by High-Technology Ventures in Canada, examined the market experience of the 124 firms sampled earlier. Some of the main stumbling blocks of many high-technology firms and innovations in the past have been the difficulties of market research, distribution, promotion and pricing. (This phase is also described in another paper (9).)

A common theme through each of these phases is the entrepreneurial management abilities of the owners and managers of these firms. The author has studied Canadian entrepreneurs in some detail (10) and believes that many technically oriented Canadian entrepreneurs do not possess the general management skills—especially in finance manufacturing and marketing—to efficiently launch Canadian innovations.

From each of these phases, it is planned to document several in-depth case studies of how some companies raise capital, manufacture products and market those products very efficiently, either using their own resources, or those of other companies. Some firms will be examples of how not to undertake certain activities, and it is hoped that, in future, other firms will be able to learn from both types of examples. Many suggestions have come from the firms themselves on how to develop innovations in Canada and to develop a better climate for such innovations.

IMPORTANCE OF THE RESEARCH

This research project is important to various levels of society in Canada, including business, government, academia and the general Canadian public. It is important to Canadians in general to foster the development of high-technology innovations by small firms in Canada to help restore Canada's position in terms of standard of living, R&D and secondary manufacturing.

The results will be important to business managers in Canada, especially those which are involved in high-technology developments themselves, to learn how to better foster innovations. Other businesses probably will be potential customers and suppliers of such firms, while financial institutions will become involved in funding and retail institutions in selling their merchandise.

Governments at all levels have been attempting to foster high-technology innovations in Canada, so the recommendations will include policy initiatives for such innovation. Specific suggestions will be made in the areas of financing, manufacturing, marketing and the management of firms in this sector.

The academic audience is obviously interested in this subject area, as illustrated by the attached bibliography and the fact that the Social Science and Humanities Research Council has singled-out innovation and entrepreneurship as two of the high-priority management-research areas for this program, and is a sponsor of this research.

RESEARCH ISSUES

Many of the research issues for this study have already been documented, but many others exist, a few of which will be examined here. In the finance area, the question of how these high-technology firms seek venture capital from a wide variety of sources was an important issue deserving intensive study. Various authors have concluded that there is a desperate need for more venture capital in Canada, especially at the start-up and small-firm end of the scale (11)(12).

Both the manufacturing and marketing areas have received some attention in previous research on innovations, but usually at the large-firm end of the scale (13)(14). There has been relatively little research done on how small firms innovate, especially in terms of the financial, manufacturing and marketing problems faced by such firms. Recommendations from successful firms and learning from the mistakes of the unsuccessful firms will heavily influence these results. Current government-funding programs, innovation centers (15) and policy initiatives were examined in terms of their effects on high-technology innovations in Canada.

Other issues included examining what happens to those firms which fail in their efforts to innovate and why they failed (16), since some of the firms involved in the study are undoubtedly unsuccessful and may eventually fail.

SELECTION OF THE SAMPLE

The first phase involved establishing a definition of high-technology firms to obtain their participation in the study. We decided to ask these firms to select themselves on the basis of whether they undertook research and development on products which they would consider innovative or use complex technologies. In addition, we wanted firms which manufactured such products themselves or subcontracted the manufacture out to other firms. This definition eliminated such businesses as computer-software firms, marketing distributors of other firms' products, and service firms using high-technology products produced by someone else. All of these firms probably would fall within other definitions of high technology.

Approximately 500 firms were contacted by mail and asked to participate in the study. Of these, 192 agreed to participate, either by responding to a mail questionnaire (119), a telephone interview (50), or an interview (23). The telephone and office interviews were completed, but only 51 firms responded by completing the written questionnaires, for a total of 124 responses.

Firms were located by using various directories, industry lists, government publications and trade shows. In addition, firms were asked to suggest the names of other firms which they felt we should approach. The interviews gave a much better opportunity for in-depth questions about the firm's business and are highly recommended to other researchers. Even telephone interviews give far superior results compared to written questionnaires, and were much cheaper to conduct than personal interviews.

CHARACTERISTICS OF THE SAMPLE SURVEYED

The firms surveyed in this study were in a variety of different industries, Figure 1. The majority of the firms (44 per cent) were in communications and computer-related fields, with the remainder being in a widely scattered variety of other applications. The types of research and development conducted by these firms is analyzed in Figure 2, where most of the firms describe themselves as being involved in the development of entirely new technology. While 40 per cent of the firms claim to be doing that type of research and development, another 20 per cent said they were conducting ongoing research on the improvement of existing applications. The remainder were split into the development of new microprocessors in computer applications or new sensing devices and remote systems for a variety of industrial applications.

It is interesting to note that the percentage of sales devoted to research and development is relatively high in these firms, as one would expect, with a mean of 28 per cent of sales being spent on R & D. However, this is biased by a number of firms which spend close to 100 per cent of their sales, either because they have low sales or are in the early stages of development. The median percentage of sales devoted to R&D was 13 per cent, which illustrates the skew of the distribution. Several firms claim to be spending more than 100 per cent of sales on research and development, either because they had no sales or because they are at a very low level of sales, having recently started selling their products, while still devoting large amounts of money to research and development.

Figure 3 illustrates the location and ownership of the firms surveyed. The vast majority (52 per cent) were located in Southern Ontario, while another 27 per cent were located in other parts of Ontario. This is because the location of most of the high-technology companies in Canada is Ontario, combined with the fact that the researcher was based in Ontario and had much easier access to companies located there. Only 11 per cent of the firms came from British Columbia, with 10 per cent of them being based in other provinces.

Figure 3 also illustrates the ownership of the firms interviewed, 90 per cent of which were Canadian-owned, independent firms. A further 4 per cent were Canadian subsidiaries and the remaining 6 per cent were foreign-owned subsidiaries. The size of the firms in the sample is measured on a variety of scales, Figure 4. The sales volume illustrates that the firms seem to be fairly large, with an average of nearly $6-million in sales, but this is skewed by the fact that several very large firms are represented in the sample. The median is probably a better measure here and it was almost exactly $2-million in sales. Also, the size of the management team seems large on average, but this is skewed by the large firms, with a maximum of 200 managers employed, and a median of four managers a company is probably much more representative of the sample. The same is true of the equity capital issued and the amount of debt held by these firms, where the median figures of $150,000 in equity and $100,000 in debt are probably more representative than the mean values of $1.5-million in equity and nearly $1-million in debt. The number of employees is likewise skewed by the large firms, with a maximum of 2,100 employees, so that the mean value of 88 employees is not nearly as representative as the median of 22. Finally, the number of shareholders in the firm was skewed by the several public firms in the sample, with a maximum of 3,800, giving a biased mean number of

126, rather than the median value of 3, which showed how small the ownership really was for most of the firms. In fact, for the majority of the firms, only one individual held the majority of the equity.

Figure 5 contains a summary of several other characteristics of the firms in question. The first of these is the educational background of the founder. The immediate observation is that the founders of these firms are very well-educated, with degrees in Engineering and Science predominating, and relatively few of them not having a university education. However, this is both an advantage and a problem, since the vast majority of the management people we interviewed seemed to be far more oriented towards the technical side of the business, because of their education and experience, than they were to the general management areas of finance, marketing and production. This is illustrated further by some of the issues and problems that are discussed in the functional area sections which follow. However, it is a general conclusion of this research that most of the firms that we interviewed, especially the smaller ones in the sample, had management teams which were highly technically oriented in terms of their background, but which were relatively poorly prepared in terms of their general management experience. Even those which had previous experience with larger firms usually had such experience in technical areas, rather than in areas of general management. This usually caused problems, since working for a larger firm does not usually give one much experience in terms of raising capital, marketing highly specialized product lines or solving problems of converting from the prototype stage to full production.

The second issue explored in Figure 5 was whether their product line had evolved. Since most of these firms are relatively young and had stayed in the same business, 62 per cent of them stated that the product line had remained essentially the same, with only new developments as R & D could produce them. However, a surprising 26 per cent of the firms stated that they had been in the consulting business before they got into the high-technology field, where they were currently involved. The final portion of Figure 5 lists the position of the person responding to the study, and 77 per cent of respondents were president or owner of the firm.

FINANCING OF HIGH-TECHNOLOGY FIRMS

The next section of the survey was concerned with the sources of the financing and particular financing problems faced by the high-technology firms interviewed in our sample. Figure 6 illustrates a summary of the sources of funds used at various stages of the development of these firms. We divided the stages into pre-startup, which we defined as before their first sale; startup or the first year; development for years 2 to 5; and maturity, which was after the fifth year. Some of the firms surveyed had not progressed through all of these stages since many of them were under five years of age. In fact, the average age of the companies surveyed was 10.5 years with a median of 8.5 years.

As can be seen from Figure 6, the personal savings of the founders are the predominant source in the early stages of the company's development, while bank loans become of increasing importance as the firm develops. Similarly, government programs seem to become more predominant as the firm matures, as do most of the other sources of financing listed. It is interesting, of course, to note that the founder and his family and friends are the most important sources of capital in the pre-startup and startup stages of the business, while the banking system, trade credit, government programs, and other sources of financing gradually take over through the development and maturity stages.

Figure 7 illustrates the split of equity and debt funding by type of financing source, and the amounts obtained from these sources, both initially and currently. Here it is evident that the personal savings of the founders are the most important overall sources of equity, followed by private placements and a mixture of other sources, such as public issues for the more mature firms, investment groups, and venture capital. By far the most important debt source was bank loans, with trade credit a distant second, closely followed by customer advances. The amounts have gradually increased in every segment and are roughly double currently what they were originally for each source listed. It is also worth mentioning that the distributions of these amounts are highly skewed, so that the average values are probably biased toward the high side for most of these firms, because many of the firms are rather small and there are a few very large firms, which dominate these statistics. In fact, the median for most of these values given in Figure 7 is less than half of the mean values shown.

Figure 8 explores the issue of whether there were special terms on the financing provided by these sources, and 39 per cent of the companies surveyed responded that there were such terms involved. These were usually personal guarantees (in 55 per cent of the cases) and various operating controls (in 13 per cent of the instances). Further conditions were required changes in the management team (4 per cent) and guarantees from the parent company, where available, in another 4 per cent.

Figure 9 explores the problems observed by these firms in obtaining financing at the various stages, and 45 per cent of the respondents stated that they did have significant difficulties. The replies range from the non-co-operative attitude of the banks (in 32 per cent of the cases), poor company performance (in 19 per cent), sources questioning the need for further financing (in 11 per cent) and the usual problems of lack of collateral and lack of experience in a new business in less-frequent cases. However, the high risk and lack of a proven product line are probably understated, since many of these companies fell into these categories, but probably did not agree with the problems as stated by some of the sources of financing.

The issue of preparation of a business plan was explored in Figure 10, and 60 per cent of the respondents stated that they had prepared a business plan, while a surprising 40 per cent of them had not. Respondents stated that almost all sources had given them some instruction in what the proposals should contain. The banks were most frequently cited (by 30 per cent of the respondents), with 26 per cent stating that they received instructions from their banker on what information to provide. This dropped to lesser percentages for the other sources. However, 27 per cent of the respondents stated that all sources gave them information and they presented the business plan to every source of capital to which they went for funds. The types of information suggested were usually financial information (in 30 per cent of the cases), a marketing plan (in 15 per cent), technical details (in 15 per cent) and a general background and five-year projections by further 10 per cent segments of respondents, Figure 10.

We inquired whether they had received outside assistance in preparing their business plans or proposals and Figure 11 shows that 34 per cent of them did receive assistance, usually from accountants (44 per cent), business associates (17 per cent) and consultants (13 per cent). Government did play some role in assisting them with 9 per cent of them stating government in general, and a further 9 per cent saying that the Federal Business Development Bank gave them assistance, usually through the Counselling Assistance for Small Enterprise Program. We also asked whether the sources of assistance stated above referred them to other sources of capital and received an affirmative answer from 36 per cent of the respondents, while a further 22 per cent stated that they had received other assistance from these sources. This type of assistance ranged from how to approach sources of capital to contacts in the industry who could either help them arrange such capital or put them in touch with the right people and possible private placements of capital from individuals, groups or corporations, Figure 12.

We asked whether raising capital was a problem for the firm in general and received a response of 51 per cent in the affirmative. This illustrates that it is a recurring

10

problem in the high-technology industry in Canada and 36 per cent stated that it was mainly a problem of very cautious lenders (usually bankers) in Canada, which they saw as a major problem in obtaining funds. Another 21 per cent stated a problem of government attitudes in providing financing, especially in the high-technology areas. A further 15 per cent stated that the view of their industry and high technology in particular was a problem in the raising of financing since many lenders did not understand the industry or the technology. In addition, Figure 13 lists what the respondents say is the source of the problem and 37 per cent of them stated government attitudes or lack of incentives were the cause, while 20 per cent blamed the private sector and another 28 per cent blamed both. Only 5 per cent of them stated that there was really no problem and another 10 per cent said the present situation was acceptable, especially for those individual entrepreneurs who were willing to get out and avail themselves of all sources available.

Figure 14 lists suggestions for improving the availability of funds. The predominant suggestion, made by 39 per cent of respondents, was to rationalize government programs. In addition, tax incentives were stated as a possible cure by 22 per cent of the respondents, while 21 per cent said that more government R & D grants were needed. For the private sector, 31 per cent stated that less-conservative banks would improve the situation and 22 per cent said that more venture capital was needed in Canada, especially on the high-technology side. In addition, 11 per cent said that more advice should be available from bankers on alternative sources of financing, especially in situations where the bank could not handle a request for financing. An equal percentage stated that they wished there were more capable finance people in the firms, since they often had problems dealing with government employees who lacked an understanding of the technical issues of their high-technology products and industry, but were much more finance-oriented than the entrepreneurs.

CONCLUSIONS AND RECOMMENDATIONS
The major conclusions of this survey were that there is definitely a lack of available financing to high-technology industries in Canada, since they have particular problems in both raising financing and in finding management skilled in the financial management of the firm. Most of the managers interviewed were technically trained and had little or no skill or experience in dealing with the financing of an independent venture. However, many of them realize this and did deal with outside sources to provide them with help in putting together a business plan, locating sources of financing and looking after the financial side of the firm's management.

These conclusions illustrate that the firms responding to this survey were really well-equipped on the technical side of the business, but poorly equipped for the general management side of the operations, especially in the area of financing. It is therefore a conclusion of the survey that most of these new high-technology firms should become aware of these problems and actively recruit people who have skills on the financial side to supplement the technical skills which are usually brought in by the founders of these firms. In fact, it was found that the founders usually brought in people who were similar in background and interests to themselves, other technically oriented people, rather than trying to complement their weaknesses by hiring people skilled in the general management areas. It is a sad fact that many of the high-technology firms and the entrepreneurs in them never quite recognize the need for these general management attributes. In fact, it is probably a basic problem that these highly technically trained people do not interact well with general management types of individuals and cannot see the need for them. They tend to be over-confident in their own general-management skills, even when they have had no previous training or experience in the area.

The difficulty, of course, arises when one asks how this situation might be cured. Possible suggestions are a variety of training programs, directed at these technical entrepreneurs to help educate them in the general-management areas of running their business. But these individuals are not very favourably oriented towards more training, especially when they do not recognize the need for this general-management skill. We found that many of the sources of capital to which these firms applied for funds were currently using requirements, such as changing the management team, usually in the direction of more capable general managers, as a requirement for the provision of their funds. This was especially true of venture capitalists and other large sources of capital. Government programs should consider the adoption of a similar practice.

REFERENCES

1. Peterson, Rein, "Small Business—Building a Balanced Economy," Press Porcepic, 1977.
2. Cooper, A., "R and D is More Efficient in Small Companies," *Harvard Business Review,* June 1984.
3. Litvak, I. and C. Maule, "A study of Successful Technical Entrepreneurs in Canada", Technological Innovation Studies Program, Department of Industry, Trade and Commerce, Ottawa, September, 1972.
4. Knight, R. M., "A Study of Venture Capital Financing in Canada," Technological Studies Branch, Department of Industry, Trade and Commerce, Ottawa, June 1973.
5. Knight, R. M., and J. C. Lemmon, "A Study of Small and Medium-Sized Canadian Technology-Based Companies," Technological Studies Branch, Department of Industry, Trade and Commerce, Ottawa, September 1978.
6. Little, B., R. Cooper, and R. More, "The Assessment of Markets for the Development of New Industrial Products in Canada," Technological Studies Branch, Department of Industry, Trade and Commerce, Ottawa, December 1971.
7. Knight, R. M., *Small Business Management in Canada: Text and Cases,* Toronto: McGraw-Hill Ryerson, 1981.
8. Knight, R. M., "Manufacturing Issues in Smaller High-Technology Firms in Canada", Unpublished Working Paper, School of Business Administration, University of Western Ontario, March 1985.
9. Knight, R. M., "Marketing by Smaller High-Technology Firms in Canada", Unpublished Working Paper, School of Business Administration, University of Western Ontario, March 1985.
10. Knight, R. M., "Entrepreneurship in Canada," *Journal of Small Business Canada,* Vol. 1 No. 1, Summer, 1983.
11. Ernst and Whinney, "Capital Formation Survey of Companies Financed by Canadian Venture Capital Sources," April, 1981.
12. Wynant, L. et al., "Chartered Bank Financing of Small Business in Canada," School of Business Administration, The University of Western Ontario, 1982.
13. Cooper, R., "Winning the New Product Game—Successful Product Innovation in Canada," Faculty of Management, Montreal: McGill University, 1976.
14. Little, B., "New Products, New Markets," School of Business Administration, The University of Western Ontario, 1973.
15. Hay, R. D. and J. Bernier, "Creating New Companies in a Canadian University" in *Frontiers of Entrepreneurship Research,* Vesper, K., 1981, Babson College.
16. Knight, R., "Bankruptcies by Type of Entrepreneur in Canada" in *Frontiers of Entrepreneurship Research,* Vesper, K., 1981, Babson College.

Figure 1
Industry Sectors of Respondents

Industry	% Responding
Communications	22
Computers and Computer Access	22
Monitoring Devices	15
Computer-Assisted Design and Robotics	9
Medical Sciences	8
Marine	8
Energy	7
Research	5
Other	4

Figure 2
Type of Research and Development

Type	% Reporting
New Technology	40
On-Going	20
New Microprocessors	15
Sensing Devices	11
Remote Systems	9
Miniaturization	5

Percentage of Sales Devoted to Research and Development

Mean 28%   Median 13%

Figure 3
Location and Ownership of Firms Surveyed

Location	% Responding
Southern Ontario	52
Other Ontario	27
British Columbia	11
Quebec	6
Maritimes	3
Other	1

Ownership	% Responding
Canadian Independent	90
Canadian Subsidiary	4
Foreign Subsidiary	6

13

Figure 4
Size of Firms in the Sample

Measure	Mean	Median
Sales Volume ($000)	5787	1998
Size of Management Team (maximum 300)	10	4
Equity Capital Issued ($000)	1404	150
Number of Employees (maximum 2 100)	88	22
Number of Shareholderrs (maximum 3 800)	126	3
Amount of Debt ($000)	781	100

Figure 5
Characteristics of Firms in Sample
Educational Background of Founder

Type	% Responding
Engineering Degree	41
Business Degree	16
Ph.D.	14
Science Degree	12
Multiple Degrees	6
No Degree	4
Trade Experience	7

Initial Product Line

Type	% Responding
Same as Present	62
Consulting	26
Service	9
Other	3

Position of Person Responding

Type	% Responding
President/Owner	77
V.P.Marketing	8
V.P.Finance	5
V.P.Other	6
Other	4

14

Figure 6

Sources of Funds Used at Various Stages

Source	Pre-Startup (Before First Sale)	Startup (First Year)	Development (2nd-5th Year)	Maturity (After 5th Year)
Personal Savings of Founders	61%	31%	10%	6%
Family/Friends	13	1	2	3
Trade Credit	6	9	11	9
Bank Loans	12	32	40	31
Government Programs	4	5	13	11
Customers	8	9	8	5
Investment Groups	2	3	8	1
Private Placements	2	2	3	1
Other (individuals, American, Public issue, etc.)	12	17	22	20

Figure 7

Type and Amounts of Funding from Various Sources

Source	Equity	Debt	Average Amount Initially (000's)	Average Amount Currently (000's)
Personal Savings of Founders	64%	5%	55	133
Family/Friends	7	3	36	47
Trade Credit	2	12	59	123
Bank Loans	4	59	131	296
Government Programs	4	10	253	521
Private Placements	14	3	1 256	2 250
Public Issues	4	0	8 141	24 272
Customers	0	11	205	402
Investment Groups	5	1	402	524
Other	13	8	296	475

15

Figure 8
Special Terms on Financing Obtained

Yes—39%   No—61%

Type	% Responding
Personal Guarantees	55
Operating Controls	13
Changes in Management Team	4
Parent Company Guarantee	4

Figure 9
Significant Difficulty Obtaining Financing at any Stage?

Yes—45%   No—55%

Type	% Reporting
Banks Not Co-operative	32
Company Performance	19
Question Need for Finance	11
Lack of Collateral	7
Business New	
Lack of Experience	6
Risk Too High	4
No Product Proven at this Stage	2

Figure 10
Prepare Written Business Plan
In Search For Capital

Yes—60%   No—40%

For Which Sources	% Reporting	Receive Instructions From These Sources
All	27	17
Banks	30	26
Individuals	14	5
Government	9	17
Venture Capital	9	9
Federal Business Development Bank	4	9
Other	9	9

Types of Information	Suggested
Financial Information	30
Marketing Plan	15
Technical Details	15
Background Details	10
Five-Year Projections	10

16

Figure 11
Receive Outside Assistance
In Preparing Proposal
Yes—34%   No—66%

Assistance From	% Reporting
Accountants	44
Business Associates	17
Consultants	13
Government	9
Federal Business Development Bank	9

Figure 12
Sources of Assistance

Refer You to Sources of Capital		Assist Otherwise in Raising Capital	
Yes—36%	No—64%	Yes—22%	No—78%

Type of Assistance	% Reporting
How to Approach	50
Contacts	25
Private Placements	25

Figure 13
Is Raising Capital
A Problem In Your Business?
Yes—51%   No—49%

Type of Problem	% Reporting
Cautious Lenders	36
Government Attitudes	21
View of Industry	15
Growth Possibilities	6
Strict Covenants	6
No Proven Product	2
High Risk	2

Source of Problem	% Reporting
Government	37
Private	20
Both	28
None	5
Present Situation OK	10

Figure 14
Suggestion For Improving Availability of Funds

Suggestion	% Responding
Rationalize Government Programs	39
Tax Incenttives	22
More Government R & D Grants	21
Less-Conservative Banks	31
More Venture Capital	22
Advice from Banks	11
More Finance People in High-Technology Firms	11

17

6 NEW VENTURES AND LARGE FIRMS: THE SEARCH FOR INTERNAL ENTREPRENEURSHIP

Introduction

The popular view of the entrepreneur consists of an independent, courageous, enthusiastic and tenacious individual who seizes an idea or invention and who somehow establishes a new enterprise in order to exploit that idea commercially (Smiles, 1884; Roberts and Wainer, 1971; McCelland, 1971). However, while this 'classical entrepreneur' continues to play an important role as an initiator of innovations and founder of new business enterprises, the emergence of the large corporation, along with an increasing degree of concentration of industry, and particularly of the science intensive industries, requires the recognition and encouragement of a second type of entrepreneur, namely the 'intracorporate entrepreneur' (Rothwell, 1975a). As a company grows through exploiting its initial innovation, its management requirements change from something that is normally an idiosyncratic management style which is innovative, fluid and willing to accept high-risk developments, to one of stable management which has high administrative skills and is capable of ensuring the efficient running of the increasingly more complex organisation. Administrators, in general, tend to take a jaundiced view of risk-taking and innovation: they are often bureaucrats who tend to wish to maintain the *status quo* and to do things always 'according to the book'. The environment created, therefore, in the larger organization will often militate against innovation (particularly radical innovation) as well as against individual entrepreneurship occuring within that organization.

The measures increasingly being taken in a number of countries to stimulate new entrepreneurship and to facilitate increased rates of innovation in small firms indicate a recognition both of the problems of large firm entrepreneurship outlined above, and of the contribution small entrepreneural firms can make to high rates of industrial innovation and the growth of new technology-based industries. The Innovation Centres experiment in the US (and latterly in Canada and the Republic of Ireland) represents, perhaps, the most explicit attempt to create greater numbers of independent entrepreneurs.

But given the current structure of industry in the advanced market economies, with the preponderance of large firms, any lack of innovativeness cannot be solved solely through the creation of more entrepreneurial small firms. It would therefore seem to be of crucial importance to seek structures for the stimulation of entrepreneurship in existing large corporations. Indeed, one of the major problems for the 1980s will be that of the ability, or otherwise, of major corporations to cope with structural change and to seek regeneration through radical innovation. Considerable evidence exists to suggest that intracorporate entrepreneurs can, and in fact do, exist in large corporations, and that they play an exceptionally important role in generating successful innovations. Some of the more convincing of this evidence is presented below.

A pioneer in this field, Schon, in his paper 'Champions for Radical New Invention' (1963), suggested that the answer to the problem of overcoming the characteristic reaction of large organizations against upsetting change and innovation lies in the encouragement of 'champions' for new ideas. The champion

> must be a man willing to put himself on the line for an idea of doubtful success. He is willing to fail but he is capable of using any and every means of informal ways and pressure to succeed. No ordinary involvement with a new idea provides the energy required to cope with the indifference and resistance that major technical change requires. It is characteristic of champions of new developments that they identify with the idea as their own, and with its promotion as a cause, to a degree that goes far beyond the requirements of their job.

Schon extended this concept to define the 'production champion' who operates within the large corporation. This is an individual with considerable power and prestige in the organization, who knows how to use the company's informal system of relationships, and whose interests extend not only to the new technology embodied in the product which he is championing, but include also the marketing, production and financial aspects essential to the product's development.

More recently in the US Globe, Levy and Schwartz (1973) made a comprehensive study of ten major innovations in an attempt to determine what factors played key roles in the complex series of activities that resulted in the innovations' outstanding success. They identified twenty-one major factors which made a significant contribution to the successful conclusion of the innovations. One of these factors, which they ranked sixth in their analysis of the frequency of occurrence of the various decisive events during the innovative sequence, was the Technical Entrepreneur.

He was defined as 'an individual within the performing organization who champions a scientific or technical activity; he is sometimes also called a "product champion".' In generalizing from the case histories, Globe *et al.* stated that

> the Technical Entrepreneur, whose importance was highlighted in the study of the 'factors', is also a 'characteristic' important in nine of the ten innovations. This is the strongest conclusion that emerges from the study. In fact, in three innovations, the technical entrepreneur persisted in the face of the inhibiting effect of an unfavourable market analysis. If any suggestion were to be made as to what should be done to promote innovation, it would be to find − if one can! − technical entrepreneurs.

Further evidence was provided in the results of Langrish *et al.*'s study in the UK of eighty-four innovations which resulted in the Queen's Award to Industry in 1966/67. Langrish *et al.* (1972) isolated seven specific factors of importance in the firm's success: two of these factors related to the presence within the firm of outstanding individuals. The first of these is an outstanding person in a position of authority who makes a special contribution to the innovation (e.g. Manager, Managing Director, Technical Director or Chairman). The second type of outstanding individual is one who, for instance, is described by his colleagues as a 'mechanical genious', and who possesses some unique form of knowledge that would otherwise not have been at the disposal of the firm. The factors 'Top Person' and 'Other Person' occurred numerically more frequently than any others in explaining success, and the latter individual was particularly important in innovations which embodied large technological change.

Perhaps the most detailed study of innovation which explicitly included consideration of the role of intracorporate entrepreneurs was project SAPPHO. In its final version, SAPPHO included the comparative analysis of twenty-two successful and twenty-two unsuccessful innovations in the chemical process industry, and twenty-one successful and twenty-one unsuccessful innovations in the scientific instruments industry (Rothwell *et al.*, 1974). This study underlined the crucial importance of the 'business innovator'; the individual who was actually responsible within the management structure for the overall progress of the project.

While the business innovator was important to success in both industries, his characteristics varied between the two. In scientific instruments, where most of the innovating firms were small, the successful business innovator approximated to the classical entrepreneur and his most important characteristics were commitment to, enthusiasm for, and involvement in, the project. In chemicals, while these characteristics were important, the further characteristics of authority and power were vital. In other words, enthusiasm and commitment were simply not sufficient to ensure success, and in order to alter significantly the course of the project, the business innovator in the chemical industry, which is characterized by very large, hierarchical and often bureaucratic firms, needs to be powerful enough to shape the project himself.

The need to promote entrepreneurship within the large organization in order to stimulate innovation and maintain growth has been recognized for some time, notably in the US, where a survey conducted in the 1970s suggested that one in four of the thousand largest American corporations in 1971 has established formal or informal intracorporate entrepreneurship programmes designed to facilitate entrepreneurial activity: this is the so-called 'ventures approach'. A useful formal definition was given by Cook (1971), which is: 'Venture management is the formalization of a new corporate-level activity designed to generate new business for the large organization primarily through the use of internal resources.' Venture management, it seems, is seen as a viable alternative to acquisitions as a means of entering new business areas; it allows firms to exploit technologies which do not altogether fit into existing operations and, perhaps most importantly, it combines the flexibility and entrepreneurial abilities of the small company with the considerable advantages of size.

In this chapter we will offer a general description of the new venture operation as an added weapon in management's armoury of strategies towards innovation and growth. We do not seek to present the new venture technique as a magical formula for instant innovative success, but rather simply as another approach towards achieving technical change and economic progress within the large company, and also as an alternative to the establishment of a new independent small firm as a suitable vehicle for individual commitment and entrepreneurial endeavour. We start with a description of a number of new venture approaches that are currently being practised in the US. Also the features of a variety of approaches utilized by a single large American corporation to stimulate in-house entrepreneurial activity are outlined. We shall then describe the process of successful industrial innovation, discuss the critical roles which need to be played by individuals within the business organization in order to achieve innovative success, and define different 'classes' of innovation according to their degree and type of novelty. The various new venture approaches will then be linked to both the innovation types which they are best suited to exploit, and to the critical roles necessary for them to encompass in order to achieve success. In this way this chapter aims at an integrated approach to the problem of innovating via the new venture method. Finally, some of the problems associated with the management of new internal venture operations will be discussed.

New venture approaches*

A spectrum of new venture approaches are currently being pursued by industry, primarily in the US. Some of these are described briefly below.

(a) *Retaining and stimulating entrepreneurs*

Here the object is to maintain the organization in its present form and to attempt to encourage entrepreneurs within this framework. However, the problems of bureaucracy, interference, lack of individual freedom, etc. will generally continue to exist, and resource allocation still tends to be biased against radical new innovation.

(b) *Venture capital operation*

The firm funds new ventures in new fields outside its traditional areas of interest. This is the simplest approach to administer since it requires only a commitment of cash. The new idea being exploited, and the entrepreneurs involved, might both have originated in the firm's own R & D laboratory.

(c) *Venture nurturing*

The firm provides not only cash, but also marketing, production, distribution and R & D assistance to the new venture. Here there is a fairly high level of corporate involvement and problems of autonomy and interference might occur.

(d) *Venture packaging and sponsored spin-off*

This involves the exploitation of ideas which have arisen in the R & D laboratory but which are not suitable, or irrelevant, for exploitation by the firm internally. Here a separate small firm is set up by enthusiastic employees to exploit the idea. The corporation supplies only some of the capital: the entrepreneurs and other outside interests provide the remainder. Hence the risk is shared.

* The authors' description of the various new venture techniques owes much to a presentation given by Prof. E. Roberts (Sloan School of Management, MIT) at Queen's University, Ontario, November, 1973, entitled 'Achieving Successful Industrial Innovations'. This section is taken largely from R. Rothwell (1975b).

(e) *Joint inside–outside ventures*

This tends to be a large firm/small firm tie-up. The large firm provides the cash resources and, if appropriate, access to production facilities and to channels of distribution. The small firm provides high technology, or specialized knowledge, and aggressive entrepreneurship. Some large firm/small firm US joint ventures are listed in Figure 6.1.

(f) *Internal venture operation*

This comprises the setting-up of a new venture operation completely within the existing organization to exploit the invention. It involves setting up a new division or a new product group within a division.

Large company	Small company	Area of joint venture
American Broadcasting Company	Technical Operations, Inc.	Black and white film transmitted to colour viewing over TV
American District Telegraph	Solid State Technology	Industrial security systems
Bell & Howell	Microx	Microfilm reader
Bravo Corporation	Anti-Pollution Systems, Inc.	Molten salt pollution control systems
Elliot Machine Div. of Carrier Corporation	Mechanical Technology, Inc.	High speed centrifugal compressors
Exxon Nuclear Corp.	Avco–Everett Research Laboratory	High-energy laser uranium isotope separation and enrichment
Ford Motor Company	Thermoelectron Corp.	Steam engines for automobiles
General Electric Co.	Bolt Beranek & Newman Inc.	Hospital computer system
Johnson & Johnson Co.	Damon Corporation	Automated clinical laboratory system
Mobil Corporation	Tyco Laboratories Inc.	Long-crystal silicon solar conversion technology
Pitney–Bowes Co.	Alpex Computer Corp.	Electronic 'point of sale' check-out systems
Roche Electronics Division of Hoffman–La Roche	Avco–Everett Research Laboratory	Inflation balloon heart assist system
Wyeth Laboratories, Division of American Home Products	Survival Technology, Inc.	Self-administered heart attack drug and injection system

Fig. 6.1 Some large–small US joint ventures. *Source*: Prof. E. Roberts, Sloan School of Management, MIT.

Although initially probably having a leaning towards R & D, it will be staffed by a multi-disciplinary team containing strong elements from marketing and sales. It should be awarded a separate budget. It should enjoy a high degree of autonomy in taking day-to-day operational decisions, and should proceed with a minimum of corporative interference. It will be able to draw on the corporate R & D, production and sales departments for help and advice. The atmosphere within the new venture group will be conducive to entrepreneurship, and its organization will therefore be flexible and non-hierarchical.

Whichever of the above venture modes the large organization adopts will, of course, depend on its corporate philosophy.* There is no reason, however, why the firm should not adopt a variety of modes, or a variety of approaches within a single mode. A spectrum of venture approaches adopted by a number of major corporations is shown in Figure 6.2. Below are outlined some features of the facilities and encouragement offered to entrepreneurial individuals to facilitate new *internal* venturing in a large and highly successful North American Corporation.

Venture capital	*Inside–outside ventures*	*Composite ventures*	*Internal ventures*
Dow Chemical Company	Ford, Mobil, G.E. Johnson & Johnson	Exxon	3M Company, British Oxygen Company (now discontinued)

       —————————▶ Increasing corporate commitment.

Fig. 6.2   Venture approaches adapted by a number of major corporations.
Source: Prof. E. Roberts, MIT.

(a) *Top-down entrepreneurial encouragement*

Presidents and other exalted executives who have made their way to the top through successful entrepreneurship in turn actively encourage this. It is a case of 'follow my example' rather than 'do as I tell you'.

(b) *Multiple internal sponsors*

There are three possible sources of monetary support and sponsorship for the exploitation of new ideas. The first is the entrepreneur's own department: it is legitimate for this department to diversify into new areas. The second is the central research organization, which is empowered to sponsor new ventures. The third is the organization's new business department. The firm provides for, and indeed, facilitates, personal mobility.

* It will also depend on the firm's current range of products and its in-house technological capabilities.

(c) *Early formation of 'product teams'*

New product teams are formed very early in the venture. They contain representatives of technical, production, finance and marketing. The team members take a risk in that if the new venture is a failure, they return to their original departments, generally losing several years seniority in the process: therefore they must be enthusiastic to join the team in the first place. The new development then becomes 'our' new idea, rather than simply 'a' new idea.

(d) *Full life cycle commitment to team*

As long as a new product team meets certain performance criteria (e.g. satisfactory technical progress, satisfactory sales), then the firm maintains a continuing commitment to the team. If the team fails to meet these criteria, then the firm's support is withdrawn.

(e) *No 'minimum size' constraint*

A new product development is not discontinued because it does not have a very large potential market. Provided that the expected or actual return on investment is deemed sufficiently large, then the project will proceed.

Finally, this company actively encourages internal competition between divisions, and it ties executives' incentives systems to what it calls 'building new businesses'.

Any organization will, of course, be limited in its choice of new venture approaches by its available resources. For example it is difficult to imagine a small or medium-sized firm attempting to adopt approaches (b), (c) or (d). Indeed, Susbauer (1973) found, from his survey of a large number of companies in the US employing intracorporate entrepreneurship practices, that 'smaller companies (less than $50 million in annual sales) reported less (intracorporate entrepreneurship) programme development than larger companies.' Further, 'larger companies have a clear tendency to establish formal programmes, while smaller companies are more likely to have established informal programmes or both kinds of programmes, if they have them at all.'* It is also interesting to note that 'companies which had initiated only formal programmes felt more positive towards their

---

* Susbauer defined *formal* intracorporate entrepreneurship programmes as (1) separate division of the parent organization, (2) a separate department of a division, (3) a separate subsidiary of the parent. *Informal* systems were: (1) part of a corporate department whose purpose is to seek new investment opportunities, *one* of which may be from ideas generated internally outside of normal R & D channels, (2) a department of the R & D activity, (3) new product committee, (4) employee suggestion reward schemes which sometimes result in entrepreneurial activity.

programmes (87 per cent) than companies which had initiated informal programmes, regardless of the size of the company, and a greater percentage of larger companies felt that their efforts were successful than smaller companies (82 per cent to 63 per cent).' This probably reflects the fact that the establishment of a formal programme represents a greater explicit corporate commitment to the new venture concept right from the start.

The successful innovation process

The transformation of a new idea or technological invention into a marketable product or process requires the existence of some sort of organizational framework within which this transformation might take place. The process by which the idea passes from inception to the market place is called the *innovation process*, and the business organization (in this case the new venture operation) can be thought of as a vehicle for sustaining this process and carrying it through to completion. (After all, the new business is founded, initially at least, to exploit a particular new idea, although at a later date it will be required to act as a foundation upon which further innovations, both radical and incremental, might be constructed.) This is a useful concept since we possess considerable knowledge concerning the industrial innovation process, and about the conditions that result in commercial success. If we can describe the process of successful industrial innovation and the characteristics of successful innovators, we should be able to describe the characteristics of the new business enterprise necessary to achieve this innovative success, and relate them to the different new venture approaches. A number of factors have been determined empirically which characterize the successful industrial innovation process (Rothwell, 1977):

(a) *Understanding users' needs*

Successful innovators have a very thorough and imaginative understanding of users' needs. They gain precise knowledge concerning the conditions in which the innovation will be required to operate. They interact, where possible, with potential customers throughout the course of the project and continually update their specifications in the light of changing user requirements. They take great pains to understand, and place priority on meeting, users' requirements rather than on satisfying their own egos!

(b) *Marketing and sales*

Between 70 and 80 per cent of successful technological innovations arise in response to the recognition of a need of one sort or another. Where the innovation arises as the result of new technology, the successful innovator determines that a need exists before he proceeds with the development, and he establishes that the need is sufficiently widely diffused (i.e. that the market is sufficiently large) for the innovation to be viable. The successful innovator mounts a comprehensive advertising and sales campaign and he educates users in the right uses and limitations of the innovation; he offers a comprehensive after-sales technical support service where appropriate. The successful innovator is aware of changing market conditions and requirements and of competitive developments elsewhere.

(c) *Communications*

Successful innovators establish efficient internal and external communication networks: communications between the different functional departments within the organization are good, as are communications between the organization, the outside scientific and technological community and the market place. Successful innovations proceed in the light of perceived company strategy.

(d) *Key individuals*

Associated with successful innovations are various 'key' individuals ('product champions' or 'internal entrepreneurs'). They are enthusiastic towards the innovation, committed to it and involved with it. They afford the innovation their wholehearted support and 'push' it through to completion. Generally they require both technical and managerial expertise, which is embodied in a single, or several individuals.

(e) *Effective manufacturing procedures*

Successful innovations suffer fewer after-sales 'bugs' as a result of poor production procedures. They are designed and manufactured in a manner which is conducive to easy and speedy maintenance. Care is taken to ensure that materials used in construction are compatible with the environment in which the innovation is to function. Long term reliability is a prime factor in the original project specification.

(f) *Cash and manpower resources*

Successful innovations are allotted sufficient cash and manpower resources to enable technical problems to be solved effectively, prototypes to be built where necessary, and sufficiently large marketing and sales efforts to be mounted. At critical stages in the process, successful innovators focus resources into the innovation to facilitate its progress. Successful innovations are afforded full corporate backing right from the start.

(g) *Management style*

Successful innovations tend to arise in organizations that are flexible and capable of being adapted to facilitate the progress of the individual innovation. The management style is participative rather than centralized, consultative rather than authoritarian, and the organization is horizontal rather than vertical in structure. In short, 'organic' rather than 'mechanistic' organizations are conducive to the generation of successful innovations.

The successful innovation process just described does, of course, represent an ideal case and very few innovations, including successful ones, will perform equally well in all the seven areas listed above. Furthermore, innovation is an inherently risky process and this risk can never be completely eradicated. However, the results of project SAPPHO (Rothwell *et al.*, 1974) showed quite clearly that, on average, successful innovators out-performed failures in all the areas of competence associated with the process of innovation, and that success could rarely be explained in terms of a single factor only.

Critical functions

Having outlined the characteristics of successful innovators, and the successful innovation process, it is now possible to identify some of the *critical functions* which need to be fulfilled by individuals within the framework of the business organization in order to achieve this success (Roberts, 1977).

(i) *Creative scientist or inventor*

His primary role is to create new ideas. He is not necessary the right person to exploit them (frequently he is not, in fact, suited to exploit them!). His creativity must be channelled along paths dictated by corporate strategy and market needs rather than by personal whim.

(ii) *Entrepreneur*

His role is to champion the idea and to 'move it' through the organization. He seeks organizational support for the idea and convinces management of its worth. He is enthusiastic towards the idea and firmly convinced of its value and high market potential. He will generally be an aggressive, independently-minded individual.

(iii) *Project manager*

His role is that of administrator. He *integrates* the various differentiated functions and welds them into a continuous innovation process. (This might not be a designated individual; the function might be fulfilled by management generally.)

(iv) *Sponsor*

His role is to provide a window to the organization. He shows the entrepreneur 'the ropes'; how to obtain funds, where to seek support etc., which can be daunting tasks in the very large corporation. He will be an experienced (and perhaps not very active) senior member of the organization.

(v) *Technological gatekeeper*

He actually reads journals and he attends conferences. He provides vital technical information. He communicates outside of his immediate circle and interacts strongly with other groups within and outside of the organization. In short, he is an extremely effective transceiver of information (Allen, 1970).

(vi) *Production engineer*

He advises the R & D and design personnel on the limitations and possibilities of the production process; he advises on various preferred design procedures (e.g. use of standard modules) and the preferential use of certain materials. He oversees the manufacture of the innovation and irons out production bugs before commercial sales. He focuses attention on designing for 'makeability' (Rothewell, 1980).

(vii) *The marketeer*

He continually feeds in information concerning user needs and market changes. He specifies users' requirements. He maintains the group's awareness that the end-point of the operation is the market place. It is his input which very often initiates the search for the new innovation.

(viii) *Resource controller*

He allocates sufficient funds to the project to enable it to progress and ensures that technical, production and marketing manpower and raw material resources are available when required. He monitors costs and takes a hand in pricing procedures.

Each of these critical functions might be embodied in a separate individual, several of them may be embodied in a single individual, or several individuals may be employed in fulfilling a single function. However this might be, these functions must generally be fulfilled if the invention is to be transformed into a commercially successful new product or process. It is the function of the new business organization to provide a framework within which these various 'critical functions' might be encompassed and to integrate them into a united single operating entity.

Classification of innovation

Innovations come in a variety of shapes and sizes, and the type of organization, or the degree of organizational change, necessary to accommodate a particular innovation will depend on that innovation's degree and type of novelty. A classification of innovations is given below, along with the required organizational change to see each innovation type through to fruition (Collier, 1974).

	Scale of innovation	*Appropriate organizational change*
Type 1	Present product Present technology Present market	This is a product improvement and can be easily accommodated within the existing organization.
Type 2	New product Present technology Present market	Can again be developed within the existing organization with the formation of a new project team in the R & D department.
Type 3	Present product Present technology New market	Again, existing organization more or less maintained. Marketing must learn the idiosyncracies of new customers and perhaps a new sales team will be formed.
Type 4	New product Present technology New market	In this case, a new product group might be established, staffed primarily by R & D and marketing personnel. Manufacturing can still be done in company's existing department. Conventional firms might simply form new R & D project and sales teams.
Type 5	New product New technology Present market	Again a new product group might be established but staffed primarily by R & D and manufacturing personnel. Group may utilize the firm's existing marketing and sales department. Alternatively, a new

106   NEW VENTURES AND LARGE FIRMS

	Scale of innovation	*Appropriate organizational change*
Type 5 (cont.)		venture group might be established depending on the degree of novelty embodied in the 'new' technology.
Type 6	New product New technology New market	Represents a new business to the company. A completely new business organization (new venture company) might be established, or a new division formed within the existing organization.

It is quite clear from the above that a new venture operation is appropriate only when the project represents the generation of a new area of business for the firm.

The appropriate new venture approach

So far a spectrum of new venture approaches which are in current usage has been considered, the characteristics of the successful innovation process have been described, the critical functions associated with successful innovators have been listed, and a typology of innovations has been developed. It is now possible to bring these factors together and to associate the different new venture approaches with the particular innovation types they are best suited to exploit, and to the various critical functions which they must contain. This is achieved in Table 6.1 which will, it is hoped, serve as a guide in assisting management to choose the approach most appropriate to the particular task in hand.

The management of new internal ventures

The venture approach that demands the greatest corporate commitment, and which is perhaps the most difficult to pursue successfully, is the new internal venture. The establishment of a new and fairly autonomous work group within an existing organizational framework will create a number of problems of both a political and administrative nature, particularly when the company is employing this technique for the first time. It is necessary, therefore, when embarking on a new internal venture scheme, to approach it with much caution and to be armed with a great deal of forward planning and prepared alternative strategies. The composition of the new venture team, its leader, and its place within the existing company structure,

Table 6.1   New venture approach

	Retaining and stimulating entrepreneurs	Venture capital operation	Venture nurturing	Venture packaging and sponsored spin-off	Joint inside–outside ventures	Internal venture operation
Innovation type	a,b,c	f	d,e	f	e	d,e,f
Critical function						
(a) within new venture	—	i, ii iii, v vii	ii, iii	i, ii iii, v vi, vii	i, ii v	i, ii ii, v vii
(b) shared	—	viii	i, iv v, vi vii, viii	viii	iii, viii	iv, vi viii
(c) within parent	i to viii	iv	—	iv	v, vi vii	—

Table 6.1. Tabulates the six new venture approaches and shows for each approach:
1. the innovation types it is best suited to exploit:
    a. present product, present technology, present market
    b. new product, present technology, present market
    c. present product, present technology, new market
    d. new product, present technology, new market
    e. new product, new technology, present market
    f. new product, new technology, new market
2. the critical functions contained completely within it, the critical functions which are shared between it and the original company, and the critical functions which are retained by the original company:
    i – creative scientist or inventor
    ii – entrepreneur
    iii – project manager
    iv – sponsor
    v – technological gatekeeper
    vi – production engineer
    vii – the marketeer
    viii – resource controller

are all factors of extreme importance in determining the success or failure of the venture. Comments concerning these issues are given below.

The new venture team

The new venture team will, initially at least, in most instances be development-oriented. However, it must contain a balance of R & D, market, production and administrative skills. Team members may be part-time or full-time depending on the venture system chosen and on the availability of resources. There might be a combination of both part-time and full-time members with a small full-time core — or leader — and a varying number of part-time members from other divisions, brought in when necessary, and especially at critical phases in the development. Members should be enthusiastic and committed towards the venture. Their probable rewards for success and possible penalties for failure must be made clear at the outset. Where the firm is dealing in a completely new market area, marketing expertise should, when possible, be brought in from outside.

It is probable that there is a minimum threshold of resources below which the venture team will not be effective, although this will of course depend on the nature of the project. Jones and Wilemon (1972) examined the characteristics of venture teams in twenty-four large US corporations listed in 'Fortune 500'. The average size of these teams was about ten full-time members, with the number of part-time members varying from none to fifty. Clearly the full-time/part-time membership system affords a high level of flexibility and allows the firm to focus large resources on the project when necessary. Maintaining a relatively small core member-ship ensures that the enthusiasm for, and the commitment to, the project are not diluted.

The leader

The post requires a fine balance between youth and experience. Prior work will probably relate to the basic character and objective of the new venture team, which are to take a new technology or idea and to exploit it commercially. Probable backgrounds are R & D, engineering management, new product development, corporate planning. He will have a desire for independent action, but will be committed towards the organization and the innovation. He will possess the ability to work with and motivate people. He will probably adopt the 'confrontation' approach when resolving conflict within his team, or between them and the rest of the corporate body, rather than the 'smoothing' or 'forcing' approaches.* Jones and Wileman (1972) looked at the characteristics of the venture managers in

---

* See, for example, Rubenstein, Barch and Douds, 'Ways to Improve Communications between R & D Groups.' *Research Management*, Nov. 1971: '. . . the confrontation approach is one which involves an open exchange about the causes of intergroup conflict, and efforts are directed towards reaching a useful and mutually acceptable decision rather than forcing one side's solution or smoothing over the situation.'

their sample of twenty-four US corporations. They were generally in their early forties; 24 per cent held a technical degree, 32 per cent had a background in R & D, 16 per cent in engineering and 24 per cent in corporate planning. Von Hippel (1977), in his study of twelve new venture operations in the US, found similar characteristics for venture managers. He then goes on to make the important point, however, that 'We do not know whether these characteristics of venture managers differ from the characteristics of other classes of managers at the parent company. We do know that age level shows no differential correlation between success and failure.'

Finally Schrage (1965), in his study of R & D entrepreneurs, found that the successful person was high in achievement motivation and low in power motivation. This result was supported in the work on the motivation of fifty-three successful R & D entrepreneurs by Warner and Rubin (1969), who found the prime motivation was a high need for achievement which was much more significant than the need for power. These results, taken with the earlier discussion on the characteristics of successful product-champions/business-innovators, suggest that it is not power *per se* (or the search for power) that is important, but rather the power, or ability, to affect favourably the progress of his 'pet' project to achieve a successful outcome, that motivates the product-champion. The point is that the venture approach can provide the venture leader with this very opportunity, i.e. the power to guide the course of 'his' new venture.

Corporate support

The new venture operation must be given — and must be seen to be given — the support of top management. It helps if venture leaders are appointed by top management, which goes some way to ensuring the co-operation of others within the organization. When necessary, the support of the other operating divisions must be willingly given. The venture leader's level and range of authority must be precisely delineated at the outset. The role of the new venture group and its relationship within the organization must be spelt out clearly by top management, in order to help circumvent suspicion and unfounded jealousy on the part of other employees.

The corporation must also persist in its support. According to Roberts (1979), a corporation must be willing to commit itself to a minimum period of five years for just *beginning* to 'grow a new business'. This is seen to be one of the most important factors in the phenomenal success of the 3M Corporations' venture operations during the past thirty years. Further, except in the case of joint ventures with smaller firms, the large company

110   NEW VENTURES AND LARGE FIRMS

might have to wait for up to ten years or more before it receives any significant income. This is clearly a problem during an era of high economic uncertainty and generally high inflation rates.

Autonomy

There is little sense in striving to create a new venture group which is designed to foster an atmosphere conducive to committed entrepreneurship and innovation, if management attempts to force it to conform with traditional operating procedures. The group must be confronted with the minimum of bureaucratic red-tape and interference, and be allowed the maximum degree of flexibility in its approach to the project in hand. However, it must be subject to independent assessment whereby its progress is monitored, and its aims checked against corporate and market requirements; it must not be allowed to persevere, and even 'grow like Topsy', simply by virtue of its own momentum. The team must, however, having been given clear and unambiguous objectives, be allowed as much operational autonomy as is practicable.

Discussion

There is, it seems, a growing awareness on the part of many large corporations — especially in the US — of the need to seek novel organizational forms in order to stimulate innovation and growth through internal entrepreneurship. As the new and science-intensive industries mature and become increasingly concentrated, the environment created in the large corporations which make up these industries can become less and less suited to individual commitment and entrepreneurial endeavour. As a result of this there has been a tendency for aggressively entrepreneurial and independently-minded individuals to leave the sometimes stifling atmosphere of the large company to establish their own small firms. A relatively new organizational concept, which is designed to combine the massive resources and varied skills of the large corporation, with the flexibility and personal involvement of the small firm, is the new venture group. There are a variety of new venture approaches currently being pursued in industry, particularly in the US,* and the appropriate organizational form chosen will depend on the company's corporate strategy, the level of its resources and on the nature of the innovation under development.

---

* For a description of the new venture approach as practised by a major UK company, see J. Gardner, 'Innovation through new ventures: new venture concept in BOC', *R & D Management*, vol. 2, no. 2, February 1973.

THE SEARCH FOR INTERNAL ENTREPRENEURSHIP   111

There is, as yet, little empirical evidence available concerning success rates among new venture operations, or of their levels of success in relation to other organizational forms utilized in parallel by firms during innovation; there are, indeed, reported some notable examples of failure.* Nevertheless, what limited evidence there is available suggests that, by and large, organizations employing the new venture approach feel that their attempts to create entrepreneurially vital activities in their companies are worthwhile.

Table 6.2 lists the reasons for the failure of twenty-one new venture approaches derived from interviews with top corporate management and with venture managers (Hlavacek, 1974). It can be seen that while the top corporate managers emphasized mainly financial problems, the venture managers placed greater emphasis on problems of internal conflicts. Further, while both groups emphasized the major problem of too small a potential market for the product, only the corporate managers mentioned technical problems. The general picture that emerges is one of caution and lack of long-term commitment by corporate management, and of internal friction and resistance to change experienced by venture managers in their dealings with other, more conventional, corporate departments.

The most popular form of venture management currently pursued in the US is joint small firm–large firm ventures (see Figure 6.1). Here the small firm generally supplies the dynamism, vigour, commitment and technology (i.e. supplies the entrepreneurship function), while the large firm supplies access to capital and to a comprehensive network of distribution, sales and after-sales servicing. Because of the very different behavioural characteristics of large and small firms, such a relationship can be fraught with problems. Two of the major problems, identified by Roberts (1979), are:

— small companies are prepared to, and indeed, often are forced to, take on-the-spot decisions, whereas large corporations often take months, if not years, to resolve their collective minds;
— small companies will shake hands on a deal, while large corporations employ a battery of lawyers to produce lengthy, and often complex, agreements.

Problems can also arise when the large firm, which is accustomed to selling often rather mature, standardized products, attempts to market highly innovative products using the same after-sales servicing network.

* For example, Du Pont's Corfam – see A. B. Robertson, *The Lessons of Failure*, MacDonald, 1974.

Table 6.2 Reasons given for the failure of 21 new internal ventures

TOP CORPORATE MANAGEMENT		VENTURE MANAGERS	
Reason for failure	Frequency*	Reason for failure	Frequency*
Sunk costs became too great	8	Market was too small	7
Market was too small	8	Distribution problems	6
Did not fit distribution system	8	Conflicts with divisional managers	6
Technical problems	6	Impatient top management	4
Wrong venture manager	6	Resistance from existing sales force	4
Drain on corporate–divisional profits	5	Marketing research inaccurate	4
Low return on investment	5	Budget too small	3
Conflicts with divisions	5	Inexperienced venture team	2
Termination of federal funds	2	Termination of federal funds	2
Weak lobbying effort	1	Decline in corporate profits	1
		Venture team too small	1

* In several cases, multiple responses were given.
Source: J. D. Hlavacek, 'Towards more successful Venture Management', *Journal of Marketing*, Vol. 38, No. 4, October 1974.

With radical new products there is a need to train customers in the right uses and limitations of the product, and to mount a speedy and efficient operation. Service personnel used to looking after standard products might experience difficulty in properly handling the new, high technology product, within existing structures and practice. Clearly, to handle the new product successfully requires some reorganization of the existing service network, which might meet with some resistance on the part of established corporate service management.

An alternative form of large firm–small firm relationship mentioned earlier is that of sponsored spin-off. General Electric, for example, established some ten years ago the Technical Ventures Operation. The main aim of TVO is to assist the commercialization of promising new product ideas which would otherwise not be exploited in-house, and it operates by bringing together the new technology, entrepreneurially-oriented individuals and capital; the capital derives both from GE and external sources of venture funds (Ben Daniel, 1973).

Finally, going back to the new internal venture, it is worthwhile repeating that this approach is not a magical formula for success via small firm-type entrepreneurship. Rather, it is one more weapon in corporate management's armoury of methods for achieving successful technological innovation. It does, however, appear to be particularly well suited to the stimulation of in-house entrepreneurship and to the exploitation of radical innovations that represent a new area of business for the large firm. It represents an explicit attempt to marry the 'human' advantages of the progressive small firm (dynamicism, flexibility, entrepreneurship) to the considerable advantages of scale enjoyed by the large corporation.

References

Allen, T. J. (1970), 'Communication Networks in R & D laboratories', *R & D Management*, *1*, 14.

Ben Daniel, B. J. (1973), 'The Technical Ventures Operation' (mimeo), General Electric Co., Schenectady, New York.

Collier, D. M. (1974), 'Research Based Venture Companies and the Links between Market and Technology', *Research Management*, May, pp. 16-20.

Cook, F. (1971), 'Setting Up Venture Operations', *Innovation*, No. 25, October, pp. 23-37.

Globe, S., Levy, G. W. and Schwartz, M. (1973), 'Key Factors and Events in the Innovation Process', *Research Management*, July.

Hlavacek, J. D. (1974), 'Towards more Successful Venture Management', *Journal of Marketing*, Vol. 38, No. 4, October, pp. 56-60.

Jones, K. A. and Wileman, D. L. (1972), 'Emerging Patterns in New Venture Management', *Research Management*, Vol. 15, No. 6, November, pp. 14-27.

Langrish, J. *et al.* (1972), *Wealth from Knowledge*, London, Macmillan.

McCelland, D. C. (1971), *The Achieving Society*, New York, Van Nostrand.

Roberts, E. B. (1977), 'Generating Effective Corporate Innovation', *Technology Review*, Vol. 80, No. 1, Oct./Nov., pp. 27-33.

Roberts, E. B. (1979), Seminar on New Ventures, McKinsey and Co., London, February; reported in C. Lorenz, 'Venture Management: 3M Show the Way', *Financial Times*, Tuesday, 20 February.

Roberts, E. B. and Wainer, H. A. (1971), 'Some Characteristics of Technical Entrepreneurs', *IEEE Trans. on Engin. Management*, EM-13, 3.

Rothwell, R. (1975a), 'Intracorporate Entrepreneurs', *Management Division*, *13*, 3.

Rothwell, R. (1975b), 'From Invention to New Business via the New Venture Approach', *Management Division*, *13*, 1.

Rothwell, R. (1977), 'Characteristics of Successful Innovation and Technically Progressive Firms', *R & D Management*, 1977.

Rothwell, R. (1980), 'It's not (just) what you make, it's the way you make it', *Design*, March.

Rothwell, R. *et al.* (1974), 'SAPPHO Updated: Project SAPPHO Phase II', *Research Policy*, No. 3, pp. 1-34.

Schon, D. A. (1965), 'Champions for Radical New Inventions', *Harvard Business Review*, March/April, pp. 77-86.

Schrage, H. (1966), 'The R & D Entrepreneur: Profile of Success', *Harvard Business Review*, Nov./Dec., pp. 56-69.

Smiles, S. (1884), *Men of Invention and Industry*, London, J. Murray.

Susbauer, J. C. (1973), 'U.S. Intracorporate Entrepreneurship Practices', *R & D Management*, *3*, 3.

von Hippel, E. (1977), 'Successful and Failed Co-operative Ventures: An Empirical Analysis', *Industrial Marketing Management*, Vol. 6, pp. 163–74.

Wainer, H. A. and Rubin, I. M. (1969), 'Motivation of R & D Entrepreneurs: Determinants of Company Success', *Journal of Applied Psychology*, Vol. 53, June, pp. 178–84.

Employment and Regional Growth

[21]

Cambridge Journal of Economics 1982, 6, 167–184

The Emilian model: productive decentralisation and social integration

Sebastiano Brusco*

Introduction

The following essay presents a dynamic analysis of the interaction between the productive structure, the labour market, and the principal political institutions in Emilia-Romagna.

There are at least three reasons why, in recent times, many economists have focused their attention on the economy of the region (Bagnasco and Messori, 1975; Bagnasco, 1977; Filuppucci, 1978; Capecchi *et al.*, 1979).

The first is that over the last fifteen years Emilia-Romagna has had an economic performance distinctly better than many other regions in Italy, and has shown itself more resilient to crisis.

Secondly, the industrial structure which developed in Emilia-Romagna, and which is the basis for its economic performance, may also be found in other parts of Italy, so that the study of Emilia is of general interest and its results may help to understand the working of industrial districts elsewhere in Italy.

Finally, in Emilia-Romagna almost all local authorities, including the regional government, are controlled by the communist party, often in alliance with the socialist party. The region, therefore, represents a kind of test for a coalition of left wing parties in Italy which is of broader European interest.

The superior economic performance of Emilia-Romagna

Table 1 compares both the participation rate and the unemployment rate in Emilia-Romagna and in Italy as a whole over the last twelve years.

According to ISTAT (the Central Statistical Office), which generally underestimates these figures, the rate of participation in the labour force reached almost 46% in 1980, 6% higher than the national average. The contrast is even more striking if Emilia is compared with Southern Italy where less than one third of the population participates in the labour force.

On the other hand, the rate of unemployment is in general lower in Emilia-Romagna than in Italy. More detailed figures would also show that recessions reach Emilia later than other regions, and their effects are more temporary.

Two other indicators also show the superiority of economic performance of Emilia-Romagna when compared with the rest of Italy.

* Università degli studi di Modena. This article originally appeared in *Problemi della transizione*, 1980, no. 5, pp. 86–105, and has been translated and abridged by Jonathan Zeitlin and Diego Gambetta.

0309–166X/82/020167 + 18 $03.00/0

168   S. Brusco

Table 1. *Participation rate and unemployment rate in Emilia-Romagna and in Italy, 1971 to 1980 (percentages)*

	Participation rate				Unemployment rate			
	Emilia		Italy		Emilia		Italy	
	Old series	New series	Old series	New series	Old series	New series	Old series	New series
1971	42·7	n.a.	36·2	38·4	2·7	n.a.	3·2	5·4
1972	41·2	n.a.	35·5	37·9	3·0	n.a.	3·7	6·4
1973	42·2	n.a.	35·5	38·0	2·9	n.a.	3·5	6·4
1974	42·4	n.a.	35·7	38·0	2·3	n.a.	2·9	5·4
1975	42·5	n.a.	35·7	38·1	2·9	n.a.	3·3	5·9
1976	42·3	n.a.	35·9	38·5	2·8	n.a.	3·7	6·7
1977		44·8		38·9		5·2		7·1
1978		44·8		38·9		5·7		7·2
1979		45·0		39·4		5·9		7·6
1980		45·9		39·9		5·7		7·6

Source: From 1970 to 1976 see ISTAT, *Rilevazione trimestrale delle forze di lavoro*; from 1977 to 1980 see ISTAT, *Rilevazione trimestrale delle forze di lavoro—nuova serie.*

From 1970 to 1979, the rate of growth of money income per head in Italy was 17·15% per year: in Emilia-Romagna over the same period income grew at an annual rate of about 18·5% (Unioncamere, 1981). Consequently, Emilian income rose from an already favourable position in 1970 to 5·6 million lire per head in 1979 compared with the average Italian income of 4·4 million per head. Moreover, the provinces of Modena and Reggio had in 1979 an income per head of 6·2 and 6·0 million lire respectively, and were the second and the fourth richest provinces in Italy (whereas in 1970, in the classification of the richest provinces, they occupied the 17th and the 12th position respectively).

Another interesting indicator is the amount of exports which originate in the region. Table 2 shows that the share of Emilian exports in total Italian exports continued to increase, almost without interruption, from 1963 to 1980.

Table 2. *Exports from Emilia-Romagna, as a percentage of total Italian exports*

1963	1964	1965	1966	1967	1968	1969	1970	1971
6·0	6·3	6·3	7·0	7·0	6·5	7·1	7·7	7·9

1972	1973	1974	1975	1976	1977	1978	1979	1980
8·1	7·9	7·5	8·6	8·4	8·8	8·8	8·9	9·4

Source: Unioncamere, *Statistiche provinciali dei movimenti valutari inerenti alle importazioni e alle esportazioni.*

The characteristics of Emilia

There are no great differences between Emilia-Romagna and Italy in the distribution of the labour force among sectors and among industries (see Tables 3 and 4). More significant are the differences in other aspects of the region's industrial structure, in particular the size distribution of firms. Table 5 shows that the proportion of the labour force employed in small productive units is always greater in Emilia than in Italy as a whole.

But the most significant point is that these small firms, often with less than 10 employees (see Table 5), are frequently grouped in relatively small zones according to their product, and give rise to monocultural areas in which all firms have a very low degree of vertical integration and the production process is carried on through the collaboration of a number of firms. In these areas only a proportion of the small enterprises market finished goods; the others work as subcontractors, executing operations commissioned by the first group of firms. Production has become widely decentralised as more and more firms which previously manufactured their own components increasingly resorted to outside suppliers. Despite union opposition, 'putting out' is now a common phenomenon.

There are many possible examples of these industrial districts: knitwear in Modena; clothes and ceramic tiles in Modena and Reggio; cycles, motorcycles and shoes in Bologna; buttons in Piacenza; tomato canning and ham in Parma; pig breeding in Reggio Emilia. But it would be a mistake to think that this phenomenon is confined to the production of

Table 3. *Employees by sector, 1980 (percentages)*

	Emilia	Italy
Agriculture	15·8	14·1
Industry	38·6	37·6
Services	45·6	48·3
Total	100·0	100·0

Source: ISTAT, *Rilevazione trimestrale delle forze di lavoro—nuova serie.*

Table 4. *Employees by industry, 1971 (percentages)*

	Emilia	Italy
Food and tobacco	11·3	7·6
Textiles	7·4	10·3
Clothing and shoes	11·4	12·2
Wood and furniture	7·8	7·5
Engineering	38·7	40·6
Non-metal minerals	11·5	6·1
Chemical	4·9	7·5
Paper and printing	3·5	4·4
Others	3·5	3·8
Total	100·0	100·0

Source: ISTAT, *5° Censimento generale dell'industria e del commercio, 1971.*

170   **S. Brusco**

Table 5. *Employees in manufacturing industries, by size of the establishment, 1971 (percentages)*

	Emilia	Italy
Up to five employees	20·5	17·6
6–9	7·3	5·8
10–19	10·4	8·4
20–49	14·7	12·5
50–99	12·7	10·2
100–249	15·3	13·2
250–499	8·4	9·0
500 and more	10·7	23·3
Total	100·0	100·0

Source: ISTAT, *5° Censimento generale dell'industria e del commercio, 1971.*

consumer goods. Industrial districts are also common in engineering: the production of automatic machinery and packaging machinery in Bologna; of agricultural machinery and oleodynamic apparatus in Modena and Reggio; of woodworking machine tools in Carpi; of food processing machinery in Parma. In these cases, the industrial districts are less clearly defined, since they form specialised parts of the engineering sector where component producers supply the manufacturers of a wide range of finished products. This concentration of small firms also extends to the service sector and is found widely on the Adriatic riviera to which four million foreign tourists come every year.

It is also notable that there is a clear connection between the proliferation of small enterprises and the use of 'black' labour. This concept has been given many definitions (Frey, 1975). It has been applied to situations where social welfare contributions are evaded and again to cases where labour is paid lower wages than the minimum set by national agreement, works in substandard conditions, or does not receive agreed levels of supplementary bonuses and holiday pay. However defined, black labour is extremely common in Emilia-Romagna, and underpayment, tax evasion and the extraordinary flexibility of labour are all important features of the productive system.

The economy of the region is also characterised by a high income per head of the labour force engaged in agriculture (in 1971 Emilian agriculture gave work to 8·6% of all Italian agricultural workers, and produced 11·5% of the total Italian agricultural product); by active and increasingly strong cooperatives, which although concentrated in food and construction exert a powerful influence on the social and productive structure as a whole; and by a limited presence of wholly or partially state-owned enterprises.

The following sections of this paper consider various aspects of the region's industrial system—the industrial structure and industrial relations. Particular attention is paid to dynamic interactions between these, the market and the government in order to study their impact on the region's economy.

Inter-firm relations

Recent research in the Faculty of Economics at the University of Modena sheds significant light on the relations between different types of firms in this industrial structure (Brusco and Malagoli, 1981). This study focuses on the garment industry in Modena, Reggio

Emilia and the adjacent provinces, as a sector marked by an extremely low level of vertical integration. It shows that in Modena and Reggio the artisanate considered as a legal category can be divided economically into three groups: half are homeworkers inscribed under the category of artisans purely for the purpose of evading taxes and social welfare payments; one-quarter produce on their own account, having direct relations with the market for finished goods; and a final quarter are subcontractors. It is important to note that many of the independent artisans put out a good deal of the components of the finished product both to the other artisans and to the numerous female homeworkers of the region. In order to understand this structure, one must also consider the larger industrial firms of the region. Half of these enterprises undertake internally only the preparation of samples and the packing and distribution of the garments, while the bulk of the work is decentralised. The other half perform directly at least some of the work, though even these also decentralise an often substantial part.

In the neighbouring provinces, the picture is totally different. There the artisans producing on their own account constitute only 8% of the total, while the larger firms are in most cases owned by entrepreneurs from Modena and Reggio. To interpret these findings, it is necessary to consider together Modena and Reggio on the one hand and the neighbouring provinces on the other. Those artisans with direct access to the market need the dependent artisans of the neighbouring or secondary provinces as a bulwark for their own productive structure. The relationship between Modena and Reggio on the one hand and the neighbouring provinces on the other thus appears to be that of metropolis to colony, and the two together constitute a single system.

It would be tempting to interpret the relationship between the purchasers of components and their subcontractors in monopsonistic terms, as if, in other words, the enterprises producing on their own account were price makers able to compel the subcontractors to accept extremely low profits. But this is untrue, as we will see more fully below. Here it suffices to stress that the market between the two parties is almost invariably competitive. The great majority of subcontractors in fact have the ability to switch customers, if the prices offered are too low, and there is no collusion among the latter strong enough to enforce artificially low prices.

The sources of decentralisation

The principal sources of the movement towards decentralisation of the productive structure in Emilia, and in Italy more generally, are twofold. The first cause can be found in the rise of trade union power since the 1960s. Since the victories of the late 1960s, the union has acquired enough strength in the large firms to make redundancies almost impossible; to protect their shop-floor representatives and to force the employers into plant-level bargaining; to exercise a certain degree of control over working conditions; and sometimes even to impose changes in the organisation of work. Since these developments did not take place to the same extent in the smaller firms, it is only natural that the large employers sought to offset the effect of unionism by shifting production towards the small firm sector. Thus it is no coincidence that the process of vertical disintegration gathered force in Italian industry towards the end of the 1960s.

The second cause can be found in the emergence since the mid-1960s of a significant demand for more varied and customised goods, produced in short series, alongside that for standardised goods. Among the examples of this trend one can point to the much greater number of versions of each model of car than existed fifteen years ago; a multiplying of styles

172   S. Brusco

in clothing and shoes; a growth in the publication of new books and magazines; and an increase in the varieties of furniture, refrigerators and sewing machines. Before the market experienced this evolution, these goods were most often produced according to the techniques originally developed by Taylor and Ford. Many of the components used in these products were made with specialised machinery, the so-called transfer machines, which were designed for the production of a single part, and which were therefore both very productive and very costly. These products were put together on elaborate assembly lines, designed in such a way that each operation was often to be completed in less than thirty seconds. Assembly lines, too, were highly costly, since they were both expensive to build, and required large amounts of planning, work study and running-in time. Both types of technology were restricted to large industry: transfer machinery because of its cost and rigidity, and assembly lines because of their dimensions alone.

The advantages of mass-production technology were reduced by the diversification of the product market and the competition in terms of quality and variety which this implies. The new demand requires more flexible, even if less productive, machinery than the transfer machines, as well as methods of assembly in which tasks are less fragmented so that slightly more diverse products can be assembled. This flexible technology is much less expensive than its predecessor and, more importantly, it is quite compatible with the needs of small firms.

This trend in turn affects investment goods. Without going into much detail, one should note that the construction of sophisticated machine tools was synonymous with that of transfer machines, which were custom-built in small series or single examples. For this reason they were particularly suitable for production with a fragmented structure, insofar as the small firms possessed the relevant know-how. During the past few years, however, the shift in consumer demand has cut down the demand for these machines. What will happen in the future will depend both on the extension of the current standardisation of components and on the diffusion of numerically-controlled machine tools which may be produced in long series. It seems probable in either case, however, that even in the investment goods sector there will remain space for short runs and therefore for small firms.

Alongside the increase in unionisation and changes in demand which have provoked the fragmentation of the industrial structure, there is another element which without acting directly constitutes a necessary condition allowing the process to occur without reduction in productivity. The sectors in which decentralisation is particularly marked are those in which it is possible to fragment the productive process without having recourse to an inferior technology. For example, the Morini motorcycle plant in Bologna has 100 employees and produces an average of 20 motorcycles per day. Most of the workers in the plant are engaged in assembly, on lines on which the tasks are not very subdivided. Except for the camshaft and the engine mounting, all of the components are put out: the frame, the tank, the shock absorbers, the handlebars, the brakes, the gears and the wheels; almost the whole machine is produced by subcontractors. And the key point is that they are produced with precisely the same techniques which would have been used had the firm decided to make them directly.

In other words one should bear in mind that, despite the increase in the scale of production in the 1950s and 1960s, with certain technologies there is no advantage in producing all the components of a product under a single roof: whether they produce similar or different pieces, twenty lathes have substantially the same productivity if they are gathered together or dispersed in separate buildings. This is what economists mean when they assert that economies of scale should be calculated in the first instance for phases of production, and that the economies which result from the juxtaposition of similar operations are often negligible

(Brusco, 1975; Muller, 1976). It should be noted, therefore, that generally the sectors in which this type of industrial structure prevails are those characterised by limited economies of vertical integration. Where these conditions do not hold, as in the ceramic tiles sector, decentralisation is nearly non-existent or assumes purely legal forms.

Even if it is accepted that for many industries the importance of technical economies of scale has often been overstated in the past, it might still be objected that there exist nonetheless both indivisibilities in the administrative work of firms and significant pecuniary economies of scale. Thus small firms might experience difficulties in book keeping, in obtaining raw materials, and in obtaining credit at the same price paid by larger firms with greater bargaining power. But in this context it is extraordinary to observe how the artisans and small entrepreneurs of Emilia-Romagna have overcome these difficulties by creating associations to provide these administrative services and to coordinate purchasing and credit negotiations, thus establishing on a co-operative basis the conditions for achieving minimum economic scales of operation. These associations, which cover the whole region, prepare the pay slips, keep the books, and pay the taxes of the small firms, giving to the latter the expertise of a large office in administration and accountancy at a minimal price. Furthermore, these associations also establish technical consultancy offices, consortia for marketing and the purchase of raw and semi-fabricated materials and, most importantly, co-operatives which provide guarantees for bank loans which can thus be obtained at the lowest possible rate of interest.

Industrial relations

Turning to the field of industrial relations, the first premise of the analysis is that the industrial structure, as we have already suggested, is divided into two segments by the size of the firms. In the 'primary' sector, the trade union has two main characteristics. First of all, it is extremely strong: there labour legislation is almost always respected; trade union representatives are recognised on the shop floor; plant bargaining yields wages above those negotiated at national level, and seeks—with intermittent success—to influence the organisation of work and to establish job ladders within the firm; finally, there is a tradition of popular mobilisation which in practice enables the unions to block any factory closure. The strength of the unions both depends on and is illustrated by the fact that in Emilia, by contrast to Piedmont and Lombardy, the 'primary' sector extends downwards to include all enterprises with more than 30 employees, so that roughly half of the labour force is unionised. Secondly, the union is generally 'reasonable'; it does not bid up wages too strongly in plant bargaining and is prepared to be flexible, even if within fairly strict limits, in enforcing contractual provisions concerning layoffs, overtime, and health and safety regulation; finally, it does not put forward over-bold projects of work reorganisation within the factory.

These characteristics of trade unionism in Emilia ensure a prompt, and generally non-violent, resolution of industrial disputes. The point at which agreement will be reached is usually recognised by both parties in advance, since it can be easily derived from the going rate for plant settlement in the country. It is precisely the strength of the union and its flexibility which guarantee at the same time that the negotiations will produce a satisfactory result without concessions and that the terms of the agreement will be enforced without subsequent flare-ups of localised conflict or idleness among the workers. Thus even though the union exercises a real control over working conditions in the plant, the employer enjoys a secure climate which makes possible a greater degree of planning of the volume of production and investment.

174   S. Brusco

In the 'secondary' sector, in contrast, everything works differently. But before going on to examine the 'rules of the game' in this segment of the labour market, it is necessary to draw attention to the heterogeneity of those to be found within it. Besides the artisans working on their own account and the subcontractors we have already discussed, there can be found four main groups. First, highly skilled workers, often specialised in maintenance work, who have registered as artisans in order to free their wages from the limits established in the national agreements, but who continue to perform exactly the same job during the same hours as before. Second, the various types of homeworkers: those already mentioned who are forced by their bosses to register as artisans in order to evade social security payments; those whose position has been regularised according to recent labour legislation; and those whose position remains 'irregular', some highly qualified and others without any particular skill, whether elderly or from the South. Third, moonlighters and pensioners who have returned to work, who often agree with the employer to evade all social security payments and divide the proceeds. And finally, women and students who, in evasion of all controls, accept seasonal, temporary, and precarious work of every kind.

In this world the dispersion of wages is extremely high, extending from the maintenance workers registered as artisans who can earn twice as much as their factory fellows, to the elderly or immigrant homeworkers who get less than one-third of what they would receive in the factory. Here there is little evidence of the struggle for egalitarianism which has formed so noteworthy a part of the history of the Italian unions. The Emilian unions attempt to regulate wages, unlike their counterparts elsewhere, by making collective agreements with the artisanal associations, which in turn press their members to regularise the working conditions of their employees and to respect the contracts; certain recent legislation has a similar intention (Malagoli and Mengoli, 1979). But the level of wages is fundamentally determined by three factors: the level of demand for the product; the intensity of labour; and finally the level of skill.

In this sector, moreover, redundancies are possible. Here firms are able to hire and fire as the volume of orders changes, both because legislation against unfair dismissals does not apply to firms with less than 15 employees and because of their scanty unionisation. In this sector all variations in the level of output are translated into variations in employment. By contrast, as a recent study shows, the large firms fear that a subsequent recession will leave them unable to dispose of surplus manpower and they therefore refrain from hiring unless they install new machinery (Brusco, Giovannetti and Malagoli, 1979).

The segmentation of the labour market

The two labour markets which correspond to these two types of firms are, in general, linked and movement from one to the other is possible. There are, to be sure, significant numbers of workers who are unable to gain access to the 'primary' sector: elderly or immigrant women; middle-aged peasants; and at least for a time recent agricultural immigrants working in small firms with particularly unhealthy working conditions. But when demand is expanding, anyone accustomed to factory life and able to work intensively, even if not very skilled, can find work where he or she pleases. And each worker is ultimately able to choose in which segment to work. Under such conditions of increasing demand, wage differentials between the sectors narrow markedly and choices between them are not determined by earnings. For women, their family situation is the most important consideration, while the central influences for men are such factors as preferences concerning the atmosphere in large and small factories, possibilities of acquiring skills, and networks of personal or family contacts.

Many young people, in these conditions, are able consciously to choose a temporary or part-time job, or to decide to work at whatever job, however disagreeable. This choice is possible in some cases because of the level of family income which ultimately guarantees subsistence; in other cases, it is based on a light-hearted trade-off of lower earnings against shorter hours of work. Often, this latter attitude springs from a sharp critique of the capitalist use of labour-power; always, it depends on the expectation that it will be possible to find a job when necessary.

For highly skilled workers, it is possible not only to choose the plant, but also to decide to go into business for themselves. The latter choice, while it brings a higher income, also requires longer and more intensive hours of work. Thus the question for the worker is whether or not to opt for more work and higher earnings. What is striking is not how many become artisans, but how many of those who are able do not. This is ultimately a further sign of the health of this regional economy.

If instead the labour market should become depressed, the situation would change significantly. The less skilled workers would experience much more difficulty in changing segments; then the absence of collective bargaining and of union guarantees would make themselves sharply felt. The very flexibility which currently constitutes an advantage for this sector would become an insurmountable obstacle to the organised defence of employment. The effects of a crisis would be much less for the highly skilled workers whose bargaining power gives them greater means of self-defence.

No major recession has struck Emilia-Romagna since the 1960s, and the system has easily absorbed the effects of the central bank's credit restrictions. However, some indication of what might happen in recession can be seen from what happened during the downturn in the garment industry in 1974, when many homeworkers were left without work, while those who were employed suffered cuts in real and even money wages. The black economy of the South indirectly suggests what might happen in recessionary conditions. There the overall level of unemployment is so high that even when the product market is booming individual bargaining gives rise to wages well below those agreed nationally, to frequent evasions of social security payments, and to very poor working conditions (David and Pattarin, 1975; Botta *et al.*, 1976).

In conclusion, the possibility of mobility from one segment of the labour market to the other depends on the same factors which determine wages: skill, the intensity of work, and the state of the product and labour market.

Mechanisms of labour market adjustment

Certain channels exist whereby the power to shed labour is transmitted between the small and the large firm sectors so that the system as a whole retains its flexibility. There are two main mechanisms, which are complementary rather than alternatives. The garment sector provides the most clearcut example of the first of these. There the impact of a fall in demand for the products of a particular firm depends on its level of vertical integration: where this is high, such a fall in demand will produce unemployment; where it is low, the workers employed in subcontracting firms will simply receive their orders from more successful competitors. To follow the process in more detail: when the level of integration is highest, each firm circulates its collection of samples through its own agents; collects and executes the orders; finishes, packs and sends the final product. When the level of integration is lowest, the firm which had prepared the samples and received the order will execute it through subcontractors from whom it will collect the final product for despatch.

176   S. Brusco

Now suppose that (1) in both cases firms are sufficiently numerous to guarantee competition; (2) that the total demand for garments is constant, so that orders lost by one firm are taken up by another; (3) that all commissioning firms belong to the primary segment, and all subcontractors to the secondary; (4) finally, that subcontractors are able to shift easily from the production of one model to that of another.

We can now see what would happen in both cases when the styles offered by a firm are rejected by the market. In the first case (high vertical integration) the crisis in the firm will hit all the workers involved in the various phases of production. If orders fall to zero, they will have to be made redundant, even if they will be hired soon afterwards by the more successful firms. In this case the system has reached a new equilibrium by redistributing workers among firms, requiring a certain number of redundancies, which by hypothesis are tense and difficult for the firm concerned.

Under similar assumptions, we can now consider what would happen in the second type of structure, i.e. one which is characterised by a minimal degree of vertical integration. This time the firm struck by the crisis does not employ weavers, cutters, stitchers, pressers and finishers; it employs only people working on prototypes, and workers in packing and despatching goods. Only these workers directly employed by the firm will be made redundant. The vast majority of the workers actually producing the garment would continue to work as before for the subcontracting firm which employs them directly. The work which is no longer coming to the subcontractor from the firm whose styles have been rejected by the market will simply be replaced by that commissioned by its more successful competitors. In this case, too, the system imposes some redundancies in order to find its equilibrium, but these are fewer than in the preceding one, and are made by firms which have fewer employees for the same gross turnover. The equilibrium has been restored not so much through a shift in manpower as through a shift in orders. The response to a downturn has been rendered that much easier.

In presenting the second mechanism to which we initially referred, our simplifying assumptions will be to some extent opposed to those employed in describing the first. Here the global movement of demand and the type of price-formation mechanism operating in this sector will be unimportant; it is rather assumed that the subcontractors are *unable* to shift their production. The only assumption which remains as before is that the commissioning firms belong to the primary segment and the subcontracting firms to the secondary one.

We can now illustrate the second mechanism with an example. Imagine a firm with 1000 employees in which a decrease in production of 10% would provoke 100 redundancies. This level of redundancies would be highly problematic in the primary segment. Imagine instead a firm which decentralises 80% of the same volume of production, which would therefore be left with 200 workers. This firm would still belong to the primary sector, while the other 800 workers would be scattered among the small enterprises of the secondary sector. This time a fall in production of 10% would require 20 redundancies in the primary sector and 80 in the secondary. The first poses no great problems, both because 20 workers are few in absolute terms and because the union is weaker in a firm with 200 employees than in one with 1000. The other 80 redundancies would pose no problems at all since they belong to the secondary sector. In this case, too, it is ultimately the secondary sector which absorbs the tensions coming from the large firms. The difference is that in this case the small firms perform this role by assuming responsibility for the major portion of the redundancies, while in the first case they coordinate the flow of subcontracted labour from the less to the more successful firms.

We can add four observations in order to clarify what has been said so far. First, the link between the two segments of the labour market has an important implication: all attempts to impose rigidities on the secondary sector would immediately reverberate on the system as a whole. Any successful initiative, whether by the unions or by public policy, which aimed to limit the small firms' power to hire and fire would automatically rigidify the manpower management of the large enterprises. It seems as if there is, therefore, a clear alternative between two objectives, both desirable: that of maintaining the system's flexibility, and that of limiting the small enterprises' power to make workers redundant when they want.

There is only one way to avoid the dilemma of ensuring primary conditions of employment in all Emilian firms and yet preserving the flexibility of the system as a whole in a situation where demand is uncertain. To achieve such a result it would be necessary to construct a new secondary sector of firms and workers outside the region. Beyond the need to find manpower which has become ever more scarce in Emilia, this is to some extent the significance of the extension of decentralisation to the Veneto, the Marche, and even Puglia. The internal contradictions of Emilia gradually become in this way external ones, which other regions have to face and resolve.

Secondly, it often happens in some productive activities that the great majority of firms cluster in the secondary sector, irrespective of the role played by the enterprise. This is, for example, the case of knitwear in which 50% of the 'parent' firms (i.e. those with direct access to the market for finished goods) have less than 30 employees. This state of affairs reaches its limits in Prato, a Tuscan town with an analogous industrial structure, where the commissioning firm very often has no employees other than the proprietor, the so-called *impannatore* who designs the fabric and commissions the spinning, weaving, and finishing from other other enterprises.

Thirdly, it will be useful to dwell for a moment on the difference between the mechanisms discussed above and another interpretation of decentralisation as a sort of 'productive lung' for the commissioning enterprises (Paci, 1975). There it is assumed that short period variations in the demand for the product of the commissioning firm may lead from time to time to the expulsion of certain operations from the factory and their subsequent recall. In this case, variations in the level of vertical integration of the firm are understood as conjunctural manoeuvres. In our view, this practice is difficult to realise, and it has no place in the mechanisms of the 'Emilian model'.

Finally, it is necessary to ask how frequently each of our hypothetical mechanisms of labour market adjustment might actually occur. As will be apparent from the assumptions on which they are based, the answer depends on two main considerations. The first is the demand for the product: the longer and more frequent the recessions, the more often the second mechanism will operate. The other consideration points instead towards the technology used by the subcontracting firms and the ease with which they are able to shift their production.

How plausible is this hypothesis that Emilian firms are easily able to shift from one product to another? In this context we should note there are variations between the production of components and assembly and in the experience of individual sectors. In the knitwear industry, for example, there are virtually no difficulties in switching models, neither in the production of components nor in assembly; in that of women's clothes, the production of components is highly flexible, whereas the adaptation of assembly lines poses some problems, though these are easily resolved; in the food industry, the flexibility is also very high. More careful attention should be paid to the engineering sector. Generally, components are more flexible than assembly and this is the reason why decentralisation is more prominent in the former. It should be noted that in this case a subcontracting firm can easily shift not only models but also subsectors: a firm producing stamped metal has no problem in switching from the production of, say, gas stoves to that of chair frames. Single-purpose machine tools, as remarked earlier, have next to no flexibility, whereas that of numerically controlled machine tools is extremely high. Finally, the flexibility of assembly lines is itself very variable: it is least where tasks are very fragmented and greatest where each position is assigned longer operations. Given the diversification of demand, this capacity to adapt easily to different products becomes synonymous in practice with the capacity to produce in short series at competitive costs.

In conclusion, the hypothesis that it is possible to shift quickly and easily from one product to another is certainly true for many firms and in many industries. And this fact is closely related to the capacity of Emilian firms to produce in short series.

The solidity of the industrial structure

The capacity of the 'Emilian model' to resist foreign competition, in particular that of Third World countries, is rooted in three main factors. First of all, flexibility in the use of manpower. We can add to what has been observed earlier that this feature of the industrial structure becomes all the more important when compared to the rigidity of industrial structures, such as, say, that of Milan, which are dominated by large firms. Second, there is the rather high technical level of the machinery employed. The flexible use of labour facilitates the introduction of innovations, even when they are labour-saving. As we observed earlier, when demand is expanding wages in the primary and secondary segments of the labour market are more or less the same; there is, therefore, no possibility for firms to recoup with low wages the low productivity of their machinery. It will be remembered that most markets, including those for semi-finished products, are highly competitive and this too speeds up the adoption of more sophisticated machinery. There is evidence, moreover, that in the most industrialised regions small firms experience no disadvantage relative to large ones in raising credit (Guglielmi, 1978; Filippi, 1979).

Finally, the solidity of the 'Emilian model' derives from the fact that this type of industrial structure more than any other fosters the skills and initiatives of its entrepreneurs in a variety of ways. In the first place, it spurs their emergence. The number of artisans or even major entrepreneurs previously employed as workers is very high, particularly as foremen, maintenance workers, and coordinators of putting-out networks. For each of these groups, their knowledge of some part of the productive process facilitates their passage to independent work. Even easier in some sectors, particularly that of garments, is the transition from subcontracting to direct contact with the market. Many subcontractors through their relations with their customers learn how to prepare samples, come into contact with the network of distribution, and eventually reach the point where they can circulate samples on their own. If these are well received they will produce a few copies within the firm and will put out the rest. At the same time, they will continue to work as subcontractors, thus avoiding undue risks. The system therefore operates as a 'forcing' ground for entrepreneurship.

Second, by using the foresight and imagination of so many artisans and entrepreneurs, this productive structure is able to offer an extraordinary variety of products, many of them novel, which cleverly interpret the needs of consumers and the shifts in their tastes. The garment sector is an obvious example. It is sufficient to realise that it would be impossible for a few large firms to produce the enormous range of styles which are created by the hundreds of small firms. An idea, seen at a Parisian or Florentine fashion show, can be reworked in a multitude of workshops. And in this way thousands of options are offered to domestic and foreign buyers. But more important examples can be cited from the investment goods sector, such as machines which dispense railway tickets, pack cigarettes and medicine capsules, or clean the streets; the extraordinary variety of agricultural machinery, from light tractors to fruit-harvesting platforms; or the many sophisticated hydraulic devices used in servo-mechanisms. These are all cases in which new needs are satisfied by a multitude of competing small firms which emulate and imitate each other and which as a result can give shape to new ideas with a speed that would be unthinkable in larger enterprises.

Finally, the small firms' capacity to develop new products and to devise new machines is enhanced both by the proximity of so many entrepreneurs engaged in similar activities and by the extensive collaboration between skilled workers and technicians within each firm (Brusco and Sabel, 1981). This phenomenon, which is particularly characteristic of monocultural areas, should be emphasised since it undercuts the conventional idea that research is only what scientists and technicians do in the laboratories of the big firms and not the on-the-job creativity of ordinary people who know their own needs. For instance, in the ceramic tile industry, the machines which move the tiles uninterruptedly along the glazing lines, or which detect breakages through the use of sonic waves, were not the product of formal research, but were rather developed through the collaboration of the tile firms with a number of small engineering firms.

Emilia: an 'interstitial' case?

The idea of 'interstices' is connected with a view of the world in which goods can be divided into two groups. The first group consists of goods produced in long series by large firms with highly subdivided labour; strong economies of scale mark such production processes. The second group reverses these characteristics, and is accordingly neglected by the large firms. As a result, their production, concentrated in small firms, is considered 'interstitial'. In such a classificatory system, the first type of goods are usually but often implicitly considered technologically advanced and the second backward. To this view is often added the assumption that goods produced in long series in large factories can only be reproduced with great difficulty in the Third World, in contrast to those of the second type, and are therefore less exposed to competition from developing countries. This has led some observers to conclude that the second type of production is ultimately destined to disappear from the advanced countries.

As we have seen, however, many goods produced in short series are nonetheless the fruit of enterprises which employ advanced technology and have some real market power. The simplest example is that of investment goods, which are often produced in short series or even on a one-off basis. The limit case, among these goods, is that of transfer machines, the robots used at Fiat, or the special pieces used in chemical plants; but, among Emilian products, this is true also of many automatic machines, machine tools, agricultural machines, and those used in ceramic tile production and food processing.

It is also true, to be sure, that some goods produced in short series are vulnerable to competition from Third World countries: for instance, the garment and knitwear industries, which on occasion suffer from the influx of Rumanian jackets and Indian T-shirts, or the producers of toys and stoves who face competition from Hong Kong and Poland. But on the whole it can be noted in most cases that the products of the underdeveloped countries are aimed at the bottom of the market. In other words, it seems possible to counteract the competition from these countries by shifting production up-market. These types of goods can only be produced with difficulty by such countries because of their distance from the consumers, their consequent difficulty in predicting shifts in tastes, and the low skill-level of their workforces.

180   S. Brusco

The history of the Italian monocultural area is precisely the history of this specialisation and movement up-market. This is the case of ceramics in Sassuolo, or to choose a case from outside Emilia, of textiles in Prato. This process can, of course, lead to a progressive narrowing of the market, and an attendant contraction of the industry and its labour force. So far, though, the process seems to go slower than is commonly expected, either because, as in Prato, sidelines have been found to make up the lost ground or because, as we have already seen, consumer demand for quality and variety is becoming increasingly pronounced. This slow expansion in the market for sophisticated products goes alongside the need to produce in shorter series and therefore to find a means of controlling the labour force different from that developed by Fordism. All this naturally increases the space in which the small firm can operate efficiently. In conclusion, therefore, the notion of interstices seems to be weak and of limited value.

Agriculture

We can now turn our attention to the relation between industry and agriculture. There is a basic distinction to be made in this regard. Agriculture has not been able to survive in the Appenine mountains which mark the southern boundary of the region. To varying degrees, therefore, the mountains have lost their population and, to schematise a bit, only those areas which can attract tourists have managed to maintain their per capita income relative to that of the region as a whole. By contrast, the Po valley, which includes the most fertile soil in Italy, has been able to dispute with industry the labour force it requires. As a consequence, the incomes of many agricultural workers, including the day labourers, are often comparable to those of their industrial counterparts. This prosperity constitutes the principal feature of Emilian agriculture even though there remains a stratum of poor peasants which some estimate at one-third of the total agricultural labour force (Brusco, 1979).

The general prosperity of agriculture in the region can be ascribed to three main causes. First, there is the extraordinary fertility of the soil. Yet this is not a sufficient cause, since there are areas in Campania and Puglia which are even more fertile but less prosperous. The second reason is the presence of co-operatives which heavily influence the market for a wide variety of agricultural products. The diffusion and strength of co-operatives which sell Emilian agricultural products directly to consumers throughout Italy has eliminated the parasitic middlemen who still flourish in other regions. The co-operatives even manage to obtain for their members a share in the profits of the food processing industry. It is for this reason that the regional government has quite correctly chosen them as its main channel for influencing the agricultural sector, to such an extent that since its creation at the beginning of the 1970s the region has directed more than 20% of its total agricultural expenditure towards co-operatives.

It should be noted in passing that this practice of co-operative work has had its impact on industry as well. While there are no co-operative firms as such outside construction, it is plausible to suppose that these traditions of co-operation have influenced those associations of artisans and small entrepreneurs of which we have already spoken.

Finally, and most importantly, the superiority of Emilian agriculture can be explained by the transformation of agrarian property relations since the war. Of all Italian regions, Emilia-Romagna was one of those in which sharecropping was most widely practiced in 1947. In the province of Modena, this type of contract covered 70% of the soil. Its decay, due more to the growth of industry than to legislation, has had deep repercussions. Many of the old landlords, whose estates often included ten to twenty sharecroppers' plots, once freed from this system have unified them into a single capitalist farm. Some of the minor landlords, almost always belonging to the urban bourgeoisie, have preferred to keep their farms as a second activity run by a salaried manager. All the remaining proprietors, large and small, have sold their land to the peasants. These sales, which were in some cases preceded by a period of rental, have selected out a wide stratum of highly skilled peasants.

The situation, therefore, has evolved along radically different lines to those of the southern regions. There, apart from the effects of the agrarian reforms, the importance of large and medium landed property has remained unchanged; the only modifications of agricultural techniques have been those linked to irrigation; the small properties freed by migration have in practice remained blocked and often uncultivated. In Emilia, where as we have seen, the land market has been extremely active, a major part of the capital accumulated through the sale of large estates was invested in the growing industrial sector. The initial capital of many engineering, ceramic, textile, and food processing firms was drawn from this source. A final example of the integration of agriculture and industry in Emilian development can be seen in the growing tendency for workers and artisans who are employed in the towns to go to live in the countryside, where they engage in a certain amount of part-time farming.

The state and local government

The central state administration appears to play a lesser role in this region than in others. First of all, tax collection is less effective here than elsewhere, both as regards firms and private households. One might expect that in such a fragmented productive structure the longstanding deficiencies of Italian public administration might be even more striking than elsewhere. One might expect, in other words, that something similar to what happens to the trade unions (or by that token to the central statistical agencies) might happen to the state: the smaller the unit in question, the less such institutions will be able to control it. If this were true it would follow that Emilia-Romagna contributes less to the state than the other rich regions of the country. In this sense, then, it would be as if there were a transfer of income from these regions to Emilia. On the other hand, it is necessary to recall that the state also contributes less to Emilia since there are fewer public and semi-public enterprises there than in other regions.

In the case of public works, too, the absence of sound data makes any conclusions speculative. It seems certain, however, that the 'red belt' is discriminated against in terms of the distribution of public funds and credit concessions. Today perhaps this bias has eased off and is less pressing than in the past: there is no doubt, however, that such discrimination has never troubled the public conscience of the Christian Democratic Party. Another phenomenon, however, acts in the opposite direction: the extraordinary efficiency of Emilian municipal government in organising public interventions, no matter how complex; in providing financial resources; and in mobilising local forces, including Christian Democrats, in support of demands directed to the state.

A specific case may serve to exemplify this political efficiency, peculiar in Italian terms. The river Panaro, which separates the province of Modena from that of Bologna, had flooded thousands of acres of Modenese land several times between 1966 and 1973. These disasters were due to the absence of adequate flood-gates. The intervention which should have been planned by the Ministry of Public Works was instead prepared by the provincial administrations of Modena and Reggio Emilia, and was ready by 1972. The Ministry had accepted it but by 1976 nothing had happened. When the river flooded in this year for the fifth time, the municipal government of Modena convoked an assembly in the city square of its citizens and

182   S. Brusco

those of the other affected towns; with the collaboration of *all* the MPs of the province so much pressure was brought to bear on the Ministry of Public Works that the funds for the long-planned flood-gates were released within fifteen days.

There is no doubt in fact that the efficiency of local government has markedly raised the real wages of Emilian workers, and has improved the quality of life. Using the minimal, even non-existent, spaces provided by a hazy legislative framework, the local governments have managed to implement policies unheard of in the rest of Italy. Two areas of intervention stand out in this respect. The first is that of social services: for example, in Reggio Emilia and Modena, nursery schools can absorb the entire demand for their services, in sharp contrast to the situation elsewhere, particularly in the South. Thus it is striking that in Bologna there are enough places in creches and nursery schools for 25% and 65% of the respective age groups; in Naples, by contrast, the corresponding figures are only 1·5% and 4% (Capecchi and Pugliese, 1978).

The second is that of urban planning and control of speculative building development. After some initial mistakes, the local governments have opted for a policy of controlled development. All possible legal instruments from expropriation and agreements to threats and inducements have been used to control the price of commercial property. As a consequence the Emilian cities have a higher proportion of publicly and co-operatively funded accommodation and lower house prices than elsewhere in Italy. The new neighbourhoods are often architecturally undistinguished but the proportion of green space per inhabitant is certainly quite high. The low price of property not only benefits private households but also promotes the prosperity of local firms. By planning for artisanal districts this policy allows small firms to buy lofts at relatively reasonable prices, and thus promotes their growth.

In other areas, too, the municipal administrations are active. Despite a certain delay they are attempting to control pollution as much as possible. They are creating a network of psychiatric consultation centres and family counselling centres. A wide range of cultural initiatives have been launched, ranging from opera to theatre to rock concerts. Finally, particularly in the past few years, attempts have been made to revive the old urban centres from which traffic has long been excluded.

Summary and conclusions

In conclusion, let us re-examine the principal component parts of the 'Emilian model' and their relation to the operation of the system as a whole. First, agriculture in this region has emerged strengthened from the reorganisation of the past two decades. Some poor peasants remain who have not been able to establish an independent farm from the collapse of sharecropping. But these groups are destined to disappear. The regional labour market is too tight to permit a rigid compartmentalisation, and the next generation is more prone to acquire industrial skills. In any case, the presence of agricultural co-operatives makes this sector rather cohesive, and certainly more resistant to recessions than elsewhere.

Second, there is a 'primary' industrial sector with advanced technology, innovative ability, high wages, and considerable union presence. Its only limitation comes from restraints on redundancies. The industrial relations system, however great its powers of mediation, imposes serious rigidities on the employers, and it is in this context that the third component of the 'Emilian model' finds its place. The 'secondary' industrial sector, consisting of small firms, shares with the 'primary' sector its advanced technology, its innovative capacity and its ability to compete on the world market, and at least when business is good pays similar wages to most of its workforce. The true role of this sector, therefore, at least in periods of expansion, is to return flexibility in the use of labour to the entire productive structure, rather than to exploit cheap labour and so make possible the use of backward machinery. There is, however, another mechanism by which the system as a whole escapes the rigidity imposed by the unions in the larger firms: the putting-out of work to other regions, in which the classic secondary labour market characteristics of low pay and backward machinery can to some extent be found.

Finally, all this takes place under the watchful eye of a local government which helps to raise real wages and to improve the quality of life. The state on the other hand, for better and for worse, plays a lesser role than in other regions.

This complex productive apparatus gives the worker a wide range of choices and opportunities: to the more skilled the opportunity to go into business for themselves; to others the ability to choose in which firm to work; and to young people the possibility of alternating periods of work with periods of 'life'. The work force can be set along a continuum with two opposite poles: artisans working to the limit of their capacity to earn a high income, and youth prepared to trade off low wages for short hours of work. More generally, therefore, it can be stated that each worker is able to decide how to divide life between work and leisure in a context which measures precisely the amount of labour expended and converts it into income.

From this above all comes the widespread certitude that this system is rich in opportunities for all, and that everyone is ultimately the master of his own fate. Such certitude is amongst the basic elements of the political consensus enjoyed by those who have attempted to guide and control this development process. For the same reason, however, there is little sympathy for those who do not share the basic values of the system and hostility and even contempt for those who criticise it from outside.

Cohesion and closure have been reinforced by the virtuous circle fuelled by the continuous prosperity of the past two decades. Flexibility and entrepreneurship produce high rates of growth, which push up family incomes; high incomes permit increased education and the accumulation of skills; and local government keeps the environmental consequences of development within tolerable limits. This circle depends on one basic condition: 'when you work you work, without cheating yourself or anyone else'.

Thus cultural as well as economic factors lead us to emphasise the freer role played by market forces in Emilia and the more authentically capitalist character of its development as compared to other Italian regions. This can be seen in the extensive role played by individual initiative; in the system's capacity to regain the flexibility lost to the unions in the large factory by segmenting the productive structure and exporting its contradictions; and in the relative absence of the national state, both in terms of public spending and tax collection. To a certain extent, however, this absence of the state has been compensated for by the initiatives of those few efficient public institutions more closely linked to the civil society of the region. Thus there has been realised in Emilia a harmonious mixture of discordant elements, but one whose complexity makes it difficult to take it as a model: efficient institutions despite the absence of the state, and active trade unions which control only half of the labour force.

So long as demand continues to expand, this social and productive structure will face only the problem of integrating into itself those who declare themselves to be outside it. But some doubt remains that this system might react badly to a deep and prolonged recession. Consider for example what happened to Turin in response to the Fiat redundancies in October 1980, and what would happen in Emilia if the success of a new Mary Quant were to

184   S. Brusco

create as many redundancies among knitwear workers. In Turin the clash between employer and resistant workers was clear cut and was moderated by special state unemployment funds and so the situation was controlled.

In Emilia, unless the local entrepreneurs could quickly copy and improve on the new styles (which could well happen), the dynamic interaction of the parts of the industrial district which guarantee a flexible response to the product market could quickly deteriorate in a competitive scramble for orders. This, in the condition where trade unions only partially control the labour market, could put downward pressure on wages, and cause a reduction of prosperity and a dismantling of the productive structure upon which that prosperity is based.

Bibliography

Bagnasco, A. 1977. *Tre Italie: la problematica territoriale dello sviluppo*, Bologna, Il Mulino
Bagnasco, A. and Messori, M. 1975. *Tendenze dell'economia periferica*, Torino, Valentino
Botta, P., Fonte, M., Improta, L., Pugliese, E. and Ruggero, F. 1976. La struttura del settore calzaturiero a Napoli, *Inchiesta*, no. 23
Brusco, S. 1975. Organizzazione del lavoro e decentramento produttivo nel settore metalmeccanico, *Sindacato e piccola impresa* (a cura della FLM di Bergamo), Bari, De Donato
Brusco, S. 1979. *Agricoltura ricca e classi sociali*, Milano, Feltrinelli
Brusco, S., Giovannetti, E. and Malagoli, W. 1979. *La relazione tra dimensione e saggio di sviluppo nelle imprese industriali: una ricerca empirica*, Modena
Brusco, S. and Malagoli, W. 1981. Disintegrated firms and industrial districts: the case of the knitwear industry in Italy, paper presented at the Third Conference of the International Working Party on Labour Market Segmentation, mimeo, Modena
Brusco, S. and Sabel, C. 1981. Artisan production and economic growth, in Wilkinson, F. (ed.), *The Dynamics of Labour Market Segmentation*, London, Academic Press
Capecchi, V. *et al.* 1979. *La piccola impresa in Italia*, Bari, De Donato
Capecchi, V. and Pugliese, E. 1978. Bologna Napoli: due città a confronto, *Inchiesta*, no. 34–36
David, P. and Pattarin, E. 1975. Retroterra rurale e condizione operaia femminile: il settore della maglieria, *Inchiesta*, no. 20
Fillippi, E. 1979. La struttura finanziaria delle medie imprese italiane, *Thema*, no. 4
Filippucci, C. 1978. L'occupazione ed il valore aggiunto in Emilia-Romagna: un'analisi disaggregata per settore di attività economica, *Statistica*, no. 3
Frey, L. (ed.) 1975. *Lavoro a domicilio e decentramento dell'attività produttiva nei settori tessile e dell'abbigliamento in Italia*, Milano, Angeli
Guglielmi, M. 1978. I problemi finanziari dello sviluppo della piccola e media impresa—un confronto regionale, *Orientamenti nuovi per la piccola e media industria*, no. 9
ISTAT, *5° Censimento generale dell'industria e del commercio—1971*, Roma
ISTAT, *Rilevazione trimestrale della forze di lavoro*, Roma
ISTAT, *Rilevazione trimestrale delle forze di lavoro—nuova serie*, Roma
Malagoli, W. and Mengoli, P. 1979. Lavoro a domicilio e artigianato nel comparto della maglieria, *Città e regione*, no. 5
Muller, J. 1976. La dimensione dell'impresa e l'integrazione verticale, *Rivista di Economia e Politica Industriale*, no. 2
Paci, M. 1975. Crisi, ristrutturazione e piccola impresa, *Inchiesta*, no. 20
Unioncamere 1981. *Il reddito prodotto nelle provincie italiane nel 1979*, Roma
Unioncamere, *Statistiche provinciali dei movimenti valutari inerenti alle importazioni e alle esportazioni*, Roma

[22]

Volume XXVIII
THE JOURNAL OF INDUSTRIAL ECONOMICS
December 1979
No. 2

THE FOUNDERS OF NEW MANUFACTURING FIRMS: A NOTE ON THE SIZE OF THEIR 'INCUBATOR' PLANTS*

P. S. Johnson and D. G. Cathcart

In an article in this *Journal* in 1955 Beesley [2] put forward the proposition that larger plants may provide better incubator environments than smaller ones for stimulating the growth of entrepreneurial aspirations in their work forces. Employees of such plants would thus be more likely to set up in business on their own account. In comparing the north-west and south-west zones of the West Midlands, he suggested that the higher rate of formation in the metal industries in the former might have been attributable in part to the fact that they had relatively more larger plants; this 'may have given the zone as a whole more experience of management techniques'.[1] On the other hand, however, other writers (e.g. Cooper [3]) have suggested that there are good grounds for holding the opposite view. It is, for example, more likely that employees of smaller plants will have greater contact with individuals who have themselves set up in business. They will gain greater familiarity with the types of market that could be served by a new business, which in the early years at least is almost inevitably going to be small. They are also likely to obtain greater all-round experience in the running of a business. While these arguments in favour of the small unit as an incubator have been put forward mainly in the context of technological spin-off, i.e. the formation of new enterprises in science-based industries, they are not specific to it and could have more general applicability.

The effect of plant size on fertility in terms of new business formation is not of academic interest only. The absolute size of plants has been increasing in the UK over a fairly long period (Prais [9, pp. 51–4]) and it would be useful to know whether this trend is likely to have any effect on the rate of

---

* The research on which this note is based was financed by the Nuffield Foundation and the SSRC. The help of both are gratefully acknowledged. We would also like to thank Adrian Darnell for his helpful comments on an earlier draft.

[1] It is worth noting that Beesley implicitly assumes that the high rate of formation in a given industry may in part be attributable to favourable incubator characteristics within the *same* industry. The obvious implications of this view is that the founders were previously employed in that industry. He thus ignores the possibility that founders may *cross* industrial boundaries when setting up in business. We have shown [6] that almost one-third of the founders covered in our study—see section I in the text—moved out of the industrial order in which they were previously employed when setting up. (At MLH level the movement was understandably much higher.) However as mentioned in the conclusion to this note, the fact that the *majority* of founders stayed within the same order has implications for the way in which studies on inter-industry differences in new business formation may be interpreted.

new firm formation. This rate is of industrial significance since there is a good deal of evidence—based largely on case studies—to suggest that new firms have often played an important part in introducing innovations and stimulating competition; see for example Freeman [4, p. 14].[2]

This note provides some evidence on variations in fertility across different sizes of incubator plant in the Northern Region of the UK. Although there are considerable differences between the industrial structure of the Northern Region and that in other parts of the UK, there are no grounds for supposing that plants of *a given size* in this region differ markedly in their characteristics from those of plants elsewhere. In the first section we outline the sources of our data, and in the second we present some results.

I. SOURCES OF DATA

This study covers the incubator plants of the founders of 74 manufacturing firms formed in the Northern Region in recent years. 'New' was interpreted in a fairly strict way—only businesses, none of whose principal founders was a sole proprietor, partner or major shareholder in any other business at the time of formation were included. (A 'principal founder' was one without whom the business would not have been formed. Many new businesses had several such founders.) Thus we concentrated very much on the business starting up from scratch.

The main source of information used to identify the relevant businesses was a regional newspaper which regularly publishes details of all new incorporations where the registered office and/or the address of at least one of the directors was in the Northern Region.[3] All incorporations occurring in 1971, 1972 and 1973 were scrutinized and those which appeared likely, on the basis of the published information, to be in manufacturing were contacted for further information. This led to the exclusion of a number of businesses on the grounds either that they were not in manufacturing or that they were not 'new' in the sense defined above. The 74 businesses were established by 115 principal founders.

The data have obvious limitations. For example, unincorporated businesses are excluded, as are companies which did not give the relevant addresses at the date of incorporation. However they were the best available and from the limited cross-checking we were able to do with other sources, it does appear that the final list is not seriously deficient. All the companies were 'live'; attempts to trace dead businesses proved abortive.

[2] G. C. Allen writing in 1961 [1] claimed that such firms 'have been responsible for a considerable part of the industrial expansion of the last fifty years' (p. 28).

[3] The information is supplied to the newspaper by a London agent. Correspondence with the newspaper and the agent confirmed that within the stated criteria, the lists were comprehensive. It is perhaps worth noting that the date of incorporation was not treated in the study as synonymous with that of formation. The latter was defined as the year in which the first full-time employee was taken on. For a fuller discussion of the data see Johnson and Cathcart [6].

THE SIZE OF INCUBATOR PLANTS   221

Information on the size of the incubator plant (at the time the founder left) was sought through interview and correspondence with each company. In most cases the information was checked through correspondence with the incubator itself. Eighteen per cent of the incubators were in non-manufacturing and 10% were located outside the region.

II. SOME RESULTS

Table I summarizes the data on fertility by incubator plant size. The data cover only those incubators which are both in manufacturing and in the Region. The measure of fertility used is the number of new business equivalents (NBEs) per thousand employees. The NBE of any given founder is the reciprocal of the number of principal founders involved in establishing the relevant business (for example if a firm has two such founders, then the NBE of each founder is a half).[4] Thus each founder is weighted by a rough measure of his contribution to the formation of a new business. (Previous studies of

TABLE I

FERTILITY OF NORTHERN REGION MANUFACTURING INCUBATORS BY EMPLOYMENT SIZE

Size of plant (No. of employees)	No. of employees (000s) in the Northern Region (1972)	No. of founders	No. of NBEs	No. of NBEs per 1000 employees
1–10	8·8[a]	7	5·0	0·57
11–99	55·7	20	16·0	0·29
100–499	128·2	24	13·5	0·11
500 or over	274·4	19	9·7	0·04
Sub-total	467·1	70	44·2	0·09
Incubator size unknown		10	7·0	
Total		80	51·2	

Source: Authors' data, Business Monitor PA1001, HMSO, London, 1972, and Business Statistics Office.
[a] This figure was supplied separately to the authors by the BSO. There are considerable problems of data collection at this size level and the figure must be seen as subject to a margin of error.

founders have implied equal weights for all founders.) Using the chi-square goodness of fit test with two degrees of freedom—the two smallest size categories had to be amalgamated—we may reject, at the 1% significance level, the null hypothesis that the number of NBEs in each size band is proportionate to the number of employees in that size band, i.e. that there is no difference in fertility across the bands. Although the limitations of the data must be borne firmly in mind, it appears from the table that fertility declines with plant size.

[4] The founders of any given firm may not of course have come from the same incubator or indeed from incubators which are in the same size band.

It should be noted too that the number of principal founders per new business also appears to decline with increases in incubator plant size. The seven founders (4·5 NBEs) who moved from manufacturing incubators *outside* the region and for whom we have data, all came from plants of 200 employees or less.

The results obtained from Table I may disguise an industry effect. Some industries may be more fertile than others because, for example, their growth rate is relatively slow and employees are therefore searching more intensely for outlets in other forms of employment. Again, some industries may have an occupational structure that is more conducive to spin-off. For example, employees in industries which emphasize marketing functions may be more aware of possible opportunities for self-employment. If the industries which are fertile for these reasons also have a relatively greater number of smaller plants then the results in Table I would follow. Unfortunately our data base is not sufficiently large for us to disaggregate in any extensive way. However we are able to provide some limited data on incubators in Mechanical Engineering (Order VII) This is given in Table II below.

TABLE II

FERTILITY OF NORTHERN REGION MECHANICAL ENGINEERING INCUBATOR PLANTS BY EMPLOYMENT
SIZE

Size of plant (No. of employees)	No. of employees (ooos) in the Northern Region (1972)	No. of founders	No. of NBEs	No. of NBEs per 1000 employees
1–10	1·4ᵃ	—	—	—
11–99	8·4	6	4·5	0·54
100–499	19·1	11	7·0	0·37
500 or over	34·9	11	4·33	0·12
Sub-total	63·8	28	15·83	0·25
Incubator size unknown		3	2·0	

Source: Authors' data, Business Monitor PA1001, HMSO, London, 1972, and Business Statistics Office.
ᵃ See the similar note to Table I. Because of the level of disaggregation involved in the above table, the reservation applies with even greater force.

To apply the chi-square test to these data we were forced to reduce the size bands to two only; below and above 500 employees. We were able to reject at the 5% level the null hypothesis that the number of NBEs in both size bands was proportionate to the number of employees in that band. It seems from the sample data in the table that once more fertility declines with plant size although the absence of any spin-off in the smallest size band should be noted.

It may of course be argued that although the fertility rate in the larger plants appears to be lower, the new businesses that are formed by founders from these plants are likely to be more successful on the grounds that the founders concerned will have been able to draw on more sophisticated managerial experience in their approach to their new ventures, and will thus have been able to identify more accurately their potential markets. 'Success' can be interpreted in several ways. In this study the only satisfactory measure we have been able to adopt is the business's total employment in the fifth year after formation. Using the Kruskal–Wallis test, we are able to find support (at the 5% level) for the hypothesis that employment in this year is unrelated to incubator size. (The employment figure was weighted by the number of founders involved in each business.) Unfortunately we were unable to disaggregate the data.

III. CONCLUSIONS

This note offers some support for the hypothesis that business fertility—measured in terms of the number of new business founders per thousand employees—tends to be greater amongst smaller plants, at least over the size ranges examined. We have not found support for the proposition that the businesses formed by the founders from the bigger plants are likely to grow more rapidly in employment terms, at least in their early years.

The evidence presented is consistent with some preselection by potential founders: they may deliberately seek employment in small plants before setting up in order to gain relevant experience. Conversely, the less entre-preneurially minded may tend to go for the larger plant which provides a more secure environment. Closures among bigger plants is also less common; thus smaller plant employees are more likely to face actual or potential redundancy. This threat may make self-employment a more attractive proposition (Oxenfeldt [8]). The results are also consistent with the findings of Mansfield for the US [7] and Gudgin for the East Midlands [5] on inter-industry differences in formation rates. Mansfield showed that his measure of barriers to entry—the capital investment required to establish a firm of minimum efficient size—had a significant negative effect on entry rates. Gudgin found that variations in the percentage of employment in small plants had a significant positive effect on variations in formations across industries. Both were attempting to capture some measure of the ease with which founders could enter a given industry. (The measure used by Mansfield is almost certainly highly (negatively) correlated with the type of measure used by Gudgin.) However, given the level of aggregation at which both studies were made, the majority of founders involved probably also worked as employees in the *same* industry in which they founded their new businesses, i.e. the destination and source industries of the founders were the same (see footnote 1). Thus the measures used may also reflect differences in the capacity of the industries concerned to generate new founders. Both results are therefore consistent with the hypothesis that the larger the employment in smaller plants the higher the level of fertility.

UNIVERSITY OF DURHAM   ACCEPTED APRIL 1979

REFERENCES

[1] ALLEN, G. C., *The Structure of Industry in Britain* (Longmans, London, 1961).
[2] BEESLEY, M. E., 'The Birth and Death of Industrial Establishments: Experience in the West Midlands Conurbation', *Journal of Industrial Economics*, 4 (1) (October 1955), pp. 45–61.
[3] COOPER, A. C., 'Technical Entrepreneurship: What Do We Know?', *R&D Management*, 3 (2) (February 1973), pp. 59–64.
[4] FREEMAN, C., *The Role of Small Firms in Innovation in the United Kingdom Since 1945*, Committee of Inquiry on Small Firms, Research Report No. 6 (HMSO, London, 1971).
[5] GUDGIN, G., *The East Midlands in the Post-War Period*, Ph.D. submitted to Leicester University (1974).
[6] JOHNSON, P. S. and CATHCART D. G., 'New Manufacturing Firms and Regional Development: Some Evidence from the Northern Region', *Regional Studies*, 13 (3) (June 1979).
[7] MANSFIELD, E., 'Entry, Gibrat's Law, Innovation and the Growth of Firms', *American Economic Review*, 52 (5) (December 1962), pp. 1023–51.
[8] OXENFELDT, A. R., *New Firms and Free Enterprise* (American Council on Public Affairs, Washington, 1943).
[9] PRAIS, S., *The Evolution of Giant Firms in Britain* (Cambridge University Press, Cambridge, 1976).

[23]

Regional Studies, Vol. 18.3, pp. 221-236.

An Industrial and Spatial Analysis of New Firm Formation in Ireland

P. N. O'FARRELL* and R. CROUCHLEY†

*Department of Town Planning, UWIST, Colum Drive, Cardiff CF1 3EU,
†Department of Sociology, University of Surrey, Stag Hill, Guildford GU2 5XH, UK.

(Received April 1983; in revised form November 1983)

O'FARRELL P. N. and CROUCHLEY R. (1984) An industrial and spatial analysis of new firm formation in Ireland, *Reg. Studies* **18**, 221-236. This paper analyses the rate of indigenous new firm formation in Ireland over the period 1973-81. Evidence is presented concerning temporal trends and new firm formation, entry rates at regional and county level, and inter-industry variations in openings. Irish new firm formation rates when compared with international evidence suggest a relatively buoyant new firm sector. New firm entry rates at industry level are related to the size structure of each industry, the age of the existing plant stock, and the extent to which employment is controlled by multi-plant organizations. Spatial variations in entry rates are related to sectoral mix, the proportion of small plants in an area, the degree of urbanization and the rate of manufacturing employment change.

New firm formation   Ireland   Spatial and industrial variations   Hypothesis testing   Implications

O'FARRELL P. N. and CROUCHEY R. (1984) Une analyse industrialo-spatiale de l'établissement de nouvelles entreprises en Irlande, *Reg. Studies* **18**, 221-236. Cet article cherche à analyser le taux d'établissement de nouvelles entreprises autochtones en Irlande portant sur la période de 1973 à 1981. On présente des preuves concernant les tendances sur le temps et l'établissement de nouvelles entreprises, les taux d'entrée au niveau de la région et du comté, et les variations inter-industrielles du nombre d'ouvertures. Une comparaison des taux d'établissement de nouvelles entreprises en Irlande avec des preuves internationales laisse supposer un secteur de nouvelles entreprises lequel est plus ou moins soutenu. Dans le domaine de l'industrie les taux d'entrée des nouvelles entreprises se rapportent à la distribution de chaque industrie par taille, à l'âge de l'équipement en usage et au degré de dépendance entre l'emploi et les entreprises à établissements multiples. Les variations spatiales des taux d'entrée se rapportent à la distribution sectorielle, à la proportion de petits établissements par zone, au degré d'urbanisation et au taux de variation de l'emploi industriel.

Établissement de nouvelles entreprises   Irlande
Variations industrialo-spatiales
Tests des hypothèses   Implications

O'FARRELL P. N. and CROUCHLEY R. (1984) Industrie- und Raumanalyse der Bildung neuer Firmen in Irland, *Reg Studies* **18**, 221-236. Diese Abhandlung analysiert die Häufigkeit einheimischer Firmenneubildungen in Irland im Zeitraum 1973-1981. Beweise werden vorgelegt betreff zeitlicher Tendenzen und Neugründung von Firmen, Eröffnungshäufigkeit auf Regional- und Countyebene, und interindustrielle Unterschiede bei sich bietenden Gelegenheiten. Im internationalen Vergleich weisst die Häufigkeit von Neugründungen irischer Firmen auf einen relativ lebhaften Sektor neuer Firmen hin. Die Häufigkeit von Firmenneugründungen auf Industrieebene wird in Beziehung gesetzt zur Grössenstruktur der jeweiligen Industrie, dem Alter der vorhandenen Betriebslagerbestände, und dem Ausmass, in dem Beschäftigung durch Organisationen mit mehreren Niederlassungen überwacht wird. Räumliche Variationen in der Gründungshäufigkeit stehen in Beziehung zu sektoreller Mischung, dem Anteil kleiner Betriebe in einem Gebiet, dem Grade der Verstädterung und der Häufigkeit des Wandels der Beschäftigung in der Fertigungsindustrie.

Firmenneugründung   Irland
Räumliche und industrielle Variationen
Hypothesenprüfung   Implikationen

INTRODUCTION

During the 1970s the Irish manufacturing sector has been coming increasingly under overseas control and ownership, primarily through the process of branch plant formation, to reach a level of 34·3% of employment by 1981. Although overseas companies have bestowed a wide range of benefits upon the Irish

economy (and it is not argued that efforts to attract more should be re-directed), it nevertheless remains a key strand of Irish industrial strategy to stimulate and expand the indigenous industrial base. Between 1973-81 a total of 2,047 new industrial plants were opened throughout Ireland and *survived* until the end of the period (for definitions, see Appendix 1). These openings comprise 407 multinational branches

(MNEs) providing 32,365 jobs by 1981; 158 new subsidiaries of Irish multiplant firms (IMPs) with 7,197 jobs; and 1,482 new indigenous single plant firms (ISPs) employing 18,032. This paper focuses upon the indigenous new firm formation process and presents evidence on temporal trends in formation rates, spatial variations at regional and county level and inter-industry differences; an attempt is also made to analyse new firm formation rates both sectorally and spatially within a multivariate framework in order to identify some of the factors underlying variations in entry. Finally, policy implications of the results are discussed.

DATA

The analysis is based upon the Industrial Development Authority's (IDA) annual employment survey conducted on January 1st each year. The survey constitutes a population census of manufacturing establishments with a minimum payroll of three including owner manager(s).[1] In subsequent years, if the employment total falls below three, the plant is retained on file and the employment recorded. Prior to 1979, the employment survey only included a sample of plants in County Dublin employing less than fifty people; but data for all new firms which survived in Dublin is available for 1981. Hence, Dublin must be excluded in any national analysis of *all* new firm entries, including those which subsequently closed, but the capital may be incorporated when the objective is to study survivors only. The following data are recorded for every plant: name of firm; total male and female employees; location; product code; year production commenced; nationality; and programme under which grant aided, if applicable. The ownership variable, so fundamental to any investigation of new openings, is not recorded by the IDA employment survey and, therefore, the relevant information was collected. Ownership has been classified, in the case of surviving plants, according to their status in 1981 and, for plants which closed, their status in the year prior to closure (see Appendix 1). This means that the methodology cannot adequately account for the effects of ownership changes between the base and terminal years (t_1 and t_2). In Britain, changes in organizational status—for example, the takeover of a fast growing single plant indigenous firm (ISP) by a larger multiplant firm—is frequently associated with closure (DICKEN and LLOYD, 1978, p. 183). Takeover and merger activity is a highly infrequent phenomenon in Irish manufacturing and the classification of plants according to their organizational status in 1981 is likely to understate the contribution of ISPs to employment change to only an extremely marginal degree.

The identification of new manufacturing firms according to whatever definition is employed has always been a difficult problem for research workers (MASON, 1983). The definition employed in this Irish study is founded upon the concept of the firm as one which has no obvious parent in any existing business enterprise. This distinguishes between subsidiaries established by existing companies—both domestic and overseas—and new independent indigenous firms. Independence has been defined in legal terms recognizing, however, that many independent firms may be functionally dependent. The staff of the IDA classified the ownership variable and a test of the reliability of their classifications was conducted in 1983 when over 300 indigenous single plant firms were randomly sampled and surveyed. Only 1·5% of firms reported that they were subsidiaries of existing businesses thereby confirming the high degree of accuracy achieved by the IDA in identifying indigenous single plant firms. The date of start-up of the new independent firms is defined as the year of entry to the IDA employment survey (Appendix 1).

Name changes are monitored and recorded when they occur; but a change of nationality or product group is only picked up *immediately* in cases where these changes also involved a name change. Where a change of nationality or product group occurs but the plant's name remains unchanged, this is only recorded if noticed by the IDA regional office and subsequently reported. There is evidence to suggest that such changes within plants between 1973–80 are rare phenomena (Appendix 1).

TEMPORAL TRENDS IN NEW FIRM FORMATION BY TOWN SIZE LOCATION

The number of new indigenous firms being established each year outside Dublin averaged 134 per annum between 1973–5; then, from 1976, the rate of entry rose rapidly to peak in 1978 and fall back slightly with the onset of the current recession (Table 1). The rate of new firm formation was some 46% higher between 1976–80 than over the 1973–6 period, and this trend is manifest outside the Dublin County area. The second row of Table 1 records the number of new firms which survived until 1981 including those in Dublin. It is a less meaningful index of the annual fluctuations in entry rates because plants established in earlier years will have been vulnerable to closure for longer periods. However, it does give an approximate indication of the national trend especially since 1977 when the Small Industry (SI) programme of the Industrial Development Authority (IDA) was extended to the capital city.

Indigenous new firm formation rates are classified by town size group in Table 2 which has to be restricted to survivors only in order to include Dublin. Hence, caution must be exercised when interpreting entry rates for earlier years whose cohorts

An Industrial and Spatial Analysis of New Firm Formation in Ireland   223

Table 1. *Annual number of new indigenous single plant firms 1973–80 (inclusive)*

	1973	1974	1975	1976	1977	1978	1979	1980	Total
Total openings[1]	153	127	123	178	215	226	198	162	1,382
Survivors[2]	142	109	119	169	238	273	247	185	1,482

Notes: 1. Dublin is excluded; total incorporates survivors and new entries which subsequently closed.
2. Dublin is included.

Table 2. *Annual number of new indigenous single plant firms[1] by town size group, 1973–81*

Year	Town size group							Total
	<1500	1,501–5,000	5,001–10,000	10,001–25,000	25,001–100,000	Cork	Dublin	
1973	39	30	16	11	6	12	28	142
1974	36	25	13	8	4	5	18	109
1975	34	26	18	11	6	4	20	119
1976	62	27	30	24	5	1	20	169
1977	62	46	23	36	8	7	56	238
1978	82	56	34	23	15	4	59	273
1979	56	35	26	27	26	22	55	247
1980	47	37	21	26	20	11	23	185
Total	418	282	181	166	90	66	279	1,482
Manufacturing employment								
1973	27,374	31,253	22,783	23,290	16,484	15,289	91,494	227,967
Number of new ISPs per 1,000 manufacturing employees (1973) per annum	1·91	1·13	0·99	0·89	0·68	0·54	0·38	0·81

Note: 1. Data is for survivors only which permits inclusion of Dublin.

have been in existence for longer. It has been shown elsewhere that closure rates do not vary by town size location (O'FARRELL and CROUCHLEY, 1983) so that it may be assumed that the survivor data is a reasonable proxy of new firm formation. It is apparent that the rate of indigenous new firm formation rose sharply in 1977 (Table 1) partly because of the extension of the SI scheme to Dublin but higher rates also occurred throughout the rest of the urban system (Table 2). Buoyancy in terms of more new indigenous firms emerged somewhat later in Cork and the major provincial towns between 25,000 and 100,000. Indeed, the recent upward trend in new firm formation is somewhat more pronounced in the larger towns than elsewhere. Between 1973–7 (inclusive) the 25,000–100,000 towns (Cork and Dublin) generated 25·7% of all new indigenous firm survivors while over the 1978–80 period 33·3% of all new firms were established in these larger towns. This net shift towards the metropolitan areas is only *partly* accounted for by the extension of the Small Industry programme to Dublin in 1977. The success of the other large towns might reflect the increased spin-off of new enterprises following the considerable phase of IDA-sponsored overseas investment in places such as Limerick-Shannon, Galway and Waterford since the late 1960s. When the number of ISP survivors is expressed per 1,000 manufacturing employees (1973) per annum, there is a clear inverse relationship between the rate of indigenous new firm formation and town size. The highest rate occurs in the below 1,500 population category (1·91) and the rate falls

steadily with increasing town size so that all size groups above 25,000 have rates below the national average. The Dublin rate is only one-fifth that of the smallest communities (1,500) and about one-half of that recorded by the major provincial towns between 25,001 and 100,000 population (Table 2). A high rate of indigenous new firm formation is predominantly a rural-small town phenomenon: only 29% of the survivors were located in towns of over 25,000 although they accounted for 54% of industrial employment in 1973.

SPATIAL AND SECTORAL VARIATIONS IN NEW FIRM FORMATION

When indigenous new firm formation rates are calculated for the non-Dublin area thereby permitting the inclusion of survivors *and* new openings which subsequently closed, the national rate is 1·27 which compares with the corresponding survivors-only figure of 1·10 (Table 3). The increasing rate of new firm formation observable from 1976–7 is most pronounced in the North West, West, Mid West, South East, Kildare, Meath and Wicklow and the Midlands. The increasing rate of new firm formation observable in the Mid West region since the late seventies may partially reflect the changed role of the Shannon Free Airport Development Company to develop indigenous industry in an intensive and innovative way not hitherto attempted in Ireland. This scheme has been operating for too short a period

Table 3. Annual number of new indigenous single plant firms by region[1], 1973–81

Year	Donegal	North West	West	Mid West	South West	South East	Kildare Meath Wicklow	North East	Midlands	Total
1973	13	4	21	11	31	14	13	22	24	153
1974	6	2	9	19	25	13	23	12	18	127
1975	9	3	17	14	15	17	17	20	11	123
1976	19	9	28	14	18	18	25	31	16	178
1977	5	15	19	26	21	44	30	24	31	215
1978	12	13	20	28	13	29	60	25	26	226
1979	3	6	29	19	40	33	20	20	28	198
1980	9	11	8	21	32	25	23	23	10	162
Total	76	63	151	152	195	193	211	177	164	1,382
Manufacturing employment 1973	5,422	3,246	8,269	18,274	35,182	23,142	15,703	18,098	9,137	136,473
Number of new ISPs per 1,000 manufacturing employees (1973) per annum	1·75	2·43	2·28	1·04	0·69	1·04	1·68	1·22	2·24	1·266

Note: 1. Dublin is excluded; total includes survivors plus new establishments which subsequently closed.

Table 4. Number of new indigenous single plant firms by county, 1973–81

County	Total number of new ISPs	Number of ISP survivors	Manufacturing employment 1973	Number of new ISPs per annum per 1,000 manufacturing employees (1973)	Number of ISP survivors per annum per 1,000 manufacturing employees (1973)
Donegal	76	70	5,422	1·75	1·61
Leitrim	24	20	764	3·93	3·27
Sligo	39	39	2,482	1·96	1·96
Galway	99	86	5,182	2·39	2·07
Mayo	52	40	3,087	2·11	1·62
Clare	58	43	6,560	1·11	0·82
Limerick	77	72	8,461	1·14	1·06
Tipperary N.R.	17	15	3,253	0·65	0·58
Cork	156	142	30,407	0·64	0·58
Kerry	39	38	4,775	1·02	0·99
Carlow	25	22	2,562	1·22	1·07
Kilkenny	34	29	3,262	1·30	1·11
Tipperary S.R.	27	24	3,958	0·85	0·76
Waterford	54	48	8,847	0·76	0·68
Wexford	53	49	4,513	1·47	1·36
Dublin	–	279	91,494	–	0·38
Kildare	56	49	6,312	1·10	0·97
Wicklow	75	62	5,069	1·85	1·53
Meath	80	69	4,322	2·31	2·00
Cavan	47	40	2,796	2·10	1·79
Louth	82	65	11,790	0·87	0·69
Monaghan	48	39	3,512	1·71	1·39
Laois	20	20	1,934	1·29	1·29
Longford	23	17	1,045	2·75[1]	2·03[2]
Offaly	35	31	3,264	1·34	1·19
Roscommon	49	42	982	6·24[1]	5·35[2]
Westmeath	37	32	1,912	2·42	2·09
Total	1,382	1,482	227,967	1·27	0·81

Notes: 1. Pooling the contiguous counties of Longford and Roscommon gives a rate of 4·44.
2. Pooling Longford and Roscommon produces a rate of 3·64.

An Industrial and Spatial Analysis of New Firm Formation in Ireland   225

to enable an unequivocal conclusion to be drawn concerning its effectiveness in the Mid West relative to the less resource intensive IDA programme in the rest of the country. In Donegal and the North East, there is no strong post-1976 upward trend.

The highest rate of indigenous new firm formation per 1,000 manufacturing employees (1973) per annum is in the North West (2·43)—almost double the national average—with the West and Midlands also registering very high rates. The North East, the South East and the Mid West have very similar rates—all with a strong urban base and some tradition of manufacturing industry—but nevertheless with below average rates of indigenous new firm formation (Table 3). The lowest rate of domestic owned new business formation in manufacturing industry was in the South West region (0·69). The highest rates, therefore, are in the most rural and least industrialized regions of the country. An exception to this pattern is the relatively high rate of new firm foundation in Meath, Kildare and Wicklow, which may be partly due to the movement out of founders from Dublin, where rates of formation are extremely low, to take advantage of less congestion and cheaper sites.

A regional level of aggregation is not the most appropriate one at which to analyse new firm formation, a process which is usually highly localized (GUDGIN, 1978). Some interesting patterns emerge, therefore, when the regional rates are disaggregated by county (Table 4). Some counties, notably Leitrim, Roscommon and Longford, had such a small manufacturing base in 1973 that it was necessary to aggregate them with a contiguous county to produce rates of new firm formation which might be more validly compared with other areas. The Roscommon-Longford area has by far the highest rate of new firm formation, 4·44 firms per thousand employees per annum. It is interesting to note that their neighbouring counties in the Midlands region have much lower rates: Westmeath (2·42), Offaly (1·34) and Laois (1·29). This may be partly explained by the fact that Roscommon and Longford are in the Designated Areas with regional development grant levels of up to 60%, while in the rest of the Midlands, which is non-designated, the grant ceiling is 45%. However, other factors, such as size and sectoral mix, upon which attention will be focused in the econometric analysis, may also be partly responsible for inter-county variations in new firm formation rates.

The highest rates of new firm formation occur in a block of country south of Donegal and north of a line from Galway to Drogheda in the North West and West regions together with Longford-Roscommon, Westmeath, Cavan and Meath—all with rates of new firm formation above 2·0 per 1,000 manufacturing employees (1973) per annum (Fig. 1). These are, with the exception of the commuting zone of Co. Meath and around Galway city, predominantly rural

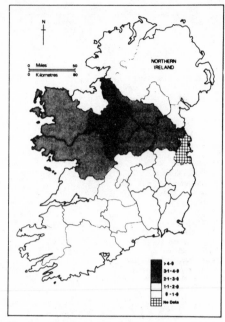

Fig. 1. *Annual number of new firms per thousand manufacturing employees (1973)*

counties.[2] By contrast, the counties of the South West, Mid-West and South East have recorded low rates of indigenous new business formation in manufacturing—less than one third of the rate achieved in the Longford-Roscommon area. The lowest rates of all were recorded in Dublin (where the survivor rate is about one-tenth of the Longford-Roscommon figure) Cork, Tipperary N.R., Waterford, Tipperary S.R. and Louth. Three of these are the most urbanized counties but the low rates in Tipperary are seemingly anomalous.

There are very considerable between-sector differences in new firm formation rates around the national average of 1·27 new firms per annum per 1,000 manufacturing employees (Table 5). The highest entry rate occurs in furniture (4·6) followed by metal trades, wood, cork and brushes, and plastics— all industries with relatively low entry barriers. The only other sectors with entry rates above the national average are printing and publishing, machinery manufacture, electrical machinery and construction, agriculture and services (Table 5). The lowest rates of entry were recorded by butter and milk products (0·09), drink and tobacco, boots and shoes, bacon and slaughtering, and hosiery. These figures demonstrate that between industry variation in new firm formation is very high: the rate of entry in furniture, for

Table 5. *Number of new indigenous single plant firms[1] by sector, 1973–81*

Sector[2]	Total number of new ISPs	Number of new ISP survivors	Manufacturing employment 1973	Number of new ISPs per annum per 1,000 manufacturing employees (1973)	Number of new ISP survivors per annum per 1,000 manufacturing employees (1973)
1. Bacon and slaughtering (4,5)	13	12	8,027	0·202	0·187
2. Creamery butter and milk products (6)	5	4	7,001	0·089	0·071
3. Grain milling and animal feed (8)	12	9	4,274	0·351	0·263
4. Bread, biscuits (9)	24	23	4,884	0·614	0·589
5. Jam, canned food, sugar, cocoa, chocolate, margarine, miscellaneous food (7,10,11,12,13)	51	41	6,525	0·977	0·785
6. Drink and tobacco (14–18)	7	6	4,930	0·178	0·152
7. Woollen and worsted, linen, cotton, jute, nylon etc. (19–21)	30	23	8,411	0·446	0·342
8. Hosiery (22)	14	8	5,317	0·329	0·188
9. Boot and shoe (23)	7	4	4,911	0·178	0·102
10. Clothing (24)	68	54	9,183	0·926	0·735
11. Made-up textiles (25)	17	15	4,815	0·441	0·389
12. Wood, cork, brushes (26,28)	78	72	3,056	3·190	2·945
13. Furniture (27)	214	197	5,813	4·602	4·236
14. Paper/paper products (29)	13	12	1,348	1·205	1·113
15. Printing and publishing (30)	42	34	3,334	1·575	1·275
16. Miscellaneous including fell-mongery and leather (31,32,47)	85	68	9,516	1·117	0·893
17. Fertilizers, paints, chemicals, soap, pharmaceuticals (33–36)	33	29	4,069	1·014	0·891
18. Glass, pottery (37)	34	30	4,138	1·027	0·906
19. Cement, structural clay (38,39)	70	63	7,410	1·181	1·063
20. Metal trades (40)	359	330	12,490	3·593	3·302
21. Machinery manufacture (41)	42	34	3,290	1·596	1·292
22. Electrical machinery (42)	62	51	5,315	1·458	1·199
23. Shipbuilding and repairs, railroad equipment, road and other vehicles (43–46)	38	33	4,383	1·084	0·941
24. Plastics (48)	41	33	1,970	2·602	2·094
25. Construction, agriculture, services (60,65,70)	23	18	2,062	1·394	1·091
Total	1,382	1,203	136,473	1·266	1·101

Notes: 1. Table excludes Dublin; there were 279 new ISPs in Dublin which served until 1981. The national rate of new firm formation for survivors including Dublin is 0·813 compared with 1·101 for the country outside Dublin.

2. Numbers in parentheses are IDA Product Codes.

example, is twenty-five times greater than in either drink and tobacco or boots and shoes. Exit rates expressed as the number of the 1973 stock of plants closing per 1,000 employees (1973) range from 1·21 (wood, cork) and 1·65 (furniture) to bacon and slaughtering (0·16) and fertilizers, chemicals and pharmaceuticals (0·17). It appears that industries experiencing high exit rates also record high rates of entry. The turnover rate of plants—i.e. entry and exit rates—is responsible for the age distribution of each industry and it has been shown elsewhere (O'FAR-RELL and CROUCHLEY, 1983) that age of young plants is related to closure (exits). Hence, sectors with high entry rates, *ceteris paribus*, will have high exit rates both because of a higher proportion of young plants

and as a consequence of size since most young plants are small and therefore more vulnerable to closure. As expected, entry rates and exit rates of new firms are quite highly correlated—$r^2 = 0·67$ for all entries—although the relationship is purely associative.

New firm formation rates: Irish and UK comparisons

The comparisons of new firm formation rates in manufacturing between Ireland and the East Midlands of England need to be interpreted with great caution and small differences should not be regarded as in any way meaningful for a number of reasons. First, comparisons are hampered by differences in data sources and survey methodologies. Second, the

An Industrial and Spatial Analysis of New Firm Formation in Ireland

227

industrial classification systems are not identical although every effort has been made to include only those groups which appear to be very similar by aggregating up from MLH level. Third, the time periods over which the annual rates are calculated are different in the two areas (Table 6). Examination of the Irish and East Midlands industry rates shows that the number of new firms per 1,000 manufacturing employees in the base year per annum in Ireland, 1·01, is considerably higher than the corresponding East Midlands figure of 0·42 (Table 6). In addition, employment generated by new firms in Ireland between 1973–81 as a percentage of base year manufacturing employment (7·9%) was substantially greater than the East Midlands 1968–75 figure of 4·1%. Specific industry comparisons reveal that the rate of new firm formation is much higher in paper products, and furniture in Ireland as it also is in printing and publishing, chemicals and pharmaceuticals, cement, structural clay and glass (Table 6). The East Midlands recorded higher rates in hosiery and footwear—industries in which there are major concentrations in this English region—and several industries, notably food, clothing, wood, cork and brushes registered very similar new firm formation levels in the two areas.

Furthermore, the number of new indigenous firms per annum in Ireland per 1,000 manufacturing employees in the *end year* is 6·20 which is considerably higher than the rates for South Hampshire (3·2), the East Midlands (3·0), Cleveland (1·3) or Scotland (1·0) (Table 7). Similarly, the impact of new firm survivors upon *end year* employment in Ireland is approximately double that for either the East Midlands or South Hampshire in the UK (Table 7).

Table 6. *Indigenous new firm formation rates*[1] *by industry: UK and Irish comparisons*

Industry	East Midlands, England 1968–75	Ireland 1973–81
Food	0·39	0·36
Drink and tobacco	0·07	0·15
Hosiery	0·36	0·19
Footwear	0·14	0·10
Clothing	0·75	0·74
Wood, cork, brushes	2·52	2·95
Furniture	1·95	4·24
Paper products	0·43	1·11
Printing and publishing	0·79	1·28
Chemicals, fertilizers, pharmaceuticals, etc.	0·27	0·89
Cement, structural clay, glass and pottery	0·27	1·01
Plastics	1·85	2·09
Total	0·42	1·01

Notes: Formation rate: number of new indigenous firms per 1,000 manufacturing employees in the base year per annum (data represents survivors only).

Sources: Ireland (this study)
East Midlands (Steve Fothergill, University of Cambridge, kindly supplied the data at MLH level).

New firm formation rates: international comparisons

It is not possible to use the measure of entry rate expressed per 1,000 industrial employees for the purposes of international comparisons because most researchers have defined entry rates per annum as a percentage of the number of firms (or establishments) in the base year. The measure used throughout this study is preferable since it reflects the process by which the population of industrial employees is the relevant indicator of the number of potential entre-

Table 7. *International comparisons of new firm entry rates*

	Entry rate per annum[1]	Employment in new firms as % of total end year employment	New firms per 1,000 manufacturing employees in end year
USA (all USA[a])	1950–58	6·9	
Canada (Ontario[b])	1961–65	6·1	
Norway[c]	1937–48	5·0	
UK: Leicestershire[d]	1947–55	3·1	
South Hampshire[e]	1971–79		3·5	3·20
Cleveland[f]	1965–76		1·8	1·30
East Midlands[g]	1968–75		4·2	3·0
Scotland[h]	1968–77		2·2	1·0
Ireland[i]	1973–81	5·7	7·5	6·20

Note: 1. Entry rate defined as number of new indigenous firms per annum as a percentage of total population of establishments at beginning of period (see text for departures from this definition in some studies).

Sources: a. CHURCHILL, 1959
b. COLLINS, 1972
c. WEDERVANG, 1965
d. GUDGIN, 1978
e. MASON, 1982
f. ROBINSON and STOREY, 1981
g. FOTHERGILL and GUDGIN, 1979
h. CROSS, 1981
i. This study

preneurs (GUDGIN, 1978, p. 136). The base measured in terms of number of firms (or plants) fails to take account of the size of the latter. However, in order to make any international comparisons, this less satisfactory measure must be used. The national studies for the USA (CHURCHILL, 1959) and NORWAY (Wedervang, 1965) refer to firms while the UK and Canadian data relate to establishments and are, therefore, more directly comparable with those for Ireland. Furthermore, the US data classified changes of ownership as births and deaths so great care must be excercised in comparing the findings. The results presented in Table 7 suggest that entry rates in Ireland are comparable with those for Norway (between 1937–48), Canada and the USA (especially when allowances are made for changes in ownership) but the UK figure is over 40% lower than the Irish one. When the employment impact of new firm survivors is considered relative to total end year employment, the Irish figure of 7·5% is approximately double those for the East Midlands and South Hampshire in the UK (Table 7).

SECTORAL VARIATIONS IN NEW FIRM FORMATION RATES: SOME THEORETICAL CONSIDERATIONS

In analysing entry rates of new firms to various industries, the conceptual framework will be derived primarily from economies since this paper is concerned with *aggregate* rates of new firm formation and not the micro-process of formation at the individual level. At the micro level, social psychologists and sociologists have developed insights into those factors which motivate a person to set up his own firm but such factors may be assumed to be randomly distributed at the aggregate inter-industry level.

The traditional economic view is to conceive of the entry of new firms into an industry as a reflection of the chances of profit making in that industry.[3] Formation rates are assumed to be a function of perceived post-entry profitability and the real or expected entry barriers so that economists have tended to ignore the supply side of entrepreneurship (STOREY, 1982, p. 3). Under the unrealistic assumptions of the static perfect competition model, new firms enter markets where prices persistently exceed long run average cost.[4] In imperfect markets, however, where pricing policy may be influenced by the entry of new firms, rates of formation may be depressed by barriers to entry. BAIN, 1956, argued convincingly that sellers in certain industries can raise prices above a competitive level without attracting new firms into the industry. There are a wide range of such barriers including: product differentiation; control over input suppliers and/or outlets; scale economies; legal and institutional factors including patents; large capital requirements; degree of seller concentration; absolute cost disadvantages and so on.

Contemporary theory of the firm, including most of the managerial models, does not incorporate any distinctive entrepreneurial function (JOHNSON and DARNELL, 1976, p. 5). There is no consensus upon the precise nature of entrepreneurship, except that it involves something more than the daily management of the firm. Included in the activities attributed to the entrepreneur have been: risk taking; combination and organization of the factors of production; leadership and motivation; long range planning; and, especially, innovation. Entrepreneurship, therefore, can and does occur within an *existing* business. Conversely, entrepreneurship and new firm formation are *not* synonymous; there are many types of new enterprise—most of which display few, if any, entrepreneurial characteristics. SCHUMPETER (1961, p. 66), however, saw a clear link between the entrepreneur (as he defined it) and the new firm, although he conceded that there were exceptions. Many, probably most, new firm founders duplicate existing production functions and orientate towards existing markets and supply sources. The new firm founder is more likely to be an adopter and imitator than an innovator; to have more in common with Marshall's organizer of factors or production than Schumpeter's creator of new products or processes.

A number of researchers (MANSFIELD, 1962; GUDGIN, 1978; and JOHNSON and CATHCART, 1979) have analysed, within a multiple regression framework, inter-industry difference in formation rates. In this study, the dependent variable Y, is defined as the number of new indigenous single plant firms per annum per 1,000 employees in industry i in the base year entering between January 1973 and January 1981. The independent variables have usually included: (1) the proportion of plants in industry i employing less than twenty in the base year (X_1); and (2) employment change in industry i over the study period (X_2). These variables are usually specified to reflect, respectively, the extent to which barriers to entry exist in any given industry and the attractiveness of industry i to potential entrants.[5] Employment in a small firm is assumed to be a better preparation for founding a business because of the wide range of task experience derived, the opportunity of regular contact with the director (who may also be the founder) and the lower level of salaries, fringe benefits and job security than in larger firms. Hence, sectors containing a high proportion of small firms will, *ceteris paribus*, generate more new founders. However, the proportion of small plants in an industry does not necessarily simply reflect entrepreneurial supply but may also mirror ease of entry (i.e. low capital requirements) or the youthfulness of an industry (CROSS, 1981, p. 168). It is hypothesized that the relationship between variable X_1 (percentage of plants in sector employing fewer than twenty persons in

An Industrial and Spatial Analysis of New Firm Formation in Ireland 229

1973) and the dependent variable (Y_1) is positive. It is not possible to disentangle all the micro-processes underlying variable X_1 within an aggregate model. The regression parameter will determine whether variable X_1 is significant; further work at the level of individual founders and their firms will be necessary to identify the mechanisms underlying it.

The extent to which new firm founders move into a different industry product category from their previous employment represents, together with the introduction of new products and processes by firms already in the region, an important element in the process of diversifying regional economies. Variable X_2, the employment change of the 1973 stock of plants in industry i, is tested against the rate of entry to verify the hypothesis that sectors experiencing growth will attract more new firms. Since a person working in industry i is more likely to identify a market gap in industry i than an individual working in j, any analysis of inter-industry formation rates must take account not only of the relative attractiveness of different industries as a *destination* for new formations (the growth rate variable), but also the relative suitability of such industries as generators of spin-off (JOHNSON and CATHCART, 1979, p. 278). The regression results may be picking up not only the attractiveness of a given industry as a destination for new founders but also its 'effectiveness' as a source industry. There is no way within this analytical framework that the two effects can be isolated. JOHNSON and CATHCART, 1979; and GUDGIN, 1978, appear to have measured employment change in all plants so that their expansion rates are dependent, at least in part, upon the rates of entry into each industry. In the absence of any strong theoretical arguments in favour of a specific functional form, a linear relationship is usually fitted (see JOHNSON and CATHCART, 1979).

$$Yi = a + b_1X_1 + b_2X_2 + e$$

Both GUDGIN, 1978, and JOHNSON and CATHCART, 1979, showed that variable X_1, was significant but not X_2—the employment change factor.

Plant dominance and industrial concentration are often viewed as factors which act to inhibit the rate of entry (CROSS, 1981, p. 167). First, the dominance of an industrial sector by a few large plants would suggest that the minimum size for efficient production is large and would, therefore, discourage entry. A second influence of large plants refers to the supply side of founders: the structure and work experience gained while working for a large organization is not conducive to entrepreneurship. A number of workers have observed that spin-off rates from smaller plants are much greater than from larger ones (JOHNSON and CATHCART, 1979; COOPER, 1971). This variable (X_3) is specified as the percentage of employment in industry i located in plants employing over 200 persons. The variable ranges from 0 (plastics) to

79.8% (electrical machinery) and is conceived as inhibiting new firm entry. The large plant size effect may be *reinforced* by the *ownership* factor (X_6). Increasing external ownership may decrease the number of risk taking managerial positions which reduces the potential supply of founders. However, this variable may also reflect demand side factors such as the greater opportunities for MNEs to achieve scale economies. It is operationalized as the proportion of employment in the sector controlled by multiplant firms (MNEs and IMPs). CROSS, 1981, p. 172, reported that the level of Scottish ownership was positively related to sectoral variations in entry rates although this result should be interpreted with some caution since it is based upon rank correlations without control for other factors. Variable X_4—the median size of new ISPs in each sector at end of first year—is included in order to test the hypothesis that the smaller the *initial* size at which a firm can become established in an industry, the easier it will be for new founders to enter. This may be regarded as a crude proxy of the capital requirements for an operation of minimum efficient size (for definition of variables see Appendix 2).

It is also hypothesized that there is an inverse relationship between median age of the 1973 stock of plants in an industry (X_5) and the rate of entry. The inclusion of age may reflect a number of processes: (1) a high turnover rate within an industry; (2) a youthful new industry (e.g. electronics) with a low average age; and (3) a direct relationship between the youthfulness of an industry and its ability to produce new firms (CROSS, 1981, p. 172). The causal mechanism is ambiguous. A host of personal and micro-environmental factors may also be important but it is expected that personality and attitudinal factors to entrepreneurship will operate randomly at an aggregate inter-industry level. Thus, the econometric analysis will permit examination of the aggregate patterns of entry and identification of some of the major influences upon it but cannot differentiate between the micro-level variables. The inter-industry analysis of entry will be conducted upon all firms[6] which entered between January 1973 and January 1981(Y_1).

SECTORAL VARIATIONS IN RATES OF NEW FIRM FORMATION: AN ANALYSIS

The twenty-five industry groups outlined in Table 5 were selected in consultation with the IDA in order to maximize product homogeneity and minimize employment size variance between industries. The latter constraint, necessary for regression analysis, prevented a more detailed disaggregation of industry groups. *A priori* theoretical reasoning and previous empirical evidence determine the order of entry of the independent variables. The value of X_1 (the percentage of plants employing fewer than twenty persons) ranges from 77% in furniture to 20% in boots and shoes; while X_2 (percentage employment change 1973–81 of the 1973 plant stock) ranges from a *decline* of 51% in woollen, worsted, linen and cotton to an increase of 95·5% in bacon and slaughtering. Some seventeen sectors declined and only eight expanded employment. Table 8 shows that X_1 (the proportion of plants employing fewer than twenty) is positively related, as hypothesized, to entry rates thereby confirming the results obtained by WEDERVANG, 1965, pp. 178–9; JOHNSON and CATHCART, 1979, p. 277; and GUDGIN, 1978, p. 166. Equation 2 is specified to reflect both the effect of X_1 and the employment change variable, X_2; the results show that X_2 is insignificant which supports the findings of other studies. Similarly, although the sign of the co-efficient X_3 (proportion of employment in establishments employing over 200) is negative, as postulated, the variable is not significant; its inclusion has a negligible effect upon the parameter and standard error of X_1 (Table 8). In the case of variable X_4 (the size of new ISPs at entry) the direction of the relationship is negative, as predicted, but the variable is not significant. The final series of hypotheses examines the rate of entry and its relationship with several characteristics of each industry. Variable X_5 (the median age of the 1973 stock) ranges in value from 4·5 years (plastics) to 35 (creamery, butter and milk; and drink and tobacco). The relationship between X_5 and Y_1 is negative, as postulated, and is significant ($p < 0·01$).

It is also hypothesized that there is a negative relationship between the percentage of employment in each industry controlled by multiplant organizations and the rate of new firm formation. The highest proportions of employment controlled by multiplants occur in paper and printing (88·4%), machinery

manufacture (84·0%) and miscellaneous (82·9%) with the lowest in furniture (15·7%), printing and publishing (15·9%) and bread and biscuits (25·8%). When variable X_6 is entered into an equation containing X_1 and X_5, it is significant with a negative directional relationship, as predicted (equation (6) Table 8). Hence, this is the best fit model with an $\bar{R}^2 = 0·76$ and the direction of all relationships as originally hypothesized.

The parameters of equation (6) Table 8 suggests that a one percentage point increase in the percentage of plants employing fewer than twenty people increases the rate of new firm formation by 0·04 per 1,000 employees per annum, having allowed for the effects of age and proportion of employment in multiplant firms.[7] This parameter is higher than the one of 0·02 reported by GUDGIN, 1978, p. 137, in the case of the East Midlands of Britain thereby implying a stronger size effect in Ireland. The coefficient of X_5, median age, suggests that a 1% rise in age of the manufacturing plant stock is associated with a lowering of new firm formation rates by 0·07 per 1,000 manufacturing employees per annum, although a causal relationship is not implied since age may reflect a number of processes. Finally, a one percentage point rise in the percentage of employment owned by multiplant enterprises reduces new firm formation rates by 0·02. An inspection of standardized residuals from equation (6) of Table 8 suggests that those sectors where indigenous new firm formation rates have been higher than those predicted by the regression equation are furniture, metal trades, plastics, and wood, cork and brushes. These are all industries characterized by very high rates of new firm formation implying that there are other factors, in addition to those included in the model, which explain their performance. One such factor is that most new firms in these industries produce products with a high bulk or weight to value ratio which for logistic

Table 8. *Regression equations with the number of new indigenous single plant firms per 1,000 employees in 1973 per annum for 25 industry groups as dependent variable* (Y_1)[1]

Equation	Equation number	$\bar{R}^2$	S.E.E.[2]
$Y_1 = -0·89 + 0·04 X_1$ $(3·04)**$	(1)	0·131	0·926
$Y_1 = -0·93 + 0·04 X_1 - 0·005 X_2$ $(2·52)*$ $(0·78)$	(2)	0·32	0·916
$Y_1 = -0·02 + 0·03 X_1 - 0·01 X_3$ $(2·52)*$ $(1·52)$	(3)	0·41	0·793
$Y_1 = 0·16 + 0·03 X_1 - 0·06 X_4$ $(1·64)$ $(0·78)$	(4)	0·32	0·926
$Y_1 = 0·42 + 0·05 X_1 - 0·06 X_5$ $(3·93)**$ $(3·05)**$	(5)	0·65	0·475
$Y_1 = 1·38 + 0·04 X_1 - 0·07 X_5 - 0·02 X_6$ $(3·20)**$ $(3·94)**$ $(2·33)*$	(6)	0·76	0·311

Notes: 1. Y_1 includes survivors and new firms which opened and subsequently closed.
2. S.E.E. = standard error of the estimate.
*Significant at $p < 0·05$. **Significant at $p < 0·01$
For each equation the figures in parentheses are t values.

reasons are subjected to little or no competition from imports (i.e. the new enterprises are relatively sheltered). Sectors with the largest negative residuals where new firm formation rates are *lower* than those predicted by the model are shipbuilding and repairs, railroad equipment and vehicles, bread and biscuits, printing and publishing, and cement and structural clay. These are clearly sectors which are more difficult to enter than predicted by the variables in the model; there are factors other than plant size, age and extent of multiplant ownership influencing rates of new firm formation in these sectors. These might include initial capital requirements, price discrimination, state of market demand, scale economies, degree of foreign competition and so on. Since the causal mechanisms underlying the statistical associations in the model are complex and not fully understood and since the number of observations is small (twenty-five), the models are of limited value for the purpose of policy prescription.

The analysis of residuals has suggested that much of the growth in new firm formation has been in business relatively sheltered from international competition.[8] It is not possible to quantify this factor precisely and incorporate it in the econometric model. However, it is apparent that one-third of new firms are in predominantly non-traded sectors of paper, printing, packaging, wood, furniture, cement, glass and clay (Table 5). Only 10% of new firms have been established in overwhelmingly traded (i.e. open to international competition) sectors such as clothing, footwear and textiles while the remainder (57%) are attributable to heterogeneous industries like metals and engineering, plastics, food and consumer goods (NATIONAL ECONOMIC AND SOCIAL COUNCIL, 1982, pp. 15–16).

The overall conclusion of this exercise is that new firm entry rates differ substantially between sectors; that entry rates are quite strongly related to the size structure of an industry but are not correlated with employment change; that the age of the existing plant stock and the extent to which the employment in an industry is controlled by multiplant organizations are also related to entry rates; and that the highest formation rates have occurred in non-traded businesses largely protected from international competition. Although all of these statistical associations with rates of entry are plausible, caution must be urged in making casual inferences.

SPATIAL VARIATION IN RATES OF NEW FIRM FORMATION: A REGRESSION ANALYSIS

An analysis of spatial variations in entry rates should help identify some of those characteristics of local economies which stimulate or inhibit the rate of new firm births. Entry rate variations have already been reported at international, inter-regional and inter-county level. Secondary data is available at county level in Ireland and so this is the smallest scale at which an analysis can be conducted. The dependent variable (Y_3) is defined as the number of new indigenous single plant firms per annum per 1,000 employees in manufacturing industry in county j in the base year (1973). Variable (Y_3) includes survivors and those firms which opened and subsequently closed.[9] Dublin is not included in the model because the size distribution of manufacturing employment in the country is not known for 1973 and, therefore, variable X_7 (proportion of total manufacturing plants employing less than twenty in 1973) could not be calculated for the Dublin area.

Some of the independent variables specified in the spatial analysis are identical or similar to those incorporated into the inter-industry model and the reader is referred to the earlier theoretical section for a discussion of these factors. It is hypothesized, as in the inter-industry model, that the percentage of manufacturing plants in county j employing fewer than twenty persons in 1973 will be positively related to the rate of new firm formation. However, although entry rates may be a function of the proportion of small plants in an area, a higher percentage of small plants may be the *result* of higher entry rates in the past. The population density of an area may directly influence the size of plants. Low population density areas attract relatively fewer large plants partly because a small town or village catchment cannot provide the quantity of labour required. Hence, less urbanized counties will possess a higher proportion of small plants. The size factor is a catch-all for several plausible influences and, therefore, care must be exercised in interpreting a significant size coefficient.

It is postulated that there is a positive relationship between the rate of change in manufacturing employment in county j, 1973–81 (X_8) and the rate of new firm formation. The expansion of a county's manufacturing base may open up new markets and increase existing ones thereby providing opportunities for new firms. Rising manufacturing employment will also increase the pool from which new founders are most likely to emerge (CROSS, 1981, p. 263).

There is evidence that large plants are poor incubators of new firm founders compared with small establishments (JOHNSON and CATHCART, 1979). Hence, it is suggested that the greater the extent to which manufacturing employment is concentrated into large plants employing over 200 persons (X_9) the lower will be the rate of indigenous new firm formation. A relatively large agricultural sector might enhance the new firm formation rate in manufacturing since farmers have direct experience of self-employment and decline of agricultural employment is continuing throughout the country thereby adding to the supply of potential entrepreneurs. It is postulated that the percentage of employment in agriculture in county j in 1971 (X_{10}) is positively related to the rate of new firm formation.

Outside the manufacturing sector itself, the greatest potential pool of new founders probably exists among the commercial and retailing business community many of whom are self-employed. It is suggested that the percentage of employment in commerce, retailing and wholesaling in county j in 1971 (X_{11}) is positively related to the rate of new firm formation and that X_{11} may be conceived as a crude proxy for the level of non-manufacturing entrepreneurship in an area.

GUDGIN, 1978, reported higher rates of new firm formation in rural areas of the East Midlands than in the older industrial towns, a phenomenon which he explained by rural districts adjacent to towns acting as overspill and by long distance commuters dwelling in rural areas preferring a location close to their homes. The form of the relationship may not be the same in Ireland where towns throughout the hierarchy have attracted significant industrial development during the past twenty years. The rural factor is investigated here by specification of an interval level variable, X_{12} (proportion of a county's population in towns of over 5,000 population), to test the hypothesis that rates of indigenous new firm formation are lower in more urbanized counties. A number of processes, in addition to those identified by GUDGIN, 1978, such as lack of alternative job opportunities, may underlie the rural–urban differential in indigenous new firm formation.

JOHNSON and CATHCART, 1979, p. 278, also demonstrated that immigrant mobile plants in the Northern Region of England were relatively poor incubators of founders of new businesses. Hence, it is postulated that areas with a high proportion of their manufacturing employment within ISPs (variable X_{13}) will generate more new manufacturing enterprises. The median age of the 1973 stock of plants in county j (X_{14}) is used to investigate the proposition that industrial areas with a young manufacturing stock will have a higher rate of entry by new indigenous enterprises than areas with a mature manufacturing stock. The hypothesis is relatively simple but again there are problems of inference. Do more recently established plants have the highest spin-off rates? A young age structure might reflect the general growth of the existing level of manufacturing activity in the area and, therefore, could be a proxy measure for general manufacturing growth (CROSS, 1981, p. 267). This factor may be controlled, however, through variable X_8.

The order in which the variables were introduced into the model was decided prior to the model fitting by *a priori* theoretical considerations and upon the basis of evidence from other research. The proportion of county manufacturing employment in plants employing below twenty in 1973 (X_7) ranges from

82% in Leitrim and 75·7% in Mayo to a minimum of 39·8% in Kildare. Variable X_7 is significant with the direction of the relationship being positive, as hypothesized (Table 9). The highest rate of manufacturing employment change between 1973–81 occurred in Longford (+130%) and Roscommon (+118%) with the lowest in Louth (−13·6%) and Monaghan (+2·4%). When this variable X_8 is fitted X_7 becomes insignificant in both models with the sign of X_8 being positive as postulated. In a model specified to include X_8 alone, the degree of correlation is quite high ($R^2 = 0.65$); no other variables are significant when added to X_8 (equation (3) Table 9). The relationship suggests that for every one percentage point rise in manufacturing employment in the county, the entry rate of indigenous new firms rises by 0·02 per 1,000 employees per annum.

The value of variable X_9, the percentage of county manufacturing employment in plants employing over 200 in 1973 ranges from 62·3% in Waterford and 61·1% in Louth to zero in Leitrim, Laois and Longford. The direction of the relationship between X_9 and the dependent is negative, as suggested, but is not significant. The proportion of the workforce employed in the agricultural sector attains a maximum in Roscommon (60·3%) and Leitrim (59·5%) and minimum in Louth (12·6%) and Waterford (22·1%). When X_{10} is added to a model containing X_8, it does not contribute to increasing the proportion of variance explained. The counties with the highest proportions employed in commerce, retail and wholesaling are Wicklow (21·2%) and Limerick (19·9%) with Leitrim (9·8%) and Roscommon (11·5%) registering the lowest percentages; indeed the striking feature of variable X_{11} is its low variance between counties. The negative relationship between X_{11} and the dependent variable is not as predicted but is not statistically significant at $p < 0.05$.

The degree of urbanization in 1976 as expressed by the percentage of a county's population resident in towns of over 5,000 population, ranges from a peak of 58·6% in Louth and 44·9% (Limerick) to zero in Leitrim, Roscommon, Longford and Cavan. The relationship between the degree of urbanization and the rate of new firm formation is significant and negative as expected (Table 9).

The proportion of manufacturing employment in ISPs in 1973 ranged from a maximum of 71·3% in Leitrim and 61·6% in North Tipperary to a very low minimum of 15·8% in Clare and 18·0% in Sligo. The relationship between X_{13} and the dependent variable is positive as predicted but is not significant. Similarly, X_{14} (the median age of the manufacturing plant stock in 1973) ranging from 26 years in North Tipperary to 4 in Leitrim, has the expected negative sign but is not significant.

The preferred model specification is that containing variables X_7 and X_{12} and not the equation with X_8 as

An Industrial and Spatial Analysis of New Firm Formation in Ireland   233

Table 9. *Regression equations with the number of new indigenous single plant firms per 1,000 manufacturing employees in 1973 per annum by county as dependent variable* (Y_3)

Equation	Equation number	$\bar{R}^2$	S.E.E.^{2}
$Y_3 = -1.73 + 0.06\,X_7$ $\quad\quad\;\;(3.29)\star\star$	(1)	0.31	1.00
$Y_3 = -0.47 + 0.03\,X_7 - 0.02\,X_8$ $\quad\quad\;\;(1.43)\star\;\;\;(3.49)\star\star$	(2)	0.69	0.45
$Y_3 = \;\;\;0.87 + 0.02\,X_8$ $\quad\quad\;\;(5.00)\star\star\star$	(3)	0.65	0.51
$Y_3 = -0.40 + 0.05\,X_7 - 0.02\,X_9$ $\quad\quad\;\;(2.39)\star\;\;\;(1.64)$	(4)	0.42	0.85
$Y_3 = -1.80 + 0.03\,X_7 - 0.05\,X_{10}$ $\quad\quad\;\;(2.48)\star\;\;\;(1.48)$	(5)	0.55	0.66
$Y_3 = \;\;\;3.12 + 0.03\,X_7 - 0.19\,X_{11}$ $\quad\quad\;\;(2.28)\star\;\;\;(1.28)$	(6)	0.49	0.74
$Y_3 = -0.03 + 0.04\,X_7 - 0.03\,X_{12}$ $\quad\quad\;\;(2.20)\star\;\;\;(2.17)\star$	(7)	0.50	0.72
$Y_3 = -1.82 + 0.05\,X_7 - 0.01\,X_{13}$ $\quad\quad\;\;(2.43)\star\;\;\;(0.95)$	(8)	0.33	0.97
$Y_3 = -0.80 + 0.06\,X_7 - 0.07\,X_{14}$ $\quad\quad\;\;(3.19)\star\star\;\;\;(1.76)$	(9)	0.39	0.88

Notes: 1. Y_3 includes survivors and new firms which opened and subsequently closed.
2. S.e.e. = standard error of the estimate.
   *Significant at $p < 0.05$.   **Significant at $p < 0.01$ ***Significant at $p < 0.001$.
   For each equation the figures in parentheses are t values.

the sole independent variable. Hence, equation (7) of Table 9 is favoured over equation (3) on grounds of *a priori* theoretical criteria and previous empirical evidence despite the fact that the latter equation has a higher $\bar{R}^2$ value; statistical criteria do not take precedence over theoretical ones. The parameters of equation (7) Table 9 suggest that a one percentage point decrease in the population of a county's population resident in towns over 5,000 population increases the rate of new firm formation by 0.03 per 1,000 employees per annum, having controlled for the effects of plant size. The same equation implies that a one percentage point increase in the proportion of plants in a county employing fewer than twenty boosts new firm formation by 0.04 per 1,000 employees per annum.

An examination of standardized residuals from equation (7) of Table 9 indicates that the counties where new formation rates are *higher* than those predicted by the regression equation including both X_7 and X_{12} are Roscommon, Sligo, Leitrim, Limerick and Louth. These are counties with some of the lowest and highest urbanization rates. Counties with the largest negative residuals where new firm formation rates are *lower* than those predicted by the model are Offaly, Laois, Kilkenny, North Tipperary, Kerry, and South Tipperary. These, with the exception of Kerry, are a block of central and south midland counties in the non-designated areas where, according to the model, higher levels of new firm formation should be expected. The contrasts between counties in the rate of new firm formation are quite large: the rates in Cork and Tipperary North Riding (0.65 and 0.64,

respectively) are some seven times lower than that of Roscommon/Longford (4.44). The fact that less urbanized areas have higher rates of new firm formation confirms the results of both GUDGIN, 1978; CROSS, 1981; and MASON, 1982. There is a need, however, to unravel the causal factors underlying the rural/urban variable. Are higher rates in rural areas, having controlled for the plant size distribution, due to a more favourable sectoral mix, cheaper land prices, the wider availability of suitable premises, the lack of many alternative employment opportunities or some other process? Subsequent research may reveal the nature of the processes responsible for higher rates of business formation in rural areas. Clearly, sectoral mix influences entry rates at county level but it was not possible to include this factor in the model since many sectors have few or no employees in some counties and therefore meaningful comparisons of inter-county variation in number of new firms per 1,000 employees cannot be drawn. However, counties with low barriers to entry sectors—such as timber and furniture—will have higher entry rates as a consequence of this compositional effect. It must be acknowledged that aggregative regression analysis identifies some of the important factors in the process of new firm formation that are amenable to measurement but will not isolate all proximate causes. New firm formation is a complex process and many factors will only emerge through in-depth investigation at micro level. Some of the inter-county variation, for example, *may* be due to the varying performance of County Development Officers liaising between the new firm founders and the IDA.

CONCLUSIONS AND IMPLICATIONS

New firm formation is important for economic development and regional differences in entrepreneurship may be a partial explanation of variations in regional economic performance. Hence, an important aim of regional policy should be to stimulate growth in locally owned plants, especially through the encouragement of new firm formation.

An analysis of new firm formation rates at the level of twenty-five industry groups indicates that between industry variation in entry is high ranging from a maximum in furniture, followed by metal trades and wood, cork and brushes with the lowest rates recorded by butter and milk products, drink and tobacco, and boots and shoes. The regression analysis indicates that there are three variables associated with the dependent, number of new indigenous firms per annum per 1,000 employees in sector *i* (1973): (1) the proportion of plants in the sector employing fewer than twenty people; (2) the median age of the sector's plant stock in 1973; and (3) the percentage of sectoral employment controlled by multiplant organizations in 1973. Furthermore, there is some evidence to suggest that formation rates have been highest in sectors relatively sheltered from international competition.

International comparisons suggest that the entry rate of new firms in Ireland is similar to those observed in Norway, Canada and the USA, although for different periods, but is perhaps 40% higher than the rate for the UK. Examination of new firm formation rates at *county* level reveals that high rates occur in a block of country south of Donegal and north of a line from Galway to Drogheda. By contrast, the counties of the South West, Mid West and South East have recorded low rates of new business formation. The analysis of new firm formation rates at county level, with number of new indigenous firms per annum per 1,000 employees in manufacturing (1973) as the dependent variable, suggests that there are two variables associated with this dependent: (1) the proportion of plants in the county employing fewer then twenty employees; and (2) the percentage of the county's population resident in towns of over 5,000 population. It appears that the number of new enterprises emerging is related to several features of the local area: the size distribution of firms; degree of urbanization; sectoral mix; and the rate of manufacturing employment change.

A relatively small proportion of new firms serve the sub-supply needs of the larger predominantly foreign companies: only 11·4% of the materials and components used by the largest New Industry sector, metals and engineering, were purchased in Ireland in 1976 (O'FARRELL and O'LOUGHLIN, 1981, p. 293) although the trend is upwards (O'FARRELL, 1982). Much of the growth that has occurred in sub-supply

industries has been in the lower skill areas, such as general welding, structural metal or packaging; indeed packaging represented over one-third of domestic purchases by the New Industry non-food sectors in 1976 (O'FARRELL and O'LOUGHLIN, 1980, p. 18). There are various supply side bottlenecks preventing the purchasing levels of foreign firms in Ireland rising to their potential of more than double the existing proportion (O'FARRELL, 1982). These bottlenecks include lack of price competitiveness, an inability to achieve and maintain quality standards and unreliability in meeting delivery date deadlines (O'FARRELL, 1982). Very few new Irish firms have been established in skill intensive sub-supply industries such as tool making, precision-casting, stainless steel valves or precision plastic moulds.

New metals and engineering firms constitute some 36% of all new businesses and most are engaged in general metal fabricating operations, metal bending and pressing, welding and repair shops, all of which typically serve local markets, and structural steel, where the economies also favour local suppliers. These businesses were founded as a response to increased demand created by plant construction, agricultural investment (farm gates and machinery) and general infrastructure expenditure (NATIONAL ECONOMIC AND SOCIAL COUNCIL, 1982). Employment generation has come almost exclusively from domestic demand; few firms have penetrated export markets. The principal opportunities for growth lie either in import substitution by providing components for MNEs or by firms currently serving only a regional or the national market exporting to the UK, the rest of the EEC or beyond. The major barriers to indigenous small firm growth are currently being investigated; they constitute a major policy problem for government and development agencies if the buoyant entry rates are to be translated into high manufacturing value added and employment. Although the rate of indigenous new firm formation in Ireland has been relatively high by international standards, and very high relative to the UK, there is evidence to suggest that most of the firms established are small concerns which are very unlikely to expand into even medium sized enterprises selling overseas.

Acknowledgements—The authors are extremely grateful to the Industrial Development Authority, Dublin, for providing the data upon which the analysis is based and for supporting the research and granting permission to publish the findings. Numerous IDA staff kindly provided information upon request; and Mr D. Flinter, Mr J. McMahon, and Mr M. Redmond contributed many useful suggestions upon an earlier draft. The normal disclaimer applies.

NOTES

1. Exclusion of firms which have never employed three or more people (including the owner-manager) will clearly

An Industrial and Spatial Analysis of New Firm Formation in Ireland 235

produce a downward bias in new firm formation rates but will have only a marginal effect upon employment arising from new firm openings.

2. There are, however, other rural counties, notably Kerry, Tipperary S.R., Tipperary N.R., Carlow and Laois which, with respect to new firm formation, performed below the national average which suggests that it is not simply a rurality factor which explains the pattern.

3. For an extensive and thorough review of the contribution of economics to the understanding of new firm formation see STOREY, 1982, pp. 47–74.

4. Due to a lack of adequate data, the profit variable cannot be tested in the empirical analysis.

5. The entry barriers literature is concerned with the prospects for self employment; scant consideration is given to the fact that a founder will usually move from an *existing* position of paid employment (or unemployment)

and that, consequently, a subjective comparison of future earnings in paid and self employment will be made (JOHNSON and DARNELL, 1976, p. 9).

6. The models fitted for survivors only data are not reported here but are available from the authors upon request. The parameters are very similar to those reported in Table 8.

7. The stability of the regression coefficients and standard errors suggests that multicollinearity is unproblematic.

8. Non-traded businesses include services localized within a region such as health care, public administration, retailing and house construction *and* manufactured goods in which the productivity improvements that can be achieved through increased scale are not great enough to offset the increased costs of distributing the product to a foreign country.

9. Models were also calibrated for survivors only and the results were very similar.

REFERENCES

BAIN J. S. (1956) *Barriers to New Competition*. Harvard University Press, Harvard.

CHURCHILL B. C. (1959) Rise in the business population, *Survey of Current Business Magazine*, May.

COLLINS L. (1972) *Industrial Migration in Ontario*. Statistics Canada, Ottowa.

COOPER A. C. (1971) Spin-offs and technical entrepreneurship, *I.E.E.E. Trans. Engin. Manag.* **EM-18**, 2–6.

CROSS M. (1981) *New Firm Foundation and Regional Development*. Gower, Farnborough, Hants.

DICKEN P. and LLOYD P. E. (1978) Inner metropolitan industrial change, enterprise structu.... .nd policy issues: case studies of Manchester and Merseyside, *Reg. Studies* **12**, 181–97.

FOTHERGILL S. and GUDGIN G. (1979) The job generation process in Britain, Research Series 32, Centre for Environmental Studies, London.

GUDGIN G. (1978) *Industrial Location Processes and Regional Employment Growth*. Saxon House, Farnborough, Hants.

JOHNSON P. and CATHCART D. G. (1979) New manufacturing firms and regional development: some evidence from the Northern Region, *Reg. Studies* **13**, 269–80.

JOHNSON P. and DARNELL A. (1976) New firm formation in Great Britain, Working Paper 5, Department of Economics, University of Durham.

MANSFIELD E. (1962) Entry, Gibrat's Law, innovation and the growth of firms, *Am. Econ. Rev.* **52**, 1023–51.

MASON C. M. (1982) New manufacturing firms in South Hampshire: survey results, Discussion Paper 13, Department of Geography, University of Southampton.

MASON C. M. (1983) Some definitional difficulties in new firms research, *Area* **15**, 53–60.

NATIONAL ECONOMIC AND SOCIAL COUNCIL (1982) *A Review of Industrial Policy*, No. 64, NESC, Dublin.

O'FARRELL P. N. (1984) Small manufacturing firms in Ireland: employment performance and implications, *Int. Small Bus. J.*, (forthcoming).

O'FARRELL P. N. (1982) Industrial linkages in the new industry sector: a behavioural analysis, *J. Irish Bus. Admin. Res.* **4**, 3–21.

O'FARRELL P. N. and CROUCHLEY R. (1983) Industrial closures in Ireland 1973–1981: analysis and implications, *Reg. Studies* **17**, 411–27.

O'FARRELL P. N. and O'LOUGHLIN B. (1980) *An Analysis of New Industry Linkages in Ireland*. Industrial Development Authority, Dublin.

O'FARRELL P. N. and O'LOUGHLIN (1981) New industry input linkages in Ireland: an econometric analysis, *Environ. Plann. A*, **13**, 285–308.

ROBINSON J. F. F. and STOREY D. J. (1981), Employment change in manufacturing industry in Cleveland 1965–76, *Reg. Studies* **15**, 161–72.

SCHUMPETER J. A. (1961) *The Theory of Economic Development*. Oxford University Press, New York.

STOREY D. (1982) *Entrepreneurship and the New Firm*. Croom Helm, London.

WEDERVANG F. (1965) *Development of a Population of Industrial Firms*. Scandinavian University Books, Oslo.

APPENDIX 1

Definitions

Establishment or plant: an identifiable unit of production engaged under a single legal entity in manufacturing activity at a distinct physical location. An establishment may be one of a number owned by a firm or enterprise but is classified separately if it has a discrete plant and work force at a specific location. Establishments may comprise one or more *technical units:* departments of a meat-packing plant which produce lard, cure bacon or canned meat are examples of technical units horizontally integrated within an establishment.

Enterprise or firm: a corporation, joint stock company, co-operative association, partnership, individual proprietorship or some other form of association. It owns and manages the property of the organization and receives and disposes of all its income; it may consist of more than one establishment.

Ownership status: the ownership variable has been classified into three categories: (1) multinational branch plant; (2) Irish multiplant branch; and (3) indigenous (Irish) single plant. Joint ventures, of which there are only some twenty-five of the 5,000 plants, were classified under the majority shareholding group. Ownership in the case of surviving plants was categorized according to their status in 1981 and, for closures, their status in the year prior to closure. In the very small number of cases where a single plant firm expands by opening a branch, thereby moving into the multiplant category, or a multiplant firm disinvests and enters the single plant group, the plants are classified according to their 1981 status.

Openings: new establishments which were in existence in 1981 but not in 1973 and their employment 'gain', as a consequence of opening, is defined as their 1981 employment. The definition of the start-up date is, to some extent, arbitrary (see MASON, 1983). In this study it is defined as the year of entry to the IDA employment survey for which the qualifying criterion is a minimum full-time employment of three, including founder or partners.

Programme under which grant aided: many grant-aided projects have received grant assistance under a number of separate programmes. In consultation with the IDA, it was decided to sort the programme classifications according to the following hierarchy. A *New Industry* grant takes precedence over all others: i.e. if a project has been in receipt of both a New Industry and a Small Industry grant, it is classified as New Industry for the purposes of the analysis. The remainder of the hierarchy, in order, is Small Industry, Re-Equipment, Shannon, Gaeltarra and Non Grant-Aided. Enterprise Development programme projects are classed as New Industry. A project is classified as grant-aided under one of the above programmes if at any time either before or after 1973 it has received a grant payment.

Relocations: relocations are an unimportant phenomenon in Irish regional employment change. Only 139 plants, approximately 2% of the stock, relocated between 1973–81. The predominant movement was an inner city–suburban shift within the Dublin conurbation and fewer than fifty *jobs* actually migrated across a *regional* boundary. Hence, inter-regional relocations can be ignored in the analysis. It is extremely important, however, to identify and account for within-region relocations because the IDA files are assembled such that when a plant closes *prior* to relocating it is classified as a *closure*; and when it re-opens at a new site it is categorized as a *new plant opening* with a different numeric code. Hence, failure to identify and adjust for relocations *within* regions would seriously bias an analysis of new firm openings by inflating the number of new firms and gross job increases arising from new openings. Relocations were identified by comparing alphabetical lists of possible relocations. A list of origins and destinations was then checked against a separate IDA listing of relocations and confirmed relocations were re-classified as permanent establishments for the purpose of deriving employment accounts.

APPENDIX 2

Definition of independent variables

X_1 = percentage of plants in industry i employing fewer than twenty persons in 1973

X_2 = rate of employment change of the 1973 stock of plants in industry i between 1973–81

X_3 = percentage of total employment in industry i located in plants employing over 200 persons in 1973

X_4 = median employment size of new indigenous single plant firms in industry i at end of first year

X_5 = median age of the 1973 stock of plants in industry i

X_6 = percentage of total employment in industry i controlled by multiplant firms in 1973

X_7 = percentage of plants in county j employing fewer than twenty persons in 1973

X_8 = rate of change in manufacturing employment in county j, 1973–81

X_9 = percentage of manufacturing employment in county j concentrated into plants employing over 200 persons in 1973

X_{10} = percentage of employment in county j in agriculture, 1971

X_{11} = percentage of employment in county j in commerce, retailing and wholesaling, 1971

X_{12} = percentage of population of county j living in towns of over 5,000 population, 1971

X_{13} = percentage of manufacturing employment in county j employed in indigenous single plant firms, 1973

X_{14} = median age of 1973 stock of plants in county j.

Part III
Culture and Economic Development

Personality and Motivation

24

CHAPTER II

THE SPIRIT OF CAPITALISM

In the title of this study is used the somewhat pre-
tentious phrase, the *spirit* of capitalism. What is to be
understood by it? The attempt to give anything like
a definition of it brings out certain difficulties which
are in the very nature of this type of investigation.

If any object can be found to which this term can
be applied with any understandable meaning, it can
only be an historical individual, i.e. a complex of
elements associated in historical reality which we unite
into a conceptual whole from the standpoint of their
cultural significance.

Such an historical concept, however, since it refers
in its content to a phenomenon significant for its unique
individuality, cannot be defined according to the
formula *genus proximum, differentia specifica*, but it
must be gradually put together out of the individual
parts which are taken from historical reality to make it
up. Thus the final and definitive concept cannot stand
at the beginning of the investigation, but must come at
the end. We must, in other words, work out in the
course of the discussion, as its most important result,
the best conceptual formulation of what we here understand by the spirit of capitalism, that is the best from
the point of view which interests us here. This point of
view (the one of which we shall speak later) is, further,
by no means the only possible one from which the
historical phenomena we are investigating can be
analysed. Other standpoints would, for this as for every

47

The Protestant Ethic and the Spirit of Capitalism

historical phenomenon, yield other characteristics as
the essential ones. The result is that it is by no means
necessary to understand by the spirit of capitalism only
what it will come to mean to *us* for the purposes of our
analysis. This is a necessary result of the nature of
historical concepts which attempt for their methodological purposes not to grasp historical reality in
abstract general formulæ, but in concrete genetic sets
of relations which are inevitably of a specifically unique
and individual character.[1]

Thus, if we try to determine the object, the analysis
and historical explanation of which we are attempting,
it cannot be in the form of a conceptual definition, but
at least in the beginning only a provisional description
of what is here meant by the spirit of capitalism. Such
a description is, however, indispensable in order clearly
to understand the object of the investigation. For this
purpose we turn to a document of that spirit which
contains what we are looking for in almost classical
purity, and at the same time has the advantage of being
free from all direct relationship to religion, being thus,
for our purposes, free of preconceptions.

"Remember, that *time* is money. He that can earn
ten shillings a day by his labour, and goes abroad, or
sits idle, one half of that day, though he spends but
sixpence during his diversion or idleness, ought not to
reckon *that* the only expense; he has really spent, or
rather thrown away, five shillings besides.

"Remember, that *credit* is money. If a man lets his
money lie in my hands after it is due, he gives me the
interest, or so much as I can make of it during that

48

The Spirit of Capitalism

time. This amounts to a considerable sum where a man has good and large credit, and makes good use of it.

"Remember, that money is of the prolific, generating nature. Money can beget money, and its offspring can beget more, and so on. Five shillings turned is six, turned again it is seven and threepence, and so on, till it becomes a hundred pounds. The more there is of it, the more it produces every turning, so that the profits rise quicker and quicker. He that kills a breeding-sow, destroys all her offspring to the thousandth generation. He that murders a crown, destroys all that it might have produced, even scores of pounds."

"Remember this saying, *The good paymaster is lord of another man's purse*. He that is known to pay punctually and exactly to the time he promises, may at any time, and on any occasion, raise all the money his friends can spare. This is sometimes of great use. After industry and frugality, nothing contributes more to the raising of a young man in the world than punctuality and justice in all his dealings; therefore never keep borrowed money an hour beyond the time you promised, lest a disappointment shut up your friend's purse for ever.

"The most trifling actions that affect a man's credit are to be regarded. The sound of your hammer at five in the morning, or eight at night, heard by a creditor, makes him easy six months longer; but if he sees you at a billiard-table, or hears your voice at a tavern, when you should be at work, he sends for his money the next day; demands it, before he can receive it, in a lump.

"It shows, besides, that you are mindful of what you

49

The Protestant Ethic and the Spirit of Capitalism

owe; it makes you appear a careful as well as an honest man, and that still increases your credit.

"Beware of thinking all your own that you possess, and of living accordingly. It is a mistake that many people who have credit fall into. To prevent this, keep an exact account for some time both of your expenses and your income. If you take the pains at first to mention particulars, it will have this good effect: you will discover how wonderfully small, trifling expenses mount up to large sums, and will discern what might have been, and may for the future be saved, without occasioning any great inconvenience."

"For six pounds a year you may have the use of one hundred pounds, provided you are a man of known prudence and honesty.

"He that spends a groat a day idly, spends idly above six pounds a year, which is the price for the use of one hundred pounds.

"He that wastes idly a groat's worth of his time per day, one day with another, wastes the privilege of using one hundred pounds each day.

"He that idly loses five shillings' worth of time, loses five shillings, and might as prudently throw five shillings into the sea.

"He that loses five shillings, not only loses that sum, but all the advantage that might be made by turning it in dealing, which by the time that a young man becomes old, will amount to a considerable sum of money." [2]

It is Benjamin Ferdinand who preaches to us in these sentences, the same which Ferdinand Kürnberger

50

The Spirit of Capitalism

satirizes in his clever and malicious *Picture of American Culture*[3] as the supposed confession of faith of the Yankee. That it is the spirit of capitalism which here speaks in characteristic fashion, no one will doubt, however little we may wish to claim that everything which could be understood as pertaining to that spirit is contained in it. Let us pause a moment to consider this passage, the philosophy of which Kürnberger sums up in the words, "They make tallow out of cattle and money out of men". The peculiarity of this philosophy of avarice appears to be the ideal of the honest man of recognized credit, and above all the idea of a duty of the individual toward the increase of his capital, which is assumed as an end in itself. Truly what is here preached is not simply a means of making one's way in the world, but a peculiar ethic. The infraction of its rules is treated not as foolishness but as forgetfulness of duty. That is the essence of the matter. It is not mere business astuteness, that sort of thing is common enough, it is an ethos. *This* is the quality which interests us.

When Jacob Fugger, in speaking to a business associate who had retired and who wanted to persuade him to do the same, since he had made enough money and should let others have a chance, rejected that as pusillanimity and answered that "he (Fugger) thought otherwise, he wanted to make money as long as he could",[4] the spirit of his statement is evidently quite different from that of Franklin. What in the former case was an expression of commercial daring and a personal inclination morally neutral,[5] in the latter takes on the character of an ethically coloured maxim

The Protestant Ethic and the Spirit of Capitalism

for the conduct of life. The concept spirit of capitalism is here used in this specific sense,[6] it is the spirit of modern capitalism. For that we are here dealing only with Western European and American capitalism is obvious from the way in which the problem was stated. Capitalism existed in China, India, Babylon, in the classic world, and in the Middle Ages. But in all these cases, as we shall see, this particular ethos was lacking.

Now, all Franklin's moral attitudes are coloured with utilitarianism. Honesty is useful, because it assures credit; so are punctuality, industry, frugality, and that is the reason they are virtues. A logical deduction from this would be that where, for instance, the appearance of honesty serves the same purpose, that would suffice, and an unnecessary surplus of this virtue would evidently appear to Franklin's eyes as unproductive waste. And as a matter of fact, the story in his autobiography of his conversion to those virtues,[7] or the discussion of the value of a strict maintenance of the appearance of modesty, the assiduous belittlement of one's own deserts in order to gain general recognition later,[8] confirms this impression. According to Franklin, those virtues, like all others, are only in so far virtues as they are actually useful to the individual, and the surrogate of mere appearance is always sufficient when it accomplishes the end in view. It is a conclusion which is inevitable for strict utilitarianism. The impression of many Germans that the virtues professed by Americanism are pure hypocrisy seems to have been confirmed by this striking case. But in fact the matter is not by any means so simple. Benjamin Franklin's own character, as it appears in

52

The Spirit of Capitalism

the really unusual candidness of his autobiography, belies that suspicion. The circumstance that he ascribes his recognition of the utility of virtue to a divine revelation which was intended to lead him in the path of righteousness, shows that something more than mere garnishing for purely egocentric motives is involved.

In fact, the *summum bonum* of this ethic, the earning of more and more money, combined with the strict avoidance of all spontaneous enjoyment of life, is above all completely devoid of any eudæmonistic, not to say hedonistic, admixture. It is thought of so purely as an end in itself, that from the point of view of the happiness of, or utility to, the single individual, it appears entirely transcendental and absolutely irrational.[9] Man is dominated by the making of money, by acquisition as the ultimate purpose of his life. Economic acquisition is no longer subordinated to man as the means for the satisfaction of his material needs. This reversal of what we should call the natural relationship, so irrational from a naïve point of view, is evidently as definitely a leading principle of capitalism as it is foreign to all peoples not under capitalistic influence. At the same time it expresses a type of feeling which is closely connected with certain religious ideas. If we thus ask, *why* should "money be made out of men", Benjamin Franklin himself, although he was a colourless deist, answers in his autobiography with a quotation from the Bible, which his strict Calvinistic father drummed into him again and again in his youth: "Seest thou a man diligent in his business? He shall stand before kings" (Prov. xxii. 29). The earning of money within the modern economic order is, so long

53

The Protestant Ethic and the Spirit of Capitalism

as it is done legally, the result and the expression of virtue and proficiency in a calling; and this virtue and proficiency are, as it is now not difficult to see, the real Alpha and Omega of Franklin's ethic, as expressed in the passages we have quoted, as well as in all his works without exception.[10]

And in truth this peculiar idea, so familiar to us to-day, but in reality so little a matter of course, of one's duty in a calling, is what is most characteristic of the social ethic of capitalistic culture, and is in a sense the fundamental basis of it. It is an obligation which the individual is supposed to feel and does feel towards the content of his professional[11] activity, no matter in what it consists, in particular no matter whether it appears on the surface as a utilization of his personal powers, or only of his material possessions (as capital).

Of course, this conception has not appeared only under capitalistic conditions. On the contrary, we shall later trace its origins back to a time previous to the advent of capitalism. Still less, naturally, do we maintain that a conscious acceptance of these ethical maxims on the part of the individuals, entrepreneurs or labourers, in modern capitalistic enterprises, is a condition of the further existence of present-day capitalism. The capitalistic economy of the present day is an immense cosmos into which the individual is born, and which presents itself to him, at least as an individual, as an unalterable order of things in which he must live. It forces the individual, in so far as he is involved in the system of market relationships, to conform to capitalistic rules of action. The manufacturer who in the long

54

The Spirit of Capitalism

run acts counter to these norms, will just as inevitably
be eliminated from the economic scene as the worker
who cannot or will not adapt himself to them will be
thrown into the streets without a job.

Thus the capitalism of to-day, which has come to
dominate economic life, educates and selects the
economic subjects which it needs through a process of
economic survival of the fittest. But here one can easily
see the limits of the concept of selection as a means of
historical explanation. In order that a manner of life so
well adapted to the peculiarities of capitalism could be
selected at all, i.e. should come to dominate others, it
had to originate somewhere, and not in isolated individuals alone, but as a way of life common to whole
groups of men. This origin is what really needs explanation. Concerning the doctrine of the more naïve historical materialism, that such ideas originate as a
reflection or superstructure of economic situations, we
shall speak more in detail below. At this point it will
suffice for our purpose to call attention to the fact that
without doubt, in the country of Benjamin Franklin's
birth (Massachusetts), the spirit of capitalism (in the
sense we have attached to it) was present before the
capitalistic order. There were complaints of a peculiarly
calculating sort of profit-seeking in New England, as
distinguished from other parts of America, as early as
1632. It is further undoubted that capitalism remained
far less developed in some of the neighbouring colonies,
the later Southern States of the United States of
America, in spite of the fact that these latter were
founded by large capitalists for business motives, while
the New England colonies were founded by preachers

55

The Protestant Ethic and the Spirit of Capitalism

and seminary graduates with the help of small bourgeois, craftsmen and yoemen, for religious reasons. In this case the causal relation is certainly the reverse of that suggested by the materialistic standpoint.

But the origin and history of such ideas is much more complex than the theorists of the superstructure suppose. The spirit of capitalism, in the sense in which we are using the term, had to fight its way to supremacy against a whole world of hostile forces. A state of mind such as that expressed in the passages we have quoted from Franklin, and which called forth the applause of a whole people, would both in ancient times and in the Middle Ages [12] have been proscribed as the lowest sort of avarice and as an attitude entirely lacking in self-respect. It is, in fact, still regularly thus looked upon by all those social groups which are least involved in or adapted to modern capitalistic conditions. This is not wholly because the instinct of acquisition was in those times unknown or undeveloped, as has often been said. Nor because the *auri sacra fames*, the greed for gold, was then, or now, less powerful outside of bourgeois capitalism than within its peculiar sphere, as the illusions of modern romanticists are wont to believe. The difference between the capitalistic and pre-capitalistic spirits is not to be found at this point. The greed of the Chinese Mandarin, the old Roman aristocrat, or the modern peasant, can stand up to any comparison. And the *auri sacra fames* of a Neapolitan cab-driver or *barcaiuolo*, and certainly of Asiatic representatives of similar trades, as well as of the craftsmen of southern European or Asiatic countries, is, as anyone can find out for himself, very much more

56

The Spirit of Capitalism

intense, and especially more unscrupulous than that of, say, an Englishman in similar circumstances.[13]

The universal reign of absolute unscrupulousness in the pursuit of selfish interests by the making of money has been a specific characteristic of precisely those countries whose bourgeois-capitalistic development, measured according to Occidental standards, has remained backward. As every employer knows, the lack of *coscienziosità* of the labourers[14] of such countries, for instance Italy as compared with Germany, has been, and to a certain extent still is, one of the principal obstacles to their capitalistic development. Capitalism cannot make use of the labour of those who practise the doctrine of undisciplined *liberum arbitrium*, any more than it can make use of the business man who seems absolutely unscrupulous in his dealings with others, as we can learn from Franklin. Hence the difference does not lie in the degree of development of any impulse to make money. The *auri sacra fames* is as old as the history of man. But we shall see that those who submitted to it without reserve as an uncontrolled impulse, such as the Dutch sea-captain who "would go through hell for gain, even though he scorched his sails", were by no means the representatives of that attitude of mind from which the specifically modern capitalistic spirit as a mass phenomenon is derived, and that is what matters. At all periods of history, wherever it was possible, there has been ruthless acquisition, bound to no ethical norms whatever. Like war and piracy, trade has often been unrestrained in its relations with foreigners and those outside the group. The double ethic has permitted here what was forbidden in dealings among brothers.

57

The Protestant Ethic and the Spirit of Capitalism

Capitalistic acquisition as an adventure has been at home in all types of economic society which have known trade with the use of money and which have offered it opportunities, through *commenda*, farming of taxes, State loans, financing of wars, ducal courts and office-holders. Likewise the inner attitude of the adventurer, which laughs at all ethical limitations, has been universal. Absolute and conscious ruthlessness in acquisition has often stood in the closest connection with the strictest conformity to tradition. Moreover, with the breakdown of tradition and the more or less complete extension of free economic enterprise, even to within the social group, the new thing has not generally been ethically justified and encouraged, but only tolerated as a fact. And this fact has been treated either as ethically indifferent or as reprehensible, but unfortunately unavoidable. This has not only been the normal attitude of all ethical teachings, but, what is more important, also that expressed in the practical action of the average man of pre-capitalistic times, pre-capitalistic in the sense that the rational utilization of capital in a permanent enterprise and the rational capitalistic organization of labour had not yet become dominant forces in the determination of economic activity. Now just this attitude was one of the strongest inner obstacles which the adaptation of men to the conditions of an ordered bourgeois-capitalistic economy has encountered everywhere.

The most important opponent with which the spirit of capitalism, in the sense of a definite standard of life claiming ethical sanction, has had to struggle, was that type of attitude and reaction to new situations which

58

The Spirit of Capitalism

we may designate as traditionalism. In this case also every attempt at a final definition must be held in abeyance. On the other hand, we must try to make the provisional meaning clear by citing a few cases. We will begin from below, with the labourers.

One of the technical means which the modern employer uses in order to secure the greatest possible amount of work from his men is the device of piece-rates. In agriculture, for instance, the gathering of the harvest is a case where the greatest possible intensity of labour is called for, since, the weather being uncertain, the difference between high profit and heavy loss may depend on the speed with which the harvesting can be done. Hence a system of piece-rates is almost universal in this case. And since the interest of the employer in a speeding-up of harvesting increases with the increase of the results and the intensity of the work, the attempt has again and again been made, by increasing the piece-rates of the workmen, thereby giving them an opportunity to earn what is for them a very high wage, to interest them in increasing their own efficiency. But a peculiar difficulty has been met with surprising frequency: raising the piece-rates has often had the result that not more but less has been accomplished in the same time, because the worker reacted to the increase not by increasing but by decreasing the amount of his work. A man, for instance, who at the rate of 1 mark per acre mowed $2\frac{1}{2}$ acres per day and earned $2\frac{1}{2}$ marks, when the rate was raised to 1·25 marks per acre mowed, not 3 acres, as he might easily have done, thus earning 3·75 marks, but only 2 acres, so that he could still earn the $2\frac{1}{2}$ marks to

59

The Protestant Ethic and the Spirit of Capitalism

which he was accustomed. The opportunity of earning more was less attractive than that of working less. He did not ask: how much can I earn in a day if I do as much work as possible? but: how much must I work in order to earn the wage, 2½ marks, which I earned before and which takes care of my traditional needs? This is an example of what is here meant by traditionalism. A man does not "by nature" wish to earn more and more money, but simply to live as he is accustomed to live and to earn as much as is necessary for that purpose. Wherever modern capitalism has begun its work of increasing the productivity of human labour by increasing its intensity, it has encountered the immensely stubborn resistance of this leading trait of pre-capitalistic labour. And to-day it encounters it the more, the more backward (from a capitalistic point of view) the labouring forces are with which it has to deal.

Another obvious possibility, to return to our example, since the appeal to the acquisitive instinct through higher wage-rates failed, would have been to try the opposite policy, to force the worker by reduction of his wage-rates to work harder to earn the same amount than he did before. Low wages and high profits seem even to-day to a superficial observer to stand in correlation; everything which is paid out in wages seems to involve a corresponding reduction of profits. That road capitalism has taken again and again since its beginning. For centuries it was an article of faith, that low wages were productive, i.e. that they increased the material results of labour so that, as Pieter de la Cour, on this point, as we shall see, quite in the spirit of the old

60

The Spirit of Capitalism

Calvinism, said long ago, the people only work because and so long as they are poor.

But the effectiveness of this apparently so efficient method has its limits.[15] Of course the presence of a surplus population which it can hire cheaply in the labour market is a necessity for the development of capitalism. But though too large a reserve army may in certain cases favour its quantitative expansion, it checks its qualitative development, especially the transition to types of enterprise which make more intensive use of labour. Low wages are by no means identical with cheap labour.[16] From a purely quantitative point of view the efficiency of labour decreases with a wage which is physiologically insufficient, which may in the long run even mean a survival of the unfit. The present-day average Silesian mows, when he exerts himself to the full, little more than two-thirds as much land as the better paid and nourished Pomeranian or Mecklenburger, and the Pole, the further East he comes from, accomplishes progressively less than the German. Low wages fail even from a purely business point of view wherever it is a question of producing goods which require any sort of skilled labour, or the use of expensive machinery which is easily damaged, or in general wherever any great amount of sharp attention or of initiative is required. Here low wages do not pay, and their effect is the opposite of what was intended. For not only is a developed sense of responsibility absolutely indispensable, but in general also an attitude which, at least during working hours, is freed from continual calculations of how the customary wage may be earned with a maximum of comfort and a

The Protestant Ethic and the Spirit of Capitalism

minimum of exertion. Labour must, on the contrary, be performed as if it were an absolute end in itself, a calling. But such an attitude is by no means a product of nature. It cannot be evoked by low wages or high ones alone, but can only be the product of a long and arduous process of education. To-day, capitalism, once in the saddle, can recruit its labouring force in all industrial countries with comparative ease. In the past this was in every case an extremely difficult problem.[17] And even to-day it could probably not get-along without the support of a powerful ally along the way, which, as we shall see below, was at hand at the time of its development.

What is meant can again best be explained by means of an example. The type of backward traditional form of labour is to-day very often exemplified by women workers, especially unmarried ones. An almost universal complaint of employers of girls, for instance German girls, is that they are almost entirely unable and unwilling to give up methods of work inherited or once learned in favour of more efficient ones, to adapt themselves to new methods, to learn and to concentrate their intelligence, or even to use it at all. Explanations of the possibility of making work easier, above all more profitable to themselves, generally encounter a complete lack of understanding. Increases of piece-rates are without avail against the stone wall of habit. In general it is otherwise, and that is a point of no little importance from our view-point, only with girls having a specifically religious, especially a Pietistic, background. One often hears, and statistical investigation confirms it,[18] that by far the best chances of economic education are found

62

The Spirit of Capitalism

among this group. The ability of mental concentration, as well as the absolutely essential feeling of obligation to one's job, are here most often combined with a strict economy which calculates the possibility of high earnings, and a cool self-control and frugality which enormously increase performance. This provides the most favourable foundation for the conception of labour as an end in itself, as a calling which is necessary to capitalism: the chances of overcoming traditionalism are greatest on account of the religious upbringing. This observation of present-day capitalism [19] in itself suggests that it is worth while to ask how this connection of adaptability to capitalism with religious factors may have come about in the days of the early development of capitalism. For that they were even then present in much the same form can be inferred from numerous facts. For instance, the dislike and the persecution which Methodist workmen in the eighteenth century met at the hands of their comrades were not solely nor even principally the result of their religious eccentricities, England had seen many of those and more striking ones. It rested rather, as the destruction of their tools, repeatedly mentioned in the reports, suggests, upon their specific willingness to work as we should say to-day.

However, let us again return to the present, and this time to the entrepreneur, in order to clarify the meaning of traditionalism in his case.

Sombart, in his discussions of the genesis of capitalism,[20] has distinguished between the satisfaction of needs and acquisition as the two great leading principles in economic history. In the former case the

63

The Protestant Ethic and the Spirit of Capitalism

attainment of the goods necessary to meet personal needs, in the latter a struggle for profit free from the limits set by needs, have been the ends controlling the form and direction of economic activity. What he calls the economy of needs seems at first glance to be identical with what is here described as economic traditionalism. That may be the case if the concept of needs is limited to traditional needs. But if that is not done, a number of economic types which must be considered capitalistic according to the definition of capital which Sombart gives in another part of his work,[21] would be excluded from the category of acquisitive economy and put into that of needs economy. Enterprises, namely, which are carried on by private entrepreneurs by utilizing capital (money or goods with a money value) to make a profit, purchasing the means of production and selling the product, i.e. undoubted capitalistic enterprises, may at the same time have a traditionalistic character. This has, in the course even of modern economic history, not been merely an occasional case, but rather the rule, with continual interruptions from repeated and increasingly powerful conquests of the capitalistic spirit. To be sure the capitalistic form of an enterprise and the spirit in which it is run generally stand in some sort of adequate relationship to each other, but not in one of necessary interdependence. Nevertheless, we provisionally use the expression spirit of (modern) capitalism[22] to describe that attitude which seeks profit rationally and systematically in the manner which we have illustrated by the example of Benjamin Franklin. This, however, is justified by the historical fact that that attitude of

64

The Spirit of Capitalism

mind has on the one hand found its most suitable expression in capitalistic enterprise, while on the other the enterprise has derived its most suitable motive force from the spirit of capitalism.

But the two may very well occur separately. Benjamin Franklin was filled with the spirit of capitalism at a time when his printing business did not differ in form from any handicraft enterprise. And we shall see that at the beginning of modern times it was by no means the capitalistic entrepreneurs of the commercial aristocracy, who were either the sole or the predominant bearers of the attitude we have here called the spirit of capitalism.[23] It was much more the rising strata of the lower industrial middle classes. Even in the nineteenth century its classical representatives were not the elegant gentlemen of Liverpool and Hamburg, with their commercial fortunes handed down for generations, but the self-made parvenus of Manchester and Westphalia, who often rose from very modest circumstances. As early as the sixteenth century the situation was similar; the industries which arose at that time were mostly created by parvenus.[24]

The management, for instance, of a bank, a wholesale export business, a large retail establishment, or of a large putting-out enterprise dealing with goods produced in homes, is certainly only possible in the form of a capitalistic enterprise. Nevertheless, they may all be carried on in a traditionalistic spirit. In fact, the business of a large bank of issue cannot be carried on in any other way. The foreign trade of whole epochs has rested on the basis of monopolies and legal privileges of strictly traditional character. In retail trade—and we

65

The Protestant Ethic and the Spirit of Capitalism

are not here talking of the small men without capital who are continually crying out for Government aid— the revolution which is making an end of the old traditionalism is still in full swing. It is the same development which broke up the old putting-out system, to which modern domestic labour is related only in form. How this revolution takes place and what is its significance may, in spite of the fact these things are so familiar, be again brought out by a concrete example.

Until about the middle of the past century the life of a putter-out was, at least in many of the branches of the Continental textile industry,[25] what we should to-day consider very comfortable. We may imagine its routine somewhat as follows: The peasants came with their cloth, often (in the case of linen) principally or entirely made from raw material which the peasant himself had produced, to the town in which the putter-out lived, and after a careful, often official, appraisal of the quality, received the customary price for it. The putter-out's customers, for markets any appreciable distance away, were middlemen, who also came to him, generally not yet following samples, but seeking traditional qualities, and bought from his warehouse, or, long before delivery, placed orders which were probably in turn passed on to the peasants. Personal canvassing of customers took place, if at all, only at long intervals. Otherwise correspondence sufficed, though the sending of samples slowly gained ground. The number of business hours was very moderate, perhaps five to six a day, sometimes considerably less; in the rush season, where there was one,

66

The Spirit of Capitalism

more. Earnings were moderate; enough to lead a respectable life and in good times to put away a little. On the whole, relations among competitors were relatively good, with a large degree of agreement on the fundamentals of business. A long daily visit to the tavern, with often plenty to drink, and a congenial circle of friends, made life comfortable and leisurely.

The form of organization was in every respect capitalistic; the entrepreneur's activity was of a purely business character; the use of capital, turned over in the business, was indispensable; and finally, the objective aspect of the economic process, the book-keeping, was rational. But it was traditionalistic business, if one considers the spirit which animated the entrepreneur: the traditional manner of life, the traditional rate of profit, the traditional amount of work, the traditional manner of regulating the relationships with labour, and the essentially traditional circle of customers and the manner of attracting new ones. All these dominated the conduct of the business, were at the basis, one may say, of the *ethos* of this group of business men.

Now at some time this leisureliness was suddenly destroyed, and often entirely without any essential change in the form of organization, such as the transition to a unified factory, to mechanical weaving, etc. What happened was, on the contrary, often no more than this: some young man from one of the putting-out families went out into the country, carefully chose weavers for his employ, greatly increased the rigour of his supervision of their work, and thus turned them from peasants into labourers. On the other hand, he would begin to change his marketing methods by so

67

The Protestant Ethic and the Spirit of Capitalism

far as possible going directly to the final consumer, would take the details into his own hands, would personally solicit customers, visiting them every year, and above all would adapt the quality of the product directly to their needs and wishes. At the same time he began to introduce the principle of low prices and large turnover. There was repeated what everywhere and always is the result of such a process of rationalization: those who would not follow suit had to go out of business. The idyllic state collapsed under the pressure of a bitter competitive struggle, respectable fortunes were made, and not lent out at interest, but always reinvested in the business. The old leisurely and comfortable attitude toward life gave way to a hard frugality in which some participated and came to the top, because they did not wish to consume but to earn, while others who wished to keep on with the old ways were forced to curtail their consumption.[26]

And, what is most important in this connection, it was not generally in such cases a stream of new money invested in the industry which brought about this revolution—in several cases known to me the whole revolutionary process was set in motion with a few thousands of capital borrowed from relations—but the new spirit, the spirit of modern capitalism, had set to work. The question of the motive forces in the expansion of modern capitalism is not in the first instance a question of the origin of the capital sums which were available for capitalistic uses, but, above all, of the development of the spirit of capitalism. Where it appears and is able to work itself out, it produces its own capital and monetary supplies as the means to its

68

The Spirit of Capitalism

ends, but the reverse is not true.[27] Its entry on the scene was not generally peaceful. A flood of mistrust, sometimes of hatred, above all of moral indignation, regularly opposed itself to the first innovator. Often—I know of several cases of the sort—regular legends of mysterious shady spots in his previous life have been produced. It is very easy not to recognize that only an unusually strong character could save an entrepreneur of this new type from the loss of his temperate self-control and from both moral and economic shipwreck. Furthermore, along with clarity of vision and ability to act, it is only by virtue of very definite and highly developed ethical qualities that it has been possible for him to command the absolutely indispensable confidence of his customers and workmen. Nothing else could have given him the strength to overcome the innumerable obstacles, above all the infinitely more intensive work which is demanded of the modern entrepreneur. But these are ethical qualities of quite a different sort from those adapted to the traditionalism of the past.

And, as a rule, it has been neither dare-devil and unscrupulous speculators, economic adventurers such as we meet at all periods of economic history, nor simply great financiers who have carried through this change, outwardly so inconspicuous, but nevertheless so decisive for the penetration of economic life with the new spirit. On the contrary, they were men who had grown up in the hard school of life, calculating and daring at the same time, above all temperate and reliable, shrewd and completely devoted to their business, with strictly bourgeois opinions and principles.

69

25

9

Entrepreneurship and the Behavior of Nonprofit Organizations: Elements of a Theory

DENNIS R. YOUNG

A fascinating divergence exists in the economic literature on nonprofit organizations between those who attempt to explain the existence of the nonprofit sector and those who model the behavior of nonprofit organizations. In particular, the rationales for nonprofits offered by Weisbrod (1975), Hansmann (1980), Douglas (1983), and others have a selfless, public-spirited quality to them. Nonprofits are seen as providers of semipublic goods, or as agents of trust for consumers whose abilities to discern quality differences are impaired. Yet those who have developed explicit models of the behavior of nonprofit organizations set quite a different tone. Scholars such as James (1983), Pauly and Redisch (1973). Niskanen (1971), Feigenbaum (1979), Tullock (1966), and Rose-Ackerman (1980) basically have assumed revenue enhancing or other self-seeking objectives on the part of management of various types of nonprofit organizations—universities, hospitals, and charities among them.

The two schools of thought are not necessarily inconsistent. One can conceive that nonprofits are established in response to particular public needs—the provision of certain public goods or the delivery of certain services that require a fiduciary relationship with the consumer. In recognition of human frailities, tax advantages are granted and certain requirements—notably the nondistribution constraint—are imposed to ensure compliance with the intended purposes. Nonetheless, some nonprofit par-

From *Nonprofit Firms in a Three-Sector Economy*, ed. by M. White, Urban Institute, Washington, D.C., 1981, pp. 135–62. The author wishes to thank John G. Simon for his encouragement, and Richard R. Nelson and Michelle J. White for their helpful suggestions. Lois Pieretti is also thanked for typing several drafts. This chapter is based on work supported by the Program on Nonprofit Organizations, Institute for Social and Policy Studies. Yale University.

ticipants severely test the imposed constraints and manipulate them toward selfish ends. In doing so, they may be more successful in ensuring their survival than their more selfless colleagues.

Such a view gives rise to the homogeneous (selfish) behavior school of economic modeling, which has enjoyed success in application to the profit-making sector (that is, the assumption of profit-maximization) and some popularity in public sector applications (for example, budget-maximizing models). The aforementioned nonprofit modeling efforts also derive their lineage from this school. However, as we shall suggest, the nonprofit sector seems considerably more complex in its behavior patterns than single objective function models assume. Furthermore, the preceding rationalization notwithstanding, the "selfish" models do not ultimately appear to be fully consistent with the more benevolent theories of existence. (If selfish behavior is pervasive, why does the public benefit rationale persist?) As an alternative, we sketch the beginnings of a theory based on the screening of entrepreneurs with a variety of objectives, operating in an environment which allows considerable room for discretion and alternative pursuits.

ENTREPRENEURSHIP

Although there is some variety in the literature in interpreting the concept of entrepreneurship, we shall abide here by the widely accepted definition of Joseph Schumpeter (1949) that an entrepreneur is an individual who carries out "new combinations of means of production." As such, the entrepreneur is distinguished from the ordinary manager in the sense that the entrepreneur is engaged in breaking new ground in his administrative or organizing role rather than engaging simply in customary managerial practice or routine decision-making. Thus, it is entrepreneurs who found new organizations, develop and implement new programs and methods, organize and expand new services, and redirect the activities of faltering organizations. Entrepreneurs are just one group of organizational participants, and thus entrepreneurship is but one determinant of organizational behavior. Nonetheless, entrepreneurship is a particularly strategic focal point for attempting to characterize the more global and externally visible aspects of organizational performance that concern economists and policymakers— for example, the extent to which expansion, innovation, self-aggrandizing, quality emphasizing, cost inflating, or socially responsive organizational behavior is exhibited, or not exhibited. The reasons for this are twofold: First, entrepreneurs often play the role of "founding fathers" of their organizations and leaders in their respective industries. As such, their personal values and motivations can be transferred to, and shape in a significant way, the organizations they are instrumental in establishing, building, or altering. Second, enterprise itself is the very means through which the global objectives of organizations are displayed. If an organization is growth-oriented, it will grow through enterprise. If it is self-aggrandizing or aspires to market dominance, these goals will be sought through the implementation of new enterprise. And if such characteristics are lacking, there will be a dearth of entrepreneurial activity.

Focusing on entrepreneurship implies, almost by definition, a behavioral rather than maximizing theory of organizational behavior.[1] In particular, since a conventional maximizing theory focuses on what managers routinely do, on a day-to-day basis within accepted rules and technical constraints, such a theoretical framework cannot accommodate the entrepreneurial function which is specifically oriented to changes in the ends and means of production. (This is why the entrepreneurial function is essentially ignored in classical microtheory.) Thus, our end product in this present exercise must necessarily be a description of the dynamic (motivational) tendencies of (entrepreneur-driven) agencies, rather than an end-state characterization of static equilibrium. (Hence, in the final section of this chapter, we consider tendencies toward organizational "trustworthiness" and "responsiveness" rather than an assessment of global, static efficiency.)

A complete entrepreneur-based behavioral theory would have several parts. In particular, the role of entrepreneurs and the incidence of venture must be placed in perspective. Thus, one must discern where entrepreneurship is likely to occur, how entrepreneurs will vary from one context to another, and how ventures conceived by entrepreneurs will be shaped and modified by environmental circumstances. Thus, despite the likelihood of a presumed wide margin of entrepreneurial discretion, a theory of nonprofit behavior must still focus on how entrepreneurs interact with their environments, rather than naively assume that entrepreneurial motives are reflected in pure form by the organizations and sectors they lead.

STRATEGY OF THEORY CONSTRUCTION

Our theory construction requires several interlocking steps. First, we must discover what motivates entrepreneurs to do what they do. Here we must squarely face the questions of modeling strategy referred to above. We could select a single dominant entrepreneurial objective that we may believe characterizes all entrepreneurs (analogous to the income maximizing notion implicit in the microeconomic theory of the firm) or we can identify a variety of objectives (for example, income, power, status, etc.), any of which might describe the driving motives of a given entrepreneur. An intermediate approach would be to identify instrumental or proxy variables which capture various entrepreneurial goals in a single index. For example, Niskanen's (1971) notion of budget-maximizing is actually intended to represent a package of status, power, and income seeking by bureaucrats. Another example is found in the theory of managerial discretion by Williamson (1967), Migué and Bélanger (1974), and others. In this literature, the corporate manager is assumed to maximize his own utility. However, the arguments of the postulated utility function include a few key variables such as organizational staff and emoluments which are designed as stand-ins for the status, income, and power objectives of management.

For several reasons, the single objective and proxy index approaches are rejected here as strategies for characterizing the motivations of nonprofit entrepreneurs. In the first place, these frameworks are basically oriented to managers. Yet, field work investigations have indicated that entrepreneurs need not always become managers of their enterprises. Indeed, sometimes entrepreneurs develop their ventures with the specific intent of turning them over for others to administer, and these nonmanagerial entrepreneurs are likely to have different motives than managerial types. [See Young (1985) and Grennon and Barsky (1980)]. Secondly, field work also suggests that entrepreneurial motivations are quite varied and not easily captured by one or two proxy indexes such as staff, emoluments, or profits. As noted below, there appear to be strong elements of belief orientation and even selflessness on the part of some important entrepreneurial characters.

Economists, of course, argue that in a competitive, profit-making sector, any variety of entrepreneurial or managerial motives is of little consequence since those who choose not to maximize profits will be driven out of business. (Note this idea is at odds with the reality of entrepreneurship which inherently involves search and experimentation as opposed to the possibility of operating on some mythical absolute norm of efficient production). This argument is hedged in a less than perfectly competitive profit sector by those of the managerial discretion school who argue that while profit-making is still of paramount importance, profit levels above some acceptable minimum may be exchanged for items of personal utility. This idea has even been extended to the public sector by Roger Parks and Elinor Ostrom (1980) who model the public sector officials as trading off a certain level of net public benefits (called a "benefits residuum") against personal utility, as proxied by staff levels.

In the nonprofit sector, there certainly seems to be a large margin of entrepreneurial "discretion." However, it is not clear that there is anything closely resembling a profit criterion or a benefits residuum to which entrepreneurs are held by market or political forces, nor is it clear that proxy indicators of personal utility (such as staff or emolument levels) can adequately capture or represent the motivations which, in general, drive entrepreneurial initiatives. (Furthermore, on a more general plane, any fixed notion of maximum or discretionary profits or benefits must be based on some precise criterion of "efficient production." As such, it is necessarily at odds with the phenomenon of entrepreneurship which itself represents the very process of defining the technological frontiers and institutional conditions upon which "efficient" operation is predicted.)

This is not to say that nonprofit entrepreneurs face no constraints or are completely unaccountable for their actions. Rather, we assert that the sources of accountability and constraints on ventures are sufficiently loose, diverse, and ill-defined, as to allow for a wide spectrum of motivations and resultant behaviors. For this reason we think it is sensible to follow a more general approach to modeling entrepreneurial motivations than a single objective or managerial discretion approach would allow. In particular, we propose to specify a set of entrepreneurial stereotypes each of which personifies an important entrepreneurial objective, such as the pursuit of income, power, autonomy, security, professional accomplishment, creative achievement, strong beliefs, or simply self-identity. With this as a basis, we hope ultimately to create a theoretical structure which will specify how entrepreneurs of different stripes become sorted into various sectors, what stimulates them to venture, what constraints inhibit their actions, and how significant a long-term imprint such enterprising leaves on their organizations and sectors.

The present chapter is limited to presentation of the first two parts of such a theory—the specification of entrepreneurial prototypes, and the nature of the selection process through which entrepreneurs are filtered into particular economic sectors. A sketch of these two elements is sufficient to provide some initial insights into the behavior of nonprofits and how that behavior may be affected by public policies that alter sectoral structure.

MODELS OF ENTREPRENEURS

Next, we postulate a set of stereotypical models that seem to capture the driving motivations and styles of entrepreneurs who conceivably may choose the nonprofit sector as their base of operations. For a fuller development of the ideas presented here see Young (1983). Young (1985) and Grennon and Barsky (1980) contain the case study materials alluded to in the discussion below.

It is important to emphasize that the following models are "pure types" in the sense that each stereotype personifies a particular variety of internal motives and drive. Naturally, most real people are more easily thought of in terms of some combination of the postulated models. The models themselves are simply analytical devices for helping to derive the behavioral implications for organizations and sectors. Thus, we will analyze the world as if it were populated with a distribution of the following characters.

The *artist* is an entrepreneur who derives satisfaction directly from the creative act, that is, his own (organizational and programmatic) constructs. There are basically two types of artist: the *architect* subtype is a builder, craftsman, or tinkerer who likes to "play" with organizational "blocks." He may view his organization as a workshop for building better structures, both physical and organizational. In one case study for example, the entrepreneur takes special pride in having nurtured a small, faltering agency into a multicampus organization featuring modern facilities, computerized record-keeping, and a unique umbrella-like organizational structure.

The *poetic* subtype is a less structured and less meticulous but more cerebral entrepreneur. He may view his agenda as a blank canvas to be filled with a painting of his own conception. In one case of a Catholic sister who established a child-care agency in the South Bronx, the venture is viewed as a personal expression of individual religious philosophy and social expression.

Both types of artist like to create, to nurture, and to see things grow. And both types seek artistic expression, need to be able to identify products (ventures) as their own work, and require the freedom to pursue their initiatives in relatively unharnessed settings without restrictive oversight.

The *professional* is highly attuned to the controversies and debates that characterize his intellectual discipline and derives his satisfaction from the pursuit and development of new ideas. He will pursue ventures at the leading edge of current professional thinking in his discipline and look to that discipline for reinforcement, recognition, and direction. In the case studies, for example, entrepreneurs of this type experiment in a careful, calculated manner with such leading edge concepts as outpatient clinical services for autistic children, and common shelter care for unmarried mothers and babies.

The *believer* is an entrepreneur who is unshakably devoted to a cause and formulates his ventures and focuses his energies primarily in pursuit of that cause. The cause may be defined (as in various case studies) as help for a particular (needy) constituency (e.g., members of an orthodox community), it may be a civil libertarian or social justice concept (e.g., fighting racial discrimination), a methodological panacea (e.g., interracial adoption), or a particular strategy of social reform (e.g., community control). Or the believer may simply have a religious resolve to be of service (as in the case of various church-based entrepreneurs and one deeply religious college professor).

The *searcher* is someone who is out to prove himself and to find his niche in the world. Often, the searcher is a young person, perhaps even moderately successful in what he is doing, but unhappy and critical in his present employment and anxious to resolve the tensions between his aspirations and uncertain self-confidence. Searchers will normally shun security to find opportunities where they can better satisfy their internal yearnings for recognition and identity. In some cases, however, the searcher may be trying to resolve a midlife crisis and attach to an institutional structure that provides a new source of direction. (In one case, a searcher-entrepreneur left his post in a university to help found a Youth Bureau. In another case, such an entrepreneur left his teaching post in a private school in New York and ultimately established a therapeutic camp in North Carolina.)

The *independent* is an entrepreneur who seeks autonomy and wants to avoid shared authority and decision-making. This may derive from strong-mindedness about how things should be done and/or frustration from working under the constraints of others. The independent basically seeks to set up an organization where he or she is his own boss, free of direct internal interference or overwhelming external constraints. (In one case, a headmaster of a private school left in conflict with his proprietor and went on to establish his own institution. In another case, the entrepreneur left his post in a state children's mental hospital to form his own child-care agency.)

The *conserver* is an organizational loyalist who carries out entrepreneurial activity (during the crisis period) in order to preserve the character and viability of his agency, with which he has long been affiliated. The loyalty of the conserver derives from some combination of personal economic interest and cherished ideas, both of which have, in his mind, become embodied in or associated with the organization itself. (In one case, a career employee who had risen through the ranks of a large child-care agency, helped initiate a new program on campus to help alleviate certain criticisms the agency was subjected to by its government funding source.)

The *power seeker* derives satisfaction from climbing to the top and gaining control over large organizations. There are essentially two kinds of power seekers:

Controllers who gain satisfaction directly from having authority over others, calling the shots, and having the security of knowing what is going on under them. Such power seekers (like the one who heads one of the largest adoption agencies in New York) prefer to run tightly, centrally controlled organizations and seek to expand those organizations only so long as they can maintain the feeling of control; and

Players who like the stage or platform their organization gives them to wield power, play high-stakes poker, and gain respect and acclaim within their organizations and in the world at large. Players are more willing to delegate authority than controllers and, hence, prefer larger and larger organizations. (In two cases, for example, entrepreneurs who have expanded two of the largest social agencies have used this base to become prominent personalities in New York public affairs.)

Income seekers are those entrepreneurs primarily driven by the motive of material reward, in the form of income, future capital gain, and perquisites of office that substitute for personal expenditure. In one nursing home case, for example, the entrepreneurs are not health or social work affiliated and view their venture basically as a business enterprise. In extreme (maximizing) form, such characters constitute the basic stereotype model implicit in the conventional theory of the firm of microeconomic theory.

Note that while the list of different entrepreneurial types is rather long, there is some overlapping and gradation of objectives from one type to another. For example, controllers may be thought of as some combination of players and independents. Furthermore, believers, poets, and professionals are similar to one another in their pursuit of concepts and ideas, albeit for different reasons and via different styles. Nonetheless, for purposes of analyzing screening decisions and behavioral implications, we find it useful to maintain the distinctions.

In order to distinguish among the qualities of entrepreneurship that we may expect to find in different parts of the economy, we postulate (in the manner of Weisbrod, 1979, and Hansmann, 1980) that a "screening process" takes place which filters the various entrepreneurial types into sectors of alternative structural characteristics. Potential entrepreneurs are presumed to make career choices early in their working lives, leading to employment in particular industries. Given this selection of industries, potential entrepreneurs are seen to further sort themselves by economic sector (profit, nonprofit, and public), by becoming employed in specific organizations.

The foregoing selection decisions are hypothesized to be based on a variety of structural characteristics of industries and sectors, as elaborated below. These characteristics may be viewed as decision variables upon which potential entrepreneurs choose careers and industries in which to work. We presume that within (wide) bounds of extant opportunity and personal talent, potential entrepreneurs select careers in industries (and sectors within industries) whose characteristics most closely accommodate their basic personality types as described above. In reality this is probably an oversimplification. That is, to some degree, personal motivations may be defined and developed within field and sector contexts rather than prior to selection (for example, one might act like a believer in one context, but an income seeker in another). However, for purposes of theory construction we assume here that the latter process is of secondary importance.

SCREENING BY FIELD OR INDUSTRY

Screening at the field or industry level can be seen to depend on four structural characteristics of industries: the intrinsic character of services produced; the degree of control by professions; the degree of economic concentration; and the social priority attached to the field.

Nature of the Service

Services can be characterized as having various degrees of social involvement, technical sophistication, and requirements for creative expression. These dimensions of service character can be seen to differentially appeal to the principal motivations represented by the postulated stereotype entrepreneurs. For example, believers will be drawn to fields like social service involving high levels of social involvement, where "causes" are clear and easy to articulate, and where "crusading" is an accepted form of behavior. Searchers might also find fields of social involvement conducive to helping them find a place for themselves, by identifying with positions on social issues or with organizations having a strongly defined social purpose. Conservers may also be disproportionately drawn to such fields because it is more likely that organizations with cherished traditions of service develop in such contexts. (The settlement house provides an example of this phenomenon.)

To the contrary, fields like medical care or research characterized by high levels of technical sophistication become the domain of the professional. Here, *believerism,* at least in blatant form, is discouraged in favor of rational discourse, methodological standards, and scientific patience and scrutiny. (Believers may operate in technical fields, espousing strongly held theories and methods, but they need to cloak these concepts in the form of rationally derived proposals.)

Technically sophisticated fields may also be attractive to artistic types of the architectural variety. Sophisticated technologies—in engineering, research, or the health fields, for example—appeal to architects and can provide them with the means to create new structures, products, and services. Thus, for example, new intensive-care or computer-research technologies become the basis for building up and reorganizing whole new organizational units.

Clearly, however, fields like the arts that emphasize creativity per se, are more likely to attract the artist entrepreneurial character, especially the poetic variety. Traditionally, for example, artistically trained personnel have been the primary management and entrepreneurial source for museums, theatre, and musical enterprise. The same creative, expressionistic urges that underlie performance in the artistic fields are likely to motivate and underwrite entrepreneurial enterprise via projects that strike out in new directions and bear messages of philosophic meaning or emotional content.

Professional Control

The degree to which organized professions control employment and maintain fundamental authority and power within a given field affects the pool of entrepreneurial talent available to that field in two ways. First, disciplinary control tends to institutionalize the nature of the service as described and protect it from degradation or corruption from extradisciplinary influences (for example, the influences of commercialism or the perspectives of other disciplines). Thus, the professions reemphasize the labeling of services as technical, helping, or creative undertakings. In part, therefore, social work is a helping profession, with its implications for self-sacrifice and public service, by self-definition of the profession itself as well as the inherent character of the work. Hence, those who would enter without this perspective are discouraged (by elders and peers) from doing so. Similarly, medicine or law are self-defined as technical professions, thereby limiting entry of those with other points of view. Finally, the arts require a creative, artistic viewpoint in a vein similar to those taken by helping and technical professions. The result is to channel, even more strongly than might otherwise be the case, believers and conservers into the helping fields, professionals into the technical fields, and artists into the creative fields.

A second important way in which professional control influences the formation of the entrepreneurial pool is through the imposition of ethical values. The altruism of the helping professions, the emphasis on intellectual honesty and technical competence of the technical professions, and the elevation of artistic expression by the creative professions, constitute only part of this ethical structure. Various professions also promulgate different values with respect to money-making and achievement of power. The helping professions by virtue of their self-sacrifice ethic will tend to deemphasize wealth and power accumulation, thus discouraging power and income seekers or moderating their desires in these dimensions. Technical professions will tend to promote income enhancement as a virtue, signifying societal recognition of their importance, competence, special skills, and investments in advanced training and education. The creative fields will be relatively neutral in these domains, neither recognizing money and power as symbols of status, nor disdaining them as sins. (The exception here is the discouragement of power seeking or income seeking undertaken at the sacrifice of originality or artistic freedom.)

In practice, of course, fields or industries are controlled by discipline-oriented professions in varying degrees. Professions do tend to seek exclusive control over particular fields or industries, but the degrees of dominance they achieve vary considerably from field to field.

INDUSTRY CONCENTRATION

Service industries in which nonprofits participate vary in the degree to which they are dominated by a few large organizations. Some fields such as day care or nursing home care are characterized by the presence of many, relatively small producing organizations, none of which represents a significant proportion of the total activity. In other fields (teaching hospitals or opera companies, for example), providers are relatively few, and activity is more concentrated in a small number of organizations (in a given locality).

Related to the question of concentration is the ease of entry into a given field for new agencies or organizations. If activity is concentrated in a few organizations, this condition may reflect relatively large capital requirements for operation which in itself represents a barrier to new entry. Or, economic concentration may reflect regulatory controls which attempt to ensure, in the absence of price competition, that facilities are efficiently utilized. Thus, government may restrict the entry of new hospitals, nursing homes, day-care centers, or foster-care agencies, to those which can demonstrate need and ensure that they will not simply dilute the occupancy of existing agencies. (The case studies in child welfare reveal numerous instances of entry impediments by city and state regulatory agencies in the form of administrative and financial requirements for incorporation and proof of need for proposed services.)

As a relevant aside, we may observe that there is a rough correlation between industry structure and the distribution of activity in a given field among profit-making, nonprofit, and public sectors. Within the service fields in which nonprofits tend to participate, there is a definite tendency for activity to become more concentrated within a few organizations as one moves from the profit-making, to nonprofit, to governmental form.[2] Government tends to locate most of the activity related to a particular function (for example, child welfare or health) within a single hierarchical structure, for example, a department of health. In contrast, the proprietary services are generally not the domain of the large corporation but rather that of the small independent operator—the doctor, the educator, or the consultant who is in business for himself or with a partner or small company. Nonprofits, partly because they are often required by government to meet various organizational standards of community involvement (e.g., advisory boards) and service regulation, tend to represent a middle ground—larger and more bureaucratic than proprietaries but smaller and more fragmented than governmental agencies. In addition, ease of entry will tend to increase as one moves from government, to nonprofit, to proprietary form, at least in terms of the governmental requirements that must be fulfilled.

The effect of industry concentration is simply to make particular fields more or less attractive to each of the entrepreneurial character types. If we assume that potential entrepreneurs have some appreciation of the current (and likely future) of the structure of the fields they select or reject, then several types of potential entrepreneurs may be screened on the dimensions of industry concentration and ease of entry.

- Independents will prefer fields which are relatively unconcentrated, where small organizations are common, and where new entry is relatively easy.
- Searchers may begin their careers in concentrated fields in which they become overwhelmed or frustrated by large organizations that impose fixed career ladders and authoritarian oversight. Ultimately, they may move to fields where new entry is possible or where many small agencies exist which may be explored for their career potential.
- Power seekers will prefer concentrated fields featuring large organizations, where opportunities abound for assuming more and more responsibility over larger and larger groups of people. Player-type power seekers will prefer more concentrated fields than controller-type power seekers, because the latter fears the feeling of losing tight control as organizations grow too large. Player types, in contrast, benefit from the larger and larger platforms (more and more notoriety) provided by bigger and bigger organizations.
- Conservers will prefer fields of modest concentration which feature organizations large, stable, and mature enough to have established traditions and provide a sense of economic security but which are not so large as to have become impersonal and institutional or mechanical in character.
- Professionals will tend to select fields which are moderately to highly

concentrated so as to provide adequate resource bases to pursue their endeavors. However, professionals may seek to avoid very highly concentrated fields if they perceive the large organizations within those fields to be inimical to the flexibility required for professional development. Professionals will also avoid fields which are so fragmented as to offer little promise of resource aggregation sufficient to support experimental activity.

• Artists will tend to select fields which exhibit a moderate to low concentration of activity. Like the professional, the artist will tend to seek sectors in which organizations have access to a resource base sufficient to support his penchant for building and program development, yet which are small enough so that new endeavors are both noticeable and identifiable as one's own product. The architect-type of artist prefers a sector that will utlimately support programs of significant size, while the poet normally prefers sectors with small agencies, preferring to be unencumbered by administrative responsibilities and constraints and free to explore a variety of ideas.

• The income seeker has no intrinsic preferences regarding the relative concentration of activity, size of organizations, or entry possibilities in a given field. Unconcentrated fields can present income opportunities through investment in the formation or building up of small enterprises, while concentrated fields may present opportunities for internal advancement in large agencies, matched by salary and benefit increases. Once having entered a weakly concentrated field, however, an income seeker may work toward its concentration, as a strategy of income maximization.

Social Priority

In terms of both the allocation of economic resources and the more elusive concept of prestige, society tends to attach greater importance and social status to some fields than others. For example, among fields in which nonprofits tend to participate, health and scientific research tend to be elevated (in the U.S. at least), while education and social service have had more precarious positions in the public's mind and in the economy. In any case, it is logical that the status of a given field will influence career choices and, hence, the types of entrepreneurs available to particular fields.

Differences in social priority among fields will have the strongest effects on two entrepreneurial types—income seekers and power seekers. Income seekers will look toward rich or expanding fields as presenting the greatest opportunities for material reward. Power seekers, especially those of the player variety, will see such fields as the locus of "where the action is." That is, they will seek the largest stage for achieving notoriety and influence over the largest and most important sets of people and resources.

Other entrepreneurial types may also be influenced in their career choice by the social status of alternative fields, but to a lesser extent than power or income seekers. Professionals and artists may see the more prestigious fields as providing stronger resource bases on which they can pursue intellectual or creative activity. Alternatively, searchers may see the higher status fields as larger vistas to explore in their efforts to find more satisfying careers.

The independent and believer types will be relatively indifferent to the social priority attached to alternative fields. The independent essentially seeks autonomy and may indeed tend to avoid fields that are in the spotlight, preferring more staid environments, although initially he may find the opportunity to establish himself in a high-status field where resources are available. The believer is even more predictable in this dimension. While fields of greater social priority may provide wider vistas for the taking up of social causes or the sponsorship of particular policies, the believer may just as well attach himself to fields he feels are underserved and require new attention by society.

SCREENING BY SECTOR

The foregoing field (industry) choice process, is one of two basic (intermingled) processes of selection through which the pool of entrepreneurial talent available for enterprise in a given sector is formed. The second process is employment choice in which individuals select organizational contexts in which to work and gain (preentrepreneurial) experience. This employment choice implies a decision on sector, that is, whether a given individual chooses to work in the commercial, nonprofit, or government sector, since any organization will necessarily fall into one of these categories. That is, once having selected a field, the potential entrepreneur will often have some choice of sector at the employment stage, since many fields are not totally dominated by a single sector. This seems especially true of fields in which nonprofits tend to participate.[3]

There is, however, a "chicken and egg" quality to the field and sector selection process. We observed earlier, for instance, how the selection by field may be strongly influenced by sectoral considerations. In particular, the predominance of a given sector in some field is likely to reflect itself in certain structural characteristics (for example, the concentration of economic activity, entry conditions, and size of organizations) upon which field selection may be based. In a similar manner, sector choice may depend on the opportunity structure of a field. That is, as a historical matter, within any given field, one sector may be larger and more vital than another, at a given point in time. The frequency of employment opportunities will vary accordingly. For example, until the mid-twentieth century when public universities began to develop, opportunities in higher education were concentrated very heavily in the nonprofit sector. In child care, a similar pattern holds, while for nursing homes, the proprietary sector developed much later than the nonprofit or public sectors.

Government funding or licensing policies often underlie these patterns. For example, some states (such as New York) refuse to certify proprietary foster care agencies. To the contrary, programs such as Medicaid have underwritten the growth of proprietary enterprise, while other legislation (for example, state higher education programs) has sponsored the development of public systems (universities).

While latent entrepreneurs of various types may have strong leanings by sector, they may have selected their fields for other reasons. If those fields are dominated by one sector or another, the potential entrepreneurs will be limited in their ability to exercise their sector preferences and will be forced to become employed in less preferred sectors. As we discuss later, the selected sector will then include motivational types that it would not otherwise attract. Given a more open opportunity structure, latent entrepreneurs would be sorted into more homogeneous motivational sets by sector.

Given some global distribution of opportunities, however, and assuming some choice of sector does obtain, there are various other factors that will tend to sort out entrepreneurial types. These factors—income potential, internal bureaucratic structure, and service ethic—tend to vary fairly systematically by sector across a wide range of fields.

Income Potential

The nonprofit sector is by definition restrained by the so-called nondistribution constraint which formally precludes appropriation of differences between revenues and expenditures as "profits," by managers or trustees. As Hansmann and others have argued, the existence of this constraint discourages income enhancing in the nonprofit sector by providing a "signal" for expected (normative) behavior and the threat of legal penalties for blatant violation.

Thus, income potential is nominally more restricted and blunted in the nonprofit sector than it is in the profit sector. To the contrary, income maximizing behavior in the proprietary sector is the prescribed norm and may be (legally) implemented directly through profits, appreciation of capital (that is, capital gains), as well as through salary and perquisite enhancement and control over input factors. Of course, the relative potentials for income enhancement between the profit and nonprofit sectors will depend on market factors, including the marketability of services and the level of competition, as well as on tax and other revenue considerations. In some fields, nonprofits can conceivably combine tax concessions and access to philanthropy, to generate income potentials in excess of proprietary capabilities. However, the appropriation of surpluses as personal income will presumably be discouraged by legal restraints and accountability to the groups (government, donors, consumers) which implicitly enforce the conditions under which such special advantages are granted.

Income potentials and (normative) expectations in the public sector are the least systematic of the three sectors. Corruption and remuneration levels of public employees tend to vary considerably over time and place. Significantly, in some parts of the public sector (for example, within the federal government and some state and large local governments) civil service and political appointee pay scales may be sufficiently attractive to warrant the attention of those whose career objectives center heavily on income enhancement. Much depends on the particular political conditions associated with given parts of the public sector, including the wealth and level of demand for public goods by the relevant constituencies, the strength of public sector unions, and the tolerance levels for corruption.

Bureaucratic Structure

Within a given field, the profit-making, nonprofit, and public sectors tend to vary according to their dependence on hierarchy and political entanglement and, hence, the flexibility, independence, and authority levels which staff members and officials can maintain. Earlier, for example, we noted the tendency of economic activity in service fields to become more concentrated and, hence, more hierarchical, as one moved from the proprietary to nonprofit to government sector.

It is not simply the dependence on hierarchy, however, that differentiates the organizational (bureaucratic) structure of the three sectors. The degree of interaction and restraint from oversight bodies, and with the body politic at large, also varies fairly systematically by sector. Agencies in each sector are normally associated with a board or council of trustees in one form or another. In the public sector, a government bureau is accountable to a legislature, or subcommittee thereof. Nonprofit agencies are normally required to have boards of directors or trustees composed of responsible community members, in whom the ultimate well-being of the corporation is entrusted. In the proprietary sector, corporate responsibility resides in a board of directors composed of shareholders, usually including the executive director himself.

Within each sector, the authority asserted by these oversight bodies varies considerably, perhaps most widely in the nonprofit sector. Nonprofit agency boards of directors are known to range from those whose officers insist on major day-to-day influence on policymaking to those which are virtually rubber stamps for the executive director. Within the public and proprietary sectors there is less variance. Legislative committees tend to assert a reasonable level of interference, if not control, over an agency's budget, and executives are normally well advised to pay homage to their legislative benefactors. In the proprietary sector, the executive usually has very strong, often dictatorial control, commensurate with his financial interest and/or ability to keep the enterprise remunerative. Thus, in general it may be asserted that the requirement of executives to share authority and to be constrained by oversight bodies increases systematically from proprietary, to nonprofit, to public sectors.

A similar spectrum obtains with respect to entanglement of a more general political nature. The proprietary agency director must be careful to cultivate certain relationships in order to secure zoning, licensing, or other approvals that he may need for operation. He may have to be careful not to arouse community opposition to his operation if he is dealing with sensitive areas such as services to the retarded or delinquent. He may also be required to follow particular rules and reporting protocols if he decides to accept government funding. However, the proprietary director will be fundamentally less entangled and constrained by political considerations and government regulation than his nonprofit or public sector counterparts.

The nonprofit agency is based on the notion of a public purpose for some constituency whether it be a particular neighborhood, ethnic or religious group, or those interested or needing a particular type of service. As such, its board of directors, staff and volunteers are more likely to have roots in this constituency and to bring a strong element of political responsiveness and responsibility to the agency itself. Even those nonprofit agencies which might be incorporated without such grassroots support will normally be required by government to constitute a board of trustees representative of the public purpose for which nonprofit status is granted. As such there will at least be a nominal sensitivity to political pressures and community interests by the nonprofit. Furthermore, in the now common case where the nonprofit receives public funds and/or is chosen by government as a vehicle for public service delivery, the nonprofit will tend to become enmeshed in the broader spectrum of political interests and regulatory requirements of the granting government agency.

By far the most overwhelming set of political constraints is faced by decision-makers and program developers in public agencies whose actions must often reflect partisan, geographic, ethnic, and other political sensitivities. Thus, new policies or program initiatives must be checked or modified for their effects on multiple groups before action can be taken.

Overall, therefore, sectoral differences in organizational structure provide differential opportunities to those potential entrepreneurs whose ultimate motives concern power, autonomy, and flexibility. In general, the public sector is the most concentrated in terms of hierarchy and outside restraint on freedom of action. The proprietary sector tends to be least intense in these dimensions. The nonprofit sector constitutes a broad middle ground.

Service Ethic

Just as the different sectors vary in the norms which they promote (signal) with respect to money-making, they also vary in the ideals or service orientation they purport to stand for. While such normative codes may not in themselves be powerful influences on behavior, their importance as signaling devices for latent entrepreneurs at the stage of employment choice cannot be ignored.

Each sector has its lofty traditions and positive self-images. In government, it is the notion of public service—devotion to country and community through the competent provision of essential services. The concept of "public interest" nominally underlies the value system for government work.

Traditionally, the profit-making sector has been the domain of the rugged individualist, the self-made man who works hard for his living and makes it on his own. It is the domain of commerce, subject to the harsh discipline of the marketplace, where activity is frankly viewed as business and only secondarily as service. It is where the fortunes may be made, but where every cent must be earned; where free enterprise holds court and government is viewed as an intrusive and corrupting influence. In the modern era of large, multinational corporations and complex entanglements between government and private industry, this image has faded, but it still maintains an essence of viability, especially in the arena of small business.

The nonprofit sector has its roots in voluntarism, charity, and community. It is a mode of organization based on the notion of voluntary mobilization of close-knit communities to assist those of its members in need or in trouble. Whether it be a social agency, hospital, or volunteer fire department, the nonprofit agency is seen to be supported by contributions, manned by volunteers or those who would work for some sacrifice in pay, controlled by community elders, and administered by those whose interests are benevolent and specifically attuned to local needs. As with the folklore imagery of other sectors, the nonprofit's idealized image has also been tarnished, as the application of this organizational device has been modified, extended, and intertwined with other sectors over time. Still, the imagery continues to bear some semblance of fact and, hence, to serve as a signal to community-minded, socially concerned idealists.

The relatively systematic differences in income potential, bureaucratic structure, and service ethic across sectors serve as screening factors at the employment stage for latent entrepreneurial types along the following basic lines:

Income seekers will tend to be attracted to the proprietary sector where the avenues for money-making are more numerous and open and where profit-making per se is a socially approved (and legal) mode of behavior. This tendency will of course be modified to the degree that the market or regulatory environment restricts financial gain in the profit sector, and/or generous income streams and salary opportunities are channeled to the nonprofit or government sectors.

Independents will also tend to gravitate to the proprietary sector because of the less overbearing requirements in that sector for shared decision-making, and accountability to others, and because the lower concentration (less hierarchy, easier entry) of activity in that sector provides greater opportunity for achieving positions of executive autonomy. This tendency will be modified to the extent that small nonprofits with rubber stamp boards in some areas are able to insulate themselves from outside pressures and, hence, attract independents. In few cases, however, will independents be attracted to government, where hierarchical and political accountability arrangements are omnipresent.

Power seekers will generally gravitate to the public sector for the same reasons that independents reject this alternative. Government exhibits major hierarchical structures and arenas of public visibility in which power seekers may climb to greater and greater heights of control and notoriety. This will be especially appealing to the player-type power seeker. The controller type of power seeker is more complex, however. While the opportunities for expanding control in the public sector appeal to him, at some level it becomes overwhelming. Major departments may be too large to control, and accountability relationships too complex to manage. The latent controller type, therefore, may decide that organizations in the nonprofit sector present more tenable alternatives.

The latent believer is an idealogue who is most likely to be attracted by the service ethic of the nonprofit or public sectors, but whose uncompromising social reform/social change attitudes are more likely to be accommodated by the less overbearing accountability structure of the nonprofit arena. Thus, the nonprofit sector is likely to employ more than its share of believers.

Conservers, too, are most likely to be employed in the nonprofit sector, for two reasons. First, conservers have a loyalty to organizations and traditions more consistent with the nonprofit and public sectors than the proprietary sector. (An exception here is the proprietary "family business" which may invoke conserver-type loyalties in the profit sector.) Second, conservers are more likely to be attracted by the smaller size and greater informality of organizations in the nonprofit sector, where traditions and personal relationships are more easily cultivated and maintained.

Like the power seekers, the two varieties of artist are also somewhat different in their likely employment preferences. Neither the poet nor architect is likely to be heavily attracted to the public sector since each desires to use activities as personal expressions of accomplishment. In the public sector, more hands are likely to stir the stew because of the greater hierarchy and complexity of accountability arrangements, with consequently less opportunity for personal identification with the product. Both artist types can be accommodated by the relatively less encumbered structure of the nonprofit sector, but the poetic type may be more confined to this sector than the architectural type. In particular, the architectural type is more concerned with the fact that he is building than what he is building. Hence, opportunities in the profit sector can be as appealing as those available in the nonprofit sector. For the poetic type, however, activity is more a matter of personal feeling and expression of values than pride of technique. The poetic type is more likely to feel inhibited by the rigor and restraint of the profit criteria than his architectural counterparts and more comfortable in the nonprofit sector where the diversity of support sources is more likely to yield organizations indulgent of diverse ideas, irrespective of direct market potential or political content.

Post-Employment-Choice Sector Mobility

By focusing on sector choice at the employment stage, we do not wish to imply that sector selection is necessarily made, once and for all, at an early stage of career development for latent entrepreneurs. Indeed for certain types, notably searchers, entrepreneurship occurs in the process of sorting out personal proclivities through employment change. Furthermore, for other entrepreneurial types, employment and sector change may represent a career pattern consistent with clear personal objectives. The most obvious example of this is the case of power seekers. The careers of power seekers are likely to exhibit a "climbing" pattern, with each successive job representing a step upward in terms of status, position, and authority over people and resources. This ladder may involve crossovers between sectors. For example, a power seeker may begin in a relatively small nonprofit agency, move to another more important one, and ultimately move into government at a high level. Or the pattern may crisscross sectoral borders several times, depending on the timing of opportunities. Because more open advancement opportunities may exist at the lower rungs of the nonprofit sector but more powerful positions at the top of the public sector, the careers of power seekers often do begin in the nonprofit sector but ultimately gravitate toward government. For reasons noted, this will tend to be more strongly the case for player than controller types.

A similar argument may be made for income seekers, with different directional patterns, however. This variety of entrepreneur may begin his career in a public agency, or perhaps nonprofit, where initial salaries may be better and where he can gain professional experience and "learn the ropes" of service provision. Later, having gained experience and perhaps accumulated some capital, he may decide to move his career into the proprietary domain. This is a common career pattern for physicians, psychologists, and academic consultants, for example. Overall, the mixed-career patterns of power seekers and income seekers complicate the basic sorting tendencies discussed earlier, by postponing and inhibiting them to a degree, rather than changing the basic directions.

Finally, it is worth reiterating certain points concerning the fineness with which potential entrepreneurs are able to match their preferences with the structural characteristics of different fields and sectors. Clearly, given the multiple dimensions on which screening decisions take place, and the relatively few distinct choices a given individual can make, the matches between entrepreneurial objectives and sectors will necessarily be imperfect. Furthermore, given the time span that may transpire between employment screening and enterprise, it is likely that some entrepreneurs will undergo changes in preferences as they become locked into particular sectors, resulting in additional matching imperfections.

IMPLICATIONS

There are several related inferences upon which we may speculate regarding the behavior of nonprofit organizations, given the nature of motivation and selection phenomena suggested in this chapter. In the most general terms, we can conclude that behavior of organizations in the nonprofit sector is not a fixed, immutable phenomenon; rather, it is a relative matter which depends substantially on both the nature of an industry and the parallel opportunities and characteristics of adjacent activity in the proprietary and public sectors as well. As such, we may surmise that public policies which affect the relative character of an industry and/or the relative opportunities among sectors, will change nonprofit behavior by altering the screening of different entrepreneurial types. Several such policies may be contemplated. For example, a policy which requires rigorous professional credentialing of managerial industry personnel may be expected to differentially screen out certain entrepreneurial types (e.g., searchers) and, hence, affect aggregate behavioral outcomes.

Of perhaps greater interest, some government policies are specifically directed toward the nonprofit sector. For example, government funding programs (such as arts funding by the National Endowment) may require nonprofit status as a condition of eligibility. Alternatively, government may simply require (as it does for child care in some states, and has been proposed for nursing homes) that all suppliers in a given industry be nonprofit. For purposes of illustrating how our theory potentially leads to empirically testable and socially relevant hypotheses, we shall briefly analyze implications of the latter policy.

Government policies which require that certain services be provided on a nonprofit basis and which proscribe the delivery of those services through other sectors, can be expected to have two possible (conflicting) effects:

1. Such policies may discourage certain entrepreneurial types from entering a given field or industry entirely; and
2. Such policies will result in a more heterogeneous entrepreneurial mix within the nonprofit sector.

Given that industry structure is only one of several important variables that we have hypothesized to screen entrepreneurial types in the choice of fields, it seems highly likely that the second of the above effects will dominate the first. Thus, for a given field, a nonprofit sector which operates in parallel with a profit-making and/or governmental sector will tend to be more homogeneous in its motivational tendencies than it would be if it monopolized the field. This could have several specific implications:

Income maximizing behavior can be expected to be more intense in nonprofit sectors which do not compete with a proprietary sector offering similar services. In such nonprofit sectors, the nondistribution constraint may be severely tested. Thus, as an empirically testable matter, we would expect that given a fixed level of policing and regulation of the nondistribution constraint, there would be a greater incidence of indirect profiteering and fraud in such nonprofit sectors. In particular, we may anticipate more indulgence in such practices as the inflation of managerial salaries and managerial self-dealing in the supply of inputs to nonprofits in this case, compared to the circumstances where the profit sector is available for parallel activity.

• Power-seeking (empire-building, expansive) behavior may be more intense in a nonprofit sector that does not compete with a public sector. Thus, as an empirical matter, we would expect to observe a growing concentration of activity in such a nonprofit sector, that is, an increasing in size and decreasing in the number of nonprofit organizations, relative to what would occur if there were a competing public sector.

• Autonomy-seeking (independent) behavior may be more intense in a nonprofit sector that does not compete with a proprietary sector. This may take the form of pressure to create new agencies within the nonprofit arena. Or, if new entry is discouraged by government controls or high cost, it may take the form of creating semiautonomous enclaves within larger, hierarchical nonprofit structures. Thus, as an empirically observable matter, we would expect to see decentralization and fragmentation of such a sector over time, manifested in terms of declining size, increasing number, and/or flattening of the hierarchical structure of member organizations, relative to what would occur if there were a competing proprietary sector.

For other types of entrepreneurial motivation, it is less clear whether confinement of industry activity to nonprofits would have a significant effect on the behavior of that sector. Artists, professionals, believers, searchers, and conservers, for example, seem likely to be fairly concentrated in the nonprofit arena, assuming available opportunities, no matter what other choices exist. Nonetheless, the sectorwide behavioral implications of these motivational types are also important. For example, in the event that the nonprofit accountability structure permits substantial internal entrepreneurial discretion, we may anticipate the following kinds of potentially worrisome patterns (in addition to those posed above for income and power seekers and independents):

• Artists of the architect variety may tend to build programs, facilities, and organizational structures beyond the requirements of client groups;
• Professionals may pursue esoteric programs of intellectual interest but marginal value to the constituent groups sponsoring the nonprofit organizations in which they operate;
• Believers and poets may lead organizations to overinvest in pet strategies, ideas, or causes, which from a more global point of view may be wasteful or misguided; and
• Conservers may delay hard decisions concerning the redirection of obsolescent policies or programs, by appealing to conservative constituent elements in their organizations and failing to provide an accurate picture of internal difficulties. Such potential behaviors raise the further policy question of how effectively the nonprofit accountability structure can control discretionary activity for those enterpreneurs screened into that sector. In particular we may inquire as to what effects particular policing initia-

tives—such as the strengthening of accountability relationships between executives and the boards of directors of nonprofit organizations, or the superimposition of community planning agencies (e.g., health and welfare councils) onto nonprofit sector decision-making regimes—may be expected to have in restraining the different varieties of potential entrepreneurial excess. Such an analysis is beyond the scope of the present paper and requires a detailed consideration of how each type of entrepreneur interacts with other constituents of the nonprofit organization. As presented above, our screening and motivation theory is essentially positive in thrust (that is, descriptive of the behavioral patterns likely to emerge under alternative policies and structural conditions). For policy purposes, however, a normative view would also be useful. In particular, we may ask if delivery of services via nonprofits produces outcomes which are in some sense more "socially desirable." This requires that we evaluate the various patterns of discretionary behavior that are predicted to take place under particular conditions of screening and policing of nonprofit constraints. Clearly, however, differentiating "unproductive" discretionary behavior from that which is nominally desirable is a very tenuous exercise. Not much can be said in the abstract, without reference to the constituent groups (clients, donors, trustees, funders) responsible for holding nonprofit organizations accountable or to some overriding social criteria. Nonetheless, the issue of potentially wayward discretionary behavior is a useful one to raise because it relates to two normative criteria of fundamental importance to researchers and policymakers concerned with the nonprofit sector. Specifically,

1. Under what circumstances can nonprofits be considered "trustworthy" in delivering services as promised and avoiding fraud and quality depreciation as strategies of self-aggrandizement?
2. Under what circumstances will nonprofits be "responsive" to demands for new, altered, or expanded services as expressed by market forces or governmental funding programs?

The motivation and screening of entrepreneurial activity is not a sufficient basis for providing a complete perspective on these questions. For example, it remains to be determined what specific conditions are responsible for igniting such initiative, what kinds of boundaries are set on enterprise by constituent and regulating groups, and how the initial intent of entrepreneurs becomes dispersed or diffused over time. But the screening and motivation processes described here may be a reasonable starting point. In particular, each variety of entrepreneur—potentially selected into or out of the nonprofit sector—has been seen to imply a particular behavior pattern (i.e., one that is more or less inspiring of trust and sensitive to current exigencies as expressed by economic demands.) Thus, policies which affect the alternative opportunities in industries and sectors may, conceivably at least, be adjusted or "tuned" to achieve some socially desired balance in these performance criteria for the nonprofit sectors or for industries as a whole.

The Behavior of Nonprofit Organizations   183

NOTES

1. This point was suggested to me by Richard R. Nelson.

2. Evidence on this matter may be gathered from scattered and spotty sources.

For hospitals in 1976, the *Statistical Abstract of the U.S.* (1978) indicates that for-profit institutions averaged 98.3 beds, compared to 195 for nonprofit, 119 for local government, and 611 for state government.

For nursing homes in 1973, Dunlop (1979) documents average sizes 69, 85, and 110 beds, for proprietary, nonprofit, and governmental, respectively.

In education in 1976, the *Statistical Abstract* (1978) indicates enrollments only for public vs. private (including nonprofit and proprietary) institutions. For elementary schools the figures are 422 public vs. 218 nonpublic; for secondary schools, 573 public vs. 324 nonpublic; for higher education, 6317 public vs. 1423 nonpublic.

For museums, size measurement is complicated by difficulties in reconciling estimates of full-time, part-time, and volunteer staff, and institutional definitions. In terms of operating budget for 1971–1972. *Museums USA* (1974) reports that private nonprofits slightly outnumber public museums in the category under $100,000, whereas the reverse holds for the $100,000–$250,000 category. Equal representation is found in the category over $250,000. In the special category of museums attached to educational institutions, a sharp differential exists between larger public and smaller private museums.

In general, better definitions are needed to effect realistic size comparisons of public, nonprofit, and proprietary activities. For example, in day care for young children, the postulated intersector size differentials would be clearer if public kindergartens were compared to nonprofit day-care centers and nursery schools, and to proprietary nursery schools and day-care homes. In museums, proprietary art galleries might be compared to nonprofit museums, to government departments responsible for public museums, and so on.

3. For example, according to the American Hospital Association (see Miller, 1980), general hospitals were distributed across sectors in 1976 as follows: 35 percent government, 52 percent nonprofit, 13 percent proprietary. For psychiatric hospitals, the figures are 59 percent, 17 percent, and 23 percent, respectively. For nursing homes the distribution is 8 percent, 19 percent, and 73 percent.

In education, according to U.S. HEW statistics in 1976 (see Miller, 1980), elementary schools split 82 percent/18 percent public vs. nonpublic, whereas secondary schools divided 87 percent/13 percent.

In higher education, according to Nielsen (1979), the division in enrollments between public and private, nonprofit institutions has gone from 50 percent/50 percent in 1950 to 78 percent/22 percent in favor of public institutions in 1977. For medical schools in 1977, the division was 57 percent/43 percent in favor of public institutions.

According to Netzer (1978), 85 percent of the arts sector (broadly defined) in terms of annual expenditure is commercial, as opposed to nonprofit or public. In museums, according to *Museums U.S.A.* (1974) for 1971–72, about 56 percent of museums were private nonprofit, compared to 34 percent government, and 5 percent attached to private educational institutions. (Proprietary galleries or exhibitions are excluded from the count.)

REFERENCES

Douglas, James. 1983. *Why Charity? The Case for a Third Sector,* Beverley Hills, Sage.

Dunlop, Burton. 1979. *The Growth of Nursing Home Care,* Lexington, Massachusetts: D.C. Heath and Company.

Feigenbaum, Susan. 1979. Some inter-industry relationships in the nonprofit sector: Theory and empirical testing. Department of Economics. Claremont Men's College.

Grennon, Jacqueline, and Robert Barsky. 1980. An exploration of entrepreneurship in the field of nursing home care for the elderly. Institution for Social and Policy Studies. Yale University. Draft.

Hansmann, Henry. 1980. The role of non-profit enterprise. *Yale Law J.* 89:835–98. Reprinted as Chapter 3 of this volume.

James, Estelle. 1983. How nonprofits grow: A model, *J. of Policy Analysis and Management,* 3:350–63. Reprinted as Chapter 10 in this volume.

Migué, Jean-Lui, and Gerard Bélanger. 1974. Toward a general theory of managerial discretion. *Public Choice,* 17:27–47.

Miller, Lohr E. 1980. A quantitative guide to the non-profit sector of the U.S. economy. Institution for Social and Policy Studies. Program on Nonprofit Organizations. Yale University. Draft.

Museums U.S.A.: A Survey Report. 1974. National Research Center of the Arts for the National Endowment for the Arts.

Netzer, Dick. 1978. *The Subsidized Muse.* Cambridge: Cambridge University Press.

Nielsen, Waldemar A. 1979. *The Endangered Sector.* New York: Columbia University Press.

Niskanen, William. 1971. *Bureaucracy and Representative Government.* Aldine-Atherton.

Parks, Roger B. and Elinor Ostrom. March 1980. Towards a model of the effect of inter- and intraorganizational structure on public bureau service outputs. Workshop in Political Theory and Policy Analysis, Indiana University. Paper no. T-80.

Pauly, Mark and Michael Redisch. March 1973. The not-for-profit hospital as a physician's cooperative. *American Economic Review.* 63:87–99.

Rose-Ackerman, Susan. 1980. United Charities: an Economic Analysis. *Public Policy* 28:325–50.

Schumpeter, Joseph A. 1949. *The theory of economic development.* Cambridge: Harvard University Press.

Statistical Abstract of the United States. 1978. U.S. Department of Commerce. Bureau of the Census. Washington, D.C.

Tullock, Gordon. 1966. Information without profit. *Papers on Non-Market Decision Making,* Blacksburg, Va.: Center for the Study of Public Choice.

Weisbrod, Burton. Toward a theory of the voluntary nonprofit sector in a three-sector economy. In Edmund S. Phelps, ed. *Altruism, morality, and economic theory.* New York Russell Sage Foundation, 1975.

———. October 1979. Economics of institutional choice. Conference on Institutional Choice and the Private Nonprofit Sector, University of Wisconsin, Madison.

Williamson, Oliver. 1967. *The economics of discretionary behavior.* Markham.

Young, Dennis R. 1983. *If Not for Profit, for What?* Lexington, Mass.: D.C. Heath.

———. 1985. *Casebook of Management for Non-Profit Organizations: Entrepreneurship and Organizational Change in the Human Services,* New York: Haworth Press.

[26]

The Economic and Social Review, Vol. 20, No. 3, April, 1989, pp. 243-255

The Leisure Factor in Entrepreneurial Success: A Lesson from the "Robber Baron" Era*

BRUCE W. ROSS
The University of Sydney

Abstract: Success in capitalist enterprise is often held to be due to hard work and in particular is usually associated with the Protestant work ethic. However, study of three major entrepreneurs — Carnegie, Rockefeller, and Morgan — reveals systematic leisure seeking and limited involvement in day-to-day business operations. It is suggested that this detachment was an ingredient in their success, enabling more effective decision making. All three relied on hard working and gifted partners but were kept informed by frequent, detailed reports. Important strategic decisions were never delegated. The major conclusion is that long hours of work are not essential for entrepreneurial success and may under certain circumstances be counter productive.

I INTRODUCTION

S uccess in capitalist enterprise has often been associated with adoption of the values of Calvinistic Puritanism and, in particular, the Protestant work ethic. Many entrepreneurs have been influenced by the teachings of Benjamin Franklin, with his emphasis on frugality and industry. There appears to be a general belief that hard work is a necessary condition for business success. However, a study of the careers of three dominant figures from the "Robber Baron" era, the so-called golden age of American capitalism — Carnegie, Rockefeller, and Morgan — shows a systematic pattern of leisure seeking and limited involvement in day-to-day business operations.

Despite the entrepreneurs' partial withdrawal their enterprises continued to

*I wish to thank Alfred D. Chandler Jr., Stephen Salsbury, Donald M. Lamberton, Flora Gill, Peter Groenewegen, Viv Hall, Warren Hogan and Gordon Mills for helpful comments. In addition the final version reflects suggestions made by an anonymous referee for this journal.

expand at very rapid rates. All three had built effective organisational structures using the partnership approach and then closely supervised the performance of their subordinates. Most importantly, each retained effective control over important strategic decisions.

This paper suggests that the time the principal decision maker spent away from routine business was an important factor in his success. Because the entrepreneurial function depends critically on the ability to perceive opportunities, excessive time spent in routine business activities may lead to less effective entrepreneurial decisions. Leisure, in particular time for reflection and thinking, is an important aspect of the creative process.

II THE WORK ETHIC

Weber (1930) identified the spirit of modern capitalism as rational and systematic profit seeking which necessitated "a hard frugality" and "infinitely more intensive work" (pp. 64-69). This spirit he saw best exemplified in the teachings of Benjamin Franklin who continually stressed the importance of hard work:

> Remember, that TIME is Money. He that can earn Ten Shillings a Day by his Labour, and goes abroad, or sits idle, one half of that Day, . . . has really spent or rather thrown away Five shillings . . .
> In short, the Way to Wealth . . . depends chiefly on two Words, INDUSTRY and FRUGALITY; i.e., Waste neither Time nor Money, but make the best Use of both. Without Industry and Frugality nothing will do, and with them, everything ("Advice to a Young Tradesman", reprinted in Labaree, 1961, pp. 306, 308).

Undoubtedly, many of the nineteenth-century entrepreneurs were strongly influenced by Franklin's example. Thomas Mellon paid direct tribute:

> I regard the reading of Franklin's *Autobiography* as the turning point of my life . . . Here was Franklin, poorer than myself, who by industry, thrift and frugality had become learned and wise, and elevated to wealth and fame. The maxims of "Poor Richard" exactly suited my sentiments (O'Connor, 1933, p. 4).

Similarly, Carnegie's partner, Henry Clay Frick, attributed his own achievements solely to his diligence:

> There is no secret about success. Success simply calls for hard work, devotion to your business at all times, day and night. I was very poor and my education was limited, but I worked very hard and always sought opportunities.

> For six years — from 1889 to 1895, when I first took hold of the Carnegie Steel business, I did not have a day's vacation. I reached the office every morning between seven and eight and did not leave until six (Forbes, 1919, p. 133).

In his analysis of the essential characteristics of modern capitalism, Sombart (1915) argued that the general pace of business forced the capitalist to work at high pressure:

> . . . the expenditure of human energy in modern business activities, extensively and intensively, is strained to the uttermost. Every minute of the day, of the year, nay, of life itself, is devoted to work; and during this working period every power is occupied at highest pressure. Everybody is acquainted with the hard-worked man of to-day. Whether employer or employed, he is constantly on the verge of a breakdown owing to overwork (pp. 181, 187).

Thus the testimony of both eminent social scientists and major entrepreneurial figures supports the view that the entrepreneur's competitive edge derives from working harder than his rivals or, at the least, that hard work is a necessary, if not sufficient, condition for business success.

It is interesting, however, to note a dissenting view from a contemporary observer of America immediately after the Civil War. Edwin Lawrence Godkin was an English journalist and lawyer who founded the weekly journal, the *Nation*. He suggested that modern business, particularly in America, was creating a new type of capitalist. Great fortunes were being made "by lucky strokes, or by a sudden rise in the value of property opened, in our day, to enterprise and speculation".

> . . . the old mode of achieving wealth and reputation in business, by slowly "working one's way up," by the practice of industry and frugality, by the display of punctuality and integrity merely, may be said to have fallen into disrepute.

In an earlier period, "the ideal trader, . . . whom Franklin had constantly in mind," was not presented with any opportunity for enterprise or speculation. "The road to fortune lay through patient, steady plodding, through early rising, plain living, small economies, and the watchful subjugation of restlessness." By contrast, distinction in commercial life was now "won by quickness and audacity, rather than by patient industry . . ." The new virtues were quickness of perception, activity, and courage. "Five out of six of the great fortunes are made rapidly, by happy hits, or bold and ingenious combinations" (Godkin, 1868, pp. 249-252; Kirkland, 1952).

246   THE ECONOMIC AND SOCIAL REVIEW

III THREE CASE STUDIES

Examination of the careers of Andrew Carnegie, John D. Rockefeller, and J. Pierpont Morgan reveals a common pattern of limited involvement in day-to-day business operations, particularly after their enterprises had passed through the early survival stage and had reached the point of take off into sustained growth.

Typically, the business had experienced an initial "surge of success" which provided the basis for rapid accumulation and internally funded growth. This released the principal decision maker from the necessity of spending long hours fighting for the survival of his firm and enabled him to concentrate on planning strategies for future growth and responding to challenges and opportunities presented by the external environment.

What is noteworthy in the cases studied is the fact that the entrepreneur disengaged himself from the enterprise to such an extent that a casual observer might be excused for regarding him as semi-retired. Typically he would be absent from the business for extended periods, either on trips abroad or staying at a summer house and only visiting the place of business when absolutely necessary.

It is significant, however, that the entrepreneur's partial withdrawal from his enterprise did not slow its growth or impede his own accumulation. Limited involvement continued while each of the three achieved national dominance in his area of activity suggesting strongly that during these periods appropriate entrepreneurial choices were being made. However the fact that the founder was frequently absent does not mean that he had abdicated the decision making role. Important strategic decisions were never delegated. In addition, all three maintained a watchdog role which anticipated modern business practice by requiring frequent and detailed reports on key aspects of the firm's operations.

Carnegie

Two major Carnegie biographers focus upon his lack of the diligence normally associated with building a great business. One describes him as an "absentee employer" (Wall, 1970, p. ix). The other points out:

> Carnegie was never a hard worker — not a hard worker, that is, in the grindstone sense; he spent at least half of his time in play, and let other men pile up his millions for him. He was the thinker, the one who supplied ideas, inspiration and driving power, who saw far into the future, not the one who lived laborious days and nights at an office desk . . . [A]fter his thirtieth year he was a roving spirit, organizing great industries, endowing them with his fire and enterprise, selecting the associates who could best transform his visionings into deeds, assuming the main

responsibility for success but leaving the drudgery to others (Hendrick, 1932, Vol. 1, p. 122).

By 1865 when, aged thirty, he left the Pennsylvania Railroad to work for himself, Carnegie had already achieved an impressive roll-call of business interests. He was principal manager of the Keystone Bridge Works, Union Iron Mills, Superior Rail Mill, and Pittsburgh Locomotive Works. He had investments in Adams Express, Columbia Oil, and Woodruff Sleeping Cars; and was also involved in banks, insurance companies, and street railways. His annual income was in excess of $50,000.

Two months after leaving the railroad, he sailed overseas on a trip which would include a five month Grand Tour of Europe. His affairs were left in the hands of his twenty-two year old brother, Tom. It was a time of great turmoil with the young nation having to readjust to peacetime conditions. The elder Carnegie wrote frequent letters home containing numerous suggestions for expansion but at the same time, with no acknowledgement of the obvious contradiction, urging extreme caution:

> We must pull up and develop the Union Mills sure . . . Am glad to see you are pushing around after trade, but my dear boy, the South is our future market . . . The Carnegie family, my boy, are destined always to be poor . . . We must work like sailors to get sail taken in.

When Tom showed signs of becoming exasperated by the pressures of business and his brother's demands, Andrew changed tack and used flattery and expressions of concern to mollify him:

> [T]he more I feel myself drinking in enjoyment, the deeper is my appreciation of your devoted self-denial and the oftener I resolve that you shall have every opportunity to enjoy what I am now doing (Wall, 1970, pp. 236-237).

Tom Carnegie never did get the opportunity to emulate his brother's example.

By the time Andrew had been abroad for four months he was already restless and wrote to his mother, ". . . feel like getting back and pitching into all kinds of business enterprises and driving things generally." However, he managed to curb his impatience and it was another five months before he returned home.

In 1867, at the age of thirty-two, Carnegie and his mother moved from Pittsburgh to New York. For the rest of his life he would live at a distance from the business activities which provided him with ever increasing wealth. This was particularly the case with the summer months. After suffering sunstroke during the Civil War he had developed a chronic intolerance for hot weather, so from early June to late October he would retire to his summer home at Cresson, Pennsylvania, high up in the Alleghenies. In later years he would spend the summer in Scotland.

The Carnegie workforce did not enjoy the same degree of leisure. A contemporary economist observed:

> No visitor to the Carnegie mills can fail to be impressed with the intensity of the effort and the strained attention evident in every department. None but the strongest could stand the terrific pace. Breakdowns were frequent at thirty-five, men were old at forty-five (Meade, 1901, p. 543).

Carnegie's lifestyle would not have been possible unless he had confidence in and could rely on the ability of his partners and managers. Throughout his career he displayed an extraordinary faculty for surrounding himself with gifted subordinates. He also maintained an intense scrutiny of their performance. Whether he was in New York or Scotland, Carnegie constantly bombarded his managers with memoranda about the most minute details of their costs. He also insisted on being supplied with complete minutes of the meetings of partners, including full voting lists. Despite this close supervision, he was unstinting in his praise of his partners' abilities:

> I do not believe that any one man can make a success of a business nowadays. I am sure I never could have done so without my partners, of whom I had thirty-two, the brightest and cleverest young fellows in the world. All are equal to each other, as the members of the Cabinet are equal. The chief must only be first among equals . . . I believe firmly in youths as executive agents. Older heads should be reserved for counsel (Hacker, 1968, p. 358).

Carnegie obviously distinguished between the degree of diligence expected from an "executive agent" and from those who provided "counsel". He stressed the necessity of his partners devoting all of their time and energy to the undertaking. When William Shinn was engaged as general manager of Carnegie's Edgar Thomson Works he retained some outside business interests. Carnegie wrote a number of pleading letters to him:

> I am naturally anxious to get all of you for E.T. I do not know your equal as an Ex. officer & I always feel with you at the helm E.T. is safe but it makes all the difference whether your entire mind is bent on the concern . . . [Y]ou should not have anything to do but run that establishment (Wall, 1970, p. 327).

He conveniently ignored the fact that his own success was very largely due to the extensive range of extraneous activities undertaken while a salaried officer of the Pennsylvania Railroad.

Carnegie's modest claim to be "first among equals" cannot be taken seriously. Even in his final year of business activity he framed the strategies which his partners implemented. From his castle in Scotland he used cables and letters to pass on very explicit "advice":

> Urge prompt action essential; crisis has arrived, only one policy open: start at once hoop, rod, wire, nail mills; no halfway about last two. Extend coal and coke roads, announce these; also tubes . . . have no fear as to the result; victory certain . . . (Allen, 1965, p. 137).

The clearest evidence of the location of ultimate decision making in the Carnegie company is seen in its eventual sale. This was effected by Carnegie simply pencilling a few figures on a slip of paper and sending it to Morgan, who glanced at it and said, "I accept." Nothing was signed until weeks later. The greatest steel corporation in the world changed hands for more than $400,000,000 and neither principal bothered to consult his partners.

Rockefeller

John D. Rockefeller freely admitted that, once well established in business, he was not what could be called a diligent business man. "The real truth is that I was what would now be called a 'slacker' after I reached my middle thirties" (Forbes, 1919, p. 299). In fact, during his whole period of active work, "which lasted from the time I was sixteen years old until I retired from active business when I was fifty-five, . . . I managed to get a good many vacations of one kind or another." He acknowledged that his ability to do this was "because of the willingness of my most efficient associates to assume the burdens of the business" (Rockefeller, 1909, p. 21).

In the days when he "seemed to need every minute for the absorbing demands of business," he would spend a great deal of time at his house at Pocantico Hills on the Hudson, "studying the beautiful views, the trees, and fine landscape effects." He conceded that his business methods differed from those of most "well-conducted merchants" because they allowed him more freedom. Even after Standard Oil moved its main operations to New York, most of his summers were spent on vacation in Cleveland and he only came to New York when his presence seemed necessary. He was thus "left free to attend to many things which interested me — among others, the making of paths, the planting of trees, and the setting out of little forests of seedlings" (ibid., pp. 22, 26).

Wherever he was John D. kept in touch with the office via telegraph wire. Each morning he received a report containing statistics such as the amount of crude on hand and shipments of refined for the previous day. In his pocket he carried a memorandum book bound in red leather:

On one page or another I would jot down what this man or that man was to do, to try, to experiment with.

And he always knew that one day that book would be brought out, and then the questioning! (Hawke, 1980, p. 98).

Rockefeller's lifestyle was facilitated by his ability to compartmentalise his thinking. Having dealt with a matter his mind could switch off, allowing him to move on to other business. "It has been that way all my life, find a problem, work at it, solve it as well as I can, put the administration in good hands, and then go on to the next" (ibid., p. 17).

He clearly perceived the advantages of his business methods and was never tempted to adopt a more orthodox approach:

> I feel sincerely sorry for some of the business men who occasionally come to see me; they have allowed their business affairs to take such complete possession of them that they have no thought for anything else and have no time to really live as rational human beings (Forbes, 1919, p. 299).

Morgan

J. Pierpont Morgan led a leisurely and privileged lifestyle with frequent trips abroad. It was his custom to leave his office at three or four and drive in Central Park or on Fifth Avenue before going home for a nap prior to dressing for dinner (Winkler, 1930, p. 136; Allen, 1965, pp. 57, 162).

At the age of thirty-three he had seriously considered retirement. He had accumulated a considerable fortune from his first partnership but his health was wretched — he suffered from headaches and insomnia and had a recurrence of the fainting spells which had prevented him serving in the Civil War. However it was just at this time that the influential Philadelphia banking house of Drexel & Co. approached him with a proposal to go into partnership in a New York office. Morgan protested his ill health and retirement plans, saying that he needed at least a year away from the pressures of business. However, the Drexel family were so keen to effect an alliance that the new firm of Drexel, Morgan & Co., opened for business in July 1871, immediately after which its managing partner sailed abroad with his family for more than a year (Allen, 1965, pp. 30-32).

While abroad he arranged the purchase of a country place, "Cragston", at Highland Falls on the Hudson. After his return it became customary for the family to spend the winter months at their New York home and the rest of the year — usually from April to October — at Cragston. During these months he always spent Thursdays at Cragston as a midweek holiday but on the other week nights occupied rooms at the Fifth Avenue Hotel. In later years he slept on his luxury yacht, the "Corsair" (ibid., pp. 55-57).

Each spring he travelled to London to maintain contact with his father's office and to take a short holiday on the Continent. Gradually these annual pilgrimages became longer and more elaborate. In 1877 the family spent almost a year abroad, chartering a steamer to go up the Nile. On later trips to Egypt Mrs. Morgan stayed at home but the travelling party usually included glamorous female companions.

The amount of time which Morgan devoted to business was further reduced by health problems. His son-in-law recalls that when he was in his early forties, "almost invariably once in every month he had a bad cold and had to spend two or three days in bed" (Satterlee, 1939, p. 191).

His attitude to work and leisure is best summed up by his reported comment that he could do a year's work in nine months, but not in a year (Allen, 1965, p. 155). His subordinates might have benefited if they had been able to follow their chief's example. By the end of the century virtually all of his early partners were dead or had retired broken in health (ibid., p. 85; Winkler, 1930, pp. 161-117). Morgan reached his seventies before he retired and lived to seventy-five. Carnegie and Rockefeller fared even better. Carnegie was eighty-three when he died while Rockefeller, after almost half a century in retirement, died at ninety-seven.

IV THE SIGNIFICANCE OF THE LEISURE FACTOR

There seems to have been a tendency to regard the leisure-seeking propensities of these entrepreneurs as an aberration, as eccentricity, or as reflecting the extent to which their success was due to the hard work of their associates and subordinates. However, I think that it can be plausibly argued that the time spent at a distance from the mundane details of business operations was an important factor in their success.

Kirzner focuses on the central role of alertness in relation to the entrepreneur and argues that profitable entrepreneurial activities are in fact "creative acts of discovery":

> The crucial element in behaviour expressing entrepreneurial alertness is that it expresses the decision maker's ability spontaneously to transcend an existing framework of perceived opportunities (Kirzner, 1985, p. 7).

To the extent that the critical factor is the ability to perceive new opportunities then, beyond a certain point, additional time spent in routine business activities may have an opportunity cost in terms of less effective entrepreneurial decision making. That such decision making does not require the commitment of prodigious amounts of time is evidenced by the fact that both Carnegie and Frick built the foundations of their business empires in their spare time while working as salaried employees.

Extensive leisure certainly provides an opportunity to "recharge the batteries". But it may do more. It permits time for thinking and reflection. The broad picture of business strategies can be reviewed and revised. This must be particularly important with proposals to diversify or to otherwise change the direction of business growth. Rockefeller certainly recognised the value of thinking time. In retirement he recalled his association with Henry Flagler:

> For years and years this early partner and I worked shoulder to shoulder; our desks were in the same room. We both lived on Euclid Avenue a few rods apart. We met and walked to the office together, walked home to luncheon, back again after luncheon, and home again at night. On these walks, when we were away from the office interruptions, we did our thinking, talking, and planning together (Rockefeller, 1909, pp. 12-13).

Undoubtedly a major factor in the success of each of the three entrepreneurs was the quality of their partners. But in many instances those partners had developed their executive skills within the business. The delegation of authority made necessary by the principal partner's absence undoubtedly contributed to that development. However, such delegation was limited both in the degree of responsibility and in time. It essentially embraced managerial rather than entrepreneurial functions and detailed scrutiny continued from a distance. Further, whenever the principal partner returned from his wanderings, he would involve himself in all details of the firm's operations.

The roles of the partners and the way in which they were recruited differed in each case. Rockefeller's partners were typically older than him; successful businessmen in their own right who had sold their businesses to Standard Oil. Morgan recruited his partners from the ranks of promising young New York bankers. Carnegie's partners were most likely to have been either early associates or young men who had risen from the ranks in the steel plants. Carnegie boasted, "Mr. Morgan buys his partners, I grow my own" (Wall, 1970, p. 665).

The differing situation with partners illustrates the danger of trying to force the analogy between the three entrepreneurs. There is obviously a common thread in each achieving dominance in a major area of American industrial activity and we have focused on their shared preference for leisure. Beyond that it is wise not to go too far. The three were basically different types. Their methods of doing business and the way in which they used leisure differed fundamentally.

Hughes describes Carnegie as "the Schumpeterian entrepreneur *par excellence*", and says that "his methods were those of ruthless and unremitting competition." By contrast, "Morgan had a passion to impose discipline and order upon everything he touched. When men came to him for help they took away orders" (Hughes, 1965, pp. 9, 12). Competition was anathema to Rockefeller and he devoted all his energy to achieving combination.

It is important not to equate leisure with idleness. For instance Carnegie used his leisure in a much more purposeful way than did Rockefeller or Morgan. He travelled around Europe inspecting plants and seeking out new processes. He then adapted and synthesised the ideas he had gathered so that they achieved a potential undreamt of by their originators.

He exemplified the genius entrepreneur, darting from one project to another with tremendous energy and flair. He was renowned for his variant of the Eureka cry, "I've got the flash!" (Hendrick, 1932, p. 204). In 1872 he arrived back from Britain to announce to his startled partners, "The day of iron has passed. Steel is king!", despite the fact that he had long opposed moving into Bessemer steel. But, as Hendrick suggests, "the discoveries that were important to Carnegie were the ones he had made himself" (ibid., p. 184).

He displayed the multi-potentiality which Koestler has observed in the great scientists. His career abounds in creative responses to challenges and opportunities, "connecting previously unrelated dimensions of experience," and achieving "the defeat of habit by originality" (Koestler, 1965, pp. 96, 706).

By contrast Morgan was not an original thinker. What he had was a remarkable capacity for judging the worth of proposals conceived by other men. An insight into his methods occurred during the Panic of 1907 when for some weeks he virtually controlled the finances of the country. The presidents of the New York banks and trust companies met at his home to formulate a rescue plan. While the bankers deliberated in the West Room, Morgan sat alone in the East Room, smoking and playing solitaire. After some hours his secretary asked, "Why don't you tell them what to do, Mr. Morgan?" He answered: "I don't know what to do myself, but some time, someone will come in with a plan that I know *will* work; and then I will tell them what to do" (Satterlee, 1939, p. 477).

V QUALIFYING THE ARGUMENT

It is important not to over-emphasise the importance of the leisure factor in entrepreneurial success. In fact Ross (1988) argued that the essence of entrepreneurial activity is "strategic commitment", which has two elements — first, strategic thought and decision and secondly, commitment based on that strategy. Successful entrepreneurs almost invariably exhibit an indomitable psychological commitment to the advancement of their enterprise. However, recognition of the necessity for commitment is not inconsistent with the observation that business leaders may benefit by occasionally or even regularly withdrawing from the routine administration of their firms.

It is also obvious that these three case studies are not of typical entrepreneurs. Quite apart from the undoubted superior abilities of these individuals, they each enjoyed the significant advantages of having gifted subordinates and functioning in an era of unparalleled growth and expansion.

A necessary condition for the development of a major entrepreneurial firm may well be the formation of an effective management team. Only with such a structure is the ultimate decision maker free to experience the luxury of substantial leisure time.

The other factor which made extensive leisure possible was the fact that none of these entrepreneurs experienced any major setbacks to the continued growth of their organisations. Entrepreneurs who are compelled to fight for the very survival of their firms will necessarily be totally preoccupied with that struggle.

It should again be emphasised that evidence of a distinct preference for leisure does not imply the absence of energy or drive. Admittedly Morgan appears to have enjoyed a rather relaxed lifestyle throughout his career, but he had the signal advantage of being launched into a thriving business through his father's patronage. By contrast, both Carnegie and Rockefeller started with nothing and demonstrated considerable tenacity and application in pursuing their business careers. However, they both established patterns of leisure taking at an early age. As noted above, Rockefeller had "a good many vacations" from the age of sixteen onwards, while Carnegie took a three month overseas holiday at the age of twenty-six, and thereafter travelled abroad almost annually.

VI CONCLUSION

The discussion in this paper does not refute the view that the Protestant work ethic was important to the success of entrepreneurs in nineteenth century America. However it does not appear that this ethic was necessarily embraced by the founders themselves. Rather its influence may have been concentrated on the emerging class of professional managers whose dedication and diligence greatly magnified the success of the founder entrepreneurs.

It is tempting to speculate as to whether the effectiveness of these managers might have been further improved if they had been able to at least partially emulate the relaxed lifestyles of their bosses. Such speculation could even be extended to Carnegie's millhands who worked twelve-hour shifts seven days a week.

The evidence presented above does not necessarily demonstrate that the typical entrepreneur of the "Robber Baron" era was a leisure seeking hedonist. Rather, by showing that three of the major figures of the age took extensive breaks from business commitments, it suggests that long hours of work are not essential for entrepreneurial success. It provides support for the view that extensive leisure, not to be understood as idle pleasure-seeking, may lead to more effective entrepreneurial decision making. Naturally these conclusions also have implications for other areas of human enterprise and decision making.

REFERENCES

ALLEN, FREDERICK LEWIS, 1965. *The Great Pierpont Morgan*, New York: Harper & Row, Perennial Library.

FORBES, B.C., 1919. *Men Who Are Making America*, 4th Edition, New York: B.C. Forbes Publishing Co.

GODKIN, EDWIN LAWRENCE, 1868. "Commercial immorality and political corruption", *North American Review*, No. 107, July, pp. 248-266.

HACKER, LOUIS M., 1968. *The World of Andrew Carnegie: 1865-1901*, Philadelphia: J.B. Lippincott Co.

HAWKE, DAVID FREEMAN, 1980. *John D.: The Founding Father of the Rockefellers*, New York: Harper & Row.

HENDRICK, BURTON J., 1932. *The Life of Andrew Carnegie*, New York: Doubleday, Doran & Co., 2 vols.

HUGHES, JONATHAN, 1965. *The Vital Few: American Economic Progress and its Protagonists*, Boston: Houghton Mifflin Co.

KIRKLAND, EDWARD C., 1952. *Business in the Gilded Age: The Conservative Balance Sheet*, Madison: University of Wisconsin Press.

KIRZNER, ISRAEL M., 1985. *Discovery and the Capitalist Process*, Chicago: The University of Chicago Press.

KOESTLER, ARTHUR, 1964. *The Act of Creation*, London: Hutchinson.

LABAREE, LEONARD W. (ed.), 1961. *The Papers of Benjamin Franklin*, New Haven: Yale University Press.

MEADE, EDWARD S., 1901. "The Genesis of the United States Steel Corporation", *Quarterly Journal of Economics*, Vol. 15, August.

O'CONNOR, HARVEY, 1933. *Mellon's Millions: The Biography of a Fortune: The Life and Times of Andrew W. Mellon*, New York: The John Day Co.

ROCKEFELLER, JOHN D., 1909. *Random Reminiscences of Men and Events*, London: William Heinemann.

ROSS, BRUCE W., 1988. "Strategic Commitment, Unknowledge and the Nature of Entrepreneurial Activity", *Prometheus*, Vol. 6, No. 2, December.

SATTERLEE, HERBERT L., 1939. *J. Pierpont Morgan: An Intimate Portrait*, New York: Macmillan.

SOMBART, WERNER, 1915. *The Quintessence of Capitalism: A Study of the History and Psychology of the Modern Business Man*, translated and edited by M. Epstein, London: T. Fisher Unwin.

THUROW, LESTER, 1976. *Generating Inequality*, London: Macmillan.

WALL, JOSEPH FRAZIER, 1970. *Andrew Carnegie*, New York: Oxford University Press.

WEBER, MAX, 1930. *The Protestant Ethic and the Spirit of Capitalism*, translated by Talcott Parsons, New York: Charles Scribner's Sons.

WINKLER, JOHN K., 1930. *Morgan the Magnificent: The Life of J. Pierpont Morgan (1837-1913)*, New York: The Vanguard Press.

27

2 The National Companies

CHAPTER 6

Lipton

THE DRIVE TO A NATIONAL MARKET

Lipton rocketed from his first shop in Stobcross Street, Glasgow, across the Scottish and then the national market with greater thrust, and certainly much more publicity, than any other retailer of his day. Despite the blaze of publicity which accompanied each new move, and the local impact of his trading methods wherever a Lipton branch opened, the rate of opening new shops was not high until his empire reached London in 1889. This forms the first phase in the history of the business—quite inseparable in style and achievement from the man himself.

Thomas Lipton opened his second shop in 1874 after three years in trade. By May 1878 there were four shops in different parts of Glasgow, with his headquarters at 21–7 High Street, and large stores in Robertson Street. In July 1878 came the first move beyond the city with the Dundee branch 'Irish Market' and, in the fanfare of the occasion, Lipton announced that he would be opening shortly in Aberdeen, Edinburgh, Greenock and Paisley: 'the success already achieved in the western metropolis by the sale of goods of the best quality at very low prices leading him to believe that his enterprise would be amply rewarded in the various towns of Scotland'. Paisley came next in June 1879— 'a branch establishment in this town will be a boon to the working classes' commented the *Paisley Herald*—and the *Paisley Daily Express*: 'The extraordinary development of Mr Lipton's business in different parts of the country has certainly been *the* feature of the Scotch provision trade during the last four or five years.'[1]

Lipton was never the man to let profitable opportunities pass

[1] *Paisley Herald*, 28 June 1879; *Paisley Daily Express*, 30 June 1879.

him by. His ruthless energy exploited every chance for expansion that came his way, so it is no wonder that, right from his first entry into trade, his business was more differentiated in some respects than his rivals. Specialisation in a few dominant lines in the provision trade he firmly maintained for almost twenty years in trade, but he sold when and where he could. From the Stobcross Street shop (where he employed only one assistant) Lipton put in a tender for, and obtained, the contract for supplying provisions to a famous Glasgow drapery store—and promptly advertised himself as their provision purveyor. By 1878 local newspapers were commenting on his large export trade in hams to the West Indies, and his lucrative contracts to hotels in different parts of Scotland and to restaurants in Glasgow (including the kitchens of the University). Opening his own stores in Scottish towns was accompanied by rising wholesale trade to country retailers. His later development of the military contract market both at home and overseas, and the massive wholesale trade in tea, which are described at more length below, thus have their foundations in the local Scottish ventures of the very early years of the business. Just as the move into manufacturing and food processing, wholesale trading was a natural move to profit from the efficiencies which the organisation of his retail trade provided. All assets were to be put to good use, and an efficient buying organisation (like efficient food-processing interests) could be made to yield advantages on the selling side more numerous than those of exploiting trade in Lipton shops. Such differentiation and expansion of enterprise had its dangers, as well as its opportunities. But these also belong to the story at a later stage.

In 1878 turnover was already running at a level of 6,000 hams, 16 tons of bacon, 16,000 dozen eggs, 10 tons of butter and 200 cheeses per week. Lipton had set up an Irish agency at Westport, County Mayo, and an egg-packing station at Clones within a few years. Up to the time he went into the tea trade in 1888–89, three-quarters of the imported produce sold by Lipton came from Ireland, where he now had developed a force of a hundred agents and several depots, his headquarters being at Ballina, County Mayo. This did not prevent him from testing the price and quality of Irish supplies against alternative sources anywhere in the world. His highly articulate letters to the *Freeman's Journal* in

98   *The Individual Companies*

1879 made pointed comparisons between the standards of some Irish butter and egg production and continental and American practice.[1] He paid his next visit to the United States, to organise a buying agency there, in August 1880 and he had taken large consignments of Canadian cheese bought from importers like R. G. Tennant & Co. of Glasgow. Meanwhile, to enlarge his Glasgow base, Lipton took over large stores and a bacon curing plant with a capacity of 10,000 sides per week, in Lancefield Street in 1879, and opened his largest prestige 'market' in 57–9 Jamaica Street—one of the best commercial sites to be found in the city.

The 1880s saw bridgeheads established in the main cities of England and Wales. At the opening of the decade there were twelve branches in the Glasgow region and turnover had risen to £200,000. The first shop in England came, with enormous publicity, at Leeds in January 1881. Then followed Liverpool (1883) when the total number was sixteen and turnover £250,000; Birmingham, Sunderland and Manchester (1885), Bristol (1886), Cardiff (1887); London (1888), Swansea, Belfast and a second London shop in 1889. These branches show the moving frontier of the business: by 1889 turnover was £1½m; there were over thirty shops and almost 1,000 employees. Halfway through the decade Lipton had begun to bill himself as 'the largest retail provision dealer in the world', while the title given him by the ecstatic *American Dairyman* had also crossed the Atlantic: 'King of the Dairy Provision Trades.' The first London shop, opened in April 1888 just opposite Whiteley's department store in Bayswater, brought the *Paddington Chronicle* to comment on the revolution in Westbourne Grove, scaring 'local buttermen out of their old and profitable prices'. Butter was offered at 1s per lb instead of the 1s 8d per lb demanded for similar quality before Lipton's market opened. Bacon retailed at 3d–6d per lb depending on the cut, and hams at 6d–7d per lb—all these being up to half prevailing prices in the traditional style 'family provision merchants'. Even the large Home and Colonial Stores branch at Islington suffered greatly for some time, when Lipton chose a site just opposite for his second London shop. Local newspaper comments on the opening of the London branches—six in 1889—

[1] *Freeman's Journal*, 27 June, 4 August, 16 December 1879; *The Nation*, 6 September 1879.

suggest that he was primarily known in the capital as a butter and cheese seller, a significant change of emphasis from the ham and bacon trade that dominated the early Glasgow shops. 'Butterine', the margarine prototype, was also being sold by 1889.

This first decade of expansion into England also saw other sides of the business develop. Lipton, far from concentrating his efforts in a single mode of operation across his own counters, threw out new enterprise at every point of the business where he thought there was profit and expansion to be had. The American business merits separate description (see below, p. 109) rapidly assuming a life of its own, independent of the demand from Lipton's British shops which first brought it into existence. It paralleled, across the Atlantic, equivalent moves at home. Thomas Lipton sought institutional trade wherever he could find it, taking military contracts, hotel and restaurant trade, and gaining the main contracts to supply the 1888 International Exhibition, which he promptly used for a new publicity campaign. His retail prices (quite apart from the wholesale terms he quickly offered) were low enough to bring independent retailers to him seeking wholesale trade. This became a growing adjunct of the business, though it awaited his entry into the tea market to develop its full scope. Then came a move towards acquiring manufacturing capacity to supply the shops. In the case of bacon and ham trade it was an almost inevitable attribute of selling on a large scale when buying direct from importers—one secret of Lipton's great success. By 1878 he had drying and curing capacity for 15,000 hams at the Robertson Street stores in Glasgow, and smoking rooms for bacon on an equivalent scale. This capacity also encouraged him to develop an agency trade in supplying country retailers, where it proved possible to buy and process bacon and ham on a larger scale than was required for his own shops. His next step was to add sausage and pie manufacture in the Lancefield Street premises in 1878, purchasing three railway provision trucks in 1889, of six tons capacity each, to get supplies to Euston for the London shops.

EXPANSION AND DIVERSIFYING

The full implications of this policy of going back to the source of supply, be it Ireland, the United States or the Antipodes, and

100   *The Individual Companies*

setting up manufacturing capacity to prepare goods for the shops, were revealed in the following decade 1889–98. Now the number of branches increased at an unprecedented rate and Lipton moved into many new lines. This new scale of trading and the growing complexity of the pattern of sales, when coupled with wholesaling in Britain and agency business abroad, brought enormous complications. With hindsight one can see that such a complex commercial and manufacturing empire, if it was to remain efficient and profitable, needed to have some restraint imposed upon it. Yet it ramified and sprouted new enterprise wherever the hope of profit led an ebullient owner. At the very least, size and diversity on the scale seen in the 1890s demanded decentralisation of management, careful cost accounting to check efficiency, a restructuring of the management. Yet the firm still ran in the old way, with Thomas Lipton in direct control of everything, appointing managers to take over the day-to-day operations but keeping all policy-making firmly in his own hands and cheerfully accepting personal responsibility for all decisions. He trained subordinates to implement his orders but not executives to exert discretion and judgment of their own. And although the tale of triumph is virtually unblemished by public criticism— being crowned indeed by an extraordinary display of confidence and adulation at the incorporation of the business in 1898—in restrospect there is no doubt that future troubles had their beginnings in this same decade 1889–98. The very scale of Lipton's achievement brought its own backlash.

Numbers of branches now grew very rapidly, particularly in the London area. By 1891 there were more than 100 branches open, turnover had increased eight times within four years and— counting all the overseas businesses—Lipton was employing more than 5,000 persons. In 1898, at the time of incorporation, he claimed to own over 400 shops (throughout the world), and to employ over 10,000 persons. By 1899 he claimed 500 shops. He had moved into the remaining regions of England—East Anglia significantly being the last. The *Grocer's Gazette* remarked in 1892 that 'nothing so smart of the kind has ever been seen in Ipswich'.[1] For Ireland, *The Grocer* complained that 'the entrance of Mr Lipton into so many important centres of Irish trade is causing much commotion'.[2] But London rapidly became the new

[1] 24 December 1893.   [2] 15 November 1890.

centre of gravity of the business, with 22 branches open there in 1892, 60 by 1895 and 72 by 1898. At incorporation there were 242 branches open in Britain with 12 more being prepared—27 in Scotland, 18 in Ireland, 125 in English provincial towns and the rest in London. Undoubtedly Lipton's decision to begin trading in tea in 1889, with the enormous success this brought at once, had much to do with this development, for London was the importing and distributing centre for all tea imports. Lipton quickly became most famous as a tea retailer in the London area. In recognition of this conquest of the national market, with all the realignments of buying, warehousing and supply lines following from this, the head offices moved to London in 1891, taking it was said, £1,000 worth of business per week away from the Glasgow post office. New headquarters were built in the following year at Bath Street, City Road, and more magnificent buildings followed in 1896.

Much the most important single boost to this expansion, perhaps more important than all other developments in the business put together, came from trading in tea. Characteristically, the most elaborate worldwide agency trade grew out of this side of the business, nucleating out of the main structure of the firm to form an enterprise in its own right, and it gave rise to the most dramatic acquisitions of the ultimate sources of supply for Lipton shops: buying tea plantations. These are important enough ventures to deserve separate attention (see below, p. 328). Here we are concerned with the place tea trading assumed in the main business. In May 1889 Lipton's entry into the tea market made headline news in Scottish papers. He began with characteristic panache. Eighty tons of tea were piped in procession from Glasgow docks to his stores, with sandwich men in Arab dress publicising the acquisition of the first Ceylon tea estates 'from the tea garden to the tea pot'. Lipton presented the London dock-strikers with 1,000 lb of tea which helped to spread the good news. He found tea prices at 3s to 4s per lb in family grocers; and retailed his own blends at 1s 2d to 1s 9d.

By the end of the year his branch in Union Street, Aberdeen, was turning over two tons of tea per week and 400 girls were packing Lipton's tea in Glasgow. Local papers in London had already started calling him 'the largest tea and coffee dealer in the

102 *The Individual Companies*

world'—a title they made ready to adopt in those years when Lipton took on any new line. Nottingham newspapers already regarded him mainly as a tea retailer. He sold four million pounds of tea in 1889, his first in the trade, and well over six million pounds in 1890, sales running at 1,200 chests per week. Over half this total was Ceylon tea. With Ceylon estates (supplying, of course, only a very small percentage of the tea sold by the firm), buying agencies in Colombo and India, a main warehouse in Mincing Lane by 1890, and 600 girls employed packing at the new City Road premises, Lipton was fully established in the new trade. The opportunities were even greater than in his other main lines, ham, bacon, cheese and butter. The trade, as he found it, was organised on traditional lines, with many intermediaries and wide margins waiting to be undercut. The market was enormously elastic, so that lower prices could invoke a vastly increased demand. Purchasing power, in terms of prices, was rising rapidly, population expanding and tea was an elemental product in staple demand in every household of the country. There were also the rising new production centres of 'black tea' in India and Ceylon to make such great expansion at lower prices possible. National sales in England in the spring of 1892 had risen to 3,000 chests (one million packets) per week. Already the blenders in City Road were basing their decisions on samples of water brought from different parts of the country. By the time of incorporation 50 tons of tea per day were moving out of City Road, a steady increase from the 200 tons per week of 1895. There were now almost 400 shops and 5,000 agents for wholesale tea selling. Many of the new branches in these years had their sales dominated by tea and the complementary line, sugar, which now also came into Lipton shops. Some in London sold only tea, sugar and cakes in their first years of trade.

The shop tea trade was already considerably augmented by contract trade with institutions, military contracts, and a wholesale trade organised through agents. A minimum order of 50 lb, for cash, was the rule, with credit trade confined to institutional contracts. Even Lipton branches were being used as centres for wholesale and contract trade at this time, which proved to be a source of much squabbling over rates of commission between branches and the head office wholesale and contract trade. Branch managers cut their own margins by offering special discounts to other retailers and agents. Naturally the wholesale grocers associations objected to doing business with head office on worse terms and threatened to outlaw Lipton's tea amongst their members. Such a threat was not to be taken seriously at this time but the internal problems created by agency and wholesale business at the branches were so great that it was abandoned.

At the same time as he was effecting a revolution in the tea trade across the world Lipton began all sorts of new ventures. He established a large bakery in Hyde Park Street, Glasgow, in 1891, to supply cakes and biscuits to his shops throughout the country and sell to independent retailers. This was also on a large scale, with the latest travelling ovens capable of producing 200 tons of cake and shortbread per week. Next came several additions to the manufacturing facilities in London. Coffee roasting, grinding and essence-making started in new premises at Old Street. Sausage-making plant, with a capacity of 60 tons per week, had been installed in the basement of the City Road premises, with a bakery for pork pies and sausage rolls adjoining. Ham and bacon curing took place at a separate site in Nelson Street (the Glasgow factory now zoning its output for branches in Scotland and the north of England). Almost a thousand people worked at the City Road premises—200 of them in the counting house. All the latest apparatus was proudly displayed for the press: electric light, typewriters, hydraulic lifts, a special post office, electric call bells, private telegraph wires, large refrigerators for rapid chilling, automatic 'drum' blenders in the tea department. National distribution now came from warehouses at four strategic import centres: Glasgow, Liverpool, London and Dublin.

A further commodity taken up in these same years, where Lipton saw a similar structure of trade and equivalent opportunities for cutting costs and developing a mass sale at lower prices, was jam. He began large-scale production at a factory in Rouel Road, Bermondsey, in 1892. The accompanying barrage of publicity, when it was extended in 1894 and rebuilt again in 1896, revealed typical objectives. Thomas Lipton was going to 'make things hum' in the jam trade. He would be selling 2 lb for the normal price of one. He had plans to grow his own fruit, devise new machinery for cutting manufacturing costs and supply pulp and jam on an agency basis in wholesale trade as well as for

Lipton's shops. There was talk of distributing Lipton's jam through the world as widely as Lipton's tea. All this happened, though not on a scale to be compared with his investment in the tea trade. Six plum farms in Kent were bought in September 1894, with the promise that there were more to follow. The factory was large enough to employ 250 persons.

In 1893 came mineral water manufacture at an Old Street factory and a confectionery factory in 1895—both on the same lines but operating on a smaller scale. Lipton also applied the same principle of controlling his sources of supply to cut out the middleman's profit to his needs in printing and packaging. The first printing works had been set up at Glasgow in 1892, employing 180 persons, with ten letterpress and three lithography machines. He then centralised all printing for the firm (they used 2,000 tons of paper annually) at the new offices in City Road in 1896, producing advertisements, tickets and posters for the shops, paper bags and stationery. There was also a large cooperage and a tin box manufactory.

Through the 1890s this wide range spread further, so that at incorporation the prospectus spoke of the following items as manufactured by the business: cocoa, chocolate, confectionery, jams, marmalade, preserved fruits, pickles, preserved meats, sauces, biscuits, cakes, coffee and cocoa essence, beef extract and fluid beef. It is not surprising that an occasional rumour went through the press that Lipton was about to start a line of steamers or make a bid to distribute daily newspapers through his shops.

ADVERTISING

The new world of retailing which was being pioneered by Lipton was marked by another important characteristic: aggressive advertising. This was so central to his trade that it deserves separate mention. Relying for success upon undercutting existing prices meant paring profit margins on each unit sale to a minimum. In turn this made expansion of the volume of trade the vital thing, to translate this fractional percentage profit into large returns. At the centre of the economics of the new style of business, therefore, lay the problem of extending the market (a quest which had not troubled the traditional-style family grocer catering

for a middle-class clientele on comfortably wide profit margins).
Advertising was thus involved in the very nature of their trade.
He who would sell to the mass market of the teeming cities had
to be a dealer in mass information and persuasion.

But the issue goes deeper than this. On the one hand the
vehicles for mass advertising were rapidly extending themselves
across the face of the new society in these same decades (indeed,
they sprang ultimately from the same world of technological
advance and social change as the multiple stores). The opportunities for their appeal to the masses advanced in step with the
necessity for it. When expansion was at its beginning, and the
numbers of shops were increasing within the area of the town or
region that saw the original foundation, the local newspaper was
the main target for advertising, apart from local posters and
various sorts of display and device at the shops. In the break-
through to national markets again, the local newspapers of the
regions in the line of advance were the main medium outside the
shops and stunts. The national press came into play only gradually, after a national sales organisation was on its way to completion and consolidation.

The drive to employ these devices owed its momentum to more
than economic incentives. Indeed, it was involved in the whole
nature of the personality of men like Thomas Lipton and owed
not a little, too, to the conscious desire on their part to emulate
American example. Most documentation on the rôle of advertising within the group of companies comes—not accidentally—
from Lipton, who kept complete files of his own press cuttings
from his first years in business. Here was self-advertisement with
a vengeance. Lipton was an ebullient, self-assertive, egocentric,
extrovert person—a bachelor who had no interests at first beyond
his business to perpetuate his name or absorb his energies and
ambitions. His personal reputation and that of his business, the
status of the name Lipton in whichever connection it was involved, were as one. Even when, after success and riches had
come, he went in for racing large yachts, the sport of kings and
magnates, that too was fairly consciously an instrument of advancing the name of Lipton upon the headlines of the world. In
some small degree ostentatious pleasure fed back momentum to
the business whose profits sustained its vast expense. More particularly was this true of his American tea company, where yachting

publicity probably obviated the need for quite expensive advertising campaigns.[1]

In the beginning, advertising was one of the many lessons brought back by Lipton from his visit to the United States in 1869. 'Every business idea, every successful move I have made', he later claimed in an expansive and uncritical moment, 'has been suggested to me by my observation of American methods.' He was speaking to an American. His inventiveness and irrepressible enterprise—even his sense of fun—ensured that all sorts of stunts were used, but the basis of his advertising in the early years lay with the local press. The *St Pancras Gazette* commented in 1892, 'his greatest ally is the newspaper'.[2] Within nine years of establishing his first shop in Glasgow in 1871, the *Grocer* (which represented the conservative side of the trade) was commenting about Lipton: 'This dealer is an inveterate advertiser in the local press, and the ludicrous cartoons which he exhibits in his shop windows have made the name of Lipton as familiar as a household word, and it is to this publicity, no doubt, he owes much of his success.'[3]

Lipton was even better known for his stunts, which were more widely current in the press even than his paid advertisements. In July 1878 several newspapers took up the report of 'Lipton's Orphans'—a legend he had painted on the flanks of two Irish porkers being driven through the streets to his market.[4] He began to parade giant American cheeses through the streets in 1881, a campaign which culminated in his offer of a five-ton monster cheese for the Queen's Jubilee celebrations in 1887.[5] The Queen declined the gift and when several towns begged it for distribution to their unemployed poor, Lipton responded with 500 lb of bacon and 2,400 eggs.

Leaflets scattered from balloons, trick mirrors reflecting a 'before and after visiting Liptons' vision, the comic pound notes

[1] A. Waugh, *The Lipton Story* (1951), p. 225.
[2] *St Pancras Gazette*, 29 October 1892.
[3] *The Grocer*, 31 July 1880.
[4] e.g. *Evening Citizen*, 9 July; *North British Daily Mail*, 10 July; *Evening News* and *Star*, 11 July 1878.
[5] These cheeses in fact represented a major move of Lipton's into large-scale cheese importing from the United States. He purchased mainly in New York State. His orders to Richardson, Beeble & Co. were large and regular enough to induce them to install special plant. In October 1886, for example, he ordered fifteen cheeses from this firm weighing between 3,500 and 5,000 lb each.

Lipton   107

(which brought him the unexpected additional publicity of a court case in 1877) verged into pantomime humour throughout the 1880s. Indeed, he became a favourite subject for Scottish music-hall comedians (always 'by permission') and one of them followed him to perform in Birmingham when the first Lipton market opened there. By 1886 he was reported to employ an artist and three assistants making cartoons to display in all his shops.[1]

An equal barrage of publicity presaged the invasion of other countries. The opening of a branch shop in Hamburg in 1893 and the general retailing of Lipton's teas in the area was accompanied by extensive advertising in German newspapers, giving biographical details of Lipton himself and descriptions of his headquarters in City Road. Constantinople, Stockholm and Copenhagen received the same treatment in 1894. In the previous year Lipton used the Chicago Exhibition as the opportunity and occasion for breaking into the Middle West. He sent an agent and a pavilion to the Fair and hung an extensive advertising campaign on this participation. In Ceylon Lipton played host to Arabi Pasha after his exile from Egypt and gained enormous publicity at the (wrong) suggestion that he might become the manager of Liptons' tea estates. Instead, the unfortunate potentate found his recommendation of Liptons' coffee and coffee essence plastered across the label on each package. Royalty and upper class patronage were sought in this country just as assiduously. Within six years of opening his first humble market Lipton possessed a letter of thanks from Lieutenant-General McPherson for a present of hams, who wrote to say that the Countess Montidjio (to whom one had been presented) agreed that they were excellent. The bid for royal favour in 1886 was rewarded eventually with the Royal Warrant for tea in 1895. In May 1897 he offered all the tea for the Princess of Wales, dinner fund for the poor. Funds for this were coming in slowly (there was opposition on the part of those who objected to 'indiscriminate' charity) until Lipton offered £25,000 to solve the problem and made an open secret of his gesture. His knighthood followed. By this time he was in the full glare of transatlantic publicity, and his name was beginning to appear, with approving comments, in *The Times* and the *Daily Telegraph*.

[1] *Dumbarton Herald*, 24 February 1886.

All this meant that, by the 1890s, Lipton was said to 'out-Pear Pears' in advertising. Expenditure had now reached £40,000 annually. A decade later the total was running between £50,000 and £60,000 annually (with occasional attempts to limit it at the lower level). However, not until February 1915 was a serious effort considered. Then a top-level advertising committee under the managing director was established to centralise and control all advertising accounts, both contracts of past accounts and budget forecasts for the year ahead. This replaced a lax system of approving an advertising 'contracts book' at directors' meetings (although even this system had some of the defects of absolute centralisation, because some individual advertisements in parish magazines were being approved—in their Minutes at least—by meetings of the board). The weekly outlays of almost £1,000 current in 1909 show that press advertising did not possess nearly the same relative importance as in the early days. Over half the total (£528 per week) was taken up with posters, electric signs and plates; hand-bills accounted for a further £100; newspapers and magazines £150; export advertising £83, among other accounts. Such a figure of almost £1,000 is made up of specific advertising expenditure and does not include the costs of commercial moves in selling some lines cheaply or having 'special' bargains, which could be understood as a general advertising cost. With national coverage of sales the costs of a competition were heavy. In 1914, for example, a tea wrapper competition, confined to the British Isles, cost over £4,000 with a further £2,000 for its publicity. New foreign markets might still bear heavy advertising costs (sometimes long before they were commercially profitable). Lipton was spending £750 p.a. in South Africa on advertising through cinemas, posters and samples. So voraciously did the virus of western example and western enterprise work its way eastwards that by the outbreak of war in 1914 a board of directors in City Road could be discussing the merits of cinema advertising in Penang.

Equivalent documentation is not possible, significantly, for the other companies, but the broad contrast between their position and Liptons' shows how much more the latter company, one might prefer to say the latter person, relied on advertising.

Immigrants, Social Mobility and Culture

28

[2]

A Theory of Immigrant Enterprise

This chapter develops a single, sustained argument for immigrants' over-representation among the self-employed and then inquires into the sources of ethnic differences in business success rates.

The Opportunity Structure

We begin with demand. For a business to arise there must be some demand for the services it offers. The initial market for immigrant entrepreneurs arises within the immigrant community itself: The immigrant community has a special set of needs and preferences that are best served, and sometimes can only be served, by those who share those needs and know them intimately, namely, the members of the immigrant community itself. Generally, those businesses that first develop are purveyors of culinary products— tropical goods among Hispanics, for example, or Oriental specialties among Asians. Businesses that provide "cultural products"—newspapers, recordings, books, magazines—are also quick to find a niche in the immigrant community. The important point about both types of activity is that they involve a direct connection with the immigrants' homeland and knowledge of tastes and buying preferences—qualities unlikely to be shared by larger, native-owned competitors.[1]

Immigrants also have special problems that are caused by the strains of settlement and assimilation and are aggravated by their distance from the institutionalized mechanisms of service delivery. Consequently, the business of specializing in the problems of immigrant adjustment is another early avenue of economic activity, and immigrant-owned travel agencies, law firms, realtors, and accountancies are common in most immigrant communities. Such businesses frequently perform a myriad of functions far above the simple provision of legal aid or travel information and reservations. As Hendricks noted in his study of Dominicans in New York City:

20   THROUGH THE EYE OF THE NEEDLE

the typical [Dominican] travel agency encompasses a host of activities which, super-ficially, at least, seem unrelated to the travel business. A typical travel agency has available translations, notary public, income tax preparation, driving instruction, real estate and rental information, foreign Spanish language periodicals, the sale of money orders, and importantly, help in the preparation of immigrant forms.[2]

To a large extent, these services are confidential, unfamiliar, and unin-telligible to the newcomer unaccustomed to American bureaucratic pro-cedures. In some cases, they may impinge on the often dubious legal status of the immigrant and his family. Whichever the case, trust is an important component of the service, and the need for trust pulls the newcomer toward a business owner of common ethnic background. To this tendency may be added a factor common to many of the societies from which the immigrants come, that is, a preference for personalistic relationships over reliance on impersonal, formal procedures; this further increases the clientele of those businesses that specialize in adjustment problems.[3]

   If immigrant business stays limited to the ethnic market, its potential for growth is sharply circumscribed, as Howard Aldrich has shown in his stud-ies of white, black, and Puerto Rican businesses in the United States and (in research conducted with Cater, Jones, and McEvoy) of Indian and white businesses in the United Kingdom. The obstacle to growth is the ethnic market itself, which can support only a restricted number of businesses, both because it is quantitatively small and because the ethnic population is too impoverished to provide sufficient buying power. Moreover, the environ-ment confronting the ethnic entrepreneur is severe: because exclusion from job opportunities leads many immigrants to seek out business opportunities, business conditions in the ethnic market tend toward a proliferation of small units, overcompetition, and a high failure rate—with the surviving busi-nesses generating scanty returns for their owners.[4]

   These conclusions may be too pessimistic in at least two respects, how-ever. First, not all immigrant communities have enjoyed so few economic resources as blacks and Puerto Ricans in the United States and East Indians in the United Kingdom. One case in point is that of New York's Jewish community in the 1920s. As Jews moved into the lower-middle and middle classes they also dispersed from the tenement districts of the Lower East Side; their search for better housing created a market for Jewish builders who evaded restrictive covenants by constructing new housing and then recruiting Jewish tenants. While the real estate and construction firms that grew up in the 1920s have since extended far beyond the confines of the ethnic market, the initial demand for housing provided the platform from which later expansion could begin. Quite the same process is being played out in New York's Asian communities today, where the housing needs of the growing Asian middle class have attracted Asian capital and stimulated the emergence of an Asian real estate industry.[5]

The immigrant market may also serve as an export platform from which ethnic firms can expand. For example, Greeks started out in the restaurant trade serving co-ethnics looking for inexpensive meals in a familiar environment. This original clientele provided a base from which the first generation of immigrant restaurateurs could branch out. More importantly, the immigrant trade established a pool of skilled and managerial talent that eventually enabled Greek owners to penetrate beyond the narrow confines of the ethnic market and specialize in the provision of "American food."[6] In the 1980s Dominican and Colombian immigrants active in the construction-contracting business in New York City appear to be playing out a similar development. Most of these immigrant business owners are engaged in additions- and-alterations work for an immigrant clientele; what leads these immigrant customers to patronize co-ethnics is not so much a search for savings as a preference for reliability, vouchsafed for by the immigrant contractor's reputation in the community to which he is linked. These initial jobs are important in two respects: they are small and therefore allow immigrants to start out at a relatively low level; in addition, the ethnic demand has supported immigrant contractors in assembling a skilled labor force and gaining efficiency and expertise, qualities that are gradually allowing them to edge out into the broader market.[7]

These examples notwithstanding, Aldrich's strictures still hold: the growth potential of immigrant business hinges on its access to customers beyond the ethnic community. The crucial question, then, concerns the type of market processes that might support neophyte immigrant capitalists. It is to that issue to which we presently turn.

Immigrant Business in the Open Market. As I noted earlier, the structure of industry is a powerful constraint on the creation of new business organizations; in that part of the economic world dominated by the demand for standardized products, scale economies, high absolute costs, and product differentiation bar the paths of entry to new immigrant concerns. But there are certain products or services where the techniques of mass production and mass distribution do not pertain. It is in these markets—those that are

22   THROUGH THE EYE OF THE NEEDLE

most often affected by uncertainty or differentiation or that are relatively small in size—where the immigrant firm is likely to emerge. Consider the cases that follow:

Low economies of scale. As an industry where the entrepreneur is likely to be his or her own boss and nothing but that, the taxi industry illustrates one path of immigrant entry into small business. The passenger alighting in Washington, D.C., is likely to step into a cab operated by an African or a West Indian; in Los Angeles, Jewish refugees from Russia are more likely to be sitting behind the wheel; in New York one finds both Africans and Russian Jews as well as Israelis and a host of other immigrants.[8]

Immigrant concentration in this field is a result of the cost structure of the taxi industry and the barriers it presents to the realization of economies of scale. Economies of scale arise when the fixed costs of any operation can be spread over larger units, as a consequence of which the average cost per unit declines. However, the importance of economies of scale depends, in part, on the ratio of fixed to variable costs.

What is distinctive about the taxi industry is that none of the most crucial cost components—wages, benefits, and gasoline—are fixed; rather, they vary directly with the number of vehicles. Consequently, the ability of the taxi operator to lower costs by building up a fleet of taxis is highly constrained. The owner of two or possibly three taxis achieves the greatest possible scale economies; by contrast, a fleet of, say, twenty to thirty cars operates at essentially the same costs as the owner-operator of a single cab. Though scale economies at the firm level are thus negligible, one can attain sizable reductions in fixed costs by keeping the vehicle under the wheel for a longer period of time. One possibility is to hire operators to keep the cab busy for two shifts and possibly more. But an alternative exists if there is a supply of owner-operators amenable to self-exploitation, in which case working long hours results in the same economies of scale. As I shall argue in a later section, immigrants' restricted opportunities will make them more likely to work long hours than natives; hence the taxi field is one in which immigrant business has grown because the characteristics of this industry are congruent with immigrants' economic orientations.[9]

Instability and uncertainty. The basic notion of economies of scale, as noted above, associates declining average unit costs with increases in the number of goods produced. However, the length of time over which the flow of output will be maintained is an equally crucial factor. Where demand is unstable, investment in fixed capital and plant is likely to be endangered. And if product requirements change frequently, the learning curve is low, since there is little time for workers to build up specialized proficiencies. Hence, when demand is subject to flux, versatility is preferable to specialization, and smaller units gain advantages over large ones.[10]

As Michael Piore has argued in his studies of economic dualism, industrial segmentation arises when demand falls into stable and unstable portions, and the two components can be separated out from one another. Where these conditions hold, one can expect an industry to be segmented into two branches: one, dominated by larger firms, that handles staple products; and a second, composed of small-scale firms, that caters to the unpredictable and/or fluctuating portion of demand. The consequence of this type of segmentation is that the two branches tend to be noncompeting; hence, where segmentation arises, it offers a sheltered position to small firms of the type that immigrants might establish.[11]

Such is likely to be the case in the garment industry. Some clothing products fall into the staple category, in which case they can almost be worn year in, year out. At the other end of the spectrum there are products whose existence is virtually ephemeral—for example, a bridal gown, which even in today's world is unlikely to be worn more than once. To be sure, most items of clothing have greater longevity than a bridal gown, but the nature of fashion is such that a dress or blouse sooner rather than later becomes out of date. Clothing purchases are also prone to various forces whose effects are often difficult to project: seasonality is one such factor (if winter is delayed, one postpones buying a coat until next year), and the overall state of the economy is another source of uncertainty (spending on fashion goods rises when one's pocket is full and falls when there is barely enough for necessities). The point is that these product-market conditions are correlated with particular types of production technology and organization: staple products involve long production runs and can be handled and merchandised by large, bureaucratized firms; those same technological and organizational features are much less suited to product markets prone to instability and unpredictable changes; consequently, these markets offer a suitable environment for small immigrant firms.

The importance of segmentation processes and their implications for immigrant business are evidenced in another industry with characteristics similar to garments—construction. One case in point is Carmenza Gallo's

24 THROUGH THE EYE OF THE NEEDLE

study of construction businesses in New York City, which shows that the building trades have provided the staging ground for new immigrant firms that specialize in residential-and-renovation work. The reason for this development is that competition with larger, native firms for the residential-and-renovation market is limited. Large construction firms dominate the market for commercial and institutional building, where the projects are large and the lead times long; by contrast, small firms predominate in the highly volatile residential and renovation sectors where the demand is highly fragmented and the dollar value of contracts is considerably smaller.[12]

Small or differentiated markets. Still another environment favorable to small immigrant firms is one in which the market is too small or too differentiated to support the large centralized structures needed for mass production or distribution. One such example is the retail grocery industry in New York City, where the structure of the market is unfavorable to the large supermarket chains that dominate the industry nationally. One crucial reason for the weakness of the chains is the complexity of the New York market, whose heterogeneous mix makes it a quagmire for national chains with cumbersome and rigid central administrations. While chains reduce distributing costs by carrying only a few basic product lines, servicing the tastes of New York's varied populace is more costly, since it requires a much more diversified line than is usually carried. Similarly, the chains attain economies of scale in overhead by centralizing administrative functions, but to ensure that ethnic tastes are efficiently serviced—for example, stocking Passover goods in stores located in Jewish neighborhoods but not in black neighborhoods or providing West Indian specialties in a Jamaican neighborhood but not in the nearby Dominican area—a shorter span of control is preferable.

Thus, not only are large-firm concentration shares lower in New York than elsewhere, but the national chains that dominate the industry in the rest of the country have ceded place instead to locally based chains whose territory is often limited to one or two of New York City's five boroughs. These local chains are sufficiently small to process information about New York's highly differentiated market segments and then service those needs appropriately. On the other hand, because they are relatively small, these local chains also lack the economies of scale needed to achieve significant market power, with the result that food retailing has been easily penetrated by smaller, ethnic concerns that compete with very considerable success against their larger counterparts.[13]

In conclusion, what distinguishes the variety of processes giving rise to immigrant business is an environment supportive of neophyte capitalists and the small concerns that they establish. Ethnic consumer tastes provide a protected market position, in part because the members of the community may have a cultural preference for dealing with co-ethnics, and in part because the costs of learning the specific wants and tastes of the immigrant groups are such as to discourage native firms from doing so, especially at an early stage when the community is small and not readily visible to outsiders. If the ethnic market allows the immigrant to maintain a business at somewhat higher-than-average costs, the other processes outlined above reduce the cost difference between native and immigrant firms. Low capital-to-labor ratios keep entry barriers low, and consequently immigrant businesses should be most common in industries where this condition prevails. Where there are problems in substituting capital for labor because changes in demand might idle expensive machines, immigrant businesses with labor-intensive processes can operate close to the prevailing efficiencies. When small markets inhibit the realization of economies of scale, small firms can achieve efficiencies close to, or better than, their large competitors and without the heavy overhead and administrative costs that the latter must shoulder.

A second characteristic of all those industries supportive of immigrant firms is that the technical barriers to entry are also low. The best example is taxis where the essential skill—driving—is one that almost everybody has. As one Russian taxi driver pointed out, entry into other fields is barred because "we have lack of communication, knowledge of law, and so on," whereas in the taxi business one can "make a living without a lot of knowledge of the industry."[14] But, in most industries, a more specific skill is required, and thus the crucial factor is whether the would-be entrepreneur can pick up the needed business know-how while still an employee. One case in point is the rehabilitation-and-renovations sector in construction: not only are jobs smaller in size, but fewer master construction skills are needed, making on-the-job training easier to obtain. A similar situation applies in another province of immigrant businesses—restaurants—where the hierarchy of skills ranges from dishwashers at the bottom to cooks at the top. Although one way of going to the top in this industry is going to a culinary school, a newcomer can also move up through observation and learning through doing: today a dishwasher, tomorrow a sandwich man; eventually, a cook.[15]

All three product-market conditions that favor small-scale enterprise— low capital-to-labor ratios, unstable product demand, and small markets— characterize the garment industry. In contrast to the rest of manufacturing,

26 THROUGH THE EYE OF THE NEEDLE

garments remains an industry where much of the labor force works in small firms; whereas only a quarter of all manufacturing workers are to be found in firms of 100 or less, clothing firms of this size contain almost half the industry's workers. Not only is average establishment size in this industry small (45 workers), but it is smaller still in the urban fashion-market centers where immigrant firms are concentrated: an average of 29 workers per establishment in New York, 26 in Los Angeles, and 21 in Miami. As an industry of small firms, apparel is also an industry where relatively little capital investment is required. Average assets per employee in the women's outerwear branch, for example, are one ninth of the level of capital investments per worker in all manufacturing industries. Because so little capital is used, the skill requirements demanded of a clothing worker are quite high; but in large measure these are also the skills required to run a garment business, and they are such that the immigrant worker can acquire them on the job.[16]

Another factor conducive to immigrant business is that the garment industry is really a conglomeration of a variety of small markets. Men's and women's clothing are distinctive industries unto themselves; within the women's branch, barriers separate the various industries—dresses and coats, blouses and sportswear, undergarments and children's wear. As evidence, specialization ratios, which measure the percent of a firm's products sold in its primary product area, tend to be very high: 94 percent in women's dresses, the high for all subindustries in the women's apparel sector; 75 percent for women's coats and suits, the lowest for all of the women's apparel subindustries. Even these ratios understate the level of specialization, since each broad product category is in turn stratified by price-line and styling characteristics. Thus, the garment industry remains the immigrant industry par excellence, and what we learn from the conditions under which immigrant garment firms have arisen should apply to the other economic fields in which immigrant capitalists have thrived.[17]

Access to Ownership

Given the existence of markets conducive to small business, the would-be immigrant capitalist still needs access to ownership opportunities. At the turn of the century, rapid economic growth created new industries, allowing immigrants to take up business activities without substantial competition from, or displacement of, natives. In fact, the garment industry offers the classic illustration of this process. As we shall see at greater length in

Chapter 3, the garment industry became immigrant-dominated because the massive tide of Italian and Jewish immigration to New York occurred just when the demand for factory-made clothing began to surge. But in the late-twentieth-century U.S. economy, growth proceeds more slowly; there are fewer opportunities for self-employment; and, until recently, the ranks of the self-employed have been diminishing. Thus, the conditions of immigrants' access to ownership positions largely depend on the extent to which natives are vying with immigrants for the available entrepreneurial slots. If these positions are coveted by natives and immigrants, then natives should capture a disproportionate share. But if the supply of native owners is leaking out of a small business industry, then immigrants may take up ownership activities in response to a replacement demand.[18]

Consider how such a replacement demand might arise for the new immigrants who have arrived in U.S. cities since the liberalization of immigration laws in 1965. In most large cities, the small business sector has been a concentration of European immigrants and their later-generation descendants. The year 1970 is the last date for which we have information for both the immigrant and the foreign-stock populations; at that time the proportion of all self-employed persons in the five largest SMSAs (Standard Metropolitan Statistical Areas) who were first- and second-generation European ethnics ranged from a high of 57 percent in New York to a low of 30 percent in Los Angeles. Both immigrants and the foreign stock were overrepresented among the self-employed in all five SMSAs; but in all five cases rates of self-employment were lower in the second than in the first generation. Thus, for European ethnic groups, their initial placement in small business was already giving way to a pattern more squarely based in salaried employment as of 1970. All the evidence suggests that this trend has since continued apace.[19]

This drift away from independent business activities is exemplified by the case of the Jews. Jews migrating from eastern Europe at the turn of the century moved heavily into small business for a variety of historical reasons: their arrival coincided with the massive expansion of small business industries; this expansion made it possible for them to utilize previously acquired entrepreneurial skills and habits and also to pursue a culturally and religiously induced preference for independence and separation; finally, the tendency to concentrate in business was reinforced by discrimination, which at the upper-white-collar level persisted well into the 1960s.[20] Assimilation, occupational advancement, and the dwindling of corporate discrimination, however, have now diluted the Jewish concentration in small business:

28   THROUGH THE EYE OF THE NEEDLE

"Jewish immigrants arrived in the big cities and took jobs as skilled workers and very small entrepreneurs; their children began to professionalize and establish themselves as white-collar workers or in more lucrative and stable businesses than those of the prior generation; and the immigrants' grandchildren competed successfully for the most desirable educational and occupational positions."[21] A variety of sources documents this shift out of small businesses. Analysis of the 1965 and 1975 Boston Jewish Community Surveys found that "while almost a quarter (23 percent) of the 1965 heads of households were self-employed outside the professions, only one in seven (14 percent) were so employed in 1975"; moreover, the ratio of business owners was higher for almost all age cohorts in 1965 than was the case in 1975.[22] Similarly, the 1981 New York Area Jewish Population Survey found consistently declining rates of self-employment from first generation to third, with much higher levels of education in the latter generation suggesting that much of its self-employment was concentrated in the professions rather than in business.[23] Finally, results from a study that examined Jews as well as a variety of Catholic ethnic groups in Rhode Island in the late 1960s, (French-Canadians, Irish, Italians, and Portuguese) show that "without exception the level of self-employment of fathers was higher than the level of self-employment of sons and the proportion of fathers of the oldest cohort who are self-employed is higher than that of fathers of the youngest cohort."[24]

As the occupational assimilation of the European ethnic population proceeds, it alters patterns of recruitment into small business. Just how this process is being played out is illustrated by a 1983 study of over 1,000 New York-area small businesses whose annual sales ranged from $500,000 to $5 million. On the one hand, the owners interviewed for this study foresaw considerable growth prospects for their businesses and expressed satisfaction with the business careers they had pursued: 55 percent said that they were "very optimistic" about their business' ability to succeed in the 1980s; 36 percent expected to create new positions within the next 12 months; 91 percent said they would choose to go into their own business if they had to do it all over again. On the other hand, these expressions of optimism and commitment were offset by a note of ambivalence regarding the businesses' future as family concerns. Only a fifth of the owners wanted their children to go into their own businesses; still fewer wanted their children to start up another business; and in considering their children's employment possibilities, the owners preferred that their children work for large rather than small concerns.

How this ambivalence affects recruitment patterns cannot be directly determined from this survey, but the data collected do show that the pool of talent entering small business has diminished. One indicator is that few new business start-ups have taken place: of the 1,057 businesses surveyed, only 9 percent had been formed between 1974 and 1983, with an additional 10 percent dating from the previous decade. Not only were there few new businesses among this group, but the small business population had greatly aged: with 52 percent of the owners surveyed 51 or older, and only 16 percent younger than 35, it appeared that few heirs were taking over these family businesses.[25] Further evidence of small business' dwindling ability to secure new recruits through established channels is attested by another study conducted in the early 1980s, focusing on 450 New York City manufacturing firms. While the results of this study pointed to the "basic vitality of most of the city's small industrial enterprises," another finding was that many otherwise viable concerns were going out of business for a variety of reasons, including sale of a small business to a large corporation, which then no longer sought to maintain the facility. A more frequent cause of business death, however, was the problem of succession:

Most often . . . small, profitable family-owned firms were closing because the owners were retiring and there were no potential buyers or family members interested in taking over the reins. We identified about 50 firms in just such a situation (out of a total of 450).[26]

What happens when a group falters in its recruitment to small business?—as is the case in New York, where the process of occupational assimilation has reduced the supply of potential business owners from the European ethnic groups that historically spawned the bulk of small entrepreneurs. One consequence is that a group's share of the small business sector inevitably declines, if for no other reason than the appallingly high death rate to which all small businesses are prone. David Birch's studies, for example, have shown that 8 percent of all firms in U.S. metropolitan areas are lost each year, which means that half of all firms in any area must be replaced every five years for the area simply to break even. For small firms and for new businesses the failure rates are higher still; indeed, the majority of new businesses do not last longer than four years.[27] Thus, as European ethnics seek out salaried employment as part of their shift toward higher positions in the social structure they are also setting up a vacancy chain. As older ethnic firms either go out of business or fail to transfer ownership to the next

30 THROUGH THE EYE OF THE NEEDLE

generation, replacement opportunities for immigrant entrepreneurs should naturally arise.

But whether immigrants are poised to take over these positions depends largely on the economic entry barriers, the nature of which I discussed in the previous section. Where those barriers are low—because capital requirements are few, optimal firm size is small, and most activities are labor-intensive—ethnic succession can be expected to take place. Just such a case is provided by the proliferation of Korean fruit-and-vegetable stores in New York City, starting in the early 1970s. As Illsoo Kim explains in his book, *The New Urban Immigrants:*

The majority of Korean retail shops . . . cater to blacks and other minorities by being located in "transitional areas" where old Jewish, Irish, and Italian shopkeepers are moving or dying out and being replaced by an increasing number of the new minorities. . . . Korean immigrants are able to buy shops from white minority shopkeepers, especially Jews, because the second- or third-generation children of these older immigrants have already entered the mainstream of the American occupational structure, and so they are reluctant to take over their parents' business. In fact, established Korean shopkeepers have advised less experienced Korean businessmen that "the prospect is very good if you buy a store in a good location from old Jewish people."[28]

One other important aspect of this retail case is that succession took place in a patterned way: while the most competitive, lower-status fields were abandoned, higher-profit, higher barrier-to-entry lines retained traditional ethnic entrepreneurs. Thus, while grocery-store ownership has passed from Jews and Italians to Koreans, the wholesalers and food processors that supply these new ethnic concerns remain almost wholly dominated by older entrepreneurial groups. This phenomenon is further indication of how economic opportunity structures condition the growth contours of an immigrant economy. But it also discloses that growth proceeds more rapidly if there is complementarity, rather than competition, between new and old small business groups. With competition, natives might seek to inhibit business growth among newcomers; and given natives' greater resources, the likelihood is good that they might achieve some measure of success. But if newcomers and old-timers are complementary, the thrust toward ethnic protectionism subsides; rather than attempting to quell business growth among the newcomers, the established groups, which benefit from their patronage, will be more likely to respond in an adaptive way.[29]

Predispositions Toward Entrepreneurship

Thus far, I have argued that there are two preconditions for the development of immigrant business: a niche in which the small business can viably function and access to ownership positions. But if there is a demand for small business activities, why do immigrants tend to emerge as the replacement group? My answer to this question is that immigrants are predisposed toward business and that they also can draw on informal ethnic resources that give them a competitive edge. In arguing this first point, I am drawing on the cultural approach; my contention about the importance of ethnic resources is distinctive in that I emphasize the fit between the immigrant firm and the environment in which it functions.

The reasons why immigrants emerge as a replacement group rest on a complex of interacting economic and psychological factors. Blocked mobility is a powerful spur to business activity. Immigrants suffer from a variety of impediments in the labor market: poor English-language facility, inadequate or inappropriate skills, age, and discrimination. Lacking the same opportunities for stable career employments as natives, immigrants are more likely to strike out on their own and to experience less aversion to the substantial risks that this course entails.[30] The limited range of job- and income-generating activities also spurs immigrants to acquire business skills. Native workers will tend not to acquire particular skills if the returns to the needed investment in education and training are lower than those for comparable jobs; by contrast, the same skills might offer the immigrants the best return, precisely because they lack access to better remunerated jobs. As Thomas Bailey has shown, this is one reason for the prevalence of immigrants in the restaurant industry, where managerial and skilled (cooking) jobs offer lower returns to investment in training than other comparable, skilled and mangerial jobs.[31] Immigrants' willingness to put in long hours—needed to capitalize a business or to maintain economies of scale—is similarly conditioned. For those without access to jobs with high rates of hourly return, such activities as driving a cab or running a store from early morning to late night offer the best available rewards for their work effort.

There are also psychological components to the entry of immigrants into small business. Much of the sociological literature has characterized the small business owner as an anachronistic type impelled by a need for autonomy and independence.[32] Auster and Aldrich note that this approach assumes that entrepreneurship reflects the decisions of isolated individuals and thus ignores the issue of why certain groups disproportionately channel

32 THROUGH THE EYE OF THE NEEDLE

new recruits into small business. Moreover, the traditional perspective also fails to account for the social pressures that condition groups and individuals for small business activity, among which the immigration process itself should be counted.[33]

The principal conditioning factor is the immigration experience itself. The process of leaving one's home to take up life in a new society is self-selective: the workers who enter the immigration stream tend to be more able, better prepared and more inclined toward risk than those who stay home. These same characteristics also give immigrants an advantage in competition with native groups in the low-wage labor market, against whom they compare favorably in terms of motivation, risk propensity, and an ability to adjust to change.[34]

Of equal importance, the immigrants' social origins alter the way in which they size up the chances of getting ahead. Michael Piore has suggested that immigrants have a more favorable view of low-level work than do natives because the migrants perceive their job's status in terms of the much-different job hierarchy of their home society.[35] Quite the same disparity would give the immigrant a distinctive frame of reference from which to assess the attractiveness of small business opportunities that open up as previously incumbent groups move on to other pursuits. Thus a young black or Puerto Rican aspiring to work as a manager behind the desk in a clean, air-conditioned bank might well look askance at the idea of taking over the candy store or grimy factory that goes vacant when its Jewish or Italian owner finally retires. Not so the immigrant, moved less by concern with unpleasant working conditions and impelled by status considerations of a different sort. In the newcomer's eyes, rather, taking over a petty proprietorship is likely to be a positive alternative to working for someone else and what is more, the best chance of getting ahead.[36]

Ethnicity as Resource. There are various dimensions to ethnicity—a common set of values and beliefs; a sense of shared identity; an interest in, or concern for, an ancestral homeland. My concern here is more with what might be called the subcultural dimension of ethnicity; that is to say, the social structures that attach members of an ethnic group to one another and the ways in which those social structures are used. These social structures consist, broadly speaking, of two parts: (1) the networks of kinship and friendship around which ethnic communities are arranged; and (2) the interlacing of these networks with positions in the economy (jobs), in space (housing), and in civil society (institutions). Migration itself takes place under the auspices of these social structures. Information about the host society (true or misleading) is transmitted through communication or personal interaction between the migrant and his or her home community, and the picture portrayed by the migrant prompts yet another native to take his chances abroad. A similar chain of events conditions the process of settlement: once arrived in the new society, who does one turn to but those friends or relatives already situated with a home and a job? To be sure, home and job are not quite as glittering as the newcomer had imagined or the settler had promised, but importantly, the settler's neighborhood is home to other compatriots, and his job is one of many similar positions where other immigrants work. Because of a preference for familiarity, the efficiency of personal contacts, and social distance from the host society's institutions of assistance, the immigrant relies on connections with settlers to find shelter and work and thus finds himself in the ethnic occupational-and-residential ghetto. Should this process repeat itself time and again, two consequences ensue. First, intense interaction within a common milieu intensifies the feeling of commonality and membership within the group. Second, there is the buildup of that critical mass needed for formal ethnic institutions—a church, a mutual aid society, perhaps a trade union, maybe a political club—which in turn serve to reinforce ethnic identity.[37]

Thus far, this is a familiar, though greatly simplified story; however, we will use it to extract several less familiar lessons. The first is that immigrants may be vulnerable and oppressed, but, because they can draw on connections of mutuality and support, they can also create resources that counteract the harshness of the environment they encounter. The second is that the social structures of the immigrant community breed organizations, both informal and formal, in a context that might otherwise tend toward anomie. The third lesson, of particular importance to the discussion that follows, is that such informal organizational resources might give immigrants an advantage against natives should the institutionalized arrangements that normally connect individuals with organizations be undeveloped and/or malfunctioning.

Now let us consider the ways in which workers are attached to jobs in small business industries and the mechanisms by which the rules of the small firm are established. The labor market in small business industries tends to be unstructured in that it contains "few, if any established institutions by means of which people obtain information, move into and out of

34   THROUGH THE EYE OF THE NEEDLE

jobs, qualify for advances in rank or pay, or identify themselves with any type of organization . . . for purposes of security or support."[38] The reasons why stable labor-market arrangements are undeveloped are various. In some instances, these conditions hold because the job is inherently temporary, as in the case of longshoring where workers are shaped up and form a work gang to unload a ship, only to return to the external labor market. In other cases, it is because skills are sufficiently general that they can be carried from one firm to another—as is the case in construction—and therefore, firms are reluctant to make an investment in training that will redound to another firm's gain. In other instances, as in the shoe industry, the firm will have a bimodal rather than a continuous distribution of skills, and the gap between the skilled and the unskilled positions is too great for on-the-job training to take place. And in all these cases, a problem is that small business industries are intensely competitive and that competition places a limit on firm size and thereby on the articulation of structured job ladders.[39]

Since small firms therefore rely on the external labor market, a chief problem is how to secure and maintain a trained labor force. One option is to lower skill levels so that the costs of training can be drastically reduced; this is the path that many small, low-wage employers in the "secondary labor market" have apparently pursued. As Piore has argued, jobs in the secondary sector "are essentially unskilled, either requiring no skill at all, or utilizing basic human skills and capacities shared by virtually all adult workers."[40] One case in point is that of the fast-food restaurant where the worker has been converted into an assembler and packer whose skills can be learned in a matter of hours.[41]

What the fast-food case also shows is that de-skilling is an alternative only when demand is standardized and tasks can then be broken down into repetitive components. However, this is the definition of mass production, and many small businesses arise in niches where specialty, not mass production, is required. One such example is construction, where new buildings are often custom-made jobs; another is the fashion segment of the apparel industry, where only small batches of highly varying products are made. In industries like these, where specialty work prevails, jobs involve a variety of tasks; the ability to adjust to changing job requirements and perform them with proficiency is precisely what is meant by skill.

Thus, the central issue confronting small firms is how to increase the probability of hiring workers who are capable of learning required skills and will remain with the firm and apply their skills there. "Hiring," as Spence has put it, "is investing under uncertainty." The problem is that the employer "is uncertain about the productive capabilities of the job applicant" prior to hiring and even for some time after the hiring decision has been made.[42] One recruitment practice widely favored in industry, precisely because it reduces this uncertainty, is to recruit through "word-of-mouth" techniques. When employers recruit by "word-of-mouth" the workers they hire tend to have the same characteristics as those friends or relatives who recommend them; employees concerned about their future tenure in the plant are unlikely to nominate "bad prospects"; and finally, new hires recruited through the recommendations of workers already employed are likely to be subject to the informal control of their associates once they are placed on the job.[43]

Consider now the possibilities in an industry like clothing or restaurants or construction, where nonimmigrants and immigrants both own firms, but the first group recruits a heterogeneous pool of workers, all of different ethnicities, while the second recruits primarily through ethnic networks. The logic of word-of-mouth recruitment is that applicants resemble the existing labor force; but, in the first case, social distance between native employer and immigrant employee makes it difficult to accurately discern the characteristics of the incumbent workers. As an example, many native employers have but the vaguest impressions of the national origins of their workers; thus, if one asks a native factory owner whether his Hispanic workers are Puerto Rican or Dominican, the answer is likely to be: "How do I know? They all speak Spanish. They're from the islands, somewhere." Furthermore, the presumption of trust inherent in the process of assembling a skilled work force through word-of-mouth recruitment is frequently weak or absent under the conditions that seem prevalent in industries that employ large numbers of immigrants and minorities. For example, personnel managers of supermarkets and department stores whom I interviewed as part of a study of youth employment complained most vehemently about the high level of theft among the largely minority, inner-city youth hired to work in their stores. "The behavior of youth is impossible," noted one personnel manager in a typical comment. "The kids steal, they eat food in the store, and they give food to their friends and relatives."[44] This recalls Elliot Liebow's finding that stealing from employers was a prevalent practice among the black street-corner men that he studied, but so was the assumption among employers that their workers would steal, resulting in a consequent reduction in the level of pay.[45]

36 THROUGH THE EYE OF THE NEEDLE

Trust is further weakened when ethnic differences separate workers from employers. In some cases, this is due to stereotyping on the part of immigrant labor and native management alike—a matter to which I shall return in greater detail below. But it may also be the case that the situational constraints provide little room for trust to develop. For instance, many immigrants in an industry like garments work under assumed names, thus making their very identity uncertain. Similarly, a work force may be prone to high levels of turnover—which may occur because of seasonality or because of frequent travel or return migration to the immigrants' home societies. Whatever the cause, high turnover will hinder the development of stable relationships on which trust might be based. A firm with high turnover is also apt to be caught in a vicious circle, since the costs of constantly hiring make it uneconomical to exercise much discretion over the recruitment process.

Now take by contrast the immigrant firm. Immigrant owners can mobilize direct connections to the ethnic community from which they come in order to recruit an attached labor force. One means of securing a labor force is to recruit family members; because the characteristics of kin, unlike those of strangers, are known and familiar their behavior is more likely to be predictable, if not reliable; furthermore, trust may already inhere in the family relationship. Thus, Korean greengrocers tend to employ family members or other close relatives in the hope of "eradicating 'inside enemies'—non-Korean employees who steal cash and goods or give away goods to their friends or relatives who visit the store as customers," probably a better solution to the problem of "inventory shrinkage" than any policy that nonimmigrant retailers have devised.[46]

Of course, while some ethnic businesses may pivot around nuclear or perhaps extended-family relationships, the average size of many businesses makes it necessary to recruit beyond the family orbit. Still, kin can be used to secure key positions. Moreover, immigrants can also hire through other closely knit networks that will bring them into contact with other ethnics to whom they are tied by preexisting social connections. For example, migration chains that often link communities in the Dominican Republic to Dominicans in New York can funnel new arrivals into ethnically dominated workplaces and immigrant-owned firms. Similarly, Chinese immigrants may gravitate toward immigrant owners who speak the same dialect as they—and thus a Toisanese-speaking newcomer may opt for a Toisanese-speaking owner as against one who only speaks Cantonese. Moreover, trust may be heightened if an immigrant culture contains mechanisms for transforming friendship relations into fictive kinship relations. For example, *compradazgo* (godparenthood) relationships between a child and godparents and between the parents and godparents are common to many Latin American societies and are seen as functional equivalents to kinship relationships. Similar relationships of fictive kinship are constructed among the Chinese.[47]

Just as newcomers turn to settlers for help in job finding, new arrivals may first seek out work in an immigrant firm, which offers the attractions of a comfortable environment and more familiar customs. Thomas Bailey, for example, reports that many immigrant restaurants in New York act as way stations for newly landed immigrants. It is commonly noted that the advantage of hiring such newcomers is that their dependence makes them likely to accept conditions with docility; but it is also the case that owners will be more likely to place trust in someone who depends on them.[48]

Ethnicity might also serve as a mechanism for mediating the strains in the workplace and providing the normative basis on which the rules of the workplace might be established. In the literature there are two conflicting descriptions of the industrial relations environment of the small firm. On the one hand, researchers working in the dual labor-market framework have argued that the small firm is riven by antagonism: supervision is tyrannical and capricious; there are no formal grievance procedures through which workers can seek redress for their complaints; and management and workers are caught in a vicious circle in which workers respond to the harsh exercise of discipline with further insubordination.[49] On the other hand, research investigating the "size effect" indicates that small firms garner favorable ratings when checked against large concerns on turnover levels, propensity to strike, job satisfaction, and a variety of other indicators.[50]

If size per se is unlikely to yield a particular industrial relations environment, these contrasting findings suggest that industrial relations outcomes are the product of the interaction of size with other factors. Compare the small concern with the large business, which is governed not only by a web of formal rules (promulgated by management or negotiated through collective agreements with unions) but also by informal understandings about how tasks are to be performed and jobs are to be allocated. Such understandings originate on the plant floor because workers, if put into stable and constant contact with one another, tend to form communities with norms, expectations, and rules of their own. These rules are often contested by management, and in unionized settings, much of the bargaining appears to center on the scope and permanence of these rules. Yet, management tends to abide

38 THROUGH THE EYE OF THE NEEDLE

by central rules and to seek change on the margins. The reasons are twofold: first, workers have the economic power to punish management for breach of the customary workplace rules; second, management, especially at the lower levels, is socialized into the rules of the workplace as well and, to some extent, belongs to the work group itself.[51]

This being said, we can now assess the possible effects of ethnicity on industrial relations patterns in small firms. As I argued above, small firms where management and labor are ethnically distinctive have difficulty stabilizing the employment relationship. One consequence of their failure to do so is that turnover tends to be too rapid to permit the formation of social groups in which customary work norms might be embedded. Moreover, even where such groups take cohesive form, social distance between management and immigrant labor tends to preclude managerial acceptance of work-group norms. In part, this lack of acceptance is a consequence of ethnic behavioral patterns that are often so divergent that simple stylistic differences are perceived in deeply threatening ways. The conditions of duress that so often confront small firms (bottlenecks, short delivery deadlines, understaffing, etc.) further contribute to antagonism. Repeated conflict over production quotas, behavioral rules, absenteeism, and instability tends to take on an explicitly racial character as management interprets workers' behavior in racially stereotyped ways. And when immigrant or minority workers are employed by members of the majority group, the economic disparities between the two groups fuel discontent with wages, personnel policies, and general working conditions, making work just another instance of inequitable treatment.[52]

By contrast, ethnicity provides a common ground on which the rules of the immigrant workplace are to be negotiated. Above I argued that the social structures around which the immigrant firm is organized serve to stabilize the employment relationship. These social structures, however, are also relationships of meaning suffused with the expectations that actors have of one another. One consequence is that authority can be secured on the basis of personal loyalties and ethnic allegiance rather than on the basis of harsh discipline, driving, and direct-control techniques. Furthermore, ethnic commonality provides a repertoire of symbols and customs that can be invoked to underline cultural interests and similarities in the face of a potentially conflictual situation. Thus, Bernard Wong describes how immigrant entrepreneurs in New York's Chinatown use ethnic symbols and customs to bind outsiders to the firm:

The [restaurant's] labor boss does a great deal to promote efficiency and esprit de corps among the staff. . . . The spirit of brotherhood is deliberately cultivated. Everyone is expected to be fair with one another. The *Yi Hei* [trusting righteousness] is welcomed. In the kitchens of many restaurants, the portrait of the God of Justice, Gwaan Gung, hangs in a visible place. Some restaurants even have an altar of Gwaan Gung to remind everyone that they should be just to each other so that the deity will not be offended.[53]

But if ethnic commonality is a device for securing the immigrant worker's loyalty, the expectations bound up in the ethnic employment exchange impinge on the owner's lattitude as well. Immigrant workers can anticipate that standards of conduct prevailing in the broader ethnic community will extend to the workplace as well. For example, Harry Herman showed in his study of Macedonians in Toronto's restaurant trade that the egalitarian traditions of Macedonia carried over into the immigrant restaurants where workers and owners regarded one another as equals. Similarly, the terms under which immigrant owners obtain kin or hometown friends as laborers may also include an understanding that the employment relationship is meant to be reciprocal. In return for the immigrant worker's effort and constancy, the immigrant owner may be expected to make a place for newly arrived relatives, to accommodate work rules to employees' personal needs, and to assist workers with problems that they encounter with the host society or else lose his labor to a competing employer.[54]

Differences among Immigrant Groups

Thus far, I have sought to explain why immigrants are overrepresented in self-employment, but one major question remains: why do some immigrants do better in business than others? The historical record shows considerable disparities in self-employment among the various European immigrant populations: Jews, for example, were far more successful in business than were the Irish, and Italians achieved higher rates of self-employment than did Poles. Similar differences hold for the newcomers who arrived in the United States between 1970 and 1980. According to the Census of Population, Koreans ranked first with 11.5 percent self-employed; lagging far behind were the Mexicans, among whom less than 2 percent worked for themselves.

Various explanations have been adduced for these differences. Let us briefly consider one widely accepted account. This hypothesis, a version of the cultural approaches surveyed in Chapter 1, suggests that high self-

40 THROUGH THE EYE OF THE NEEDLE

employment rates are largely a function of the skills acquired prior to migration and of previous exposure to an advanced market economy. One virtue of
the skills hypothesis is that it seems to do a nice job of explaining the
preponderance of Koreans among today's self-employed immigrants: Koreans
come with high levels of education (in 1980, 33 percent of the 1970–1980
newcomers reported having received a bachelor's degree); Korea is a rapidly
developing society whose competitive social system is in many ways akin to
that of the United States; and while Koreans have difficulty using their
formal and informal skills to gain entry into salaried professional and managerial positions, these same skills prove very useful in the competition for
small business positions.

The problem is that the situation of other immigrant groups does not fit
quite so neatly into the skills hypothesis. Koreans, it is true, report high
levels of education. Educational levels were considerably higher still among
Indians who came to the United States during the 1970s (63 percent of whom
reported having achieved a B.A.), yet Indians had less than half (43 percent)
of the self-employment rate of the less educated Koreans. The difference,
one might say, is that the Indians had the advantage of English-language
facility and therefore had fewer difficulties in getting jobs for which their
training qualified them, which might well be the case. But notice how
another factor has suddenly crept into the explanation and that, on conceptual grounds, language is almost certainly a component of skill. The difficulties become more grievous when one asks which group ranked number 2
among the self-employed. The answer is the Greeks, with 10.5 percent
working for themselves in 1980; but among this number 2 group, just over a
tenth of the 1970–1980 arrivals reported having a college education. The
problems are further compounded when one looks at the Chinese, similar to
the Koreans in educational background, exposure to industrialism, and
culture, and yet number 3 in the proportion working for themselves, with a
self-employment rate one half of the Koreans'. Of course, one could offer
various reasons for Greeks doing well despite their lower levels of education
and Chinese not doing as well as one might expect. However, the point of
this exercise is not to account for differences among particular immigrant
groups; rather it is to develop a general analytic framework. From this
perspective, what is wrong about the skills hypothesis is simply that it
is a single-factor explanation. The comparison among Koreans, Greeks,
Indians, and Chinese shows that a variety of factors impinge on the self-
employment process. Consequently, the most useful approach is multi-

variate, which implies that the terms of the interaction among the various factors is indeterminate. What one can do at an analytic level is to specify the variables that affect self-employment outcomes; it remains for empirical work to determine their effects on a case-by-case basis.[55]

In the broadest sense, one can separate out the conditions that influence the self-employment process into three categories: premigration characteristics; the circumstances of migration and their evolution; and postmigration characteristics. Under the former fall such attributes as skill, language, business experience, kinship patterns, and exposure to conditions (such as a high level of urbanization and industrialization) that would foster entrepreneurial attitudes. The circumstances of migration refer to the conditions under which the immigrants move, whether as temporary workers or as permanent settlers, as well as to the factors influencing their settlement type. Characteristics such as economic and occupational position, and discrimination (or the lack thereof) would fall under the postmigration rubric. It follows from the discussion above that no single characteristic—whether premigration or postmigration experience or circumstance of migration—will in and of itself determine the level of self-employment; rather, the critical factor will be how these various characteristics interact with another.

Premigration characteristics. The likelihood of succeeding in business is enhanced if an immigrant comes with skills that are useful to business success in both a general and a specific way. A good historical illustration is the case of turn-of-the-century Russian Jews who, by virtue of prior experience in tailoring, a high level of literacy, and a historical orientation toward trading, moved rapidly into entrepreneurial positions in the garment industry.[56] Since the educational level of the new immigrants is much higher than was true for the earlier immigrant waves, a considerable proportion do arrive with general skills that would be relevant for business success. As the comparison between Indians and Koreans suggested, it is not so much those immigrants with the highest or most developed general skills that will flock into business; rather, it is those whose general skills are not quite appropriate to the new context.

Relatively fewer immigrants arrive with skills that are specific to the business fields they enter. For example, New York's fur industry contains a high proportion of Greeks, both as workers and as owners, almost all of whom have come from the province of Kastoria where they were apprenticed as furriers at a relatively young age.[57] Yet the bulk of Greeks in business are

42   THROUGH THE EYE OF THE NEEDLE

active in the restaurant industry, and cooking is not a skill that most Greek males appear to have brought with them, especially when one considers that Greek restaurants mainly specialize in "American food"! Thus, the crucial issue is how skills are acquired upon arrival in the host society. One answer, which follows from our discussion of ethnicity as organizational resource, is that groups with strong informal networks will do better in transmitting skills to newcomers. However, it is also true that these informal networks are important because of the conditions in small business industries; hence, for all groups, positional factors will be an important influence on self-employment rates.

Circumstances of migration. Whether newcomers arrive as temporary migrants or as permanent settlers, migration scholars increasingly agree, is a crucial condition of mobility and integration into the host society. Michael Piore, in his aptly named book *Birds of Passage*, has argued that most labor migrations to industrial societies begin as movements of temporary workers. In Piore's view, the fact that workers see themselves as temporary migrants explains why they constitute a satisfactory work force for dead-end jobs that native workers reject: as long as the migrants maintain the expectation of return, their concern is with the accumulation of capital to be brought home and invested in a business or farm, not with the attainment of social mobility in the societies to which they have migrated. Piore's discussion of social mobility largely involves access to the structured job ladders of large organizations, rather than the attainment of business ownership. But his argument also suggests a framework for evaluating how the circumstances of migration will affect entrepreneurial success.[58]

Earlier I contended that immigrants' predisposition toward business arises out of a response to blocked mobility. A better formulation would take account of Piore's argument and note that the opportunities or obstacles to mobility are likely to lie in the eyes of the beholders. Hence, the same factors that condition temporary migrants for work in low-level, dead-end jobs will also dampen the frustration that spurs other immigrants to start up in business on their own. As long as migrants anticipate returning home, as long as their stint in the host society is punctuated by periodic trips home, as long as they evaluate success in terms of their original standard of living, they will continue to furnish a supply of low-level labor. But those same low-level jobs will be unacceptable to permanent settlers, whose ambitions extend to the positions occupied by natives as well as to the rewards generated by those positions. Consequently, blocked mobility will impinge more severely on settlers than on their counterparts among the birds of passage.

Permanence is also likely to add an edge to the settler's quest for opportunity: if one does not succeed, there is no going back. It is for these reasons that permanent immigrants, as Piore points out, have a "reputation for being more aggressive . . . than temporary migrant groups."[59] And thus the circumstances of migration breed an affinity with the requirements of entrepreneurial success: only the aggressive immigrant will be foolish or desperate enough to start up a business when anyone can observe how many new concerns fall victim to a quick but painful death.

In addition to influencing aspirations, the circumstances of migration are also likely to affect immigrants' behavior in a way that will condition the likelihood of setting up on their own. One characteristic of temporary migrants is that their settlement and work patterns are too haphazard and variable to promote the acquisition of needed business skills and are also disruptive of the informal networks that play such an important role in organizing the immigrant firm and its labor force. By contrast, we can expect permanent immigrants to be more deliberate in their quest for economic progress. One nice example of this is Philip Young's description of Korean greengrocers in New York and the foresight and planning with which they pursue their trade: they may spend months scouring the city for the best possible location, and often deliberately open stores next to supermarkets so as to capture part of the latter's walk-in trade.[60]

The alternative to this argument is the possibility proposed by Edna Bonacich—that immigrants who move as "sojourners" with a clear intention of returning home will opt for business over employment as the better way of rapidly accumulating a portable investment capital.[61] There are two major problems with this hypothesis. One is that setting up a business is a far riskier endeavor than working for someone else. If we assume that even the most entrepreneurial of sojourning immigrants begin as employees, it is likely that they will accumulate a nest egg that can either be safely banked for returning home, or it can be invested in a small business whose chance for success is always open to doubt. Faced with these options, the prudent sojourner is likely to keep on working for someone else, as Robin Ward has shown in a study of East Asian immigrants in Britain. Though Bonacich has argued that these East Asian immigrants illustrate the influence of sojourning on ethnic business activity, Ward's study shows that they are in fact more likely to prefer employment over business in areas where high wages are paid to those

44   THROUGH THE EYE OF THE NEEDLE

prepared to undertake hard and unpleasant work, resorting to business only in those cities where the available jobs are relatively poorly paid.[62]

Another condition of immigrant business activity is settlement pattern. Permanent immigrants usually either come with family or import immediate relatives shortly after settling; temporary immigrants leave family members at home. The consequence for temporary immigrants is that they must continue to funnel remittances that are needed to support relatives still living in the home country rather than use those monies to start up a business. As Kessner pointed out in his comparison of Italian and Jewish immigrants at the turn of the century, "the large sums of money sent back over the ocean to Europe drained [the Italians of] risk capital [for] investment and enterprise."[63]

Postmigration characteristics. Another factor that will exercise a strong effect on self-employment outcomes is a group's position in the economy. This factor follows from the argument made about opportunity structures, namely that certain environments are more supportive of small businesses than others. But the likelihood that immigrants will take advantage of these supportive conditions is greatest if immigrants are already concentrated in those industries where small business is the prevailing form. First, the motivation to go into business presupposes other conditions; for example, having some information about business opportunities that in turn can be used to assess the likelihood that one's efforts will be rewarded. Second, the neophyte capitalist will do better if he or she has some knowledge of the activities that the new role of ownership will entail; such knowledge is usually better if obtained at first hand rather than through indirect methods; and, as I have argued, one characteristic of those environments supportive of small business is precisely that the knowhow needed to run a business can be acquired through on-the-job training. Thus, immigrant groups concentrated in small business industries will have access to more and better information about small business opportunities and will also have more opportunities to acquire the relevant skills than those groups concentrated in industries where small businesses are not prevalent.

But emphasizing position begs the question of why groups occupy one position and not another. To some extent, this is a matter of prior skill; to some extent, purely random factors come into play, such as arriving at a time or place where small business industries generate a demand for immigrant labor. One important influence is the degree of native-language facility, and looking at the effects of language provides a good illustration of how pre- and postmigration experiences interact to affect self-employment outcomes. Immigrants who arrive in the United States with English-language facility have a broader range of employment opportunities than do those newcomers whose English is virtually nonexistent or barely serviceable; and, having a broader range of opportunities, such immigrants are more likely to find employment in industries where the organizational form tends to be large. One case in point is that of West Indians in New York, who are heavily concentrated in an industry dominated by large, bureaucratized organizations, namely, health care.[64] Once ensconsed in this environment, the next logical step is not to go out and set up one's own business. Rather, the mobility-minded immigrant might acquire course credits or a degree, enroll in the job-training program run jointly by union and management, or simply accumulate the seniority needed to move up the next rung in the job ladder. What is at work here is in part a simple reference-group phenomenon: people act on the basis of imitation and follow the norms set by their peers. But the decision to enroll in a job-training program rather than setting up one's own shop also appears as a rational decision: the hospital worker knows far more about how to move up in the hospital hierarchy than about how a business might be run. One further point is simply that positional advantages or disadvantages tend to cumulate. In the West Indian case, this means that new arrivals are more likely to seek out jobs in health care than in an industry where there are few West Indians—simply because the existing concentration of West Indians makes it much easier for newcomers to get a job. At the same time, continued concentration in hospitals means that few entrepreneurial role models are created; hence, the tendency to seek mobility through the structured career ladder of the health-care system is reinforced.

Even within a small business industry some occupations are more strategic than others in terms of providing an employee with exposure to the skills and contacts needed to start up a small business. In the garment industry, for example, the typical new manufacturing business is set up when a salesman and a textile cutter get together: the salesman has the necessary knowledge of the market, and the cutter knows the production side. In restaurants, as Thomas Bailey has pointed out, waiting is the logical occupational bridge to becoming a restaurateur: the waiter learns how to size up the customer, direct him or her to the appropriate choice, and then hustle the customer off when a new patron is ready to take the table.[65] In retailing,

46 THROUGH THE EYE OF THE NEEDLE

selling is also the point of departure for many employees who decide to start
up on their own. For prospective immigrant capitalists, the question is how
to gain access to these strategic occupations. This problem is particularly
serious because many of these occupations involve face-to-face interaction,
in which case natives' desire to maximize social distance from immigrants
will obstruct the latter's recruitment into these key positions. What is at
work is an instance of the principle of cumulative social advantage: immigrants belonging to a group whose characteristics favor business success will
also be more likely to be hired by co-ethnics and thereby gain access to
needed business skills. By contrast, those immigrants whose characteristics
are less conducive to entrepreneurship will be more likely to work for
natives, which in turn will reduce the likelihood of their gaining access to
strategic occupations.

Conclusion. This chapter developed an explanation for immigrant enterprise
that emphasized the interaction between the opportunity structure of the
host society and the social structure of the immigrant community. The demand for small business activities emanates from markets whose small size,
heterogeneity, or susceptibility to flux and instability limit the potential for
mass distribution and mass production. Since such conditions favor small-
scale enterprise, they lower the barriers to immigrants with limited capital
and technical resources. Opportunities for ownership result from the process of ethnic succession: vacancies for new business owners arise as the
older groups that have previously dominated small business activities move
into higher social positions. On the supply side, two factors promote recruitment into entrepreneurial positions. First, the situational constraints that
immigrants confront breed a predisposition toward small business and further encourage immigrants to engage in activities—such as working long
hours—that are needed to gain minimal efficiencies. Second, immigrant
firms can draw on their connections with a supply of family and ethnic labor
as well as a set of understandings about the appropriate behavior and expectations within the work setting to gain a competitive resolution to some of the
organizational problems of the small firm. While these factors lift the self-
employment rate of the overall immigrant population, levels of business
activity vary among specific immigrant groups. A group's success in attain-
ing business ownership is determined by three characteristics—its premigration experiences, the circumstances of its migration and settlement,

its postmigration experiences—and how these characteristics interact with one another.

The next two chapters focus on the garment industry itself, considering the broader economic processes operating within this industry that have created the opportunities for the new immigrant garment capitalists.

214 NOTES

Chapter 2

1. For the original formulation of the special-consumer-tastes argument, see Robert Kinzer and Edward Sagarin, *The Negro in American Business: The Conflict between Separatism and Integration* (New York: Greenburg, 1950); for a recent, quantitative assessment of the effects of culturally based tastes on business opportunities for immigrants and minorities, see Howard Aldrich et al., "Ethnic Residential Concentration and the Protected Market Hypothesis," *Social Forces* 63, no. 4 (June 1985):996–1009.

2. Glenn Hendricks, *The Dominican Diaspora* (New York: Teachers College Press, 1974), pp. 123–24.

3. Ibid., p. 124.

4. Howard Aldrich, "Ecological Succession in Racially Changing Neighborhoods: A Review of the Literature," *Urban Affairs Quarterly* 10 (1975):327–48; Howard Aldrich and Albert Reiss, Jr., "Continuities in the Study of Ecological Succession: Changes in the Race Composition of Neighborhoods and their Businesses," *American Journal of Sociology* 81 (1976):846–66; Howard Aldrich, John Cater, Trevor Jones, and Dave McEvoy, "From Periphery to Peripheral: The South Asian Petite Bourgeoisie in England," in I. H. Simpson and R. Simpson, eds., *Research in the Sociology of Work*, vol. 2 (Greenwich, Conn.: JAI Press, 1982).

5. Deborah Dash Moore, *At Home in America* (New York: Columbia University Press, 1981); Betty Liu Ebron, "Chinese-American Developers Poised to Smash Old Barriers," *Crain's New York Business*, September 9, 1985; Kirk Johnson, "Asians Galvanize Sales Activity in Flushing," *New York Times*, July 25, 1984, section 8, p. 1.

6. Theodore Saloutos, *The Greeks in the United States* (Cambridge: Harvard University Press, 1964).

7. Carmenza Gallo, "The Construction Industry in New York: Black and Immigrant Entrepreneurs," working paper, Conservation of Human Resources, Columbia University, 1983.

8. Marcia Freedman and Josef Korazim, "Self-Employment and the Decision to Emigrate: Israelis in New York City," *Contemporary Jewry*, vol. 7 (forthcoming); Raymond Russell, "Ethnic and Occupational Cultures in the New Taxi Cooperatives of Los Angeles," paper presented at the 77th Annual Meeting of the American Sociological Association, San Francisco, September 8–10, 1982.

9. Gorman Gilbert, "Operating Costs for Medallion Taxicabs in New York City," report prepared for the Mayor's Committee on Taxicab Regulatory Issues, New York City, October 1981; Edward G. Rogoff, "Regulation of the New York City Taxicab Industry," *City Almanac* vol. 15 (1980):1–9, 17–19.

10. E. A. G. Robinson, *The Structure of Competitive Industry* (Cambridge: Cambridge University Press, 1931); William Shepherd, *The Economics of Industrial Organization* (Englewood Cliffs, N.J.: Prentice-Hall, 1979).

11. Michael Piore, "The Technological Foundations of Dualism and Discontinuity," in Suzanne Berger and Michael Piore, *Dualism and Discontinuity in Industrial Society* (Cambridge: Cambridge University Press, 1980).

12. Gallo, "The Construction Industry."

13. This analysis is based on a case study of the grocery store industry prepared as part of a report on youth employment for the New York City Office of Economic Development (Thomas Bailey and Roger Waldinger, "Youth and Jobs in Post-Industrial New York" [New York, 1984]). For a similar analysis of the effects of population heterogeneity on market size and large-firm shares in the grocery store industry, see Paul Cournoyer, "The New England

Retail Grocery Industry," working paper 1121–80, Sloan School of Management, MIT, Cambridge, Mass., 1980.

14. Quoted in Russell, *Sharing Ownership in the Workplace*, p. 126.
15. Gallo, "The Construction Industry"; Bailey, "Labor Market Competition."
16. Data on establishment size and capital investment are calculated from the 1977 Census of Manufactures.
17. Data on specialization ratios are drawn from the 1982 Census of Manufactures.
18. For a similar argument based on research conducted in the U.K., see Aldrich, Cater, Jones, and McEvoy, "From Periphery to Peripheral." This work has been very helpful in my own thinking on the process and implications of ethnic succession. Aldrich et al., however, were principally concerned with the effects of residential succession on business opportunities for immigrant shopkeepers; they concluded that as neighborhoods shifted from white to Asian, the proportion of white storekeepers declined and the proportion of Asian storekeepers increased.
19. Data calculated from U.S. Department of Commerce, Bureau of the Census, *1970 Census of Population: National Origin and Language* (Washington, D.C.: Government Printing Office, 1973), PC(2)–1A, Table 16.
20. For the historical background, see Kessner, *The Golden Door*, and Moses Rischin, *The Promised City* (Cambridge: Harvard University Press, 1962); on the persistence of corporate discrimination against Jews, see the studies summarized in Nathan Glazer and Daniel Moynihan, *Beyond the Melting Pot*, 2d ed. (Cambridge: MIT Press, 1969), pp. 147–49.
21. Steven M. Cohen, *American Modernity and Jewish Identity* (New York: Tavistock, 1983), p. 21.
22. Ibid., pp. 86–87.
23. Data calculated by me from the 1981 New York Area Jewish Population Survey. I am grateful to my colleague, Paul Ritterband, for making the survey available to me.
24. Calvin Goldscheider and Frances Kobrin, "Ethnic Continuity and the Process of Self-Employment," *Ethnicity* 7 (1980):262.
25. Chemical Bank, *Small Business Speaks: The Chemical Bank Report* (New York: Chemical Bank, 1983), pp. 23–24, 38–39, 78–79.
26. New York Interface Development Project, "Proposal for a Pilot Employee Ownership Project," unpublished manuscript, 1982, p. 2; the citation summarizes the information reported in studies of five New York City industries (electric and electronic equipment, fabricated metals, plastics, machine trades, and banking) and six industrial neighborhoods (Jamaica, Woodside, Staten Island, Greenpoint/Williamsburg, East Williamsburgh/North Bushwick, Sunset Park, Long Island City) all conducted by the Interface organization for the city of New York.
27. David Birch, "Who Creates Jobs?" *The Public Interest* 65 (1981):7; Catherine Armington and Marjorie Odle, "Small Business—How Many Jobs?" *The Brookings Review* 1 (Winter 1982):17.
28. Kim, *The New Urban Immigrants*, p. 111.
29. New York City, City Planning Commission, *City Assistance for Small Manufacturers*, report prepared by the City Planning Commission, 1982; Young, "Family, Labor, Sacrifice, and Competition," p. 70.
30. Roger Waldinger, "The Occupational and Economic Integration of the New Immigrants," *Law and Contemporary Problems* 45 (1982):197–222.
31. Bailey, "Labor Market Competition."
32. C. Wright Mills, *White Collar: The American Middle Classes* (New York: Oxford, 1958).

216 NOTES

33. Ellen Auster and Howard Aldrich, "Small Business Vulnerability, Ethnic Enclaves and Ethnic Enterprise," in Ward and Jenkins, *Ethnic Communities*, p. 44.

34. Barry Chiswick, "Immigrants and Immigration Policy," in William Fellner, ed., *Contemporary Economic Problems* (Washington, D.C.: American Enterprise Institute, 1978).

35. Piore, *Birds of Passage*.

36. This point is made by Gerald Mars and Robin Ward, "Ethnic Business Development in Britain: Opportunities and Resources," in Ward and Jenkins, *Ethnic Communities*, pp. 17–18.

37. See, for example, J. S. MacDonald and L. D. MacDonald, "Chain Migration, Ethnic Neighborhood Formation, and Social Networks," in Charles Tilly, ed., *An Urban World* (Boston: Little, Brown, 1974), and Charles Tilly and Harold Brown, "On Uprooting, Kinship, and the Auspices of Migration," in Tilly, *An Urban World*.

38. Orme W. Phelps, "A Structural Model of the U.S. Labor Market," *Industrial and Labor Relations Review* 10 (1957):406.

39. In addition to Phelps, see Peter Doeringer and Michael Piore, *Internal Labor Markets and Manpower Analysis*, (Lexington, Mass.: Heath, 1971).

40. Michael Piore, "An Economic Approach," in Piore and Berger, *Dualism and Discontinuity*, p. 18.

41. Thomas Bailey, "A Case Study of Immigrants in the Restaurant Industry," *Industrial Relations* 24, no. 2 (1985):205–21.

42. A. Michael Spence, *Market Signalling* (Cambridge: Harvard University Press, 1974), pp. 2–3.

43. Doeringer and Piore, *Internal Labor Markets*; Richard Lester, *Hiring Practices and Labor Competition*, Industrial Relations Section, Princeton University, Research Report 88, 1954.

44. Thomas Bailey and Roger Waldinger, "Youth and Jobs in Post-Industrial New York," p. 55; also Roger Waldinger and Thomas Bailey, "The Youth Employment Problem in the World City," *Social Policy* (1985), pp. 55–8.

45. Elliot Liebow, *Tally's Corner* (Boston: Little, Brown, 1967); see also Michael Piore, "On-the-Job Training in a Dual Labor Market," in Arnold R. Weber, et al., eds., *Public-Private Manpower Policies* (Madison, Wis.: Industrial Relations Research Association, 1969).

46. Kim, *The New Urban Immigrants*, p. 112.

47. Hendricks, *Dominican Diaspora*, p. 31; Bernard Wong, *A Chinese-American Community* (Singapore: Chopmen, 1979).

48. Bailey, "Immigrants in the Restaurant Industry."

49. Doeringer and Piore, *Internal Labor Markets*; Richard C. Edwards, *Contested Terrain* (New York: Basic Books, 1979).

50. See Geoffrey K. Ingham, *Size of Industrial Organization and Worker Behavior* (Cambridge: Cambridge University Press, 1970), and references cited therein.

51. Doeringer and Piore, *Internal Labor Markets*, pp. 17–27; William F. Whyte et al., *Money and Motivation* (New York: Harper, 1955).

52. Gerald Suttles, *The Social Order of the Slum* (Chicago: Chicago University Press, 1968); Thomas Kochman, *Black and White Styles in Conflict* (Chicago: Chicago University Press, 1983).

53. Wong, *A Chinese-American Community*, p. 103.

54. Harry Herman, "Dishwashers and Proprietors: Macedonians in Toronto's Restaurant Trade," in Sandra Wallman, ed., *Ethnicity at Work* (London: Macmillan, 1979).

55. Data on characteristics of Greeks, Koreans, and Chinese calculated from, U.S. Bureau of the Census, 1980 Census of Population, I, Part D, Table 255.

56. Cf. Kessner, *The Golden Door*; Goldscheider and Zuckerman, *The Transformation of the Jews*.

NOTES **217**

57. Interview with Gary Kugler, Associated Fur Merchants of New York, February 1983. For an analysis of the fur industry and its labor requirements, see Roger Waldinger and Thomas Bailey, "Displacement Pressures on Manhattan Manufacturing Industries and Job Retention Strategies," Report No. 2, prepared for the New York City Office of Economic Development, 1983.

58. Piore, *Birds of Passage*, pp. 57–68.

59. Ibid., Chapter 3, esp. pp. 55–68.

60. Young, "Family Labor," pp. 64–65.

61. Bonacich, "A Theory of Middleman Minorities"; Bonacich and Modell, *The Economic Basis*.

62. Robin Ward, "Minority Settlement and the Local Community," in Bryan Roberts, Ruth Finnegan, and Duncan Gallie, eds., *New Approaches to Economic Life* (Manchester: Manchester University Press, 1985), pp. 189–209.

63. Kessner, *The Golden Door*, p. 167.

64. Employment rates for West Indians calculated from the Public Use Microdata sample of the 1980 Census of Population.

65. Bailey, "Immigrants in the Restaurant Industry."

[29]

American Entrepreneurs and the Horatio Alger Myth

SINCE 1925 a number of scholars have conducted studies of the general business elite in America.[1] Their studies have concluded that the American business elite has been predominantly native born, urban, better educated than the general population, and has originated disproportionately from higher economic classes. These conclusions are not surprising. It might have been surprising if the business elite were found to have emerged predominantly from the poor and less educated, and the immigrant, farm or working-class populations. Such origins would infer a rapid displacement of elite members, the possibility of rapid and massive disaggregation of family fortunes, and the loss of family aggrandizement as a motivating consideration in the minds of aspiring businessmen. This, however, was apparently not the case.

While these studies typically treat the business elite as a single collectivity, one such analysis by Collins, Moore, et al. examined a distinct subcategory of business leaders.[2] Their 1960-1962 study of living, innovating entrepreneurs revealed that there was validity in the traditional Horatio Alger "rags-to-riches" myth.[3] Many of their subjects had experienced childhood poverty and disrupted family lives which stimulated strong motivations for personal achievement. The purpose of this article is to appraise and perhaps to extend this

Journal of Economic History, Vol. XXXVIII, No. 2 (June 1978). Copyright © The Economic History Association. All rights reserved.

[1] Pitirim Sorokin, "American Millionaires and Multi-Millionaires; A Comparative Study," *Journal of Social Forces*, 3 (May 1925), 627-40; F. W. Taussig, C. S. Joslyn, *American Business Leaders* (New York, 1932); C. Wright Mills, "The American Business Elite: A Collective Portrait," JOURNAL OF ECONOMIC HISTORY, 5 (Dec. 1945), 20-44; William Miller, "American Historians and the Business Elite," JOURNAL OF ECONOMIC HISTORY, 9 (Nov. 1949), 184-208; William Miller, "Recruitment of the Business Elite," *Quarterly Journal of Economics*, 64 (May 1950), 242-53; Suzanne Keller, *The Social Origins and Career Lines of Three Generations of American Business Leaders* (Ph.D. dissertation, Columbia University, 1953); Frances W. Gregory, Irene D. Neu, "The American Industrial Elite in the 1870's," pp. 193-211, and William Miller, "The Business Elite in Business Bureaucracies," pp. 286-306, in William Miller, ed., *Men in Business* (Cambridge, Mass., 1955); Stuart Adams, "Trends in Occupational Origins of Business Leaders," *American Sociological Review*, 19 (Oct. 1954), 541-48; W. Lloyd Warner, James C. Abegglen, *Occupational Mobility in American Business and Industry* (Minneapolis, 1955); W. Lloyd Warner, James C. Abegglen, *Big Business Leaders in America* (New York, 1955); Mabel Newcomer, *The Big Business Executive* (New York, 1955); Seymour Martin Lipset, Reinhard Bendix, *Social Mobility in Industrial Society* (Berkeley, 1963).

[2] Warner and Abegglen's distinction between "mobile" executives and the "birth elite" is an exception to the tendency to present a single collective portrait of the general business elite. Warner and Abegglen, *Business Leaders*, especially chs. 4 and 5.

[3] Orvis F. Collins, David G. Moore, et al., *The Enterprising Man* (East Lansing, 1964).

440   *Sarachek*

line of analysis by examining the published accounts of another set of entrepreneurs.

In my account, a businessman is considered an entrepreneur if he creates a new economic enterprise; or brings an enterprise verging on economic bankruptcy and dissolution back to life as a thriving firm; or if his guidance transforms a quite small firm into a fundamentally different entity of quite different proportion; or if he creates a new enterprise from the consolidation of predecessor firms so that the consolidation is economically of different character than its predecessors. In short, I limit entrepreneurship to the narrow Schumpeterian sense of one who creates innovations de nouveau, or out of the shells and seeds of predecessor firms. I am not talking about career executives who arrive at the top of going enterprises by rising through the ranks of the corporate hierarchy.

A RESTATEMENT OF THE HORATIO ALGER MYTH

Horatio Alger's stories offer several variations on the "rags-to-riches" theme of the hero's humble origins. He is most likely rural born, but might be of urban birth instead. He might be an orphan, the son of an invalided father or the son of a hard-working poor but honest father. He is apt to be native born, but he might be foreign born instead. He may have been born to a working-class family, a middle-class family that has fallen upon hard times, or, unbeknownst to him, to a wealthy family from which he has been orphaned. His natural parents are virtuous upholders of the middle-class values of the Protestant ethic. He may encounter evil guardians and step-parents, but some time along the way he is apt to be aided by an older, well-intentioned male benefactor.

The variant of the myth used in this paper may differ in some ways from others' formulations.[4] This study explores the frequency with which entrepreneurs have experienced some type of traumatic child-hood deprivation. The trauma may be the loss of a father through death or separation. The trauma may be the child's realization that the father somehow provides a negative authority figure unworthy of emulation. Deprivation may also take the form of the father who provides a strong authority image, but expresses rejection of his son,

---

[4] Cf. Ralph Andreano, "A Note on the Horatio Alger Legend: Statistical Studies of the Nineteenth Century American Business Elite," *Business Enterprise and Economic Change,* Louis P. Cain, Paul J. Uselding, eds. (Kent, 1973), pp. 227-46; Gregory and Neu, "Industrial Elite," p. 193; Irvin G. Wyllie, *The Self-Made Man in America* (New Brunswick, 1954).

denigrating his abilities and capacities for becoming a competent and effective adult. The orphaned, rejected or ineptly fathered child may well conclude that his development and successful survival must be of his own fashioning. The opposite of the disadvantaged child is the child whose father was supportive in the sense of providing a strong and successful authority figure around which the child might model his own character development. The supportive father endeavors to train or guide his son toward a successful career. In addition to the psycho-social dimension of the father-son relationship, I describe the economic origins of entrepreneurs. The theme of the hero's disadvantaged childhood is of significance only as it relates to the possibility that such a childhood might be a source of motivation toward personal achievement. One additional motivational issue is examined even though it properly falls beyond my formulation of the Horatio Alger myth. Since it is popularly presumed that first-born children are most apt to become the family achievers, I also examine entrepreneurs' birth order positions.

THE SAMPLE OF ENTREPRENEURS

I found 187 entrepreneurs who were described in sufficient detail in published biographies and company histories to be included in this study.[5] This nonrandom method of sample selection is the only feasible means of obtaining childhood descriptions of a numerous group of entrepreneurs, almost all of whom are now deceased. Twenty-three of the entrepreneuers were born before 1800 and only 12 were born after 1899. Sixty were born during the first half, and 92 during the last half of the nineteenth century. Of those selected, 157 (83 percent) were born in the United States. Furthermore, only 31 percent of their fathers were clearly described in the literature as foreign born. Thus, like the enterpreneurs in the Collins, Moore, et al. study, and like the subjects of the general business elite studies, my group is predominantly native born.[6]

Table 1 indicates the sample's distribution of entrepreneurial activities. Since several could be classified in more than one way, I categorized the entrepreneurs according to their financially larger

---

[5] Space does not permit reproduction of the biographical bibliography here. The author will supply bibliographies upon request and at the cost of office reproduction.

[6] Collins, Moore, et al., *Enterprising Man*, 234; Mills, "Collective Portrait," pp. 22-28; Miller, "American Historians," p. 201; Gregory and Neu, "Industrial Elite," p. 197; Warner and Abegglen, *Occupational Mobility*, p. 90; Newcomer, *Big Business*, p. 43; Keller, *Social Origins*, pp. 40-41.

442 *Sarachek*

TABLE 1
NUMERICAL DISTRIBUTION OF ENTREPRENEURS
ACCORDING TO THEIR INDUSTRIES

Transportation	27	Farming & Lumbering	6
Banking & Finance	12	Land Development	5
Service	14	Manufacturing	83
Mercantile	18	Mining & Oil	18
Utilities	4		

and more extensive business ventures. My sample excludes non-whites and females. Published accounts of these entrepreneurs are very few and their experiences seem likely to have differed from those of white males. Several authors have also commented on the differences between Jewish and non-Jewish businessmen, and for that reason Jews are not included in my sample of entrepreneurs.[7] Media entrepreneurs, other than book publishers and businessmen in advertising agencies, are excluded from the sample. I assumed that book publishers and advertising enterpreneurs were primarily profit minded, while heads of other types of media (such as newspapers, magazines, radio, television and motion pictures) might possibly have been motivated more by desires to be appreciated, artistically creative, or socially influential.

THE FATHER-SON RELATIONSHIP

I first grouped the entrepreneurs according to their childhood relationships with their fathers. One category was that of "Father-Dead," which includes entrepreneurs who experienced the death of their natural fathers prior to reaching the age of sixteen.[8] Another

---

[7] Miller, "Recruitment of the Business Elite," p. 245; Newcomer, *Big Business*, p. 48; David C. McClelland, *The Achieving Society* (New York, 1961), pp. 364-67. See the following three articles in Marshall Sklare, ed., *The Jews* (Glencoe, 1960): David Goldberg, Harry Sharp, "Occupational Selection Among Detroit Jews," pp. 119-37; Nathan Glazer, "The American Jew and the Attainment of Middle-Class Rank: Some Trends and Explanations," pp. 138-46; Fred L. Strodtbeck, "Family Interaction, Values, and Achievement," pp. 147-65.

[8] *Father-Dead Entrepreneurs*
(Birth years are listed after the names)

Ivan Earnest Allen (1877)	John Deere (1804)
Cornelius Aultman (1827)	Daniel Drew (1797)
Thomas Robert Bard (1841)	George Eastman (1854)
William Henry Belk (1862)	John Murray Forbes (1813)
William Benton (1900)	John Baptiste Ford (1811)
William E. Boeing (1881)	Robert Fulton (1765)
William Tell Coleman (1824)	George Franklin Getty (1855)
Richard Teller Crane (1832)	Amandeo Peter Giannini (1870)
John Crerar (1827)	Adolphus Williamson Green (1843)
Henry Parsons Crowell (1855)	Hugh Alexander Hamilton (1890)
Samuel Cummings (1927)	James J. Hill (1838)
Glenn Hammond Curtiss (1878)	Hans Jeppesen Isbrandtsen (1891)

Horatio Alger Myth   443

TABLE 2
FATHER-SON RELATIONSHIPS OF ENTREPRENEURS

	Number	Percent of Total
Father-Dead	52	28%
Father-Separation	13	7
Father-Inadequate	32	17
Father-Rejecting	7	4
Supportive Fathers	77	41
Special Cases	6	3
Total	187	100%

group was that of "Father-Separation," which consists of entre-preneurs who experienced the commencement of at least one year's separation from their fathers prior to their sixteenth birthdays. Father-separation was not deemed to occur when the entrepreneur, rather than the parent, chose to leave the father (for example, P. Cooper, S. Brannan, C. R. Mason).[9]

"Father-Inadequate" is a category of cases in which the father appears as a predominantly negative authority figure.[10] The son may

Thomas James (1775)
Morgan Jones (1839)
Walter Knott (1891)
Frederick Kohnle (1860)
George Washington Littlefield (1842)
Samuel Lord (1802)
John William Mackay (1831)
George Mardikian (1903)
Alexander McDougall (1845)
Hugh McIlvain (1775)
Thomas Handasyd Perkins (1764)
Anson Greene Phelps (1781)
Allen Pinkerton (1819)
Henry Bradley Plant (1819)

George Palmer Putnam (1814)
John Roach (1815)
Samuel Slater (1768)
Albert Goodwill Spalding (1850)
Ellsworth Milton Statler (1863)
A. T. Stewart (1802)
Justus Clayton Strawbridge (1838)
W. Clement Stone (1902)
Israel Thorndike (1755)
Nathan Trotter (1787)
Frederick Weyerhaeuser (1834)
Josiah White (1781)
Halsey William Wilson (1868)
Oliver Fisher Winchester (1810)

[9]   *Father-Separated Entrepreneurs*

Simon Cameron (1799)
Hugh Roy Cullen (1881)
Henry P. Davison (1867)
William Crapo Durant (1861)
Carl Graham Fisher (1874)
Robert Gair (1839)
Joyce C. Hall (1891)

Robert Deniston Hume (1845)
James Joseph Ling (1922)
Robert Morris (1735)
John D. Rockefeller (1839)
James Stillman (1850)
Charles Bates Thornton (1913)

[10]   *Father-Inadequate Entrepreneurs*

John Emory Andrus (1841)
John Jacob Astor (1763)
Samuel Brannan (1819)
William Anderson Burnette (1887)
Andrew Carnegie (1835)
William Lockhart Clayton (1880)
William Colgate (1783)
Samuel Colt (1814)

Erastus Corning (1794)
Peter Cooper (1791)
Henry Gassaway Davis (1823)
Granville M. Dodge (1831)
David Eccles (1849)
James Buchanan Eads (1820)
James Fisk, Jr. (1834)
Henry M. Flagler (1830)

444 *Sarachek*

have learned from the father's example what *not* to be and what *not* to believe if he was to avoid the father's experiences and inadequacies. In some cases the son consciously rejected the father as an ineffectual failure. J. E. Andrus, S. Brannan, S. Insull, A. E. Stilwell, T. J. Watson, H. M. Flagler and G. M. Verity held such opinions of their fathers. Some fathers could not cope and became invalided or suffered mental breakdowns and severe depression. In some instances the father was dramatically rejected by society. The fathers of C. Huntington and J. C. Penney were driven from their rural churches. The inability of Huntington's father to maintain his family resulted in the local community forcibly separating his children from him and his wife. In some cases the fathers were shiftless or even drunkards. This includes the fathers of E. Corning, J. J. Astor, S. Brannan, D. Eccles, J. A. Roebling, C. Huntington and W. A. Burnette. Sometimes the fathers were so ineffectual as economic performers that the sons were forced to assume the role of their families' primary breadwinners at extremely young ages or, at the latest, very early adulthood.

Some of those in this category remembered their father with genuine fondness, but I included them here if it was apparent that the entrepreneur recognized the inadequacies of the father. G. H. Mead, J. Wanamaker, W. S. Johnson, T. Johnson, and G. M. Dodge were genuinely fond of their fathers. J. C. Penney attempted to idealize the memory of his father despite his recollection of the shame and deprivation felt during childhood. Rather than raising his family out of poverty by working his heavily mortgaged, 400 acres of rich farm land, Penney's father allowed most of the land to remain fallow while he devoted himself to his calling as an unpaid preacher. Penney's memoirs recall the shame of the hot and stinging rejection his father ultimately suffered when his parishioners excommunicated him from his own church. Subsequently, the father ran for Congress unsuccessfully three times. Penney's own economic initiatives as a child were repeatedly thwarted by his father's chastising application of moral precepts. Though cloaking his life activities under the facade of his father's teachings and christening his businesses "Golden Rule

Collis Huntington (1821)	John August Roebling (1806)
Samuel Insull (1859)	Richard Warren Sears (1864)
Tom L. Johnson (1854)	Arthur Edward Stilwell (1859)
Walter Samuel Johnson (1884)	Samuel W. Traylor (1869)
George Houk Mead (1877)	Cornelius Vanderbilt (1794)
Jeno F. Paulucci (1918)	George Matthew Verity (1865)
George Peabody (1795)	John Wanamaker (1838)
James Cash Penney (1875)	Thomas John Watson (1874)

Stores," Penney early set himself on a radically different course than
his father's aesthetic rejection of material wealth. Penny chose instead
to build an empire in retailing.

"Father-Rejecting" is a category that includes entrepreneurs whose
fathers were dominant authority figures, but who tended to thwart
their sons' efforts and impress upon their sons a sense of inadequacy
and ineptness.[11] G. W. Borg's father displayed almost no emotion or
interest in his son until he reached his teens. Then indifference
changed to continual criticism. J. W. Gates' father was several times
restrained by his wife from throwing his son out of his home. J. P.
Getty's father provided his son with a separate room and entrance to
the house; his parents' continuing distrust of his worth and business
abilities became a motivating force encouraging Getty to prove himself.

By contrast, "Supportive Fathers" were interested in the development of their sons' character and business abilities.[12] They were

---

[11]   *Father-Rejecting Entrepreneurs*

George William Borg (1887)	Jay Gould (1836)
John Warne Gates (1885)	Claibourne Rice Mason (1800)
Jean Paul Getty (1892)	William Boyce Thompson (1869)
Stephen Girard (1750)	

[12]   *Supportive Father*

Samuel Leeds Allen (1841)	Edward Ford (1843)
Philip Danforth Armour (1832)	Henry Ford (1863)
Edward Goodrich Acheson (1856)	Alfred C. Fuller (1885)
Roger W. Babson (1875)	Eugene Duncan Funk, Sr. (1867)
Michael Late Benedum (1869)	Alfred C. Gilbert (1884)
Carl D. Bodine (1881)	Armand Hammer (1898)
Paul J. Bodine (1883)	James Harper (1795)
Milton Bradley (1836)	Hayward Augustus Harvey (1824)
Joshua Loring Brooks (1868)	Fritz August Heinze (1868)
Thomas Hamilton Broyhill (1877)	Ernest Henderson (1897)
James Edgar Broyhill (1892)	Conrad Hilton (1887)
Godfrey Lowell Cabot (1861)	William Henry Hoover (1849)
Johnson Newlon Camden (1828)	Johns Hopkins (1795)
Asa Griggs Candler (1851)	Howard Hughes (1906)
Roy Diekman Chapin (1880)	Henry Edwards Huntington (1850)
Walter P. Chrysler (1875)	George Francis Johnson (1857)
Jay Cooke (1821).	J. Logan Jones (1859)
Jacob Dolson Cox (1852)	Jesse Holman Jones (1874)
William H. Danforth (1871)	Kirk Kerkorian (1917)
Walter S. Dickey (1860)	Edward Lamb (1903)
Herbert Henry Dow (1866)	Edward Hudson Lane (1891)
James Buchanan Duke (1856)	Edward Drummond Libbey (1854)
Eleuthere Irenee du Pont (1771)	James Lick (1796)
Marriner Stoddard Eccles (1890)	Charles Addison Ludey (1874)
John F. Ernsthausen (1888)	Cyrus Hall McCormick (1809)
Cyrus Field (1819)	Ernest Whitworth Marland (1874)
Harvey S. Firestone (1868)	Fred Louis Maytag (1857)
Charles R. Flint (1850)	Andrew W. Mellon (1855)

positively supportive emotionally. They were apparently not hyper-critical of their sons' abilities, nor did they tend to draw limits on their sons' initiatives. They might have been strict disciplinarians, but discipline was linked to a striving for excellence rather than punishment and limitation. They provided strong authority figures for their sons, projecting the image of competence and strength.

The final category is composed of "special cases" which cannot otherwise be categorized.[13] Thomas A. Edison and his father seem to have maintained an ambivalently tolerant neutrality. The father did not understand nor appreciably influence his son. It was the mother who devoted herself to his welfare and became the profound influence in his life. Kellogg's older brother clearly overshadowed the influence of the parents in molding this entrepreneur's character and motivations. R. G. LeTourneau's and W. S. Stratton's fathers were supportive parents, but in these cases the sons rebelled and rejected the parents' good intentions.

Since there is rarely anything ambiguous about a parent's death or separation, these two categories of father-son relationship might be proportionately overstated. There is also a strong bias in some biographies to understate the fathers' inadequacies or to describe them ambiguously. While this sort of ambiguity sometimes resulted in the deletion of an entrepreneur from the "Supportive Fathers" category, it is my belief that ambiguity more often resulted in deletion of entrepreneurs from the category of "Father-Inadequate," and in a few cases, from the category of "Father-Rejecting." Thus, these two categories are probably understated relative to the others.

As Table 2 indicates, the largest single category of entrepreneurs experienced supportive fathers. Nevertheless, 104 entrepreneurs (56 percent of the total sample) experienced the death, separation, in-

---

Edward Gideon Melroe (1892)
David Halliday Moffat (1839)
John Pierpont Morgan (1837)
Charles Steward Mott (1874)
Ralph Mueller (1877)
Orvis Marcus Nelson (1907)
Ransom Eli Olds (1864)
William Francis O'Neil (1885)
George Mortimer Pullman (1831)
David Edward Ross (1871)
Joseph Benjamin Saunders, Jr. (1901)

Josiah Ellis Saunders (1889)
Igor Ivan Sikorsky (1889)
Leland Stanford (1824)
Edbridge Amos Stuart (1856)
Charlemagne Tower (1809)
Juan Terry Trippe (1899)
William Volker (1859)
George Westinghouse (1846)
Orville Wright (1871)
Wilbur Wright (1867)

[13]

Thomas Alva Edison (1847)
Ray Hugh Garvey (1893)
Will Keith Kellogg (1860)

Special Cases

Robert Gilmore LeTourneau (1888)
Winfield Scott Stratton (1848)
Paul Starrett (1866)

TABLE 3

PERCENT COMPARISON OF STUDIES OF THE OCCUPATIONAL BACKGROUNDS
OF FATHERS OF THE AMERICAN BUSINESS ELITE[a]

Fathers' Occupations	Business Elite Studies						Entrepreneurial Studies	
	Mills[d] (1570-1879)	Gregory & Neu[e] (1870s)	Miller[e] (1900s)	Newcomer[f] (1900)	Taussig & Joslyn[g] (1928)	Warner & Abegglen[h] (1952)	This Study	Collins & Moore[i] (1960)
Workers[b]	3%	8%	2%	2%	7%	13%	5%	24%
Skilled Workers[c]	7	25	14	6	9	10	12	12
Farmers	24	13	22	21	12	9	28	19
Professionals	19	51	55	20	13	14	12	10
Business	40			51				
Owners of Businesses					34	26	37	26
Major Executives					16	15	0	0
Minor Executives					7	11	3	2
Other	6	3	7		2	2	1	6
Unknown							2	

447

[a] Figures rearranged for purposes of comparison and rounded to the nearest whole percent.
[b] Semi and unskilled workers, white collar workers and salesmen.
[c] Skilled workers, craftsmen and mechanics.
[d] Mills, "Collective Portrait," p. 32.
[e] Gregory and Neu, "Industrial Elite," p. 202.
[f] Reconstructed from Newcomer, *Big Business*, pp. 53, 55.
[g] Taussig and Joslyn, *American Business Leaders*, p. 82.
[h] Warner and Abegglen, *Occupational Mobility*, pp. 38, 45.
[i] Collins, Moore et al., *Enterprising Man*, p. 239.

adequacy or rejection of a natural father. This aggregated group of 104 entrepreneurs experienced some form of disadvantaged childhood relationship with their fathers.[14]

FATHERS' OCCUPATIONS

While sometimes acknowledging that occupational origins are at best a crude indicator of economic class, the business elite studies have used these origins to indicate the level of elite class mobility.[15] The approximation between occupation and class is of course entirely too crude to be of any real use. Success within occupations may vary enormously. The status of an occupation greatly varies through time, between regions, and between rural and urban settings. Finally, whatever the father's occupation, the father's death or separation from the family may critically influence family class membership. A tracing of entrepreneurs' fathers' occupations is useful, however, as a basis of comparison to the general business elite studies and as an indicator of the entrepreneurs' early motivational training. Fathers who pursued more than one occupation are each listed only once in Table 3, according to the occupation of greatest importance as measured in terms of the time invested and personal commitment of the father during the entrepreneur's childhood.

None of the entrepreneurs in my sample (or in that of Collins, Moore, et al.) had fathers who were major corporate executives. Few were even minor executives. These observations contrast sharply with the data of the Taussig and Joslyn study and the Warner and Abegglen analysis of the general business elite.

Otherwise, however, my sample of entrepreneurs' fathers does not appear to differ inordinately from those of the general business elite studies shown in Table 3. Indeed, my sample is strikingly similar to

[14] Entrepreneurs experiencing the death or separation of a father may experience at least two relationships with their fathers. Fifteen entrepreneurs were under five years of age when their fathers died. Thirteen "Father-Dead" and "Father-Separated" entrepreneurs experienced father-son relationships described with such lack of detail that they must be disregarded. Fathers absent due to death or separation are frequently described in less biographic detail than other fathers. Empoying *less stringent* standards of judgment than used in the rest of this paper, it appears that 21 of the remaining group of "Father-Dead" and "Father-Separated" entrepreneurs experienced inadequate fathers. These include W. Benton, S. Cameron, W. T. Coleman, D. Drew, W. C. Durant, C. G. Fisher, J. M. Forbes, R. Gair, G. F. Getty, J. C. Hall, R. Hume, F. Kohnle, J. J. Ling, A. McDougall, T. H. Perkins, A. G. Phelps, G. P. Putnam, J. Roach, J. D. Rockefeller, E. M. Statler and J. White. Two entrepreneurs, R. Morris and C. B. Thornton, experienced rejection from their fathers. The remaining 14 entrepreneurs appear to have experienced supportive fathers. These include T. R. Bard, W. E. Boeing, R. T. Crane, H. P. Crowell, S. Cummings, G. Eastman, A. P. Giannini, G. W. Littlefield, G. Mardikian, H. B. Plant, A. G. Spalding, J. Stillman, N. Trotter and F. Weyerhaeuser.

[15] Gregory and Neu, "Industrial Elite," p. 202.

Horatio Alger Myth   449

Gregory and Neu's. If the "minor executives" were added to the "owners of businesses" and independently employed "skilled workers," then 52 percent of the entrepreneurs in this study could be characterized as having fathers engaged in business. This is almost identical to Gregory and Neu's finding that 51 percent of the general business elite members functioning in the 1870s had fathers who were businessmen. The Bendix and Howton general business elite study is least like our entrepreneurial sample. Their results are not shown in Table 3 because their occupational categories were not constructed in ways that permit easy comparison.[16] If one combines Bendix and Howton's "businessmen" with their "master craftsmen and small entrepreneurs," approximately 70 percent of their business elite (born between 1831 and 1920) had fathers in this aggregated category—a far higher figure than the 52 percent in my distribution.

An interesting occupational difference is apparent in Table 4, which compares entrepreneurs who had supportive fathers with those who were disadvantaged. Workers and minor executives are more heavily

TABLE 4
OCCUPATIONAL DISTRIBUTION OF ENTREPRENEURS'
SUPPORTIVE AND DISADVANTAGING FATHERS

	74 Supportive Fathers	104 Fathers of Disadvantaged Entrepreneurs	All 184 Fathers of Entrepreneurs
Workers[a]	1	9	10
	(1%)	(9%)	(5%)
Skilled Workers[b]	8	14	22
	(11%)	(13%)	(12%)
Farmers	19	31	52
	(26%)	(30%)	(28%)
Professionals	8	12	22
	(11%)	(12%)	(12%)
Owners of Businesses	36	30	68
	(48%)	(29%)	(37%)
Minor Executives[c]	1	4	5
	(1%)	(4%)	(3%)
Other[d]	1		1
	(1%)		(1%)
Father's Occupation Unknown[e]		4	4
		(4%)	(2%)

[a] Semi and unskilled workers, white collar workers and salesmen.

[b] Independently employed craftsmen and mechanics.

[c] Middle and plant managers in business and government organizations.

[d] The individual included in this category is Pierre Du Pont who was a political appointee of national stature in France.

[e] Refers to the fathers of S. Lord, J. Crerar, J. W. Mackay, H. A. Hamilton.

[16] Reinhard Bendix, Frank W. Howton, "Social Mobility and the American Business Elite," in Lipset and Bendix, Social Mobility, p. 122.

represented among the fathers of disadvantaged entrepreneurs than among supportive fathers, while owners of businesses are both absolutely and proportionately more numerous among supportive fathers than among the fathers of disadvantaged entrepreneurs. Whether we look at supportive fathers or fathers of disadvantaged entrepreneurs, however, the majority were independently employed. The fathers' experience of being self-employed probably enhanced the sons' abilities and willingness to initiate independent economic activity. If so, it is understandable why owners of businesses would be more heavily represented among the supportive fathers. By definition, supportive fathers were most prone to train and encourage their sons' development.

ECONOMIC ORIGINS

For purposes of exploring the entrepreneurs' economic origins, I collected information on two other issues: how economically successful were the entrepreneurs' fathers? How much experience did the entrepreneurs have with poverty? In examining the biographies I used for data, I consciously focused on the verbs and nouns, rather than the adjectives and adverbs. Words like frugal, industrious, modest, poor, and successful were considered to be much less important than events such as frequent geographic and occupational moves in search of a livelihood, bankruptcy, or the necessity to terminate a son's education prematurely so that he could contribute to the family income. In this way, I tried to limit the effect of the biographers' biases on my data.

Four categories of economic achievement are listed in Table 5. "Marginal" fathers had substantial difficulty maintaining family livelihoods at minimally secure levels. An entrepreneur's father was counted as marginal even though the mother or the children earned enough to compensate for the father's inability to provide a minimal level of subsistence. The category "reasonable livelihood" covered a rather large range of economic performance. It simply meant that the father was able to maintain the family reasonably secure from the threat of destitution, but not well enough to develop much by way of economic surplus. Thus, it encompassed the stable but spartan existence of a Cape Cod farmer (P. D. Armour's father), the lives of mechanics and craftsmen (like Chrysler's and Lick's fathers), and those of store owners (H. E. Huntington's and C. A. Ludey's fathers). Roughly, the term "reasonable livelihood" is used to encompass the upper-lower class through the lower-middle and middle-middle class.

TABLE 5
ECONOMIC ATTAINMENTS OF ENTREPRENEURS' FATHERS

	Wealthy	Prosperous	Reasonable Living	Marginal	Unknown
Father-Dead	2	6	25	15	4
Father-Separated		3	5	5	
Father-Inadequate		2	6	24	
Father-Rejecting	1	3	3		
Total 104 Fathers of Disadvantaged Entrepreneurs	3 (3%)	14 (13%)	39 (38%)	44 (42%)	4 (4%)
74 Supportive Fathers	15 (20%)	22 (30%)	30 (41%)	7 (9%)	
Special Cases		1	3	2	
Total of 184 Fathers	18 (10%)	37 (20%)	72 (39%)	53 (29%)	4 (2%)

"Prosperous" meant that the father had provided the family with a sizable measure of discretionary income and more than negligible reserves of capital. This was predominantly the upper-middle class. In small towns and rural areas such families may have been considered wealthy by their neighbors, but they had yet to achieve the measure of wealth that would have enabled them to be recognized as upper class in the largest urban centers. The category of "wealthy" was reserved for the upper economic class of large-scale wealth. M. Eccles', J. P. Getty's, J. Stillman's and H. Hughes' fathers were, for example, "wealthy."

Half of the entrepreneurs with supportive fathers came from prosperous or wealthy backgrounds, while only 16 percent of the disadvantaged entrepreneurs had this sort of environment. Forty-two percent of the disadvantaged entrepreneurs had economically marginal fathers, compared to only 9 percent of those with supportive fathers. The experience of entrepreneurs with supportive fathers does not differ greatly from that of the business elite in general. Most studies report that half or more of the American business elite came from upper-middle or upper-class economic backgrounds,[17] while only 5 percent to 16 percent[18] had lower-class origins. The Horatio Alger myth may not apply to either the general business elite or to entrepreneurs who had supportive fathers, but my data suggests that it is an apt description for the disadvantaged entrepreneurs.

I defined poverty as both a near inability to meet the minimal levels

[17] Mills, "Collective Portrait," p. 30; Miller, "American Historians," p. 206; Newcomer, *Big Business*, pp. 61-64; Lipset and Bendix, *Social Mobility*, pp. 122-23.
[18] Miller, "American Historians," p. 206, and Newcomer, *Big Business*, p. 63, respectively.

of subsistence and the loss of economic standing relative to one's peers and neighbors.[19] This was a severe level of poverty rather than just a matter of low income. Poverty was not the same as marginality, as computed for Table 5. For example, an entrepreneur's father may have provided a reasonable livelihood, yet the son may have experienced genuine poverty due to the father's death or absence. Conversely, the father may have been a marginal provider, and yet the family could have been saved from poverty because of the mother's efforts, as in the case of G. P. Putnam, or because of the support of some relative, as in the case of A. E. Stillwell's father. Forty-four (42 percent) of the 104 disadvantaged entrepreneurs experienced some period of genuine poverty during childhood. Only 2 (3 percent) of the 77 entrepreneurs with supportive fathers, however, experienced poverty at some time during their childhood. Taking the entire group of 187 entrepreneurs, a total of 49 (26 percent) clearly went through a period of poverty. Thus, while severe poverty was not the norm for this sample, a quite significant proportion of these entrepreneurs did have experience with "rags" before they attained their "riches."

FIRST MAJOR JOB

The heroes of the Horatio Alger stories are forced to enter the work force prematurely at quite early ages. Table 6 summarizes the ages of entry into the work force of our 187 entrepreneurs. A job is "major" if it is full time and undertaken under the expectation that entry into the work force is permanent. An individual working his way through school would not qualify as having undertaken his first major job. One who was working in his parents' business or on their farm had not assumed his first major job, unless he undertook primary responsibility for the conduct of the family venture or appears to have made a career choice to remain with that enterprise and obtain his livelihood from it.

The collective group of 187 entrepreneurs started working sooner than the general business elite. Both the Miller study and the Gregory and Neu study found that 55 percent of their business elites assumed their first major jobs before reaching the age of 19.[20] Newcomer found that only 40 percent had assumed their first job prior to reaching the age of 20.[21] Only 31 percent of Warner and Abegglen's

---

[19] For example, J. B. Duke returned with his father to their farm following the Civil War to resume life at a subsistence level. For our purposes, this was not considered as a condition of poverty since it was similar to the condition of other southern farmers of that period and locale.

[20] Miller, "American Historians," p. 206; Gregory and Neu, "Industrial Elite," p. 203.

[21] Newcomer, *Big Business*, p. 88.

Horatio Alger Myth   453

TABLE 6
AGE AT WHICH ENTREPRENEURS ASSUMED
FIRST MAJOR JOBS

	Under 10	10-15	16-18	19 and over	Unknown
Father-Dead	3	25	12	11	1
Father-Separated	1	4	6	2	
Father-Inadequate	1	18	9	4	
Father-Rejecting	1	3	1	2	
Total 104	6	50	28	19	1
Disadvantaged	(6%)	(48%)	(27%)	(18%)	(1%)
Entrepreneurs					
77 Supportive-Father	—	12	28	34	3
Entrepreneurs		(16%)	(36%)	(44%)	(4%)
Special Cases	—	3	3	—	
Total of 184 Fathers	6	65	59	53	4
	(3%)	(35%)	(32%)	(28%)	(2%)

group of 1952 business elite members had entered work careers prior
to the age of 19.[22] By contrast, 70 percent of our 187 entrepreneurs
held their first major jobs prior to the age of 19.

Fifty-two percent of the entrepreneurs experiencing supportive
fathers entered their first major jobs before age 19, while the comparable figure was 81 percent for the disadvantaged entrepreneurs.
Thus, while entrepreneurs with supportive fathers again emerge as
similar to the general business elite, the disadvantaged entrepreneurs
were different.

I also compared the entrepreneurs according to the ages at which
they undertook their major innovational ventures. Seven disadvantaged entrepreneurs inaugurated their innovational efforts prior to
reaching the age of 18, while none of the entrepreneurs with supportive fathers did so before that age. With this exception, the distribution of ages at which different entrepreneurial types inaugurated their
innovations was similar; approximately six out of ten entrepreneurs
had launched their innovations prior to reaching the age of 30. Even
those who had experienced severe poverty during childhood compiled a similar record of early achievement.

SPONSOR-PROTÉGÉ RELATIONSHIPS

Warner and Abegglen, as well as Collins, Moore, et al., found that
successful businessmen frequently remember men other than their
fathers as being particularly influential in shaping their careers.[23]

[22] Warner and Abegglen, *Occupational Mobility*, p. 272.
[23] Op. cit., ch. 4; Warner and Abegglen, *Business Leaders* p. 79; Collins, Moore, et. al.,
Enterprising Man, pp. 109-24.

These sponsors may have aided their protégés by providing advice, personal influence, and business contacts, or material aid (for example, loans, jobs, apprenticeship, partnership, provision for formal education, et cetera).

Among the 77 entrepreneurs with supportive fathers, at least 11 (14 percent), and possibly as many as 26 (34 percent), received career aid from some sort of sponsor. For these businessmen, it would appear that outside sponsorship was unnecessary because their fathers performed the sponsorship function themselves. Among the disadvantaged entrepreneurs, however, sponsorship was more essential and prevalent. At least 42 (40 percent) and perhaps as many as 66 (63 percent) of the 104 entrepreneurs in this group were aided by some sort of sponsor. Sponsorship also varied within the subgroups of disadvantaged entrepreneurs. Between 21 (66 percent) and 27 (84 percent) of the 32 entrepreneurs experiencing inadequate fathers had sponsors, while only between 14 (27 percent) and 28 (54 percent) of the 52 who experienced the death of a father during childhood had such outside support. Perhaps entrepreneurs experiencing inadequate fathers were more prone to seek alternative male authority figures, while entrepreneurs who experienced the death of their fathers during childhood were more apt to distrust male authority figures, preferring to rely entirely on their own resources.

BIRTH ORDER

In determining birth order, I counted only siblings who survived to age 21 and who were either unborn or surviving at the time the entrepreneur reached age 21. Table 7 indicates that the largest number of our entrepreneurial group was born in the middle birth order position. This, however, says nothing about the possibility of an entrepreneur being the oldest, middle, or last child in his family. Table 8 indicates the actual frequencies of birth order, along with the frequencies expected if the data had conformed to a χ^2 distribution of 2 degrees of freedom. Only those families composed of at least three siblings are included in the data presented in Table 8. I performed a χ^2 test of the assumption that birth order and entrepreneurship are independent. The relevant null and alternative hypotheses are:

H_0: Entrepreneurship is independent of birth order.

H_1: Entrepreneurship is dependent upon birth order.

Using the data presented in Table 8, the χ^2 is 15.51. This result is significantly different than would be expected if the null hypothesis

TABLE 7
BIRTH ORDER

	Only Child	Oldest	Middle	Youngest	Order Un-determined
Father-Dead (52)	6	14	21	10	1
Father-Separation (13)	—	4	6	3	—
Father-Inadequate (32)	2	10	17	3	—
Father-Rejecting (7)	2	3	1	1	—
Supportive Fathers (77)	4	24	35	12	2
Special Cases (6)	—	—	4	2	—
Total (187)	14 (7.5%)	55 (29.4%)	84 (44.9%)	31 (16.6%)	3 (1.6%)

were true. If the null hypothesis were true, this result would occur less than 1 out of 1,000 times. This is so because at $\alpha = .001$ with 2 degrees of freedom, $\chi^2 = 13.82$. I therefore rejected the null hypothesis and accepted the alternative.

I then applied the χ^2 test to the following null hypothesis and its alternative:

H'_0: Entrepreneurship is independent of birth order with respect to the middle versus the youngest birth order positions.

H'_1: Entrepreneurship is dependent upon the birth order with respect to the middle versus the youngest birth order position.

Using the data from the second and third rows of Table 8, the calculated value of $\chi^2 = 0.29$. If null hypothesis H'_0 were true, this result would occur more than 1 out of 2 times. This is so because at $\alpha = .5$ with 1 degree of freedom, $\chi^2 = .46$. I therefore accepted the null hypothesis H'_0 and rejected the alternative H'_1. If follows that the significance of the birth order must occur between the first born position and those birth order positions which are not first born. From Table 8 it is apparent that the actual frequency of first borns among entrepreneurs exceeds the expected frequency. Thus, even

TABLE 8
DISTRIBUTION OF ENTREPRENEURIAL AND NON-ENTREPRENEURIAL
SIBLINGS IN FAMILIES OF THREE OR MORE CHILDREN

	Entrepreneurs		Non-Entrepreneurs	
	Actual	Expected	Actual	Expected
Oldest	40	24	107	123
Middle	84	99	520	505
Youngest	23	24	124	123

$$\chi^2 = \frac{\Sigma (f_o - f_e)^2}{f_e} = 15.514$$

Total = 898

though the largest number of entrepreneurs was born to middle birth order positions, within a family producing at least one entrepreneur, the oldest birth order position had the highest probability of being occupied by an entrepreneur.

These conclusions are subject to the limitation that a χ^2 test properly presumes a test sample drawn in a random fashion. My sample of entrepreneurs was drawn in a way that was not truly random. My results are meaningful, therefore, only on the assumption that the sample would have been similar if it had been drawn in a random fashion.

My study of 187 entrepreneurs indicates that a high proportion of these men experienced disadvantaged childhoods in terms of their relationships with their fathers and quite frequently in economic terms. Their backgrounds involved modest income or actual poverty. The entrepreneurs typically began to work at earlier ages than other businessmen, and they frequently benefited from association with some older male "sponsor" at some point in their careers. In these regards, my results confirm those of the Collins, Moore, et al. study.

I was also able to identify two different types of entrepreneurs. Those entrepreneurs experiencing disadvantaged relationships with their fathers appeared to fit many of the Horatio Alger "rags-to-riches" characteristics, while entrepreneurs who experienced supportive fathers seemed to have been quite similar to the general business elite. The latter group tended to come from more prosperous family backgrounds, inaugurating their careers later and making less use of nonparental sponsors than was the case with disadvantaged entrepreneurs.

Perhaps future studies using other sources will corroborate and refine these conclusions. A definitive statement about the historical process that produced entrepreneurships can only develop out of a series of such examinations drawing upon detailed biographical research. On the basis of my own preliminary treatment, entrepreneurs appear to have been significantly different in terms of family and economic backgrounds than the general business elites that have been studied by others. Important elite characteristics are overlooked by lumping all segments of the business elite into some common "collective portrait." Even among entrepreneurs, important subcategories can be observed. We must thus refine our modes of quantitative analysis if we are to achieve a better understanding of the sources of economic innovation in past and present times.

BERNARD SARACHEK, *University of Missouri—Kansas City*

Development and Decline

[30]

ENTREPRENEURSHIP AND DEVELOPMENT*

By Harvey Leibenstein
Harvard University

I

The received theory of competition gives the impression that there is no need for entrepreneurship. If all inputs are marketed and their prices are known, and if all outputs are marketed and their prices are known, and if there is a definite production function that relates inputs to outputs in a determinate way, then we can always predict the profit for any activity that transforms inputs into outputs. If net profits are positive, then this should serve as a signal for entry into this market. The problem of marshaling resources and turning them into outputs appears to be a trivial activity. From this point of view it is hard to see why there should ever be a deficiency of entrepreneurship. But there is frequently a lack of entrepreneurship. The answer is that the standard competitive model hides the vital function of the entrepreneur.[1]

My aim in what follows is twofold: to suggest a theory of the economy and of entrepreneurship in which entrepreneurship has a unique and critical role and to use this theory to indicate why entrepreneurship is a significant variable in the development process.

In a paper published in 1966 [9] I argued that there does not exist a one-to-one correspondence between sets of inputs and outputs.[2] There are three main reasons for this: contracts for labor are incomplete, the production function is not completely specified or known, and not all factors of production are marketed. I will argue that these are the basic postulates for an economy in which entrepreneurship has a distinct and critical role.

We may distinguish two broad types of entrepreneurial activity: at one pole there is routine entrepreneurship, which is really a type of management, and for the rest of the spectrum we have Schumpeterian or "new type" entrepreneurship. (We shall refer to the latter as N-

* The author would like to thank his colleagues Sam Bowles, Albert O. Hirschman, Gustav Papanek, Nathan Rosenberg, and Ray Vernon for helpful comments that led to some revisions of an earlier version. They are not responsible for the deficiencies that remain.

[1] This point is elaborated in detail in Professor Baumol's paper [3]. His quotation from Veblen is especially apt. Professor Hirschman makes similar points in [8a, pp. 2–5].

[2] See [9] for evidence of specific cases. Econometric evidence on production functions is hard to interpret. Production functions fitted for specific industries frequently have very low values for R^2. While this is consistent with the notion that there is no one-to-one correspondence between inputs and putputs, there are also many other reasons why the fits may be poor. See Marc Nerlove, "Recent Empirical Studies on the CES and Related Production Functions," in *The Theory and Empirical Analysis of Production* (N.B.E.R., 1967), p. 78.

entrepreneurship.) By routine entrepreneurship we mean the activities involved in coordinating and carrying on a well-established, going concern in which the parts of the production function in use (and likely alternatives to current use) are well known and which operates in well-established and clearly defined markets. By N-entrepreneurship we mean the activities necessary to create or carry on an enterprise where not all the markets are well established or clearly defined and/or in which the relevant parts of the production function are not completely known. In both cases the entrepreneur coordinates activities that involve different markets; he is an intermarket operator. But in the case of N-entrepreneurship not all of the markets exist or operate perfectly and the entrepreneur, if he is to be successful, must fill in for the market deficiencies. To my mind one of the main obstacles to our understanding of the entrepreneurial role lies in the conventional theory of the production function. This theory seems so reasonable at first blush that we are likely not to notice the subtle assumptions it makes. The basic culprits are the following assumptions: that the complete set of inputs are specified and known to all actual or potential firms in the industry, and that there is a fixed relation between inputs and outputs. The first assumption is implicit. To my knowledge, it is never stated explicitly, but I have not made an exhaustive search of the literature to check this. The second assumption is explicit, but it is rarely challenged.

In its usual conception the production function is considered to be clearly defined, fully specified, and completely known. Where and to whom in the firm this knowledge is supposed to be available is never stated. In fact, there are great gaps of knowledge about the production function. Points on the production function refer to well-defined inputs. To the extent that they are not completely defined in actuality, the entrepreneur must in some way make up the deficiency. Suppose that to produce a certain commodity, a certain type of machine has to be employed. If no one in the country produces such a machine and if imports are barred, only entrepreneurs who have access to information on how to construct the machine can enter the industry. The potential entrepreneur has to make up for a market deficiency. But that is not his only major function.

Important inputs not well marketed are types of management and market knowledge. Even managers of the more routine type may not be available in well-organized markets in many developing countries. Where available, their capacities may be very difficult to assess. One of the important capacities of management is the ability to obtain and use factors of production that are not well marketed. In some countries the capacity to obtain finance may depend on family connections rather than on the willingness to pay a certain interest rate. A successful entrepreneur may, at times, have to have the capacity to operate well in the political arena connected with his economic activities.

The usual characteristics attributed to entrepreneurs involve gap-filling as one of their essential underlying qualities. For example, it may be thought desirable that entrepreneurs possess at least some of the capacities to: search and discover economic opportunities, evaluate economic opportunities, marshal the financial resources necessary for the enterprise, make time-binding arrangements, take ultimate responsibility for management, be the ultimate uncertainty and/or risk bearer,[3] provide and be responsible for the motivational system within the firm, search and discover new economic information, translate new information into new markets, techniques, and goods, and provide leadership for the work group. In a world of perfect markets, if such a world were possible, each of these characteristics would be marketed as a specific service. Thus, some firms might specialize in the discovery of economic opportunities and sell this information to others. A similar remark could be made of each of the capacities mentioned above. The reason that this is not the case is because some inputs are inherently unmarketable, and some are difficult to market and are frequently unmarketed. For example, we cannot have a perfect market in risk-taking since, among other reasons, there is a "moral risk" problem in profit insurance. (The entrepreneur can intentionally do poorly and cash in on the policy.) Similarly, if the motivational system is the sum of all the human elements and their relations to each other within the firm rather than something specifically provided from outside the firm, then this element cannot be marketed. One of our basic points is that the conditions for perfect markets and the nature of some commodities are inconsistent with each other.

It is important to stress that entrepreneurial activities do not arise only because of market structure imperfections. This view gives too shallow an interpretation of the entrepreneurial role.[4] First, some gaps in markets are inherent in all cases. Second, and what is perhaps less apparent, is that the entrepreneur has to employ some inputs that are somewhat vague in their nature (but nevertheless necessary for production), and whose output is indeterminate. The provision of leadership, motivation, and the availability of the entrepreneur to solve po-

---

[3] Schumpeter [12, p. 137] is very firm on the point that the entrepreneur is not a risk bearer or uncertainty bearer: "The one who gives credit comes to grief if the undertaking fails." Furthermore, in countries with highly developed stock markets some entrepreneurs can shift the risk by selling shares.

[4] A narrow "imperfect market" interpretation of the entrepreneurial role gives the impression that markets are perfectable, say by the elimination of monopolistic influences, and that by doing so, the significant aspects of the entrepreneurial role can be eliminated thereby. This is not the view taken in this paper. The ideas of this paper are not brought out fully by thinking that the entrepreneurs' role depends only on market imperfections.

tential crisis situations, the capacity to carry ultimate responsibility for the organizational structure and the major time-binding (implicit or explicit) contractual arrangements are of this sort. Third, and most important, the entrepreneur has to possess what might be called, for want of a better term, an "input completing" capacity. If six inputs are needed to bring to fruition a firm that produces a marketable product, it does no good to be able to marshal easily five of them. The gap-filling and the "input-completing" capacities are the unique characteristics of the entrepreneur.

As we have defined the entrepreneur he is an individual or group of individuals with four major characteristics: he connects different markets, he is capable of making up for market deficiencies (gap-filling), he is an "input-completer," and he creates or expands time-binding, input-transforming entities (i.e., firms).

Entrepreneurship is frequently a scarce resource because entrepreneurs are gap-fillers and input-completers and these are scarce talents. Other things equal, the amount of gap-filling and input-completing required determines the degree of scarcity. Gap-filling is necessary because information about some inputs are unmarketable; and because private information about markets cannot always be proven and made public information. Of course, gap-filling will also be necessary where universalistic markets have not been developed, or where the inputs are, in principle, marketable but for some reason such markets have not arisen. For any given economic activity there is a minimum quantum of various inputs that must be marshaled. If less than this minimum variety is universalistically available, the entrepreneur has the job of stepping into the breech to fill the lack of marketable inputs; i.e., he must be an input-completer.

In my "X-efficiency" paper [9] I argued that neither individuals nor groups (say, firms) work as hard or as effectively or search for new information and techniques as diligently as they could, nor is effort maintained at a constant level. The nature and degree of directed human effort of a given individual is not invariable in the sense in which the characteristics of some physical inputs and their capacities may be said to be invariable. The degree of directed effort depends on a variety of factors that determine the internal motivational state of the firm and the external motivational state of the appropriate segment of the economy. Thus, under some circumstances the level of directed effort of the human inputs may be low and, as a consequence, some firms operate under a considerable degree of slack [5] [9]. Persistant slack implies the existence of entrepreneurial opportunities.

The motivational state is likely to be composed of the following elements: (1) The system of financial rewards for effort, some of which may be directly related to the quantity of output but some of the rewards may not be clearly related to output. (2) There may also be a system of rewards and "punishments" related to aspects of behavior other than the productive ones. For example, promotion within a firm may be related to personality traits or kinship or personal ties unconnected to the direct pursuit of the aims of the firm. (3) Finally, there is an interpersonal mechanism of group approval and disapproval, as well as approval-disapproval relations between individuals in different relative hierarchical statuses that normally influence productive behavior. The sum of these relationships is essentially the motivational state of the system. It seems clear that the degree and nature of directed effort will depend on the motivational state. This is especially likely to be true for nonroutine aspects of directed effort such as those involved in the introduction of technological change.

There is a significant relation between the entrepreneur's perceptive capacity and the fact that firms operate under some degree of slack [9]. The existence of slack and the fact that not all inputs are marketed means that the market signals for profit opportunities are blurred. Since there is no one-to-one correspondence between inputs and outputs, a knowledge of output price and input prices can no longer yield the necessary signals. On the other hand, an error in perception can be partially counterbalanced by increased effort in marshaling resources and in operating the plant.

It is noteworthy that the traditional theory does not explain the existence of firms as time-binding entities. The theory presented here suggests that since the production function is incomplete, firms become valuable storehouses of detailed experience and knowledge. In part, this means that successful firms are entities that house successful motivational systems that can be retained only through a scheme of renewable contractual arrangements of different time durations. It is in this way that the firm captures some of the long-term benefits of previous gap-filling and input-completing conquests.

A way of looking at the essential elements is to visualize the economy as a net made up of nodes and pathways. The nodes represent industries or households that receive inputs (or consumer goods) along the pathway and send outputs (final goods and inputs for the other commodities) to other nodes. The perfect competition model would be represented by a net that is complete, that has pathways that are well marked and well defined, that has well-marked and well-defined nodes, and one in which each element (i.e., firm or household) of each node deals with every other node along the pathways on equal terms for the same commodity. In the realistic model we have in mind there are holes and tears in the net, obstructions (knots) along the pathways, and some nodes and pathways, where they exist, are poorly defined and poorly marked or entirely unmarked from the viewpoint of elements of other nodes. We may refer to this net as impeded, incomplete, and "dark" in contrast to the unimpeded and "well-lit" net that represents the competitive model. Of course, a portion of the real economy net may very loosely approximate the "unimpeded" net of the perfect competition model. Entrepreneurs working in the well-defined, non-hole, non-obstruction part of the net carry out routine entrepreneurial-managerial activities, while those that operate on the impeded, incomplete, and dark parts carry out N-entrepreneurial activities. Entrepreneurial activities will make some portions of the net less impeded through extending markets (i.e., creating new pathways) but may make others more so through the creation of monpolies, or the creation of other obstacles (e.g., high entry costs) where they previously did not exist. Inventions and the creation of new knowledge will to some extent extend the net to vague and incomplete areas, but other inventions may substitute relatively well-defined pathways and nodes for those which were ill-defined and obstruction-laden previously.

II

Although there is no universally accepted theory of development we can point to two important elements in the process: (1) Per capita income growth requires shifts from less productive to more productive techniques per worker, the creation or adopton of new commodities, new materials, new markets, new organizational forms, the creation of new skills, and the accumulation of new knowledge. (2) Part of the process is the interaction between the creation of economic capacity and the related creation of demand so that some rough balance between capacity growth and demand growth takes place. The entrepreneur as a gap-filler and input-completer is probably the prime mover of the capacity creation part of these elements of the growth process.[5]

We now know that development is not simply a process of physical and human capital accumulation in the usual sense. If that were all that were involved, then development would simply be a function of the willingness to save. Experience has shown that this is not the case. The work of Solow and others [1] [2] [13] have shown that growth cannot be explained by the contributions of the increase in standard inputs. The work of Chenery and Strout [4] emphasizes that the degree of capital absorption can be a significant constraint to growth in developing

[5] The basic idea is that firms do not operate on their production possibilities frontier. In part, the internal motivational state of the firm determines the degree to which actual output is less than the production possibilities frontier output. Thus, costs per unit of output are not minimized. The size of the difference between actual costs and true minimum costs offers opportunities for those entrepreneurs who think they can produce at lower costs.

countries. The existence of and need for gap-filling and input-completing capacities could explain why standard inputs do not account for all outputs and why capital absorption should be a problem. Economic planning experience in many countries reveals that there is frequently a considerable divergence between plan targets and results. This divergence may be partly explained by the fact that enterpreneurship is not a normal input whose contribution can be readily determined, predicted, planned for, or controlled.

We now sketch briefly some of the basic strands of a theory from which the concept of the entrepreneur as a gap-filler and input-completer derives.

The demand side is determined by the following: (1) The maximal production possibilities set in the sense of maximum knowledge. By maximum knowledge we mean that the techniques are known somewhere in the world—knowledge that is conceivably obtainable although it may be at an exceptionally high cost. (2) We deduct from the large maximal possibilities set the subset of techniques in use and those techniques that contain the following basic characteristics: they are actually known in detail without anything more than routine search activities and the inputs required for production are marketed on a routine basis. (3) What is left is that portion of the maximal production possibilities set which forms the potential opportunities for gap-fillers. Now, gap-filling and input-completing activities are usually costly. Taking these costs into account and calculating the expected prices of marketed inputs and potential outputs, each element in the gap-filling opportunity set can be associated with a set of potential profits or losses (depending on who does the gap-filling). We reduce the gap-filling opportunity set to those possibilities that are associated with expected yields of positive net profits. This set is likely to be very much larger than what will actually be pursued by entrepreneurs. The gap-filling opportunity set is likely to be non-unique since the costs associated with gap-filling depend on the specific entrepreneur that attempts to take advantage of the opportunity. The sequence in which gap-fillers choose opportunities will determine the degree to which any one turns out to be profitable. In addition, the degree of effort put forth by different enterpreneurs and the same entrepreneur at different times will vary, depending on the personality, circumstances, and the motivating influences that exist at the time. Thus, the association between gap-filling opportunities and profitable opportunities is not likely to be a unique one-to-one correspondence.

The supply side is determined by the following: the set of individuals with gap-filling and input-completing capacities, the sociocultural and political constraints which influence the extent to which entrepreneurs take advantage of their capacities, and the degree to which potential entrepreneurs respond to different motivational states, especially where nontraditional activities are involved. Clearly, the personality characteristics of entrepreneurs are important. Apart from gap-filling and input-completing capacities, the potential entrepreneurs' response to opportunities will depend on their preference for certain modes of behavior as opposed to others. Thus, the entrepreneurial personality theories developed by Hagen [6] and McClelland [10] which connect nurture to the creation of entrepreneurial drives are significant elements on the supply side. Last, but not least, the alternatives open to individuals are important, since we must take into account opportunity costs of entrepreneurial acts.

In such a theory growth would depend, in part, on the degree of routine entrepreneurship, the degree to which gaps and impediments in markets exist, and the quality, motivations, and opportunity costs of the potential gap-fillers and input-completers available.

It is not possible at this stage to develop a complete and detailed model of economic development and entrepreneurship. One reason for this is that we do not have, at present, a theory of obstructed, incomplete, and "relatively dark" economic systems. However, it may be useful to sketch briefly the broad outlines of what such a model might contain if further research proved successful.

The model, if it were successfully developed, should enable us to describe the the motivational state that arises from any given state of the impeded system and the reactions to the motivational state. That is, the model should show the links between the maximal opportunity set and those opportunities that are actually perceived and pursued by entrepreneurs. We now attempt to specify the links that are likely to be involved: (1) The input gaps are in part determined exogenously. (2) Given the input gaps, and the opportunity set, the interfirm motivational state should determine the degree to which firms expand in response to the pull of profit opportunities and the push of the fear of falling behind competitive firms. The interfirm motivational state itself is determined by the number of firms in the industry, the nature of the market structure, and the energy and aims of the entrepreneurs within these firms, which in turn determines the degree of competition between firms. The interfirm motivational state is unlikely to be sufficient to determine how any specific firm behaves. Among the intervening elements is the perceptive mechanism of the firm which determines the way in which firms receive, filter, and process market information and the degree to which firms become aware of changes of relative competitive status. (3) Thus, the intrafirm motivational state, whose constituents we have described above, determines how firms react to the activities of competitors, and to changes in the opportunities the firm faces. The intrafirm motivational state depends in part on the organizational structure of the firm and in part on the rate of change of manpower (especially managerial personnel) within the firm. The basic notion here is that as new individuals enter the firm, the existing equilibrium between decision-makers and their reactions to each other and to external opportunities may change so that the intrafirm motivational state changes accordingly. Of course, this last depends also on the degree to which new management personnel are similar or different in their capabilities and attitudes from those that they replace. (4) Finally, the input-completing and gap-filling capacities of the potential entrepreneurial pool determines the response of members of this pool to changes in opportunities and motivational states. An important aspect of the abilities involved is both the perception of economic opportunities and the capacity to assess such opportunities. These are presumably determined in part by factors exogenous to the system such as those involved in nurture, informal training, experience, as well as formal education of individuals. In sum, the model should in some way enable us to specify the relations of the links mentioned to the nature of economic states so that we can determine entrepreneurial reactions to changes in the economic state.

It might be helpful to classify N-entrepreneurs into different categories and determine each category's responsiveness to a given motivational state. Probably a significant part of such a model would be the interaction of different types of entrepreneurs to each other's activities (i.e., imitation, linkages, followers on "cleared" pathways, knowledge spread, etc.). Each period the response of the N-entrepreneurs to the motivational state creates a new state of the system and changes the motivational states in subsequent periods. At the same time it changes the supply of N-entrepreneurs in subsequent periods since some of those that enter foreclose their availability on subsequent occasions. Thus, the impulses created by entrepreneurial acts lead to sequences of entrepreneurial activities and changing opportunities which influence the pattern and rate of growth.[6] In addition, basic secular factors would have to be taken into account, since each year some potential entrepreneurs retire and others enter, while, at the same time, inventions lead to changes in the technical frontier and add new elements to the impeded and incomplete part of the market net.

III

To be of interest a theory needs some conjectures to tell us how some basic elements in the theory behave. Hence, to add some interest to this

---

[6] It would be interesting to see under what assumptions we could derive from such a model the growth promoting backward linkages suggested by Professor Hirschman [7] [8].

paper, I will hazard the following, all of which are on an "other things equal" basis: (1) The greater the rate of growth desired, the greater the quantum of gap-filling and input-completing capacities required. (2) The supply of active gap-fillers depends on opportunity costs. (3) The greater the assets of the group related to the gap-filler by kinship or friendship ties, the greater the gap-filling capacity of the entrepreneur involved. (4) Differential gap-filling and input-completing capacities are a critical element in explaining the differential rewards of entrepreneurs. (5) The routinization of gap-filling activities reduces the rewards of entrepreneurs.

There are a set of theories about entrepreneurship which revolve around the notions that in underdeveloped countries entrepreneurs prefer traditional industries, that their behavior is tradition-bound, and that they face overriding institutional obstacles. Yet, developing countries have periods of low growth and other periods of rapid growth. My conjecture in this connection is that in fact traditionalism is not the critical element but that the motivations present—e.g., the profit rates —are such that those with gap-filling capacities are willing and able to exert themselves under some motivational circumstances and reduce the degree of exertion under others. Thus, the ebb and flow of low and high growth rates can be explained without positing institutional rigidities that would appear to be almost impossible to overcome.

Two related elements that come to mind are the facts that entrepreneurs frequently come from groups which have fairly large extended families who are often engaged in trade and that they are disproportionately recruited from elements of the population that in some sense or other are looked upon as "outsiders." The extended family aspect can be explained by the fact that gap-filling capacities depend in part on kinship relations in which there is a much higher degree of trust and through which one can draw on more diverse capacities than exist on a universalistic basis. While there are many aspects to the outsider part of the phenomena, part of it, perhaps, can be explained by the fact that to the extent that outsiders are restricted from some economic opportunities, their opportunity costs as entrepreneurs are likely to be lower than other portions of the population, and hence they more readily engage in entrepreneurial activities compared to "insiders" whose opportunity costs are higher. However, not all outsiders become entrepreneurs since low opportunity costs can only be a facilitating and not a sufficient condition for entrepreneurship.

I realize that I run the risk of being charged, to use Professor Baumol's phrase, with offering nothing more than a taxonomy. I want to suggest that this is not the case—that the characteristics of the world described in this paper and the specified nature of the entrepreneurial role is such that it does lead to potentially interesting conclusions for development problems.

Our basic assumptions are as follows: (1) Motivation internal to the firm is a basic input that is not marketed. (2) There always exists some degree of slack (or excess capacity) due to low X-efficiency. (3) To bring any enterprise into fruition requires the marshaling of a minimum quantum of inputs. (4) Some inputs are "nonexhaustible" in the usual sense; that is, they do not necessarily decrease with use. Indeed, in some cases the opposite may be the case. Knowledge and motivation are two inputs of this type.

Some possible conclusions derivable from our assumptions are as follows:

1. While entrepreneurship may be scarce because of a lack of input-completing capacities, some entrepreneurial characteristics may in fact be in surplus supply; that is, they are unused simply because of the lack of the input completing capacity. In addition, some may be unused because the motivational state does not bring forth an adequate entrepreneurial response. As a consequence, it is possible that in some cases, small changes in the motivational state or in the reduction of market impediments may turn entrepreneurial scarcity into an abundant supply.

2. Our analysis of entrepreneurship requires us to reconsider the literature on investment criteria. Since investment can alter the market impediments and hence alter the supply of entrepreneurship, we must consider such possible side effects in our investment criteria. Thus, a lower profit investment that releases entrepreneurial energies and capacities may be more fruitful in the long run than a higher profit investment, if profit is calculated apart from the side effects we have just mentioned.

3. Some types of input creation which would normally appear to be functional may in fact be dysfunctional when the side effects are taken into account. For example, some types of higher education provided to potential entrepreneurs may be dysfunctional in that it increases the opportunity costs of potential entrepreneurs and may as a consequence decrease the supply of entrepreneurship.[7]

4. The theory suggests that training can do something to increase the supply of entrepreneurship. Obviously, not all characteristics of entrepreneurs are trainable. However, since entrepreneurship requires a combination of capacities, some of which may be vital gaps in carrying out the input-completing aspect of the entrepreneurial role, training can eliminate some of these gaps. For example, it may be difficult to train people to spot economic opportunities, but it is possible to train them to

[7] Somerset Maugham's story of the illiterate verger is an illustration of this possibility.

assess such opportunities once perceived. Similarly, certain managerial skills are trainable, but without them new firms might not survive because of their inability to overcome initial managerial difficulties.

For policy purposes, the theory suggests that development economists focus their attention when concerned with specific countries on studying the gaps, obstructions, and impediments in the market network of the economy in question and on the gap-filling and input-completing capacities and responsiveness to different motivational states of the potential entrepreneurs in the population.

REFERENCES

1. M. Abramovitz, "Resources and Output Trends in the United States Since 1870," *A.E.R.*, May, 1956.
2. O. Aukrust, "Investment and Economic Growth," *Prod. Meas. Rev.*, Feb., 1959.
3. W. Baumol, "The Entrepreneurship in Economic Theory," *A.E.R.*, May, 1968.
4. H. B. Chenery and A. M. Strout, "Foreign Assistance and Economic Development," *A.E.R.*, Sept., 1966, p. 686.
5. R. M. Cyert and J. G. March, *A Behaviorial Theory of the Firm* (Prentice-Hall, 1963).
6. E. E. Hagen, *On the Theory of Social Change* (Irwin, 1962).
7. Albert O. Hirschman, *The Strategy of Economic Development* (Harvard Univ. Press, 1951).
8. ———, *Development Projects Observed* (1967).
8a. ———, *Journeys Through Progress* (1963).
9. H. Leibenstein, "Allocative Efficiency vs. *X*-Efficiency," *A.E.R.*, June, 1966.
10. D. McClelland, *The Achieving Society* (Princeton, 1961).
11. G. F. Papanek, *Pakistan's Development* (Cambridge, 1967).
12. J. A. Schumpeter, *The Theory of Economic Development* (Harvard Univ. Press, 1951).
13. R. Solow, "Technical Change and the Aggregate Production Function," *Rev. of Econ. and Statis.*, Aug., 1957.

[31]

Industrial Organization and Entrepreneurship in the Developing Countries: The Economic Groups

Nathaniel H. Leff*
Columbia University

I. Introduction

The subject of industrial organization has not received much attention in the analysis of postwar economic development. This neglect has occurred despite the importance of industrial organization for such questions as efficiency in production and investment and, especially, for transmitting the external economies which are believed to play a central role in the development process.[1] By contrast, the topic of entrepreneurship in less-developed economies has been discussed extensively, if not always in satisfactory theoretical terms.[2] As William Baumol expressed it a decade ago, despite the entrepreneur's "acknowledged importance . . . [he is] one of the most elusive characters in the cast that constitutes the subject of economic analysis . . . [and has] virtually disappeared from the theoretical literature."[3] This conceptual elusiveness is especially unfortunate for the analysis of the developing economies, in which entrepreneurship is likely to be more necessary for output expansion and structural change than in the more developed countries.

* I am grateful to Tuvia Blumenthal, Neil Chamberlain, Frank Edwards, Ronald Findlay, David Felix, Harvey Leibenstein, Richard Porter, Frederic Pryor, Kazuo Sato, and Julian Simon for helpful comments on an earlier version of this paper. I also thank the Faculty Research Program of the Columbia Business School for financial support; and the Department of Developing Countries of Tel-Aviv University, where the first draft of the paper was written, for the use of its research facilities. I bear sole responsibility for any deficiencies in the paper.

[1] Paul N. Rosenstein-Rodan, "Problems of the Industrialization of Eastern and South Eastern Europe," *Economic Journal* 53 (June 1943): 202–11.

[2] For an indication of the large volume of professional literature addressed to the subject of entrepreneurship and economic development, see the bibliography in Flavia Derossi, *The Mexican Entrepreneur* (Paris: OECD Development Centre, 1972), pp. 409–28.

[3] William Baumol, "Entrepreneurship in Economic Theory," *American Economic Review* 58 (May 1968): 61–71; quote from p. 64.

Economic Development and Cultural Change

Industrial organization and entrepreneurship are of course related.[4] Accordingly, this paper attempts to make some analytical progress by considering these two subjects together. We will proceed by drawing attention to and analyzing a pattern of industrial organization in the developing countries which has important effects on the functioning of these economies, particularly on the conditions which affect investment and production decisions. This pattern of industrial organization, which I shall call "the group," is distinct from other forms of capitalist organization in the less developed countries which have been more widely noted and discussed; for example, the public sector corporation, the broadly held public company, the family owned company, and the multinational corporation. Despite its existence as a phenomenon which appears in many developing countries and despite its pervasive economic effects, which we shall discuss below, the group has received surprisingly little generalized analysis. Some aspects of the group phenomenon have been noted before, usually in observations for individual less developed countries. Also, most observers have focused on one or two features of the groups, such as their monopoly power or their political connections. However, relatively little effort has been directed to conceptualizing the groups in more general analytical terms, and analyzing the implications for economic development, industrial organization, and entrepreneurship.[5]

II. The Economic Groups

In many of the less developed countries a significant part of the domestic and privately owned industrial sector, and particularly the activities which use relatively modern and capital-intensive techniques, is organized in a special institutional pattern. Following the Latin American term, we may call this structure the "group," although this pattern of economic organization is also common, with different names, in Asia and Africa. Documentation on the structure and scale of group activities in many less developed countries is sparse. This is not surprising, for collection of data on a phenomenon usually requires that its existence first be noted in the professional literature and a conceptual framework be developed to analyze it. Such a general framework has previously not been developed for the groups. Nevertheless, on the basis of presently available materials, the following generalizations can be advanced.[6]

---

[4] Cf. the comment by W. A. Lewis: "We have no good theory of entrepreneurship because we have no good theory of monopoly," cited by Baumol, p. 68.

[5] The present paper concentrates on the causes of the group structure and on its positive effects on the functioning of the less developed economies. Pernicious effects and their policy implications are discussed in my "Monopoly Capitalism and Public Policy in the Less-developed Economies," mimeographed (1978; available from the author).

[6] For some published sources which discuss aspects of the groups (often in different terms), see, e.g., W. Dean, *The Industrialization of São Paulo* (Austin:

Nathaniel H. Leff

The group is a multicompany firm which transacts in different markets but which does so under common entrepreneurial and financial control. More generally, this pattern of industrial organization has two essential features. First, the group draws its capital and its high-level managers from sources which transcend a single family. The capital and the managers may come from a number of wealthy families, but they remain within the group as a single economic unit. The group's owner-managers typically include some (but by no means all) members of the family within which the group's activity originated. However, what distinguishes this institution from the family firm and what gives it the resources for greater scope is the fact that owner-managers from other families also participate. Participants are people linked by relations of interpersonal trust, on the basis of a similar personal, ethnic, or communal background.[7]

Second, somewhat like the *zaibatsu* in pre–World War II Japan, the groups invest and produce in several product markets rather than

University of Texas Press, 1969), pt. 1; A. Lauterbach, "Management Aims and Development Needs in Latin America," *Business History Review* 42 (Winter 1968): 558–59; Derossi, esp. pp. 97–115 and 158–93; François Bourricaud, "Structure and Function of the Peruvian Oligarchy," *Studies in Comparative International Development* 2 (1966): 1–15; Robert T. Aubey, "Entrepreneurial Formation in El Salvador," *Explorations in Entrepreneurial History*, vol. 6 (November 1969), esp. pp. 272–76; D. W. Stammer, "Financial Development and Economic Growth in Underdeveloped Countries: Comment," *Economic Development and Cultural Change* 20 (January 1972): 318–25; Andrew J. Brimmer, "The Setting of Entrepreneurship in India," *Quarterly Journal of Economics* 69 (1955): 553–76; G. Rosen, *Some Aspects of Industrial Finance in India* (Glencoe, Ill.: Free Press, 1962), chap. 1; E. K. Hazari, *The Corporate Private Sector* (Bombay, 1966); Gustav Papanek, *Pakistan's Development* (Cambridge, Mass.: Harvard University Press, 1967), pp. 67–68; Thomas A. Timberg, "Industrial Entrepreneurship among the Trading Communities of India," Harvard University Economic Development Report no. 136, mimeographed (Cambridge, Mass.: Harvard University, July 1969), pp. 1–126; Hannah Papanek, "Pakistan's Big Businessmen," *Economic Development and Cultural Change* 21 (October 1972): 1–32, esp. 17–32; Lawrence J. White, *Industrial Concentration and Economic Power in Pakistan* (Princeton, N.J.: Princeton University Press, 1974); and Harry Strachan, *The Role of Family and Other Groups in Economic Development: The Case of Nicaragua* (New York: Praeger Publishers, 1976). (The page references cited below to Strachan's work refer to his D.B.A. thesis, Harvard University, 1972.) I have also been informed by Steven Resnick, K. S. Lee, and Jose Buera that a similar pattern exists in the Philippines, South Korea, and the Dominican Republic, respectively. Also, on the basis of his field experience in Asia and Africa, Richard Porter has written to me that the groups are common in other countries of Asia and Africa. These materials, as well as my own interviews conducted in the course of fieldwork in less developed countries, constitute the basis for the statements advanced in the text.

[7] The groups I am discussing are, for reasons of their comparative advantage and private returns, largely in the "modern" sector of the economy. Another type of group, often purely ethnic and without capabilities in modern technology, sometimes operates as an informal financial intermediary in activities where "organized" sources of finance are scarce in less developed countries (see, e.g., William Baldwin, "The Thai Rice Trade as a Vertical Market Network," *Economic Development and Cultural Change* 22 [January 1974]: 179–99).

Economic Development and Cultural Change

in a single product line. These product markets may be quite diverse, ranging, for example, from consumer durables to chemicals to steel rolling. These activities have sometimes been selected on the basis of forward or backward integration. In other cases, new investments have been made in product markets which are unrelated but in activities where the group's technical and managerial capabilities are applicable as inputs.[8] Large groups have also established banks and other financial intermediaries to tap capital from sources outside the immediate members of the group.[9] Finally, the groups usually exercise a considerable degree of market power in the activities where they operate.

In some respects the groups' diversified activities obviously resemble the American conglomerates. However, for microeconomic reasons discussed below, they developed indigenously and independently in the less developed countries.[10] It is also important to note that in many less developed countries the assets of the larger individual groups run to tens of millions of dollars. Taken together, they comprise a significant perecentage of the modern industrial sector, particularly of that portion which is not owned by public sector firms or by multinational corporations.

Reliable documentation on the extent of group activities is not available for many countries; and in developing countries with a substantial stock of direct investments by multinational corporations it would be easy to underestimate the groups' quantitative importance. This is because their investment strategy involves portfolio balance through diversification in different activities; consequently, they do not concentrate their investments in a single industry. By contrast, foreign-based multinational corporations can also diversify their portfolios interna-

---

[8] For a similar pattern in more developed countries, see Edith T. Penrose, *The Theory of the Growth of the Firm* (New York: Basil Blackwell, 1959), chaps. 5 and 7. Cf. also with G. B. Richardson's distinction between expansion into activities which are "complementary" to or "similar" to a firm's initial activities (see his paper, "The Organization of Industry," *Economic Journal* 82 [September 1972]: 887–92).

[9] In some cases, the reverse sequence has occurred: from a group's establishing a bank to entry into nonfinancial activities. Derossi (p. 178, n.) remarks that in addition to the banks which belong to industrial groups in Mexico the same can be said of 41 of the country's 44 *financieras* (investment banks).

[10] In some respects these reasons are similar. Thus the groups' pattern of diversifying to utilize slack resources is similar to the expansion path documented by Alfred D. Chandler for American firms (see, e.g., his *Strategy and Structure: Chapters in the History of Industrial Enterprise* [Cambridge, Mass.: M.I.T. Press, 1962], pp. 102–3, 432, 448). By contrast, the emergence of the groups in the less developed countries owes less to the conditions of tax and capital-market legislation, which were important in the United States. On the latter, see Jon Didrichsen, "The Development of Diversified and Conglomerate Firms in the United States, 1920–70," *Business History Review* 46 (Summer 1972): 202–19. Didrichsen has also emphasized the importance of economies of scale to imperfectly marketed skills (see the discussion in Sec. III below).

Nathaniel H. Leff

tionally.[11] Because of the groups' interactivity diversification, multinational corporations are often the largest firms within specific industries. The foreigners' position as the dominant firm within individual industries may divert attention from the groups' large overall assets within the industrial sector as a whole.

Despite data limitations, some figures convey an idea of the groups' scope. In Nicaragua, Strachan reports that in the early 1970s four groups accounted for 35% of all loans and investments of the total financial sector and a much larger share of loans and investments in the private financial sector.[12] In Pakistan in 1968, 10 groups controlled 33% of all assets of private, Pakistani-controlled firms in the modern manufacturing sector; and 30 groups controlled 52%.[13] These assets were held in a wide range of diversified activities.[14] Similarly, in India the largest four groups held 17% of the assets of public and private companies in 1958 and the largest 20 groups, 28%.[15] As regards diversification, data for 37 of the largest Indian domestically owned groups show an average of five activities per group.[16] Excluding the two largest groups (Tata and Birla), the average was still four activities per group.

A more detailed picture of the size and diversification of groups in a developing economy is available from a 1962 study in Brazil.[17] These data on the assets and diversification of Brazilian groups in 1962 are presented in table 1. Although these data convey an idea of the size of groups in Brazil, for a number of reasons table 1 tends to understate the importance of the groups. First, the study considered only the groups' own capital, excluding external resources which they could mobilize. The balance-sheet data utilized may also underreport true asset values, both to reduce tax payments and because of accounting lags during inflation. The study was also confined to the four most industrialized states of Brazil's south, thereby omitting groups located elsewhere in the economy. Finally, the data of table 1 relate to 1962, before the large economic expansion which began after 1967. An update of these data

---

[11] In some cases where multinational corporations operating in developing countries have generated cash flow in excess of profit-remission constraints, they have also followed a pattern of interactivity investment within the local economy. This behavior reflects the same causes as those affecting the groups (see Sec. III below).

[12] Strachan, pp. 80–81.

[13] White, p. 65.

[14] Letter from Gustav Papanek, May 6, 1969.

[15] Hazari, chap. 2, as cited in White, p. 71.

[16] These figures on group participation in different activities were computed from data presented in Timberg, pp. 88–104.

[17] Maurício Vinhas de Queiroz, "Os grupos multibilionarios," *Revista do instituto de ciências sociais* (Rio de Janeiro) 2, no. 1 (January 1965): 47–77; Luciano Martins, "Os grupos bilionarios nacionais," ibid., pp. 79–115. I am grateful to Marcio Teixeira for bringing this data source to my attention.

Economic Development and Cultural Change

TABLE 1

Own Assets and Diversification of Private, Locally Owned Groups
in Four States of Brazil, 1962

	Asset Class ($ Million)		
	2.5–10	>10	>25
Groups (*N*)................	144	24	5
Average companies per group (*N*)	8*	21	N.A.

Sources.—Maurício Vinhas de Queiroz, "Os grupos multibilionarios," *Revista do instituto de ciências sociais* (Rio de Janeiro) 2, no. 1
(January 1965): 47, 50, 64; Luciano Martins, "Os grupos bilionarios
nacionais," ibid., p. 86.
    Note.—The asset figures are in 1962 dollars, converted from cruzeiros
at an exchange rate of 400 cruzeiros per dollar. N.A. = not available.
    * Sample estimate.

would undoubtedly show a much larger scale for the assets of groups in
Brazil.

Bearing in mind the size and diversity of groups and their importance in the private, domestically owned modern sector of the economy,
we will consider and discuss below the effects this feature of industrial
organization has on the functioning of the developing economies. First,
however, let us analyze the causes of the group structure.

III. Causes of the Group Pattern of Industrial Organization

The group pattern of industrial organization is readily understood as a
microeconomic response to well-known conditions of market failure in
the less developed countries. In fact, the emergence of the group as an
institutional mode might well have been predicted on the basis of familiar
theory and a knowledge of the environment in these countries.

The group can be conceptualized as an organizational structure for
appropriating quasi rents which accrue from access to scarce and imperfectly marketed inputs. Some of these inputs, such as capital, might be
marketed more efficiently, but in the conditions of the less developed
countries they are not. Some of these inputs are inherently difficult to
market efficiently; for example, honesty and trustworthy competence
on the part of high-level managers.[18] Finally, substantial private gains
can accrue from *not* marketing some inputs, for example, information
generated in one group activity which is relevant for (actual or potential)
investment and production decisions elsewhere in the economy.

The absence of markets for risk and uncertainty also helps explain
another feature of the groups' pattern of expansion—their entry in diversified product lines. This pattern may appear to be due exclusively to
the relatively small size of the domestic market for many manufactured

[18] Harvey Leibenstein, "Entrepreneurship and Development," *American Economic Review* 58 (May 1968): 72–83.

Nathaniel H. Leff

products in the less developed countries. More important, however, for reasons of portfolio balance, diversification has an obvious appeal in economies subject to the risks and uncertainties of instability and rapid structural change. The groups' practice of choosing new investments on the basis of backward and forward linkages also stems in part from an effort to alleviate risk and uncertainty. Vertical integration has been sought to avoid being dependent on a monopolist or oligopolist for materials inputs, or on an oligopsonist for the group's output. In conditions where both parties must make specific and long-lived investments, bilateral oligopoly involves serious risks and uncertainties concerning future quantities, qualities, and prices for inputs and for outputs. In addition, vertical integration can avoid the transactions (bargaining and enforcing) costs which intricate arm's-length negotiations would entail.[19]

These conditions which lead to gains from vertical integration are well known from the more developed countries.[20] They are likely to be more severe, however, in the less developed countries. The probability of having to confront strong market power is greater in these economies whose domestic markets are often too small to accommodate more than a few sellers and buyers for many intermediate products.[21] Also, in relatively large and open economies such as those of the more developed countries random fluctuations in the components of overall market demand for specific intermediate products may be offsetting. The less developed economies, however, are too small and often too closed to enable the law of large numbers to have this smoothing effect, and make more predictable the total market demand for individual intermediate products.

The institution of the group is thus an intrafirm mechanism for dealing with deficiencies in the markets for primary factors, risk, and intermediate products in the developing countries. In this perspective, the group pattern of industrial organization fits closely into the theory of entrepreneurship and development formulated by Harvey Leibenstein.[22]

Leibenstein has suggested that entrepreneurship in less developed countries involves the opening of channels for input supply and for marketing of output in situations where a routinized market mechanism does not exist. In the absence of such "intermarket operators" some input and/or output quantities, qualities, and costs would be so beclouded by risk and uncertainty that investment and production in these activities

[19] Oliver E. Williamson, "The Vertical Integration of Production: Market Failure Considerations," *American Economic Review* 61 (May 1971): 112–23.

[20] George J. Stigler, "The Division of Labor Is Limited by the Extent of the Market," reprinted in his *The Organization of Industry* (Homewood, Ill.: Richard D. Irwin, Inc., 1968), pp. 136–38.

[21] Reliance on international trade to complement the domestic market might be another possibility. However, in addition to problems often posed by overvalued exchange rates, foreign trade often involves—or is perceived to involve—substantial risks and uncertainties of its own in the less developed countries.

[22] See n. 18 above.

Economic Development and Cultural Change

would not take place. With their access to nonmarketed inputs and with their pattern of vertical integration, however, the groups create a channel both for mobilizing and for allocating such inputs and outputs. In fact, the group can perhaps best be understood as an institutional innovation for internalizing the returns which accrue from interactivity operations in the imperfect market conditions of the less developed countries. What has happened in effect is that the groups have appropriated as gains the quasi rents of the output which Leibenstein envisaged would otherwise be foregone due to imperfect factor markets and insufficient entrepreneurship.

Not only does the group pattern of industrial organization provide the "real life" correspondence to Leibenstein's theory of entrepreneurship, but it also suggests some analytical extensions. First, the group constitutes a pattern of industrial organization which permits *structure* rather than gifted individuals to perform the key interactivity function of entrepreneurship. Another departure from earlier theoretical expectations is that with the institution of the group some factors and products flow within the *firm* rather than through the market.

IV. Other Explanations

The preceding discussion has explained the group pattern of industrial organization largely as an institutional innovation for overcoming—and reaping the benefits from—imperfect markets in the less developed countries. We must also consider some other interpretations of this phenomenon.

Thus it has been suggested that the group structure arises mainly because of political connections which permit special access to government dispensations of, for example, import licenses.[23] Groups undoubtedly do benefit from government largesse in the form of import licenses, bank charters, and tax and investment credits; but this is hardly an "alternative" explanation. For one thing, the groups' entrepreneurship and the externalities which they internalize (see below) help explain why particular government favors may have higher present value for groups than for other firms and, consequently, why the groups can outbid others in acquiring political favors and connections.[24] More generally, I do not believe that political influence per se is a *sufficient* reason for the emergence of the group pattern of industrial organization.[25] If the reader

[23] See, e.g., White, p. 17.

[24] For a more general framework on this topic, see my "Corruption and Economic Development," *American Behavioral Scientist* 3 (December 1964): 8–14.

[25] Cf. Hannah Papanek's comment: "Although political influence obviously played an important role in the development of the Big Houses, it was not in itself sufficient for large-scale growth of the enterprises" (p. 17).

Nathaniel H. Leff

judges otherwise, however, political connections can readily be conceptualized as an imperfectly marketed input.

It may also be suggested that the group structure is due to no more than imperfect access to capital and that the highly skewed distribution of wealth common in less developed countries simply means that the very rich take a pervasive role in industrialization. I find this explanation insufficient on a number of grounds. First, it fails to explain why only a small percentage of individuals and families in the traditional wealthy class establish groups. Also, some groups have been founded by individuals who were initially not in the high-wealth brackets.[26]

The emphasis I have placed on the importance of conditions other than preferential access to capital alone as an explanation for the groups[27] is supported by other features of their structure.[28] The groups do not operate simply as financial trusts or holding companies; rather, they maintain active entrepreneurial participation in their manifold activities. The existence of structures similar to groups in the public sector of some less developed countries provides further evidence that more than imperfect access to capital underlies the group pattern of industrial organization. Public sector companies in the less developed countries generally face less stringent conditions of capital supply than do private firms. Nevertheless, where legislation has permitted, some public sector companies have also operated with diversified investment and production activities similar to those of private groups.[29]

V. The Groups and Entrepreneurship
The existence of large-scale, diversified firms is a familiar phenomenon in advanced capitalist economies. What have we gained from noting that a similar phenomenon, in the special form of the groups, is also present in the developing countries?

First, the group pattern of industrial organization has helped relax entrepreneurial constraint which, in the first postwar decade, many observers expected would limit the pace of economic development in the

[26] Hannah Papanek (ibid.) has also noted the "modest antecedents of some of the big businessmen in Pakistan today."

[27] Cf. George Stigler's comment that the phrase "imperfections in the capital market" has too often been employed as a substitute for analysis of other relevant conditions (see his "Imperfections in the Capital Market," *Journal of Political Economy* 75 [June 1967]: 287–92, reprinted in *The Organization of Industry*).

[28] Strachan (p. 111) reports that in the Nicaraguan groups people who can contribute only capital but not special management skills to group activities are gradually excluded from participation. He has also noted another piece of information which reduces the importance of preferential access to capital as a sufficient condition for the group structure. He points out that Costa Rica, where the banking system has been nationalized since the late 1940s, has groups which operate in modes similar to those of Nicaragua, with its privately owned banking system.

[29] An example is the Pertamina company in Indonesia.

Economic Development and Cultural Change

underdeveloped countries. Thus, this institution has permitted "pure" Schumpeterian entrepreneurship to become effective. This is because the group provides the capital and the technical and managerial resources which are necessary to transform "innovativeness and alertness to opportunities"[30] into actual investment and production decisions. The institution of the group also facilitates economies in the use of scarce entrepreneurial resources. Economies of scale to entrepreneurship can be appropriated as able individuals are utilized to their full potential in the group's large and diversified activities. In addition to such "central office" effects, the groups increase entrepreneurial mobility, for they can deploy entrepreneurial resources to specific intragroup companies as opportunities arise.

Perhaps even more importantly, the group *structure* itself reduces the amount of enterepreneurial capacity which is required per unit of innovative decision making. Thus the groups' partcipation in many different activities increases information flows and reduces uncertainty surrounding investment and production decisions.[31] More generally, the groups embody in their structure and expansion path a number of suggestions which have been advanced on theoretical grounds for economizing on entrepreneurship in developing countries. As noted earlier, the group performs the Leibenstein entrepreneurial function of overcoming deficiencies in important factor and product markets. In addition, as we have seen, the groups expand along a path of backward and forward linkages, with investment decisions taken in function of economic and technological complementarities. Thus the groups have in effect implemented at the micro level the development pattern which Albert Hirschman proposed as an optimizing *macro* strategy for economies where entrepreneurship is scarce.[32]

Note finally a subjective, motivational feature which also increases the groups' orientation toward the investment and economic expansion aspects of entrepreneurship. The groups' top managers are often aggressive "empire builders." However, these managers lack some standard criteria for evaluating their performance, either for purposes of their own self-assessment or, perhaps even more important subjectively, for com-

[30] For a discussion of these aspects of entrepreneurship, see I. M. Kirzner, *Competition and Entrepreneurship* (Chicago: University of Chicago Press, 1973), pp. 39–57.

[31] In terms of John Harris's decision-theory conceptualization of entrepreneurship, the reduced uncertainty caused by the group pattern of industrial organization leads to a shift of the action set toward the origin and a rise in the probability that a given profitable investment will be implemented. For Harris's model of entrepreneurship, see his paper, "Entrepreneurship and Economic Development," in *Business Enterprise and Economic Change: Essays in Honor of Harold F. Williamson,* ed. Louis Cain and Paul Uselding (Kent, Ohio: Kent State University Press, 1973).

[32] Albert O. Hirschman, *The Strategy of Economic Development* (New Haven, Conn.: Yale University Press, 1958), pp. 42–43.

Nathaniel H. Leff

parison with rival groups. Thus, the deficiencies of formal capital markets in the developing countries prevent the use of share-prices in the stock market as an evaluative mechanism. And problems of accounting in these inflationary environments also preclude utilizing the group's overall rate of return on capital as a yardstick. In this context, two figures which are more readily available take on a special appeal as a performance measure: the size of a group's turnover and, relatedly, the rate of sales growth over time. This approach leads to a bias toward sales maximization, subject to a profit constraint, in the group's operations. The inefficiencies associated with such a management orientation are well known.[33] In the present context, however, this orientation also reinforces a group's propensity for entrepreneurial expansionism.

VI. Other Beneficial Effects on the Developing Economies
In addition to entrepreneurship, the group pattern of industrial organization also makes a difference in terms of other positive effects on the functioning of the developing economies. Not only does the group provide an institution for mobilizing capital from a pool which extends beyond the resources of a single family, but it performs a similar function for higher-management personnel as well. Such an enlargement of the base from which human resources can be recruited is especially important in the less developed countries. This is because mobilization and utilization of these human resources is in any case severely limited, due to the fact that top management is often selected only from within the circle of people who have at least some participation in ownership. The separation of ownership from control has not occurred on a large scale in the indigenous private sector of these economies.[34]

Furthermore, the group's internal relations of interpersonal trust permit the formation of larger top management teams than would otherwise be possible.[35] This facilitates effective communication and delegation of authority and enables firms to overcome organizational constraints

[33]William J. Baumol, *Business Behavior, Value and Growth* (New York: Harcourt, Brace & World, 1959), pp. 49–50.

[34] As discussed below, the groups' activities may suffer from some forms of inefficiency. It would be easy to attribute this to nepotism and to the lack of separation of ownership from control. Many of the groups' top managers are, however, professionally trained. In addition, the keener motivation and vested interest of owner-managers may increase the pressures for superior performance. In the United States, there is some evidence of better performance in firms which are owner controlled rather than management controlled (see R. J. Monsen, J. S. Chiu, and D. E. Cooley, "The Effect of Separation of Ownership and Control on the Performance of the Large Firm," *Quarterly Journal of Economics* 82 [August 1968]: 435–51; and Harvey Leibenstein, "Organization or Frictional Equilibria, X-Efficiency, and The Rate of Innovation," *Quarterly Journal of Economics* 83 [November 1969]: 614–15).

[35] Interpersonal trust among the top owner-managers of the group is so important in these environments that Strachan (pp. 4, 22–25) considers it one of the central features of this pattern of industrial organization.

Economic Development and Cultural Change

on size and efficiency.[36] As a result, group firms can achieve economies of scale which might otherwise be foregone and can attain output levels and rates of growth within individual activities which would be beyond the scope of family-owned firms.[37]

The group pattern of industrial organization also affects rates of return to capital and the rate of capital formation in the less developed countries. The groups' capacity to marshall the managerial and technical resources necessary for entry into new activities mitigates downward pressures on rates of return to capital which would otherwise occur if firms were restricted to their existing activities. The groups' power in product markets probably also leads to a higher rate of return.[38] In addition, the diversification in the groups' activities reduces portfolio risk. Both individually and a fortiori, in interaction, these risk and rate-of-return conditions caused by the group pattern of industrial organization probably lead to a higher rate of investment than would otherwise prevail.

Further, investments made along lines of vertical integration permit the group to internalize economies which would otherwise be external to the firm and its individual activity. Thus, in addition to increasing the volume of capital formation, the group pattern also leads in this respect to a (socially) more optimal allocation of investment.[39] With their interactivity investment allocations, the groups provide a previously unsuspected mechanism for capital mobility between activities. In fact, to some extent the groups approximate the functioning of a capital market in the less developed countries.[40] The pattern of investment and production

[36] See Penrose, pp. 28–29. On the special aspects of this managerial problem in developing countries, see Peter Kilby, *Entrepreneurship and Economic Development* (New York: Free Press, 1971), pp. 26–29.

[37] This has also been noted by White (p. 33). His data for Pakistan (pp. 150–51) indicate that group firms there experienced faster growth than nongroup firms. This result obtained even when the size of original equity investment, which was also larger for group firms, is held constant.

[38] Studies with U.S. data, for example, have indicated a strong positive relation between a firm's rate of return and its market power, as measured by its market share within an industry (see, e.g., W. G. Shephard, "The Elements of Market Structure," *Review of Economics and Statistics* 54 [February 1972]: 25–37. This relation holds even when barriers to entry are low [p. 31]). For a less developed country, Pakistan, White (pp. 145–46) has presented evidence showing a positive relation between industry concentration ratios and industry rates of return. William J. House reports similar results for Kenya (see his paper, "Market Structure and Industry Performance: The Case of Kenya," *Oxford Economic Papers* 25 [November 1973]: 405–19).

[39] In discussing their investment decisions, group firms usually express themselves in terms of the need to provide input and output quantities for complementary group activities rather than in terms of prices and rates of return. This need not be as irrational as might first appear. In effect, such decisions involve using the primal rather than the dual solution of an implicit linear programming optimizing model.

[40] White (p. 33) has also noted aspects of the groups' capital market activities. An extended analysis is presented in my "Capital Markets in the Less-developed Countries: The Group Principle," in *Money and Finance in Economic*

Nathaniel H. Leff

decisions taken in cognizance of backward and forward linkage effects helps explain the speed of the adjustment process with which interrelated investment opportunities have been taken up in less developed countries.[41] Finally, the coordination of investment and production decisions by the groups has both reduced the need for, and lessened the burden on, government planning of the modern sector in developing countries.

The preceding discussion has noted some of the ways in which the group pattern of industrial organization improves the efficiency of the less developed economies. However, the groups also create some serious distortions. These involve inefficiency within the group, interfirm and intersectoral distortions, and finally, political-economic effects on overall development patterns. In effect, the groups have taken factor-market imperfections in the less developed countries and transmuted them into product-market imperfections. In the process, rapid industrial growth has often occurred, but the groups have also created a special form of monopoly capitalism in the less developed countries. The associated distortions raise important problems for public policy in the less developed countries. However, that subject is so large that it requires another paper.[42]

VII. Conclusions

This paper has drawn attention to and analyzed a neglected feature of industrial organization which has far-reaching effects on the economies of many less developed countries, the group. As noted, the groups have their origin in well-known market imperfections of the less developed countries. Mobilizing imperfectly marketed inputs, and reducing uncertainty and risk with their diversified and vertically integrated activities, the groups in fact constitute the "intermarket operators" on which Leibenstein's theory of entrepreneurship has focused. Further, in addition to its effects on entrepreneurship, the group pattern of industrial organization also permits less developed economies to relax institutional constraints in the allocation of capital and of managerial resources. Consequently, domestic, privately owned firms can enter and can attain efficient scale in activities which might be beyond the scope of a private, locally owned firm. And because of the groups, the modern sector in many less developed countries is far less "fragmented"—both in a static and a dynamic sense—than might be expected from accounts which have not been

Growth and Development, ed. Ronald I. McKinnon (New York: Marcel Dekker, Inc., 1976).

[41] This has also been noted, in different terms, by Albert Hirschman, "The Political Economy of Import-substituting Industrialization in Latin America," *Quarterly Journal of Economics* 82 (February 1968): 1–32.

[42] See my "Monopoly Capitalism and Public Policy in the Less-developed Countries."

Economic Development and Cultural Change

aware of this pattern of industrial organization.[43] Having described the costs of factor-market imperfections in the less developed countries, economists should hardly be surprised that an institution like the group emerged to appropriate the gains to overcoming these distortions.

This paper has also provided an example of the now well-documented point that economic theory can be relevant beyond the more advanced countries where it was first developed. Thus, standard microeconomic concepts help explain the emergence of the group institutional pattern, a phenomenon which might easily be attributed exclusively to sociocultural or political conditions. Understanding the economic basis of the group is not equivalent to justifying the institution, however, and indeed is a necessary step for reforming it. Our focus in this paper on the groups' effects in mitigating factor-market imperfections should not divert attention from the product-market distortions and serious problems for public policy which this pattern of industrial organization also creates.

The group institutional form clearly resembles some features of industrial and corporate organization in the more developed countries. The similarities to the conglomerate and to the large-scale multidivisional company are evident. Moreover, some of the causes of the group pattern also overlap with those which Oliver Williamson has discussed in his work on the theory of the firm in the more advanced economies.[44] Further, as we have seen, some aspects of the microeconomic and managerial reality in the advanced sector of the less developed economies are fairly similar to those of the more developed economies. Consequently, if adapted to recognize differences such as the absence of a formal capital market, the economics of the modern firm may be more applicable to the advanced sector of the developing countries than might have been assumed. And because of the similarity in patterns of industrial organization, oligopoly theory can clearly be helpful in modeling some features of price, output, and capacity decisions in the modern sector of the developing economies.

Finally, although we have discussed some aspects of the groups in the developing countries, many important questions obviously remain unanswered. One wonders, for example, why groups or a similar pattern of industrial organization has not emerged with equal frequency in all development contexts, both contemporary and historical. Similarly, it

---

[43] See, for example, Ronald McKinnon's description of "the fragmented economy," in chap. 2 of his *Money and Capital in Economic Development* (Washington, D.C.: Brookings Institution, 1972).

[44] See Oliver E. Williamson, *Markets and Hierarchies: Analysis and Antitrust Implications* (New York: Free Press, 1975), and particularly his emphasis on the importance of small numbers, bounded rationality (uncertainty), informational asymmetry, and opportunism (and hence the need for trust).

Nathaniel H. Leff

would be useful to have much more quantitative information on the scale and diversification of group activities and on the size distribution of groups in individual countries and its change over time. These may clearly be related to particular phases of development and government development strategies. Provision of answers to these questions and filling in our picture of the groups must await the collection of detailed statistical data. As noted earlier, however, collection of data requires that attention be drawn to a phenomenon and that a conceptual framework be elaborated to analyze it. Hopefully, the present paper will help serve this prior need.

[32]

The Entrepreneur and the British Economy, 1870-1914

By D. H. ALDCROFT

I

In the last two or three decades much new work has appeared on the period 1870 to 1914 which has tended to confirm earlier suspicions that, whilst the British economy was growing fairly rapidly in absolute terms, its relative position *vis-à-vis* the world economy was deteriorating and that British industrial and commercial performance left much to be desired. British rates of growth of production, exports and productivity were slower in this period than in the early Victorian years, and compared unfavourably with growth-rates abroad, especially with those of Germany and the United States.[2] In their quantitative assessments of the British economy most economists have been more concerned with analysing the changes in growth-rates and economic variables and accounting for such changes in terms of their interaction without examining fully the basic factors which motivate changes in the variables themselves.[3] But as Kuznets has recently pointed out it is difficult to explain the course of economic change purely in terms of economic variables given the wide variety of other conditioning factors which must be taken into account.[4] Undoubtedly there are many factors, both economic and non-economic, which affected the course of British economic history in this period, but one of these in particular, that of British enterprise, has so far received comparatively little attention. The chief purpose of this article is to put forward the hypothesis that Britain's relatively poor economic performance can be attributed largely to the failure of the British entrepreneur to respond to the challenge of changed conditions.

Although little is known about the origins and activities of British business leaders in this period[5] (and for this reason the subsequent analysis will of

---

[1] I should like to thank Dr R. H. Campbell, Dr P. L. Payne and Mr R. B. Outhwaite for reading various drafts of this article and offering many valuable suggestions. The author, however, is alone responsible for the views expressed herein.

[2] See, for example, E. H. Phelps Brown and S. J. Handfield-Jones, 'The Climacteric of the 1890's: A Study in the Expanding Economy', *Oxford Economic Papers*, Oct. 1952; E. H. Phelps Brown and B. Weber, 'Accumulation, Productivity and Distribution in the British Economy, 1870–1938', *Economic Journal*, June 1953; D. J. Coppock, 'The Climacteric of the 1890's: A Critical Note', *The Manchester School*, Jan. 1956; J. R. Meyer, 'An Input-Output Approach to Evaluating the Influence of Exports on British Industrial Production in the late 19th Century', *Explorations in Entrepreneurial History*, Oct. 1955; D. C. Paige, *et al.* 'Economic Growth: The Last Hundred Years', *National Institute Economic Review*, July 1961.

[3] Two useful correctives have been written. See W. A. Lewis, 'International Competition in Manufactures', *American Economic Review*, 1957, and J. Saville, 'Some Retarding Factors in the British Economy before 1914', *Yorkshire Bulletin of Economic and Social Research*, May 1961.

[4] S. Kuznets, 'Quantitative Aspects of the Economic Growth of Nations: VI, Long-Term Trends in Capital Formation Proportions', *Economic Development and Cultural Change*, July 1961, p. 56.

[5] See C. Erickson, 'The Recruitment of British Management', *Explorations in Entrepreneurial History*, Oct. 1953, p. 63.

114   D. H. ALTCROFT

necessity be highly impersonal) there is ample evidence, both in contemporary and recent literature, to suggest that British businessmen were weighted down by complacency, conservatism and antiquated methods from the 1870's onwards.[1] Thus in 1902 McKenzie wrote:[2] 'If our workmen are slow, the masters are often enough right behind the times. In spite of all recent warnings, there is a stolid conservatism about their methods which seems irremovable. Even great houses which have the name of being most progressive, often enough decline to look into new improvements.' Four years later Shadwell, in his *Industrial Efficiency*,[3] echoed the same refrain, whilst in 1915 Veblen decided that Britain was paying the penalty for having been thrown into the lead and that British industrialists were burdened with 'the restraining dead-hand of their past achievement'.[4]

Much of the contemporary literature possibly tended to exaggerate the true position, yet Hoffman writing in the early 1930's was hardly less severe in his condemnation of British industrialists and merchants.[5] More recently two American authors, Landes and Hoselitz, have remarked on the apparent failure of British enterprise in this period,[6] whilst Musson in his reappraisal of the Great Depression has made some equally critical remarks about British enterprise.[7]

Moreover, studies of individual business firms confirm the belief that entrepreneurial initiative and drive were flagging particularly before 1900.[8]

It would appear therefore that the British entrepreneur had lost much of the drive and dynamism possessed by his predecessors of the classical industrial revolution. In a short article it will be impossible to treat the subject as extensively as one would wish. It is intended therefore to analyse four aspects which are relevant to the question in hand – technological progress, methods of production, scientific research and technical education, and commercial methods. Having demonstrated the shortcomings of Britain's entrepreneurs under these heads an attempt will be made in the last section to account for their deficiencies.

[1] Toynbee wrote critically of British industrialists: 'If one were to single out the point in which Great Britain has been most at fault one would put his finger on the conservatism of our captains of industry who have idolized the obsolescent techniques which had made the fortunes of their grandfathers', *A Study of History* (abridged), p. 330, quoted in J. Jewkes, 'The Growth of World Industry', *Oxford Economic Papers*, Feb. 1951, p. 9, note 4.

[2] F. A. McKenzie, *The American Invaders* (1902), p. 230.

[3] A. Shadwell, *Industrial Efficiency* (1906), vol. 2, esp. p. 453.

[4] T. Veblen, *Imperial Germany and the Industrial Revolution* (1939 ed.), p. 132.

[5] R. J. S. Hoffman, *Great Britain and the German Trade Rivalry, 1875–1914* (1933), esp. p. 80.

[6] D. S. Landes, 'Entrepreneurship in Advanced Industrial Countries: The Anglo-German Rivalry', *Entrepreneurship and Economic Growth*, papers presented at a conference at Cambridge, Massachusetts, Nov. 1954; B. F. Hoselitz, 'Entrepreneurship and Capital Formation in France and Britain since 1700', *Capital Formation and Economic Growth*, a report of the National Bureau of Economic Research, 1955, Princeton Univ. Press; cf. H. Whidden, 'The British Entrepreneur: 1899 to 1949', in *Change and the Entrepreneur* (Harvard Univ. Press, 1949), p. 43.

[7] A. E. Musson, 'The Great Depression in Britain, 1873–1896: a Reappraisal', *Journal of Economic History*, June 1959, pp. 199–228.

[8] See especially, C. Wilson and W. Reader, *Men and Machines: A History of D. Napier and Son, Engineers Ltd., 1808–1958* (1958), p. 56; S. Marriner, *Rathbones of Liverpool, 1845–73* (1961),pp. 128–31; F. E. Hyde, *Blue Funnel: A History of Alfred Holt and Company of Liverpool from 1865–1914* (1957), p. 55, and W. G. Rimmer, *Marshalls of Leeds, Flax-Spinners, 1788–1886* (1960), pp. 252–3.

II

It is suggested that technical progress is a more important factor in economic expansion than capital accumulation. Though relationships do exist between industrial growth and investment there is no close correlation between the two and it is not possible to explain differences in the rates of growth between countries simply in these terms. The statistics relating to Britain, America and Germany for the period 1870–1914 do not, for instance, permit such facile generalizations.[1] At one time it was fashionable to argue that capital was the major source of growth, but it has since been realized that high rates of investment do not necessarily produce high rates of growth and vice versa. Given favourable market opportunities faster growth can of course be achieved by increasing investment in existing techniques (e.g. the duplication of production facilities), but eventually there comes a time when additions to the capital stock yield diminishing returns. When this stage is reached only the willingness to invest in new technology will produce an acceleration in the rate of growth. Then capital accumulation is no longer an independent variable, but is determined by the rate of technical progress. In other words, in the long run although technical change will be facilitated and have wider repercussions with more capital formation it is technical progress which in the final analysis generates changes in the investment variable and which is the major force producing growth. There is a further point in the argument to consider. Technical progress includes more than the use of new machines and the a option of new processes; it can in the widest sense of the term cover a whole host of improvements such as better methods of organization and the use of more skilled labour. In fact it is relatively easy to raise productivity by using existing resources in a more efficient manner, for as Professor Williams points out 'there is tremendous scope for growth through better industrial housekeeping'.[2] And since better resource utilization requires little or no additional outlay in capital it follows that capital accumulation need play no part in raising growth-rates. Thus, even in the short run, technical progress can hold the key to faster growth. Empirical investigation has shown that these assumptions are largely correct. Cairncross, Salter and Kuznets, to name only a few, have demonstrated the importance of technical progress as opposed to capital accumulation as a determinant of growth.[3] In a study of the American economy Urquhart found that technical change was the most important single factor in raising productivity between 1850 and 1950.[4]

If this hypothesis is accepted, then we are obliged to show that Britain's rate of technical progress was inferior to that of either Germany or America.

---

[1] See Kuznets, *loc. cit.* and 'Population, Income and Capital', *Economic Progress*, edited by L. H. Dupriez and D. C. Hague, 1955, pp. 37–9.

[2] B. R. Williams, 'Technical Innovation: The Key to Faster Growth', *Times Review of Industry*, Dec. 1962, p. 5.

[3] A. K. Cairncross, *Factors in Economic Development* (1962), esp. p. 107; W. E. Salter, *Productivity and Technical Change* (1960), p. 98; S. Kuznets, *Six Lectures on Economic Growth* (1959), p. 30. For useful summaries of the position see Williams, *loc. cit.* and C. Clark, *Growthmanship* (1962, Hobart Paper 10).

[4] M. C. Urquhart, 'Capital Accumulation, Technological Change and Economic Growth', *The Canadian Journal of Economics and Political Science*, Nov. 1959, p. 423.

116   D. H. ALDCROFT

For the moment we will abandon the all-embracing concept of technical progress and concentrate our attention on the adoption of new machines and processes to produce both old and new products.

The evidence suggests that Britain lost her former technological leadership in a number of industries. The failure to adopt new techniques, that is new machinery and other cost-reducing innovations, as rapidly as our competitors was one of the chief reasons for the fact that British export price indices were generally above European and American levels and ultimately for the decline in the rate of growth of the economy.[1] A few examples will serve to illustrate this point.

Between 1886 and 1913 Britain lost her position as leading producer and exporter of iron and steel.[2] In a recent comparative study Orsagh has shown that not only did Britain have a lower rate of conversion of pig-iron into steel than either America and Germany but also that between 1883 and 1910 German and American prices of iron and steel fell by 20 and 14 per cent. respectively whilst British prices were roughly one-third higher.[3] This deteriorating position can be attributed largely to the failure of British iron and steel makers to keep abreast of modern developments. Although steel capacity more than doubled in the couple of decades before 1914 there was no significant change in technical practice. Britain was slow to modernize her plant [4] or to adopt new processes for steelmaking and coking. The more extensive use of the 'direct' process of steelmaking (that is liquid pig conversion direct to steel) could have resulted in considerable economies, whilst the adoption of by-product recovery ovens for coking would have permitted greater utilization of waste gases and by-products. Yet in 1913 less than 28 per cent of the iron intended for steelmaking was sent in liquid form to the converters, whereas as early as 1900 some 75 per cent of German steel was made by the direct process.[5] Similarly in modern methods of coking Germany was well ahead; in 1909, 82 per cent of her coke was produced in by-product recovery ovens compared with only 18 per cent in Britain.[6] In fact at nearly every stage of the productive process British manufacturers lagged behind their rivals with the result that '. . . few British works, if any, are modern throughout in equipment and practice, with coking ovens, blast furnaces, steel furnaces and rolling mills adjacent to one another, and making full use of waste gases'.[7] No doubt the difficulties of the industry were enhanced by the shifting pattern of and deterioration in coal and ore resources,

---

[1] See C. P. Kindleberger, 'The Terms of Trade and Economic Development', *The Review of Economics and Statistics*, Feb. 1958, p. 77, and K. Martin and F. G. Thackeray, 'The Terms of Trade of Selected Countries, 1870–1938', *Bull. of the Oxford Univ. Institute of Statistics*, Nov. 1948, p. 376.

[2] For details see J. C. Carr and W. Taplin, *History of the British Steel Industry* (1962), pp. 230–35, and T. H. Burnham and G. O. Hoskins, *Iron and Steel in Britain, 1870–1930* (1943), pp. 30–31.

[3] T. J. Orsagh, 'Progress in Iron and Steel; 1870–1913', *Comparative Studies in Society and History*, Jan. 1961, pp. 219–21.

[4] In the 1890's Andrew Carnegie told British steelmakers what he thought was wrong with their trade: 'Most British equipment is in use twenty years after it should have been scrapped. It is because you keep this used-up machinery that the U.S. is making you a back number', quoted in F. Thistlethwaite, *The Great Experiment* (1955), pp. 211–12.

[5] D. Burn, *The Economic History of Steelmaking, 1867–1939* (1961 ed.), p. 222, note 4.

[6] Carr and Taplin, *op. cit.* p. 211.

[7] Committee on Industry and Trade: *Survey of Metal Industries* (1928, H.M.S.O.), p. 27.

but personal deficiencies are alone responsible for the failure to adapt. As Orsagh says: 'A lack of *enterprise* was responsible for the continued existence of small, relatively inefficient, independent works; just as a lack of enterprise was responsible for the failure to innovate at a more rapid pace. The British entrepreneur, to judge by his behaviour, was unlike his German and American counterparts.'[1]

The iron and steel industry was not, of course, the only culprit. The failure to adopt labour-saving machinery in the coal industry was partly responsible for the decline in productivity from the 1880's onwards. In 1924 only 19 per cent of British coal output was cut by machinery compared with 70 per cent in America where productivity rose by 50 per cent between 1890 and 1914.[2] Admittedly the less favourable geological structure of British mines and the existence of a plentiful supply of cheap labour hardly provided an incentive to mechanize, but as Taylor points out, 'The achievements of Scotland and West Yorkshire, modest as they may seem by American standards, are sufficient to suggest that the explanation of the slowness of innovation in Great Britain is to be sought as much in the entrepreneurial as in the strictly technological field'.[3] In the tinplate trade the position was much the same, particularly after 1891 when the Americans made rapid progress in this field. 'Like that of the British coal industry, the prosperity of the tinplate industry was founded on unchanged organization and unaltered technique. The lessons of the post-McKinley depression went unregarded and little was done to develop marketing facilities, to improve technique, to lower costs, or to adapt the structure of the industry to improve its competitive ability'.[4] Similarly the adherence to traditional techniques in the cotton industry was accompanied by diminishing returns. In contrast the efficiency of the American cotton industry increased considerably in this period because of the greater willingness to adopt new machinery particularly the automatic loom which reduced weaving costs by about one-half.[5] Even shipbuilding is open to criticism for much of the equipment in British yards was less advanced than that in America or Germany, and indeed by 1939 the industry was badly out of date.[6] In fact, generally speaking, by 1914 there was hardly a basic industry in which we held technical superiority except perhaps pottery.[7]

[1] Orsagh, *loc. cit.* p. 30.

[2] *Report of the Royal Commission on the Coal Industry* (1925), Cmd. 2600, 1926, p. 122. The proportion mechanically conveyed was even smaller.

[3] A. J. Taylor, 'Labour Productivity and Technological Innovation in the British Coal Industry, 1850–1914', *Economic History Review*, Aug. 1961, p. 58.

[4] W. E. Minchinton, *The British Tinplate Industry, a History* (1957), p. 71.

[5] M. T. Copeland, 'Technical Development in Cotton Manufacturing since 1860', *The Quarterly Journal of Economics*, Nov. 1909, pp. 144–47.

[6] S. Pollard, 'British and World Shipbuilding, 1890–1914: A Study in Comparative Costs', *Econ. Hist. Rev.* 1957, p. 436; L. Jones, *Shipbuilding in Britain* (1957), p. 90.

[7] English potters, though conservative themselves, were often decades ahead of U.S. potters in the adoption of better methods. An ingenious reason for the less satisfactory progress in America has been put forward by one writer, in that many of the workmen and managers came from England to the U.S. and 'in the process of transplanting English processes and attitudes in American industrial soil, the undesirable features seemed to take root more vigorously than the desirable ones', H. J. Stratton, 'Technological Development of the American Pottery Industry', *Journal of Political Economy*, Oct. 1932, p. 668.

The position would not have been so bad had the lag been confined simply to the basic industries, but in fact we were behind in developing the new industries. It was foreign enterprise, and not British, which contributed most to the development of chemicals, machine tools, scientific instruments, motor-vehicles and electrical manufacture. By 1914 Britain was easily surpassed by America or Germany in these industries and often we were dependent on those countries for a substantial proportion of our domestic consumption of these commodities. The performance of the chemical industry was perhaps the most disappointing, since Britain had once been the dominant producer. In the latter half of the nineteenth century, however, our position was rapidly undermined and by 1913 this country accounted for only 11 per cent of world production compared with 34 per cent for America and 24 per cent for Germany, whilst Germany's exports of chemicals were nearly twice those of Britain. The worst branch was synthetic dyestuffs in which Germany had virtually a world monopoly and supplied Britain with some 90 per cent of her total consumption.[1] The position of the other industries gives little grounds for satisfaction. Needless to say the comparative neglect of the new industries was particularly unfortunate since these were the potential growth industries and had an important part to play in the economy. Moreover, the resultant over-commitment to the basic industries was an important factor intensifying the difficulties of the British, and particularly the Scottish, economy in the inter-war years.

III

One of the reasons for the slow progress made in both the old and new industries was the lack of appreciation by industrialists of the importance of science and technology and its application to industry. This was particularly true in the case of such science-based industries as iron and steel, chemicals and electrical engineering, the progress of which was dependent to a large extent upon scientific and technical expertise.[2] But the fact was that British economic supremacy had been built up by a nation of 'practical tinkerers' [3] and British industrialists were strikingly reluctant to depart from 'rule-of-thumb' methods and seemed even proud of the fact that they carried out little original research or employed few technicians. 'The only research British entrepreneurs would readily sponsor was that which led quickly to immediate and practical results. They thought in terms of training clever mechanics rather than engineers, and laboratory analysts instead of chemists.'[4] As late as 1904 a leading Sheffield steelmaker was saying that there was a feeling in the industry that young men with engineering and science degrees had spent too much time in theory to have the

---

[1] I. Svennilson, *Growth and Stagnation in the European Economy* (1954), pp. 165, 290, 292–3.

[2] As early as the 1870's the 'lack of a highly intelligent class of workmen to carry out the practical details was held responsible for the fact that many valuable inventions in the steel industry had been abandoned in England', H. J. Habakkuk, *American and British Technology in the Nineteenth Century* (1962), p. 154.

[3] Landes, *loc. cit.* p. 8.

[4] J. J. Beer, *The Emergence of the German Dye Industry* (1959), p. 20.

necessary workshop experience and that degrees stood in the way of obtaining good positions in the industry.[1] This attitude was typical of most British industries [2] and it stands out in sharp contrast to that of abroad, particularly Germany, where '. . . one of the most fundamental and important causes of the present prosperity of the German nation is the close relations which exist in that country between science and practical affairs'.[3] Indeed, much of the success of Germany (and to a lesser extent America), especially in the newer industries, can be attributed to the systematic and organized application of science to industry, the thorough system of technical education under State auspices and the co-operation between academic institutions and industry.[4] As one director of a German iron and steel works pointed out: 'We can compete and make profits because of the scientific basis of our manufacture and the technical education of our workpeople . . . every one of our foremen and managers has had two years' special education at the cost of the firm – a technical and scientific education.'[5]

Britain had little to compare with the scale and provision of university and technical education in Germany [6] which ultimately provided an army of technicians and scientists for the new science-intensive industries. Just before the first World War Britain had only 9,000 full-time students compared with around 58,000 in Germany, a figure not reached in this country until 1938. In addition, Germany had 16,000 polytechnic students, whereas there were only 4,000 taking comparable courses in Britain.[7] In view of these figures it is not surprising that German industry was able to recruit a far larger number of scientists than British industry. In 1901, for example, there were some 4,500 trained chemists employed in German works compared with fewer than 1,500 in the United Kingdom, and the ratio of university graduates in German and British chemical works was in the range 4 to 1. Moreover, German chemists were generally superior in training and quality than their British counterparts.[8] Similarly, it was estimated that in 1912 eleven polytechnic schools were supplying German industry with 3,000 engineers per annum.[9] By contrast, in Britain the annual number of students graduating with first and second class honours in science and technology (including mathematics) in universities

[1] C. Erickson, *British Industrialists: Steel and Hosiery, 1850–1950* (1959), p. 36.
[2] See W. H. G. Armytage, *A Social History of Engineering* (1961), p. 214; F. A. Wells, *The British Hosiery Trade: Its History and Organization* (1935), p. 182; S. B. Saul, 'The American Impact on British Industry, 1895–1914', *Business History*, Dec. 1960, p. 24.
[3] E. D. Howard, *The Cause and Extent of the Recent Industrial Progress of Germany* (1907), p. 145.
[4] But in Britain, 'The phenomenal wealth of the British middle classes throughout the nineteenth century led to the development of a highly individualistic science organized seriously, but somewhat chaotically, by men of science themselves, including an unprecendently large number of wealthy amateurs', J. Bernal, *Science and Industry in the Nineteenth Century* (1953), p. 142.
[5] S. J. Chapman, *Work and Wages*, Part 1, *Foreign Competition* (1904), p. 78.
[6] Marshall reckoned that, apart from Scotland, British education lagged behind that of Germany in some respects by more than a generation. A. Marshall, *Industry and Trade* (1919), p. 97.
[7] D. S. L. Cardwell, *The Organisation of Science in England* (1957), p. 156. It was estimated that in 1900 the number of day students per 10,000 population was 5·0 in U.K., 7·9 in Germany and 12·8 in U.S.
[8] W. M. Gardner, *The British Coal-Tar Industry* (1915), pp. 222–3; *Report on Chemical Industry in Germany*, Cd. 430, 1901, pp. 38 *et seq.*
[9] H. Hauser, *Les méthodes Allemandes d'Expansion Economique* (Paris, 1915), p. 43.

in England and Wales was only 530 and but a small proportion of these had received any training in research.[1] Yet even this was probably an improvement from what had gone before. In 1872 a British deputation visiting Germany and Switzerland found that all the universities and colleges in England together contained less students taking up research and the higher branches of chemistry than a single German university, that of Munich.[2]

Britain's backwardness in technical education is not difficult to explain. For one thing there was, as we have already noted, a widespread indifference among British manufacturers to the value of employing properly trained workers, no doubt partly on account of the fact that they themselves, apart from a few notable exceptions such as Lowthian Bell, had no more than a limited knowledge of science, and partly because the skilled craftsmen available satisfied their limited requirements. It was this lack of support for such education which 'goes far to explain the relatively slow progress in technical instruction compared with Germany'.[3] There is, of course, the other side to the question. It can be argued that it was the deficiencies of the British educational system as a whole which were at fault. In particular, the neglect of scientific studies in public schools and elementary schools and the failure to organize a system of secondary education until the turn of the century produced generations of employers who were in no position to appreciate the importance of qualified men. Furthermore, since for much of the nineteenth century the basic educational system in Britain left much to be desired, it is plausible to assume that there were relatively few industrial workers who had received sufficient elementary education to enable them to benefit from a course in technical instruction.

Whatever the line of causation there can be no doubt that poor educational facilities were ultimately responsible for the paucity of properly qualified men in industry and this in turn limited the range of opportunities open to British business men. It also provides an explanation as to why so little basic industrial research was carried out in this country compared with Germany where 'the mutual interaction between research and manufacture became extraordinarily close'.[4] The Germans made every effort to break down the basic raw materials in order to find new derivatives which could be utilized for the manufacture of new products. Such painstaking and persistent research by highly qualified technologists and scientists enabled Germany to exploit her resources fully and to acquire superiority in a wide range of industries including engineering, chemicals and precision instruments.[5]

People in Britain were not oblivious to the fact that this country was falling behind in technical education and scientific research. In fact the fear of

---

[1] *Report of the Committee of the Privy Council for Scientific and Industrial Research for the Year 1915–16,* Cd. 8336, 1916, p. 8.

[2] S. Smith, *The Real German Rivalry* (1916), quoted in Marshall, *op. cit.* p. 97, note 1.

[3] S. F. Cotgrove, *Technical Education and Social Change* (1958), p. 28; see also Cardswell, *op. cit.* p. 167.

[4] R. A. Brady, 'The Economic Impact of Imperial Germany: Industrial Policy', *Journal of Economic History,* Supplement, 1943, p. 117.

[5] This point is brought out clearly by Beer, *op. cit.*; see also L. F. Haber, *The Chemical Industry during the Nineteenth Century* (1958).

German competition produced increasing demand for some improvement[1] and from the 1880's onwards some attempt was made both by the government and industry to remedy the situation. Nevertheless, progress was painfully slow and by the early twentieth century much lost ground remained to be covered. Firms were often too small to carry out adequate research even if the value of applied science had been fully appreciated, whilst industrial leaders still tended to regard technically trained people with scepticism. By 1914 fewer than 10 per cent of the steel industry's leaders had either technical school training or university education in science.[2] It was not until the demand of the first scientific war (or the 'engineers' war, as Lloyd George called it) made action imperative that any really serious attempt was made to fill the deficiency in this field.

IV

As we pointed out earlier, capital accumulation is not necessarily the ultimate criterion of growth. Identical values of capital may in fact contribute to widely different amounts of product depending upon the way in which that capital is utilized. The Americans and later the Germans were to show that it was not just capital intensity or the volume of resources alone which was responsible for greater output and high efficiency, but the utilization of the various factors of production, and above all capital, in the most economical way possible that was the clue to their success. Large-scale mass production of standardized goods secured maximum output at minimum costs. 'Probably in no other country in the world', wrote the Board of Trade *Journal* in 1901, 'is the principle of division of labour carried out to a greater extent, or with greater success, than it is in the United States. That the results obtained justify the theory is too evident everywhere to be disputed.'[3] Failure to emulate such methods where possible meant that in some industries British costs were unnecessarily high. This put Britain at a competitive disadvantage in world markets and ultimately resulted in loss of foreign orders.[4]

The uneconomical use of resources was most apparent in those industries which were slow to adopt modern methods of production and organization, notably machine tools and engineering in which Britain rapidly lost ground to her rivals. As *The Times Engineering Supplement* observed as late as 1915 the organization and methods of production in some of these factories was almost as defective as the machinery.[5] Britain, the pioneer of machine tools, was rapidly outdistanced by America and by the 1880's it was said that the price of machine tools in the U.S. had fallen to half that of the equivalent British tools.[6] From that date onwards Germany made rapid strides in this field too

---

[1] For this influence and its effects see the excellent article by G. Haines, 'German Influence upon Scientific Instruction in England, 1867–1887', *Victorian Studies*, March 1958.

[2] Erickson, *op. cit.* p. 39.

[3] Quoted in R. H. Heindel, *The American Impact on Great Britain* (1940), p. 222.

[4] For examples see *Engineer*, 7 Apr. 1899 and B. C. Browne, 'Our American Competitors', *National Review*, June 1899, pp. 568–80.

[5] *Times Engineering Supplement*, 28 May 1915.

[6] H. J. Habakkuk, *American and British Technology in the Nineteenth Century* (1962), p. 107.

and by 1913 her exports of machine tools were four times greater than those of Britain.[1] The secret of the American and German success in machine tools was due to the fact that they concentrated on the production of large quantities of one or two standard tools in large, highly specialized and efficiently equipped plants. In contrast, in Britain a very large number of relatively small and inefficient firms existed producing a multiplicity of articles and some of them 'seemed to take a pride in the number of things they turn out'.[2] Costs of production in Britain could have been reduced appreciably if many of the older works had been well planned on a large scale, equipped with plant of the most efficient kind and if the character of the production had been standardized. But in fact there was 'generally an absence of totally new works with an economic lay-out', and it was not until the war 'opened the eyes of manufacturers to the advantages of manufacturing in large numbers instead of ones and twos',[3] that British machine-tool makers made any serious attempt to streamline their methods of production.[4]

An important factor which inhibited the development of cheap motor-car production in this country was the excessive number of small firms producing innumerable designs of cars. Before 1913 nearly 200 makes of car had been placed on the market and of these over 100 had disappeared.[5] In a recent, excellent article[6] Dr Saul has illustrated the weaknesses of the early firms in the industry. A large number of small firms each producing their own individual products and with 'a disastrous inability to see the technical as well as the commercial side of the American approach', made little attempt to combine to adopt more efficient methods of production. As Saul observes: 'The vital absentees from the British industry were the men with a deep knowledge of modern machine tools and the production methods that went with them. The American industry, in marked contrast, had many such engineers . . . In Britain the engineers were obsessed by the technical product rather than by the technique of production.' Britain therefore failed to produce a cheap popular car largely because of the wasteful use of resources. By 1914 no manufacturer had managed to produce more than one car per man per annum. Yet as early as 1904 Ford was producing 1700 cars with 300 men.[7]

Similar complaints were made about other industries, namely that antiquated methods of production hampered progress. The success of the German electrical industry, for instance, was attributed to the fact that production of electrical apparatus was consolidated in the hands of some few influential

---

[1] *Engineering*, 11 Sept. 1914, p. 335.

[2] *Report of the Departmental Committee on the Engineering Trades after the War*, Cd. 9073, 1918, p. 10.

[3] Cd. 9073, *op. cit.* p. 8 and *Report of the Engineering Trades (New Industries) Committee*, Cd. 9226, 1918, p. 18.

[4] See *Engineering*, 14 Mar. 1919, pp. 355-8. Shortly after the war twelve of the main firms in the industry pooled their manufacturing interests in an attempt to apply the principle of mass production by standardizing design and limiting the range of tools produced by each firm. The scheme achieved considerable success and great improvements in workshop organization were effected by it. For details see *The Times Trade Supplement*, 21 Aug. 1920, p. 605 and 4 Feb. 1922 (Industrial Yorkshire Section), p. 15.

[5] G. Maxey and A. Silberston, *The Motor Industry* (1959), p. 12.

[6] S. B. Saul, 'The Motor Industry in Britain to 1914', *Business History*, Dec. 1962, pp. 22-44.

[7] *Ibid.* pp. 43-44.

syndicates, which, with branches in almost all countries of Europe and well organized selling facilities, were able to take the lead in nearly every department of electrical manufacture. The cheapness and excellence of certain German products made in immense numbers to standardized forms and patterns was said to be a barrier to successful rivalry in this country, where quantities of such articles ordered were relatively small and where almost every electrician required his own sizes and patterns.[1] Likewise the early American electrical manufacturing industry was surprisingly modern in its methods of production and organization.[2]

It may of course be contended that the larger home market, especially in America, gave greater scope for mass-production techniques. This argument can, however, be carried too far. In some cases, e.g. the car industry, the size of the market was important though it did not necessarily constitute the vital force in determining methods of production. If anything it was the nature of the market rather than its size which was the crucial factor.[3] But regardless of favourable market opportunities there is no getting away from the fact that American employers and their workers were far more willing to accept new methods of procedure to improve efficiency than their British contemporaries. The tinplate industry provides a useful illustration of this point. When the Americans began to produce their own tinplate the market for it was considerably less than the British one. Yet by the early 1890's American tinplate workers were producing more from each mill than their Welsh counterparts, not because they had different machinery but simply because the productive facilities were organized in a more efficient manner. 'A Welsh emigrant', it was said, 'would have recognized the machinery of an American mill in 1890, but he would have been a stranger to its arrangement and operation. Therein lay the contribution of American industrial technology to the manufacture of tinplate.'[4]

V

The reduced rate of industrial growth has been attributed by some writers to the fall in the rate of growth of exports. Meyer, in an input-output analysis, concludes that the total effect, indirect as well as direct, of a decline in export growth upon the U.K. economy was more than sufficient to account for the slower rate of industrial production.[5] Coppock[6] arrives at much the same conclusion and suggests that this reduced the incentive to invest. On the other hand, Kindleberger, in a recent paper, argues that this hypothesis is incorrect since it assumes that the pattern of exports would remain unchanged and concludes that 'the causation ran from the economy to exports, rather than the

[1] *The Times Engineering Supplement*, 29 Jan. 1915, p. 13 and 29 Oct. 1915, p. 192.
[2] H. C. Passer, 'Electrical Manufacturing Around 1900', *Journal of Economic History*, 1952(4), p. 394.
[3] See below.
[4] C. W. Pursell, 'Tariff and Technology: The Foundation and Development of the American Tinplate Industry, 1872–1900', *Technology and Culture*, Summer 1962, p. 280.
[5] Meyer, *loc. cit.* pp. 17–18.
[6] Coppock, *loc. cit.*

other way'.[1] Whatever the line of causation the fact is that Britain suffered a relative decline in her rate of growth of trade and this ultimately must have affected her pattern of industrial growth. By 1913 Britain's share of world trade in manufactures was 25·4 per cent compared with 37·1 per cent in 1883; between these two dates Germany increased her share from 17·2 to 23 per cent and the U.S. from 3·4 per cent to 11·0 per cent.

To some extent this decline was inevitable for a number of reasons: the increasing industrialization abroad, the relative stagnation of trade during the Great Depression, the erection of tariff barriers and the use of unfair commercial practices by foreigners. But to attribute everything to these factors would be misleading. Nor would it be totally correct to accept without qualification Lewis's proposition that the British export organization was over-committed to selling textiles, rails and consumer goods to primary producers and less suited to selling steel and machinery to the rich and expanding markets of Europe.[2] It is true that Britain shared less in the expansion of the European market in this period and concentrated more of her exports on the Empire, though by 1911–13 her share of exports going to Empire countries was no more than in the middle of the nineteenth century.[3] On the other hand, the Americans and Germans were just as adept at exploiting the protected European market as they were at gaining entry to the markets of the more underdeveloped countries where traditional goods were most in demand. Thus in a group of 15 manufacturers the British exports to protected foreign markets between 1895 and 1907 increased by 44 per cent whilst those of Germany and America increased by 125 per cent and 500 per cent respectively. The same exports to identical markets in the British Empire registered an increase of 91 per cent for Britain as against 129 per cent and 359 per cent for Germany and the U.S.A. During this period American manufactured exports to Empire countries increased at a faster rate than those of Britain, especially to the British West Indies and Canada. By 1913 Americia was slightly ahead in the West Indies and her exports to British North America were about three times greater than those of Britain.[4] Again, whilst German exports to Europe rose faster than Britain's (1890–1913), and by 1913 Germany was selling more to nearly every European country (and to America) than Britain, she was also expanding her trade more rapidly with many underdeveloped countries, e.g. Russia, Latin America and Turkey.[5] Thus by 1913 Germany monopolized the Russian market, her exports to that country being almost four times those of Britain.[6]

Insofar as Britain was committed to selling traditional goods in traditional markets it stemmed from the character of her production, namely the failure to shift resources from the older basic industries into new lines of production as

[1] C. P. Kindleberger, 'Foreign Trade and Economic Growth: Lessons from Britain and France, 1850–1913', *Econ. Hist. Rev.* XIV (1961), pp. 293–8.

[2] W. A. Lewis, 'International Competition in Manufactures', *American Economic Review*, 1957, p. 583.

[3] Kindleberger, *loc. cit.* p. 296.

[4] Heindel, *op. cit.* pp. 143, 164, 167.

[5] Hoffman, *op. cit.* p. 132 ff.; see also R. Schüller, 'Die Handelspolitik Grossbritanniens', *Zeitschrift für Volkswirtschaft, Sozialpolitik und Verwaltung*, 1908, pp. 149–78; E. Crammond, 'The Economic Relations of the British and German Empires', *Journal of Royal Stats. Soc.* July 1914, esp. pp. 788–91.

[6] J. E. Gay, 'Anglo-Russian Economic Relations', *Econ. Jl.* June 1917, pp. 316–17.

rapidly as America or Germany. According to Tyszynski's calculations Britain was on balance a net loser in the share of world trade gained in new products over the period 1899–1937.[1] But even more important was the failure all along the line to adapt commercial procedure to meet the needs of the time. Industrialists and traders were finding it not only difficult to sell new goods in new markets but they were also finding increasing difficulty in selling traditional goods in established markets. If Britain was behind the times in technique and methods of production she was even further behind the times in her selling methods. 'In marketing, as in manufacturing, England was clinging, in a changing world, to methods and types of organization which had been formed in the days of her supremacy.'[2]

The weaknesses of the English commercial system were emphasized in the Diplomatic and Consular Reports. Few of these reports praised British commercial ingenuity. In fact the general opinion among the consuls stationed abroad was that to maintain commercial supremacy British firms and traders would have to adapt themselves more to the requirements of their customers. Some of the main criticisms included the disinclination of traders to supply cheaper goods, to study the customers' wishes properly or to adopt the metric system in calculations of weights, measures and currency. As the consul reporting from Naples declared: 'It can never be too impressed upon British trade that all goods for sale on the Continent should be marked in metres and kilogs., and all catalogues sent to the Continent should be in a language "understanded of the people".'[3] Another frequent complaint made was the scarcity of British trade representatives abroad. British commercial travellers were generally few and far between and in some countries, for example Spain, the *bona fide* British traveller was almost unknown.[4] For example, the number of travellers entering Switzerland in 1899 on behalf of Britain was a mere 28 compared with 3,828 for Germany and 1,176 for France.[5] Nor was it unusual for the British travellers, few as they were, to be ignorant of the customs and languages of the countries they represented. 'It is pitiable', remarked Her Majesty's Consul at Naples, 'to see the British commercial traveller stumbling along with an interpreter, while his German competitor is conversing fluently, and one is still more sorry for him when his patterns and samples are marked with British weights and measures.'[6] Other criticisms included the poor packing of goods and inadequate credit facilities, many British firms finding it difficult to compete with foreign firms which were backed by their own trade banks.[7]

On the other hand much of the success of Germany and America in the export field was based on their efficient sales policies. They paid as much

---

[1] New products include chemicals, electrical goods, motor vehicles and industrial equipment. H. Tyszynski, 'World Trade in Manufactured Commodities, 1899–1950', *The Manchester School*, Sept. 1951, p. 290.

[2] G. C. Allen, *British Industries and their Organization* (1935 ed.), p. 19.

[3] Chapman, *op. cit.* I, pp. 250–1.

[4] *Opinions of H.M. Diplomatic and Consular Officers on British Trade Methods*, Cd. 9078, 1898, p. 6; *Diplomatic and Consular Reports*, nos. 4772 and 4776, Cd. 5465 (165/169), 1911, p. 6.

[5] Chapman, *op. cit.* I, p. 253.

[6] Cd. 9078, *op. cit.* p. 6.

[7] *Diplomatic and Consular Report*, no. 5004, Cd. 6005 (177), 1912, p. 33.

attention to selling and distribution as they did to production. By organizing foreign commerce, establishing direct-selling agencies and sending highly qualified travellers all over the world to ferret out openings for business they virtually created their own markets. The whole commercial policy of Germany was said to be directed towards the encouragement and extension of foreign trade. There were a number of organizations such as the Commerce Defence League and the Export Bureau of the German Export Bank which sent German agents abroad and supplied information on foreign markets to member firms.[1] Some of the larger American firms established nation-wide systems of sales agencies and employed salesmen who were technically competent.[2] In contrast the British approach was essentially conservative and individualistic, and at times apathetic and indifferent. There was a general lack of co-operation among British manufacturers for marketing purposes whilst the small scale of the typical firm rendered it difficult to establish selling organizations and agencies for dealing with foreign markets. For distribution purposes British firms relied heavily on the traditional merchanting system which all too frequently provided an inadequate reflection of the needs of her customers. British firms and merchants seemed almost hostile to the adoption of intensive and dynamic selling methods of their competitors which so clearly paid results.

On the other hand, it was alleged that the system of commercial intelligence was more efficient in America and Germany than that provided by the British Government for traders in this country. The foundation for this criticism is somewhat slender. Britain's consular service improved considerably in this period particularly after 1899 when the Board of Trade established its Commercial Intelligence Branch which provided an ever-increasing supply of information in the interests of British trade.[3] But as Platt has shown in a recent article in this journal,[4] it was more often the case that British firms did not avail themselves of the services of the Department to the extent they might have done. In 1913 it was estimated that only just over 1,500 firms took full advantage of the Board of Trade's information.[5] Platt suggests that the major reason for this neglect was the fact that British manufacturers 'already enjoyed the advantage of a considerable network of commercial agencies abroad'. This may well be true, but it in no way lifts the burden of responsibility from British manufacturers, for it was these very institutions which were slow to adapt themselves to the changing needs of the time.

It is not improbable that British commercial deficiencies were one of the main reasons for the failure to acquire new markets and the loss of old customers. As late as 1912 it was reported from Roumania that 'There is no doubt, were

[1] Watchman, 'Some New Facts about German Commercial Tactics', *The National Review*, Mar. 1910, pp. 83–6; H. Birchenough, 'The Expansion of Germany', *Nineteenth Century*, Feb. 1898, p. 189.
[2] See Passer, *loc. cit.* p. 392; E. M. Bacon, 'Marketing Sewing Machines in the Post Civil War Years', *Bulletin of the Business Historical Association*, June 1946, pp. 90–4.
[3] *Report to the Board of Trade by the Advisory Committee on Commercial Intelligence*, Cd. 4917, 1905, pp. 3–4.
[4] D. C. M. Platt, 'The Role of the British Consular Service in Overseas Trade, 1825–1914', *Econ. Hist. Rev.* XVI (1963), pp. 494–512.
[5] *Report on the System of British Commercial Attachés and Commercial Agents*, Cd. 3610, 1907, p. 2; *Report to the Board of Trade by the Advisory Committee on Commercial Intelligence*, Cd. 6779, 1913, p. 5.

proper representation to be secured, that British merchants would increase, instead of losing, the trade they already do with the country in machinery, textiles, ironwork, paints, chemicals, clothing, hats, boots, machine and other tools . . . merchants might do worse than pay a personal visit to the country.'[1] Orders and markets were lost through the wilful neglect of British firms and traders to cater for the needs and wants of their customers.[2] For example, in 1883 New Zealand ordered 20 locomotives from England only two of which were delivered at the end of eighteen months. The order was subsequently transferred to an American works in Philadelphia. Here they were not only completed in three and a half months but the finished product was better suited to the New Zealand railways and cost £400 each less than the English ones.[3] Many instances can be given to show how the Germans beat the English merchants by adapting their wares to the wants and prejudices of the customers. To quote just one example. The Brazilians disliked the black paper in which English needles were wrapped and therefore the Germans offered inferior needles in bright red paper and captured the entire market.[4] Nor was the question of ornamental packing as unimportant as it might seem, for it was alleged that 'a large proportion of the remarkable growth of the export trade of Germany is attributed by many authorities to the tasteful decoration of their goods by enterprising manufacturers'.[5]

VI

In the foregoing analysis we have demonstrated the existence of entrepreneurial sluggishness over a wide sector of Britain's industrial economy. A more difficult task is to explain why entrepreneurs behaved in the way they did. Some of the reasons, notably the attitudes adopted towards education and research, have already been touched upon. In a general article of this nature it will be impossible and even inappropriate to dwell upon all the specific factors relating to each industry. Consequently attention will be focused on the more important factors of general applicability. The author apologizes now for any glaring omissions.

First of all we may say that the general economic climate or public opinion in Britain was not conducive to change or to the acceptance of new ideas to the same extent as in America where 'society in the nineteenth century was basically predictable for innovations in producers' goods because it was not a society hostile to cheaper and better methods of production',[6] or as in Germany where efforts on the part of manufacturers were envisaged as a struggle

[1] *Consular and Diplomatic Report*, no. 5102, Cd. 6665 (60), 1913, pp. 7–8.
[2] See A. Lambert, 'Neglecting Our Customers', *Nineteenth Century*, Dec. 1898, pp. 940–56.
[3] E. B. Dorsey, *English and American Railroads Compared* (1887), p. 105.
[4] Howard, *op. cit.* p. 90, note (1).
[5] Cd. 9078, *op. cit.* p. 6.
[6] W. P. Strassmann, *Risk and Technological Innovation: American Manufacturing Methods during the Nineteenth Century* (1958), p. 185. Sawyer stresses the importance of social and cultural factors in economic development: 'Both the prevailing creed and the open structure of society were surely mightily at work in the development of this era, in the release and channeling of men's energies', J. E. Sawyer, 'The Social Basis of the American System of Manufacturing', *Journal of Economic History*, 1954 (4), p. 369.

for the 'rebirth and unity of the Fatherland'.[1] Part of the lethargy of British manufacturers may be explained by the lack of response from the demand side. In general Americans, and to a lesser extent Germans, were more responsive to change, that is they were more willing to purchase large quantities of standardized relatively cheap goods rather than 'aristocratic goods of high individual quality'.[2] Society, or in other words demand, was, at least in America, as Habakkuk has observed, more malleable and less stereotyped than in this country and could therefore be moulded more easily to the pattern most appropriate to high rates of growth.

But it would be unwise to lay too much stress on market opportunities as Habakkuk has done, for lack of response from the demand side was certainly not the sole explanation. Demand can be stimulated from the supply side by the initiative of manufacturers through the introduction of new products or by energetic selling methods. Yet in these respects British industrialists took the line of least resistance and were extremely reluctant to accept the challenge of new conditions. It is quite evident that many entrepreneurs adopted a very complacent attitude towards their businesses, particularly on the commercial side where the 'take it or leave it attitude' has persisted even up to this day.[3] Was this because they were drunk with the achievements of their past performance and were content to live on their ancestral capital? Was Veblen right when he suggested that Britain was burdened with the restraining dead-hand of her past achievement and that the maturing British economy and social structure brought recourse to conspicuous waste? [4] Support for his hypothesis is not lacking. 'We are suffering from a surfeit of commercial and maritime prosperity', a contemporary wrote in 1902, 'a prosperity which has been our monopoly for so long that we are unable to realise that it must inevitably be threatened, and may conceivably be taken away from us.' [5] Recent historians have intimated that the accumulation of sufficient wealth was inimical to progress since it allowed the pursuit of leisure interests outside the business.[6] Burn, in his study of the steel industry, lays considerable stress on the 'indolence and apathy engendered by phenomenal success', and the corrupting influence of fortune on heirs to an industrial dynasty.[7] As succeeding generations of businessmen began to acquire new interests and sought to advance themselves in society, the restless strive to maximize profits ceased. In South Wales 'the tinplate maker had little incentive to pursue wealth. With a modest sum it was comparatively easy to

[1] Landes, *loc. cit.* p. 19.

[2] E. Rothbart, 'Causes of the Superior Efficiency of U.S.A. Industry as compared with British Industry', *Economic Journal*, Sept. 1946, p. 386.

[3] See *The Guardian*, 10 June 1962.

[4] Veblen, *op. cit.* pp. 131–43.

[5] Y. Capel, 'England's Peril', *Westminster Review*, Feb. 1902, p. 963. This point has been confirmed as regards the shipping industry by S. G. Sturmey in his recent book *British Shipping and World Competition* (1962), p. 399.

[6] Thus referring to the Rathbone family Miss Marriner writes: 'The family had made sufficient wealth to allow them to pursue their own interests and they were not keen enough to try to adapt their methods to new conditions', Marriner, *op. cit.* p. 131. Cf. Landes, *loc. cit.* p. 19 and W. G. Rimmer, *Marshalls of Leeds, Flax-Spinners, 1788–1886* (1960).

[7] Burn, *op. cit.* pp. 298–301.

become a prominent member of local society and to enjoy a comfortable standard of living . . . The tinplate makers of South Wales were therefore easily satisfied and had little incentive to expand production or to attain leadership in the industry.' [1] Landed estate, the great status symbol of the nineteenth century, became the most coveted possession of Victorian entrepreneurs. Hence business affairs tended to become of secondary importance as second and third generations moved from the 'furnace to the field'.[2] In engineering the Boultons, in linen the Marshalls, in cotton the Strutts and in brewing the Bests, all attempted to raise their social standing in this way. As Thompson says 'Clogs to clogs in three generations was matched as a piece of folklore by the saying that the third generation makes the gentleman'.[3]

Whether this theory would bear general application remains to be seen, but it has been suggested that at least in a technical sense Britain was handicapped by an early start.[4] Briefly the argument is that technical innovation was more expensive in Britain because of the greater cost of writing off accumulated plant and equipment, and innovation in one sector or process often created bottlenecks which could only be relieved by innovation throughout the remaining sectors. In other words, capital was highly interrelated and this made it difficult to replace single components of a productive process on a one-at-a-time basis.[5] Thus modernization in the cotton industry was hampered by the unsuitability of many sheds for highly mechanized equipment.[6] The unprogressive nature of British railways in this period [7] has been attributed to the fact that much of their capital is so highly interrelated. Limits were set to the increase in the size of locomotives, coaches and waggons by the height of bridges, the short radius of curves and by the whole layout of stations, docks and works. The chairman of the Caledonian Railway was not exaggerating when he said 'there is not, at the present time, a single shipping port, iron and steel work, or gaswork, or any work in Scotland, capable of dealing with a waggon of a carrying capacity of 30 or even 20 tons of coal, and there are not half a dozen collieries in Scotland whose appliances for separating coal are capable of admitting a waggon of the height of a 30 ton waggon'.[8]

It cannot be denied that there is much truth in this argument, but it seems extremely doubtful whether it could serve as a general explanation as to why progress in British manufacturing industry was slower than in other countries.

---

[1] Minchinton, *op. cit.* p. 106.
[2] A. Briggs, *Victorian Cities* (1963), p. 69.
[3] F. M. L. Thompson, *English Landed Society in the Nineteenth Century* (1963), pp. 129–31.
[4] There is an extensive literature on this subject. See F. J. R. Jervis, 'The Handicap of Britain's Early Start', *The Manchester School*, Jan. 1947, pp. 112–22; M. Frankel, 'Obsolescence and Technical Change in a Maturing Economy', *American Economic Review*, June 1955, pp. 296–314; C. P. Kindleberger, 'Obsolescence and Technical Change', *Bull. of the Oxford University Institute of Statistics*, Aug. 1961, pp. 281–97, and E. Ames and N. Rosenberg, 'Changing Technological Leadership and Industrial Growth', *Economic Journal*, Mar. 1963, pp. 13–31.
[5] Ames and Rosenberg, *loc. cit.* p. 123.
[6] Salter, *op. cit.* p. 85.
[7] According to Paish 'Our railways have been content to go on working by the antiquated methods of thirty or forty years ago, and have neglected to take advantage of the experience of the American lines', G. Paish, *The British Railway Position* (1902), p. 12.
[8] *Ibid.* p. 117.

First because it implies that manufacturing technique must have been at a very primitive stage in America and Germany for them to have had any great cost advantage over Britain when contemplating the introduction of new methods or machinery. Second, it tends to ignore the fact that plant and equipment were older in this country which should in theory have provided an added incentive to scrap. And lastly, it would seem to imply that innovation in one process, e.g. cotton spinning, would be more expensive and difficult in Britain because of the resulting repercussions on other branches of the productive process. But there seems to be no obvious reason why capital should have been more highly related in this country than elsewhere.

A more convincing argument is the one regarding the different endowment of factors of production. The lag in the utilization of new techniques can be regarded partly as a reflection of an economy's supplies of factors of production relative to its labour force. Thus, according to Salter, 'When real investment is cheap relative to labour, standards of obsolescence are high and the capital stock is up-to-date; when real investment is dear, rapid adjustment is uneconomic and the capital stock consists largely of outmoded equipment'.[1] In America the abundance of land and scarcity of labour stimulated industry to install labour-saving machinery or use capital-intensive techniques whereas in Britain factor endowments favoured accumulation with existing techniques.[2] In other words, a widening of capital was more appropriate in the British case rather than a deepening of capital as in America, though in the latter case there is some doubt as to the extent of the capital-deepening process.[3] In a number of industries the different costs of factors of production can account for the rate of growth in capital equipment. Taylor, for instance, has noted that cheap labour hardly provided an adequate incentive to technical change in the coal industry.[4] In turn cheap coal retarded research into fuel economy and delayed the introduction of electricity as a new source of power. Again the main reason for the more rapid adoption of ring spindles and automatic looms in the American cotton industry was because they were more economical of labour and hence more suited to the American conditions than the British.[5] Similarly it can be argued that the relative abundance of skilled craft labour in this country compared with America made it less imperative for British manufacturers to adopt automatic machinery and mass-production methods. The cost incentive apart, it is important to remember the differing attitudes of American and British labour towards technical change. The American worker was far more receptive to new ideas and actually abetted the process of technical change,[6] whereas 'an English workman finds it almost impossible to imagine that the adoption of labour-saving methods could result in higher wages and more employment'.[7] Although the introduction of new methods and machinery

---

[1] Salter, *op. cit.* p. 69.
[2] See Rothbart, *loc. cit.* p. 386 and Habakkuk, *op. cit.* p. 141.
[3] On this point see A. Hansen, 'Economic Progress and Declining Population Growth', *American Economic Review*, Mar. 1939, p. 7.
[4] Taylor, *loc. cit.* p. 63.
[5] Copeland, *loc. cit.* pp. 129–47.
[6] Strassmann, *op. cit.* p. 186.
[7] Chapman, *op. cit.* I, pp. 176–77.

in Britain does not seem to have met with quite the same amount of opposition from employees as during the first half of the nineteenth century, it does appear that the lack of enthusiasm and the difficulty which manufacturers met in reducing piece-rates to the extent warranted by the increased productivity due to labour-saving machinery made British manufacturers less willing than their counterparts across the Atlantic to introduce new machinery and methods.[1]

One factor of relevance which we have not discussed in any great detail is the structure of the firm. The typical unit in British business was often the small firm dominated by family control. This tended to limit the flexibility of management and reduced the ability of firms to acquire the means to undertake large-scale expansion. Dr Sturmey has shown how the domination of family control bred conservatism in shipping resulting in an industry 'heavily biased towards maintaining the *status quo* and ill-adapted to showing flexibility to meet the enormous changes of the inter-war period.'[2] Rimmer, in his study of Marshalls the flax-spinners, lays great stress on this point. He maintains that the relative decline of the Leeds flax industry was not simply due to tariffs, imported flax and high wages but 'more important was the neglect, indifference, defeatism, even open hostility within firms based on the family'.[3] The difficulties of the small firm are well known. The wartime committee on scientific research observed that ' . . . the small scale on which most industrial firms have been planned is one of the principal impediments in the way of the organization of research, with a view to the conduct of those long and complicated investigations which are necessary for the solution of the fundamental problems lying at the basis of our staple industries'.[4] That the small firm was at a comparative disadvantage is not, I think, disputed; the important point is to establish why this was so. It may be argued that the tradition of self-financing contributed to the prevalence of small and medium-sized plants in may industries which in America and Germany were organized in large undertakings and this in turn can explain why in certain fields British industry was less productive and progressive than American and German industry.[5] On the other hand, it cannot be argued that it was a shortage of capital as such that kept firms small or that the London capital market, with its concentration on gilt-edged and foreign issues, was unaccustomed to financing domestic issues.[6] The success of raising finance of companies which secured a public quotation, such as Brunner Mond and Co., Lever Brothers [7] and some of the steel companies,

---

[1] Habakkuk, *op. cit.* p. 136; see also E. H. Phelps Brown, *Growth of British Industrial Relations* (1959), pp. 94–96.

[2] Sturmey, *op. cit.* p. 397.

[3] Rimmer, *op. cit.* p. 253.

[4] Cd. 8336, 1916, *op. cit.* p. 25.

[5] See Hoselitz, *op. cit.* p. 331.

[6] This is the point Lewis and Saville make. See also H. Foxwell, 'The Financing of Trade and Industry', *Economic Journal*, Dec. 1917.

[7] In 1894, when Levers issued their first block of capital to the public, four times the amount required was subscribed. By 1911 the firm had raised £6¼ million in the market. C. Wilson, *The History of Unilever* (1954), I, pp. 45 and 122.

refutes this latter point.[1] Rather the line of causation was the other way round. Domestic capital went into gilt-edged and foreign issues not because of the inability of the capital market to finance home industrial issues but because of the paucity of domestic issues in which to invest or because English firms were on too small a scale to attract the issue houses. Firms remained small through lack of finance only insofar as family entrepreneurs were reluctant to enter the capital market for fear of letting in 'foreign' control.[2] Only this can explain why by 1914 nearly 80 per cent of British companies were private ones the dominant feature of which was the absence of any appeal to the general public. This reluctance to share control may also explain why the banks played relatively little part in the long-term financing of industry notwithstanding the conservative nature of the banks themselves. In this respect British manufacturers were obviously at a disadvantage with their competitors, particularly Germany, where the link between the banks and industry was especially strong. Nor was the question merely one of long-term finance. Time and again British industrialists and traders lost ground to their competitors because of their poor credit facilities for which the banks were partly to blame. As one witness to the Committee on Shipping and Shipbuilding after the war put it: [3] 'Our experience is that there is a want of elasticity and lack of enterprise in our British banks which have hampered us, especially in dealing with foreign customers. We have found that foreign banks are much more helpful to their clients in assisting their enterprises.'

In some cases, particularly where development was interdependent, a lag in one industry retarded the progress of others. The late development of the aluminium industry can be partly attributed to the electrical lag whilst the slow growth of motor-car production explains why the most intensive phase in the development of the British rubber industry was about a decade later than in America.[4] Likewise the manufacture of electricial products was dependent upon the extension of the power supply which was held up for a time by the vested interests of the municipalities in gas. Occasionally, too, unfavourable legislation made things more difficult. The absence of a compulsory working clause in the British patent law until 1907 led to the exploitation of many inventions abroad especially in the field of chemicals.

Obviously it would be difficult – probably impossible – to find a single answer, even for one industry, to account for the unprogressive behaviour of British industrialists in this period. There are a host of interrelated factors, general and specific, economic and non-economic which have a bearing on the matter and

[1] Saul in his article on the early motor industry comes to much the same conclusion. In their recent book on *The Stock Exchange* (1962), Prof. E. V. Morgan and W. A. Thomas make no suggestion as to the inefficiency of the Stock Exchange in this respect. On the contrary, they state rather proudly that 'the combination of Stock Exchange and promoters provided a system which gave birth to many companies still flourishing today and which, in the twenty years prior to 1914 channelled more than £1,000 million of investment into British industry and commerce' (p. 139).

[2] Cf. Sturmey, *op. cit.* pp. 397–98. Even after companies became public there was sometimes a noticeable reluctance to offer shares to the public. See J. H. Clapham, *An Economic History of Modern Britain*, vol. 3, p. 204.

[3] *Report*, Cd. 9092, 1918, p. 30.

[4] W. Woodruff, 'The Growth of the Rubber Industry of Great Britain and the United States', *Journal of Economic History*, 1955 (4), p. 383.

it would be rash to conclude that any one of them had a preponderating influence. Nevertheless, the force of tradition dies hard with the British people and
this more than anything else seems to have influenced the outlook and actions
of British industrialists and their employees. So long as it was possible to make
an honest penny British entrepreneurs were content to jog along in the same
old way using the techniques and methods which their ancestors had introduced.
As one American commented after observing skilled Welsh tinplate workers,
'They know their business but when you ask them why they do a certain thing
in a certain way they say, "Because my father did it, and my grandfather
before him", and therefore they think they have to do it in the same way.'[1]
Fifty years of industrial pre-eminence had bred contempt for change [2] and had
established industrial traditions, in which the basic ingredients of economic
progress, science and research, were notably absent. And the longer this change
was delayed the more difficult it became for manufacturers to sanction and
their workers to accept a break with established traditions.

VII

In concentrating our attention on the role of the entrepreneur we have ignored
many of the factors which influenced the rate of growth of the British economy
between 1870 and 1914. This is not meant to imply that such factors were of no
importance. Some of them, such as the impact of the great depression, tariffs,
population changes, and government activity, probably have an important
bearing on the more favourable outcome of economic change abroad than in
Britain. Nor must we forget the fact that Britain's relative decline was partly
inevitable, since it was inconceivable that she could maintain her early nineteenth-century growth-rates indefinitely or that she could retain her commanding role in the world economy in the face of rapid economic progress elsewhere.
As a League of Nations study pointed out: 'It is axiomatic that a country
which is a pioneer in industrial and commercial development should lose in
relative position as other countries follow suit, even if it gains in absolute
terms.' [3]

   On the other hand, what we have tried to illustrate in this article is that
changes in economic variables stem largely from entrepreneurial decisions.
Insofar as these decisions and the action arising from them were inconsistent
with the needs of the time, then to that extent British growth indices compared
less favourably with those of our competitors. The relationship is a simple one
depending on our working hypothesis adopted earlier that technical progress
(in the widest sense of the term) is one of the major determinants of economic
expansion. In this period innovations, technical advances, economies of scale

[1] Pursell, *loc. cit.* p. 280.
[2] In 1930 a governmental report noted that 'the very success of the Lancashire cotton industry
in developing efficient methods in the conditions of the past . . . is today responsible in part for a
disinclination to explore new possibilities and try new methods, many of which have already been
exploited with success, for example, in the southern parts of the United States and in Japan', *Report
of the Committee on the Cotton Industry*, Cmd. 3615, 1930, para. 39.
[3] League of Nations, *Industrialization and Foreign Trade* (1945), p. 109.

and factor substitution were confined to a small sector of the economy and were slow to mature. The effects on productivity movements were adverse, unit costs were raised and rates of growth retarded. The conclusion, therefore, is inescapable: that the British economy could have been made more viable had there been a concerted effort on the part of British enterprise to adapt itself more readily.

Fortunately certain considerations can be put forward to redeem the entrepreneur's character. There can be no suggestion that entrepreurial dynamism was non-existent at this time. Progressive types such as Lever and Beecham and some of the early manufacturers in the car and chemical industries would make a suggestion such as this untenable. In fact it is possible to argue that there was far too much individual enterprise and insufficient co-operative action between firms and industries.[1] Moreover, it seems likely that entrepreneurial lethargy was more evident before 1900 than afterwards. By the turn of the century foreign competition had awakened the interest of some industrialists and in the decade or so before the First World War some attempt was being made to recover lost ground.

Many of the points raised in this article have been of a highly controversial nature and the conclusions offered are at best tentative. Much further research is required into the history of individual firms and industries before a final judgment can be passed. Nevertheless, the author's purpose will have been achieved if it stimulates inquiry into some of the more neglected aspects of our industrial and commercial history of this period.

University of Glasgow

---

[1] I should like to thank Dr P. L. Payne for drawing my attention to this point. The early motor-car industry provides a typical case. Of the 393 firms founded before 1914, 280 had ceased to exist by that date. Saul, *Business History* (Dec. 1962), *loc. cit.* p. 23.

33

5

The entrepreneur and technological change

L. G. SANDBERG

Whenever the performance of a group, organisation or country falls short of widely held expectations, the leaders of that group, organisation or country are likely to be branded as incompetent, venal or both. By the same token, success will result in high praise and widespread admiration for the leaders. Sometimes such condemnation or adulation is warranted: often it is not. Circumstances may well be more important than any contribution made by leaders. Pointing out such circumstances, however, is not always a rewarding task. Those who note that failure or decline was beyond the power of any leader to prevent are 'apologists', while those who credit success to fortunate circumstances are likely to be considered 'small-minded' or 'petty'. This proclivity to condemn or praise certainly includes the economic arena, and does not only concern government economic policy. Business leaders, managers and 'entrepreneurs' are also fair game. (In this chapter, 'entrepreneur' refers to anyone who has responsibility for a firm's decisions concerning choices of technology, rates of investment and scrapping, research expenditures, etc. This group includes individual owner-managers, hired managers and individual or groups of corporate officials.)

It should not be surprising, therefore, that Britain's relative economic decline in the period before the First World War (see chapter 1), elicited a storm of criticism of the British entrepreneur. Journalists, sociologists and economic historians, both at the time and subsequently, have devoted great effort to describing and explaining the shortcomings of those economic weaklings. If only business leadership had been competent, it is argued, the British economy would have fared much better. A fine example of this attitude is the assertion of Burnham and Hoskins in *Iron and Steel in Britain, 1870–1930*: 'If a business deteriorates, it is of no use blaming anyone except those at the top' (1943: 271).

Much of this criticism, naturally enough, consists of unflattering comparisons with the competition, principally America and Germany. Entrepreneurs there are generally praised for their aggressive and innovative behaviour. It is noteworthy, however, that even American and German sectors and regions judged to have performed badly (i.e. where output grew slowly or declined) are also alleged to have been the victims of poor leadership. In the case of the

100

troubled American railroads, for example, a study of management recruitment and practices concludes that they 'clung to ossified and outmoded managerial practices after the industry reached maturity [circa 1900]' (Morris 1973: 317). This judgement, incidentally, compares unfavourably with that of a companion study of British railway management. The latter notes that 'after 1890 there was a slight increase in inter-company movement [of executives], probably a reflection of a growing interest in new ideas in management' (Gourvish 1973: 298–9). Similarly, the previously lionised New England cotton textile managers were roundly condemned when they succumbed to Southern competition after the First World War, and the American coal mining industry, a world-wide example of efficiency before the First World War, was found seriously wanting in managerial performance by the Coal Commission of the 1920s (McCloskey & Sandberg 1971: 90). Finally, a study of the apparently retarded introduction of the diesel engine in America concludes that 'entrepreneurial shortcomings are the most apparent cause of the diesel's early failure in America'. Blame for this particular failure is awarded jointly to the American and German participants (Lytle 1968: 143).

The problem of 'technological backwardness'

By far the most common charge raised against allegedly sub-standard entrepreneurs, British, American or whatever, is some version of 'technological backwardness'; that is, a failure to encourage, appreciate and take rapid advantage of advances in technology. The worst offence of this kind is to have installed economically obsolete equipment in new plants. Other common charges include continuing to operate obsolete equipment after it should have been junked and ignoring new, presumably profitable, opportunities that arose from the advance of technology.

The principle reason for the prevalence of this particular charge is the observation that firms, national industries and even whole national economies that are declining, absolutely or relatively, will almost always have a less modern stock of equipment than will firms, national industries or national economies that are growing rapidly. This is true virtually regardless of the reason for the decline. It is, of course, certainly true if the decline is in fact the result of a failure to keep up with the advance of technology. It will also be true, however, if some industry in a given country (e.g. British cotton textiles) is declining because technological advance has shifted international comparative advantage in that industry to some other country (e.g. Japan). (See ch. 13.) In an extreme case, the British industry may not adopt the new technology at all, either because the old technology is better given Britain's factor endowments, or because Japan's new comparative advantage is so great that Britain is better off abandoning the industry. An apparent technological lag is also likely to emerge in a declining industry even if the decline itself has nothing whatever to do with technological change.

Before discussing the possible economic impact of 'technological backwardness', some preliminary observations are needed. First of all, it must be stressed that it is by no means always harmful to a nation for some branches of its industry to decline or even vanish. This is obvious if the product itself has become obsolete (e.g. covered wagons), but it may also be true if the local industry is destroyed by foreign competition. The theory of comparative advantage makes it clear that all countries gain simultaneously by concentrating on the production of those goods and services where they have the lowest relative costs. Such specialisation is the basis of international trade. Comparative advantage, however, is not a static relationship. As technical change occurs and as a country accumulates relatively large stocks of physical and human capital (the education, experience and skills of its work force), its comparative advantage changes from one set of economic activities to another. Thus, Britain had a comparative advantage in the production of cotton textiles before the First World War, but has it no longer. Today she has a comparative advantage in more capital-intensive – where the capital is both human and physical – manufacturing and service industries than textiles.

Generally speaking, a country is well advised to let its economy adjust to the dictates of comparative advantage. Failure to do so is likely to result in ever larger sections of the economy requiring ever larger subsidies and tariffs, thus becoming an ever heavier burden on the rest of the economy. Government policies to ease the pain of such adjustments, but not to prevent them, may however be justified.

The managers of an industry, such as British cotton textiles, that is in inevitable decline face a difficult task. They have to junk technically well functioning equipment and dismiss workers whose skills and experience have now become worthless – effectively leaving them as middle-aged or elderly unskilled workers. To invest in new, modern equipment would not, however, be a sound strategy. While it would no doubt keep the industry operating, though at a loss, somewhat longer than otherwise, the economy as a whole would be the poorer for it.

Another point is that installing the most modern technology available is not always a sound policy. The very latest in equipment frequently is plagued by 'bugs', and time and experience (not necessarily yours) is needed before it becomes profitable to operate. An example of such a case in Britain in this period is the experience of G. Z. de Ferranti. The financial troubles experienced by his ambitious electrical enterprises stemmed to a large extent from his insistence on operating at the very frontier of technology (Byatt 1968: 248–9).

The case of de Ferranti raises the more general question of the criteria by which the behaviour of industrial entrepreneurs are to be judged. It seems likely that

102

de Ferranti's pioneering work, even including his mistakes, was socially, although not privately, profitable; the knowledge his work created was a valuable public good. He and his financial backers paid for its production but most of the benefits accrued to others throughout the world. Unintentionally de Ferranti and his backers became public benefactors.

Although there are those who argue that entrepreneurs should be judged on the basis of their total contribution to society, this is not a sound criterion. Entrepreneurs cannot reasonably be expected to take benefits and costs affecting others into account. That is properly the function of government.

What criteria, then, should be used to evaluate managerial performance? The most reasonable criterion, at least as a first approximation, is the management's success in maximising the present value of their enterprise; that is, the discounted value of expected future profits. An inevitable difficulty is that such a measure cannot rely exclusively on hindsight, and a judgement must sometimes be made as to whether an entrepreneur should reasonably have been able to foresee later developments in technology or market conditions.

What are the principal economic consequences for the firm and, more importantly, for the national industry and the whole economy, when entrepreneurs fail to meet this standard of competence? By definition, a managerial error, such as investing in the wrong technology or failing to junk obsolete equipment or failing to take advantage of a profitable investment opportunity, is only a failure if it reduces the present value of the expected flow of future profits of the firm. Thus, managerial mistakes must reduce profit levels below what they would otherwise have been. What happens beyond that point, however, depends greatly on the market structure in which the firm is operating.

If the firm is part of a competitive industry, as was the case with most British firms between 1860 and 1914, then the principal question is how the other firms in the industry act. If a given error is limited to a single firm, then for all practical purposes the consequences would also be limited to that firm. The firm would simply operate at sub-normal profits, or at a loss, until the mistake was corrected. Bankruptcy, of course, might intervene, in which case the new owners would be able to rectify the error (e.g. throw out obsolete equipment). The loss of production in an industry resulting from mistakes by one firm, or even a limited number of firms, could easily be offset by new entry or increased production by other firms.

If, however, all the firms in the industry made the same mistake, then the situation would be quite different. The efficiency loss caused by the collective error would now be much larger – roughly by a multiple of the number of firms involved. On the other hand, the cost of these errors might be shifted away from the owners of the firms. In the absence of foreign competition, in fact, each firm might even be as well, or conceivably even better, off with *everybody* making the mistake rather than with *nobody* making it. The loss caused by inefficiency would then be borne by someone else; the consumers of the industry's output and the suppliers of raw materials are the most likely candidates for the role of victim.

Some degree of foreign competition is, however, the rule rather than the exception. If it can be assumed that the foreign producers made the right decisions while all the local producers made the wrong decision, then international competition would force at least part of the inefficiency loss back onto the local producers and probably onto local owners of specialised factors of production (including workers owning skill and experience) used in the industry. The output of the local industry would naturally be lower than would otherwise have been the case. If this forces a reduction in the *absolute* size of the local industry, unnecessary readjustment costs would also be imposed on the participants in the industry.

This scenario, however, seems unlikely. If one or two local firms made the right technological decision, even if by pure dumb luck, their business should prosper and their profits should grow. This, in turn, should cause the other local firms to reconsider, and, if possible, rectify their mistake.

A historical example of such market pressure has been found by a recent student of the pre-First World War British bicycle industry. Commenting on the rapid adoption of new technology in the industry he notes: 'If such a training [an engineering apprenticeship] instilled conservative instincts in its recipients [the bicycle industry entrepreneurs], it was countered by the competitive system which enforced a progressive code of conduct' (Harrison 1969: 302).

This analysis has to be modified somewhat for industries that involve rent-yielding natural resources. These are industries such as coal mining when the value of the coal exceeds the costs of extraction. Firms with superior natural resources can survive some managerial failure by absorbing the losses out of their rental income. In addition, the market signals coming from competitors who have made the right decision will be obscured for two reasons. First, the usefulness of a technological innovation is likely to vary between firms depending on the precise nature of the natural resource being worked; some coal deposits are more suited to mechanical cutting than are others. Second, the increased profits reaped from a proper technological choice can easily be obscured by the presence, or absence, of pure economic rents. This is especially the case if the adoption of new technology has only prevented the total abandonment of relatively low quality resources.

The likelihood of large loss through managerial error increases in the absence of free competition. The fewer the number of firms in the industry, the less effective are the self-corrective forces of the market. The worst case is clearly a single firm monopoly, regardless of the sources of the monopoly, whether that source is economies of scale, cartel organisation or patents. Whatever the props of a monopoly, it has monopoly rents to waste and at least no domestic competitors to worry about. Equally important, the smaller the number of independent decision makers, the more likely it is that no one will stumble on the right choice, thereby setting a successful example for others to emulate. Inefficiency may, however, create a profitable take-over opportunity for alert outsiders; stubbornly inefficient owners are likely to be bought out by more rational entrepreneurs.

A further point is that managerial incompetence cannot make all sectors of a country's economy internationally uncompetitive simultaneously, or at least not for very long. International trade in goods and services is controlled by comparative, not absolute, advantage. Thus, sectors with *relatively* little loss from managerial incompetence may well have their international competitiveness *enhanced*.

Even if it is possible to navigate these theoretical shoals and arrive at an acceptable estimate of the cost to the British economy resulting from entrepreneurial errors, a final problem remains. To test the key hypothesis of the 'entrepreneurial failure' school: 'that Britain's relatively poor economic performance (1870–1914) can be attributed largely to the failure of the British entrepreneur to respond to the challenge of changed conditions' (Aldcroft 1964: 113), it is necessary to establish some standard for the performance of a country's entrepreneurs as a group. Perfect entrepreneurial behaviour is not likely to have been achieved in Germany or America in this same period, or in Britain in earlier periods. Thus a measure of the cost of entrepreneurial mistakes in Britain between 1860 and 1914 only has meaning if it can be compared with similar measures for other periods and countries.

Clearly we do not now have, nor are we likely ever to have, enough information to calculate a final and definitive measure of the role of the British entrepreneur during the 1860–1914 period. Nevertheless we have a good deal of information on entrepreneurial behaviour concerned with technological choice in a number of important industries. Enough information exists, in fact, to permit us to come to a preliminary conclusion on the role of the entrepreneur.

The information available comes from two types of studies. The first type concerns the general economic performance of British firms and industries during the 1860–1914 period. These studies deal with such matters as the rate of growth of output of the firm or industry, their ability to deal with foreign competition, the rate at which they adopted new technology and their rate of productivity growth (either of labour productivity (output per worker) or total factor productivity). Total factor productivity is a much more sophisticated concept (and much more useful to economists) than labour productivity, but it is also more likely to suffer from measurement errors. (See ch. 1.)

The virtually unanimous conclusion reached by the authors of this type of study in cases where the firm or industry has maintained its international competitiveness, has rapidly adopted new technology and has displayed rates of productivity growth similar to German and American competitors, is that the quality of management was good. This is usually an appropriate inference. It is conceivable, however, that there were aspects of the situation which gave a special, unnoticed, advantage to the British industry and thus that it should have performed even better than it did.

The reaction when the firm's or industry's performance is disappointing is more varied. On the one hand, there is the reaction typified by Burnham and Hoskin's assertion quoted at the beginning of the chapter. At the other extreme is the reaction of a recent investigator of the Welsh coal mining industry in the period 1850–1914. After noting the relatively slow rate of mechanisation in the industry, he claims that: 'Had cutters and conveyors been more necessary to the industry in South Wales and had they justified their adoption in terms of factor costs then there can be no doubt they would have been adopted sooner' (Walters 1975: 297).

In most cases, however, the response is more muted. It usually consists of an impressionistic list of extenuating circumstances for the disappointing perform-ance, followed by the conclusion that the leadership of the firm or industry cannot, nevertheless, entirely be excused from blame. Since none of these various conclusions are proven they cannot be accepted; for all we know, there may or may not have been an element of entrepreneurial failure present.

The other type of study tries explicitly to determine how appropriate was some technological or investment choice made by British, and sometimes American, entrepreneurs. The questions which are asked are, for example. given the economic environment in which it operated was it profitable for the British cotton industry to install machine type X rather than type Y, was it profitable for the British chemical industry to keep operating its Z process equipment for making alkali products after, say, 1890; did British ship owners replace sailing ships by steam ships in a way compatible with profit maximisation? The choice of exactly which such questions should be subjected to quantitative analysis has, in effect, largely been made by the proponents of the 'entrepreneurial failure' hypothesis. It is usually a set of decisions that they have branded as examples of entrepreneurial incompetence that has been chosen for study.

If the choices facing the decision makers at the time are correctly specified and the appropriate data (factor prices, interest rates and the characteristics of the technical alternatives) are obtained, such an analysis will allow us to determine whether or not the decision which was made was economically sound. It may also permit a quantitative estimate of the loss resulting from possible mistakes.

Following a brief discussion of the role of technical training, the rest of this chapter will summarise the evidence currently available on the behaviour of British entrepreneurs relative to technological change in a number of industries between 1860 and 1914. The survey is not complete in its coverage, either in terms of industries discussed or including every scrap of evidence available on the

106

industries which are mentioned. An attempt has, however, been made to be exhaustive with regard to studies of the second type just described, except that agriculture is treated in chapter 8.

Technical training and productivity growth

It is often alleged that part of Britain's productivity growth lag after 1870 (see chapter 1), stemmed from inadequate levels of technical training. The alleged low British level of such training is contrasted with reports of higher levels in other countries, especially Germany. Although it was largely governmental authorities in these other countries who provided this technical training, the ultimate blame for Britain's supposed failure is normally laid on the private sector. The claim is that prejudices against employing technically trained workers prevented the emergence of a demand for technical training financed by the government (Landes 1969: 344–6).

This contention raises theoretical considerations similar to those associated with 'technological backwardness'. Given competitive labour and product markets and assuming that technical training really is very valuable, then, if only a few firms make the right choice and hire technically trained workers, the profits of these firms will increase sharply. This will provide a signal for others to follow and firms who hold out will be placed at a disadvantage. Thus since at least some firms hired technically trained workers and since the British economy was highly competitive, it is difficult to believe that an irrational opposition to technical training could have been a major hindrance to economic growth.

In fact, however, closer examination of the facts indicates that the principal difference between Britain and Germany was the nature, not necessarily the extent, of technical training. In Germany it consisted largely of formal, full time class work, while in Britain it consisted of apprenticeship training supplemented by part time, especially night classes. Several possible reasons, other than irrationality, can be suggested for this difference. Most important, Britain had a larger corps of experienced and skilled industrial workers and more large-scale enterprises. These conditions made apprenticeship training more feasible in Britain. It might even be said that Germany, being less able to provide apprenticeship training, was forced to adopt more formal, group oriented methods of instruction. Certainly the expense, particularly in terms of forgone earnings and production, is greater with full time class work than with apprenticeship training combined with night classes (Floud 1976a: 9–11).

Survey of industries

The iron and steel industry

The large-scale production and widespread use of first iron and then steel was a major aspect of industrialisation and industrial growth during the nineteenth century. Britain led the way in both production and consumption. As late as 1880, Britain produced twice as much pig iron as Germany and more than the United States; her per capita consumption was three times as high as in those countries. After 1880, however, there was little growth in Britain and rapid advance elsewhere. Before the First World War, Germany produced twice as much and the United States over three times as much pig iron as Britain and both had distinctly higher levels of per capita consumption.

British pig iron production, in fact, did not exceed its 1882 level until 1896 and only exceeded it by 20 per cent in 1913. Figures on steel production were somewhat more encouraging. Steel production in Britain grew almost as rapidly as in the United States until 1890. After that year, the growth rate dropped to approximately 3 per cent per annum.

Britain's share of world production and world exports fell sharply. In 1875–79, Britain produced 46.0 per cent of the world's pig iron and 35.9 per cent of the world's steel. By 1910–13, these shares had been reduced to 13.9 per cent and 10.3 per cent. The virtual stagnation of her exports meant that Britain's share of world iron and steel exports declined rapidly. Although Britain exported almost five times as much tonnage as Germany in 1880, Germany had pushed ahead before the First World War. In addition, Britain had by then become the world's largest importer of iron and steel (Payne 1968: 72, 78, 85).

These developments were viewed with considerable alarm by contemporary observers. Iron and steel was an important industry. Its gross output (less coal and imported ore) amounted to 11.6 per cent of Britain's GNP in 1871 and 10.3 per cent in 1881, but only 5.8 per cent in 1901 and 6.4 per cent in 1907. In 1880, iron and steel ranked second to cotton textiles among British industries, but by 1907 it had fallen to eighth place (Deane & Cole 1962: 226–7).

As these events unfolded, the British iron and steel industry was subjected to increasingly shrill, sometimes even hysterical, criticism. Admonitions came from the whole spectrum of audible opinion – from journalists to academic economists. The latter, in a relatively moderate vein, noted that while Britain's share of the industry was bound to shrink, it was not bound to shrink so much. More aggressive and innovative leadership could certainly have prevented the relative decline from being so precipitous. The critical view of the industry's leadership before and after the First World War was confirmed in scholarly circles by two major studies of the industry (Burn 1940 and Burnham & Hoskins 1943). Both of these works, but especially the latter, were highly critical of the management of British iron and steel.

108

These critics present a long bill of particulars against the industry. Consistently heading the list is the British industry's unquestioned lag in adopting the basic (as opposed to acidic) process of steel making and the slow development (presumably related to this) of the phosphoric ores found in Lincolnshire and Northamptonshire. Among other popular allegations are a failure properly to integrate production, neglect of possible fuel economies, neglect of electrical metallurgy and neglect of continuous rolling (Levine 1967: 39–42).

Only very recently, principally in the work of McCloskey (1973), has a serious effort been made to evaluate these alleged entrepreneurial failures. This work consists of a detailed and quantified analysis of the alleged 'failure' rapidly to expand basic steel production together with studies of productivity growth rates and levels in various branches of the British and American iron and steel industries.

As to the alleged neglect of the phosphoric ores, McCloskey is able to show that the users of pig iron (principally steel producers) were paying the same price for pig iron made of this ore as for similar pig iron made from other ores. Thus the product was correctly valued in the market. Secondly, he shows that there were no larger but unexploited potential profits available to investors in that branch of the industry than elsewhere. Thus there were apparently no irrational prejudices against the ores or against investing in their exploitation (*ibid*: 57–67).

McCloskey rejects the charge of general irrational neglect of the basic open hearth process on other grounds. He notes that the spread of open-hearth basic steel making was very rapid in Britain after 1900, the year that saw the commercial introduction of the Talbot tilting furnace. This furnace was designed to deal with the problem of slag accumulation which was particularly serious for the open hearth process, and especially bad in Britain where scrap, which generates no slag, was relatively expensive and therefore little used. Thus the Talbot furnace was particularly well suited to the production of basic open hearth steel in Britain and its more rapid adoption in Britain than in Germany is consistent with rational behaviour by steel entrepreneurs in both countries (*ibid*.: 68–72).

The results of calculations of factor productivity change do not, at least at first glance, seem as favourable to the British cause. British productivity in pig iron production and in Bessemer steel rails grew rapidly until shortly after 1880 and then stagnated, in the case of pig iron all the way into the 1930s. The results for open hearth steel ship plates, a major product in this period, seem more promising. They indicate a substantial rate of productivity growth until the middle of the first decade of this country.

In America, on the other hand, productivity growth continued, at least in pig iron and open hearth steel, after it had stopped in Britain. Furthermore, the study undermines the explanation which is sometimes offered; that the British steel industry's productivity lagged behind that of her competitors as a result of an ageing stock of captial. This ageing, in turn, resulted from the relatively slow growth of British demand (Temin 1966). While such a relationship between growth of demand, age of equipment and rate of productivity change can exist, it was simply not very important in this particular case.

The data on productivity growth is put into quite a different light, however, by two further considerations. First, if the halt in productivity improvement was the result of entrepreneurial failure, it seems strange that the collapse should have occured twenty years earlier in some branches of the industry than in other. More important, not until shortly before the First World War did American total factor productivity reach British levels. In other words, more rapid productivity growth in America before that point only reduced the existing British lead. This observation is consistent with the hypothesis that British entrepreneurs were usually quick in adopting the new technology available up to the 1880s (1905 for open hearth steel), and that productivity growth ceased at that point because the possibilities of available technology had been exhausted in Britain. Thus, British entrepreneurial behaviour after the 1880s appears to be poor only because it had been so good previously. To compound the irony, the Americans now look good because they previously were laggards. These findings tempt one to propose an 'entrepreneurial failure' explanation for the American industry's 'productivity failure' before the First World War (McCloskey 1973: chs. 6 & 7).

Still, it is disturbing that American productivity continued to grow well past British levels. This development raises questions about British interwar entrepreneurship (without proving that it was poor), and throws a shadow backwards onto the Edwardian period. British steel managers may well have encountered productivity ceilings in some sectors in the 1880s, but they also seem to have been slow off the mark when new opportunities for productivity improvement became available once more. The fact that the Americans did not catch up until shortly before the First World War, furthermore, does not guarantee that new opportunities had not opened up somewhat earlier. The Americans give no evidence of ever having hit a ceiling, implying that they were somewhat below it even as they passed their immobile British rivals.

The engineering and electrical goods industries

The engineering and electrical goods industries are of prime importance to any modern, industrialised economy. In Britain, the various branches of the engineering industry jointly passed cotton textiles to become Britain's largest manufacturing industry in terms of value added before 1900. The electrical products industry, entirely dependent on a newer technology, was much smaller but it also was growing very rapidly.

The experiences of the various and diverse branches and firms of these

110

industries during the pre-First World War period have recently been much studied. This work has concentrated on matters such as the rate of growth of total output per worker, the rate of adoption of new technology, the degree of competitiveness with foreign rivals and with profitability. Quantitative studies of particular technological choices or the rate of total factor productivity growth have not appeared.

The major, overall result of this work is that the performance of the branches and firms varied tremendously. Thus, among the older established engineering trades, textile machinery building in particular, and especially spinning equipment, fared very well indeed. The producers of steam engines and turbines and heavy machine tools also enjoyed a considerable degree of success. Lower grades, however, are given to the producers of railway locomotives and rolling stock and to some types of machine tools (Saul 1968: 191–209). The traditional clock making industry met virtually total disaster (Church 1975b). Among the new trades, similar diversity is to be found. Sewing machine and bicycle producers are usually given high marks, while makers of motor cars and agricultural equipment were less successful. In the production of engines, gas and semi-diesels did well while the use and manufacture of the regular diesel engine made relatively little progress (Saul 1968: 209–26).

On a more general plane, there is disagreement as to whether the widespread adoption of American production techniques by the British engineering industry in the 1890s involved the elimination of an existing, uneconomic technological lag. On the one hand, it is sometimes argued that these methods were superior well before this time but that the British industry only adopted them when large-scale American exports penetrated the British market. The alternative hypothesis is that the techniques were in fact not superior earlier. The influx of American products occurred more or less immediately once American technology became economically superior – and it was then rapidly adopted in Britain. The advantage in this contest seems to lie with the latter position (Floud 1974).

In the case of the electrical goods industry, there is first the problem of the relatively slow adoption of electrification in British industry. While the question of possible irrationality has not been definitely settled, it is clear that British manufacturing was relatively heavily concentrated in fields such as textiles, where there was little or no advantage in electrical driving. It is also clear that the electrification that did occur in Britain was, as rational calculation would dictate, concentrated in industries such as engineering and shipbuilding where its advantage was greatest (Byatt 1968: 243). As to the various branches of electrical goods manufacturing, once again there was a great diversity in performance. The most successful branch of the industry in Britain was electrical cables and related telegraphic equipment. Electrical machine building and, especially, light bulb manufacturing, performed less well (*ibid.*: 258–66).

The standard conclusion drawn from this variation in performance among

branches of these industries in Britain is that the successful branches are evidence
of good entrepreneurship and the weaker ones are examples of poor
entrepreneurship. The suggestion is thus that any theory of consistently poor
British entrepreneurial behaviour has been disproved, but that poor entrepreneurship did exert some drag on the performance of the economy. Are such
conclusions justified?

If it is *assumed* that the single, or at least the dominant, determinant of success
or failure by a branch of the engineering industry in some country is the quality
of entrepreneurship, then the relative quality of entrepreneurship between
countries in engineering can be determined by counting successes and failures
in each country. In fact, however, it is clear that other variables, such as the
nature of demand and the supply of experienced and skilled labour, also play
important roles in the performance of branches of the industry in various
countries. Empirical support for a belief that entrepreneurship is not everything
is readily available. One example is the experience of the two divisions of Siemens
Brothers (the English subsidiary of a Germany company). Their dynamo factory
did very poorly (in fact it was 'the most unprofitable factory in the industry' –
despite 'close control' from Berlin) as did this whole British branch of
manufacturing. The cable division, on the other hand, shared in the general
prosperity of British cable manufacturing (*ibid.*: 255–6, 262–3). Another example
can be found in the history of British clock manufacturing. As this branch was
forced to the wall, principally by Swiss competition, a number of British clock
manufacturers, including the largest firm, shifted successfully to other branches
of metal working (Church 1975b: 628–9).

This type of evidence, in fact, is compatible with the opposite belief, namely
that the supply of managerial talent is infinitely elastic. Since this assumption
means that managers of constant (and presumably good) quality will always be
available, other factors must determine the success of a firm, branch or industry.
Abundant evidence is available, however, indicating that entrepreneurial skill
makes a great difference to the performance of different firms engaged in the same
line of business. It is reasonable to believe that some variation in entrepreneurial
talent also exists, and makes a difference to performance, among branches of
industries and even in whole industries. Furthermore, if factors other than
entrepreneurship affect the overall success of a branch of industry, then the most
favoured branches and industries will also tend to attract the best entrepreneurs.
The ability to recognise opportunity is certainly part of good entrepreneurship.
This tendency, of course, will reinforce the other factors and will increase
international specialisation between branches of a given industry and between
industries.

Thus, the varying degrees of success of different branches of the British
engineering and electrical goods industries are compatible with the belief that
these British industries had both good and bad entrepreneurs. It is not possible,

however, to conclude that British management in this industry was better or worse than in other countries simply by counting the number of successful branches in each country. The same factors that affect the likelihood of success between various branches of the engineering industry within a country may also affect the likelihood of success in the industry in general. It may have required greater ability to achieve a given degree of success in the British engineering industry than, let us say, in the German one. This would also imply that a smaller percentage of Britain's supply of skilled entrepreneurs would be attracted to the engineering industry.

The chemical industry

The role played by scientific research and innovation in the chemical industry has frequently caused it to be viewed as more important than is indicated by its share of national value added or industrial employment. Indeed, the production of sulphuric acid has, on occasion, been used as an index of a country's level of industrialisation.

Thus it is not surprising that the performance of the British chemical industry was viewed with great concern in late-Victorian and Edwardian Britain. By some standards, at least, the industry performed quite well. In fact, in terms of employment, the industry grew faster between 1881 and 1911 than any other industrial group in Britain, with the single exception of the public utilities. By the latter year, the industry employed 2.7 per cent of the manufacturing labour force. Four years earlier the chemical industry had contributed 3 per cent of Britain's total net industrial output (Richardson 1968: 279–80).

Clearly any failure in terms of output growth was a relative one. The problem was that the chemical industry was growing even faster, and reaching higher absolute levels of output, in Germany and the United States. In 1913, Britain produced an estimated 11 per cent of world chemical output while Germany and the United States accounted for 24 per cent and 34 per cent respectively (*ibid.*: 278).

What is more striking, however, is the degree to which there was national specialisation among various types of chemical products. Germany, for example, was totally dominant in dyes, drugs and photographic chemicals and the United States led the way in electrochemicals. Britain did well in soap (the province of one of the period's truly great entrepreneurs in industrial organisation and retailing: William Lever of Lever Bros. and Unilever), paints, coal tar intermediates and explosives (*ibid.*: 280).

Despite British success in some fields, the slower overall rate of growth, and the total failure in other fields, particularly dyestuffs, resulted at the time, and ever since, in a flood of criticism of the industry's performance. The principal specific charges are usually: first, the prolonged retention of the Leblanc process in alkali production, despite the superiority of the Solvay process; second, the retention of the lead-chamber process rather than the adoption of the contact process in sulphuric acid production; third, the failure of British research and development (R & D) to keep up with Germany in dyes and drugs. The last of these charges is part of a more general claim that the British industry underemployed scientists and underinvested in research.

The first two of these allegations have been subjected to careful quantitative analysis. The question posed was: At what point in time should the old processes (Leblanc and lead-chamber) have been abandoned by profit maximising entrepreneurs? The most likely answers are in 1897 for the Leblanc process and not before 1914 for the lead-chamber process.

Before 1897 the British Leblanc producers had merged in 1890 to form United Alkali Producers (UAP). In Britain, their chief competition came from Brunner Mond, who held the Solvay patent rights for Britain until they expired in 1886. Despite the profitable example of Solvay production by that firm, and the expiration of the patent, UAP retained its Leblanc capacity in soda ash until 1902 and did not abandon its other Leblanc alkali lines until the First World War. The estimated profit lost to UAP resulting from this retention of economically obsolete equipment, discounted back to 1890, ranges between £1.9 million at 3 per cent interest and £0.9 million at 6 per cent. The sensitivity of these calculations to interest rates is apparent from the result that at 8 per cent the loss would have been zero (Lindert & Trace 1971a, b).

It does seem that UAP made a technological error in keeping its obsolete Leblanc process equipment working some years too long. However, given the modest size of the loss, the error could hardly have been a major blow to the nation; less than £2 million does not seem a very large loss to stem from an error which is usually described as one of the worst examples of 'entrepreneurial failure' in Britain before 1914. It is also interesting to note that UAP had a considerable amount of market power. While other Solvay firms, even in Britain, set an example of greater profitability, UAP was not under nearly as much pressure to do things right as is a firm operating in a competitive environment.

The problem of judging Britain's alleged failure to invest sufficiently in chemical R & D in general, and in the dye field in particular, has not yet been satisfactorily solved. In principle, underemployment of chemists and under-investment in R & D means that the employment of chemists and investment in R & D should yield unusually high returns. Those firms who invested relatively most in such activities should have tended to be the most profitable. This may indeed have been the case, but no convincing evidence on the subject is available.

A somewhat different perspective on Germany's success in dyes and drugs results from looking at the high degree of product specialisation in the industry as a whole. Dyes and drugs were highly research intensive and Germany had, thanks to its educational system, a relatively large supply of scientists and

114

research oriented University chemistry departments. Combining this with the generally admitted shortcomings of the British patent system (there was no effective requirement that foreign patent holders either themselves utilise or license their inventions in Britain), the Germans may well have had a relative advantage in this sector. In a complex technology, furthermore, once someone gets ahead, they usually get increasingly hard to catch. British chemical firms may have been wise, thereby displaying good entrepreneurship, to stay out of Germany's chemical specialties. In fact, the generally praised American industry produced even less in the way of dyes than did the British.

The cotton textile industry

It should hardly be necessary to remind the reader of the importance to the British economy of the cotton textile industry, from the start of the industrial revolution to the disastrous collapse of the industry during the interwar period. Not until the end of the nineteenth century was the industry replaced (by the combined engineering trades) as the leading British industry in terms of value added. In exports, the record is even more impressive. Having constituted an amazing 50 per cent by value of all British exports in 1830, the industry's share slowly declined, but still amounted to 24.1 per cent in 1913. Although the growth rate of the industry was slower after the middle of the century than before, its consumption of raw cotton doubled between 1860, or 1870 for that matter, and the all time record year of 1913 (Sandberg 1974: ch. 1).

Given the industry's admirable record in terms of output and exports right up to the First World War, it is not surprising that contemporary criticism of the industry's management was limited to social, not economic, questions. The rapid decline of the industry during the interwar period, however, resulted not only in criticism of the industry's management at that time, but also produced a very critical reassessment of entrepreneurial behaviour during the period before the First World War. As far as scholarly opinion was concerned, the poor performance of the pre-First World War cotton textile industry became an accepted fact with the publication in 1933 of *Increasing Return* by G. T. Jones. Jones calculated what he called a 'real cost' index (the exact inverse of a total factor productivity index) for the Lancashire cotton industry which showed no improvement whatsoever in the industry's efficiency between 1885 and 1910. Indeed, he found a slight *decline* in efficiency between 1900 and 1910 (Jones 1933: 117, 274).

The key specific charges which were levied against the pre-First World War British cotton managers were that they were unduly slow in adopting the ring spindle in spinning and virtually ignored the automatic loom in weaving. The principle advantage of the ring spindle over the older competing technology, the mule spindle, was that it could be operated by unskilled (largely female) labour, while the mule required the services of skilled (largely male) operatives. Thus the ring spindle saved on labour costs. The principal disadvantage of the ring was that, to make a given fineness (or 'count' – the count is the number of 840 yard hanks per pound of yarn) of yarn, it required a longer staple and usually more expensive cotton than did the mule. This did not matter for low count yarn because even short staple cotton was long enough for low count rings. At higher counts and qualities, however, there was a raw material cost differential between the two technologies.

In the United States, except at extremely high counts (above 100), the labour saving of the ring more than compensated for the extra cotton cost. In Britain, the relatively very large supply of skilled mule spinners considerably reduced the labour cost saving available from the ring. As a result, the ring was superior for counts up to about 40 while the mule was superior for counts above 40. The situation in France and Germany appears to have been similar to that in Britain. An examination of actual behaviour confirms that cotton entrepreneurs were responding rationally to this situation in all four countries. Except for a very few, extremely high count, installations American entrepreneurs installed only rings in new plants, while British, French and German entrepreneurs installed mules for counts above a point somewhere around 40, and rings for counts below that point (Sandberg 1974: ch. 2). A related problem concerns the rate of replacement of technically well-functioning British low count mules with rings. The economics of replacement are obviously different from those of choosing a technique for a totally new installation. In the latter case, the technology with the lowest total cost is superior. In the former case, the old, existing technology should only be replaced if the *total* cost of the new technique is less than the *variable* cost of the old technique. On a set of what appear to be reasonable assumptions concerning the costs of replacing mules with rings in existing plants, it seems that British managers behaved rationally in this regard also. As would be expected, the rate of replacement of mules with rings was more rapid in America than in Britain (*ibid.*: ch. 3).

The principal advantage of the automatic loom was that it enabled each operator to tend more looms, thereby reducing the labour costs per unit of output. The principal drawback was that they were much more expensive than plain looms, thereby raising the capital costs per unit of output. An analysis of conditions in the United States and in Britain indicates that the likely saving in labour costs outweighed the increase in capital costs in the United States, but not in Britain. Thus, American entrepreneurs should have installed automatic looms in new weaving sheds while British entrepreneurs should have avoided the automatic loom entirely. In fact, of course, that is overwhelmingly what they each did. The argument that automatic looms were not installed in Britain because they were incompatible with existing weaving sheds is not applicable to this period. Automatic looms were not installed for good reasons, even in new

116

sheds (*ibid.*: ch. 4). Furthermore, these calculations of the profitability of the automatic loom in Britain are based on conditions before the First World War. The situation was much worse after the war. A massive installation of automatic looms would have greatly increased the losses experienced by the industry during the interwar period. The inevitable and painful dismantling of the British cotton textile industry would have been no less inevitable and even more painful.

While the British cotton entrepreneurs apparently responded properly to these innovations in spinning and weaving, there is no doubt that their world-wide introduction hurt Britain's relative position in the industry. That is always the case with innovations that are more suited to conditions abroad than at home. The ring spindle, in particular, seriously reduced the value of Britain's large stock of human capital which was embodied in her corps of skilled mule spinners.

Nevertheless, it does seem strange that the efficiency of the Lancashire cotton textile industry, as reported by Jones, should actually have declined between 1900 and 1910, particularly since the period witnessed a substantial increase in labour productivity in the industry. An investigation of the Jones index, however, reveals that these peculiar results depend on some highly questionable procedures and data. Most important, Jones' method of joining two series of cotton cloth prices in 1899 is unacceptable. Substituting a more reasonable technique eliminates the peculiar drop in efficiency claimed for the post 1900 period. Instead, a more reasonable recalculation of the index results in a continuation after 1900 of the modest rate of efficiency growth that Jones himself reported for the 1885–1900 period. While this rate is not as rapid as that estimated for Massachusetts, the two can be reconciled without reliance on 'entrepreneurial failure' in Britain (Sandberg 1974: ch. 5).

The coal mining industry

The coal mining industry was a giant in the British economy during the 1860–1914 period. The value of its output was equal to about 3 per cent of GNP in 1860 and 7 per cent in 1913. Employment rose from 350000 in 1870 to 940000 in 1907. These data give a picture, not only of a large industry, but of one that is experiencing rapid growth. This is confirmed by the increase in tons of coal produced from 83 million in 1860 to 287 million in 1913. Exports rose over the same interval from seven million tons to seventy-three million tons (Taylor 1968; Deane & Cole 1962: ch. 6; Mitchell & Jones 1971: ch. IV).

Despite these impressive figures, concern about the health of the industry was frequently expressed at the time, and the performance of the industry during the period has been the object of a great deal of retrospective criticism. To some extent, this criticism stems from the even more rapid growth of the industry in Germany and America. Even more disturbing, however, was the decline in labour productivity recorded by the industry starting in the 1880s. British output

Entrepreneurship

per man year increased from 270 tons in 1874–78 to 319 tons in 1879–83 and 1884–88 and then declined to 257 tons in 1908–13. In the other European countries, output per man peaked later and had only stagnated, or declined very slightly, by 1908–13. These developments left labour productivity in Britain in 1908–13 at the same level as that in Germany and somewhat above the French and Belgian levels. In America, however, there was continuous advance in labour productivity, leaving the American level well above that in Britain and the other countries (Taylor 1968: 46).

Various factors may have contributed to the sharp drop in British labour productivity. It is reported that the hours of work declined, absenteeism increased and the average quality of the rapidly expanding labour force declined. It is noted second that the coal was subjected to better preparation at the pit head, thus improving the quality of the product. Perhaps most important of all, the quality of the remaining untapped coal deposits was deteriorating; Britain had, with perfect rationality, mined her most accessible coal first. Germany's later start somewhat delayed the point of increasing costs due to thinner, more fractured and deeper seams, while America was still opening up new, high quality coal fields. Finally, it has been frequently stressed that the British industry was much slower to mechanise, particularly with mechanical coal cutters, than was the American industry. The two interrelated questions about the quality of British coal mining management that emerge from these observations are: one, whether the lag in mechanisation behind America was a sign of technological backwardness; two, whether Britain's lower, and declining, level of labour productivity can be explained without recourse to 'entrepreneurial failure'.

The direct quantitative analysis of the first of these questions is made extremely difficult by the varying geological conditions between, and within, the various coalfields. As a result, most of the discussion of the problem is of a qualitative and impressionistic nature. For example, the leading historian of the British coal mining industry argues that the fact that some British coal fields installed coal cutters faster than some others is, in itself, a reflection on the management of the laggards. At the same time, however, he reports that the leading fields had a relatively large number of narrow seams, the kind which benefited the most from mechanical cutters (Taylor 1961: 60–1). Such evidence says nothing at all about the appropriateness of the overall rate of introduction of coal cutters. It does imply, however, that the British coal managers were rational enough to introduce mechanical cutting first into those mines where it did the most good.

In another study, the same author raises another type of argument. Although he cannot show that the British coal mine operators were unwise in not installing more coal cutters, he nevertheless wonders about their motives: 'Insofar as unwillingness to persevere with the coal-cutter was symptomatic, not of a rational assessment of its potentialities, but of the operation of the conservative tendencies in the industry, its consequences could be far reaching' (Taylor 1968:

118

59–60). This is pure speculation. The author cannot show that there was anything wrong with the behaviour of the coal managers. He grants that they 'may well' have made 'the right choice', but he then adds that *if* they did it for the wrong reason then that is a bad sign. While in a sense this is true, such hypothesising proves nothing.

One further attempt has been made to reconcile the difference in labour productivity in the British and American coal mining industries. This study begins by noting that in 1907 the British industry used about the same number of horsepower per worker as the American industry did in 1909. This implies that the much greater depths of the British mines had increased capital per worker to levels similar to those in America even without mechanical coal cutters. Since American wages were much higher than British wages, this, in turn, implies that Britain was substituting capital for inferior natural resources. Using estimates of the response (elasticity) of output per worker to seam thickness and depth, the study makes a reasonable case that the difference in natural resource quality explains the difference in levels of output per worker (McCloskey 1971a: 289–95).

The mercantile marine

One of the most important and successful sectors of the British economy between 1860 and 1914 was the mercantile marine. Throughout that period approximately one third of total world tonnage was of UK registration. This fraction, in fact, considerably understates Britain's share of world shipping capacity. British ships were much more modern than world average. Almost 4 per cent of the UK fleet was sold abroad each year. Thus, for example, in 1914 85 per cent of all UK registered ships had been built since 1895 (Aldcroft 1968a: 326–7).

Given this performance, it is not surprising that the management of the British merchant marine has been virtually exempt from the kind of criticism levelled against other British entrepreneurs. The reason for including the sector in this chapter is thus simply that a quantitative study has been made of the most important technological decision facing all shipping entrepreneurs during this period, the shift from sail to steam. This shift occurred gradually, starting with the construction of the *Claremont* in 1807 and it was not yet complete at the end of our period. It began with routes where frequent refuelling stops could be made, then continued to routes requiring longer and longer open water crossings. On each route, passengers and perishable goods were the first to be carried by steam and durable bulk cargoes were the last.

The explanation for this process lies in the continuous improvement in the fuel economy of marine steam engines. As fuel consumption per mile fell, fuel costs declined; more important, a smaller part of the ship's cargo space was taken up by fuel supplies. Thus it became economical to travel greater and greater distances without refuelling. To the extent that bunker coal was in any case obtained from Britain, it became economically feasible to use steam ships further and further away from Britain. Thus it is that the grain trade between Australia and Britain around the Cape was the last bastion of the sailing ship. The quantitative study made of this process concludes that the actual timing of these shifts agrees well with the predictions of a decision model using the relative costs of steam and sail. Shipping entrepreneurs apparently responded with alacrity to the changing relative profitability of sail versus steam on various routes (Harley 1971). A more recent but similar study of the adaptation of motor ships by the British mercantile fleet after the First World War does, however, detect an uneconomic lag. The authors of this study blame this lost opportunity on a prejudice in favour of coal and on the excessive claims of the British steam turbine producers (Henning & Trace 1975: 385).

Conclusion

This industrial summary is incomplete. It does not contain everything we know about British entrepreneurship and technical change between 1860 and 1914, much less everything we might like to know. Still, what is known on the subject is far from trivial and, generally speaking, it is unfavourable to the hypothesis of 'entrepreneurial failure'. While some examples of 'technological backwardness' and other types of failure have been found, and more undoubtedly remain to be found, it is not established that the failure rate was any higher than in other countries, including the United States and Germany, during the same period or than in Britain during earlier periods. Much less has it been shown that the British 'entrepreneurial failures' in this period exceeded those in Germany and America by so much that they can materially have contributed to Britain's relative economic decline.

What is perhaps most damaging to the 'entrepreneurial failure' hypothesis is the fact that a large percentage of the serious alleged specific mistakes invariably listed by supporters of the hypothesis (the failure to adopt ring spinning, automatic weaving, basic steel making, Solvay processing of alkalis and mechanical coal cutting) have been carefully studied and the resulting failure yield is very modest indeed. To re-establish the hypothesis, it must be argued that the failures were of a more subtle and insidious kind.

Thus, to the question: 'Did "entrepreneurial failure," and especially "technological backwardness", play a significant role in Britain's relative economic decline?' the answer must be: 'Probably not.'

120

Suggestions for further reading

The case for 'entrepreneurial failure' in Britain is made by Aldcroft (1964), Landes (1969) and Levine (1967). A set of industry studies that can best be described as neutral on this issue are found in Aldcroft (1968b). Generally sceptical industry case studies are included in McCloskey (1971b). British iron and steel and cotton textile entrepreneurs, respectively, are exonerated in McCloskey (1973) and Sandberg (1974). A more general defense of the British entrepreneur is presented in McCloskey and Sandberg (1971).

34

8

An overview and an assessment

It is a very difficult country to move, Mr. Hyndman, a very difficult country indeed, and one in which there is more disappointment to be looked for than success.
—Disraeli to H. M. Hyndman (1881)

Now we ask ourselves more and more if the so-called progress we see going on about us at breakneck speed is what we really want. This is the age of the international companies – the commercial dinosaurs that stride from continent to continent. It is the age of supertankers, superstores, supersonic flight. The only thing which for many is not super is life itself.
—*Folkestone Herald* (31 July 1971)

The cultural domestication of the industrial revolution
At the time of the Great Exhibition of 1851, Britain was the home of the industrial revolution, a symbol of material progress to the world. It was also the home of an apparently triumphant bourgeoisie. Observers like Carlyle and Marx agreed in pointing to the industrialist as the new aristocrat, a figure that was ushering in a radically new order and a new culture. Yet they were misled. From the time of their assertions, social and psychological currents in Britain began to flow in a different direction.

By the nineteen-seventies, falling levels of capital investment raised the specter of outright "de-industrialization" – a decline in industrial production outpacing any corresponding growth in the "production" of services.[1] Whether or not such a specter had substance, it is true that this period of recognized economic crisis in Britain was preceded by a century of psychological and intellectual de-industrialization. The emerging culture of industrialism, which in the mid-Victorian years had appeared, for good or ill, to be the wave of the future, irresistibly washing over and sweeping away the features of an older Britain, was itself transformed. The thrust of new values borne along by the revolution in industry was contained in the later nineteenth century; the social and intellectual revolution implicit in industrialism was muted, perhaps even aborted. Instead, a compromise was effected, accommodating new groups, new interests, and new needs within a social and cultural matrix that preserved the forms and even many of the values of tradition. Potentially disruptive forces of change were harnessed and channeled into supporting a new social order, a synthesis of old and new. This containment of the cultural revolution of industrialism lies at the heart of both the achievements and the failures of modern British history.

The new society created by the later Victorians rested on a domestication of the wilder traits of earlier British behavior; the riotous populace, the aggressive and acquisitive capitalists, and the hedonistic aristocrats of the Georgian world became endangered, if not extinct, species of Englishmen. Their descendants were more restrained, more civilized, and also more conservative, in that they now had an established and secure place in the social order, or, in the case of the aristocracy, had come to terms with social change and re-cemented their place in the status quo. By Victoria's death, British society had weathered the storms of change, but at the cost of surrendering a capacity for innovation and assertion that was perhaps the other face of the unruliness and harshness of that earlier Britain.

In particular, the later nineteenth century saw the consolidation of a national elite that, by virtue of its power and prestige, played a central role both in Britain's modern achievements and its failures. It administered the most extensive empire in human history with reasonable effectiveness and humanity, and it maintained a remarkable degree of political and social stability at home while presiding over a redistribution of power and an expansion of equality and security. It also presided over the steady and continued erosion of the nation's economic position in the world. The standards of value of this new elite of civil servants, professionals, financiers, and landed proprietors, inculcated by a common education in public schools and ancient universities and reflected in the literary culture it patronized, permeated by their prestige much of British society beyond the elite itself. These standards did little to support, and much to discourage, economic dynamism. They threw earlier enthusiasms for technology into disrepute, emphasized the social evils brought by the industrial revolution, directed attention to issues of the "quality of life" in preference to the quantitative concerns of production and expansion, and disparaged the restlessness and acquisitiveness of industrial capitalism. Hand in hand with this disparagement went the growth of an alternative set of social values, embodied in a new vision of the nation.

The dominant collective self-image in English culture became less and less that of the world's workshop. Instead, this image was challenged by the counterimage of an ancient, little-disturbed "green and pleasant land." "Our England is a garden," averred the greatest poet of Imperialism; another Imperialist, a poet laureate, celebrated England at the height of Imperial fervor for its "haunts of ancient peace"; and an anti-Imperialist socialist has inspired his readers with the aim of making England once again, as it had been before the industrial revolution, the "fair green garden of Northern Europe." The past, and the countryside – seen as inseparable – were invested with an almost irresistible aura. These standards and images supported a very attractive way of life, geared to maintenance of a status quo rather than innovation, comfort rather than attainment, the civilized enjoyment, rather than the creation, of wealth.

British political opinion bore the imprint of the aristocracy long after the demise of the aristocracy's power. The politicians, civil servants, churchmen, professional men, and publicists who did so much to shape modern British political opinion and policy moved in a climate of opinion uncongenial to the world of industry. Most of them showed a striking fondness for gentry tastes and standards, making such tastes an essential part of the modern British style of government. Political calls for economic growth went against the grain of the values and style of life actually believed in by most politicians and civil servants, as well as by the rest of the elite.

Industrialists themselves were far from immune to this antiindustrial culture; like others, they breathed it in ever more deeply the higher they rose in social position. The new British elite was open to industrialists, if they adapted to its standards. With few exceptions, they were ready to do so, although such adaptation required a degree of disavowal of their own former selves and their very function in society By modeling themselves – in varying proportions – upon civil servants, professional men, and men of landed leisure, industrialists found acceptance at the upper reaches of British society. Thus, the famed "Establishment" and its consensus was created. Social integration and stability were ensured, but at a price – the waning of the industrial spirit.

Postindustrialism or de-industrialism?

The peculiar pattern of British social and cultural history has involved both benefits and costs. Which, however, has predominated? Has this pattern been on balance a fortune or a misfortune for Britain? And what signposts to the future – if any – does this cultural history set out?

Many, within and without Britain, have praised the cultural path thus taken. Even the business historian D. C. Coleman was at pains to point out in his argument for the importance of the gentlemanly ideal that he was not *criticizing* its sway:

> If, by some unlikely magic [Victorian and Edwardian businessmen] had turned themselves into single-minded, constantly profit-maximizing

entrepreneurs, what sort of world might have resulted? If it is true that one of the costs of Public Schools producing "first-class administrators" was some lag in industrial advance, how can we know that the price was not worth paying?[2]

Others, on both Left and Right, have thought the gain certainly more than worth the price. The *Times* spoke for many of them in 1971 when it reflected on the lack of enthusiasm for "wealth, as such," and found it good. "The secret hope of Britain," it concluded,

> is indeed that the monetary obsession has penetrated our society less deeply than it has others. There are probably still more people in Britain who will give total effort for reasons of idealism than for reasons of gain.[3]

A peculiar English gift for the "quality" rather than the "quantity" of life was claimed as early as 1907, by the cosmopolitan novelist Ford Madox Ford. "The especial province of the English nation," he reflected, "is the evolution of a standard of manners . . . The province of the English is to solve the problem of how men may live together."[4] Around the same time, foreign visitors (particularly Americans) began to note the pleasantness and relaxed quality of English life. Arthur Shadwell, an Edwardian "efficiency expert," reported: "An American gentleman said to me one day: 'We are a tearing, driving, scheming lot here. The Englishman leads a tranquil, happy life, and I for one envy him'."[5] The direct descendant of this nameless American was the *New York Time*'s London correspondent during the later sixties and early seventies, Anthony Lewis, who observed in a farewell "love letter": "There is a larger reality than the pound and inflation and the GNP. It is life, and the British are good at that."[6] Some have gone even further in their admiration, and see the British as pioneering new forms of "postindustrial society." John Kenneth Galbraith, interviewed on the BBC, told his hosts that

> your real problem is that you were the first of the great industrialized nations, and so things happen here first. You are living out the concern for some more leisurely relationship with industrial life that the other people have been discussing for 50 years or more.[7]

To Bernard Nossiter, London correspondent for the *Washington Post* during the 1970s, "Britons . . . appear[ed] to be the first citizens of the post-industrial age who are choosing leisure over goods on a large scale," and he heartily approved of their choice.[8]

However, others have sounded a more somber note, portraying rustic-gentlemanly values as sliding imperceptibly into decadence. Donald Horne expressed it with the vehemence of an expatriate:

> Kindness, tolerance and love of order become snobbery, woolliness and love of the past. Effortless ease becomes the ease of not making

any effort to do anything. Gentlemanly intuitive wisdom becomes the inability to make up one's mind. Doing the decent thing comes to mean that there should be no sharp clash of attitudes, no disagreeable new beliefs, that might disturb someone. The sense of fairness becomes the belief that competition is unfair: it might benefit some new person, but it might also harm some old person.[9]

This point of view was expressed succinctly by Lord Nuffield in 1959, when he called Britain a "nation in semi-retirement."[10] Others have shared Nuffield's perception of a failure of national energies, adaptability, or will. One of the most eloquent and earliest was C. P. Snow, who in the same year, 1959, delivered this warning to his fellow members of the British governing class:

> More often than I like, I am saddened by a historical myth. Whether the myth is good history or not, doesn't matter; it is pressing enough for me. I can't help thinking of the Venetian Republic in their last half-century. Like us, they had once been fabulously lucky. They had become rich, as we did, by accident. They had acquired immense political skill, just as we have. A good many of them were tough-minded, realistic, patriotic men. They knew, just as clearly as we know, that the current of history had begun to flow against them. Many of them gave their minds to working out ways to keep going. It would have meant breaking the pattern into which they had crystallised. They were fond of the pattern, just as we are fond of ours. They never found the will to break it.[11]

Nearly two decades later, Snow's Venetian analogy seemed more relevant than ever to the Marxist Tom Nairn. "The House of Lords," he complained in 1977,

> is a better gauge of British futures than IBM. Underneath the ceaseless speechifying about new starts, the dominant dream is of a Venetian twilight: a golden-grey steady state where staid arts and moderate politics join to preserve the tenor of things English. The true impulse is not really to "catch up" with the greater, evolving world outside, but to hold one's own somehow, anyhow, and defend the tribe's customs and weathered monuments.[12]

Sixteenth-century Venice, of course, had nothing equivalent to North Sea oil; but similar windfalls to other nations, when unreinforced by a favorable social environment, have had little lasting effect. The classic historical example is seventeenth-century Spain. The historian J. H. Elliot laid responsibility for that nation's decline at the feet of its ruling class, which

> lacked the breadth of vision and the strength of character to break with a past that could no longer serve as a reliable guide to the future... At a time when the face of Europe was altering more rapidly than ever before, the country that had once been its leading power proved to be lacking the essential ingredient for survival – the willingness to change.[13]

The vision was given literary form when one of Britain's best contemporary writers, known previously as a novelist of personal relations, was impelled by the crisis of the seventies to explore the condition of the national spirit. Margaret Drabble had become increasingly concerned by what seemed to her to be negative and retreatist social values,[14] and in her novel *The Ice Age* portrayed an English elite in a state of psychic and moral exhaustion. Returning to the moralist tradition of the early Victorians, Drabble sought within her dark canvas for sources of renewal, and was unafraid to court ridicule by calling upon John Milton and his vision of "a noble and puissant Nation, rousing herself like a strong man after sleep." *The Ice Age* summed up one view of the "condition of England."

It has also been argued that the pleasant vision of English "post-industrialism" is a mirage; that the quality of life cannot be readily opposed to the quantity or even their constituents easily separated.[15] Recent studies of public opinion, moreover, suggest that, as Rudolf Klein has regretfully put it, "altruism appears to be largely a function of economic prosperity."[16] A no-growth society does not seem likely to be a more humane, more tolerant, or even more comfortable society. One recalls Edward Heath's 1973 warning:

> The alternative to expansion is not, as some occasionally seem to suppose, an England of quiet market towns linked only by trains puffing slowly and peacefully through green meadows. The alternative is slums, dangerous roads, old factories, cramped schools, stunted lives.[17]

"Modernization": un-English?

To mention Edward Heath is to raise the question of whether this national culture can be – or is being – changed. The gentlemanly consensus of "domesticated progress" began to come under strain in the early 1960s, as the continental economic surge sowed anxiety about national decline in the minds of British observers. These anxieties brought the issue of modernization into the political arena. Beginning in 1964, this new issue played an important role, at least rhetorically, in every general election. The general election of 1979, in particular, was fought around the question of national economic decline. In a historic exchange, whose outlines were first perceptible in 1970, the Labour party stood for English tradition, the status quo, and "safety first," whereas the Conservatives – their leader especially – gave the calls for sweeping change. "I am a reformer," Margaret Thatcher announced, "and I am offering change."[18] The Conservative victory gave Britain a leader well known for her resolve to reverse the pattern of the past century. Thatcher indeed seeks, as her opponents charged, to "turn the clock back" – to restore nineteenth-century economic dynamism by reintroducing the disciplines and incentives of the market.

If the argument of this book is valid, the outcome of Thatcher's crusade may turn on how successful methods like lowering marginal tax rates and restricting the money supply will be in altering cultural attitudes formed over many years.[19] The least tractable obstacle to British economic "redevelopment" may well be the continuing resistance of cultural values and attitudes. A recent survey of British attitudes toward money and work commissioned by *New Society* revealed a nation "remarkably unambitious in a material sense":

> Very few sincerely want to be rich. Most people in Britain neither want nor expect a great deal of money. Even if they could get it, the vast majority do not seem prepared to work harder for it: most of our respondents thought we should work only as much as we need to live a pleasant life...It seems clear that the British today prefer economic *stability* to rapid economic growth.[20]

Indeed, the 1970s saw in Britain (as elsewhere) a *reaction* against the calls of the 1960s for modernization and growth. Edward Heath, after painfully imposing the gospel of efficiency upon the Conservatives, failed even more painfully to impose it upon the nation. The acute Labor Minister Richard Crossman commented on Heath's difficulties with "the traditional Right" in the sixties: "The policy he is putting across seems to me to be attractive only to young and thrusting businessmen" – no prescription for successful politics.[21] "Technophobia," as two journalists put it in 1967, persisted in the grass roots of the Tory party.

> What[ever] aspirations the present leadership may have [they warned]...the party traditionalists take little account of doctrines of business efficiency, and largely loathe the Americans who invented most of the concepts. How lonely the evangelistic Mr. Marples looks in the Tory Party when he tries to convince the ranks of the devoted that their concern is with technology and business efficiency, and how curious has been his fate! What applause there was for Mr. Angus Maude's "for Tories simply to talk like technocrats will get them nowhere"![22]

Nonetheless, Heath pushed on, seeking to break the psychological resistance, within and outside the party, to modernization. He described Britain in December 1969 as "a Luddite's paradise...a society dedicated to the prevention of progress and the preservation of the status quo." He seized the surprise Conservative victory in 1970 as a mandate for the transformation of Britain, announcing to the first party conference after the election that "we were returned to office to change the course of history of this nation – nothing less." More and more Heath saw the root problem facing him as psychological: the shortsighted tendency of his countrymen to "prefer comfort to progress."[23] Yet it was by no means clear how this tendency could be changed by government. Heath was soon labeled a "radical" and a "divisive" figure,[24] and most of his initial program was abandoned, gutted, or proven ineffective even before his government was swept away in the wake of the 1973-4 confrontation with the miners.

After a taste of Heath's crusade, in February 1974 the public found more appealing the Labour campaign, which, despite the party program's pledges of nationalization and redistribution, was remarkably conservative in spirit. The party leadership had moved from promising in 1964 to reshape Britain in the "white heat of a new technological revolution" to pledging a decade later an end to "divisiveness," a taming of the "ruthless, pushing society," and "a quiet life."[25]

In office, Harold Wilson, and especially his emollient successor, James Callaghan, followed the tone set by the general election, seeking above all to promote social harmony and stability, and cushioning the social fabric and the economic status quo from the stresses of change. The modernizing rhetoric of the 1960s, evoking Joseph Chamberlain and Lloyd George, was gently laid to rest, and the spirit of Stanley Baldwin hovered over Downing Street. Both Wilson and Callaghan, in contrast to Heath, acquired farms and were often photographed there, appearing in Baldwinesque fashion as men of the country. For both men these farms (neither was a serious agricultural enterprise) maintained a link to what Callaghan's wife called "the peasant in us."[26]

Many intellectuals and publicists took the two Conservative electoral defeats in 1974 as a repudiation of "growthmania." Christopher Price, a Labour MP, was one of a number who argued that "Labour is now the natural party to rein back" from such misguided zeal. The "ancestral virtues" of the party, which had provided a "moral authority" during the Attlee-Cripps era of austerity, could now again, Price argued, do good service.[27] In the sixties, he later reflected, whatever party, "The message was the same: 'Out with the old, on with the new.' New towns, new tower blocks, new supersonic planes, new motorways. And if a few greenhouse windows were broken to let Concorde fly, if good houses were torn down for roads and redevelopment, too bad. 'You couldn't make omelettes...' Now it is all suddenly different." Novelty had soured, and "bigness" – which, Price recalled, "some Socialists had been preaching against for a century" – had become unfashionable. Price set out a "non-economic" agenda for what he called a socialist political program. Its aim was to protect the existing "social and environmental fabric of Britain" – its "pleasant, fraternal, convivial" character, and its countryside. "All this," he conceded, "may sound negative." Well and good. "Labour has always been used to start things. I suspect its role in the future will be more concerned with stopping them."[28]

After 1974, educated opinion seemed more disillusioned than ever with "progress." Ramsay Macdonald's biographer, David Marquand, found Macdonald's antimaterialism freshly relevant: "Ten or fifteen years ago," he remarked in 1977, "Macdonald's warning that the quality of life might be sacrificed in the pursuit of material prosperity, and that socialists might lose sight of their non-material objectives in the struggle for votes, could be dismissed as a piece of sentimental obscurantism. It cannot be dismissed so easily today."[29]

A new cultural phenomenon came of age in the 1970s: explicit and organized opposition to the results of technical and material advance. This was of course part of a development embracing the entire industrialized world, where antigrowth and antitechnology movements had taken root among left-wing university students and had become a force to be reckoned with in public life. In Britain, this general movement took on a more popular and nationalistic form. The ranks of English critics of progress extended far beyond the universities or the Left; these critics tended to see their mission as inseparable from English patriotism – to save traditional English life from unwelcome change. The great variety of new or resurgent causes taken up in the late sixties and early seventies, from environmentalism to historical preservation to the Campaign for Real Ale, constituted a nonpartisan "movement to protect English culture."[30] As Marquand argued (all the more powerfully for being a well-known critic of the Left): "The issue of the future is small against big, community against *anomie*, peace-of-mind against rate-of-growth, grass roots against tower blocks, William Morris against both Sidney Webb and Henry Ford."[31]

Perhaps the chief literary embodiment of this spirit of resistance was the immensely popular poet laureate John Betjeman, who was more widely read than any previous laureate. Betjeman extended the pastoral nostalgia of his predecessors, John Masefield and Alfred Austin, to suburbia, now an integral part of Old England. His writing disparaged the new and evoked the security of old, familiar things. The public responded with enthusiasm to his Tory "longing for the simplicity of irremovable landmarks."[32] This longing moved the Left as well as the Right: The *New Statesman* in 1973 hailed Betjeman's denunciation of urban redevelopment. "At last," it announced in its front-page leader,

> a Poet Laureate has expressed the nation's feelings. This week Sir John Betjeman observed that destroying the surroundings in which people live – and which they like, and are accustomed to – amounts to straightforward robbery. It is stealing the people's property, said Sir

John; exactly the same as being burgled. In some ways, maybe worse. You can buy substitutes for the contents of a house. A familiar narrow street, with its obscure chapel, tree and corner shop, is irreplaceable.[33]

Similarly, the socialist playwright and critic Dennis Potter wrote with approval in the Sunday *Times* (London) that "Betjeman is the surviving proof that it is all right, after all, to be an Englishman. He stands at the wrought-iron gates, ready to hold back the flood."[34]

The identification of "English" with "holding back the flood" of change had been made familiar by that widely read man of the Left, J. B. Priestley, who had by the 1970s become a popular authority on the national character. He reveled in attacking the modernizers, arguing in 1970 that they failed to understand that, as he had implied as early as 1949, the modern world was "alien to the English temperament." It was natural and good that the English did not take readily to its characteristic activities. "We are instinctively opposed," he announced, "to high-pressure industry and salesmanship, wanting something better than a huge material rat race." The nation's future, Priestley urged three years later, hung upon resisting "change for change's sake."[35]

At the end of the day, it may be that Margaret Thatcher will find her most fundamental challenge not in holding down the money supply or inhibiting government spending, or even in fighting the shop stewards, but in changing this frame of mind. English history in the eighties may turn less on traditional political struggles than on a cultural contest between the two faces of the middle class.

8. An overview and an assessment

1. See Frank Blackaby, ed., *De-Industrialization* (London, 1978); see also Peter Jenkins, "A Nation on the Skids," *Manchester Guardian Weekly*, 8 October 1978, and [Paul Barker], "Europe's Merseyside," *New Society 46* (14 December 1978), 623.
2. "Gentlemen and Players, " *Economic History Review*, series 2, 26 (1973), 115.
3. "What is the British Disease? " the *Times* (London), 29 April 1971.
4. *The Spirit of the People* (London, 1907), 151.
5. *Industrial Efficiency* (London, 1906), *II*, 459.

6. "Leaving the Village," *International Herald Tribune*, 2 August 1973. See also Lewis's comparison of English and American life, in which England comes out, for all its faults, the home of "human values" ("Notes on the New York Skyline . . . ," *Atlantic*, June, 1971, 58-62).

7. Quoted in Krishan Kumar, "A Future in the Past? " *New Society 42* (24 November 1977), 418-19. See the reflections by Christopher Price, MP, provoked by Galbraith: "A Dunce as Prizewinner," *New Society 39* (3 March 1977), 452-3.

8. *Britain – A Future That Works* (Boston, Mass., 1978), 100.

9. *God is An Englishman*, (Sydney, Australia, 1969), 71.

10. Quoted by R. R. James, *Ambitions and Realities: British Politics, 1964-1970* (London, 1972), 293.

11. *The Two Cultures and the Scientific Revolution* (New York, 1959), 42.

12. "The Politics of the New Venice," *New Society 42* (17 November 1977), 352.

13. *Imperial Spain, 1469-1716* (London, 1963), 378. This was a failure, he stressed elsewhere, of a society, and not of a handful of leaders: "Behind this inert government . . . lay a whole social system and psychological attitude which themselves blocked the way to radical reform" ("The Decline of Spain" [1961], in *The Economic Decline of Empires*, ed. Carlo Cipolla [London, 1970], 185). "Spanish Main Gold," as Peter Jenkins recently remarked, "was to Castille what North Sea oil may prove for Britain – the agent of de-industrialization" ("Going Down with Great Britain," *Harper's*, December, 1979, 28).

14. See the *Guardian*, 26 November 1973.

15. See, for example, Wilfred Beckerman, *In Defense of Economic Growth* (London, 1974).

16. Review of James Alt, *The Politics of Economic Decline* (Cambridge, 1979), in *New Society 50* (8 November 1979), 332.

17. Preconference message to Conservative party workers, 28 September 1973, quoted in Sunday *Telegraph*, 30 September 1973.

18. Quoted in *Manchester Guardian Weekly*, 22 April 1979.

19. See, for a similar argument during the election compaign, Peregrine Worsthorne, "Do British Want to Lose Their Chains? " Sunday *Telegraph*, 8 April 1979, 16.

20. Tom Forester, "Do the British Sincerely Want to Be Rich? " *New Society 40* (28 April 1977), 158, 161.

21. *The Diaries of a Cabinet Minister* (New York, 1976), *I*, 351.

22. Glyn Jones and Michael Barnes, *Britain on Borrowed Time* (Harmondsworth, 1967), 268. Maude saw himself as keeper of the Tory conscience, and denounced preoccupation with economic growth as no part of the Conservative tradition. Echoing R. H. Tawney, he labeled it (in *The Consuming Society* [London, 1967]) a "fetish" producing "a sterile cycle of increasing production for increasing consumption of increasingly trivial things."

23. Anthony Lewis, "The Radical of 10 Downing Street," *New York Times Magazine*, 14 March 1971, 46.

24. See David Marquand, "Compromise Under Attack," *New Society 16*, (5 November 1970), 829, and Paul Johnson, "Ted Heath's Britain," *New Statesman 83* (18 February 1972), 196.

25. See David Butler and Dennis Kavanagh, *The British General Election of February 1974* (London, 1974), 125-6, 162-3; David Butler and Michael Pinto-Duschinsky, *The British General Election of 1970* (London, 1971), 169; and Robert Rhodes James, *Ambitions and Realities: British Politics,*

1964-1970 (London, 1972), 220, 239. See the suggestive analysis of the key words and phrases used by the candidates by Shelley Pinto-Duschinsky, "A Matter of Words," *New Society* 27 (7 March 1974), 570-1. Wilson continued this winning line in the October election: "What the people want," he affirmed, "what every family needs, is a bit of peace and quiet" (David Butler and Dennis Kavanagh, *The British General Election of October 1974* [London, 1975], 134).

26. Quoted in *People* (New York), March, 1977, 32.

27. "The Politics of Austerity," *New Statesman* 87 (3 May 1974), 607-8. The decade of the forties was harked back to as a model by a number of left-wing writers. It now seemed an age of elevating austerity and common purpose, before prosperity opened the floodgates of selfishness and the frantic pursuit of artificial wants. Mervyn Jones, novelist and regular contributor to the *New Statesman*, greeted the year 1975 ("A New Year Salute," *New Statesman* 89 [3 January 1975], 3-4) with a reassurance that prolonged zero growth was all for the best: "I never believed that human happiness can be measured in gross national product per capita." He and others, he recalled, had spent the fifties deploring the pursuit of affluence; they were right then, and should hardly be despondent now that "the affluence show is closed down," at least "for the time being." "There have been," he went on, "only two periods in my lifetime that justified a positive pride in being a citizen of this country: the war, and the early post-war years." In Attlee's Britain, for all the shortages, "the number of people who felt deprived, who got nothing of value out of life, was surely less than it is now." (The irony of such nostalgia is inescapable if one looks at a cartoon in the 4 October 1944 issue of *Punch*, in which a scene of a queue of shoppers draws the [humorous] observation from a bystander, "I suppose in about thirty years' time people will insist on describing this as the good old days." [Precisely on the nose!]).

28. "Labour After the Defeats," *New Statesman* 92 (12 November 1976), 659-60.

29. *Ramsay Macdonald* (London, 1977), 462.

30. Lincoln Allison, "The English Cultural Movement," *New Society* 43 (16 February 1978), 358-60. Allison offered a "culturist manifesto": "Join the organisations which oppose harmful modernization and development. Do it thoughtfully but with determination. Protect your communities. Learn ancient skills. Renovate old houses. Defend quality, whether of beer or of landscape; the substitutes rarely satisfy. In doing so you will reward not merely yourself, but your society."

31. "Farewell to Westminster," *New Statesman* 93 (7 January 1977), 2.

32. Anthony Hartley, *A State of England* (London, 1963), 129n.; see also Clive James, "Supplier of Poetry," *New Statesman* 88 (22 November 1974), 745: "The urge to preserve supplied him with his most important creative impulse."

33. *New Statesman* 85 (23 February 1973), 253.

34. Quoted in Allison, "English Cultural Movement," 360.

35. *The Edwardians* (London, 1970), 289; *The English* (London, 1973), 242.

Name Index